Human Resources Management
for Effective Schools

Human Resources Management for Effective Schools

THIRD EDITION

John T. Seyfarth

Virginia Commonwealth University

Allyn and Bacon

Boston • London • Toronto • Sydney • Tokyo • Singapore

Series Editor: *Arnis E. Burvikovs*
Series Editorial Assistant: *Matthew Forster*
Manufacturing Buyer: *Julie McNeill*
Cover Designer: *hannusdesign.com*
Production Coordinator: *Pat Torelli Publishing Services*
Editorial-Production Service: *TKM Productions*
Electronic Composition: *TKM Productions*

Library of Congress Cataloging-in-Publication Data

Seyfarth, John T.
    Human resources management for effective schools / John T. Seyfarth.--3rd ed.
      p. cm
    Rev. ed. of: Personnel management for effective schools. 2nd ed. c1996.
    Includes bibliographical references and index.
    ISBN 0-205-33363-X
      1. School personnel mamagement--United States. 2. School management and organization--United States. I. Seyfarth, John T. Personnel management for effective schools. II. Title.
    LB2831.5 .S46 2002
    371.2'01'0973--dc21   2001046449

To Susie and Chuck

Contents

4 *Obtaining Information and Evaluating Applicants   41*

5 *Selecting Administrative and Support Personnel   59*

Preface

This third edition bears a new title, and its contents reflect the impact that technology is bringing to our lives. The new title, *Human Resources Management for Effective Schools,* is more in keeping with current usage, but the book continues to emphasize the connection between sound human resources practices and student learning. When the first edition of this book appeared in 1991, the idea that decisions about hiring, evaluating, and rewarding employees could have a major impact on student achievement was accepted but seldom acted on. Today, that is no longer the case; administrators at the school and district levels understand the importance of these decisions for student learning and act accordingly.

This change has come about in part because of the adoption of new policies by the various states, including standards for student achievement. Once policymakers specify what students at each grade level are expected to know, teachers are held accountable for helping students acquire that knowledge and administrators are held accountable for selecting competent teachers and facilitating their work. The measure of teacher success becomes student performance. Administrators, principals, and supervisors are expected to help teachers improve their skills and overcome the roadblocks that hinder their success.

Efforts are also being made in some states to adopt higher standards of teacher quality and to develop valid predictors of teaching potential. Methods currently used for that purpose (primarily standardized tests) have not been well accepted by teachers, and it is not clear whether tests are able to accurately identify good teachers. While better methods of selection are being developed, the task of determining which applicants promise to be successful teachers remains a matter of judgment on the part of human resources administrators and principals. Needless to say, no educator is infallible in that regard. All principals have had the experience of hiring a teacher they thought would be outstanding who failed to live up to his or her early promise, and they have also had the opposite experience of hiring a candidate with little promise who turned out to be hard working and successful.

The point is not only that teacher selection is an art and not a science, though that is probably true, but since we know that certain practices more often lead to sound decisions about personnel than other practices, selecting teachers involves exercising judgment based on research, public policy, and closely held values.

Expectations among the general public for schools in the United States are rising, and whether school personnel are able to meet those hopes will determine whether public schools in this country will continue to thrive or wither and die. As expectations rise, the work of teachers, principals, and counselors becomes more difficult and demanding. Nowhere is the pressure to do a better job more keenly felt than among principals and human resources administrators. This book is written in the hope that it will serve a useful purpose in helping these individuals better understand their jobs and perform them more effectively.

The third edition contains much new material, and some older material has been deleted. Two new case studies are included, and the legal chapter has been expanded to include more information about state legislation. That chapter also reports on recent court decisions that human resources administrators should know about. The popular "Suggested Activities" and "Plan of the Chapter" features are retained, and a new feature, "Online Resources," has been added. Like other fields, human resources management is expanding so rapidly that it is difficult to keep up. The websites cited in the Online Resources section will help human resources personnel and students stay abreast of new developments in the field. Much of the content from the former chapter on technology has been incorporated into other chapters. Another change made possible by technology is the inclusion of supplemental material for the book online at the Allyn and Bacon website, www.ablongman.com/edleadership. This new website provides links to many useful sites, chapter objectives, test questions, and activities.

Acknowledgments

It is not possible to acknowledge all those who have contributed to the development of this book over the years. A host of colleagues—school practitioners, graduate students, and university faculty—have provided me with insights and materials that have enhanced my perception of human resources management in the schools.

I thank the following reviewers for their helpful comments: Michael Cunningham, Marshall University; Prudence Gushwa, Minnesota State University; and James Tate, Southwestern Oklahoma State University.

John T. Seyfarth
Richmond, Virginia

Human Resources Management for Effective Schools

1

Human Resources Management and Effective Schools

This book is about managing people in schools. Its objective is to make prospective and practicing school administrators aware of the wide range of activities covered by the term *human resources management* and to present the best of current practice in personnel work. Effective personnel practices are prerequisite to bringing about improved student learning, and all decisions relating to selection, placement, evaluation, development, promotion, and termination of employees should be made with that outcome in mind.

School administrators whose responsibilities include any aspect of human resources management will be interested in this book. All of the activities of personnel department staff members involve personnel management, and many of the duties of principals and assistant principals also fall under that heading. When a principal interviews an applicant for a secretarial position, plans a staff development program for faculty, or evaluates a counselor's performance, he or she is engaging in human resources management. The importance of the principal's role in human resources decision making is increasing as school districts move toward wider implementation of site-based management and decentralization of responsibility for some personnel decisions to the school level.

Most personnel decisions have either a direct or indirect impact on the quality of instruction. When a decision is made to employ a teacher, counselor, or aide, when a new personnel evaluation procedure is implemented, or when a compensation plan is adopted, there are likely to be implications for the quality of instruction. The potential impact of personnel decisions on instruction should be taken into account at the time these decisions are made. Our knowledge of teaching and learning is not yet extensive enough that we can always predict with a high degree of confidence what effects such decisions will have. However, as a result of advances in research on teaching, we are able to make these decisions now with much more confidence than was possible even a few years ago.

The book rests on three assumptions. The first of these is that capable teachers are essential to achieving quality education and that such teachers will always be in short supply. The supply of teachers fluctuates, depending on a number of factors, including salaries and demographic characteristics of the college student population, but the number of "good" teachers in the teacher pool will always fall short of the demand.

The second assumption holds that effective management of human resources requires thoughtful application of learned knowledge and skills. Some people are fond of saying, "I know a good teacher (or secretary, counselor, or social worker) when I see one," implying an intuitive ability to judge teaching success that is contradicted by research on the predictive validity of teacher selection criteria. Studies show that the ability to predict success in teaching requires a good deal of knowledge and perhaps some luck. Relying on strictly intuitive judgments when the number of applicants is large will almost certainly result in mediocre selection decisions, at best.

The third assumption is that proficiency in identifying and selecting quality teachers is not sufficient to solve the problems of teacher recruitment and retention if working conditions in schools are such that able teachers are induced to leave. Identifying and employing persons with the ability to become effective teachers is only the beginning. Principals and supervisors must create conditions in schools that facilitate teachers' work and help them to achieve success.

Plan of the Chapter

Important changes are taking place in our attitudes about the management of organizations. This shift has occurred in response to the growing realization among business and political leaders that U.S. firms face intense competition from global corporations. However, this rethinking of management practices is not limited to commercial enterprises. Government and public organizations, including schools, are also adopting new methods and philosophies of administration in order to extend scarce resources and respond to criticisms of low quality and inefficient services.

This chapter provides the conceptual framework for the book. The chapter reviews the school reform efforts of recent years and shows how an emphasis on decentralized decision making and new attention to quality are changing the way schools are run. The following topics are dealt with in this chapter: (1) model of school learning, (2) educational reform, and (3) organizational effectiveness.

Model of School Learning

The model of school learning around which this book is organized is depicted in Figure 1.1. The model assumes that student learning is directly related to teachers' classroom behavior. That behavior is influenced by: (1) teachers' knowledge of effective teaching techniques, the subject they teach, and appropriate ways of moti-

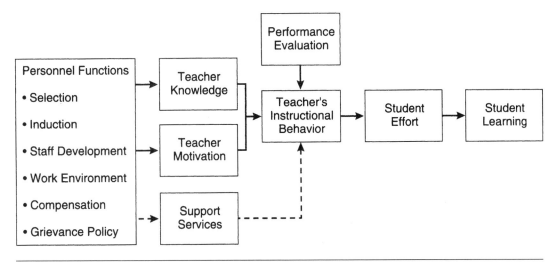

FIGURE 1.1   Relationship of Personnel Functions to Student Learning

vating students; (2) teachers' motivation to perform effectively on the job; and (3) availability of support services to enhance teachers' and students' efforts.

Human resources managers help influence the quality of instruction in schools by the functions they perform. Recruitment, selection, induction, and staff development help ensure that members of the instructional staff are qualified and knowledgeable. Other functions, including development of equitable compensation policies and a grievance resolution mechanism, help maintain teacher morale and motivation. Finally, performance evaluation provides feedback to commend effective staff members and identify areas of needed improvement for others. Personnel administrators are also responsible for staffing support services such as guidance and counseling, technology, home/school visitation, and instructional supervision. These personnel provide both direct and indirect assistance to teachers.

Thus, human resources management is an essential function for creating and maintaining the conditions necessary for effective learning to occur. However, the key to effective instruction is the teacher. As shown in Figure 1.1, teachers' instructional practices stimulate student motivation and effort, resulting in student learning. The teacher's classroom practices are influenced, in turn, by his or her motivation and knowledge of the content and by what is learned from ongoing evaluation of the teacher's performance. The availability of support services reinforces teachers' efforts by providing information about and support for students.

Educational Reform

The educational reform movement that began in the early 1980s prompted efforts to change the organization and operation of schools. The warning by the National

Commission on Excellence in Education (1983) that poor-quality schools were a threat to the nation's security prompted action by the states to attempt comprehensive school reforms. Two concepts lay at the heart of these reform strategies: decentralization and expanded participation in decision making, A reform that incorporates both ideas is school-based management.

School Decentralization

The two types of decentralization are horizontal and vertical. A school district is horizontally decentralized when authority is distributed among personnel in the district office. Assistant superintendents, supervisors, coordinators, and other specialists assume increased responsibility for specific decisions. Vertical decentralization occurs when authority is delegated downward in an organization. School-based management is an example (Brown, 1991).

The assumption behind vertical decentralization is that staff members in the schools understand students' problems and needs and are in a better position to make correct decisions about the use of resources than district staff members. Decentralization frees educators at the school site to take initiative to create effective responses to the educational needs of students (Martin, 1993). Administrators become facilitators, and other staff members' roles are expanded to include policy making and governance (Milstein, 1993).

Decentralization is not easily accomplished, and it entails costs as well as benefits. It requires district-level staff members to change the way they view their roles and it requires them to adopt a service orientation. Such a change is likely to be resisted, since many who are affected by decentralization struggled to attain their positions and are unwilling to surrender their authority and influence easily (Wissler & Ortiz, 1988).

Organizations tend to become recentralized over time, and the success of decentralization depends on maintaining mechanisms that counter the drift toward recentralization (Wissler & Ortiz, 1988). Other problems that are encountered when authority is delegated downward include teachers who prefer not to participate in school governance decisions, principals who are unwilling to share their power and become facilitators and mediators, and absence of a pool of skilled people able to establish and maintain a cooperative work environment (Milstein, 1993).

Advocates of downward decentralization argue that administrators should delegate decisions about instructional methods and procedures to teachers since "no one knows better how to do a job than the person who does it." However, that statement is only true when workers are well informed about the relative advantages and disadvantages of alternative ways of performing a job. For that reason, redesigning jobs to permit jobholders to make decisions about work methods should be accompanied by staff development programs to prepare individuals to exercise that responsibility wisely (Lawler & Mohrman, 1991).

For all of the potential problems, there is general agreement that vertical decentralization can help reduce the bureaucratic control that many feel intensifies the problems of the schools. That has led to the introduction of school-based management, an arrangement that entails delegating authority over certain decisions to teachers and administrators in the schools.

School-Based Management

Almost one-fourth of school districts responding to a nationwide survey in 1989 reported they had adopted school-based management (SBM), and an additional one-fourth were considering doing so (Prasch, 1990). A more recent National Education Association (1991) survey showed that about 30 percent of local association presidents who responded reported that the districts in which they worked had some form of SBM.

School-based management constitutes a significant departure from the bureaucratized, centralized system of school governance that emerged during the Progressive Era in the United States (Snauwaert, 1993). For the first seven decades of the twentieth century, schools and school districts were consolidated into fewer and fewer units. The number of school districts dropped from 128,000 in 1932 to 15,000 in 1990, and the number of public elementary schools fell from 233,000 in 1932 to 44,000 in 1991 (*Historical Statistics*, 1975; McDowell, 1993).

The move toward fewer and larger districts and schools was undertaken primarily for reasons of efficiency, and although the residents of many communities were unhappy to see their schools closed, they agreed to the restructuring because of promised benefits for students. Many students had to travel great distances to school after consolidation took place, but the schools they attended were larger and better equipped, the teachers were better trained, and programs were more comprehensive than those in the schools they left.

However, consolidation had disadvantages as well as advantages. It increased the influence of educational bureaucracies, encouraged lack of responsiveness, and hampered accountability. School-based management has been proposed as a remedy for the dysfunctional features of centralized school bureaucracies. It is promoted as a way of increasing flexibility, accountability, and productivity in schools (Brown, 1991). One superintendent described SBM as goal driven, needs responsive, results oriented, and teamwork/group operationalized (Prasch, 1990).

Under SBM, decisions that have traditionally been made by district office administrators are delegated to school councils or committees. Part of the appeal of SBM is the belief that it restores the essential mission of schools—instruction of students—to the center of educators' attention and it conveys a philosophy that all other activities of the district exist to support that mission (Prasch, 1990).

Features of SBM.   Among the defining features of SBM plans are site-based budgeting to allow alternative uses of resources; governance committees composed of teachers, parents, and community members; increased autonomy in choice of staffing configurations and selection of personnel; power to modify the school's curriculum to serve specific needs of students; a process for obtaining waivers of local or state regulations; and an expectation for an annual report on progress and school improvement (Cawelti, 1989). Not all plans incorporate all of these features, but a school must have some of them in order to be considered an SBM school.

Districts differ in the types of services they choose to decentralize. Some districts delegate decisions about particular parts of the budget but not about personnel or curriculum; some decentralize certain aspects of the curriculum; and others decentralize other decision areas. Other services are usually handled centrally. Purchasing is normally centralized, but teachers are encouraged to participate in decisions about the types of instructional materials and equipment to be purchased. Some experts recommend centralizing payroll, legal services, transportation, and food services (Prasch, 1990).

Site-based management frequently involves decentralization of the services provided by instructional coordinators and subject specialists. These individuals may be called on to provide help with staff development and training or to assist teachers with instructional or management problems. In some cases, schools that use these services pay a fee for them (Brown, 1991).

Advantages of SBM.   A number of advantages and disadvantages of SBM have been identified. The claimed advantages include better programs for students; full use of human resources; higher-quality decisions; increased staff professionalism, satisfaction, loyalty, and commitment; development of staff leadership skills; clear organizational goals; improved communication; support for staff creativity and innovation; greater public confidence; enhanced fiscal accountability; and higher student achievement (David, 1989; Prasch, 1990).

Benefits from site-based decision making cited by respondents to the National Education Association (1991) survey were increased involvement of employees in decisions and improved coordination of programs and activities within schools. One local president cited as a benefit the fact that all participants come to meetings as equals. Others indicated that trust among teachers, parents, and administrators had risen, lines of communication had opened, and morale had improved. "Because more people have access to the decision-making apparatus, there is more room for new initiatives and addressing problems," according to one association president (National Education Association, 1991, p. 17).

An advantage of SBM that is mentioned more often than any other is increased flexibility in use of resources. In Cincinnati, which recently adopted SBM, instructional leadership teams in 14 elementary schools decided to eliminate the position of librarian and hire an additional teacher instead. An assistant superintendent in the district noted that schools are legally required to have teachers but that decisions about hiring other support staff are made by each school (www.slj.com/article/news/19991018_6625.asp).

Disadvantages of SBM.   Disadvantages of SBM mentioned most frequently include increased workloads for teachers and administrators, less efficiency, diluted benefits of specialization, uneven school performance, greater need for staff development, possible confusion about new roles and responsibilities, and coordination difficulties (Prasch, 1990).

A common complaint about SBM is that the planning process is highly time consuming, particularly during the first year of implementation (Brown, 1991). As a result, some teachers choose not to participate. They believe that the amount of time devoted to the tasks associated with site-based decision-making projects lessens their instructional effectiveness (National Education Association, 1991; Chapman, 1990).

Principals in schools with SBM assume new relationships with staff members. With professional staff, principals discontinue the role of overseer and operate on the assumption that teachers know their jobs. Only when a teacher proves to be indifferent or incompetent does a principal intervene to provide direct supervision. In many SBM schools, principals also assume a new role with noncertified personnel, such as custodians and food service workers, who become part of the decision-making process in the school (Prasch, 1990).

In districts with school-based management, personnel decision making is altered in significant ways. Human resources staff members become facilitators, collecting and sharing information and coordinating activities of applicants and school staff members who interview them and decide whom to hire. District personnel staff members may be asked for information about legal requirements or for advice about what factors should receive most weight in selecting teachers, but they play a less active part in the final decision than is the case with more traditional forms of governance.

Organizational Effectiveness

A persistent dilemma for organizations is managing the factors that influence performance in such a way that employees are able to make progress toward attaining the organization's goals. Performance is influenced by three factors: employee knowledge and ability, employee motivation, and the environment of the workplace. When those factors are satisfactory—that is, when employees have the knowledge and ability to perform their jobs and are motivated to do their jobs well, and when the work environment facilitates employees' efforts—then superior results are likely to be achieved and the organization will be regarded as effective (Rowan, 1996). Many characteristics and outcomes have been used as indicators of organizational effectiveness, including productivity, efficiency, profit, accidents, employee absenteeism, turnover, job satisfaction, and evaluations by external entities (Campbell, 1977). Ratings of the effectiveness of schools are usually based on efficiency, equality, or quality (Glasman, 1986).

Taxpayers' organizations and political leaders demand efficiency in use of resources; civil rights groups and parents argue for equality; and parents and employers who hire the schools' graduates seek quality. Most of the time the schools are able to maintain a balance in pursuit of these outcomes, but occasionally public opinion swings so strongly in favor of one of the three that the others are in danger of being neglected.

Efficiency as a Goal

Efficiency was the dominant theme in school administration during the early years of the twentieth century, when the new profession of educational administration was charged with the task of preparing the schools to accommodate a flood of students from immigrant families. Pressed by rapidly rising enrollments and limited resources, administrators turned to the corporate world to find ways to accomplish the task they had been assigned. From industry they borrowed the spirit, if not the methods, of scientific management. Efficiency continued to be emphasized in schools until the emergence of the human relations movement helped to achieve balance in the schools during the 1930s.

Equality as a Goal

The emphasis on equality came into prominence with the U.S. Supreme Court's decision ruling that segregated schools violated the constitutional rights of minorities (*Brown* v. *Board of Education*, 1954, 1955). Interest in equality of educational opportunity broadened during the 1970s to include not only racial minorities and females but also students with mental and physical disabilities. The Education for All Handicapped Children Act mandated far-reaching changes in programs serving people with disabilities; it also required expansion of services and added safeguards to protect procedural rights of students.

Quality as a Goal

Quality of school programs is an issue that has received periodic attention from citizens and legislators, often in connection with national crises. The National Commission on Excellence in Education (1983) aroused the nation's concern when it declared that the United States was threatened by a rising tide of mediocrity as a result of the deteriorating quality of education. The Commission's report was one of many such studies that appeared about that time and that sounded similar themes.

Ironically, it was the publication of a study entitled *Equality of Educational Opportunity* (Coleman, 1966) that launched the debate on school effectiveness. The focus of the study was equality, as the title declared, but it had a good deal to say about educational quality as well. The study concluded that schools contributed relatively little to students' academic achievement and that most of students' cognitive growth could be accounted for by family background factors. These findings were disputed by critics who claimed that the research design and statistical treatment of the data magnified the impact of family factors on student achievement and diminished the schools' contributions to learning.

Process-Product Research

Process-product research was aimed at identifying teaching strategies that consistently produced increased student achievement without regard to the content being taught or the age of the students. The findings from this body of research yielded insights into which teaching practices were most effective and led to prescriptions for teaching behaviors and instructional strategies that teachers were expected to implement in their classrooms (Wideen, Mayer-Smith, & Moon, 1996).

The term *direct instruction* is the name given to the model of instruction that emerged from the process-product research. Direct instruction consists of a series of teacher-directed activities, beginning with review, followed by presentation, guided practice, feedback, and independent practice (Rosenshine & Meister, 1995).

The direct instruction model is a blueprint for effective teaching, and teachers who follow the model in their teaching on a consistent basis can be expected to increase student achievement. However, as Hamachek (1999) points out, there is a difference between *effective* teaching and *good teaching.* Whereas effective teaching is determined by whether students actually learn what they are taught, good teaching is related to teachers' classroom behavior.

A number of factors must be considered in evaluating "good" teaching. One of these is pace. *Pace* refers to how much content is covered during a lesson. Teachers tend to rely on the reactions of a small group of students, often referred to as a *steering group.* These are students whom the teacher believes should be able to grasp most of the content presented at the prevailing pace. Typically, the steering group consists of students who are average or slightly below average in ability and who are selected because their teachers believe that the pace at which they are able to learn will also accommodate most other students (Anderson & Torrey, 1995).

Other characteristics of "good" teachers are warmth and responsiveness, or behaviors that show kindness and consideration for students and peers; enthusiasm, defined as a high level of energy and an optimistic attitude; intellectual ability, including curiosity about the world combined with mastery of a wide repertoire of instructional skills; and accountability, or the acceptance of responsibility for students' behavior and the belief that all children can learn (Hamachek, 1999).

Maintaining an orderly classroom has long been accepted as another mark of "good" teaching, since orderly classrooms are essential for student learning to occur. Teachers are expected to accept responsibility for managing student behavior without having to rely excessively on administrators for help (Emmer, 1995). Although the process-product research paradigm has had a far-reaching effect on instructional practices in schools, the research is not without limitations.

Limitations of the Research

Many process-product studies have been conducted in urban elementary schools, and it is not clear whether similar results would be obtained in other types of schools. The studies involve identifying correlations between school characteristics and learning outcomes, a method that does not permit cause-effect conclusions.

Another limitation of process-product research is the narrow definition of *effectiveness* used. In most of the studies, schools identified as effective are selected on the basis of higher-than-expected achievement test scores. This is a relative definition that can lead to a situation in which a school that is considered effective may have test scores that are equal to those of a school that is not rated effective. The definition also permits instability in effectiveness, since a school may be rated effective one year and ineffective the following year (Bossert, 1988).

A third weakness of the studies is that important school outcomes are ignored. Researchers concentrate on one outcome (student achievement) while overlooking other types of goals schools seek to accomplish (Bossert, 1988). From a research standpoint, the strategy is wise, but it has the effect of limiting the usefulness of the findings. In spite of these deficiencies, however, the research on effective schooling has enlarged our knowledge of what constitutes effective schools and how to achieve improved quality in our schools.

Summary

Human resources management has a direct impact on schools' instructional effectiveness by decisions about recruitment, selection, induction, evaluation, and development of instructional staff members. The effectiveness of schools is determined by student achievement, following learning standards developed by the states, as measured by standardized tests. Process-product research led to extensive reforms in teaching practices in schools. Later, state-developed achievement standards were introduced and attention focused on ways of decentralizing decision making and involving more people at the school level in decisions that affect student learning. *School-based management* is the term used for the practice of allowing teachers, administrators, and parents to make certain decisions about allocation of human and material resources.

References _____

Anderson, L., & Torrey, P. (1995). Instructional pacing. In L. Anderson (Ed.), *International encyclopedia of teaching and teacher education* (2nd ed., pp. 212–214). Tarrytown, NY: Pergamon.

Bossert, S. (1988). School effects. In N. Boyan (Ed.), *Handbook of research on educational administration* (pp. 341–352). New York: Longman.

Brown v. *Board of Education of Topeka*, 347 U.S. 483 (1954).

Brown v. *Board of Education of Topeka*, 349 U.S. 294 (1955).

Brown, D. (1991). *Decentralization: The administrator's guidebook to school district change.* Newbury Park, CA: Sage.

Campbell, J. (1977). On the nature of organizational effectiveness. In P. Goodman & J. Pennings (Eds.), *New perspectives on organizational effectiveness* (pp. 13–55). San Francisco: Jossey-Bass.

Cawelti, G. (1989, May). Key elements of site-based management. *Educational Leadership, 46,* 46.

Chapman, J. (1990). School-based decision making and management: Implications for school personnel. In J. Chapman (Ed.), *School-based decision-making and management* (pp. 221–244). London: Falmer.

Coleman, J. (1966). *Equality of educational opportunity* (Vol. 1). Washington, DC: U.S. Government Printing Office.

David, J. (1989, May). Synthesis of research on school-based management. *Educational Leadership, 46,* 45-47, 50-53.

Emmer, T. (1995). Teacher managerial behaviors. In L. Anderson (Ed.), *International encyclopedia of teaching and teacher education* (2nd ed., pp. 219–223).Tarrytown, NY: Pergamon.

Glasman, N. (1986). *Evaluation-based leadership: School administration in contemporary perspective.* Albany: State University of New York Press.

Hamachek, D. (1999). Effective teachers: What they do, how they do it, and the importance of self-knowledge. In R. Lipka & T. Brinthaupt (Eds.), *The role of self in teacher development* (pp. 189–224). Albany: State University of New York Press.

Historical statistics of the United States. Colonial times to 1970. (1975). Washington, DC: U.S. Department of Commerce, Bureau of the Census.

Lawler, E., & Mohrman, S. (1991). High-involvement management. In R. Steers & L. Porter (Eds.), *Motivation and work behavior* (5th ed., pp. 468–477). New York: McGraw-Hill.

Martin, L. (1993). *Total quality management in human service organizations.* Newbury Park, CA: Sage.

McDowell, L. (1993). *Public elementary and secondary schools and agencies in the United States and outlying areas: School year 1991–92.* Washington, DC: U.S. Department of Education, National Center for Education Statistics.

Milstein, M. (1993). *Restructuring schools: Doing it right.* Newbury Park, CA: Corwin.

National Commission on Excellence in Education. (1983). A *nation at risk: The imperative for educational reform.* Washington, DC: U.S. Government Printing Office.

National Education Association. (1991). *Site-based decision making: The 1990 NEA census of local associations.* Washington, DC: Author.

Prasch, J. (1990). *How to organize for school-based management.* Alexandria, VA: Association for Supervision and Curriculum Development.

Rosenshine, B., & Meister, C. (1995). Direct instruction. In L. Anderson (Ed.), *International encyclopedia of teaching and teacher education* (2nd ed., pp. 143–149). Tarrytown, NY: Pergamon.

Rowan, B. (1996). Standards as incentives for instructional reform. In S. Fuhrman & J. O'Day (Eds.), *Rewards and reform: Creating educational incentives that work* (pp. 195–225). San Francisco: Jossey-Bass.

Snauwaert, D. (1993). *Democracy, education, and governance.* Albany: State University of New York Press.

Wideen, M., Mayer-Smith, J., & Moon, B. (1996). Knowledge, teacher development and change. In I. Goodson & A. Hargreaves (Eds.), *Teachers' professional lives* (pp. 187–204). London: Falmer.

Wissler, D., & Ortiz, F. (1988). *The superintendent's leadership in school reform.* New York: Falmer.

2

Planning for Staffing Needs

Planning represents an effort to anticipate and shape the future. The process of planning involves identifying a desired future state, assessing conditions and trends that may influence the organization's ability to achieve that state, and developing strategies to reach the goal. Few organizations are successful for very long without planning.

This chapter addresses several issues related to planning in schools. Evidence suggests that schools will continue to be at a competitive disadvantage vis-à-vis other employers in seeking to attract and retain well-qualified personnel (Pounder, 1987). For that reason, it is important to anticipate staff needs and to plan carefully to recruit, select, and retain employees with the qualifications to help the district achieve its goals.

Plan of the Chapter

This chapter deals with the following topics: (1) strategic planning and (2) determining staff needs.

Strategic Planning

Strategic planning is a process through which stakeholders in an organization work together to assess the internal and external environments, identify an organizational mission and goals, and develop strategies for achieving the goals. Seldom do all members of an organization agree about the group's values and priorities, and one purpose of strategic planning is to help create a consensus around critical values (Sybouts, 1992).

Strategic planning originated in industry but has been widely adopted by schools and other public service organizations (Conley, 1993). The process begins with the preparation of a mission statement, which is a declaration of a district's commitment to certain academic, social, and career outcomes for students and teachers (Sybouts, 1992). Each school's mission statement must be compatible with the district's mission. Once a mission statement has been agreed on, goals and strategies are developed to specify how the school or district proposes to achieve the vision described in the mission statement. Exhibit 2.1 shows examples of school mission statements.

A strategy known as *visioning* is used to help members develop consensus on values and goals. Employees organized into teams address five basic questions about the organization's future (Fear & Chiron, 1990):

- Where are we today?
- Where do we want to go?
- How are we going to get there?
- Who is responsible for what?
- How much will it cost and what are the benefits?

Planning is an attitude as well as an activity, and all members of the organization must be participants in order for an activity such as visioning to succeed (Hussey, 1985). In school districts, a task force made up of representatives from all levels of the workforce take the lead in planning. In schools with site-based management, the school council or parent/teacher committee has that responsibility.

Much long-range planning relies on a rational approach to preparing for the future. Planners collect data on a variety of indicators that show how well the organization is succeeding in achieving its goals and then develop strategies for improving performance where needed. Here are some examples of indicators that are used to show how well a school district and the schools within it are doing in achieving their stated goals:

- Percentage of students reading at or above grade level
- Percentage of students achieving passing scores on tests of core subjects
- Enrollment in advanced placement classes and average scores on AP exams
- Average attendance figures

EXHIBIT 2.1   *Model School Mission Statements*

It is the mission of *Northwest Public Schools* to equip students with the knowledge, skills, and attitudes they need to question constantly, communicate effectively, think logically, and act responsibly.

The mission of the *Mission Heights School District* is to provide educational opportunities that promote a desire for learning in all students and to prepare them to be responsible, productive citizens in a diverse and dynamic society.

The mission of *Lafayette School District No. 2* is to prepare young people to value learning and to be successful in their life's work through a partnership between the schools and the families they serve.

- Dropout rate by ethnic group and economic status
- Average scores on Scholastic Assessment Test (SAT) or American College Test (ACT)
- Number and percent of graduates entering college and receiving academic scholarships

If specific goals have been set for the district, it is a straightforward task to monitor the progress toward achieving them. It is the trend over time that is important, since figures for one year tell little. If a district adopts a goal that all children will read at grade level by the end of third grade, the annual data report should show steady progress toward reaching that result. If achievement trends show no change or even drop from one year to the next, that is a signal that action is needed.

Critical Issues Analysis

Strategic planning operates on two assumptions—that the future evolves from the present and that it will be different from the present (Hatten & Hatten, 1988). Planners use a process called *environmental assessment* to identify trends that are evident in the external environment that have implications for the organization's ability to accomplish its mission. One technique used to produce an environmental assessment is critical issues analysis. *Critical issues analysis* begins with planners identifying potential critical issues and submitting each one to a test. The test involves three questions (Wilkinson, 1986)*:

1. Will the issue affect the performance of the organization?
2. Will it require allocation of organizational resources?
3. Can the organization reasonably expect to control or exert significant influence on the impact the issue has on the organization's performance?

If the answer to all three questions is *yes*, then the issue is a critical one. Consider these examples of issues that might be considered by the faculty of a school engaged in developing a strategic plan:

1. The school's dropout rate has begun to rise in the past few years after a period of stable or declining figures.
2. The school's faculty has half a dozen key members, including two department heads, who will retire within three years and who must be replaced.
3. The district is considering redrawing school boundary lines; the proposed plan would shift 250 students to other schools and bring in a group of about 120 new students, for a net loss of 130 (out of 1,200)
4. Enrollment increases in middle schools will result in overflow classes in some schools in the coming school year.

*Various citations from Wilkinson (1986) on pages 14–17 are reprinted with permssion. G. Wilkinson, "Strategic Planning in the Voluntary Sector," in J. Gardner, R. Rachlin, & H. Sweeny (Eds.), *Handbook of Strategic Planning* (New York: Wiley, 1986), copyright © 1986. Reprinted by permission of John Wiley & Sons, Inc.

5. Some teachers want the school to adopt a student conduct code that would mandate specific penalties for violations of certain rules. The current code allows some discretion in enforcing rules, and some teachers think that discipline is uneven.

Wilkinson's (1986) test questions will be applied to these five problems to decide which ones qualify as critical issues.

Testing Issues

Question 1: Which issues will affect the performance of the school? Loss of key faculty members and crowding in middle schools could affect the school's performance on key indicators. Changing the school's boundary lines might also have an impact on student achievement, either positive or negative. A student conduct code might reduce disruptive behavior and help increase student achievement. Since dropout rate is an indicator of school performance, that will also have an effect on the school's standing.

Question 2: Which issues will require allocation of resources? All five issues potentially could involve allocation of resources. The proposed change in boundary lines could result in the loss of teaching positions, and reviewing applications and interviewing teachers to replace those who retire will require some staff time. Increased enrollment in middle schools may require the purchase of mobile classrooms. If a decision is made to attempt to lower the dropout rate or develop a new code of student conduct, those actions will require allocation of staff time.

Question 3: On which issues can the school expect to have an impact? On two of the topics—hiring replacements for retiring faculty and implementing a student conduct code—the school can expect to have a major impact. On redrawing boundary lines, dealing with increased enrollment, and lowering the school's dropout rate, the school's impact will be limited.

Using Wilkinson's (1986) test, two issues (loss of key faculty members and a new student conduct code) qualify as critical items because all three questions are answered in the affirmative. For one issue (proposed changes in boundary lines), two questions were answered affirmatively. These results suggest that the potential loss of faculty members from retirement and the implementation of a new student conduct code should enter into the school's planning.

Futures Wheel

To help assess the probable impact of critical issues, planners prepare a futures wheel for each critical issue. An advantage of the futures wheel is that it helps planners trace the impact of an event two, three, or even four stages beyond the immediate results.

Figure 2.1 shows an example of a futures wheel illustrating how increased enrollment will affect the school program. One immediate outcome is that space will be unavailable for some classes, including science labs and possibly art. Another likely result is that the cafeteria schedule will have to rethought *and* lunch periods extended or shortened. Overcrowding can lead to more conflict among students and can degrade the quality of the school climate. On a more positive note, because of increased enrollments the middle schools should acquire additional staff members and increased allocations for supplies and equipment.

Ranking Issues

When the futures wheel has been completed, participating planners discuss the range of opportunities and threats posed by each issue under examination and rank them on three dimensions: probability, impact, and imminence. Probability and impact are rated on 10-point scales. For *probability,* a rating of 1 indicates that the rater believes the event is highly improbable, whereas a rating of 10 reflects a judgment that it is highly probable. For *impact,* 1 indicates negligible impact, whereas 10 indicates a judgment of major structural change. For *imminence,* a 3-point scale is used, with judges rating how soon a development is predicted to occur. Rating choices are near term (up to one year), medium term (next three years), and long term (next five years) (Wilkinson, 1986).

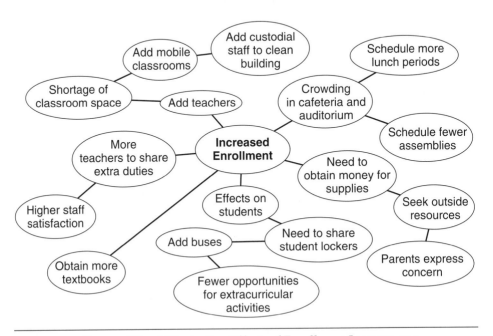

FIGURE 2.1   **Futures Wheel Illustrating Effects of Enrollment Increase on a Middle School**

Issue Brief

When the ratings have been compiled, the planners identify six to nine issues that are perceived as being most likely to occur, having the greatest impact on the organization, and being most imminent. For each of the issues selected for detailed examination and analysis, an issue brief is prepared, containing the following information (Wilkinson, 1986):

1. Title and definition of the issue
2. Identification of threats and opportunities related to the issue
3. Identification of driving influences—environmental forces that give the issue momentum and force
4. Potential outcomes of alternative scenarios
5. Impact on the organization of each of the scenarios
6. Planning challenges—a set of "need to" statements setting out the overall actions required of the organization to maximize opportunities or minimize threats

An example of an issue brief for the problem of increasing enrollments appears in Exhibit 2.2.

Exhibit 2.2   *Sample Issue Brief*

 I. Title
 Increasing enrollment in middle school

 II. Challenges and opportunities
 Challenge: Increased enrollment causes further crowding of facilities, creating a shortage of classroom, laboratory, cafeteria, and locker space. Increased enrollment creates additional work for custodians and other staff members. Increased enrollment makes it less likely that students will be selected to play on athletic teams. Increased enrollment will likely precipitate student conflict.
 Opportunity: Additional teachers and staff members will be allocated to the school. Money budgeted for instructional supplies will increase, and student fees will increase.

 III. Driving forces
 Population growth

 IV. Prospects
 Worst case: Space limitations will force cutbacks in instructional programs, resulting in loss of learning. Increased crowding will cause a deterioration in the quality of school climate.
 Best case: The crowding problem will be solved by redrawing school zones. Space will be adequate to maintain a high-quality instructional program. The quality of school climate will remain high.

Internal Organizational Assessment

An internal assessment describes the internal environment of an organization. An internal assessment for a school includes major strengths and weaknesses, the nature of the student body, school climate, financial restraints or resources, staff resources or limitations, facilities, equipment, internal politics, and school policies (Sybouts, 1992).

A variety of information about students appears in an internal assessment, including the number of students by gender, age, and socioeconomic levels. The assessment also notes trends related to grade-point average (GPA), honors, test scores, behavior, attendance, dropout statistics, rate of college attendance, and participation in school programs (Mauriel, 1989; Sybouts, 1992).

An internal assessment also contains information about the number of teachers, their level, and the quality of their training, experience, and competence; working relationships among teachers; type, quality, history, and reputation of the school's or district's programs; and the number and types of buildings, equipment, playgrounds, and stadiums (Mauriel, 1989).

The internal assessment also includes information about programs offered by the school or district, including test scores, enrollments in elective courses, course evaluation data from student and parent surveys, and awards received by students participating in debates, tournaments, and contests. Another measure of program quality is the percentage of graduates who are admitted to selective colleges and college attendance and completion rates (Mauriel, 1989).

It is advisable to select a few goals and to focus efforts on achieving those rather than try to accomplish a large number of objectives (American Association of School Administrators, 1983). When a goal is agreed on, it should be tested for consistency with the mission statement, and one or more strategies for achieving the goal should be identified (Sybouts, 1992). Two examples of human resource goals for a school are shown here with accompanying strategies.

Goal No. 1:   Develop and implement a plan for teacher evaluation that enables teachers to grow professionally and increase their effectiveness and maintain high job satisfaction.

Strategy: Appoint a committee to review criteria for evaluating teaching effectiveness now used by other schools and to present recommendations to the school council for proposed criteria to be used in this school.

Strategy: Appoint a committee to identify sources of information for evaluating teaching effectiveness using the criteria previously approved and to develop and test procedures for collecting the information. The committee's findings will be presented to the school council for approval.

Goal No. 2:   Implement a policy to permit teachers to develop individual professional development plans.

Strategy: Solicit opinions from teachers regarding the feasibility of individual professional development plans and their suggestions for operation of the program.

Strategy: Select volunteers to contact schools that have such plans in operation in order to obtain information about them and identify problems encountered in implementing the plans.

Strategy: Appoint a committee of teachers to review information obtained from teachers and from other schools and to make general recommendations for a policy.

Using results from the internal and external assessments, planners prepare a strategic plan for the district that contains both short-term (1 to 3 years) and long-term (4 to 10 years) goals. Key outcomes that should be addressed in the plan are (Lewis, 1983):

1. Instructional programs and services
2. Student learning and growth
3. Human resources
4. Financial resources
5. Physical resources
6. Community involvement and relations
7. Organizational management
8. Performance evaluation and training

Determining Staff Needs

A common form of planning in schools is to prepare enrollment projections that enable administrators to anticipate future enrollments and recruit and hire teachers and other personnel needed to staff the schools. Achieving a high degree of accuracy in enrollment projections is important. Underestimating enrollments may mean that class sizes will have to be increased, whereas overestimating results in more teachers hired than are needed. Accurately estimating enrollment requires a good bit of skill as well as luck. The more long range the prediction, the greater the possibility for error.

The U.S. Department of Education projects total school enrollments of 34.4 million students in 2003, rising to 35.0 million in 2005, and dropping slightly to about 34.8 million in 2009 (National Center for Education Statistics, 2000). National projections of school enrollments are useful for deciding on federal education policy, but they are not very helpful in making hiring decisions at the local level. Enrollment trends vary widely across the country, and one locality may be gaining students while another is losing enrollment. Local school administrators must anticipate these swings and take them into account in planning for personnel needs.

Colleges and universities graduate more teachers than are actually needed to staff the schools, but only about 6 out of 10 college graduates who prepare to teach actually take jobs in the field. Of those who do enter teaching, between one-third and one-half leave the profession in the first five years to pursue other careers or raise a family (National Governors Association, 1999).

Data from the School and Staffing Study (Ingersoll, 1996) indicated that the greatest teacher shortages in recent years were in math, science, and special education. Some 21 percent of secondary schools reported having difficulty hiring special education teachers, 18 percent of the schools experienced shortfalls in the number of math teachers, and 15 percent of the schools found physical science teachers in short supply. Other subjects in which teacher shortages were reported included life science, English, and English as a Second Language (ESL).

Because of the difficulty in finding qualified applicants, states and districts have devised innovative ways of recruiting qualified applicants. Massachusetts offers $20,000 signing bonuses paid over four years to teachers who meet certain criteria (National Governors Association, 1999). The South Carolina Teaching Fellows Program was created by the General Assembly of that state in 1999. It provides fellowships for up to 200 high-achieving high school seniors who receive $6,000 per year for up to four years in return for agreeing to teach in the state for a comparable length of time (South Carolina Center for Teacher Recruitment, 2000). The Department of Defense works with school districts in a collaborative "Troops to Teachers" program that provides financial assistance to former military workers and school districts to help prepare defense workers for careers in education (Taylor, 1994).

Long-term predictions on school enrollments in the United States made in the early 1960s proved to be far from accurate because those who made them used assumptions that turned out to be faulty. Planners assumed that the birthrate would continue unchanged for the foreseeable future. They failed to anticipate the advancements in birth control that made family planning easier and more practical. As a result, the birthrate dropped and so did school enrollments. Enrollment projections are only as accurate as the assumptions on which they are based.

Cohort Survival Method

The method that is used most often to predict future enrollments is called the *cohort survival method.* The word *cohort* originally referred to a division of soldiers in the Roman army. It has since come to mean any group of people who begin a venture together. People who were born in the same year or who were initiated into a college fraternity at the same time are examples of cohorts. For purposes of predicting school enrollments, we consider a cohort to be any group of students who start school together. A cohort may lose members when individuals move away or drop out of school, or gain members when students transfer into a school.

The cohort survival method is based on the assumption that the future will be like the past. For the short term, that is usually a safe assumption. Drastic changes in population do not normally occur within the space of a year or two, nor do people's habits change quickly. However, in school districts near military bases or in communities with industries that are sensitive to economic fluctuations, relatively large variations in enrollment can occur with no advance warning.

The cohort survival method is most accurate in districts in which school enrollments are relatively stable or in which enrollment trends are consistent. The method is less accurate in predicting enrollments for districts with fluctuating enrollments (Alspaugh, 1981). The accuracy of any prediction diminishes as the distance from the predicted event increases. Predicting enrollments one year in advance is more accurate than predicting enrollments 5 or 10 years ahead. There are two reasons for loss of accuracy over time. Unforeseen events can affect school enrollments, and errors in predicting near-term enrollments compound over time, creating ever-larger distortions.

Persons who calculate enrollment projections for school districts try to limit error to less than 1 percent of actual enrollments. A 1 percent error rate means that for a projection of 1,000 students, the actual enrollment will fall between 990 and 1,010, and that for a projection of 10,000 students, the actual enrollment will fall between 9,900 and 10,100. For small errors, districts are usually able to accommodate the difference by increasing (or decreasing) class sizes slightly or hiring an additional teacher or two. However, larger errors have more significant repercussions.

If enrollments exceed the projection by just 100 students, a district may have to employ several additional teachers and locate space for that many more classes. If projections call for more students than actually enroll, the district may be responsible for paying salaries for some teachers who are not needed.

Most districts that use cohort survival analysis prepare separate projections for each school and then combine them to obtain a district total. Since most districts now maintain automated enrollment data, it is fairly simple to carry out the necessary calculations at the district office. The results are usually reviewed by principals, who are sometimes aware of impending events, such as a plant closing or construction of a new subdivision, that will affect their schools' enrollments. With this information, adjustments are made and the final predictions prepared. Projecting an accurate district total is somewhat easier than predicting correct enrollments for individual schools since district enrollments are generally more stable.

Projecting First-Grade Enrollment

In preparing enrollment projections for kindergarten, data on the number of births 5 years earlier are used. In the example shown in Table 2.1, projections over a 5-year period in a district with increasing enrollments are averaged to obtain the mean enrollment ratio. In actual practice, enrollment figures for 10 years or even more are used in the calculations. Using more years produces more reliable estimates (Schellenberg & Stephens, 1987).

Retention Ratios

To project enrollments for grades 2 through 12, a retention ratio is calculated by dividing each year's enrollment at a given grade level by the previous year's enrollment at the next lower grade level. This procedure is repeated for each of five years prior to the current year. A mean retention ratio is obtained, and the mean is mul-

TABLE 2.1 *Developing Kindergarten Enrollment Projections for a District with Increasing Enrollments*

1 Birth Year	2 Live Births	3 Starting Year	4 Enrollment	5 Enrollment Ratio
1991	2073	1996	2019	.9740
1992	2097	1997	2044	.9747
1993	2105	1998	2069	.9829
1994	2118	1999	2093	.9882
1995	2121	2000	2136	1.0071
1996	2206	2001		

Step 1: Divide the enrollment (col. 4) by the number of live births five years earlier (col. 2) to obtain the enrollment ratio (col. 5). The enrollment ratio for 1997 is 2044/2097 = .9747. A ratio greater than 1.00 means that the number of kindergarten students exceeded the number of births five years earlier.

Step 2: Add the enrollment ratios and divide by 5 (.9740 + .9747 + .9829 + .9882 + 1.0071 = 4.9269; 4.9269/5 = .9854). This is the mean enrollment ratio.

Step 3: Multiply the number of live births five years earlier by the mean enrollment ratio to obtain the projected enrollment for the 2001 school year (.9854 ↔ 2206 = 2174).

tiplied by the current year's enrollment in the next lower grade level to obtain the enrollment projection for the upcoming year. This procedure is illustrated in Table 2.2, using hypothetical data to project enrollments in grade 7 for a district with decreasing enrollments. When projected enrollments are obtained for all grades, they are added to the kindergarten projections to obtain the projected districtwide total enrollment.

When enrollment trends are evident, allowance should be made by adjusting the projection either up or down. If the enrollment ratio has increased each year for the previous five years, there is a good chance that it will continue to increase (although perhaps at a declining rate), and using the average for the previous five years will underestimate the enrollment. On the other hand, if the trend shows a decline over a five-year period, the enrollment ratio is likely to overestimate enrollments. Depending on the direction and magnitude of the trend, an adjustment of the final enrollment figure may be needed.

Most administrators prefer to underestimate rather than to overestimate enrollments because the potential cost to the district is smaller in the case of underestimates. Enrollments that exceed projections slightly can often be accommodated by increasing class sizes, but once a teacher has been hired there is no way that the money for his or her salary and benefits can be recaptured (unless a contingency clause has been included in the contract).

TABLE 2.2 *Developing Seventh-Grade Enrollment Projections for a District with Decreasing Enrollments*

1	2	3	4	5
	6th-Grade		7th-Grade	Retention
Year	Enrollment	Year	Enrollment	Ratio
1995	2964	1996	2847	.9605
1996	2496	1997	2391	.9579
1997	2473	1998	2378	.9616
1998	2280	1999	2132	.9351
1999	2144	2000	2117	.9874
2000	2057	2001		

Step 1: Divide the seventh-grade enrollment by the previous year's sixth-grade enrollment to obtain the retention ratio (col. 5) for a given year. The retention ratio for 1996 is 2847/2964=.9605.

Step 2: Find the sum of the five retention ratios and divide by 5 (.9605 + .9579 + .9616 + .9351 + .9874 = 4.8025; 4.8025/5 = .9605). This is the mean retention ratio.

Step 3: Multiply the number of students enrolled in grade 6 in 2000–2001 by the mean retention ratio to obtain the projected number of seventh-grade students for 2001 (2057 ↔ .9605 = 1976).

A sizable one-time increase or decrease in the retention ratio affects the mean ratio and may bias enrollment estimates. For example, in Table 2.2 the ratio for 1999 (.9351) is lower than the other figures and is probably an aberration. When it is used to calculate the mean retention ratio, the obtained figure will be likely to underestimate actual enrollments. When this happens, an adjustment can be made to correct the estimate.

Determining Staff Allocations

School systems rely on enrollment projections to determine how staff resources will be allocated. Teachers, aides, counselors, librarians, and assistant principals are assigned on the basis of the number of students expected to enroll in each school. If the enrollment projections indicate that a school will have an increase in enrollment, a decision must be made whether additional staff are needed and, if so, in which positions or grade levels. Schools that lose students may have to give up positions.

Information about resignations and retirements are taken into account, and a determination is made on the number of employees who must be employed, transferred, or laid off. If additional staff members are needed, action is taken to initiate interviews with qualified applicants.

In recent years, school districts have begun to look at other factors in addition to enrollment in deciding how to allocate personnel. One plan is to award points to a school based on the types of students with particular needs. Schools might receive 1 point per student, with additional points for each child on free lunch, each child with a disability, or each child who is gifted. Some districts grant additional faculty resources for schools with high mobility.

Staffing arrangements in site-managed schools are generally determined by the principal and teachers of the school, who have the option of reconfiguring staff to better meet the needs of the students. The faculty in a school might decide, for example, to hire fewer teachers and more aides or to do without an assistant principal in order to gain an additional teacher or several aides. Such a system provides a way to allocate staff that is equitable, and it lets each building control the configuration of staff to meet its needs.

Summary

Planning is an effort to anticipate and prepare for the future by mobilizing an organization's resources to attain a desirable future state. In strategic planning, a school identifies its goals and resources and develops strategies for attaining them. Strategic planners carry out a critical issues analysis by identifying forces that are expected to affect the school's operation, require allocation of resources, or that can be influenced by the school. Following analysis and discussion, selected issues are chosen for further study and a brief is prepared for each issue.

One of the important tasks in human resources planning is projecting staff needs. This involves projecting enrollments and determining the number of personnel needed to staff the schools. Procedures are set in motion to recruit and select additional staff or, if enrollments are dropping, to reduce staff size.

The cohort survival method is the most widely used technique for projecting enrollments. This method is most accurate when school enrollments are stable or trends are consistent; it is least accurate when enrollments fluctuate.

Suggested Activities

1. Interview a school administrator to find out in which fields the supply of teachers falls short of demand. Investigate to learn what programs are in place or are being planned to ease the shortage.

2. A scan of the external environment assesses such factors as demographics, cultural climate, family structure, and the influence of other institutions and agencies. Choose a school that you are familiar with and write a paragraph describing the changes you anticipate in the external environment of that school during the next five years.

3. In preparing an internal organizational assessment for a school, strategic planners consider student achievement data, program offerings, enrollment projections, de-

mographic characteristics, dropout rate, staffing, teachers' experience and educational background, and facilities and equipment. Select one of these factors and write a paragraph or two describing that feature for a school with which you are familiar.

4. Prepare a futures wheel showing the effects of the adoption of a new student conduct code with specified penalties for violation of school rules.

5. Prepare an issues brief for the topic of adopting a new code of student conduct.

Online Resources

The following websites are resources for districts seeking teachers and contain recommendations for actions that districts can take to increase their applicant pool.

National Commission on Mathematics and Science Teaching for the 21st Century (www.ed.gov/americacounts/glenn)
> This site, which contains the report of a citizen's panel headed by former Senator John Glenn, recommends ways of increasing the nation's supply of teachers of mathematics and science. Among other ideas, the panel recommended summer institutes, more financial aid, and better pay for teachers.

National Teacher Recruiting Clearinghouse (www.recruitingteachers.org)
> The Clearinghouse brings individuals seeking teaching jobs and districts attempting to locate qualified applicants together. It provides links to departments of education and advice to districts on websites for recruiting and retaining teachers.

Teach for America (www.tfanetwork.org/tfa2/join_our_corps/home.asp)
> Teach for America is a corps of recent college graduates with academic majors who commit two years to teach in underresourced urban and rural public schools.

Teacher Advancement Program (www.mff.org/tap/tap.taf)
> The Teacher Advancement Program, sponsored by the Milken Family Foundation, employs a comprehensive and systemic strategy for addressing recruitment, training, induction, professional development, compensation, performance evaluation, and career advancement.

References

Alspaugh, J. (1981, Summer). Accuracy of school enrollment projections based upon previous enrollments. *Educational Research Quarterly, 6,* 61–67.

American Association of School Administrators. (1983). *Planning for tomorrow's schools.* Arlington, VA: Author.

Conley, D. (1993, April). *Strategic planning in practice: An analysis of purposes, goals, and procedures.* Paper presented at the annual meeting of the American Educational Research Association, Atlanta. (ERIC Document Reproduction Service No. ED 358530).

Fear, R., & Chiron, R. (1990). *The evaluation interview* (4th ed.). New York: McGraw-Hill.

Hatten, K., & Hatten, M. (1988). *Effective strategic management: Analysis and action.* Englewood Cliffs, NJ: Prentice Hall.

Hussey, D. (1985). *Introducing corporate planning.* Oxford: Pergamon Press.

Ingersoll, R. (1996). *Teacher supply and demand in the U.S.* Paper presented at the annual meeting of the American Statistical Association, Orlando, FL. (ERIC Document Reproduction Service No. ED 415229).

Lewis, J., Jr. (1983). *Long-range and short-range planning for educational administrators.* Boston: Allyn and Bacon.

Mauriel, J. (1989). *Strategic leadership for schools.* San Francisco: Jossey-Bass.

National Center for Education Statistics. (2000). *Digest of education statistics, 1999.* Washington, DC: U.S. Department of Education.

National Governors Association (1999). *Teacher supply and demand: Is there a shortage?* [On-line.] Available: www.na.org/pubs/issueBriefs/2000/000125Teachers.asp.

Pounder, D. (1987). The challenge for school leaders: Attracting and retaining good teachers. In W. Greenfield (Ed.), *Instructional leadership: Concepts, issues, and controversies* (pp. 287–301). Boston: Allyn and Bacon.

Schellenberg, S., & Stephens, C. (1987). *Enrollment projection: Variations on a theme.* Paper presented at the annual meeting of the American Educational Research Association, Washington, DC.

South Carolina Center for Teacher Recruitment. (2000). [On-line.] Available: www.scctr.org.

Sybouts, W. (1992). *Planning in school administration: A handbook.* New York: Greenwood.

Taylor, T. (1994). *Troops to teachers. Guidelines for teacher educators.* (ERIC Document Reproduction Service No. ED 366591).

Wilkinson, G. (1986). Strategic planning in the voluntary sector. In J. Gardner, R. Rachlin, & H. Sweeny (Eds.), *Handbook of strategic planning* (25.1–25.23). New York: Wiley.

3

Preparing for Personnel Selection

Selecting school personnel involves matching applicants' qualifications to selection criteria. To the extent that a good match is achieved, employees will be successful in their work. However, when an applicant is placed in a position that does not fit his or her qualifications, the individual will experience frustration and will not do high-quality work.

Plan of the Chapter

This chapter presents a model of the selection process and explains how selection criteria are developed and applied to identify qualified applicants for vacant positions. Chapter 4 examines how information about applicants is obtained and evaluated. The following topics will be discussed in this chapter: (1) a model of the selection process, (2) identifying selection criteria, (3) job-specific selection criteria for teaching, (4) selecting personnel for other positions, and (5) recruiting candidates.

A Model of the Selection Process

The selection process has four objectives: (1) to ensure that individuals selected to work for an organization possess the knowledge, skills, and abilities to perform their jobs effectively; (2) to help individuals make informed decisions about whether to accept an offer of employment; (3) to create a sense of commitment to the organization on the part of new employees; and (4) to commit the organization to provide the support necessary for newly hired employees to succeed. A sound selection process results in hiring employees who possess the knowledge, skills, and abilities needed in the job for which they are hired and who are committed to the organization (Lawler, 1992).

To achieve the first objective, the employer identifies criteria related to successful performance on a job. Job-specific criteria are the knowledge, skills, and abilities that are integral to success in a specific position. Nonjob-specific criteria are characteristics that contribute to success in many different jobs. Knowledge of and ability to apply the principles of physical conditioning are examples of job-specific criteria for an athletic coach, just as ability to use a power saw is a job-specific criterion for a carpenter.

Nonjob-specific criteria are attributes that contribute to successful performance in many jobs. Examples of nonjob-specific criteria are the ability to express ideas clearly, regular attendance on the job, avoidance of alcohol and drug abuse, a positive attitude toward the job, and willingness to work cooperatively with other employees.

By assessing indicators of the selection criteria, an employer rates applicants for the position and hires the person whose qualifications best match the selection criteria. An example of an indicator of knowledge of the principles of physical conditioning is successful completion of a course on that topic, and an indicator of skill in word processing is the ability to type a document using a specified word-processing program with acceptable speed and with few errors.

Figure 3.1 graphically depicts the selection process. Individuals applying for a teaching job must meet certain basic criteria before their individual qualifications are considered. All states require that applicants be certified to teach before they are

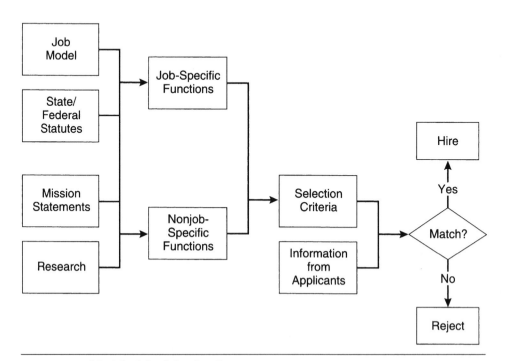

FIGURE 3.1   Model of the Selection Process

hired, but when teachers are in short supply, states may issue temporary or emergency certificates to help districts fill vacancies. Most school districts now require that applicants hold a major or minor in their teaching field, and some require that successful applicants must have taken and passed one or more tests covering knowledge of basic skills, knowledge of the teaching field, and familiarity with effective teaching practices.

The Americans with Disabilities Act (ADA) has brought about changes in the selection process by introducing the concept of *essential functions.* These are tasks that are fundamental to a particular job and that an employee must be able to perform in order to be considered qualified for the position.

Selection decisions have traditionally hinged on considerations of worth—that is, an individual's ability to make a contribution that is valued by the employer. If several candidates for a position were equally qualified, the candidate who was able to meet other needs of the employer, in addition to those required in the job for which he or she was applying, was hired (Scriven, 1990).

For example, an applicant for a teaching position who had experience in coaching tennis or field hockey might be chosen over an equally qualified applicant who lacked coaching experience, even though coaching was not required in the position. Under ADA, an employer who rejects an applicant with a disability who is able to perform the essential functions of a position, with or without accommodation, and hires an applicant who is not disabled, on the basis that the person hired can perform certain peripheral functions, violates the law (Jacobs, 1993). Thus, the legislation forces employers to concentrate in selection of employees on job-specific criteria.

The identification of essential functions is achieved by analyzing information from the same sources that are used to identify selection criteria (job model, state and federal statutes, mission statement, and findings of related research; see Figure 3.1). The job model specifies the results that a jobholder is expected to accomplish and describes conditions under which the work takes place. State statutes spell out mandatory preparation and licensing requirements for personnel, and research identifies school characteristics and teacher attitudes and behaviors associated with increased student learning.

Determining whether a particular task is an essential function of a job involves consideration of three factors: the tasks that the position exists to perform, the number of employees available to perform a task, and whether a person hired for the position is chosen for his or her ability to perform the task (Fersh & Thomas, 1993). Consider a high school counselor whose primary duties include counseling students and providing information to help students choose a college or make vocational plans. On three or four occasions each year, the counselor visits nearby middle schools to counsel middle school students on the transition to high school. One applicant for the position is confined to a wheelchair and is unable, without help, to travel to other schools.

Can the district reject the applicant who has a disability in favor of someone who is physically able to travel? The answer probably depends on whether visiting middle schools is considered an essential function of the job. Since little of the counselor's time is devoted to that task and the counselor is not chosen primarily on the basis of his or her ability to do it, it is unlikely that these visits would be considered an essential function. Moreover, since it is possible to make an accommodation by assigning some other employee to visit the middle schools or by providing assistance for the counselor to make the trip, no rational basis exists for rejecting the applicant who has a disability.

Job-specific criteria are given more weight in the selection process under ADA than was true before that law was enacted. However, nonspecific criteria are still part of the picture, since some attributes are important to success in any undertaking. Employees who are regular in attendance, who are cooperative with other workers and with supervisors, and who are able to do their jobs without close supervision are usually successful in whatever tasks they undertake. Employers need to exercise care, however, to avoid using nonjob-specific criteria that are peripheral to successful performance.

Identifying Selection Criteria

The primary source of information about the selection criteria for a position is a job description or job model. A *job description* identifies the position and describes the duties and responsibilities associated with it. The description usually gives some information about the school and the district in which the vacancy occurs. It includes a list of qualifications required in the position, and it may describe resources available to the incumbent.

Rochester (New York) schools use a generic job description for teaching positions (Haller, 1987). The description identifies the job goal as helping students "to learn subject matter and/or skills that will contribute to their development as mature, able, and responsible men and women" (p. 184).

Among the performance responsibilities for teachers identified in the Rochester job description are the following: planning programs that meet individual needs, interests, and abilities of students; creating an environment that is conducive to learning; guiding the learning process toward achievement of curriculum goals; establishing clear objectives and communicating those objectives to students; employing appropriate instructional methods and materials; evaluating students and providing progress reports as required; diagnosing learning abilities and disabilities of students on a regular basis; working cooperatively with staff, superiors, and community; assisting in implementing the school's rules of behavior; maintaining order in a fair and just manner; maintaining and improving professional competence; and attending meetings and serving on committees as appropriate.

The Rochester document is based on the assumption that all teaching jobs in a district are alike. In fact, teaching positions vary, depending on the subject and grade level taught and the school environment. Teaching a fifth-grade class in an elementary school with a multiethnic student population is a different experience, and requires different skills, than teaching English in a college preparatory high school. The results that are expected and the resources that are available to assist teachers in the two situations differ. Position descriptions that are specific to a particular school or job can help to target the selection process and increase the probability of making successful staffing decisions.

Writing a Job Model

An alternative to the traditional job description has been developed by Dailey (1982). The job model is an improvement over position descriptions because it focuses on results and makes it possible to focus the selection process on choosing an employee who can achieve those outcomes.

The job model presents a realistic picture of the job, including both its attractive and unattractive features. If a position is located in a school in an old building with out-of-date equipment and few supplies, the job model states those facts. If parents are cooperative and supportive of teachers, that too is reported. An effort is made to avoid presenting only the positive features of a position, since once a teacher is hired he or she soon becomes aware of the less attractive features of the situation and must be able to produce results in spite of them. Employees who are informed in advance of both the negative and positive features of a new position more often experience feelings of satisfaction than those who are told only the good news about the job (Wanous, 1980).

An example of a job model for the position of high school Spanish teacher is shown in Exhibit 3.1. The job model consists of three parts. The section entitled "Results Sought" describes the outcomes the Spanish teacher is expected to accomplish. This section is the heart of the job model because it helps to focus the search on the important task of identifying a candidate who can achieve those results. "Job Environment" describes characteristics of the school and community that are likely either to facilitate or hinder performance. Interviewers use the information in this section to investigate applicants' ability and willingness to overcome barriers and to use resources effectively to achieve specified results. Applicants use the information to weigh their feelings of adequacy to face the challenge presented by the position.

The "Priority Actions" section of the job model describes tasks that must be performed on the job. These may be actions that lead directly or indirectly to accomplishment of the results described under "Results Sought," or they may be actions that help other persons in the school accomplish the results for which they are responsible. Examples of priority actions that might be required of a teacher are covering required curriculum content and assessing and reporting to parents on students' academic progress.

The first step in constructing a job model involves identifying the results sought. Schools are organizations with multiple and ambiguous goals. It is not easy in such organizations to reach consensus on results sought. The recommended procedure is to ask four or five persons who are familiar with the job to complete the following statement: "A person in this job is effective if he or she produces the result that . . . " (Dailey, 1982). Each contributor writes eight endings for the sentence and ranks these eight outcomes from most important (rank 1) to least important (rank 8).

To help in writing these statements, Dailey (1982) has offered this advice: "A 'result' should be a very *tangible* effect of work *useful to someone else* and contribut-

EXHIBIT 3.1   *Job Model: High School Spanish Teacher (Levels 1 and 2)*

Results Sought

1. Students listening to a speaker describing familiar activities in Spanish are able to answer questions about the main ideas of the presentation in Spanish (level 1) and about details of the presentation in Spanish (level 2).
2. Students carry on a brief conversation with a Spanish-speaking person discussing daily events at home or school using limited vocabulary (level 1) or more extensive vocabulary (level 2).
3. Students write a brief (one-page) essay using regular verbs, present tense only (level 1) or both regular and irregular verbs, present and past tenses (level 2) on a familiar topic, when provided a stimulus in Spanish.
4. In English (level 1) or in Spanish (level 2) students present oral reports on elements of Hispanic culture, including religion, dress, history, and literature.
5. Students who complete one level are prepared to succeed at the next higher level.
6. Parents are familiar with their children's progress in Spanish and afford themselves of the opportunity for conferences with the teacher as needed.

Job Environment

The job is located in a high school in a rural/suburban area near a city of approximately 125,000 people. The school enrolls 1,200 students from low- and middle-income families; about one-fifth of the students are Black, Hispanic, or Asian. About 60 percent of the school's graduates attend college. Three foreign languages (French, German, and Spanish) are offered by the school. Level-1 classes typically have 25 to 30 students, and level-2 classes usually have between 20 and 25. Instructional materials that are integrated with the textbook, including audio- and videotapes and transparencies, are available for teachers' use.

Priority Actions

The successful Spanish teacher must speak and write Spanish fluently and must be able to motivate students from diverse backgrounds to apply themselves to the study of the language. The teacher must plan and present instruction that will enable students to attain facility in speaking and writing Spanish and must be able to diagnose students' deficiencies and provide appropriate instructional remedies. The teacher must be available to meet with students who request additional help and to confer with parents concerning their children's performance. The teacher must be able to work with teachers from other schools to develop the curriculum and select instructional materials.

---

ing to the organization's reason for existing." Some educators focus on instructional strategies rather than results or outcomes of instruction. Statements such as "allow for individual differences" and "plan stimulating activities" describe actions, not results. Although these actions may lead to desirable outcomes, they are not tangible effects of work that are useful to others. Action statements belong under "Priority Actions."

The 6 to 10 statements that appear most often on contributors' lists are compiled under the "Results Sought" heading of the job model. Exhibit 3.2 shows examples of actions and corresponding results for several positions. Note that the

EXHIBIT 3.2   *Examples of Actions and Results Sought*

Action	Results
Assistant principal manages textbook ordering, inventory, and storage	Textbooks are available in sufficient quantities when needed
Child care provider encourages children to take part in group activities	Children interact comfortably with peers in group activities
Football coach coordinates activities of assistant coaches	Assistant coaches understand their own and others' duties and work together effectively
English teacher covers material in the approved curriculum	Students demonstrate mastery of material in the approved curriculum

results described in Column 2 of the exhibit are tangible effects that are useful to someone else. Textbooks are available for students' use, children play together in groups, assistant coaches work together, and so on. The actions described in Column 1 contribute to attaining those results, but they do not appear in the "Results Sought" section of the job model.

To prepare a description of the job environment, several individuals who are familiar with the position are asked to list forces that facilitate or hinder performance. The three most important facilitating forces are ranked +1 to +3, and the three most important hindering forces are ranked –1 to –3. These lists are then combined into a narrative statement under the heading "Job Environment." The description of the job environment should be a straightforward report of the factors that new employees will encounter in the position, including both positive and negative features.

Finally, a description of job demands is prepared by asking four or five persons who are familiar with the position to answer the questions that appear in Exhibit 3.3. When the results of this exercise are compiled, that information is written in narrative form and included in the section entitled "Priority Actions." The information generated by these three exercises is combined into a job model. Ideally, a separate job model is prepared for each vacancy, but that is not always practical. In those cases generic job models may be written for groups of positions (early childhood, special education/mentally retarded, high school physical education, and so on).

Job-Specific Selection Criteria for Teachers

Teachers are hired to help students learn. They are expected to perform other duties as well, including maintaining records of students' attendance and academic accomplishments, serving on curriculum committees, and carrying out various

EXHIBIT 3.3   *Questions to Help in Writing Job Demands*

---

1. How important is it that the person in this position be able to perform the following activities?
   a. Make presentations to parent or community groups
   b. Prepare detailed lesson plans
   c. Meet with parents to discuss students' progress
   d. Lead a discussion about various aspects of the school's programs
   e. Lead a team of other professionals in planning and carrying out an assigned task
   f. Develop solutions to unique problems and obtain support to implement them
   g. Deal with children who are rowdy and disorderly
   h. Plan instruction for children who are mentally or physically disabled
   i. Maintain accurate records of money, supplies, or student work
   j. Arrange public displays or performances of students' artistic work
   k. Develop and present instructional demonstrations
   l. Collect money or raise funds for special projects
   m. Monitor the school cafeteria, hallways, and parking lots
   n. Maintain a high degree of student involvement in academic tasks
   o. Conduct committee meetings to assess progress of students in special placements
   p. Arrange placements for students in community commercial businesses and government agencies
   q. Assist students in acquiring job information
2. How important is it that the person who fills this job have motivation of the type described in each statement?
   a. Wants to produce a stable level of performance and be satisfied to work within routines
   b. Desires goodwill and affection from people and cares a great deal about having close relationships
   c. Wants to acquire and use influence and to exercise leadership
   d. Wants to set objectives in order to measure progress toward a better way of doing things
   e. Wants to acquire new or more intense experiences or to try new activities and ventures

---

Items listed under question 2 are from *Using the Track Record Approach: The Key to Successful Personnel Selection* by C. A. Dailey, 1982, AMACOM, New York.

managerial responsibilities. All of these are job-specific criteria, but none is more important than helping students to acquire knowledge, skill, and attitudes of respect for self and others.

The Interstate New Teacher Assessment and Support Consortium (INTASC), a collaborative effort involving the Council of Chief State School Officers and other groups, has developed a set of principles for beginning teachers that constitute useful criteria for teacher selection. These INTASC principles are based on research on teacher effectiveness and relate to the core task of teaching—presenting instruction that results in student learning—while ignoring other less central aspects of the teacher's role. Exhibit 3.4 shows the 10 INTASC principles.

EXHIBIT 3.4   *INTASC Principles for Beginning Teachers*

Principle 1: Teacher understands the central concepts, tools of inquiry, and structures of the disciplines and creates learning experiences that make subject matter meaningful for students.

Principle 2: Teacher understands how children learn and develop and provides learning opportunities to support their intellectual, social, and personal development.

Principle 3: Teacher understands how students differ in their approaches to learning and creates instructional opportunities that are adapted to diverse learners.

Principle 4: Teacher understands and uses a variety of instructional strategies to encourage students' development of critical thinking, problem solving, and performance skills.

Principle 5: Teacher uses individual and group motivation and behavior to create a learning environment that encourages positive social interaction, active engagement in learning, and self-motivation.

Principle 6: Teacher uses knowledge of effective verbal, nonverbal, and media communication techniques to foster active inquiry, collaboration, and supportive interaction in the classroom.

Principle 7: Teacher plans instruction based on knowledge of subject, students, the community, and curriculum goals.

Principle 8: Teacher understands and uses formal and informal assessment strategies to evaluate and ensure the continuous intellectual, social, and physical development of the learner.

Principle 9: Teacher is a reflective practitioner who continually evaluates the effects of his or her choices and actions on others (students, parents, and other professionals in the learning community) and who actively seeks out opportunities to grow professionally.

Principle 10: Teacher fosters relationships with school colleagues, parents, and agencies in the larger community to support students' learning and well-being.

Source: Council of Chief State School Officers. *Model Standards for Beginning Teacher Licensing and Development: A Resource of State Dialogue* (1992). Available online: www.ccsso.org/intascst.html.

Because of the extensive amount of research on effective teaching, we know a great more about what to look for in prospective teachers than was true even 10 years ago. The behaviors shown in Exhibit 3.4 have been shown repeatedly to be related to teachers' ability to bring about increased student learning. Nevertheless, even with improved understanding of what makes a teacher effective, identifying individuals with potential to be effective is problematic.

If you are considering an individual for a teaching position, how do you know how much he or she knows about the subject matter or whether he or she has the ability to communicate clearly, motivate students, and maintain their interest? Some common sources of information about applicants may give clues, but there is no absolutely reliable answer to those questions. A college transcript reveals quite a bit about the extent and quality of one's knowledge, and references from previous supervisors can yield information about an applicant's instructional skill. However, if the applicant is a beginner, references are less useful. For these individuals, a statement of teaching philosophy may yield insight into the attitudes and beliefs that will shape their behavior as a teacher. All of these sources, and others, should be used to collect information and arrive at a sound selection decision.

It has not been uncommon in the past for teacher selection decisions to be made without careful consideration of valid selection criteria, in part because the criteria were not available. The attitude of those who made these decisions was "If he/she doesn't work out, we can always find a replacement." Fortunately, we now recognize the shortsightedness of that approach. Finding a suitable replacement for a teacher who doesn't work out is a difficult undertaking, and even more important, the time lost before a satisfactory replacement is found cannot be recovered. Students who are taught by a marginal teacher suffer learning losses that are seldom made up.

So the effort must be made to find ways of determining which applicants possess the critical skills necessary to ensure student learning. Chapter 4 investigates the types of information available to help human resources personnel make selection decisions.

Selecting Personnel for Other Positions

One of the most difficult tasks administrators face is finding qualified substitute teachers. This is always a challenge, and as the supply of qualified full-time teachers shrinks, substitutes are often pressed into taking full-time assignments, making it even more difficult to locate individuals who can fill in for a teacher who is absent. It is not unusual for a principal to hire a substitute teacher who is not fully qualified for the assignment because no qualified substitute is available. Some communities have the benefit of a pool of retired teachers who can be called on to substitute; graduate students and their spouses are another valuable source of substitutes in districts located near a university.

The most common complaints about substitutes is that they lack knowledge of the curriculum or are not well prepared to work with children with special needs. Teachers and administrators agree that requiring substitute teachers to participate in training before they are hired as substitutes would be desirable, but district administrators are reluctant to adopt such a policy unless other districts in the area do the same (Tannenbaum, 2000).

Administrators and teachers can take actions to encourage teacher substitutes to return to their schools. Some actions that are recommended are asking regular teachers to leave assignments along with extra work for students who finish early. Substitutes appreciate receiving a clear explanation of school rules and procedures, accurate seating charts, and a guide to emergency procedures. Some substitutes also like to have the names of students they can depend on for information. To improve communication between teachers and substitutes, some schools now provide a form on which each can report suggestions, problems, or commendations that are then forwarded to the principal and transmitted to the other party (Tannenbaum, 2000).

Some personal attributes are important in many jobs. Among them are emotional maturity, self-discipline, tough-mindedness, and ability to plan. *Emotional maturity* is important for all persons who come in contact with children, including teacher aides, bus drivers, custodians, and clerical personnel. An emotionally mature person exhibits patience with children whose behavior can occasionally be trying and is able to maintain firm boundaries without feeling intimidated or reacting impulsively. An emotionally immature individual lacks the perspective to be able to look beyond his or her own needs in order to understand and respond to the needs and concerns of the child. Emotional maturity is especially vital for those who work with children who have problems of social adjustment or who are emotionally disturbed.

Self-discipline is important in jobs in which individuals work with minimal supervision and must schedule their work around frequent interruptions. Receptionists and secretaries, for example, need to possess self-discipline in order to persist in completing tasks in spite of interruptions from the telephone or from visitors. Custodians need self-discipline since they work without close supervision and must assume responsibility for monitoring heating and cooling equipment, changing lightbulbs, and, when the need arises, shoveling snow from school sidewalks, without being directed to do so.

Tough-mindedness refers to the ability to judge a situation objectively without excessive sentimentality and to persist in pursuing a course of action intended to correct a problem in the face of personal criticism. It is a trait that is especially important in those who are in personnel work or who deal with abusive individuals. Social workers who must initiate court action against families that keep their children out of school without good cause must be tough-minded and persistent in continuing to press these families to abide by the law.

Among the few jobs in which planning is not important are those that involve waiting on customers or manufacturing products on an assembly line. In those jobs, planning is usually done by someone else. In schools, planning is critical for success. Individuals in support positions must plan in order to have supplies on hand they need in their work, and they must plan the use of their time so they will be able to finish work on schedule.

Recruiting Candidates

Recruiting applicants is an essential part of the selection process. No vacancy should go unfilled for lack of applicants, but districts with noncompetitive teacher salaries or less-than-desirable working conditions often have difficulty attracting qualified applicants in sufficient numbers and quality. In virtually all districts, certain subject specialties are in short supply and extraordinary efforts may be required to reach and inform potential applicants about these jobs.

Advertising and recruiting are a necessary part of the selection process in most districts. Even districts that have an abundance of applicants recruit in order to increase the diversity of the applicant pool. Human resources personnel visit college campuses and professional meetings regularly to interview students who are nearing the completion of their program of studies and to talk with practicing teachers who may be interested in relocating. Advertisements in local and national newspapers, at professional conferences, and on the Internet are also common. Some examples of school districts that advertise job vacancies online appear in the Online Resources section at the end of this chapter. Personal contacts offer another way to find applicants.

In advertising teaching vacancies, school districts promote the advantages they offer, whether it is quality of life, variety of instructional programs, or high salaries. School districts located near beaches or mountains prepare brochures showing the recreational opportunities available to their employees; districts with generous fringe benefits advertise that fact, and those with small class sizes emphasize that advantage. Many school districts hope to attract people who are committed to teaching or who are seeking a challenge. These appeals are sometimes worded as an opportunity to "make a difference," "change lives," or "reach the hard to reach." The Peace Corps' slogan, "The hardest job you'll ever love," is an example of an appeal to these exalted aspirations. The slogan attracts people who are willing to endure hardship in order to make a contributions to others.

Summary

Selection of personnel involves matching applicants to the selection criteria for a position. A basic objective of the selection process is to ensure that individuals who are hired possess the knowledge, skills, and abilities to perform effectively. The Americans with Disabilities Act holds employers responsible for evaluating applicants on the job-specific criteria for a position and their ability to perform the job, with or without accommodations, without regard to physical or mental disabilities. The job-specific and nonjob-specific criteria that are essential for success on a job are the basis for selection decisions.

Selection criteria for a position are obtained from a job description or job model and other sources, including state and federal statutes. A job model lists results sought in a job along with descriptions of the job environment and priority actions. A result is a tangible effect of work that is useful to someone else and that helps accomplish the unit's mission.

Among the criteria shown by research to be related to effective teaching are organizing and managing classes effectively, motivating students to learn, communicating information effectively, and maintaining student involvement in instructional activities. Among the selection criteria for support positions are emotional maturity, self-discipline, initiative, and tough-mindedness.

Suggested Activities _____

1. Work in teams to write a job model about a position held by one member of the group. Designate one individual to be a "resource person" and interview that person to obtain information.

2. Write an advertisement for a publication, such as *Education Week*, for the job you developed for Question 1. Point out features of the employing district and of the job that you believe would appeal to prospective applicants.

3. Obtain a job description for a support position (counselor, school psychologist, visiting teacher, etc.). Use it to identify selection criteria and indicators for the position.

4. For the job you currently hold, list job-specific criteria that could be used to choose a replacement for you. Identify sources from which information about the criteria you choose could be obtained. Which sources are most reliable? Least reliable?

Online Resources _____

Online recruiting is the newest method for reaching prospects. Districts with websites typically list vacancies for both teaching and support personnel, and some provide an online application form for those interested in applying. Websites of some of these districts are listed here.

Miami-Dade County Public Schools (http://dcps.dade.k21.fl.us/pers/)
  Miami-Dade County lists vacancies for teachers as well as administrators and noninstructional personnel.

Milwaukee Public Schools (www.milwaukee.k12.wi.us/hr/hrhome.htm)
  Milwaukee Public Schools provides information about open positions at this site.

Seattle Public Schools (www.seattleschools.org/area/employment)
  The Seattle Public Schools site permits job hunters to search a list of vacancies by grade or subject and school. It also includes listings for substitute teachers.

References _____

Dailey, C. A. (1982). *Using the track record approach: The key to successful personnel selection.* New York: AMACOM.

Fersh, D., & Thomas, P. (1993). *Complying with the Americans with Disabilities Act: A guidebook for management and people with disabilities.* Westport, CT: Quorum.

Haller, E. (1987). Teacher selection in the city school district of Rochester. In A. Wise, L. Darling-Hammond, D. Berliner, E. Haller, P. Schlechty, B. Berry, A. Praskac, & G. Noblit (Eds.), *Effective teacher selection: From recruitment to retention—Case studies* (pp. 153–187). Santa Monica, CA: Rand.

Jacobs, R. (1993). *Legal compliance guide to personnel management.* Englewood Cliffs, NJ: Prentice Hall.

Lawler, E. (1992). *The ultimate advantage: Creating the high-involvement organization.* San Francisco: Jossey-Bass.

Mood, A. M. (1970). Do teachers make a difference? In *Do teachers make a difference?* (pp. 1–24). Washington, DC: U.S. Government Printing Office.

Scriven, M. (1990). Teacher selection. In J. Millman & L. Darling-Hammond (Eds.), *The new handbook of teacher evaluation* (pp. 76–103). Newbury Park, CA: Sage.

Tannenbaum, M. (2000, May). No substitute for quality. *Educational Leadership, 57,* 70–72.

Wanous, J. P. (1980). *Organizational entry: Recruitment, selection, and socialization of newcomers.* Reading, MA: Addison-Wesley.

4

Obtaining Information and Evaluating Applicants

Selection decisions involve collecting information about the types and amount of knowledge, experience, and personal qualifications required in a position. Those details are then matched with information about the applicants, and the person whose qualifications most closely match the requirements for the position is hired. Chapter 3 dealt with writing a job model and using it to identify the essential functions and selection criteria for a position. This chapter explains how information about applicants is gathered and evaluated.

Plan of the Chapter

Evaluation of applicants begins with the collection and verification of information about applicants for a position. This chapter focuses on sources of information about applicants for teaching positions, including applications, transcripts, references, and tests. Several types of interviews are discussed, and research findings on employment interviews are presented. The chapter also contains information on criminal background checks and examines the effects of transfer policies on student achievement. Websites of organizations that help recruit teachers or that provide background information on criminals are listed.

Sources of Information about Applicants

The district personnel office is responsible for gathering information about prospective employees, even in districts with school-based management. Initial screening of applicants is done by district-level staff members, and information gathered about qualified applicants is made available to decision makers in the schools.

There are five principal sources of information about applicants, and each is a potential contributor of data about applicants' qualifications. This information is used to determine whether the applicant meets the selection criteria for the position and is able to perform the essential functions of the job, with or without accommodation. The five information sources are the application form, transcripts, references, tests, and interviews.

Application Form

The application form should provide space for applicants to supply information about their educational background, including professional certification. It should also request information on the applicant's work history, including jobs held, dates of employment, and, for the most recent positions, the name of a person who is familiar with the individual's work and who is willing to provide a reference. The application form should provide enough information about an applicant that a selection committee can tell whether the individual is able to perform the essential functions of the position (Herman, 1994).

Questions that are not related to qualifications for performing a job should not appear on the application form since such information may be used for discriminatory purposes. Districts may ask about conviction of a crime if it pertains to a bona fide occupational qualification or business necessity, but inquiries about an applicant's arrest record should be avoided (*Education Law*, 1989). Questions dealing with race or ethnic background, religion, sex, or age should not be asked, although that information may be collected anonymously on preemployment inquiry forms. The legal ramifications of requesting this type of information are discussed in more detail in Chapter 12.

Other questions that are likely to be suspect are inquiries related to marital status or name of spouse, maiden name of female applicants, questions about the number and age of children or plans to have children, child care arrangements, organizational memberships, whether an applicant's spouse objects to the applicant's traveling, and whether an applicant is the principal wage earner in the family (*Education Law*, 1989). Employers are safe in asking if an applicant has commitments that would interfere with regular attendance on the job and, if language fluency is a requirement on the job, whether the applicant is able to read, write, or speak other languages.

Employers may ask if an applicant is over 21 years of age and whether he or she is a citizen of the United States. Noncitizens may be asked if they hold a valid work permit issued by the U.S. Immigration and Naturalization Service. Rather than ask applicants questions about their medical condition, employers are advised to describe the nature of the essential functions required on a job and ask applicants whether they will be able to perform those tasks and what accommodations, if any, they will need in order to perform them (Jacobs, 1993).

Transcripts

Some districts have attempted to simplify the application process by dropping the requirement that transcripts be submitted with the application. It is important that a transcript be obtained at some point in the selection process, however, in order to verify that the individual has indeed completed an approved course of study and received a college degree. Imposters have succeeded in posing as teachers, ministers, and physicians without holding a degree and, in a few cases, without ever having attended college. An official transcript bearing an embossed seal from the issuing institution is acceptable as valid evidence of an applicant's having attended that institution.

The transcript provides useful information about an applicant's academic achievements and course of study. Although a high grade-point average is no guarantee that an applicant will be successful in the classroom, other things being equal, individuals who do well academically in college generally achieve better results with children than those who are average or below.

References

Administrators often discount letters of references since many of them are one-sided, praising the applicant's strong qualities and avoiding mention of any faults. One reason principals supply positive references for teachers whose performance may have been marginal is a fear of legal action. A teacher who is denied a job opportunity because of a negative reference from a former principal may seek a legal remedy. About half the states have immunity laws that protect administrators who give a negative reference for a former employee from being sued for defamation. Principals in states without such immunity may be unwilling to make any comment at all about a former teacher, either in writing or on the telephone. The desire to avoid legal entanglements has also resulted in some school districts adopting policies that limit the information they release about former employees to dates of employment and positions held (Drake, 1989). However, in spite of legitimate questions about the validity of information from references, most districts require applicants to submit the names of three or four individuals who are acquainted with their work. In some districts, the application form for a professional position specifically requests the names of supervisors in all previous positions.

Tests

The use of tests to screen prospective teachers is not new, but the practice has become more common in recent years as about four-fifths of the states have established minimum scores to determine which individuals will or will not be issued teaching certificates.

Teachers' associations generally acquiesce in testing prospective teachers but oppose testing employed teachers. The National Education Association (2000) adopted a resolution stating that "competency tests must not be used as a condition of employment, license retention, evaluation, placement, ranking, or promotion of licensed teachers."

One professional group has identified a set of principles that it believes should be followed when test scores are used for selection decisions (Association of Teacher Educators, 1988). Among these principles were the following:

1. Tests should be validated for the purpose for which they are to be used. A test used for selection should therefore be validated for that purpose.
2. Tests should have a rational relationship to the job to be performed. That means that tests should be chosen to measure knowledge of subject or teaching techniques.
3. Cut-off scores on tests should be determined by an accepted empirical procedure rather than by arbitrary means.
4. Individuals should not be rank-ordered on the basis of test scores unless strong evidence exists that the test possesses criterion validity (that is, accurately predicts future performance).
5. Test scores should not be used to discriminate against a group or individual.

Interviewing for Selection

Interviews are used almost universally in employee selection, in all types of organizations. However, even though they are widely used, interviews are no more valid—and perhaps are less valid—than other ways of gathering information. Among the problems with interviews are the following:

1. Temporal placement of information influences interviewers' judgments. Positive information received early in the interview relates to more favorable judgments, and negative information results in less favorable judgments (Rowe, 1989).
2. Interviewers attach more weight to unfavorable information than to favorable information, but the reason is not clear. Some believe interviewers use negative information to narrow the list of applicants, thereby simplifying their jobs, but one author suggested that the attention to negative information indicates that interviewers are sensitive to the personal and organizational costs of hiring unqualified applicants (Rowe, 1989).
3. Interviewers may be subject to subconscious bias. Comparing an applicant with other persons who were interviewed earlier is called a *contrast effect* and is one of several biases that influences interviewers' judgments. Another is the *halo effect,* in which an interviewer's attitude about one characteristic influences ratings on all characteristics (Webster, 1982). A third source of bias is social merit considerations, discussed on the next page.
4. Interviewers use only a limited number of dimensions in judging an applicant (Zedeck, Tziner, & Middlestadt, 1983).

Interviews are subject to the same legal scrutiny as written tests (Arvey, 1979). However, of the more than 8,000 employment practices cases reported between 1979 and 1987, fewer than 1 percent involved complaints about interviews. Nevertheless, interviewers should be aware that when courts do examine interviewing practices, questioning techniques are often a subject of scrutiny. Questions should be job relevant, and the same questions should be asked of all applicants (Campion & Arvey, 1989).

Poor reliability is a problem with certain types of employment interviews. When two interviewers come to different conclusions about an applicant—one recommends hiring the applicant, and the other recommends against—that is an indication of lack of reliability in the interview. Structured or semistructured interviews are more likely to produce agreement because all interviewers ask the same questions and attach the same weights to various pieces of information (Whetzel & McDaniel, 1999).

The best results are obtained when individuals who conduct interviews are trained in their use and are familiar with the legal requirements governing employee selection. Topics that were described as inappropriate for use on application forms should also be avoided during interviews (Campion & Arvey, 1989).

Increasing Validity of Interviews

The validity of the interview as a selection device depends in large part on the interviewer's skills. Skills of interviewing can be learned, and training should be provided for those who screen applicants for teaching positions. One of the most important skills for interviewers to possess is the ability to put applicants at ease. This is done by greeting the applicant warmly and helping to make him or her feel comfortable by talking briefly about a topic of mutual interest. Good interviewers avoid using words that are likely to create a defensive attitude on the part of an applicant. They also use body language to communicate their interest in what the applicant is saying and are sensitive to messages communicated by the applicant's body language (Moffatt, 1979).

Those who are adept at their work develop the skill of using implied or embedded questions. Implied questions involve paraphrasing or repeating what the applicant has said and then pausing. This is interpreted by the interviewee as a cue to elaborate. An example of an embedded question is this statement by an interviewer: "I am curious about the reasons for your statement that teaching second-graders is tougher than teaching high school students."

It is important to guard against bias in selection decisions. Interviewers can learn to avoid contrast and halo effects, but avoiding social merit bias is more tricky. A *social merit factor* is a trait or characteristic that inclines people to view another individual favorably or unfavorably. Social merit factors are the basis for one's initial attraction to other people in social situations. Individuals who are taller than average or who are strikingly attractive or who are graduates of prestigious universities are likely to be regarded by others more favorably than those who lack those advantages. Similarly, someone who has a poor complexion or a speech impediment is likely to be evaluated less favorably by other people than someone without those disadvantages. Social merit factors ordinarily have little to do with an individual's ability to perform effectively in a job, but interviewers may be influenced unconsciously to rate an applicant more or less favorably because of them.

Interviewers must be somewhat skeptical in order to be effective, since applicants who are eager to make a good impression are likely to be tempted to embellish the truth or omit negative information altogether. Conventional wisdom suggests that a person who is lying will give himself or herself away because of nervousness, but in fact, many people are able to lie without appearing at all nervous to a casual observer. Interviewers must rely on other means of detecting omissions and exaggerations. One such method that trained interviewers use when they suspect lack of truthfulness is to continue asking questions. The more questions an applicant must answer, the more difficult it becomes to continue to conceal the truth (Vrij, 1999).

Other methods interviewers use to tell whether an applicant is truthful are internal consistency, the amount of unfavorable information provided, and clear evidence of exaggeration. *Internal consistency* refers to the absence of conflicting or contradictory answers. Since most people have encountered some unpleasant experiences on the job, a complete *absence of negative information* may mean that an applicant is withholding information. *Exaggeration* is the opposite of withholding information—it involves blowing up positive accomplishments to make them appear more significant than is warranted (Fear & Chiron, 1990).

Interview validity can be increased by use of the *behavior description interview technique* (Janz, 1989). In this approach, the interviewer asks questions about actual events an applicant has experienced in previous jobs or elsewhere. An individual's behavior in a previous situation is a more reliable predictor of how the person will act in similar situations in the future than responses to questions about hypothetical events. Focusing on an applicant's past behavior or track record is based on the principle that "a person can do again what he or she has done in the past" (Dailey & Madsen, 1980, p. 147).

The track-record approach somewhat mitigates the problem, which is inherent in what-would-you-do-if types of questions, of social desirability responses (Latham, Saari, Pursell, & Campion, 1980). A *socially desirable response* is one that an applicant believes will be more acceptable to the interviewer than a more honest response. Such responses may be given when an individual stands to gain something of value by creating a favorable impression on another person.

Asking an applicant to tell about a time when he or she took a particular kind of action or responded in a particular way to a problem situation reduces the possibility of the applicant's relying on socially desirable responses. For example, an interviewer might ask an applicant for a teaching position, "Tell me about a time when you helped a young child learn a new skill." Even persons who have no previous teaching experience may have taught a younger sibling to ride a bicycle or fly a kite. Descriptions of such incidents reveal a good deal about the kind of teacher a person will make.

If the applicant has taught, the possibilities for asking questions of this type are endless. The interviewer might ask, "Tell me how you taught your fifth-graders about the frontier in American history" or "How do you explain the concept of valence to your chemistry students?"

Sample Questions

Some sample questions that can be used in an interview to focus on past behavior are:

1. "Tell me about a time that you helped a child learn a new word in reading."
2. "I see that you have experience using the McGraw-Hill reading program. I'd be interested in how you used these materials in the classroom."
3. "Middle school students often find math to be dull. Can you tell me what you have done to increase student interest in math?"
4. "What techniques have you used that work well in helping tenth-graders improve their writing skills?"
5. "I'd like to hear about unusual materials you have used in your art classes."
6. "Discipline is always a challenge for teachers. What techniques do you rely on to keep order?"

For an applicant who has not held a full-time teaching position, questions that refer to student teaching or substitute teaching may be used. Substitute teachers often must rely on lesson plans prepared by absent teachers, so their responses to questions such as these may not be as reliable as indicators of future behavior as responses from teachers who have held full-time assignments.

Other questions that may be useful in assessing an applicant's potential teaching effectiveness are those that deal with working with colleagues, supervisors, administrators, and parents. An interviewer might ask, "What would you do if you wanted to introduce a new activity into a class you were teaching but had heard that the principal was opposed to the idea?" (Haberman, 1987).

Questions that are motivated by a bias on the part of the interviewer should not be asked of an applicant. Areas that are protected by antidiscrimination legislation are especially to be avoided unless questions deal with skills or knowledge that are essential for successful performance on the job. Some simple examples of questions that are not recommended are those dealing with an applicant's age, marital status, number and ages of children, and religious affiliation. Asking about age might suggest a bias against older people; questions about marital status and children could reveal a bias against women; and inquiring about religious affiliation might reveal a bias against certain religions. The University of Wisconsin–Milwaukee Office of Diversity/Compliance (1999) maintains a website that lists questions that for legal or ethical reasons should be avoided during employment interviews.

Setting the Stage

The interviewer sets the stage for the interview by letting the applicant know what types of questions to expect and how the selection decision will be made. If the interviewer plans to take notes, that fact should be mentioned before formal questioning begins.

Rating the Applicant

Research has shown that note taking improves the interviewer's ability to recall information about the applicant later (Webster, 1982). Detailed note taking can be a distraction, but writing key words and phrases rather than complete statements minimizes the disruptive effect and allows the interviewer to accurately reconstruct the interview later. It is common practice to use a checklist or rating scale to evaluate applicants immediately following the interview. An example of a rating scale that can be used for this purpose is shown in Exhibit 4.1. The example draws on the job-specific criteria for teaching from Exhibit 3.4.

Before an applicant is hired, an effort should be made to determine whether he or she has a criminal record. Failure to check can be a potentially serious error. Some states now require all applicants for teaching positions to be fingerprinted and to submit to a criminal background check (Abercrombie, 1998). Criminal databanks with information about persons convicted of child abuse, kidnapping, and other violent crimes are now available in most states, and the U.S. Department of Justice, through its National Sex Offender Registry Assistance Program, leads an effort to make information on all sex offenders available to local law-enforcement officials. Also, private firms can be hired to conduct preemployment background checks on applicants, including their criminal history, employment and credit history, drug screenings, and education verification. A list of companies that perform these services can be located on the Internet by entering "employee background" or "employee screening" in a search engine.

EXHIBIT 4.1   *Applicant Rating Form*

Rate the applicant from 1 (low) to 5 (high) on each item.

	(Circle One)				
• Knowledge of subject matter	1	2	3	4	5
• Oral communication ability	1	2	3	4	5
• Enthusiasm for teaching and learning	1	2	3	4	5
• Maturity of judgment	1	2	3	4	5
• Ability to motivate students	1	2	3	4	5
• Choice of instructional methods	1	2	3	4	5
• Relationships with parents and co-workers	1	2	3	4	5
• Belief in students' ability to learn	1	2	3	4	5

Even the most careful screening does not always identify potential child abusers. In the past it was not uncommon for a school district to allow an employee to resign rather than face arrest and trial for a misdemeanor involving children. In addition, criminal agencies sometimes make mistakes and an individual criminal record is lost or inadvertently destroyed (*Hiring the Right People,* 1994).

A person should not be considered guilty on the basis of an accusation alone, but if such a charge has been made against an applicant, it should be investigated and the accused given a chance to answer the charge (Hyman & Snook, 1999). Even when there is no indication that an individual has been accused or convicted of criminal activity, it is good personnel policy to question omissions or inconsistencies on the application form and to check with previous employers. Missing dates on work records and reluctance to furnish the names of previous supervisors should be investigated further. Such warning signs usually turn out to be simply oversights, but it is better to investigate and find nothing than not to and wind up with a problem employee (Hughes & Ubben, 1989).

Some districts now require applicants to sign an affidavit swearing that they have not engaged in behavior that would preclude them from being hired to work in a school. An example of one such affidavit is shown in Exhibit 4.2.

EXHIBIT 4.2 *Applicant Affidavit*

I have not at any time pleaded guilty to or been convicted of any of the acts listed below, and I have never been terminated from a position or threatened with termination for committing any of these acts:

- rape or sexual assault
- drug or alcohol abuse
- sexual harassment
- molesting or sexually exploiting a child
- indecent exposure

Have you ever been accused of any of these actions? _____. If yes, explain below the circumstances and disposition of the charges.

Date_____   Signature_____

Date _____   Witness _____

Types of Interviews

In a structured or standardized interview, all applicants for a job are asked the same set of prepared questions. The interviews are sometimes conducted by a team of interviewers who keep detailed notes on applicants' responses. There are several advantages to structured interviews. Notes from the interviews can be valuable in case legal action is initiated against the district for discrimination in hiring (Herman, 1994), and the structured format helps ensure that important topics are covered.

Screening Interview

For most professional positions, at least two interviews are held before a selection decision is made. The first is a screening interview, which is used to judge an applicant's personal and professional qualifications. If the applicant has the required qualifications, then he or she may be invited to take part in a selection interview.

The application is used as the basis for the screening interview. Only candidates who are clearly not qualified should be eliminated at this time. Candidates about whom there is a question should be given an opportunity to proceed to the selection interview, since some of them may be found to have strengths that compensate for certain weaknesses (Drake, 1989). Structured questions are usually used for screening interviews.

Selection Interview

The selection interview is used to help decide whether a qualified applicant is suited to fill a specific job vacancy. Selection interviews are longer, more intensive, and less structured than screening interviews. The questions asked by interviewers in the selection interview cover much the same material as the screening interview, but they are more specific and probing. In the selection interview, principals and teachers are interested in knowing whether an applicant possesses the professional skill and experience to perform the essential functions of a job and the personal qualifications needed for a good fit.

The selection interview is the time to examine in detail an applicant's views about various facets of the job for which he or she is being considered. To do this, interviewers use probes to encourage candidates to describe, expand, and elaborate on previous answers. Some examples of interview probes are (Moffatt, 1979):

- "I'd like to hear more about your thinking on that subject."
- "I'm not sure what you have in mind."
- "Why do you feel that way?"
- "Could you elaborate?"
- "Would you describe that in more detail?"
- "Tell me more."

Examples of interview questions that can be used to elicit information about the job-specific criteria for teaching identified in Exhibit 3.4 are shown in Exhibit 4.3.

Perceiver Interview

A *perceiver interview* is a type of structured interview in which identical questions are asked of all applicants. When used to select teachers, the purpose is to identify those who will be effective in helping to increase student achievement. Questions in the perceiver interview deal with three types of content: (1) values and philosophy of life (example: "Give reasons why you believe teaching is an important job"); (2) one's style of interacting with other people (example: "Do you prefer to work on a project as a member of a team or independently on your own?"); and (3) analysis of problematic situations that might be encountered in teaching (example: "How would you work with a student who loves to read and does well in his schoolwork but seems to have no friends?").

Critical Incident Interview

An approach to a structured interview developed for business organizations can be adapted for use in teacher selection interviews (Latham, Saari, Pursell, & Campion,

---

EXHIBIT 4.3   *Interview Questions for Selecting Effective Teachers*

Criterion: Is able to organize and manage a class effectively
Question: What classroom rules do you usually establish for students, and how do you introduce and explain the rules?

Criterion: Is able to motivate students to learn
Question: When you introduce a topic that is not a favorite with students, what do you do to build and hold their interest?

Criterion: Is able to communicate information effectively
Question: When you give an assignment that students are not familiar with, how do you make sure they understand what is expected?

Criterion: Is able to maintain student involvement in instructional activities
Question: How do you determine whether students understand new material, and what do you do if you find that they do not understand?

Criterion: Believes in the educability of all children
Question: What have you done in the past when you have had students who were not learning?

Criterion: Has extensive knowledge of subject
Question: What have you learned recently about the subject you teach that you did not know before, and how did you learn it?

1980). It is especially valuable with applicants who have not previously taught. This technique assumes that human behavior is goal oriented and that individuals choose behaviors with the intention of achieving certain results or outcomes. (This is also an assumption of goal theory, which is discussed in Chapter 6.)

The technique involves identifying critical incidents that are likely to be encountered by an employee on the job. For a teacher, critical incidents might include a student who is disrespectful or disruptive, a situation in which a teacher is seeking to encourage critical thinking on the part of students through use of higher-order questions, or a child's difficulty in grasping new material. Each critical incident is described in a written narrative. The interviewer asks the applicant to read the narrative and indicate what action he or she would take if confronted with the situation described. The interviewer scores the applicant's response against benchmark answers prepared by a group of knowledgeable individuals who are familiar with the job. If the critical incidents highlight situations that are likely to be experienced in a specific position, applicants' responses can yield useful cues to probable behavior on the job.

After the incidents have been selected, a team consisting of four to six teachers and administrators prepares "benchmark" responses to be used as an aid to scoring applicants' answers. The three benchmark responses represent excellent answers (scored 5), average answers (scored 3), and poor answers (scored 1). A response with a benchmark score of 5 represents the most complete response to the problem. It is an answer that would be given by an experienced teacher and takes into account all or most facets of the problem. A response rated 5 shows sensitivity, action aimed at resolving the problem, and a clear sense of professional responsibility. A response with a benchmark score of 1 represents a very limited response to the problem described in the narrative. It is an answer that might be given by a teacher with limited experience and knowledge of teaching or by a teacher who, despite having teaching experience, displays questionable judgment or lack of sensitivity. Such a response uses very little of the information provided in the narrative. The suggested plan of action is incomplete or addresses superficial aspects of the problem.

An example of a critical incident involving a child who tried out for the school soccer team but was not selected is shown in Exhibit 4.4, along with three benchmark responses. Applicants' answers to a problem such as this will vary, and the benchmark responses are used as guides to help interviewers score actual responses.

It is common practice for interviewers to pose hypothetical questions about incidents that teachers sometimes face and ask applicants what they would do in a similar situation. There are several important differences between that practice and the critical incident technique described here. First, a critical incident depicts a realistic but ambiguous problem with more than one possible response. It usually involves issues that teachers deal with on a daily basis.

Second, the critical incident approach yields insights into the applicant's thinking and judgment. The strongest applicants use the information from the critical incident to formulate a hypothesis and develop a plan of action based on testing the hypothesis. In the 5-point response to the problem in Exhibit 4.4, the teacher

EXHIBIT 4.4   *Example of a Critical Incident*

Troy is a sixth-grader who transferred to Fielding Middle School this year from out of state. Troy is small for his age, but he behaves aggressively with other children, perhaps partly out of a desire to win the approval of classmates. He recently tried out for the school soccer team and has just received the news that he was not selected. He is very disappointed, especially since a classmate, Eric, was chosen for the team. The students initiate a discussion about the process by which players are selected.

"They only have one tryout, and if you have a bad day, you don't get picked," Joseph says, who also tried out but failed to win a spot on the team.

"Troy should have been picked," Eric says. "He's good. Besides he played last year on the Wombats team."

"I think he should be picked, too," Joseph adds.

"The coach just didn't like me," Troy says. "I knew he wouldn't pick me. Besides, I don't want to play on the stupid team. I bet they don't win any games."

"I think the students ought to vote on who plays for the team," Valerie says. "They know who the good players are better than the coach."

Eric gives her a look of disgust. "The coach usually picks good players," he says, "but Troy should have been on the team instead of Jerry Wilkins. Jerry's fast but he can't score."

This is an opportunity for a discussion of being a good sport and respecting decisions of people in positions of responsibility. How would you proceed?

Benchmark Response 1 (1 point): I would tell Troy that he feels bad because he didn't get picked and that he should congratulate his classmate who was picked and not feel bitter.

Benchmark Response 2 (3 points): I would tell the class that at one time or another all of us will have the experience of not being chosen when we think we should have been. The way to handle those feelings is to be happy for those who got selected and work harder so maybe next time we will be picked.

Benchmark Response 3 (5 points): I would ask the students to think of reasons why coaches are responsible for choosing players and what criteria they are likely to use when making those choices. I would ask if it's possible a coach might make a mistake and, if so, if that should be held against him. I would ask what a student who was not selected for the team might do to overcome his disappointment.

---

acknowledges Troy's feelings and invites the students to help him consider constructive ways of dealing with his disappointment. In the 1-point benchmark response, the teacher downplays Troy's feelings.

Transfer Policies and Student Learning

According to figures from the National Center for Education Statistics (1992), about 20 percent of teachers hired by public schools are first-time teachers. Slightly more than one-fourth reenter teaching after an absence, and the remainder are transferring from other teaching positions.

Employees seek to transfer from one school to another for a number of reasons. Some want to transfer for convenience, whereas others seek to move to schools with better programs, facilities, or equipment. Still others hope to work with particular teachers or administrators or want to be assigned to a school with school-based management.

In many districts an effort is made to act on transfer requests before decisions are made to hire new teachers. This allows teachers who are already employed by the district to have the first choice of vacancies. Such a policy is helpful in sustaining teacher morale, but it can create problems when selection decisions are delayed while employed teachers are given the option to interview for vacancies.

Preference in Transfers

Some districts have policies that specify that teachers seeking transfers must be placed before new hires are made (Darling-Hammond, Wise, Berry, & Praskac, 1987). In other districts, the bargaining agreement gives transferring teachers the right to select the school in which they prefer to teach, subject only to the condition that teachers choose in order of seniority, with the most senior teacher having first choice (Haller, 1987).

Policies that give employed teachers the right of first refusal for available vacancies can delay decisions on selection and thereby prevent the district from issuing contracts to promising applicants. For that reason, some districts attempt to solve the problem of delay by issuing open contracts to qualified candidates. An open contract secures a commitment from the teacher but leaves the district the option of making a placement decision at a later time. A potential problem with this tactic is that the more highly sought after teachers may choose to sign with a district that offers an immediate placement decision.

Delays in offering teaching contracts can occur for a variety of reasons in addition to transfers. Whatever the reason, delays increase the likelihood that a district will lose out to other districts in the competition for teaching talent. A common reason for delays in making selection decisions is uncertainty regarding need, which is a factor when enrollment projections are unavailable or are suspected of being inaccurate, when finances are tight, or when late resignations are expected.

Caution in hiring teachers who may turn out not to be needed is important when the potential cost to the district can reach $50,000 per teacher, including salary and benefits. However, if experience has shown that the number of teachers needed consistently exceeds earlier projections, a district may offer a limited number of open contracts to promising applicants. This prevents the loss of teachers with strong qualifications to competing districts.

Equity in Transfer Practices

Placement and transfer decisions almost always raise questions of equity in the distribution of teacher talent. A district that relies solely on seniority in deciding transfer requests risks having all of its experienced teachers located in the most desirable schools, except for the individuals who principals reject. The end result of such a policy is maldistribution of teacher talent, with the most experienced teachers located in the more desirable schools and those with the least experience assigned to the less desirable schools. These are oftentimes schools with large proportions of children from poor and minority families. Staffing these schools exclusively with inexperienced teachers risks loss of learning.

Of course, experience is not necessarily synonymous with ability, and many inexperienced teachers are very capable, but the problem with open transfer policies is that the most able teachers do not remain long in schools that have little to offer in the way of rewards and prestige. In a profession in which there are limited opportunities for vertical mobility, teachers gravitate toward schools with better teaching conditions, a reputation for quality programs, or better facilities. This can create a problem for administrators who may be left with no alternative other than staffing less popular schools with beginning teachers.

Summary

Information about prospective employees is collected by the district office from five principal sources—application form, transcripts, references, tests, and interviews. The information is used to determine whether an applicant can perform job-specific functions.

Application forms and interviews are the most widely used methods for collecting information about applicants, but tests of knowledge of subject and methods of teaching are used in most states.

Interviews are more reliable when interviewers are taught methods of avoiding bias. A common but subtle form of bias is giving preference to certain individuals on the basis of social merit factors.

Critical incident interviews ask applicants to describe how they would handle realistic, work-related problems. The applicant receives a detailed description of the problem, and his or her answer is scored by comparing it to benchmark responses. This technique originated in industry and is especially valuable for assessing applicants' judgment.

Teacher transfers in schools are common, and they can affect the quality of instruction. A sound policy on teacher transfers maintains a balance of experienced and inexperienced teachers in all schools in the district.

Suggested Activities _____

1. On the Internet locate application forms for a teaching position from three or four school districts and compare them. Can you identify a legitimate purpose for all the questions that are asked? Are any questions missing that should be included?

2. Work together with one or two other persons to write a critical incident for use in interviewing applicants for a teaching position. Identify the grade level and/or subject taught. When you finish writing the incident, write 1-point and 5-point benchmark responses.

3. Suppose you are the principal of a school and one of your teachers, whose spouse is being transferred to a position in another city, asks you to write a letter of reference. You have misgivings because the teacher is not effective. Discuss your ethical responsibilities in this situation and tell what you would do.

4. Read the following responses of two teacher applicants to interviewers' questions. What do the responses tell you about the applicants? If you were the interviewer, what follow-up questions would you ask each applicant?

   Q: Tell me about yourself.

   Applicant 1: I was born and raised in Seattle. I have two sisters and come from a normal, happy family. One of my sisters is a teacher, and the other is working on her MBA. I was very active in sports in high school and college and still play tennis when I can. I am married with two children. My husband is a CPA. I am creative and enthusiastic and love to get children excited about learning.

   Applicant 2: I love teaching and don't remember a time when I didn't want to teach. I love working with young children and helping them progress socially and mentally. I taught third grade in Illinois for five years before we moved here. My own daughter was in my class the last year I taught there. That was fun. I believe now I might like to change to a higher grade level—maybe fourth or fifth. I think I'd like to work with children who are a little more mature.

5. Read Case Study I (at the end of the book) and answer the questions that follow the case study.

Online Resources _____

The organizations and agencies listed here sponsor efforts aimed at attracting and retaining teachers and providing information to assist in teacher selection.

South Carolina Center for Teacher Recruitment (www.scctr.org)
> In 1999 the South Carolina General Assembly funded the Teaching Fellows Program. Its mission is to recruit talented high school students into teaching by providing fellowships for high school seniors who exhibit high academic achievement. Fellows agree to teach one year in South Carolina for each year they receive a scholarship.

Teach for America (www.tfanetwork.org/tfa2/join_our_corps/home.asp)
> A national corps of recent college graduates with academic majors commit to teach two years in underresourced urban and rural public schools.

Teacher Advancement Program (www.mff.org/tap/tap.taf)
> The Teacher Advancement Program, sponsored by the Milken Family Foundation, addresses recruitment, training, induction, professional development, compensation, performance evaluation, and career advancement.

California Center for Teaching Careers (CalTeach)
> CalTeach is an interactive recruitment network maintained by the State of California Institute for Education Reform, 6000 J Street, Sacramento, CA 95819–6018. It provides information for persons considering a teaching career and gives districts an opportunity to advertise vacancies or search resumes for qualified applicants. Email address: calteach@csulb.edu.

Recruiting New Teachers (www.recruitingteachers.org)
> This site gives information on how to find and retain teachers and provides links to state departments of education.

U.S. Department of Justice Bureau of Justice Statistics (www.ojp.usdoj.gov/bjs/pubalp2.htm)
> This site contains an extensive list of Department of Justice publications dealing with crime statistics and prevention. Among the titles of particular interest to school administrators are *School Crime, Students' Reports of School Crime, Summary of State Sex Offender Registries, Sex Offenses and Offenders,* and *Child Victimizers: Violent Offenders Their Victims.* Most of the publications can be downloaded.

References

Abercrombie, K. (1998, April 29). Right to teach in California denied without prints. *Education Week,* p. 5.

Arvey, R. (1979). Unfair discrimination in the employment interview. *Psychological Bulletin, 86,* 736–765.

Association of Teacher Educators. (1988). *Teacher assessment.* Reston, VA: Author.

Campion, J., & Arvey, R. (1989). Unfair discrimination in the employment interview. In R. Eder & G. Ferns (Eds.), *The employment interview: Theory, research, and practice* (pp. 61–73). Newbury Park, CA: Sage.

Dailey, C., & Madsen, A. (1980). *How to evaluate people in business.* New York: McGraw-Hill.

Darling-Hammond, L., Wise, A., Berry, B., & Praskac, A. (1987). Teacher selection in the Montgomery County Public Schools. In A. Wise, L. Darling-Hammond, D. Berliner, E. Haller, P. Schlechty, B. Berry, A. Praska, & G. Noblit (Eds.), *Effective teacher selection: From recruitment to retention—Case studies* (pp. 52–92). Santa Monica, CA: Rand.

Drake, J. (1989). *The effective interviewer: A guide for managers.* New York: AMACOM.

Education law: Vol. 2. (1989). New York: Matthew Bender.

Fear, R., & Chiron, R. (1990). *The evaluation interview* (4th ed.). New York: McGraw-Hill.

Haberman, M. (1987). *Recruiting and selecting teachers for urban schools.* Reston, VA: Association of Teacher Educators.

Hakel, M. (1982). Employment interviewing. In K. Rowland & G. Ferris (Eds.), *Personnel management* (pp. 129–153). Boston: Allyn and Bacon.

Haller, E. (1987). Teacher selection in the city school district of Rochester. In A. Wise, L. Darling-Hammond, D. Berliner, E. Haller, P. Schlechty, B. Berry, A. Praska, & G. Noblit (Eds.), *Effective teacher selection: From recruitment to retention—Case studies* (pp. 153–187). Santa Monica, CA: Rand.

Herman, S. (1994). *Hiring right: A practical guide.* Thousand Oaks, CA: Sage.

Hiring the right people. (1994). Malibu, CA: National School Safety Center. (ERIC Document Reproduction Service No. ED 411397).

Hughes, L., & Ubben, G. (1989). *The elementary principal's handbook: A guide to effective action* (3rd ed.). Boston: Allyn and Bacon.

Hyman, I., & Snook, P. (1999). *Dangerous schools: What we can do about the physical and emotional abuse of our children.* San Francisco: Jossey-Bass.

Jacobs, R. (1993). *Legal compliance guide to personnel management.* Englewood Cliffs, NJ: Prentice Hall.

Janz, T. (1989). The patterned behavior description interview: The best prophet of the future is the past. In R. Eder & G. Ferris (Eds.), *The employment interview: Theory, research, and practice* (pp. 158–168). Newbury Park, CA: Sage.

Latham, G., Saari, L., Pursell, E., & Campion, M. (1980). The situational interview. *Journal of Applied Psychology, 65,* 422–427.

Moffatt, T. (1979). *Selection interviewing for managers.* New York: Harper & Row.

National Center for Education Statistics. (1992). *The condition of education, 1992.* Washington, DC: U.S. Department of Education.

National Education Association. (2000). *NEA 2000–2001 resolutions.* Available online: www.nea.org/cgi–bin/AT–resoutionssearch.cgi

Rowe, P. (1989). Unfavorable information and interview decisions. In R. Eder & G. Ferris (Eds.), *The employment interview: Theory, research, and practice* (pp. 77–89). Newbury Park, CA: Sage.

University of Wisconsin–Milwaukee Office of Diversity/Compliance. (1999). *Questions to avoid during employment interviews.* Available online: www.uwm.edu/Dept/OD_C/interviews.html

Vrij, A. (1999). Interviewing to detect deception. In A. Memon & R. Bull (Eds.), *Handbook of the psychology of interviewing* (pp. 317–326). New York: Wiley.

Webster, E. (1982). *The employment interview: A social judgment process.* Schomberg, Ontario, Canada: S.I.P.

Whetzel, D., & McDaniel, M. (1999). The employment interview. In A. Memon & R. Bull (Eds.), *Handbook of the psychology of interviewing* (pp. 213–226). New York: Wiley.

Zedeck, S., Tziner, A., & Middlestadt, S. (1983). Interviewer validity and reliability: An individual analysis approach. *Personnel Psychology, 36,* 355–370.

5

Selecting Administrative and Support Personnel

Finding qualified candidates to fill vacancies in schools is an ongoing challenge in most schools and districts. This chapter examines the procedures used to fill vacancies in administrative and support positions in schools and describes the duties performed by the individuals who hold those jobs. Finding the right people for these positions is critical in order for schools to run smoothly and offer effective instructional programs.

District office personnel, current principals, and those who contemplate becoming principals will be interested in the topic of selection of principals and assistant principals, for both personal and professional reasons, and in the material on selecting aides, counselors, substitute teachers, and clerical personnel out of professional interest.

Plan of the Chapter

Teachers are indispensable in schools, but schools also depend on the people filling other roles in order to function smoothly and effectively. This chapter examines the processes involved in selecting administrative and support personnel for schools. It contains the following sections: (1) selection procedures, (2) selecting administrators, (3) managerial motivation, (4) progress toward equity, and (5) selecting other support personnel.

Selection Procedures

Selection procedures for administrative and support personnel parallel the procedures in teacher selection. The steps are:

1. Prepare a job model or job description.
2. Announce the vacancy.
3. Conduct a preliminary screening of applicants and eliminate those who are not qualified.
4. Conduct first-round interviews with selected candidates.
5. Select finalists and conduct second-round interviews with them.
6. Announce the selection decisions and notify unsuccessful applicants.

Preparing a Job Model

The preparation of a job description or job model follows an analysis of the position to identify major tasks performed on the job or results expected. Information for the analysis may be collected either from interviews with those who currently hold the position or from questionnaires completed by them (Gatewood & Feild, 1987). The use of a job model or job description is important in defining the parameters of the search and selection process and in avoiding the problem of misperception of the position (Jentz, 1982).

The items in Exhibit 5.1 make up a generic list of duties that are commonly performed by elementary school principals, but the responsibilities associated with

EXHIBIT 5.1 *Duties of Elementary Principal*

1. Carries out policies of the board in such a way as to achieve and maintain the school's instructional effectiveness
2. Effectively utilizes resources of the district to enhance the school's instructional effectiveness
3. Plans and implements the instructional program of the school in cooperation with teachers, supervisors, and parents
4. Maintains complete and accurate records and monitors the instructional program of the school by reviewing indicators of instructional effectiveness
5. Works with district office staff and members of the school staff to recruit, interview, and select personnel for the school
6. Supports teachers by means of classroom visits, conferences, and evaluations of performance
7. Provides or obtains assistance to help teachers overcome identified instructional problems
8. Recognizes individual teachers and students for significant accomplishments in teaching and learning
9. Obtains resources for and provides support and direction to enable school personnel to continue their professional development
10. In cooperation with teachers and parents, develops and implements a code of student conduct in order to create a school climate conducive to learning
11. Meets with parents to provide information and review and resolve concerns
12. Establishes and implements a process for prompt requisitioning of materials and equipment and informs personnel about the procedures
13. Oversees maintenance and cleaning of the building

an actual position will vary from district to district and even from one school to another within a district. Duties of middle and high school principals are similar to those of elementary school administrators, except that secondary administrators usually deal with a larger number of people and activities. Secondary school administrators also spend more time planning and monitoring student activities than their elementary or middle school counterparts.

Preparing a list of duties such as those in Exhibit 5.1 is the first step in developing a job model for an elementary school principal. The list of duties is then converted to an inventory of results sought, and, finally, descriptions of the job environment and priority actions are added. A similar procedure would be used to develop job models for a middle or high school principal, assistant principal, counselor, media specialist, teacher aide, and school secretary.

Announcing the Vacancy

Most districts announce all administrative, supervisory, or counseling openings to current employees in order to give those who may be interested the opportunity to apply. Some negotiated agreements contain a clause requiring that teachers be notified of administrative and counseling vacancies. An issue of concern to individuals who are interested in moving up is whether vacancies are filled from within the district or from outside. Some school districts have ironclad policies of filling all vacancies from within, whereas others hire the most qualified candidate, regardless of location. Consistently hiring from within the district has the advantage of helping maintain high teacher morale, but it runs the risk of developing inbred thinking. Hiring outsiders often brings fresh thinking into the system.

Advertising administrative openings outside of the immediate locality is common. Publications such as *Education Week* and metropolitan newspapers such as the *New York Times* regularly carry announcements of openings for school administrators. State and national professional associations for administrative and counseling personnel also maintain lists of openings in their respective fields.

Screening the Applicants

Preliminary screening of applicants consists of checking the application form to be sure it is completely filled out and determining that the applicant has the necessary educational qualifications for the position and, when applicable, that he or she holds appropriate professional certification. Also at this time any tests that may be required are administered and scored.

Interviewing and Checking References

A number of suggestions for conducting selection interviews with teachers were presented in Chapter 4. Most of the advice presented there applies equally to interviewing for administrative and support positions. The number of first-round interviews varies with the position and the number of applicants. For a principalship, it is not uncommon for 10 or more candidates to be invited to first-round interviews. For the position of teacher aide or secretary, there may be no more than 2 or 3 candidates. First-round interviews are intended to narrow the field to the most promising prospects, and if there are only a small number of applicants for a position, one round of interviews may be all that is needed. Discussion of selection criteria for each of the support positions will be presented later in this chapter. If needed, second-round interviews are conducted with the candidates whose qualifications appear to most nearly match the requirements of the position.

At this point, references are contacted and asked about the applicants' work record and performance in previous positions. They may also be asked to verify the accuracy of information furnished by the applicant. The final step is to check appropriate criminal justice databanks in order to verify that applicants still under active consideration have not been convicted of a crime that would disqualify them from holding the position.

Announcing Decisions

Completion of second-round interviews is normally followed in short time by an announcement of the selection decision. The decision may be delayed if two equally strong prospects are vying for the position or if none of the finalists appears qualified. In the latter case, the decision may be made to reopen the search and interview additional applicants.

When a decision is made to hire an individual, that person normally receives word promptly, but the mail moves more slowly for those who were not chosen. Courtesy dictates that all active applicants (that is, those who participated in second-round interviews and have not withdrawn) are informed when the decision is made, but this practice is by no means universally observed.

Applicants from within the district who made the list of finalists should receive a personal communication, either in the form of a letter or a telephone call, informing them of the reasons they were not chosen and suggesting ways they might improve their chances of selection in the future. Those who are unlikely to receive serious consideration for future openings should be notified tactfully of that fact and encouraged to pursue other opportunities. Candidates from outside the district should be informed when a decision has been made and encouraged to apply again in the future if their qualifications warrant that.

Selecting Administrators

Finding satisfactory replacements for administrative personnel who retire or resign and filling new administrative vacancies are high-priority activities in all school districts. With the growing use of school-based management and continued emphasis on improving school programs, the process of screening and selecting administrators is changing. Parents, teachers, and other employees of the school board are playing a more active role in the selection of administrators, on the assumption that those who help choose a leader will be responsive to that individual and work harder to ensure his or her success than those who have no voice in the selection.

Choosing a principal is an especially important decision because of the principal's potential influence on the quality of the instructional program in a school. In some districts with school-based management, principals are chosen by a local committee that includes teachers and parents, whereas in other districts, the committee makes a recommendation but does not make the final selection. Either method can result in high-quality choices if committee members are well informed with regard to the qualities that are desirable for principals.

It is becoming difficult to attract strong leaders into the principalship, since fewer people are willing to accept the heavy workload and heightened level of responsibility that contemporary principals must shoulder. Principals are responsible for the safety of teachers and students, and they are accountable for prudent management of expensive facilities and sizable budgets. A typical workday for a principal begins early in the morning and does not end until late evening, after a basketball game, PTA meeting, or parent conference is concluded. Teachers are increasingly reluctant to apply for administrative jobs because many of them have decided that the modest increase in salary is not worth the added responsibilities and longer working hours.

The shortage of qualified applicants for positions as principals is not likely to ease soon, and efforts are underway in a number of states involving several professional associations to inform policymakers about the shortage and to initiate action to encourage more competent individuals to pursue careers as educational administrators. Some states have provided funding for professional development programs for administrators, and a number of school districts have taken steps to "grow their own" leaders by providing scholarships to promising teachers who are interested in becoming school principals (Million, 1998).

Administrative internships are used in many districts to provide opportunities for teachers to gain firsthand experience with administrative duties and to learn more about district policies and procedures. The position of administrative aide, which involves half teaching and half administrative duties, is a popular type of internship. Positions such as administrative aide are assessment positions—jobs high in visibility that permit decision makers in the district to observe and evaluate an individual's potential for advancement (Gaertner, 1978/1979).

Districts are also beginning to use a variety of methods to collect information that will permit more valid inferences about applicants' potential leadership abilities. Simulations, written exercises, and situational questions are being used to assess candidates for the principalship and other administrative positions (Anderson, 1988).

School-based management places more responsibility for the quality of instructional programs on principals. It also requires that the process by which principals and assistant principals are selected receive more thought and attention than they have received in the past.

Selection of Principals

Most principals began their careers as teachers. Many of the skills that help one succeed in the classroom are useful in carrying out the responsibilities associated with the principalship. However, successful teachers do not always make successful principals—a fact that should be kept in mind in choosing administrators.

Principals are responsible for eight major functions related to the operation of the school. These duties may be delegated to other members of the administrative team or even occasionally to teachers, but the principal bears ultimate responsibility for the duties to be being carried out in a timely and effective manner. Principals and assistant principals should be selected on the basis of demonstrated evidence of successful previous performance or the potential for successful performance in these eight areas (Baltzell & Dentler, 1983):

1. Organization of the school setting
2. Resource and logistical management
3. Staff supervision
4. Staff evaluation
5. Staff development
6. Student discipline and safety
7. Instructional improvement and accountability
8. Spokesperson or symbolic agent of both school and district

The eight functions are described in the paragraphs that follow, and suggestions are made for assessing applicants on each. In all cases, the strongest predictor of success is evidence of previous successful experience in a similar setting. Assessing applicants who have had no previous administrative experience and must be judged on the basis of their potential is one of the most difficult selection decisions administrators make. Many school districts now assign teachers who aspire to become administrators to part-time or temporary duties in which they have the opportunity to demonstrate their managerial abilities without having the responsibilities of a full-time position.

Organization of the School Setting.   This function involves establishing lines of authority and communication and clarifying responsibilities within a school. It is an indispensable part of effective management. Leadership experience outside of education, including volunteer work, can be useful for assessing an individual's prospects for success in this area. Those who evaluate applicants' qualifications should pay particular attention to experiences that involve coordinating or directing the activities of other adults. Some examples are serving as a volunteer coordinator for Boy Scout or Girl Scout programs, directing a United Way or other community agency fund drive, and organizing volunteer workers in community musicals, theater groups, rescue squads, and the like.

Experiences in education that are valid indicators of organizational ability include overseeing the reorganization of a department, in particular the merging of two or more specialties into a single organizational unit. The main considerations are the extent of an individual's contribution to the effort and its success.

Resource and Logistical Management.   Principals are expected to manage fiscal accounts, supervise the distribution and use of equipment and supplies, and oversee the maintenance of the school building. These are managerial responsibilities that have implications for instructional effectiveness of the school. Teachers have similar responsibilities but on a much smaller scale. Few applicants will have had experience in this area unless they have held a managerial position inside or outside of education.

Staff Supervision.   Supervision includes efforts to facilitate teachers' work. Other than department heads and those who have worked as administrative aides, most teachers have had little or no experience in supervising their colleagues. However, some have supervised teacher aides. In assessing supervision of aides, decision makers should consider the length, frequency, and quality of that supervision. These factors can be judged from teachers' self-reports if confirmed by other teachers or school administrators.

Summer school administrative assignments are another means by which teachers who aspire to become administrators demonstrate their supervisory ability. Ordinarily only a limited amount of supervision is carried out during summer school, but an administrator who supervises informally over a cup of coffee is demonstrating the potential for success in that area.

Staff Evaluation.   In some districts, department heads are involved in teacher evaluation, and in a few cases, teachers even take part, but most teachers have had no experience with that responsibility. Some questions that can be asked of applicants for an administrative position that will help assess their readiness to evaluate teaching are:

1. What evidence would you look for in observing a fifth-grade teacher to show that students understand the material that is being presented?
2. How would you determine whether a teacher has diagnosed students' needs before presenting a lesson?
3. How would you judge whether a homework assignment given by a teacher whom you are observing is suitable for the students?
4. How could you tell during an observation how well a teacher is monitoring students' learning?
5. What would you look for as evidence that a teacher uses technology effectively in the classroom?

Staff Development.   Staff development is examined in detail in Chapter 8. With school-based management, principals are assuming more responsibility for planning and presenting staff development programs. However, this is an area in which even some persons with administrative experience are novices. In fact, some teachers have had more experience as trainers and peer coaches than the principals of their schools.

An applicant with little experience in planning or conducting staff development programs might be asked to describe some programs that he or she felt were particularly effective and to identify reasons for their effectiveness. Other evidence that can be deduced from an interview includes the applicant's self-identified developmental needs and aspects of program design about which the candidate is especially enthusiastic. An important factor in this area is the individual's knowledge of human and material resources that can be used in planning staff development programs. A strong candidate should be able to identify several nationally known staff development programs.

Student Discipline and Safety.   The principal is ultimately responsible for student discipline and safety, but success in this area is dependent on his or her ability to develop among the teachers a shared sense of responsibility for the task. The most obvious indicator of future effectiveness in this area is the teacher's own record in the classroom. A teacher who successfully manages behavior of students in one classroom without being unduly repressive probably will be able to manage discipline on a schoolwide basis. However, there are important differences in the two settings. The teacher maintains a relationship with all students he or she teaches, whereas an administrator must administer discipline to students whom he or she knows only slightly.

The role of police officer is one that teachers dislike but one that administrators are often required to fill. Applicants with a strong aversion to that role will derive little satisfaction from serving as an assistant principal. Ideally, applicants for administrative positions should have experience in working with all types of children, including those from a variety of cultural backgrounds, children with physical, mental, or emotional disabilities, and children who are gifted and talented.

Instructional Improvement and Accountability.   Principals often are expected to take the lead in implementing instructional improvement in their schools. This involves achieving increased student learning within an existing or redesigned curriculum framework. Knowledge of instructional materials and various teaching methods and familiarity with the research on effective teaching (described in Chapter 1) are indicators of potential success in this area. Another criterion for assessing the ability to effect instructional improvement is knowledge of subject. A teacher who lacks comprehensive knowledge of a teaching field is unlikely to bring about instructional improvement.

Spokesperson or Symbolic Agent.   The spokesperson presents the organization's programs and point of view to the media and the public. Teachers rarely have the opportunity to serve as spokesperson for a school or district, but some perform a spokesperson role as part of the responsibilities involved in chairing district or association committees. An individual who serves as a delegate to professional conferences or who serves as union negotiator acquires valuable experience as a spokesperson. Poise and the ability to articulate a position are important for success in this area.

An individual's ability to function effectively as a spokesperson can be inferred from oral communication skills as well as from evidence of sensitivity to the views of others. Leaders are frequently required to summarize the views of groups with divergent opinions as a way of bringing about consensus on an issue. The ability to understand and verbalize a variety of positions on an issue, including those that differ from one's own, is a valuable asset to a school administrator. Evidence of this skill can be obtained from questions in which the candidate is asked to describe two divergent positions on an issue of current interest and to explain the strengths and weaknesses of each.

Selection of Assistant Principals.   The selection of assistant principals has been characterized as "haphazard" and not guided by coherent policies and criteria (Hess, 1985). The assumption has been made that the principal is ultimately responsible for the administration of a school and that an assistant principal's lack of expertise can be compensated for by the principal's greater knowledge and skill, based on greater experience. Assistant principals are sometimes viewed as apprentices learning the job of principal from an experienced administrator who serves as a role model for the newcomer. In Kentucky, all beginning principals serve as interns in their first year as a principal. They are evaluated by a committee composed of the superintendent, a university professor, and a mentor principal (Kirkpatrick, 2000).

However, most school districts now expect assistant principals to be contributing members of the administrative team immediately upon their appointment. Successful instructional programs require the "energy, talent, and commitment of a great many actors within each school building" (Spady, 1985, p. 118), including assistant principals. Aspirants to administration are expected to learn the skills of the trade by means of district- or university-sponsored internships (Baltzell & Dentler, 1983).

The assistant principal reports directly to the principal of a school and carries out duties assigned by him or her. These often have to do with maintaining the stability of the school as an organization, as opposed to attending to improving and strengthening the instructional program of the school (Reed & Himmler, 1985). One of the assistant principal's most important duties is to maintain order and discipline.

Assistant principals are generally required to develop an activity calendar and establish a master schedule (Reed & Himmler, 1985). In some schools, they plan and coordinate orientation and assignment of new teachers, student teachers, and teacher aides, and participate in supervising and evaluating certificated staff. Assistant principals are also responsible for building maintenance, inventories of supplies and equipment, ordering and maintaining textbooks, and managing student attendance (Educational Research Service, 1984). In short, there is very little that principals do that is not also done by assistant principals.

Given the scope and importance of the evolving role of the assistant principal, the selection criteria for the position should be the same as those used in selecting principals. The differences in the selection criteria used for the two positions usually have to do with depth and length of experience, with the principal expected to have more varied experience, and with counterbalancing qualifications. That is, an effort is usually made to select an assistant principal whose subject field and administrative experiences complement rather than duplicate those of the principal.

Use of Tests for Selection of Administrators

Written Tests.   About one-fourth of the states in the United States now require candidates for the position of principal to complete a written examination (Egginton, Jeffries, & Kidd-Knights, 1988). One such examination is the School Leaders Licensure Assessment (SLLA) developed by the Educational Testing Service in cooperation with state departments of education in several states. Some states have developed their own tests, either independently or with the assistance of a testing firm, and a few large-city school districts have adopted testing procedures to help screen prospective administrators. Some of the tests now in use combine written exercises with in-basket exercises. On in-basket exercises, an examinee responds to telephone messages, memoranda, letters, and emails similar to those that principals might receive. In addition to imposing testing requirements, some state legislatures have introduced additional educational requirements for prospective school administrators, and others have mandated internship programs.

Assessment Centers.   Many school districts increasingly rely on assessment centers to help in the selection of school principals, and some states now require aspirants for school administration to successfully complete an assessment center procedure. An assessment center is a series of exercises that simulate problems that might confront a school principal. Candidates record the decisions and actions they would take and are evaluated by a team of assessors who observe them in the process of carrying out a variety of simulated tasks (Gatewood & Feild, 1987).

The best known and most widely used assessment procedure was developed by the National Association of Secondary School Principals (NASSP). Participants in the NASSP centers are rated on 12 attributes (McCall, 1986). These attributes are described in Exhibit 5.2.

Although assessment procedures are considered tests in the technical sense, they avoid many of the objections that are raised to selection tests because they possess both construct and criterion validity. *Construct validity* refers to the accuracy with which an instrument measures psychological structures, functions, or traits (Landy, 1985). Assessment measures have construct validity because of the close match between the simulated tasks candidates are asked to perform and the actual work of school principals.

EXHIBIT 5.2   *Skills Assessed in NASSP Assessment Centers*

1. *Problem analysis*
    Ability to analyze information to identify the important elements of a problem
2. *Judgment*
    Skill in identifying and acting on educational priorities; making sound decisions with the information at hand
3. *Organizational ability*
    Skill in planning, scheduling, and controlling the activities of others; skill in using resources
4. *Decisiveness*
    Ability to recognize that a decision is required and making it
5. *Leadership*
    Skill in recognizing that a group requires direction and in involving others in solving problems
6. *Sensitivity*
    Skill in perceiving the needs and concerns of others and responding in a caring, supportive way
7. *Stress tolerance*
    Ability to perform under pressure without loss of effectiveness
8. *Oral communication*
    Ability to verbally express one's thoughts clearly and persuasively
9. *Written communication*
    Ability to write clearly and persuasively
10. *Range of interests*
    Knowledge of a broad range of subjects; involvement in activities that are unrelated to the job
11. *Personal motivation*
    Desire to perform well in situations that challenge one's abilities
12. *Educational values*
    Commitment to a coherent set of educational priorities

Source: "Twelve Skill Dimensions: Professional Benefits" by D. S. McCall, January 1986, *NASSP Bulletin, 70,* pp. 32–33. Reprinted by permission. For more information concerning NASSP services and/or programs, please call (703) 860-0200.

Criterion validity refers to the power of a test to predict performance on a particular job. Participants in assessment centers receive ratings in 12 areas in addition to an overall placement recommendation. A number of studies have shown that assessment center ratings are positively correlated with performance in a variety of jobs. A study of the relationship of performance of school administrators to assessment center ratings reported similar results (Schmitt, Noe, Meritt, & Fitzgerald, 1983). The dimensions most highly and consistently correlated with job performance of administrators were (1) leadership, (2) oral communication, (3) organizational ability, (4) decisiveness, (5) judgment, and (6) problem analysis. Ratings of school climate were not correlated with principals' performance on the assessment center tasks.

Managerial Motivation

Although there is no single set of criteria that can ensure accurate selection of principals, applicants who have motivations that are similar to those of managers are somewhat more likely than persons without such motivations to succeed in managerial roles. Two well-researched psychological characteristics that identify managerial motivation are the need for power and the need for achievement (Stahl, 1983).

Need for power is not, as the name suggests, a desire to behave in dictatorial ways toward other people. It refers to the satisfaction that an individual receives from persuading others of the validity of his or her ideas. It might more accurately be called a "need for interpersonal influence" rather than need for power.

Need for achievement refers to the inclination to set challenging goals and strive to reach them. Individuals with this characteristic receive gratification from accomplishing demanding tasks or striving toward challenging goals. People with high need for achievement prefer goals that challenge their abilities but that they can, with hard work, expect to achieve.

In most research involving these two constructs, a projective instrument, the thematic apperception test, is used to assess an individual's placement on the achievement and power scales. Stahl (1983) developed a reliable paper-and-pencil test to measure these traits. He demonstrated that persons who hold positions as managers or who possess leadership qualities are more likely to score high on managerial motivation than nonmanagers and engineering students. Stahl operationally defined *managerial motivation* as consisting of a combination of high scores on both need for achievement and need for power. There is no difference in the incidence of managerial motivation based on gender or race. Women and minorities are equally as likely as men and whites to score high.

One trait that was found not to be related to managerial motivation was *need for affiliation.* This refers to an individual's desire to be liked and accepted by other people. One reason for the absence of an association between the two variables may be that managers occasionally need to take actions that are unpopular with those who work for them. Persons with high need for affiliation are often uncomfortable when faced with that prospect.

Reasons for Choosing Administration

A number of reasons have been advanced to explain the discrepancies in the number of females, as compared to the number of teachers, in administrative positions. Among the explanations are limited opportunities for socialization of women into administrative roles, limited visibility, and inaccessibility to informal networks (Yeakey, Johnston, & Adkison, 1986). It has also been suggested that women prefer jobs that allow them to devote time to home and family and that teaching is better suited than administration to the dual roles of careerist and homemaker (Shakeshaft, 1987).

Individuals choose to seek a career in school administration for a variety of reasons. Men and women cite different factors when they are asked to identify the attractions of an administrative career. Women cite financial factors more often than men, and women are more likely than men to give altruistic reasons for being attracted to administration. Women, much more often than men, cite the appeal of the work as a reason for their interest in administration. The opportunity to develop and use personal abilities is mentioned by both sexes about equally often (Adkison, 1985).

The Adkison study is rather dated and involved a relatively small number of administrators in one school district, and so the results should be interpreted with care, but the findings provide a clue that might help explain why more women do not apply for administrative positions. Almost 23 percent of the female respondents but only about 7 percent of male respondents cited altruistic reasons for wanting to be administrators. An example of an altruistic reason is to help children learn. Individuals with that motivation may feel they can accomplish their goal in the classroom as well as in the principal's office. For a woman who is already uncertain about her chances for promotion, such a rationalization would be easily accepted.

Need for Sponsorship

Women in positions of leadership more often than men cite the importance of encouragement from sponsors in attaining their positions. For these women, sponsorship of a relatively powerful superior appears to play a similar function in career advancement that informal networks provide for men. However, some experts suggest that sponsorship is no less critical for men than for women to advance in educational administration (Ortiz & Marshall, 1988). They argue that sponsorship limits competition and that "women have not enjoyed the benefits of the sponsorship process" (p. 126). They suggest that teaching and administration have evolved into separate, gender-specific occupations with different agendas and viewpoints.

Women who receive the support of a sponsor tend to be older than their male counterparts, since the accomplishments that bring about the recognition needed for sponsorship take time. They are also more oriented to instruction, having spent a good many years teaching and serving in quasi-administrative roles related to instruction. From the point of view of selecting promising administrative leaders for effective instruction, individuals who have demonstrated excellence in teaching and other instructional assignments over time represent a pool of talent that schools have yet to use to full advantage.

Those who make selection decisions in schools have an opportunity to bring about instructional improvement by identifying and encouraging teachers with leadership potential to apply for positions as department head, assistant principal, principal, and supervisor. It is clear that some of these people will not apply unless they are encouraged to do so and receive support from those with influence over the final selection.

Progress toward Equity

The number of women and minorities serving as school administrators in the United States continues to be disproportionately small compared to their presence in the teaching force, but some progress has been made in achieving a better balance. The proportion of public school principalships held by women more than doubled between 1979 and 1994, rising from about 15 percent to nearly 35 percent (Adkison, 1985; Zheng & Carpenter-Hubin, 1999). Central city schools were most likely to be headed by women in 1990 (41 percent), and rural areas and small towns had the fewest female school administrators (34 percent of suburban schools and 22 percent of rural and small town schools) (National Center for Education Statistics, 1993b). Female administrators are much more common in elementary schools than in secondary schools.

The number of African American principals in public schools in the South dropped sharply in the late 1960s and early 1970s as a result of desegregation of schools in that region, and the disparity in numbers of African American principals continues in the South and nationally. In 1990–91, only about 7 percent of all public school principalships were held by African Americans. They were found most often in central cities and in schools with large minority enrollments (National Center for Education Statistics, 1993b).

Selecting Other Support Personnel

Schools hire a wide variety of support personnel to help teachers work with students and provide various types of services to children and their families. Exhibit 5.3 lists some of the titles held by people in support positions in schools. Employees in these positions receive annual salaries in some cases but more often are paid on an hourly, daily, or weekly rate. The amount of education required for these jobs varies from high school to postgraduate, and pay and benefits vary accordingly.

Among the school personnel who have an important impact on instructional programs are psychologists and social workers, guidance counselors, library/

EXHIBIT 5.3 *Examples of Support Personnel Employed in Schools*

Adult education and literacy specialist	Equipment repair assistant
Athletic trainer	Maintenance
Behavior technician	Media specialist
Bus driver	Paraprofessional
Bus route coordinator	Secretary
Child nutrition worker	Social worker
Custodian	Teacher aide
Educational psychologist	Teacher assistant

media specialists, instructional aides, substitute teachers, and secretaries. Selection criteria for these positions are described in the sections that follow.

School Social Workers

School social workers, also known as visiting teachers, were introduced in schools in the early 1900s. They were added to school staffs to improve communication between families and the schools and to provide assistance to teachers and administrators in working with children who had academic, social, or emotional problems or whose home conditions posed a potential threat to their security and well-being.

Social workers perform liaison functions with community agencies, including social welfare organizations, law enforcement agencies, and medical service providers. If a child is in trouble with the police, a social worker will contact the police to find out what the child's offense was and will work with the family to obtain legal representation and help prevent a future recurrence. A social worker may also be called on to appear as a witness in court proceedings against families that refuse to send children to school or are suspected of neglect or abuse.

Typically, social workers work with individual students who have been referred by teachers for such problems as poor attendance, behavior problems, suspected abuse or malnutrition, social maladjustment, or health problems. They may be asked to investigate the home life of a child who falls asleep in school or who comes to school without lunch money. Often, social workers quietly collect food or clothing for children whose families are not able to afford to buy them, or they may put the family in touch with a church or individual who can offer assistance.

Specialized training prepares social workers to use a variety of psychological techniques and casework methods to alleviate problems of children and families. They need to have strong communication skills and must be able to work effectively with a variety of people in situations that may be dispiriting or even dangerous (Allen-Meares, Washington, & Welsh, 1996).

Social workers are expected to be proactive child advocates and must be able to work effectively with families that may be suspicious or even hostile. They must maintain good working relationships with personnel in community services agencies, churches, and the courts. Among the criteria to look for when hiring a school social worker are the desire to help children, the ability to confront recalcitrant parents and officials, and the courage to take action to remove children from deplorable home conditions when necessary.

School Psychologists

Psychologists first appeared in schools near the beginning of the twentieth century. One of the first duties they were assigned—and one on which they continue to spend a good deal of time—is performing diagnostic services for special education placement. Psychologists report that, on average, they devote about 70 percent of their time to assessment activities; 20 percent is spent consulting with parents, teachers, administrators, and other professionals; and 10 percent is allocated to direct intervention with students (Fagan & Wise, 1994).

They also assist in administering, scoring, tabulating, and interpreting the results of standardized tests; help teachers to develop diagnostic tests; and offer advice on preparing instructional materials for students with particular learning needs. Psychologists are frequently asked to conduct professional development sessions for teachers on instructional strategies for children with learning disabilities, attention deficit disorder, and/or mental retardation.

A candidate for a position as school psychologist needs to have extensive professional preparation, including a master's degree or Ph.D. Among the important personal qualities necessary for success as a psychologist in schools are warmth, empathy, and ability to relate easily to a wide variety of people. Psychologists must be familiar with a wide range of psychological and diagnostic instruments and be able to administer and interpret the results of these tests. They need to be well organized and behave at all times in an ethical manner. Communication skill and adaptability are other necessary qualities.

At one time, teaching experience was considered as a requirement for school psychologists. In recent years, however, many states have eliminated that requirement and place greater emphasis on preparation and skill as a psychologist.

Guidance Counselors

The number of counselors in public elementary and secondary schools increased from about 14,600 in 1958 (Digest of Education Statistics, 1989) to 88,607 in 1996. However, even though counselors are more common in schools now than in the past, there is not total agreement about their role. Teachers, students, parents, and principals all have opinions about an appropriate role for counselors, but they sometimes disagree.

A study of role expectations held for middle school counselors by the four groups found that parents and students held similar expectations and that teachers and principals held similar expectations. Parents and students viewed the counselor as primarily responsible for helping students with problems. Teachers and principals, on the other hand, thought of the guidance function as only part of what the counselor does; they attached equal importance to administrative tasks such as record keeping and scheduling (Remley & Albright, 1988).

Another study compared counselors' perceptions of their own role to principal's perceptions. The respondents in this case were counselors and principals in elementary, middle, and junior high schools in one midwestern state (Bonebrake & Borgers, 1984). The researchers found a high degree of agreement among the two groups in their ranking of 15 tasks performed by counselors.

Guidance Counselor Functions.   School guidance counselors perform eight vital functions in schools. These functions demonstrate the variety of activities that counselors are involved in and the number of groups with which they work:

1. Counselors collect and record information for student records.
2. Counselors communicate with teachers and specialists about students with learning or emotional problems.
3. Counselors confer with families who request assistance with children's academic, health, and social problems.
4. Counselors meet with individuals and groups of students to discuss class schedules, educational and career planning, and academic and interpersonal problems.
5. Counselors collect follow-up data from graduates on their educational and career experiences since graduation.
6. Counselors coordinate special student services provided by specialists such as psychologists and social workers.
7. Counselors write letters of reference for students seeking admission to institutions of higher education or applying for jobs.
8. Counselors coordinate state or district testing programs and assist in administering tests and interpreting results to students and families.

Individual counseling provides students with an opportunity to have professional assistance in a caring, nonevaluative environment to solve problems and make decisions. Group guidance is developmental and preventive in nature. In group counseling, the counselor facilitates interaction among members of a group of students who are attempting to solve common developmental problems. Counselors may also train teachers to provide group guidance services.

Secondary school counselors assist students in making career plans and selecting courses appropriate for those plans, and provide guidance on how to meet high school graduation requirements. Career guidance and counseling is an organized group program that helps students prepare to select a career and enter the world of work.

Counselors often help to coordinate services provided by school and community agencies for a child. They serve as liaison from the school to community agencies and handle requests for information from community individuals and groups. Counselors also perform a public relations service by informing parents and members of the community about guidance and counseling programs and services.

Factors that are considered in selecting counselors are the recency and quality of training and, in particular, exposure to a well-planned and comprehensive internship. Positive personal qualities are especially important for counselors because of the closeness of the relationship between the counselor and the students with whom he or she works.

Traits that have been identified as essential to success in counseling include accurate empathic understanding, communication of respect, warmth, sincerity, and specific expression (Herr, 1982). Depending on the nature of the assignment, other criteria will be added to those essentials. Additional qualifications include knowledge of occupational opportunity structures, knowledge of requirements for entry into various occupations, and the ability to relate effectively to parents and teachers.

Skills in which counselors are most likely to need additional training, as determined by a survey of experts, are counseling students from single-parent families, consultation skills with teachers, small-group counseling, and planning a comprehensive career development program. More than three-fourths of respondents identified those as critical training needs of school counselors (Comas, Cecil, & Cecil, 1987).

Given the emerging demographic profile of schools, the first task (counseling children from single-parent families) is one that counselors increasingly will be called on to perform. Other skills identified by the experts in which counselors are in need of training are ethical standards, drug abuse and alcohol counseling, parent education (Comas et al., 1987), and violence in the schools. All of these are areas about which interviewers may want to question counselor applicants during the selection process.

Library/Media Specialists

As the use of instructional technology has become more common in schools, the role of the media specialist has increased in importance. The title *media specialist* is intended to convey a sense of the emerging role of librarian. In addition to such traditional tasks as maintaining collections of a variety of sources of information, librarians now are expected to be familiar with current and constantly changing ways of storing and retrieving information.

This requires that they understand the operation of computers and be able not only to access information but also to train others to use the software by which accessibility is gained. To some extent at the present time and to a much greater degree in the future, library/media specialists will be expected to provide support for teachers who wish to develop instructional software and to help solve the problems that arise in the process of using individually developed or commercially produced programs.

Two attributes should be given primacy in the selection of media specialists. The first is an attitude that encourages students and teachers to use the media center and its materials extensively and often. Usage creates extra work for the staff, since books, magazines, records, compact disks, filmstrips, fiche, recorders, and projectors that are taken from shelves and drawers must be returned to them. However, care should be taken to hire media specialists who will welcome usage of the media center as an indicator that the center is contributing to the vitality of the instructional program.

The second attribute to be looked for in a prospective media specialist is recent training. A person need not have just graduated in order to have up-to-date knowledge about instructional technology, but it is certain that anyone who completed their training more than three or four years previously and who has not had recent refresher training since graduating is out of date. This is one field in which training must be almost constant in order for a person to remain in touch.

Instructional Aides

Instructional aides represent the largest group of support personnel in schools. They provide a variety of services for teachers and students. More than 30 states have established guidelines for hiring instructional aides. Although few states require certification for instructional aides, most require that they have at least a high school education. Many districts now provide district-sponsored in-service education programs for aides. Professional groups recommend that training provided for aides should include the following topics: developmental characteristics of children, learning principles and instructional strategies, behavior management strategies, and strategies for maintaining a safe and secure environment in the classroom. Los Angeles provides training for teams consisting of teachers and aides who work together, and Albuquerque (New Mexico) and Cleveland (Ohio) give financial aid and time so that aides can take college work to help them advance on the career ladder (*Roles for Education,* 1997).

Instructional aides in Denver tutor students who need assistance with reading and work with others on computer-assisted supplemental mathematics. Norfolk (Virginia) schools train aides to serve as liaisons to parents of "at-risk" children. They plan workshops for parents, make home visits, and perform other services. Instructional aides in some districts are represented on school councils, participating in making decisions about the curriculum and instructional practices (*Roles for Education,* 1997).

The list of duties that aides perform to assist teachers is limited only by the teacher's imagination and the aide's abilities. Aides do everything from helping to fill out report cards, to planning and presenting plays, to tutoring students, to mixing paints (Nielsen, 1977). The job description for elementary school aides published by Kent (Washington) School District lists six functions of aides (Educational Research Service, 1984):

1. Assists teacher in management of student arrival and departure activities
2. Provides staff with clerical assistance such as typing, filing, duplicating, recording information, and organizing materials for distribution
3. Assists with personal needs of students
4. Supervises students at the elementary level during play periods and recess periods in and out of classrooms
5. Performs supportive tasks for a certified teacher that are primarily non-instructional in nature
6. Performs other duties as assigned

The list contains no mention of aides being involved in instruction, but in many classrooms, teacher aides extend instruction by the use of follow-up strategies to reinforce what students have been taught. Research indicates that aides can perform this role as effectively as teachers if they receive appropriate training (Love & Levine, 1992).

Aides are more common in elementary schools and special education classrooms than in other settings. In special education classes, aides assist teachers by attending to the physical and emotional needs of children who have disabilities.

The preferred candidate for the job of aide is someone who will be able to take directives from teachers but who does not need to wait to be told what to do. Experience with children is an advantage.

Substitute Teachers

Human resources administrators report that it is becoming more difficult to find good substitutes for teachers who are absent from their jobs. Because of the short supply of teachers in certain subject fields, some former substitutes have been pressed into full-time service, whereas others are limiting their substitute work because of difficult teaching conditions, heavy paperwork demands, and uncooperative students. Schools that provide support are the most likely to be able to find substitute teachers when they need them.

Respondents in a recent study reported that substituting is most apt to be an enjoyable experience in schools in which teachers are helpful, materials are easily located, and the teacher leaves lesson plans and suggestions for activities for students who finish their work early. All teachers, including substitutes, appreciate having well-behaved students; substitutes also like to have the names of two or three dependable students who are familiar with homework assignments and the classroom schedule. Survey respondents also reported that being informed about classroom rules, routines, and emergency procedures and having seating charts made their work easier (Tannenbaum, 2000).

Some schools use a report form to be completed by both the substitute and regular teacher. On the form, the substitute teacher can report how much material was covered, whether any problems arose, and note questions raised by students. The regular classroom teacher uses the form to thank the substitute or to make special requests (e.g., that furniture and supplies be put back in place next time). Both teachers see the other's report, and the principal also reviews them. In this way, two-way communication is maintained and the principal is alerted to any problems that may have arisen (Tannenbaum, 2000).

Few districts provide training for substitute teachers, although many school administrators believe that some training would be useful. An orientation session to familiarize substitutes with the district curriculum and workshops on teaching children with disabilities are mentioned often as needed innovations, but because of the competition for substitutes, districts hesitate to unilaterally impose training requirements (Tannenbaum, 2000).

Districts that have developed successful strategies for locating and retaining substitute teachers are usually happy to share their ideas with professional colleagues. Some of the strategies that have worked can be found on the website for the Substitute Teaching Institute at Utah State University, Logan. See the Online Resource section at the end of this chapter for the address of the website. Ideas for attracting substitute teachers that have worked include offering higher pay, longevity pay, provision of partial benefits, and discounts on merchandise in local stores.

Secretaries

A school secretary's is often the first voice heard by parents and others who call the school, the first person to whom new students talk, and the first individual contacted by visitors to the school (Drake & Roe, 1986). Secretaries are often known by more students than any other single individual, with the exception of the classroom teacher and possibly the principal. Given the nature of this position and the extent of the secretary's contacts with the public, teachers, and students, careful selection for this position is critical.

It has been estimated that there are four million school secretaries in the United States and that 99 percent of them are females. Their duties can be classified into five categories (Rimer, 1984):

1. Public relations (greeting visitors, explaining school rules and policies to parents of new students, dealing with community organizations and special groups)
2. Student services (attending to nonlearning needs of students; performing as nurse, friend, disciplinarian; possessor of supplies and information)
3. Clerical (filing, typing, answering the telephone, record keeping, maintaining staff and student records, requesting or sending student information, writing letters, making announcements, operating office equipment, and maintaining office supplies)
4. Financial (collecting money, writing checks, making deposits, bookkeeping, filling out requisitions)
5. Office management (maintaining an attractive and businesslike environment and supervising clerical employees and student workers)

It should be clear from the foregoing that the secretary is first and foremost a public relations expert. In schools with more than one clerical employee, one serves primarily as gatekeeper, providing or denying access to the principal, receiving and transmitting telephone messages, and dealing with walk-in or call-in requests from students and teachers. The second employee then is assigned to handle clerical duties and office management chores and, when needed, to assist the head secretary with information requests.

A necessary qualification for the position of secretary is the ability to tolerate frequent interruptions without undue frustration. Regardless of the importance of the task being worked on, the secretary is expected to put it aside to handle a request from a student or teacher. Rarely is the secretary able to finish a task without being interrupted at least once. To work in such an atmosphere requires patience, flexibility, and a sense of humor. Some of the tasks that secretaries perform, most notably financial record keeping and check writing, require an atmosphere that permits concentration. In order to keep errors to a minimum, it is necessary to provide an opportunity for the secretary who performs those chores to retreat to a quiet, out-of-the-way room where there will be no interruptions. When selecting a secretary, it is important to recognize that not all individuals operate effectively in an atmosphere as busy as school offices often are. Care must be taken to select the person who can tolerate the noise and confusion without undue feelings of stress.

Because of their location in the center of the school's information flow, secretaries obtain considerable confidential information about teachers and students. Caplow (1976) noted that employees who have access to the manager of an organization and who possess information about other organization members acquire power that exceeds that allocated to them by the organization chart. He warned that such power can be a source of organizational problems and thus urged managers to keep the power of their assistants in check.

Summary

Successful schools depend on the quality of the personnel who run them. Besides teachers, schools require administrators, counselors, secretaries, teachers' aides, substitute teachers, and other support staff. The selection process for these positions is similar to that used to select teachers, beginning with preparation of a job model or job description and announcement of the vacancy. Administrative vacancies receive priority attention in school districts because of the critical nature of the position. Principals perform eight functions, including organizing the school setting, supervising and evaluating teachers, supervising student discipline and safety, and encouraging instructional improvement. These functions should form the basis for assessing applicants for administrative positions.

Selection of assistant principals has been a neglected area, but with increasing attention to the importance of the principalship for school effectiveness, more care is being taken to select well-qualified assistants. People who possess managerial motivation (high need for achievement and power) generally gravitate toward positions of leadership. Minorities and women have made progress in increasing their representation in administrative ranks in school districts in recent years, but they are still underrepresented in comparison to their presence in the teaching force. The number of counselors in schools has grown rapidly. Counselors provide a variety of services, including personal and group counseling and career guidance.

Suggested Activities

1. Interview an assistant principal and prepare a list of duties performed or results expected on the job. Compare duties performed by assistant principals to those performed by the principal.

2. In developing board policy on evaluation of teaching personnel, it is advisable to be flexible on certain issues and specific on others. Examine a policy statement on evaluation, paying particular attention to the following elements and tell whether the policy defines practice narrowly or allows some leeway.
    a. Number of observation visits by principal
    b. Allowing teachers to evaluate their colleagues
    c. Naming personnel who may observe classes and which ones may not
    d. Timing of classroom observations and requiring advance notice
    e. Establishing a deadline for completing the evaluation process
    f. Establishing an appeals procedure for teachers who feel they have been rated too low
    g. Determining remedial actions for teachers who receive unsatisfactory ratings

3. Form three-member panels to debate the question: Should administrators be selected from within the district or recruited from outside the district? Cite evidence to support your position.

4. Write a letter of application for the position of school principal. Select two or three of the eight functions of principals described in this chapter and explain how your educational and work experiences have prepared you to perform those functions.

Online Resource

Substitute teachers generally receive little attention from researchers. The site shown here is devoted to substitute teachers.

Substitute Teaching Institute, Utah State University, Logan (http://subed.usu.edu)
The Institute helps school districts develop policies and best practices for recruiting, screening, training, and evaluating substitute teachers. The website contains information of value to administrators who are responsible for obtaining substitute teachers and for the teachers themselves.

References

Adkison, J. (1985). The structure of opportunity and administrative opportunities. *Urban Education, 20,* 327–347.

Allen-Meares, P., Washington, R., & Welsh, B. (1996). *Social work services in schools* (2nd ed.). Boston: Allyn & Bacon.

Anderson, L., & Gardner, C. (1995). Substitute teachers. In L. Anderson (Ed.), *International encyclopedia of teaching and teacher education* (2nd ed., pp. 367–369). Tarrytown, NY: Pergamon.

Anderson, M. (1988). *Hiring capable principals: How school districts recruit, groom, and select the best candidates.* Eugene, OR: Oregon School Study Council.

Baltzell, D., & Dentler, R. (1983). *Selecting American school principals: A sourcebook for educators.* Washington, DC: National Institute of Education.

Bonebrake, C., & Borgers, S. (1984). Counselor role as perceived by counselors and principals. *Elementary School Guidance and Counseling, 18,* 194–199.

Caplow, T. (1976). *How to run any organization.* New York: Holt Rinehart.

Comas, R., Cecil, J., & Cecil, C. (1987). Using expert opinion to determine professional development needs of school counselors. *The School Counselor, 35,* 81–87.

Digest of education statistics. (1989). Washington, DC: U.S. Office of Education.

Drake, T., & Roe, W. (1986). *The principalship* (3rd ed.). New York: Macmillan.

Educational Research Service. (1984). *Job descriptions in public schools.* Arlington, VA: Author.

Egginton, W., Jeffries, T., & Kidd-Knights, D. (1988, April). State-mandated tests for principals— A growing trend? *NASSP Bulletin, 72,* 62–65.

Fagan, T., & Wise, P. (1994). *School psychology: Past, present and future.* New York: Longman.

Gaertner, K. (1978/1979). The structure of careers in public school administration. *Administrator's Notebook, 27*(6), 1–4.

Gatewood, R., & Feild, H. (1987). *Human resource selection.* Chicago: Dryden.

Herr, E. (1982). Discussion. In H. Walberg (Ed.), *Improving educational standards and productivity* (pp. 99–109). Berkeley, CA: McCutchan.

Hess, F. (1985). The socialization of the assistant principal from the perspective of the local school district. *Education and Urban Society, 18,* 93–106.

Jentz, B. (1982). *Entry: The hiring, start-up, and supervision of administrators.* New York: McGraw-Hill.

Kirkpatrick, R. (2000, September). Recruiting and developing candidates for principal. *NASSP Bulletin, 84,* 38–43.

Landy, F. (1985). *Psychology of work behavior.* Homewood, IL: Dorsey.

Love, I., & Levine, D. (1992). *Performance ratings of teacher aides with and without training and follow-up in extending reading instruction.* Paper presented at the annual meeting of the American Educational Research Association, San Francisco. (ERIC Reproduction Service No. ED 349294).

McCall, D. (1986, January). Twelve skill dimensions: Professional benefits. *NASSP Bulletin, 70,* 32–33.

Million, J. (1998, April). Where have all the principals gone? *NAESP Online.* Available online: www.naesp.org/comm/pr0498.htm.

National Center for Education Statistics. (1993a). *Digest of education statistics.* Washington, DC: U.S. Department of Education.

National Center for Education Statistics. (1993b). *Schools and staffing in the United States: A statistical profile, 1990–91.* Washington, DC: U.S. Department of Education.

National Center for Education Statistics. (1994, January). Public and private school principals: Are there too few women? *Issue Brief,* pp. 1–2.

Nielsen, E. (1977). *Instructional aides.* Redwood City, CA: San Mateo County Office of Education. (ERIC Document Reproduction Service No. ED 238824).

Ortiz, F., & Marshall, C. (1988). Women in educational administration. In N. Boyan (Ed.), *Handbook of research on educational administration* (pp. 123–141). New York: Longman.

Reed, D., & Himmler, A. (1985). The work of the secondary assistant principal: A field study. *Education and Urban Society, 18,* 59–84.

Remley, T., Jr., & Albright, P. (1988). Expectations for middle school counselors: Views of students, teachers, principals, and parents. *The School Counselor, 35,* 290–296.

Rimer, A. (1984, Fall). Elementary school secretary: Informal decision maker. *Educational Horizons, 63,* 16–18.

Roles for education: Paraprofessionls in effective schools. (1997). Washington, DC: U.S. Department of Education.

Schmitt, N., Noe, R., Meritt, R., & Fitzgerald, M. (1983). *Validity of assessment center ratings for the prediction of performance ratings and school climate of school administrators.* (ERIC Document Reproduction Service No. ED 236777).

Shakeshaft, C. (1987). *Women in educational administration.* Newbury Park, CA: Sage.

Spady, W. (1985). The vice-principal as an agent of instructional reform. *Education and Urban Society, 18,* 107–120.

Stahl, M. (1983). Achievement, power and managerial motivation: Selecting managerial talent with the job choice exercise. *Personnel Psychology, 36,* 775–789.

Tannenbaum, M. (2000, May). No substitute for quality. *Educational Leadership, 57,* 70–72.

Yeakey, C., Johnston, G., & Adkison, J. (1986). In pursuit of equity: A review of research on minorities and women in educational administration. *Educational Administration Quarterly, 22,* 110–149.

Zheng, H., Carpenter-Hubin, J. (1999). *Exploring gender differences in America's school administrator workforce: Statistical evidence from national surveys.* Paper presented at the annual meeting of the American Educational Research Association. (ERIC Document Reproduction Service No. ED 432817).

6

Motivation of Personnel

Individuals who work with other human beings make daily decisions that reflect their beliefs about how to motivate people. These private theories of motivation may be simple or elaborate, primitive or sophisticated, based on research or personal experience, yet everyone has a personal theory of motivation on which he or she acts when working with others. The purpose of this chapter is to investigate three of the most widely accepted theories of motivation and to consider the implications of these theories for managing human resources in schools.

Plan of the Chapter

This chapter suggests ways of applying what is known about motivation to the problem of improving instructional effectiveness in schools. The chapter covers the following topics: (1) meaning of work motivation, (2) expectancy theory, (3) equity theory, (4) goal-setting theory, (5) job satisfaction in teaching, and (6) job satisfaction and teacher turnover.

Meaning of Work Motivation

The factors that influence people in choosing an occupation and in carrying out the tasks associated with a particular job have been studied by organizational psychologists for many years. Most of the research on motivation in the workplace has taken place in industrial settings. Nevertheless, much of what has been learned can be applied to those who work in schools.

Work motivation consists of a set of forces "that originate both within as well as beyond an individual's being, to initiate work-related behavior, and to determine its form, direction, intensity, and duration" (Pinder, 1984, p. 8) and as having to do with "the conditions responsible for variations in the intensity, quality, and direction of ongoing behavior" (Landy, 1985, p. 317). By combining elements of these descriptions, we arrive at a definition that is suitable for our purposes.

Work motivation refers to conditions responsible for variations in the intensity, quality, direction, and duration of work-related behavior. Variations in the quality of work produced by employees may arise from either motivational or knowledge differences. If an employee is not achieving satisfactory results, it is necessary to ascertain whether the problem originates with lack of motivation, lack of knowledge, or both.

Psychologists have advanced several theories to explain how people become motivated to perform a job and what factors within the individual or in the work setting influence the level of motivation experienced. Three theories are of particular interest to school administrators because of their potential for improving our understanding of work motivation among teachers. The three theories are:

1. *Expectancy theory:* Advocates believe that people are motivated by the opportunity to earn incentives.
2. *Equity theory:* Advocates believe that people expect a balance between effort expended and rewards received and lose motivation when that balance is missing.
3. *Goal-setting theory:* Advocates believe that people are motivated to achieve identified goals.

Each theory has its own implications for administrative action. An administrator who believes that employees are motivated by expectancy will attempt to identify and distribute incentives to increase teacher motivation. One who believes in equity theory will try to provide more generous rewards to employees who work hard and withhold some rewards from those who put forth less effort. Administrators who subscribe to goal-setting theory will attempt to identify long- and short-range goals that are personally meaningful to employees and help the employees to achieve those goals.

These theories are described in more detail in the following sections.

Expectancy Theory

Expectancy theory is based on the premise that workers perform tasks to gain incentives and that motivation is a function of the value of the incentive to the individual. Vroom incorporated three concepts into his model of expectancy motivation—valence, instrumentality, and expectancy—so the theory is sometimes referred to as VIE theory (cited in Pinder, 1984).

1. *Valence* refers to the positive or negative feelings attached to work outcomes. For example, money received for performing a job has positive valence for most workers, whereas working in a dirty environment has negative valence. For teachers, student success has positive valence. Some work outcomes that

have negative valence for teachers are unnecessary paperwork and being required to monitor hallways, restrooms, and bus-loading areas.

2. *Instrumentality* refers to the perceived connection between a work outcome and some object or event that has positive valence for an employee. An employee must believe that something he or she does on the job will lead to a desirable result in order for motivation to occur. According to the theory, a teacher who has been asked by the principal to serve on a textbook committee will be more motivated to serve if he or she believes that by doing so, something pleasant will be forthcoming. The teacher must believe that the task (serving on the committee) is instrumentally related to an incentive he or she values. That might be the principal's approval, or it might be the opportunity to improve the instructional program.

3. *Expectancy* refers to the employee's perception of the probability of successfully achieving a work outcome. In the preceding example, the teacher who has been asked to serve on the textbook committee may decide not to do it if she believes that she lacks the requisite knowledge and skills, since she would not expect to be able to perform the task satisfactorily.

Glatthorn (1995) summarizes these three factors in terms of teachers' beliefs: "I can perform successfully" (expectancy), "The actions I take will achieve the results I want" (instrumentality), and "The results I achieve will be recognized by rewards that I value" (valence). He notes that in the United States, teachers are motivated by intrinsic rewards, such as the satisfaction of seeing students learn, whereas in some other countries, teachers place more value on salary and other extrinsic rewards.

Expectancy theory suggests that instrumentality is a function of an individual's estimate of the probability that he or she can achieve certain results. When one's success is tied to the performance of others, as it is in programs that reward groups of teachers, then instrumentality is the sum of the individuals' estimates of success. In such a program, each teacher considers not only his or her ability to accomplish desired results but must also attempt to determine whether other teachers will be successful. In that situation, instrumentality will be influenced by cohesiveness among teachers and the level of confidence they have in one another (Kelley, 1998).

Work outcomes include tasks performed on the job, but they may also include *opportunities*. For example, the chance to attend a workshop to improve one's skills is a work outcome, but most of us would not refer to it as a task. This distinction is important because with it we can use expectancy theory to help explain why teachers are sometimes not motivated to participate in staff development activities.

Expectancy theory is illustrated in Figure 6.1. The figure shows how a work situation leads to a condition of motivation or lack of motivation for an employee. The employee considers a work outcome, which might be an in-service program offering instruction on a new way to teach music. The teacher asks first, "Can I achieve the work outcome?" This might involve several other considerations, including "Do I have the time to take this in-service class?" "Is Tuesday afternoon a convenient time for me?" "Can I learn the material?" If the answer to any of these questions is *no*, the teacher will not be motivated for this particular work outcome.

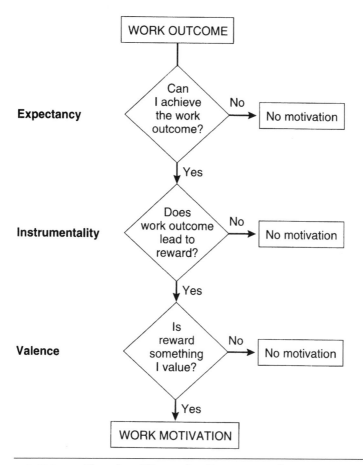

FIGURE 6.1   **Flowchart Illustrating Expectancy Theory**

If the answer to all of the questions is *yes,* the teacher moves to the next decision block.

At this point, the teacher considers whether there is an incentive to perform the outcome. The music teacher in the example might decide that the workshop could result in her acquiring new instructional techniques that would increase student interest in music or help her get a better job. If one of these outcomes has positive valence for the teacher, then she will be motivated to attend the workshop.

Consider another situation: A district offers a salary increment to teachers who agree to teach in schools with concentrations of low-achieving students. A teacher considers first whether he or she can perform the task. If the job involves working with children with learning problems, the teacher may decide that he or she lacks the necessary skills. However, if the teacher feels able and qualified to do the job and the salary increment is attractive, he or she will be motivated to accept the offer.

Ethical Question

Some psychologists have commented recently that the use of rewards and incentives as motivators raises ethical questions. Some have also challenged their effectiveness in increasing motivation. Kohn (1993) stated, "Rewards, like punishments, can usually get people to do what we want for a while. In that sense, they 'work.' But my reading of the research, corroborated by real-world observation, is that rewards can never buy us anything more than short-term compliance" (p. 784).

Kohn (1993) has written specifically about motivating learners, but he believes that similar conclusions apply to other situations. He argues that when incentives are used to change behavior—whether to persuade people to quit smoking or to wear seatbelts—the use of incentives works as long as rewards are forthcoming, but when the rewards are withdrawn, individuals revert to earlier behaviors.

Those who have ethical objections to incentives suggest that their use amounts to an effort to control people's behavior, and they are opposed to that because they feel that it denies individuals the right of free choice. The debate about the use of incentives will continue, since both sides are convinced that they are correct. In the meantime, the use of incentives in the workplace will probably continue. Those who supervise personnel in schools will need to consider the ethical implications of their actions and adjust their behavior accordingly.

Rewards and Incentives

For an incentive to have an effect on performance, it is necessary that the employee anticipate receiving it and understand that certain performance standards must be met in order to qualify to receive the reward. Anticipation differentiates *rewards* from *incentives,* terms that are often and incorrectly used interchangeably (Mitchell, Ortiz, & Mitchell, 1983).

Incentives are of three types: material, solidary, and purposive (Clark & Wilson, 1961). *Material incentives* are tangible rewards, such as money and prizes, awarded to employees who attain specified levels of performance. *Solidary incentives* come from association with members of a group. Peer acceptance and support are examples of solidary incentives. *Purposive incentives* are rewards that are related to the purpose for which an organization exists. Giving teachers a greater voice in decisions about their work is an example of a purposive incentive.

Examples of incentives under the three categories identified by Clark and Wilson (1961) are:

Material Incentives
1. Fewer extra-duty assignments
2. Financial assistance

Solidary Incentives
1. Recognition or praise for performance
2. Assistance and support from peers

Purposive Incentives
1. Assignments that utilize special knowledge and skills
2. Opportunities for professional growth and development

Guidelines for Applying Expectancy Motivation

Using expectancy theory to motivate teachers is more likely to succeed if administrators follow these guidelines:

1. Select incentives that are valued by teachers. Schools make relatively little use of purposive and solidary rewards, even though teachers generally respond positively to them. Direct financial incentives to teachers seem to have promise for attracting teachers to specific assignments, such as schools with large numbers of non-English-speaking students or schools located in neighborhoods with a high rate of crime. They can also be used to achieve specific goals, such as raising achievement test scores. However, financial incentives do not work as well in raising the overall level of quality of teaching performance (Johnson, 1986). These issues will be discussed in more detail in Chapter 10.
2. Be sure that teachers understand the instrumental connection between work outcomes and incentives. If the connection between the work outcome and the incentive is not clear, no motivation will occur. Some merit pay programs fail because teachers do not understand what they must do to earn the merit increase.
3. Select work outcomes that are attainable. Teachers must believe that a work outcome is attainable in order for expectancy to affect their work behavior. Choosing work outcomes that are beyond the reach of most teachers defeats the purpose of using rewards and incentives.
4. Make incentives available to all teachers but allow the individuals to decide whether to seek them. Do not use incentives to achieve work outcomes that are expected or required of all employees. For example, teachers should not be offered incentives for being on time to school.
5. Make sure that teachers who achieve designated work outcomes receive the associated reward.

Equity Theory

Equity theory can be illustrated by a story about a man who has just bought a new car at what he feels is a bargain price. The man searched for a dealer who would consider an offer and then negotiated with the salesperson to get the best deal possible. After considerable effort, he succeeded in buying the automobile with the equipment he wanted at a price substantially below the list price. A week later, he tells a friend about his good fortune and learns that the friend has that day bought an identical car from the same dealer at an even lower price.

The car buyer's evaluation of his own performance changed when he learned that his friend had been more successful than he. In the same way, workers evaluate the rewards they receive by comparing them to the rewards garnered by others in similar jobs (Adams, 1965). Thus, a teacher who receives a $1,000 salary increment will feel satisfied if other teachers received a similar amount but dissatisfied if other teachers received more.

To whom do employees compare themselves in making equity judgments? According to equity theory, an interpersonal standard is the basis for judgment. Individuals compare their effort/reward ratio to that of other employees in similar jobs. If the ratios are equal or nearly so, individuals feel satisfied, but they are likely to be dissatisfied if they feel they are working harder or receiving fewer rewards than coworkers in similar jobs (Goodman, 1974).

Reducing Tension

Equity theory also suggests that if Allan and Barry both work equally hard but Allan receives a promotion and Barry does not, both will experience feelings of psychological tension. They may try by various means to allay the tension, including cognitive distortion. For example, Barry may tell himself, "Maybe Allan works harder than I thought" or "Allan talks a lot about how hard he works, and the boss believes him."

A second way to relieve psychological tension is to change one's inputs. Barry may decide not to work so hard, or he may elect to change his priorities on the job in order to devote more effort to activities that are rewarded. He may also act to change the comparison. One way to do that is to tell himself, "Allan may be a better salesman, but I'm a better manager." Or he may say, "A promotion is not worth it if I have to neglect my family to get it." Finally, Barry may leave the job altogether.

Allan may experience some of the same tension that Barry feels, and if so he will probably react in some of the same ways. For example, he might distort reality by telling himself, "I always thought Barry was kind of lazy." Or he may decide to change his inputs by working less hard in order to avoid further alienation from Barry.

Equity theory helps one to understand teachers' opposition to merit pay and other forms of performance-based compensation. Since most of these programs rely on principals' ratings to determine which teachers will receive salary increases, teachers fear that principals may reward their favorites and ignore all others. Teachers seem to be less concerned about inequities in the single salary schedule than they are about possible inequities in performance-based compensation plans.

Equity theory assumes that employees have accurate information about the amount of effort their colleagues expend, but in education that assumption is often faulty. Since teachers seldom observe one another's work directly, they lack complete information about the work habits of others. Nevertheless, they form judgments about which of their colleagues work hard and which do not, basing those conclusions on inconclusive evidence, such as how late a teacher stays at school and whether he or she takes work home.

Even though an employee may be misinformed about how hard colleagues work, it is the beliefs one holds that provoke the responses predicted by equity theory. Thus, the perception of inequity has the same effect on employee behavior as actual inequity.

Guidelines for Applying Equity Motivation

Using equity theory to motivate teachers is most likely to be successful when administrators follow these guidelines:

1. Differentiating rewards on the basis of performance will increase productivity but may also increase intragroup conflict. If harmonious relations and minimal conflict are important, distribute rewards equally among members.
2. Whenever possible, give all employees the chance to work toward rewards, but if rewards are offered to some groups and not others, make certain that the individuals understand and accept the reasons for the differentiation. Providing clerical assistance to employees who serve on a curriculum revision committee is acceptable, but providing such assistance to coaches who already receive a salary increment is likely to be perceived as inequitable.
3. Achieve a balance between the effort required and the value of the reward. Rewards that are of little value should be more easily attained than those that are of greater value. In education, the cost of incentive programs is always a concern. Costs may be capped by limiting the number of incentive awards given, but a more equitable approach is to increase the amount of effort required to gain a reward, so that fewer people try for them.
4. In education, perceived inequities most often arise in connection with evaluating performance. If no objective and valid way of measuring performance exists, managers are vulnerable to charges of unfairly rewarding favorites. To avoid the charge, appoint a committee of teachers to set standards for deciding which individuals shall receive rewards.

Goal-Setting Theory

One reason that games are highly motivating is because they have clear and challenging goals. Whether playing bridge, video games, or touch football, participants understand the objective of the activity and enjoy the challenge of trying to attain it. A number of psychologists contend that clear-cut and challenging goals are as effective for motivating people in work settings as in recreational situations. Locke and Latham (1984) suggest that people gain a sense of accomplishment and efficacy from attaining goals, provided the goals are sufficiently challenging and success is not either impossible or meaningless.

Goal-setting theory has been shown to work in psychological laboratories as well as actual work environments when the goals are accepted by the people involved. Studies have shown that individuals who were assigned more challenging goals outperformed those who received moderately difficult or easy goals. Also, individuals who were given specific goals did better than those who were given vague admonitions such as "Do your best."

Goal setting is a form of self-leadership. Organizations use a variety of external control mechanisms for influencing employee behavior, including evaluation, rules and policies, and supervisory oversight. In recent years, however, organizations have begun to place more emphasis on internal controls. By working to achieve commitment by employees to the organizational mission and goals, it is the hope of these organizations that the need for external mechanisms of control will diminish.

Self-leadership refers to an inclination by an employee to engage in behaviors that contribute to the accomplishment of an organization's mission and that are performed in the absence of any external constraint (Manz, 1986). Employees engage in self-leadership because they are committed to the goals and purpose of the organization that employs them. In schools with school-based management, self-leadership assumes greater importance because these schools do not have access to the full range of external controls on employees that are available to districts with centralized administrative structures.

Locke and Latham (1984) stated that goals are motivating for employees even though they were not involved in setting them. Teachers may differ from other employees in that respect, however, since teachers believe that setting instructional goals is an important function of their jobs. Goals that are set by the administration are more likely to be accepted by teachers if the principal justifies the choice of goals and offers to provide support to members in attaining those outcomes.

Guidelines for Applying Goal-Setting Motivation

When goal setting is used as a motivational device for employees in schools, the following principles should be kept in mind:

1. There is some evidence that goal setting works better when employees are confident of their ability to achieve goals (Carroll & Tosi, 1973). Supervisors may need to provide interpersonal support for employees who lack confidence in their ability to achieve a goal. Individuals who are new to the job may be especially uneasy about identifying performance goals.
2. Performance goals should reflect the outcomes envisioned in the school's strategic plan and mission statement. Other documents that can be helpful in formulating goals are job models and incentive pay plans or career ladders.
3. A way should be found to measure progress toward individual or group performance goals and to share the findings. Detailed feedback helps in several ways. It reduces uncertainty concerning which behaviors are most appropriate in the pursuit of goals, and it provides information about the relative importance of various goals (Ashford & Cummings, 1983). Feedback is more

likely to be perceived accurately if it follows the performance without delay, is positive, and is given relatively frequently (Ilgen, Fisher, & Taylor, 1979). The motivational value of feedback is influenced by the extent to which it conveys to the recipient a sense of competence.

4. Employees will be more committed to performance goals that are chosen consensually by members of work teams.

Using Goal Setting for Evaluation

Goal setting is commonly used in schools as part of the evaluation process. Teachers choose annual goals and are evaluated on their success in achieving them. In such programs, it is advisable for principals and teachers to discuss how goal attainment will be measured and to set a date for achieving the goals (Locke & Latham, 1984). The time limit is ordinarily one year, but interim reviews of teacher performance at periodic intervals during the year are recommended. Teacher evaluation schemes that involve teacher-selected outcomes are reviewed in more detail in Chapter 9.

Guidelines for Goal Setting in Evaluation

When goal setting is used as an adjunct to teacher evaluation, the following guidelines should be considered:

1. Individual teachers should select goals that help advance the school's established mission. The principal can help by reviewing individuals' goals for compatibility with the objectives of the school.
2. Since individuals vary in their abilities and stage of professional development, some variance in goal difficulty is to be expected. However, employees should be advised to maintain a reasonably comparable level of difficulty in the goals they select. If one individual chooses very challenging targets while another picks only easy ones, the effect will be to create feelings of inequity and demotivation.
3. When an organization asks employees to identify performance goals, it should commit itself to help the employees achieve the goals they choose. To avoid the frustration and discouragement that arise from seeking unrealistic results, employees should be advised to select attainable goals, and supervisors should work to obtain the resources employees need in order to achieve them (Katzell & Thompson, 1990).
4. Employees should be assisted to write goal statements that are clear and concise, describe measurable outcomes, and require a significant and continuing effort. Since most goal statements represent a year's work, a problem that is sometimes encountered is that the goals are too modest. A goal that can be accomplished within a month or two is not sufficiently challenging. Employees often think of goals as being an addition to their normal workload. In fact,

the goal statement should incorporate the activities that are part of normal responsibilities.

5. Employees are understandably concerned about the possibility of being penalized if they select goals that are too difficult and they fail to achieve them. That fear can be reduced by giving individuals an opportunity to revise their goals if it turns out they are unable to accomplish as much as they had expected.

Job Satisfaction in Teaching

A persistent question in the minds of administrators and organizational psychologists has to do with the relationship between job satisfaction and performance. It is frequently assumed that by creating conditions that increase employees' levels of satisfaction, we will obtain increased productivity, but the evidence for a connection between the two is not strong.

The median correlation from studies that examined the relationship between satisfaction and performance was about 0.14 (Vroom, 1964). In practical terms, that means that when an employee's level of satisfaction increases, the job performance will improve slightly, or that when job performance improves, job satisfaction levels will rise a little. The direction of the cause-effect relationship is not clear. Some experts believe that satisfaction results from performance rather than the other way around (Lawler & Rhode, 1976).

Two explanations for the low correlation between satisfaction and productivity have been advanced. One is that in many jobs productivity is determined by the speed at which an assembly line moves or a machine operates. Employees' feelings do not influence the machines' speed (Fincham & Rhodes, 1988). A second explanation is that employees may feel satisfaction for reasons that are unrelated or negatively related to productivity. For example, a vendor in a sports stadium might prefer to watch sporting events rather than sell popcorn and peanuts. Watching teams play reduces sales but increases the employee's feelings of satisfaction with the job.

Satisfaction and Self-Concept

The relationship between performance and satisfaction is thought by some to be mediated by self-concept; that is, when the work requires the use of abilities an individual values, then performance and satisfaction will be associated. On the other hand, a worker who performs well at a task that requires the use of talents the individual does not value will experience little or no increase in satisfaction (Vroom, 1964). This explains why teachers derive relatively little satisfaction from performing routine tasks such as monitoring hallways, cleaning blackboards, and supervising cafeterias. For most of us, the skills required to carry out these tasks are not those that we think of as an integral part of our self-identity.

Some psychologists have concluded that self-esteem is not affected by either success or failure. They describe self-esteem as a positive way of experiencing self when a person is fully engaged and is using his or her abilities to achieve a valued outcome. These psychologists believe that people must learn how to achieve esteem for themselves, by attempting challenging tasks and working hard to achieve their goals (Dweck, 1999).

Sources of Satisfaction in Teaching

The level of satisfaction a person experiences with his or her work is related to three attributes having to do with his or her adaptability and expectations. *Career resilience* refers to the ability to adapt to new situations, even when they are discouraging or restrictive. More resilient individuals tend to be high in need for achievement and willingness to take risks and are able to work either independently or cooperatively, as the situation requires. *Career insight* and *career identity* are also related to the ability to derive satisfaction from one's work. A person with career insight is realistic about the career he or she has chosen and neither overestimates nor underestimates what is possible to accomplish. Career insight helps a person establish realistic career goals based on an accurate assessment of his or her strengths and weaknesses and the possibilities inherent in the job (London, 1998). Career insight often changes over time as a worker becomes more familiar with the organization for which he or she works. During their first few years in the classroom, beginning teachers have unusually high expectations of what they will be able to accomplish. They soon learn to temper those expectations in order to more closely match the realities of the teaching situation (Blase, 1990).

Career identity is the extent to which one defines oneself by work. People with strong career identity are likely to be more involved with the job and the profession and place a high value on the opportunity for recognition and a leadership role (London, 1998). A worker who has high career identity and who works for an employer who does not reward effort and loyalty will likely not be very happy in the job.

Schein (1990) introduced the concept of career anchor as a way of explaining the factors that motivate people in the search for and performance on a job. Among the career anchors he identified are technical aspects of the work; managerial aspects of the work, including opportunities to analyze and solve problems and to help people work together; job security and long-term commitment to the organization; the need to build or create an enterprise; setting one's own schedule and pace of work; challenges, such as overcoming major obstacles; and balancing career and lifestyle, such as spending time with family or friends (Schein, 1990). The anchor is the meaning or purpose a person seeks through a job, and if a person finds a job that allows him or her to achieve that purpose, then he or she is likely to feel a sense of satisfaction. A teacher who prefers a managerial anchor would look for opportunities to move into a supervisory or administrative position, whereas one who gravitates toward a challenge anchor might choose to teach children with disabilities. A teacher who is motivated by technical aspects of the job would enjoy having the opportunity to develop multimedia presentations or create a course to be taught online.

For most teachers, satisfaction from their jobs arises from the opportunity to perform tasks that they believe are socially significant and that yield intrinsic satisfactions. Of 10 sources of satisfaction from teaching identified by teachers in a study, the 4 highest ranked were intrinsic rewards (Plihal, 1981). The 10 items are listed in Exhibit 6.1.

The principal is an important actor in creating conditions that lead to teacher satisfaction. One study reported that teachers are more satisfied with their work when principals have "a firm sense of professional autonomy" and "regard their staff members as competent, independent professionals" (Morris, 1981, p. 1). Schools with large proportions of satisfied teachers were compared with schools in which the proportion of satisfied teachers was smaller. It was found that principals of the schools with fewer satisfied teachers more often reported that "poor teaching or teachers" was a problem in the school, than was the case in schools with more satisfied teachers (Morris, 1981, p. 4).

Sources of Dissatisfaction in Teaching

There are several sources of dissatisfaction in teaching of which principals and other personnel administrators should be aware. Some dissatisfaction is inherent in the work, but some is amenable to change.

One source of teacher dissatisfaction is simple boredom. Teaching becomes highly repetitive after a short time, and for some people repetition leads to boredom. During the first year in the classroom, teachers have the benefit of novelty. Everything is new and much must be learned. Beginning with the second year, the teacher begins to repeat activities and content, and after a few more years, the teacher has done everything at least once.

EXHIBIT 6.1   *Sources of Satisfaction for Teachers*

- Knowing that I have "reached" students and they have learned
- Enjoyment of experience and/or use of skills
- Development of personal skills (mental and physical)
- The activity itself: the pattern, the action, the world it provides
- Friendship and companionship
- Chance to use influence
- Respect from others
- Time (especially summers) for travel and holidays
- Security of income or position
- Salary

Source: J. Plihal, *Intrinsic Rewards of Teaching*. Paper presented at the annual meeting of the American Educational Research Association, 1981. ERIC Document Reproduction Service No. ED 200599.

This repetitiveness, while in some ways a lifesaver for overworked teachers, is also the source of boredom. Some teachers seem to be able to avoid becoming bored, possibly because of the nature of the subjects they teach, but boredom is an occupational hazard for many. Administrators can help relieve boredom by providing stimulating staff development programs, providing for conference travel and sabbatical leave, and arranging transfers to new situations for teachers who request them.

Another source of dissatisfaction that is prevalent in teaching is interruptions and distractions. Teachers complain frequently about intercom announcements that interrupt their classes, but they also feel distracted by visitors and paperwork (Plihal, 1981). Principals in many schools have taken steps to reduce the number of interruptions. Some allow announcements only once a day except for emergencies.

Another cause of frustration for teachers is lack of teaching resources. In many districts there is simply not enough money to permit teachers to purchase the maps and charts, filmstrips and viewers, paper and scissors that they need in order to teach in the way they prefer. One-half of the teachers interviewed in a study reported that the teaching materials in their schools were "poor" or "barely adequate" (McLaughlin, Pfeifer, Swanson-Owens, & Yee, 1986). Unfortunately, administrators often have little control over budgets, other than to request the money to purchase needed materials and supplies.

Teachers who are assigned to teach subjects that they are not qualified to teach or for which they lack interest are likely to cite that as a cause of frustration and dissatisfaction. Administrative decisions to assign teachers to teach courses for which they have inadequate preparation create incompetence (McLaughlin et al., 1986). Although it may not be possible to avoid misassignment of teachers in every case, it is possible to reduce the number of instances.

Teacher selection procedures should be reviewed if schools frequently find themselves short of teachers in certain fields. Problems are most likely to arise in fields with an undersupply of teachers, such as science and mathematics, and in fields that are affected by enrollment fluctuations. Changing selection procedures to give preference to teachers who are certified in more than one teaching field and helping teachers to acquire additional endorsements in fields with teacher shortages can help alleviate the problem.

Many teachers feel dissatisfied because of the pervasive sense of failure they experience in trying to work with children who have suffered deprivation either because of family failures or poverty. Teachers report that they are forced to take on parenting roles in order to respond to the needs of children from single-parent or dual-career families. Working with students who are learning disabled in mainstreamed settings and large classes are other sources of frustration for many teachers (McLaughlin et al., 1986). Unfortunately, administrators have relatively limited resources with which to attack the problems of poverty and neglect. The needs of children such as these far exceed the resources available to assist them. It may be of some help for administrators to stress to teachers the need to adopt realistic expectations. Suggestions for administrative actions that will help address teacher dissatisfaction arising from the sources discussed are shown in Exhibit 6.2.

EXHIBIT 6.2   *Administrative Responses to Teacher Dissatisfaction*

Source of Dissatisfaction	Administrative Action
Boredom	Rotate teaching assignments Provide workshops and seminars on new content and methods Provide educational leave
Interruptions	Schedule announcements once a day Use volunteers to reduce teacher responsibility for fund raising Train teachers in classroom management
Misassignment	Provide support for training teachers assigned out of field Examine qualifications of all teachers and reassign accordingly Consider changes in curriculum Provide supervisory support for teachers out of field
Lack of Resources	Obtain support from other sources Reallocate instructional budget to most needed items Encourage sharing of supplies
Working with At-Risk Children	Frequent praise "Time out" for teachers to help them reduce stress Expert supervisory assistance

Job Satisfaction and Teacher Turnover

Attrition is an important problem in teaching, as it is in many occupations. It has been estimated that about 13 percent of teachers leave the profession or change jobs each year (National Center for Education Statistics, 1998). Attrition is highest among young teachers. It is estimated that about one-half of new teachers in urban schools leave during the first five years (Streisand & Toch, 1998).

Teachers as a group are more satisfied with their work than people in most other occupations (Rodman, 1986), but their satisfaction is affected by the conditions of their work. A study in Great Britain found that the more discipline problems beginning teachers encountered, the more likely they were to leave teaching (Veenman, 1984). Some teachers leave the profession because they are discouraged by what they perceive as a lack of success in the classroom, and others decide that they are not temperamentally or intellectually suited for the job. Not all teachers leave because of dissatisfaction, however. Some teachers leave involuntarily because of enrollment declines or changes in their family situation.

Inadequate salary was the most frequently cited reason for leaving teaching by those who had taken jobs in other fields in one of the few studies of the topic.

Some 60 percent of respondents named that factor. Most of the individuals who left the profession had improved their financial situation as compared to a group of persons who were still teaching (Metropolitan Life Insurance Company, 1985).

Working conditions, including lack of input, nonteaching duties, and paperwork, were second in frequency of mention in the Metropolitan Life (1985) survey; they were named by 36 percent of the former teachers. Student-related reasons ranked third in frequency of mention, named by 30 percent of the respondents (Metropolitan Life Insurance Company, 1985).

There is evidence that academically able teachers are more likely to leave the profession as compared to those with less academic ability (Schlechty & Vance, 1981). The reason is not clear, but it is possible that teachers with higher levels of ability have more career options than less able individuals.

Organizational Correlates of Attrition

There has been very little research on organizational features of schools that are related to higher levels of teacher turnover. In one of the few studies that has been done, it was found that of the organizational characteristics studied, compensation factors were most strongly related to retention. Four of five items dealing with compensation were negatively correlated with teacher turnover. The items were higher beginning salaries for teachers, teachers paid for service on curriculum committees, teachers' hospital insurance premiums paid by the district, and summer employment available for teachers (Seyfarth & Bost, 1986).

Some evidence indicated that working conditions are positively correlated with teacher retention. In districts in which educational leaves for teachers were available and in which teachers helped select other teachers, teacher retention was higher, as compared to districts without those features. Interestingly, tuition payments for graduate study were associated with higher rather than lower teacher attrition (Seyfarth & Bost, 1986).

If a workplace allows employees to have fun and if people have a feeling of belonging, they are usually reluctant to leave. Some commercial firms do a better job than school districts in devising ways to hold employees, and school administrators might consider borrowing some of their ideas. Two actions taken by commercial firms that have helped reduce worker attrition are creating websites on which employees can post their gripes and classifying email so that employees can skip routine messages to save time. Messages that everyone is expected to read are labeled "first class." "Second class" messages are ideas and suggestions that others have found work well, and "no class" is for humor, puzzles, and classified ads. To encourage employees to "have a life" outside of the job, a Cincinnati firm displays photographs of its employees engaged in their favorite weekend activities. The photos help to heighten a feeling of family and have also turned out to be a potent recruiting device (Harris & Brannick, 1999).

A large drug retailer makes a video available to managers to show prospective employees. The video stresses the importance of a positive attitude and shows employees who have gone out of their way to help customers. The video shows all aspects of the operation of a drugstore, ranging from unloading trucks and stocking merchandise to helping customers find merchandise (Harris & Brannick, 1999).

Demographic Correlates of Attrition

Several demographic factors correlate with employee retention. Among those that have been shown to be related to attrition are length of service, age, level of skill, and education level. Workers who are younger, who have been with an employer a shorter length of time, and who have fewer skills and less education are more likely than employees without those traits to leave their jobs (Price, 1977). School districts that employ relatively large numbers of young teachers can expect to have higher than average turnover rates. However, teachers with higher levels of education are more, rather than less, likely to leave their jobs. That may be the result of increased awareness of job opportunities among teachers who hold advanced degrees.

Teacher turnover may be an indicator of teachers' lack of satisfaction with their jobs or have to do with factors in their personal lives or the economy. Many of the teachers who leave classrooms do so because of family reasons, either to bear or care for children or to move with a spouse to another locality. There is not much that principals and personnel administrators can do to reduce attrition that is related to family factors. However, in order to be able to understand fully the causes and implications of teacher attrition, it is necessary to collect detailed information on teacher mobility and the reasons for it.

In some districts, teachers who resign from their jobs are interviewed or asked to complete a questionnaire explaining their reasons for leaving. Although the validity of this information is debatable, it is an important source of data about an area of human behavior in which our knowledge is very limited. Unexplained increases in turnover may reveal previously unsuspected morale problems. An investigation is called for if turnover rates increase suddenly, particularly when the increase occurs among groups of teachers with normally low attrition.

Turnover generally refers to employees who leave a company or district altogether, but information about teacher transfers can also give clues about teacher motivation. Teachers transfer from one school to another in order to find more pleasant working conditions or greater convenience.

At the district level, a transfer has no effect on the overall composition of the teaching force, but at the school level it does. If an experienced teacher in a school is replaced by a less experienced one, the net result may be a decline in instructional effectiveness within the school. Principals should therefore be concerned with discovering the true reasons for teachers' requests for transfer and their decisions to leave the profession.

Not all attrition is to be deplored. Both from an individual point of view and from the point of view of the district, some is necessary and desirable. Individuals who discover that they have made the wrong career choice should be encouraged to seek other outlets for their talents.

The profession erects relatively few barriers to those who seek to become teachers. It is argued by some that ease of entry is desirable for reasons of equity (Sykes, 1983), but the training of individuals who are not intellectually or temperamentally suited for teaching imposes on both the individuals and the districts that employ them the cost of correcting earlier errors of choice and judgment.

Summary

Motivated and knowledgeable teachers are essential elements of effective schools. Motivation refers to conditions responsible for variations in the intensity, quality, direction, and duration of work-related behavior. Expectancy theory explains variations in motivation as attributable to responses to the opportunity to earn rewards. Equity theory holds that motivation is affected by perceptions of fairness, and goal-setting theory suggests that people are motivated to achieve identified goals. It is often assumed that satisfaction is positively correlated with performance on the job, but the evidence shows that the correlation is weak. Happy employees are not necessarily outstanding performers. For teachers, satisfaction is related to reaching children, whereas dissatisfaction arises from factors that impede effective teaching.

Suggested Activities

1. Suppose you are the principal of a school located in an inner-city neighborhood. Many of the students are from single-parent families, and most do not expect to go to college. The school staff consists of two groups—older teachers who have taught at the school for years and younger teachers who have recently begun replacing teachers who retire. The young teachers work hard but are sometimes discouraged by the difficult conditions in which they work and by the negative, defeatist attitudes of older teachers. A businessperson in the neighborhood offers you $5,000 to be spent to help teachers in the school. There are two conditions: The money must be spent on teachers and must be used to help improve student achievement. You may choose to allocate the money among teachers in any way you choose. You may give all of the money to one teacher, divide it equally, or divide it among teachers who submit the best proposals telling how they would use the money to achieve the donor's goals. Write a letter thanking the businessperson for the gift and explaining how you have decided to distribute the money. Using one of the motivation theories discussed in this chapter, give reasons why you believe your plan will achieve the desired results.

2. Some examples of actions that have been taken by commercial firms to make the workplace more attractive to workers in order to reduce attrition were described in this chapter. Pair with another student and see how many ideas the two of you can think of in 15 minutes to help reduce teacher attrition in schools. Propose ideas that are feasible and not cost prohibitive.

3. Evaluate the following performance goals proposed by teachers. Use the criteria provided and decide whether the goal is acceptable as written or if it needs to be

revised. Specify on which, if any, criteria the goal is deficient. *Criteria:* (a) Clarity (Is it clear what the teacher must do to achieve the goal?); (b) Relevant (Is the goal related to the teacher's assignment and to the school's mission?); (c) Realistic (Does the teacher possess the necessary authority and resources to accomplish the goal?); (d) Measurable (Is it possible to measure the teacher's progress toward achievement of the goal?); and (e) Challenging (Is the goal sufficiently challenging?)

Goals:

(1) I want to improve my attendance record this year and to reduce the number of times I am absent from school.

(2) My goal this year is to diagnose my students' performance more often so that I can plan to better meet their needs.

(3) I plan to do more extensive planning this year, including weekly and daily lesson plans in all subjects.

(4) I plan to set a faster pace this year so that I will be able to cover more material by the end of the year.

Online Resources

A wealth of material on topics bearing on worker motivation can be accessed online. Much of this material is geared to business but can be adapted to schools.

Workforce (www.workforce.com/index.html)
> This site provides information on topics having to do with motivation, including employee incentives, compensation plans, and satisfaction. The site is oriented to business users, but much of the material can be applied in educational settings. Free membership includes an email newsletter.

ERIC Digests (www.ed.gov/databases/ERIC_Digests)
> ERIC is a widely used database that is the source of information, reports, and research related to education. Each year, between 100 and 200 new digests are published, containing syntheses of recent research on topics of general interest. The full text of most of these digests is available online. Among the topics covered in recent digests are beginning teacher induction programs, elementary teacher supply and demand, and teacher evaluation.

Brookings Institution (www.brookings.org)
> This searchable database holds an extensive collection of materials related to public policy issues, including education. The Brown Center on Education Policy (www.brook.edu/gs/brown/brown_hp.htm) provides access to policy papers expressing a variety of points of view on educational issues.

References

Adams, J. S. (1965). Inequity in social exchange. In L. Berkowitz (Ed.), *Advances in experimental social psychology* (Vol. 2, pp. 267–299). New York: Academic Press.

Ashford, S. J., & Cummings, L. L. (1983). Feedback as an individual resource: Personal strategies of creating information. *Organizational Behavior and Human Performance, 32,* 370–398.

Blase, J. J., Jr. (1980). *On the meaning of being a teacher: A study of the teacher's perspective.* Unpublished doctoral dissertation, Syracuse University, Syracuse, NY.

Carroll, S., & Tosi, H. (1973). *Management by objectives: Applications and research.* New York: Macmillan.

Clark, P. B., & Wilson, J. Q. (1961). Incentive systems: A theory of organizations. *Administrative Science Quarterly, 6,* 129–166.

Dweck, C. (1999). *Self-theories: Their role in motivation, personality, and development.* Philadelphia: Psychology Press.

Fincham, R., & Rhodes, P. (1988). *The individual, work and organization.* London: Weidenfeld and Nicholson.

Glatthorn, A. (1995). Teacher development. In L. Anderson (Ed.), *International encyclopedia of teaching and teacher education* (2nd ed., pp. 41–46). New York: Pergamon.

Goodman, P. (1974). An examination of referents used in the evaluation of pay. *Organizational Behavior and Human Performance, 12,* 170–195.

Harris, J., & Brannick, J. (1999). *Finding and keeping great employees.* New York: AMACOM.

Ilgen, D. R., Fisher, C. D., & Taylor, M. S. (1979). Consequences of individual feedback on behavior in organizations. *Journal of Applied Psychology, 64,* 349–371.

Johnson, S. (1986, Summer). Incentives for teachers: What motivates, what matters. *Educational Administration Quarterly, 22,* 54-79.

Katzell, R., & Thompson, D. (1990, February). Work motivation: Theory and practice. *American Psychologist, 45,* 144–153.

Kelley, C. (1998, May). The Kentucky school-based performance award program: School-level effects. *Educational Policy, 12,* 305–324.

Kohn, A. (1993). Rewards versus learning: A response to Paul Chance. *Phi Delta Kappan, 74,* 783–787.

Landy, F. J. (1985). *Psychology of work behavior* (3rd ed.). Homewood, IL: Dorsey.

Lawler, E. E., & Rhode, J. G. (1976). *Information and control in organizations.* Pacific Palisades, CA: Goodyear.

Locke, E. A., & Latham, G. P. (1984). *Goal setting: A motivational technique that works!* Englewood Cliffs, NJ: Prentice Hall.

London, M. (1998). *Career barriers: How people experience, overcome, and avoid failure.* Mahwah, NJ: Erlbaum.

Manz, C. (1986). Self-leadership: Toward an expanded theory of self-influence processes in organizations. *Academy of Management Review, 11,* 585–600.

McLaughlin, M. W., Pfeifer, R. S., Swanson-Owens, D., & Yee, S. (1986). Why teachers won't teach. *Phi Delta Kappan, 67,* 420–426.

Metropolitan Life Insurance Company. (1985). *Former teachers in America.* New York: Author.

Mitchell, D. E., Ortiz, F. I., & Mitchell, T. K. (1983). *Work orientation and job performance: The cultural basis of teaching rewards and incentives.* Riverside, CA: University of California.

Morris, M. B. (1981). *The public school as workplace: The principal as a key element in teacher satisfaction* (Technical Report No. 32). Los Angeles: University of California, Graduate School of Education.

National Center for Education Statistics. (1998). *The condition of education, 1998.* Washington, DC: U.S. Department of Education.

Pinder, C. C. (1984). *Work motivation: Theory, issues, and applications.* Dallas: Scott, Foresman.

Plihal, J. (1981). *Intrinsic rewards of teaching.* Paper presented at the annual meeting of the American Educational Research Association. (ERIC Document Reproduction Service No. ED 200599).

Price, J. L. (1977). *The study of turnover.* Ames: Iowa State University Press.

Rodman, B. (1986, May 7). Teachers' job satisfaction seen greater than that of other college graduates. *Education Week,* p. 4.

Schein, E. (1990). *Career anchors.* San Diego: University Associates.

Schlechty, P. C., & Vance, V. (1981). Do academically able teachers leave education? The North Carolina case. *Phi Delta Kappan, 63,* 106–112.

Schlechty, P. C., & Vance, V. (1983). Recruitment, selection and retention: The shape of the teaching force. *The Elementary School Journal, 83,* 469–487.

Seyfarth, J. T., & Bost, W. A. (1986, Fall). Teacher turnover and quality of working life in schools: An empirical study. *Journal of Research and Development in Education, 20,* 1–6.

Streisand, B., & Toch, T. (1998, September 4). Many millions of kids, and too few teachers. *U.S. News & World Report.* Available online: www.usnews.com/usnews/issue/9809124teac.htm.

Sykes, G. (1983). Public policy and the problem of teacher quality: The need for screens and magnets. In L. S. Shulman & G. Sykes (Eds.), *Handbook of teaching and policy* (pp. 97–125). New York: Longman.

Veenman, S. (1984). Perceived problems of beginning teachers. *Review of Educational Research, 54,* 143–178.

Vroom, V. H. (1964). *Work and motivation.* New York: Wiley.

7

Induction

People who are hired to fill a job they have not previously held have many questions about the work and the organization that will employ them. For those who are entering a field for the first time, the questions focus on job duties and expectations, income, opportunities for advancement, fellow workers, and one's superiors. Some of these questions are answered in the interview or in orientation sessions, but many are not. Unfortunately, most employers provide little information to help employees feel comfortable in their new work setting. What the new employee learns is usually acquired from other employees, varies in accuracy, and reflects the attitudes of those employees toward the employing organization.

Plan of the Chapter

Organizations that provide planned induction programs for new employees increase the chances that those employees will obtain accurate information about the job and the organization and that they will be more satisfied and productive as a result. Identifying the purposes of induction programs for teachers and principals and suggesting ways of planning programs that will help meet their needs for information are the goals of this chapter. The chapter is written for principals and district staff members who work with new teachers. The following topics are examined: (1) expectations and teaching reality, (2) purpose and types of induction programs, (3) content of induction programs, (4) mentors and teacher induction, (5) induction and career development, (6) administrative leadership for induction, and (7) induction for administrators.

Expectations and Teaching Reality

One of the reasons mentioned most frequently by educators for choosing a teaching career is a special interest in working with children or young people (Jantzen, 1981). Other reasons mentioned frequently are "a life-long opportunity to learn," "an opportunity for exercising individual initiative," and "the opportunity for service to mankind." In their choices of reasons for choosing a teaching career, students reveal their expectations for their lives as teachers. To the extent that these expectations are fulfilled by their experiences in the classroom, these teachers are likely to feel satisfied with their choice of career, but if their expectations are not met, they may feel disappointed and even cheated.

The New Teacher

Few periods in the lives of young teachers compare in importance with the first year in the classroom (Johnston & Ryan, 1983). It is a time of transition, and many of these teachers are on their own for the first time in their lives. They face the tasks of learning a new and challenging job, finding a place to live, locating transportation, and making friends. Beyond that, many young teachers are only beginning to learn who they are and what they wish to become. Any new job involves rites of passage, and for young teachers, the first job involves a passage from being dependent to independent and the start of a journey of discovery about themselves (Schempp, Sparkes, & Templin, 1999). This is a time when beginning teachers learn what behaviors are appropriate to their work roles and become aware of the unwritten values, norms, and operating procedures that guide interactions among staff members (Smylie, 1995).

During their first year in the classroom, many teachers find that the idealistic expectations they held for the job are dashed. They discover that instruction requires endless hours of preparation, usually at the end of an exhausting day of teaching, and that this preparation interferes with their social lives. They also find that students are not as eager to learn as they had expected them to be (Blase, 1980).

New teachers often find the role of classroom disciplinarian a difficult one to assimilate. One new teacher wrote:*

> My biggest worry now is keeping a straight face. I just cannot seem to keep from laughing at the kids. Partly, I'm sure, it's just me—but I'm sure other new teachers face the same problem. I cannot seem to get mad at them and I laugh many times when I shouldn't. I guess I lack a detachment which can only come with time. (Morris, 1968, p. 10)

Within a few weeks, the same teacher was writing:

> All of my problems with my third period class seem to be concentrated on one boy. The problems are not all his fault but he personifies them. I really believe that it is physically impossible for him to stay quiet and in his seat for a whole period. This one kid has really gotten to me!! To top it off, he is in my homeroom and I have to face him for a solid 90 minutes right in the middle of the day. (Morris, 1968, p. 11)

Source: "Diary of a Beginning Teacher" by J. Morris, October 1968, *NASSP Bulletin, 52,* pp. 10, 11. Reprinted by permission. For more information concerning NASSP services and/or programs, please call (703) 860-0200.

Many beginners are surprised to realize that the stern admonitory tones they have heard other teachers use and that they had thought they would never adopt become second nature to them after they have been teaching a few months. They also see their fantasies of being friends with their students fade in the cold light of classroom reality. This experience of dissonance between the expectations one brings to a new job and actual experiences at work are not limited to teaching. New entrants into most occupations report similar experiences. A term that has been applied to this experience is *reality shock.* Two types of factors have been cited as leading to reality shock (Veenman, 1984).

Personal causes have to do with the individual. They include personality characteristics that are not suited to teaching and attitudes that are uninformed and out of place. Situational factors that contribute to reality shock include inadequate professional preparation, teaching assignments for which the new teacher has no prior preparation, lack of materials and supplies, absence of clear instructional objectives, isolation, overcrowded classes, and a school climate that is not conducive to instruction (Huling-Austin, 1986; Veenman, 1984).

Purpose and Types of Induction Programs

Academically able teachers are more likely to leave the profession as compared to those with less academic ability. A study conducted in a southeastern state found that 71 percent of white teachers with NTE scores at the 10th percentile remained in teaching for at least five years, compared with just 56 percent of those who scored at the 90th percentile (Murnane, 1996).

A composite profile of a teacher who is most likely to leave the profession is a male secondary school teacher with less than five years of experience who works a second job. This teacher is likely to report that his first year in the classroom did not go well, and he often works in a school in which the majority of students are of a different ethnic background than his. He is also likely to feel that the principal does not give him much support (Betancourt-Smith, Inman, & Marlow, 1994).

A well-planned induction program might help reduce attrition among new teachers who fit this profile. If these teachers had a better first-year experience as a result of an induction program that also showed them that the principal cared about their welfare, more of them might remain in the profession longer. There is, in fact, some evidence that well-planned induction programs do help to retain new teachers. A pilot induction program in California lowered attrition among new teachers from 37 percent to 9 percent over a five-year period. School districts in Ohio and New York achieved similar results with their induction programs (Curran, Abrahams, & Manuel, 2000).

A survey by the National Science Teachers Association found that 90 percent of science teachers named isolation from peers as a limitation on their professional growth. Recently, a program has been initiated on the Internet to bring science teachers into contact with one another. The site is maintained by Genentech Corporation and features an idea exchange, online discussions of science issues, a list of classroom activities for science classes, and access to scientific specialists (Weld, 1998).

Changing conditions in education that have made teaching more difficult and stressful have underscored the need for well-designed induction programs. Among the conditions that make teachers' work more difficult today than in the past are the increasing numbers of at-risk children in the schools, the establishment of a pre-scribed curriculum with results measured by scores on standardized tests, and the introduction of new technologies that teachers are expected to master (Mager, 1992)

Five purposes for induction programs for beginning teachers have been iden-tified: (1) to improve teacher effectiveness, (2) to encourage promising new teachers to remain in teaching by offering support and assistance, (3) to promote the profes-sional and personal well-being of new teachers, (4) to communicate district and school cultures to beginning teachers, and (5) to satisfy state mandates (Hirsh, 1990a).

The definition of *induction* used in this book is a planned program designed to facilitate the process by which new teachers in a school acquire the social and technical knowledge and skills they need to perform effectively in their work roles and interpersonal relationships (Smylie, 1995). Three distinct types of induction programs are in use in the schools: orientation programs, performance improve-ment programs, and state-mandated induction programs.

Orientation Programs

The simplest of these three types of induction programs consists of orientation ses-sions to introduce new teachers to the school and the community. These programs provide information about the district, help new employees to become better acquainted with the community in which they will be working (Kester & Marockie, 1987), explain performance expectations and help new employees to learn what is expected of them on the job, provide some emotional support, promote employees' personal and professional well-being (Huling-Austin, 1986), and clarify the organi-zational hierarchy (Pataniczek & Isaacson, 1981). These programs tend to be of short duration, and the emphasis is on information dissemination.

About 80 percent of first-year teachers in one study reported they participated in orientation sessions of one kind or another (Pataniczek & Isaacson, 1981). Orien-tation sessions are not always well received by teachers. Although the teachers in the study reported that they valued the information they received, many felt that equally good results could have been achieved by providing the information in a faculty handbook. One administrator described traditional orientation programs as boring to old-timers and confusing to beginners (Hunt, 1968).

Performance Improvement Programs

The second type of induction program incorporates some of the features of the first type and also seeks to help new members learn the culture of the school (Schlechty, 1985). Some of these programs have multiple objectives, whereas others have limited scope and narrowly focused goals. Two of the most important of the objectives identified for this type of induction program in schools are helping beginning teachers to improve their instructional effectiveness and reducing attrition of new teachers (Huling-Austin, 1987).

Among the topics that are likely to be especially useful for beginning teachers seeking to improve their instructional effectiveness are workshops at which discipline and classroom management procedures are explained; conversations with subject-area specialists who provide an orientation to the district curriculum and help locate resources and share lesson plans and tests; explanations of performance assessment procedures; and assistance in preparing a professional development plan (Hirsh, 1990b). This type of program often continues over a semester or a full year. In addition to receiving information about the school and the district, participants usually receive individualized assistance with their teaching from an administrator, supervisor, or, increasingly, another teacher.

The simplest type of assistance consists of responses to requests for help. More complex kinds of assistance include classroom observations combined with feedback. These observations may be provided by other teachers but are separate from the normal evaluation procedures. Mentoring programs are included in this category. They are characterized by intensive involvement of an experienced teacher with a beginner and may deal with many facets of the new teacher's experiences (Anderson & Shannon, 1988).

State-Mandated Induction Programs

The third type of induction program operates under state mandate and requires beginning teachers to demonstrate mastery of specified teaching competencies. This type of program is primarily evaluative in nature, but in some of these programs, evaluation is combined with limited assistance.

In some states, beginning teachers are required to demonstrate that they possess certain teaching competencies in order to receive a permanent teaching certificate. In most of these programs, an assessment or assistance team is designated to work with one or more beginning teachers. Usually, the team includes among its members one principal and one experienced classroom teacher. Some programs provide training for the team members, although the training is often brief and may be limited to use of a particular classroom observation instrument. Team members observe the beginning teacher and may give feedback on the teacher's performance along with recommendations on corrective actions.

Content of Induction Programs

The content of induction programs in schools is often based on surveys of problems and needs identified by beginning teachers. The most comprehensive review of this research was Veenman's (1984) report. He summarized findings from 83 studies published in North America, Europe, and Australia. The 10 most frequently perceived problems from these 83 studies are listed here in order of frequency of mention.

1. Classroom discipline
2. Motivating students
3. Dealing with individual differences
4. Assessing students' work (tie)
5. Relations with parents (tie)
6. Organization of classwork (tie)
7. Insufficient materials and supplies (tie)
8. Dealing with problems of individual students
9. Heavy teaching load resulting in insufficient preparation time
10. Relations with colleagues (Veenman, 1984, pp. 154–155)

Competent mentor teachers can assist beginning teachers with most of the problems on Veenman's list, but some of the problems require administrative action. For example, a mentor teacher might help a beginning teacher deal more effectively with classroom discipline and student motivation, but the mentor teacher would likely be unable to help solve problems related to lack of materials and supplies or heavy teaching load, since those factors usually result from policy decisions.

There is some evidence that the kinds of assistance beginning teachers actually seek are different from the needs they identify on questionnaires. One study found that requests for assistance with classroom discipline constituted only 5.2 percent of beginning teachers' requests for assistance from mentor teachers, although it headed the list of problems cited by beginning teachers in the studies reviewed by Veenman (1984) (Odell, Loughlin, & Ferraro, 1986–87). That was the lowest frequency of seven assistance categories.

Beginning teachers most frequently requested assistance with instruction (35 percent), followed by system requests (20.6 percent) and resource requests (14.5 percent). System requests had to do with "information related to procedures and guidelines of the school district" (p. 53), and resource requests were related to "collecting, disseminating, or locating resources for use by the new teacher" (p. 53) (Odell et al., 1986–87).

These results suggest that teachers respond to questionnaires from a different frame of reference than has been assumed. Their responses may indicate which problems teachers believe are most critical to their success as a teacher, not necessarily those for which they are most likely to seek help. The findings also show that when a new teacher does not ask for assistance with a particular problem, it does not necessarily indicate that he or she feels comfortable with that situation. There is a good deal of evidence that teachers refrain from asking for help if they believe such requests will be interpreted as evidence of lack of teaching competence. New teachers may not ask for help with classroom discipline yet nevertheless welcome and profit from any assistance that is made available.

Supplementing Preservice Training

Induction and staff development programs must sometimes provide training that was not incorporated into the new teacher's preservice preparation. As more schools adopt school-based management, it will be necessary for teachers to receive training in the leadership skills required by the added responsibility that structure requires. Many preservice programs presently offer little or no preparation in assuming leadership roles (Stallings, 1984).

Principals' leadership styles vary from laissez faire to directive, and teachers must learn to accommodate themselves to a variety of styles as administrators come and go or as teachers themselves transfer from school to school. Very few preservice programs address differences in principals' leadership styles, nor do they prepare new teachers to adapt to these different approaches. Induction is an appropriate time to help beginning teachers identify and respond in an appropriate way to the leadership behaviors of principals and supervisors with whom they work. In some schools, a small group of influential teachers exert leadership, and beginning teachers must be able to recognize such coteries and be able to work effectively through them (Stallings, 1984).

Other groups that new teachers must learn to take into account in their work include parents and professional organizations. Parents are more interested and involved in school affairs in some districts than in others, but in no school is it wise to ignore parents. Professional organizations are much more powerful in certain districts than in others, but they too are a force of which new teachers should be aware (Stallings, 1984).

Mentors and Teacher Induction

Induction programs in schools serve several different purposes, as noted earlier. The design of the program depends on the purpose for which the program was established. One of the most popular components of induction programs is the mentor teacher. This position goes by a variety of names, including *buddy teacher, support teacher, cooperating teacher,* and *teacher advisor.* Several studies have shown that mentor teachers have been instrumental in helping beginning professionals acquire increased teaching competence (Zahorik, 1987).

Mentor teachers perform a variety of functions to help new teachers feel at home and learn their jobs. They introduce the new teachers to others on the staff, provide copies or handbooks and curriculum guides, explain grading and discipline policies, and often help set up the classroom (Tickle, 1994). Mentors also provide political information and advice to their mentees, help them make contacts, and provide information to help with career decisions (Anderson & Shannon, 1988).

One of the reasons for the success of mentors is that teachers are accustomed to seeking help from colleagues. Most teachers prefer to talk to another teacher when they have a question rather than seek assistance from a supervisor or administrator (Pataniczek & Isaacson, 1981). In part, the preference for conferring with other teachers is related to convenience. It is usually easier to locate another teacher than to find a supervisor or administrator, and new teachers are often afraid that asking for help from the principal may raise questions in the administrator's mind about their competence. To avoid that possibility, some teachers avoid asking for help, or they go to a teacher whom they think they can trust (Schempp, Sparkes, & Templin, 1999).

Districts that have introduced high-quality mentoring programs have found that attrition rates for new teachers dropped more than two-thirds from their previous levels (Darling-Hammond, 1999). A study of mentoring reported that teacher mentors cited two factors that they regarded as their most useful contributions to beginning teachers: providing support and encouragement and informing new teachers about school and district policies, procedures, and paperwork (Ganser, 1993).

When mentors and new teachers were asked what qualities were most important for individuals who work with beginning teachers, the list of most-mentioned attributes included experience, sensitivity, approachability, and a calm manner (Tickle, 1994). The complete list appears in Exhibit 7.1.

Training Mentor Teachers

Training for mentor teachers is an important part of a successful induction program. The complexity of the skills required to function effectively in a support role should not be underestimated. It is sometimes assumed that teachers who perform well with children will be equally effective as mentors to adults (Wagner, 1985). Unfortunately, that is not always true.

Even when training is provided, "school systems cannot expect that experienced teachers will be able to provide effective assistance to beginners in a systematic way" (Thies-Sprinthall, 1986, p. 13). It seems safe to say that training that

EXHIBIT 7.1   *Essential Qualities of Effective Mentors Identified by Mentors and Beginning Teachers*

Professional Qualities	Personal Qualities	Tutorial
Credibility as a teacher	Empathetic	Accessible
Experience	Sensitive	Positive constructive nature
Continuous learner	Non-judgmental	Supportive/encouraging
Open to learning from colleagues	Approachable	Honest
	Sense of humor	Reliable
	Good listener	
	Calm manner	
	Optimistic	

Sources: The Induction of Teachers: Reflective Professional Practice (p. 179) by L. Tickle, 1994, London: Cassel. Copyright © by Les Tickle. Reprinted with permission. "The Good Mentor" by J. Rowley, May 1999, *Educational Leadership, 56,* pp. 20–22. Reprinted with permission of the Association for Supervision and Curriculum Development. Copyright © 1999 by ASCD. All rights reserved.

is brief and superficial is not likely to have much impact on the ability of mentor teachers to affect the behavior of beginning teachers. The training they receive should be designed to convey the knowledge and skill they will need in working with beginning teachers. Two of the important skills are knowledge of a variety of teaching models and the ability to explain and demonstrate the conditions under which each is appropriate (Thies-Sprinthall, 1986).

Quality mentoring programs are expensive to develop and operate, but they have a high probability of helping to retain young teachers. The features that distinguish a high-quality program from one of less quality include released time for mentors, a reasonable caseload, and compensation for the mentor. These and other features of well-designed programs are shown in Exhibit 7.2.

Induction and Career Development

Commercial and industrial organizations in particular emphasize the career development aspect of induction. In some firms, mentors are assigned to new employees and serve as sponsors to help the new worker establish informal networks inside and outside the company. Mentors also serve as teachers, and they are particularly helpful in assisting beginners to understand the organization's culture, including both written and unwritten rules and norms. They provide feedback on both performance and interpersonal relations and allow learners to test their assumptions about the organization. Mentors occasionally play devil's advocate by challenging an employee's perceptions or behavior. Finally, mentors play the role of coach by sharing their own career histories and struggles as a way of providing emotional support to beginning employees who experience difficulties in getting their ideas accepted (Farren, Gray, & Kaye, 1984).

Career Development in Schools

Some public school induction programs incorporate career development features. For example, the state of California has enacted legislation under which local school boards may elect to initiate a mentor program with state financial support. The leg-

EXHIBIT 7.2   *Features of High-Quality Mentoring Programs*

School site administrators understand and support the mentoring program.
Mentors are provided for all beginning teachers.
Mentors are chosen using district criteria and receive training.
Mentors receive released time to work with new teachers.
Mentors are assigned reasonable caseloads.
Mentors are paid for work with beginning teachers.
Mentors are evaluated on effectiveness.

Source: "State-Initiated Induction Programs: Supporting, Assisting, Training, Assessing, and Keeping Teachers" by E. Fideler, Winter 2000, *State Education Standard, 1* (1), 12–15.

islation requires that mentors be credentialed and experienced classroom teachers who have demonstrated exemplary teaching ability as indicated by effective communication skills, subject-matter knowledge, and mastery of a range of teaching strategies, and are recommended by a teacher-dominated selection committee (Wagner, 1985). Mentors are appointed for terms of up to three years, during which time they teach a reduced classload and receive a stipend in addition to their regular salary. For most teachers in programs such as these, the opportunity to gain critical experience and acquire new skills outweighs the importance of added fiscal benefits.

Administrative Leadership for Induction

Principals play a key role in the success of induction programs in their schools. They act as facilitators by leading discussion groups or arranging for space, materials, and speakers. Principals also help facilitate induction by assigning mentors to new teachers and scheduling classes so that mentors and their charges have common planning periods. Principals who are committed to continuous learning serve as models for teachers in their schools and encourage new teachers to take advantage of the opportunities provided by induction (Payne & Wolfson, 2000).

One of the problematic aspects of programs that use mentors is helping experienced teachers to overcome a reluctance to comment on their colleagues' work. One author (Zahorik, 1987) made the following observation:

> Teachers must come not to fear exposing their classroom practices. They must see that knowledge of their classroom behavior by others as well as by themselves is essential to improvement....Changing teachers' views of teaching is obviously a difficult and lengthy process, but it seems to be an unavoidable first step to developing collegiality, improving instruction, and making teaching satisfying work. (p. 395)

Principals can help by encouraging all teachers to be more open in their teaching and by reassuring those who are observed by colleagues that they will not be evaluated on the basis of collegial observations.

Induction programs are subject to failure when unreasonably high expectations are held for them. They cannot be expected to overcome problems related to resource scarcity or policy limitations. Induction does not remove the need for ongoing staff development activities aimed at raising or maintaining the quality of the instructional program, and it does not take the place of performance evaluation.

Principals should be aware of the danger that induction may make poor teachers feel good about doing a poor job (Huling-Austin, 1986). Other potential problems arise when teachers without supervisory training or experience attempt to assist beginning teachers in improving their instructional practices or when narrowly defined instructional models are prescribed for all teachers, leading to standardized practice (Thies-Sprinthall, 1986).

Induction is not a substitute for instructional leadership. Clearly defined performance expectations are essential for effective instruction, and induction programs cannot take the place of that ingredient. Principals are sometimes surprised to hear teachers report that performance expectations are not clear, since they are clear to them. What is needed is continuous reinforcement of behavioral expectations as employees learn new roles (Kurtz, 1983).

Recommendations for Principals

Even in districts without formal induction programs, principals can anticipate and remove some of the obstacles to effective teaching that are frequently encountered by teachers who are in their first year of teaching. The following practices will help beginning teachers attain success during their first year in a school (Kurtz, 1983):

1. Plan special in-service sessions for beginning teachers throughout the school year with timely topics addressing the concerns of that group. Information is timely if it is presented when teachers need it. If presented before the need arises, the information is likely to be disregarded; if it is presented afterwards, it is worthless.

Beginning teachers want help in evaluating student work and assigning grades, but a presentation on that topic will be more successful if presented about halfway through the first grading period than if it is scheduled for the opening of school or the week grades are due.

2. Pair beginning teachers with experienced teachers, matching individuals for subject taught, physical proximity, and teaching philosophy. In some districts, the bargaining agreement places limits on the types of activities that teachers may be asked to participate in and the amount of time they may commit to such activities. Within the contract's limitations, attempt to involve teachers who are warm and supportive and who have demonstrated they are effective at producing student learning. Spell out what is expected of the support teacher, but avoid asking that individual to perform as a mentor unless training is provided.

3. If the school has a mentor program, plan to meet periodically with mentor teachers to review their experiences working with beginning teachers and, when necessary, to identify general problems that need attention.

4. Avoid allowing beginning teachers to end up with only the courses and students more senior teachers do not want. If the bargaining agreement permits it, limit new teachers' preparations to the fewest number possible and assign students who are known to be disruptive to more experienced teachers. Be aware, however, that this action may be controversial, since some experienced teachers will resent being imposed upon and will accuse beginners of not carrying their load.

5. Exercise care and judgment in making extra-duty assignments in order to avoid jeopardizing the teaching effectiveness of beginning teachers. The first year in the classroom is a demanding experience, and most beginning teachers require large amounts of preparation time. Burdening new teachers with extra-duty assignments will make it much more difficult for them to be effective in bringing about student learning.

6. If an induction program is offered, schedule sessions for beginning teachers separately from the sessions for experienced teachers but give beginners the opportunity to attend both. Administrators who are responsible for the programs should choose content that is relevant to teachers' needs. Refer to the research by Veenman (1984) and Odell, Loughlin, and Ferraro (1986–87), presented earlier in this chapter, for ideas on relevant content.

Induction for Administrators

Most administrators learn the skills they need on the job in informal ways, either by trial and error or by observing an experienced administrator. Some are fortunate enough to begin their careers working with an experienced educator who is able to articulate issues that need to be considered as decisions are made, and who is willing to assist the beginner by talking through each new type of problem as it arises.

Principals who work with an assistant principal who has had no previous administrative experience should plan to spend time with the new assistant outlining duties and discussing the teachers' expectations of administrators. A useful guide on how to conduct such an induction activity is provided by Jentz (1982).

Interviews

Among the steps Jentz (1982) has recommended are helping the new assistant principal to learn more about the school's culture and procedures by scheduling him or her to conduct interviews with individuals with whom the assistant principal will be working in the coming months. For example, if the assistant is expected to help prepare the school's budget, interviews would be scheduled with the school bookkeeper and with the district business officer. The assistant principal would also want to talk to several department heads about budgeting, purchasing procedures, and handling of payments and fees.

These interviews serve several purposes. First, they allow the assistant to make initial contacts with individuals with whom he or she will be working in the future. Second, they serve to acquaint the assistant principal with existing rules and procedures as they are interpreted by the individuals involved and alert him or her to problems that may exist in the implementation of the rules. Since policies are sometimes ignored in practice, it is a good idea as well for the new administrator to read the district's policies on fiscal accounting in order to learn "what the book says."

Third, the interviews convey to those upon whom the administrator must rely for assistance when developing the budget that the assistant principal is interested in their opinions. This will facilitate future working relationships. Similar interviews can be conducted in connection with other duties for which the administrator will have responsibility.

Preparing Work Plans

Beginning assistant principals can also be helped by preparation of detailed work plans for the year. Jentz (1982) recommended preparing a chart that shows each of the major policy areas for which the assistant principal is responsible (e.g., budget, teacher absence, student enrollment, student discipline, and so on) arrayed along one dimension and a calendar on the second. Deadlines for completion of specific tasks related to each of the policy areas are noted.

In a separate document, Jentz (1982) recommended listing a detailed sequence of steps that must be accomplished in carrying out the duties assigned to the assistant. For example, one step in preparing a budget is to notify department heads of the date for submission of a tentative budget request along with guidelines for preparing it.

The principal very likely will not have the time to prepare this chart for the assistant, but the assistant should be asked to keep a record of the steps involved in carrying out major duties and to prepare a copy for the principal. This record can later be typed and kept for future referral.

Summary

Induction involves planned activities developed for the purpose of acquainting new employees with an organization and equipping them with knowledge, skills, and attitudes to enable them to function effectively and comfortably in the work setting. Three types of induction programs are common in public schools: orientation, performance effectiveness, and state mandated. The first year of teaching is a transitional year for many teachers, and for some the experiences in the classroom create reality shock.

Mentor teachers can help reduce the impact of reality shock by giving new teachers a sounding board and a source of advice and suggestions. Mentors who are selected with care and trained to perform the functions of the role can be of value in helping new teachers to deal with the problems they encounter. The most frequently mentioned problem areas identified by new teachers include student discipline, motivating students, and providing individual assistance.

Administrators should be aware of potential problems in implementing teacher induction programs and should be aware that induction does not reduce the need for instructional leadership and does not replace performance evaluation responsibilities of principals. In schools with no formal induction program, principals can make life easier for first-year teachers by appointing a support teacher to assist the new teachers and by relieving new teachers of extra-duty assignments and unnecessarily heavy teaching duties.

Induction for administrators should provide the individual with the opportunity to learn about the responsibilities of the position by talking to people with whom he or she will work. Specific guidelines on major tasks are helpful to those who are new to an administrative job.

Suggested Activities

1. Prepare a five-minute talk to welcome new teachers to your school and to give them a brief history of the school and the community.

2. Working with a classmate, one of you interview a person who has recently completed the first year of teaching, and the other interview a person who recently served as a mentor for a beginning teacher. Ask each individual what he or she perceives as the advantages and disadvantages of mentoring for themselves and for the person with whom they worked. Compare the answers and report your findings to the class.

3. From *the Dictionary of Occupational Titles* select an occupation about which you have little knowledge. Suppose you have been selected for a job in that occupation. Write five questions you would like to have answered in an induction program. How many of your questions might also be asked by a beginning teacher? (The *Dictionary of Occupational Titles* is published by the U.S. Department of Labor and is available in most libraries.)

4. Prepare a plan for a semester-long induction program for new teachers. Specify instructional objectives for each session and identify a possible presenter.

Online Resources

Mentoring and induction programs for new teachers have received great attention in recent years. Websites with information on those topics are shown here.

New York State Education Department (www.emsc.nysed.gov/development)
This site contains suggestions on how to find time for mentoring programs, including scheduling classes to allow for common planning time and hiring retired teachers as replacements for teachers who are mentoring or being mentored.

Miami-Dade County Public Schools (http://mdcps.dade.k12.fl.us/pers/toc.htm)
This website contains information about Miami-Dade County Public Schools. Topics include wages, benefits, certification, professional development, National Board standards, and code of ethics. This site could serve as a model for districts that are in the process of constructing or updating their websites.

Education Week (www.edweek.org/sreports/qc00/templates/chartcfm?slug=intro-cl.htm)
This article gives information about the 28 states that provide funds for or require induction programs.

National Governors Association (www.nga.org/pubs/IssueBriefs/2000/000125Teachers.asp)
Information about teacher induction programs in several cities and states is available on this site.

References_____

Anderson, E. M., & Shannon, A. L. (1988, January/February). Toward a conceptualization of mentoring. *Journal of Teacher Education, 39,* 38–42.

Betancourt-Smith, M., Inman, D., & Marlow, L. (1994). Professional attrition: An examination of minority and nonminority teachers at risk. (ERIC Document Reproduction Service No. ED 388639).

Blase, J. J., Jr. (1980). *On the meaning of being a teacher: A study of the teachers' perspective.* Unpublished doctoral dissertation, Syracuse University, Syracuse, NY.

Cornett, L., & Gaines, G. (1992). *Focusing on student outcomes: Roles for incentive programs.* Atlanta: Southern Regional Education Board. (ERIC Reproduction Service No. ED 358058).

Curran, B., Abrahams, C., & Manuel, J. (2000). Teacher supply and demand: Is there a shortage? *National Governors Association Reports Online.* Available online: www.nga.org/Pubs/IssueBriefs/default.asp.

Darling-Hammond, L. (1999, Fall). Solving the dilemmas of teacher supply, demand, and standards. *Quality Teaching, 9* (1), 3–4.

Farren, C., Gray, J. D., & Kaye, B. (1984, November/December). Mentoring: A boon to career development. *Personnel, 61,* 20–24.

Fideler, E. (2000, Winter). State-initiated induction programs: Supporting, assisting, training, assessing, and keeping teachers. *State Education Standard, 1* (1), 12–15.

Ganser, T. (1993). *How mentors describe and categorize their ideas about mentor roles, benefits of mentoring, and obstacles to mentoring.* Paper presented at the annual meeting of the Association of Teacher Educators, Los Angeles. (ERIC Document Reproduction Service No. ED 354237).

Hirsh, S. (1990a, Fall). New teacher induction: An interview with Leslie Huling-Austin. *Journal of Staff Development, 11,* 2–4.

Hirsh, S. (1990b, Fall). Designing induction programs with the beginning teacher in mind. *Journal of Staff Development, 11,* 24–26.

Huling-Austin, L. (1986, January/February). What can and cannot reasonably be expected from teacher induction programs. *Journal of Teacher Education, 37,* 2–5.

Huling-Austin, L. (1987). Teacher induction. In D. M. Brooks (Ed.), *Teacher induction: A new beginning* (pp. 3–23). Reston, VA: Association of Teacher Educators.

Hunt, D. W. (1968, October). Teacher induction: An opportunity and a responsibility. *NASSP Bulletin, 52,* 130–135.

Jantzen, J. M. (1981, March/April). Why college students choose to teach: A longitudinal study. *Journal of Teacher Education, 33,* 45–48.

Jentz, B. (1982). *Entry: The hiring, start-up, and supervision of administrators.* New York: McGraw-Hill.

Johnston, M. J., & Ryan, K. (1983). Research on the beginning teacher: Implications for teacher education. In K. R. Howey & W. E. Gardner (Eds.), *The education of teachers: A look ahead* (pp. 136-162). New York: Longman.

Kester, R., & Marockie, M. (1987). Local induction programs. In D. M. Brooks (Ed.), *Teacher induction: A new beginning* (pp. 25–31). Reston, VA: Association of Teacher Educators.

Kurtz, W. H. (1983, January). How the principal can help beginning teachers. *NASSP Bulletin, 67,* 42–45.

Mager, G. (1992). The place of induction in becoming a teacher. In G. DeBolt (Ed.), *Teacher induction and mentoring: School-based collaborative programs* (pp. 3–33). Albany: State University of New York Press.

Morris, J. (1968, October). Diary of a beginning teacher. *NASSP Bulletin, 52,* 6–22.

Murnane, R. (1996). Staffing the nation's schools with skilled teachers. In E. Hanushek & D. Jorgenson (Eds.), *Improving America's schools: The role of incentives* (pp. 241–258). Washington, DC: National Academy Press.

Odell, S. J., Loughlin, C. E., & Ferraro, D. P. (1986–87, Winter). Functional approach to identification of new teacher needs in an induction context. *Action in Teacher Education, 8,* 51–57.

Pataniczek, D., & Isaacson, N. S. (1981, May/June). The relationship of socialization and the concerns of beginning secondary teachers. *Journal of Teacher Education, 32,* 14–17.

Payne, D., & Wolfson, T. (2000, October). Teacher professional development—The principals' critical role. *NASSP Bulletin, 84,* 13–21.

Rowley, J. (1999, May). The good mentor. *Educational Leadership, 56,* 20–22.

Schempp, P., Sparkes, A., & Templin, T. (1999). Identity and induction: Establishing the self in the first years of teaching. In R. Lipka & T. Brinthaupt (Eds.), *The role of self in teacher development* (pp. 142–161). Albany: State University of New York Press.

Schlechty, P. C. (1985, January/February). A framework for evaluating induction into teaching. *Journal of Teacher Education, 36,* 37–41.

Smylie, M. (1995). Teacher learning in the workplace: Implications for school reform. In T. Guskey & M. Huberman (Eds.), *Professional development in education* (pp. 92–113). New York: Teachers College Press.

Stallings, J. A. (1984). Implications from the research on teaching for teacher preparation. In R. L. Egbert & M. M. Kluender (Eds.), *Using research to improve teacher education* (pp. 128–145). Washington, DC: ERIC Clearinghouse on Teacher Education.

Thies-Sprinthall, L. (1986, November/December) A collaborative approach for mentor training: A working model. *Journal of Teacher Education, 37,* 13–20.

Tickle, L. (1994). *The induction of new teachers.* London: Cassell.

Veenman, S. (1984). Perceived problems of beginning teachers. *Review of Educational Research, 54,* 143–178.

Wagner, L. A. (1985, November). Ambiguities and possibilities in California's mentor teacher program. *Educational Leadership, 43,* 23–29.

Weld, J. (1998, March). Attracting and retaining high-quality professionals in science education. *Phi Delta Kappan, 79,* 536–539.

Zahorik, J. A. (1987). Teachers' collegial interaction: An exploratory study. *Elementary School Journal, 87,* 385–396.

8

Professional Development for Educational Personnel

All personnel functions have a direct or an indirect impact on school effectiveness, but none has a greater potential effect than professional development and training. Professional development provides opportunities for teachers and other professional and support personnel to acquire new skills and attitudes that can lead to the changes in behavior that result in increased student achievement.

However, despite its promise, professional development often fails to achieve the results that planners hope for and expect. This chapter examines some of the reasons that professional development is less successful than it might be and reviews how these programs are changing in response to shifting expectations and the emergence of new organizational forms in schools.

Plan of the Chapter

This chapter addresses these topics: (1) functions of professional development, (2) characteristics of effective professional development, (3) planning for professional development, and (4) professional development for administrators and support personnel.

Functions of Professional Development

Professional development has been defined as any activity or process intended to improve skills, attitudes, understandings, or performance in present or future roles (Fullan, 1990). The definition emphasizes one aspect of professional development—to effect change—but ignores another purpose, which is to secure compliance with district policies and procedures (Evertson, 1986). Schlechty and Crowell (1983) called the latter the maintenance function of professional development. They explained that this function refers to activities intended to "keep things from get-ting worse" (p. 55) by reminding people "of what it is assumed they already knew but have forgotten" (p. 56).

Incorporating this idea into the preceding definition results in a more accurate description of professional development. In this book, *professional development* is defined as any activity or process intended to maintain or improve skills, attitudes, understandings, or performance of professional and support personnel in present or future roles.

Types of Change

Change may occur in more than one way. Change in the way work is performed is referred to as *technological change* (Schlechty & Crowell, 1983). Examples of techno-logical change include revisions in the curriculum content and the introduction of new ways of delivering instruction, such as using television or computers. Changes in the design of programs as well as changes in the ways students are managed and motivated also fall under the rubric of technological change.

Changes in the way people relate to one another are referred to as *structural changes* (Schlechty & Crowell, 1983). Structural change may involve a reassignment of duties or a change in the way power and authority are allocated in schools. Addi-tion of new positions, such as teacher aide, or changes in responsibilities and rewards, such as those that occur when a career ladder is introduced, are examples of structural changes (Schlechty & Crowell, 1983). Site-based management is another example of a structural change. Some structural changes are aimed at empowering teachers, but some authorities are skeptical of the value of these changes for improving student learning (Geisert, 1988).

Thus, professional development may be used to support technological or structural change or to serve a maintenance function. A change of one type may lead to change of the other kind. Introduction of certain technological changes in schools leads to alterations in power and authority relationships. When a school purchases computers for students' use, it is introducing a technological change, but the new technology may also trigger structural changes, as teachers begin to develop coop-erative working arrangements in order to facilitate access to the machines.

Accommodating Teachers' Needs

People have different needs as they attempt to implement the two types of change, and it is necessary to design development programs that accommodate these needs. When they implement new teaching methods or content, teachers want specific and practical suggestions on how the new technology will work, to see demonstrations of it, and to be allowed to try it out in a threat-free environment and receive feed-back. They prefer to adapt new techniques to their situations rather than implement them whole. Finally, teachers want to be convinced that the strategy they are being asked to adopt is superior to that they have been using.

In the case of structural change, employees need to have a clear conception of how the change will affect them. Changes that are perceived as altering relations among people have the potential to reduce security and are likely to be resisted unless teachers are convinced of the need for the change. The preferred presenter of a technological change is someone with expertise in the new technology, whereas the preferred presenter of structural change is someone who is trusted by those who will be affected. Expertise is less important in this case than a reputation for honesty and fairness. Thus, for a session involving structural change, a presenter might be an administrator in whom teachers have confidence and who can help allay feelings of threat aroused by the proposed alterations in roles, responsibilities, and relationships.

Characteristics of Effective Professional Development

Many of the professional development opportunities to which teachers have access do not incorporate the latest findings about what makes such programs effective. According to a recent study of professional development programs funded under Title II of the Elementary and Secondary Education Act (the Eisenhower Program), the majority of teachers who participated were involved in traditional types of activities. The median number of hours spent on a single activity was 15, and most teachers (64 percent) were involved in activities that lasted one week or less. Only about 20 percent of those surveyed took part in activities that included collective participation (Birman, Desimone, Porter, & Garet, 2000).

Current research has shown that brief workshops for teachers on topics chosen by district administrators and supervisors are not the most effective way of bringing about change in instructional practices. A more effective approach, according to the research, is to avoid brief workshops dealing only with technical skills in favor of a more intensive approach that deals with teachers' knowledge, experience, and beliefs, in addition to teaching techniques (Lieberman, 1999).

Research and experience have led to the conclusion that cooperative learning activities that emulate what takes place in classrooms are the surest way of having an impact on teaching practice. In these activities teachers take on the role of learner and experience how an explanation or demonstration by a skilled facilitator enhances their understanding of new material and how the discussion of relevant topics with colleagues increases their interest and motivation. Facilitators model for teachers the techniques that research and experience have shown to be effective. They pose open-ended questions about content and provide opportunities for teachers to work on activities that allow them to think as a scientist, mathematician, historian, or author (Cutler & Ruopp, 1999).

A number of other recommendations have been made recently to improve the quality of training programs in schools. These include devoting more attention to helping teachers learn about and use techniques that assess students' understanding of subject content and identifying areas in which additional instruction is needed. Suggestions have also been made that development programs should provide opportunities for teachers to engage in professional conversations with their colleagues about problems encountered in their teaching (Morocco & Solomon, 1999).

Teachers acquire knowledge about teaching from a variety of sources, of which professional development is only one. Reading, coursework, conversations with colleagues, and work with students are other sources from which teachers gain new insights, expand their knowledge, and add to their repertoire of skills. One writer distinguishes between "inside" and "outside" knowledge. *Outside knowledge* comes from consultants, conferences, and books, whereas *inside knowledge* is learning that is gained from conversations with and observations of colleagues and from one's own experience in the classroom. Teachers tend to view outside knowledge as abstract and theoretical. It is advisable for planners to maintain a balance between the amount of inside and outside knowledge presented and to seek to blend information from these sources into a meaningful configuration to increase teacher interest and comprehension (Lieberman, 1999).

Feedback and Support

Research is clear on the need for feedback and support for teachers who are implementing new classroom practices. The principal is an important source of this support. Both teacher learning and behavior changes are more likely to occur when the principal is supportive of the change (Sparks, 1983).

Support from other teachers is also important. Peer coaching is a technique designed to be used by teachers and administrators to help other teachers learn new teaching behaviors. Teachers receive training in a new technique, including information about the skills and strategies and the rationale for their use. They practice the new technique in their classrooms while a coach observes. Afterwards, the observer-coach critiques the teacher's performance, demonstrates the technique, and makes suggestions for improvement. The teacher and coach then discuss appropriate ways to use the new strategy. Using coaching triads rather than pairs increases the amount of feedback each participant receives and reduces the "mutual admiration society" aspect that sometimes occurs when two teachers coach one another (Duttweiler, 1989).

Coaching offers several advantages that are not found in more traditional professional development arrangements. Because teachers who are coached are likely to spend more time practicing new strategies and are more likely to receive immediate feedback on their performance, behavioral change can be expected to occur. Joyce and Showers (1988) claimed that coached teachers use newly learned techniques more appropriately than teachers who do not have the benefit of coaching. They also suggested that coached teachers retain their knowledge of new techniques longer and have a clearer understanding of the purpose and uses of the strategies.

Showers (1985) reported that coached teachers show much higher levels of behavior change than teachers who receive the same training without coaching, but other researchers have not found the same results (Sparks, 1983). The effectiveness of coaching probably depends on the coach's skill, the complexity of the behavior being learned, and the teacher's receptiveness to change.

Peer observation alone appears to be about as effective as peer coaching in producing behavior change among teachers when it is carried out in an atmosphere of trust. There are several reasons for this. Peer observers pick up ideas that they use in their own teaching, and they often become more aware of their own teaching behavior as a result of watching others teach. Observing also helps to free teachers from the psychological isolation that pervades many schools (Sparks, 1983).

Congruence and Ease of Adoption

Teachers are more likely to adopt strategies for use in their classrooms when they fully understand them and when the strategies are congruent with their teaching philosophies. Difficulty of implementing new techniques is another consideration that influences teachers' decisions. If the time and effort required to learn or use them are excessive, teachers are unlikely to adopt them (Doyle & Ponder, 1977).

Some of the most effective programs are those in which a school district and a university reach an agreement under which the university offers coursework tailored to meet an identified need of teachers in the district. One example was the Houston Teaching Academy, which offered a program to prepare teachers to work in inner-city schools (Arends, 1990).

In Maryland, the University of Maryland and Montgomery County Schools cooperated to form the Minority Teacher Education Project. The district hired minority individuals with bachelor's degrees as teacher aides and gave them released time to participate in a two-year program at the university that led to their receiving a teaching credential (Arends, 1990).

College work is especially valuable for teachers who are assigned to teach out of their field or who entered teaching through an alternative certification route. In 1991, 39 states provided for alternative certification of teachers in at least some specialty areas. As a rule, teachers with alternative certification have a strong background in a content area but are not as well grounded in pedagogy. Many of them need coursework in instructional methodology and human learning. Teachers who came through a traditional teacher preparation program some years ago or who have been reassigned to a new teaching field often need additional training in a content area (National Center for Education Statistics, 1993).

The numbers of individuals who are teaching out of their field are not large. Even in special education, a field of chronic shortages, the majority of teachers are fully certified. Nevertheless, the lack of expertise among these teachers can be a significant area of need to be addressed by professional development.

Other resources available to developers are state departments of education, which usually have on their staffs specialists in the major subject fields who can be called on for information about instructional materials and in-service ideas. In some localities, curriculum centers are also available to help schools meet developmental needs of teachers. In whatever form professional development is offered, planners need to offer instruction in both content and process (Mell & Mell, 1990).

Most teachers would like to find methods and materials that produce better results than those they are using, and they are inclined to try innovations that promise to do that (Guskey, 1986). For staff developers, the implications of those facts are clear. They should select strategies that have been shown to be effective in increasing student learning and should plan workshops to include clear explanations and demonstrations showing how the techniques work.

The research reviewed in this section provides direction for administrators who are responsible for planning and coordinating professional development programs. The characteristics associated with more effective programs are those that should be incorporated into development programs for teachers.

Planning for Professional Development

Due to the increasing cost of professional development, district superintendents are anxious to see evidence that the programs are producing the desired results. Productive programs are brought into being by careful planning, including consideration of three factors: assignment of responsibility, design of the program, and evaluation and follow-up.

Responsibility

Results-oriented professional development places responsibility for professional growth on teachers rather than on the district. Lawyers and doctors have a commitment to update continually their knowledge of new developments in their fields. But it has been the practice in education that district administrators assume most of the responsibility for determining what kinds of professional development activities teachers need. Teachers participate in planning and may present materials to their colleagues, but as a rule they are not expected to assume responsibility for their own growth (Tucker & Codding, 1998).

Results-oriented professional development is keyed to the school's goals and involves teachers and principals interacting to determine what knowledge, skills, and information they need to help students reach performance standards. This approach requires teachers to search for practices that have been shown to be effective in other settings and to adapt them to their own schools (Tucker & Codding, 1998).

A decision that must be made is whether to operate professional development as a centralized or decentralized activity. Some districts offer a unified program for all teachers, whereas others leave decisions on the content, format, and timing of developmental activities to the staff of each school.

School-Based Programs.   In districts with site-based management, much of the responsibility for staff development programs is delegated to the school; mandatory districtwide in-service programs cease to exist. The primary function of district staff members shifts from initiation and organization of training sessions to facilitation and support of activities initiated at the school level (Duttweiler, 1989; Smylie & Conyers, 1991). This change is accompanied by a shift in resources, with schools assuming responsibility for administering professional development budgets (Shanker, 1990).

Principals and teachers share the leadership for planning and presenting development activities for professional staff members at the school. The principal focuses attention on development by informing staff members of opportunities for professional growth, by distributing professional and curriculum materials to them, by seeking staff members' opinions about current issues related to their work, by increasing staff members' awareness of new developments, and by encouraging teachers to try new practices (McEvoy, 1987).

The idea of assigning responsibility for development to faculty members in each school is based on the belief that "the individual school is the most viable unit for effecting educational improvement" (Goodlad, 1983, p. 36). Goodlad admits that this position cannot be defended on the basis of research or common practice but calls it "a reasonable working hypothesis" (p. 39).

Several claims for the superiority of decentralized programs are made by proponents. One is that school-based programs, by directly involving teachers in decisions about program content and format, lead to higher levels of interest and commitment. Advocates also claim that site-based programs increase collaboration among and between teachers and principals (Howey & Vaughn, 1983), that site-based programs are more flexible, and that program offerings are more relevant and practical than offerings in programs that are centrally directed.

Decentralized programs also have potential disadvantages. One of the main drawbacks is the heavy demand they make on the time of the principal and teachers who are involved in planning and presenting training workshops. Most principals feel they already have too little time for instructional leadership responsibilities, and adding more duties further complicates that problem. School-based programs are also somewhat less efficient than centralized operations since some duplication across schools is unavoidable.

Staff developer is a new role for most teachers, and although most who attempt it have credibility with their colleagues and are successful, problems are occasionally encountered. Moving from teacher to development leader in the same school can be difficult, and some teachers prefer not to attempt it. Further, in schools with strong individualistic cultures, the lack of cohesiveness can threaten the success of school-based development programs (Joyce, 1990).

The arrangement recommended in this book is to encourage school faculties to plan their own development activities when they have identified specific objectives that apply to the school and that are most appropriately addressed at the school level. A centralized option should also be available for schools that are not prepared to undertake their own effort.

Time for Professional Development.   Teacher time for development falls into four categories (Moore & Hyde, 1981). *Salaried work time* includes all hours during which teachers are on duty. *Released time* includes periods during which substitutes are hired to release teachers from teaching duties. *Stipend time* is time outside of regular work hours during which teachers participate in professional development and are paid a salary supplement. *Personal time* is time that is teachers' own. Negotiated contracts often limit the use of teachers' personal and stipend time for professional development. It is important to check the contract before scheduling activities during those times.

Use of teachers' personal time for developmental purposes is the least costly option for the district, but it is also the least feasible. Some teachers are willing to use their own time to work toward a master's degree, but few willingly participate in professional development activities on their own time. A better approach is to schedule occasional activities during work time before and after school, keeping in mind that teachers prefer to reserve this time for planning, conferring with parents, personal errands, and housekeeping. The other two options (stipend time and released time) are feasible options and are about equally costly.

Design of the Program

In designing in-service activities for teachers, planners must take into account three factors: form, duration, and participation.

Form.   *Form* refers to structure and content. Professional development may involve groups—as in traditional workshops, teacher networks, and task forces— or it may feature individual activities, such as mentoring, individual research projects, and internships. The size of training group appears to have little effect on the outcomes of training, but the composition of the group does seem to make a difference. More learning occurs when elementary and secondary teachers receive training together than when they are separated (Wade, 1984/1985).

Objectives of Professional Development.   The outcomes of professional development for teachers can be changes in knowledge, behavior, or attitudes for individuals or groups. A single activity may have objectives of several types, but the more different outcomes the planners envision, the more complex the venture becomes and the harder it is to ensure that the desired results will be obtained. Exhibit 8.1 summarizes examples of objectives of the three types for both individuals and groups.

Objectives may be stated either as individual or group outcomes. An example of an individual objective is: "All participants will demonstrate familiarity with five techniques for teaching thinking skills to students in the grade level or subject they teach and will commit themselves to try all five techniques in their classes within one month." A group objective could be stated in the following way: "Participants will collectively identify methods of increasing time on task that have worked in their own classes and will agree to try at least two new methods in their classes and discuss the results with colleagues within one month."

EXHIBIT 8.1   *Individual and Group Objectives of Professional Development*

Individual Objectives

Behavior	Improved skill in assessing students' needs
	Improved ability to present instruction
Attitude	Increased confidence as a teacher
	Increased satisfaction in teaching
	Stronger commitment to teaching
Cognition	Increased knowledge of subject
	Changed beliefs about teaching
	Increased knowledge of educational trends
	Better understanding of school values and mission

Group Objectives

Behavior	Increased willingness to share and participate
	Greater interest in collaborating with other teachers to develop curriculum and teaching strategies
Attitude	Increased mutual trust
	Growth of team spirit
	Feeling of belonging
Cognition	Able to evaluate the effectiveness of group work
	Increased skill in analyzing group functioning
	Growing consensus on educational values

Source: School Effectiveness and School-Based Management: A Mechanism for Development by Y. Cheng, 1996, London: Falmer. Reprinted by permission.

Plan Content.   Once the objectives of the program are selected, the decision about content is simplified. Both objectives and content should take into account the realities of the school as an organization and a social system and should recognize the teacher as a person and professional. Professional development programs are often presented with little or no thought given to school norms and teacher role relationships that affect the implementation of new technologies (North Dakota State Department of Public Instruction, 1986).

Some examples of topics related to improving instruction are the social climate of the school, revision of particular curriculum areas, teaching strategies, use of technology, student learning styles, and teaching students with special needs (Joyce & Showers, 1988). The research on effective schools suggests other possible topics, including time on task, behavior management, organization and grouping, lesson design, instructional sequencing, and teacher expectations (Mohlman, Kierstad, & Gundlach, 1982). Brookover and associates (1982) described 11 professional development modules on a variety of topics, including effective learning climate, grouping, classroom management, cooperative learning, and use of assessment data.

When planning professional development programs that involve technological change, it is important to bear in mind that teachers are not likely to be persuaded about the value of a new technique until they have seen for themselves that it works. If a technique works without being unduly costly of teachers' time and effort, they will be more likely to embrace it than if it is unproven. Staff developers should therefore concentrate on selecting strategies that have been shown to work and should offer assistance and support for teachers who are trying the new procedures.

Teachers are more likely to try new ideas when the presentation focuses on concrete practices rather than theoretical issues. Attention to specific rather than global teaching skills is also helpful. Presenters who have credibility with teachers and those who address teachers' personal concerns related to adopting the change are more likely to be successful in achieving teacher support for change (Guskey, 1986).

Planners should take maximum advantage of the resources available to them. An important source of assistance for professional development is local colleges and universities. At one time colleges and universities were the primary providers of professional development for school personnel, but today, with most school districts having developed their own programs, few teachers rely exclusively on colleges and universities for developmental opportunities (Little, 1990). Nevertheless, coursework should not be overlooked as one component of an effective professional development program.

To assess individual priorities, employees may be asked to identify their own growth needs, or supervisors, principals, and department heads list areas in which teachers ask for assistance. Exhibit 8.2 shows a survey instrument for collecting information from teachers to supplement data from other sources, including test results, evaluation reports, audits, and accreditation studies (Kramer & Betz, 1987).

The content of in-service programs usually consists of subject matter knowledge, the processes by which children learn, or generic teaching techniques. A key to raising student achievement is ensuring that teachers have a sophisticated understanding of the subject they teach and are well informed about the processes by which students learn the subject (Birman et al., 2000).

Teachers who have a thorough understanding of their subject are able to answer crucial questions that enable them to diagnose students' comprehension and plan instruction accordingly. Some of the questions teachers need to be prepared to answer are Which concepts are most important for students to understand? What beliefs, conceptions, or misconceptions do students hold about the subject? and What instructional activities or techniques will increase children's curiosity about the subject matter (Solomon & Morocco, 1999)?

The National Board for Professional Teaching Standards has identified the knowledge, skills, and dispositions needed by teachers and has asked teachers to demonstrate that they meet those standards. National Board Certification is volun-

EXHIBIT 8.2   *Assessment of Developmental Needs of Teachers*

Directions: The information you provide will be used in planning for staff development activities in the district. Please answer all questions thoughtfully and truthfully.

1. How many years (total) teaching experience do you have?
2. What grade level(s) do you teach?
3. What subject(s) do you teach?
4. What is the highest degree that you hold?
5. When did you last take a college course in your subject specialty?
6. With which of the following groups would you prefer to attend a staff development workshop?
   - ❐ Teachers from your own school
   - ❐ Teachers from other schools in this district
   - ❐ Teachers from other districts
   - ❐ Mixed groups, including teachers and administrators from this district
   - ❐ Mixed groups, including teachers and administrators from other districts
7. What is your preference of day and time for professional development sessions?
8. From the following list, select the three workshops you would be most interested in attending.
   - ❐ Time on task
   - ❐ Classroom organization and management
   - ❐ Classroom climate
   - ❐ Learning styles
   - ❐ Teacher-made tests
   - ❐ Higher-order thinking
   - ❐ Using technology in the classroom
   - ❐ Effects of teacher expectations on student achievement
   - ❐ Curriculum revision
   - ❐ Lesson design
   - ❐ Teaching students with special needs
   - ❐ Preparing an individualized educational plan
   - ❐ Teaching gifted children
   - ❐ Site-based management
   - ❐ Assessing student performance
   - ❐ Working with parents and the community
9. Can you suggest presenters for any of the topics on the list? (If so, list the name of the topic and the presenter.)
10. Would you be willing to serve as a workshop leader presenting a topic in which you have received previous training? (If yes, give your name and school and the topic you can present.)

tary for teachers who wish to establish credible professional credentials. Teachers must prepare a portfolio and participate in assessment activities in order to achieve board certification (Jenkins, 2000).

Methods of Presentation.   Development workshops are likely to be most successful when they incorporate four components: (1) presentation of theory, (2) demonstration of a teaching strategy, (3) initial practice, and (4) prompt feedback (Showers et al., 1987). The more complex the behavior being taught, the greater is the need for a training design that incorporates all four elements. The addition to the first two elements of the opportunity to practice and receive performance feedback dramatically increases the likelihood that teachers will retain and use what they learn (Showers et al., 1987). Practice and feedback appear to be especially important when the behavior being learned is unfamiliar to the learner (Sparks, 1983).

Sessions that are planned for beginning teachers should use a structured, directive approach. Teachers with more experience prefer to learn ways to add variety to their teaching and favor a collaborative approach (Burden & Wallace, 1983).

To prepare teachers to use specific instructional techniques, the following format is recommended (Stallings, 1985):

1. *Baseline/pretest:* Teachers are observed for target teaching behaviors. Profiles are prepared showing how frequently each behavior is used. From the profiles, teachers consult with supervisors and set goals.
2. *Information:* Information is provided to participating teachers linking research and practice. Teachers are checked for understanding.
3. *Guided practice:* Teachers adapt the new techniques one at a time to their own context and style. After trying the new methods, they assess them and are provided feedback from peer observers. Leaders obtain a commitment from participants to try the new method in their own classes and provide support and encouragement for the change.
4. *Postest:* Teachers are observed again and a new profile is prepared. Teachers set new goals and assess the training program for effectiveness.

Duration.   Although some studies have reported that the length of training sessions has no statistically significant relationship to the effectiveness of professional development, it is reasonable to believe that more time is needed to learn material that is high in complexity as compared to simpler material (Sparks, 1983). A scheduling plan that has been shown to produce good results is a series of brief (three-hour) workshops spaced at intervals of two or three weeks over a period of several months (Mohlman, Kierstad, & Gundlach, 1982). Presenting small amounts of new material at each of several sessions rather than crowding all of it into one or two meetings helps teachers gradually integrate the new practices into their existing routines. Teachers also find it easier to cope with concerns aroused by change when the innovations are presented at a more leisurely pace (Sparks, 1983).

Participation.   The context in which development activities take place has an important bearing on the extent to which teachers are likely to see new methods and materials as relevant to their situation and make the decision to try them out. Among other things, context covers the location of training sessions, the quality and comfort of the physical facilities, and the availability of appropriate learning aids. Another important aspect of context is the participants themselves. A session in which a single representative from each school takes part is a very different experience from one in which all the teachers from a school are simultaneously involved. A session in which all participants are beginning teachers is very different from one in which teachers from all levels of experience are on hand (Birman et al., 2000).

Collective participation (that is, all or most of the teachers from a single school participate) enables teachers to discuss concepts and problems that arise in implementing new strategies. Collective participation may also contribute to development of a shared professional culture (Birman et al., 2000).

Evaluation and Follow-Up

Evaluation of professional development programs is often carried out as an afterthought with little or no advance planning. Time spent in planning the evaluation will yield increased confidence in the findings. A comprehensive evaluation plan involves assessing four outcomes of professional development (Wade, 1984/1985). Exhibit 8.3 shows sources of data for a comprehensive evaluation of a professional development program.

The initial presentation of a new program or technique is only the first step in implementing change. Providing regular feedback to teachers who are charged with implementing the model and providing sustained support and follow-up after the initial training are critical elements of an effective professional development program (Guskey, 1986). Feedback can be provided by other teachers who have had sufficient training in the technique to be able to guide their peers in its use.

Professional Development for Administrators and Support Personnel

Professional development for administrators does not receive much attention in most school districts. Principals who wish to grow professionally can usually find the necessary financial support, and their schedules are flexible enough to permit them to be away from their buildings for training purposes. However, many districts do not require or even encourage principals to engage in professional development activities (Hallinger & Greenblatt, 1989).

The principal's job is a demanding one; in most schools, principals have very little time that is not already committed. Moreover, most principals feel a sense of responsibility to be available in case a problem should arise in their schools. Some

EXHIBIT 8.3   *Information to Be Collected in a Comprehensive Evaluation of Professional Development Programs*

Outcome	Items
Teacher Reactions	Convenience of time and day of session Convenience of the location Comfort of the room Ability of presenters to make concepts clear and to maintain interest Presenters' knowledge of subject Appropriateness of the content for teachers' own schools or classrooms Probability of using strategies presented in the workshop Estimated need for feedback and follow-up
Teacher Knowledge	Teachers' estimates of their knowledge of subject before and after attending session Pre- and posttest to measure knowledge gain Desire to learn more about the subject
Behavior Change	Teachers' estimate of frequency of use of new strategy one month after attending session Data from classroom observers showing frequency of use Teachers' estimates of difficulty of use (time involved, student understanding and receptivity) Teachers' estimates of likelihood they will continue to use strategy
Student Learning	Results of experimental research on student gains in classes with teachers using new techniques, compared to students in classes with teachers using old techniques Students' estimates of amount they learn when teachers use new versus old techniques Data from classroom observers on student interest and participation in classes using new versus old techniques

principals feel that taking time for their own growth and development is selfish and deprives children and teachers of their attention.

Principals who take advantage of professional development opportunities for themselves report that they do so because it helps them to grow and learn or helps them avoid burnout. One principal commented, "It's very important to me to continue to learn. It's self-satisfying, it makes me feel good about myself." Another stated, "[I] need energy from outside, otherwise I'd be burned out or bored out" (Hallinger & Greenblatt, 1989, p. 71).

Periodic surveys of principals' and supervisors' needs can help those responsible for professional development to provide sessions that will help principals and supervisors to feel better prepared to deal with the dual responsibilities of school management and instructional leadership. Perennial issues of concern to both groups include evaluation of teaching performance, supervision of teachers, and conducting postobservation conferences. Other topics appear periodically as issues of interest. In one survey of principals, the following topics received frequent mention (Olivero, 1982):

1. *School climate:* Principals were interested in learning how to analyze school morale and in being able to understand the relationship between climate and school policies. Principals expressed a need to be able to take action to develop more positive climates in their schools.
2. *Team building:* Principals asked to learn more about use of interpersonal skills to achieve improved collegial relations among teachers in their schools.
3. *Internal communications:* Principals hoped to improve two-way communication among staff members and with students, community members, and other district personnel.

A newly emerging form of professional development for principals involves peer conversations aimed at helping principals to perform more effectively in their leadership roles. Small groups of administrators use structured protocols to look at their work and that of their students. A moderator convenes the group, explains the rules, and helps keep the conversation on the topic. The rules help prevent one or two participants from monopolizing the conversation by requiring that speakers take turns and listen attentively when others are speaking. Time is allowed for presenting work, listening without commenting, and giving and receiving feedback (Mohr, 1998).

The results of administrators' performance in assessment centers can also be used as a source of data on professional development needs of this group. A study of assessment center results for 94 practicing and aspiring principals found that the administrators were rated highest in group leadership and oral communication and lowest in problem analysis and creativity. The results indicated that improvement was needed in instructional leadership skills for practicing principals and in organizational ability for aspiring principals. Professional development opportunities in instructional leadership, group leadership, and organizational ability were readily available to the aspiring and practicing principals who participated in that study, but training opportunities in resourcefulness, decisiveness, creativity, and judgment were limited (Elsaesser, 1990).

Individualized Development Plans

Because individual needs and interests vary, the ideal approach to professional development is to allow each individual to design a program uniquely suited to his or her needs and interests. The Nebraska Council of School Administrators has developed such a plan, called the Nebraska Professional Proficiency Plan (Joekel, 1994), which permits administrators to plan their own professional development agenda.

Under the plan, an administrator works with a mentor to develop an individualized plan that includes, among other things, a list of career goals, descriptions of personal strengths and areas of needed improvement, and identification of one immediate goal. With the assistance of the mentor, the administrator brainstorms and lists activities that will help him or her to achieve the immediate goal and develops a means to monitor accomplishment of tasks leading to the goal (Joekel, 1994).

The administrator compiles a performance portfolio to document his or her progress toward attainment of the goal. After reviewing the portfolio, the mentor approves or recommends refinements or additional evidence. Upon completion of the individual development plan, the administrator and mentor submit a report to the state Council of School Administrators, which, after approving the report, issues a certificate of accomplishment (Joekel, 1994).

Career Counseling for Administrators

Most businesses provide extensive in-service training for their managers because they believe that it is a good investment for the individual as well as for the firm, but education lags in this regard (Daresh, 1987). Many corporations provide career counseling services to managers, but few school districts do so. The decision to leave the classroom in order to take an administrative position is a major change in career direction. Most people who consider such a career change would like to have the opportunity to discuss the decision with a sympathetic listener. Career counseling could help individuals consider all aspects of a decision more carefully and result in better quality decisions.

Some districts now arrange for prospective administrators to take part-time administrative assignments as a way of assessing their administrative potential. For the individual, such an arrangement is a growth experience; through it he or she learns what the job is like and acquires experience that can be used at a later time. The district receives the individual's services and acquires information about his or her performance.

Some new ideas are being tried in administrator in-service. One of these is a program that focuses on analyzing real-life problems. Participating administrators write short reports that describe an actual administrative problem and tell how the problem was handled. These reports become the focus of discussions that permit other administrators to relate how they have handled similar situations in the past and to suggest alternatives that might be tried. State departments of education have recognized the need for improvements in administrative development, and some now sponsor administrative academies that offer training for superintendents and other administrators (Daresh, 1987).

Some districts now recognize that many growth experiences are available to administrators other than those represented by traditional staff development. An example of one such approach is provided by Elam, Cramer, and Brodinsky (1986). It is a growth chart on which an administrator makes a record over the course of a year of a variety of activities in which he or she has participated that have led to professional growth. Some of the categories include reading, writing, research, conventions, conferences, meetings, speeches, association or community activities, travel, college courses, visits to other schools or businesses, and participation in cultural activities.

Suggestions for improving in-service training for administrators are similar to those for teachers. Planners are advised to personalize staff development activities by focusing program content on areas of identified need and providing opportunities for participants to build on their experiences as administrators. Demonstration, modeling of new skills, and providing opportunities for practice both in the training session and on the job are other recommendations. Performance feedback is important while a new skill is being learned. Administrative training should provide for both personal and professional growth and should be related to identified district instructional goals. Training should be cumulative, with sessions designed to build on previous offerings (Pitner, 1987).

Training for Staff Support Personnel

Some school districts operate comprehensive training programs that provide in-service opportunities and college courses for clerical and paraprofessional personnel. Such a program is offered to personnel in Los Angeles schools, where teachers' aides are able to participate in a program leading to an associate or baccalaureate degree from a local college. Employees who complete a bachelor's degree in an approved teacher preparation program are hired by the district as teachers. The Los Angeles school district also offers in-service training for clerical and crafts employees. These classes focus on skills development, including clerical skills, student discipline for bus drivers, computer operation, and food service operation (DeVries & Colbert, 1990).

Summary

Professional development refers to any activity or process intended to maintain or improve skills, attitudes, understandings, or performance of professional and support personnel in present or future roles. It has a significant potential for influencing instructional effectiveness. Research on effectiveness of professional development programs has yielded findings related to length and scheduling of training sessions, and size and composition of the group. In districts with school-based management, responsibility for professional development is being delegated to schools. Planning for a professional development program in a school begins with creation of a planning committee and the completion of a needs assessment. A comprehensive program should include developmental opportunities for administrators and training for support staff.

Suggested Activities

1. Interview the training director of a company or agency other than a school. Some examples of agencies you might contact are a health department, social service agency, bank, electric or gas utility, or hospital. Find out who is served by the training program, the type and frequency of offerings, and the background and qualifications of the training staff. Compare the program in the agency you study to the professional development operation in a school district.

2. Imagine you are the principal of a school and write a memorandum to the director of professional development in your district, arguing in favor of initiating a plan to introduce teacher coaches into all schools. Support your arguments with evidence from published research or statements of knowledgeable experts and suggest ways of implementing the teacher coach program.

3. Plan a three-hour in-service session for principals on a topic of your choice. Prepare an outline of the activities to be included and the handouts, tapes, films, or transparencies that will be used.

Online Resources

The sites listed here contain a wealth of information that will be helpful in planning professional development activities.

Eisenhower Program (www.edgov/inits/teachers/eisenhower/title.html)
   The Eisenhower Program supports professional development programs for teachers of mathematics and science. This site contains a summary of a report evaluating Eisenhower-supported professional development activities in five states.

National Staff Development Council (www.nsdc.org)
   This site has links to a report on professional development for principals and lists of Council publications. The emphasis is on "how to" strategies for professional development. There is also a self-assessment test to help planners determine where their school district stands and information on standards for professional development programs for school personnel.

North Central Regional Educational Laboratory (www.ncrel.org/pd)
   This site links to pages with information on tools for planning professional development programs and a resource center. There are also descriptions of model programs nationwide and discussions of issues in planning for professional development.

References

Arends, R. (1990). Connecting the university to the school. In B. Joyce (Ed.), *Changing school culture through staff development* (pp. 117–143). Alexandria, VA: Association for Supervision and Curriculum Development.

Birman, B., Desimone, L., Porter, A., & Garet, M. (2000, May). Designing professional development that works. *Educational Leadership, 57,* 28–32.

Brandt, R. (1996, March). On a new direction for teacher evaluation: A conversation with Tom McGreal. *Educational Leadership, 53,* 30–33.

Brookover, W., Beamer, L., Efthim, H., Hathaway, D., Lezotte, L., Miller, S., Passalcqua, J., & Tornatzky, L. (1982). *Creating effective schools: An in-service program for enhancing school learning climate and achievement.* Holmes Beach, FL: Learning Publications.

Burden, P. R., & Wallace, D. (1983, October). *Tailoring staff development to meet teacher needs.* Paper presented at the Association of Teacher Educators meeting, Wichita, KS. (ERIC Document Reproduction Service No. ED 237506).

Cheng, Y. (1996). *School effectiveness and school-based management: A mechanism for development.* London: Falmer.

Cutler, A., & Ruopp, F. (1999). From expert to novice: The transformation from teacher to learner. In M. Solomon (Ed.), *The diagnostic teacher* (pp. 133–161). New York: Teachers College Press.

Daresh, J. C. (1987). Administrator in-service: A route to continuous learning and growing. In W. Greenfield (Ed.), *Instructional leadership: Concepts, issues, and controversies* (pp. 328–340). Boston: Allyn and Bacon

DeVries, R., & Colbert, J. (1990). The Los Angeles experience: Individually oriented professional development. In B. Joyce (Ed.), *Changing school culture through staff development* (pp. 203–217). Alexandria, VA: Association for Supervision and Curriculum Development.

Doyle, W., & Ponder, G. (1977). The practicality ethic and teacher decision-making. *Interchange, 8,* 1–12.

Duttweiler, P. (1989, Spring). Components of an effective professional development program. *Journal of Staff Development, 10,* 2–6.

Elam, S., Cramer, J., & Brodinsky, B. (1986). *Staff development: Problems and solutions.* Arlington, VA: American Association of School Administrators.

Elsaesser, L. (1990, April). *Using assessment center results to determine subsequent staff development activities for principals.* Paper presented at the annual meeting of the American Educational Research Association, Boston. (ERIC Document Reproduction No. ED 318763).

Evertson, C. (1986). Do teachers make a difference? Issues for the eighties. *Education and Urban Society, 18,* 195–210.

Fullan, M. (1990). Staff development, innovation, and institutional development. In B. Joyce (Ed.), *Changing school culture through staff development (pp.* 3–25). Alexandria, VA: Association for Supervision and Curriculum Development.

Geisert, G. (1988, November). Participatory management: Panacea or hoax? *Educational Leadership, 46,* 56–59.

Georgia State Department of Education. (1990). *School-focused staff development guide.* Atlanta: Author.

Goodlad, J. (1983). The school as workplace. In G. Griffin (Ed.), *Staff development* (pp. 36–61). Chicago: University of Chicago Press.

Guskey, T. (1986, May). Staff development and the process of teacher change. *Educational Researcher, 15,* 5–12.

Hallinger, P., & Greenblatt, R. (1989, Fall). Principals' pursuit of professional growth: The influence of beliefs, experiences, and district context. *Journal of Staff Development, 10,* 68–74.

Howey, K., & Vaughn, J. (1983). Current patterns of staff development. In G. Griffin (Ed.), *Staff development* (pp. 92–117). Chicago: University of Chicago Press.

Jenkins, K. (2000, May). Earning board certification: Making time to grow. *Educational Leadership, 57,* 46–48.

Joekel, R. (1994, January). Nebraska Professional Proficiency Plan. *Design for Leadership: Bulletin of the National Policy Board for Educational Administration, 5,* 5–7.

Joyce, B. (1990). The self-educating teacher: Empowering teachers through research. In B. Joyce (Ed.), *Changing school culture through staff development* (pp. 26–40). Alexandria, VA: Association for Supervision and Curriculum Development.

Joyce, B., & Showers, B. (1988). *Student achievement through staff development.* New York: Longman.

Kramer, P., & Betz, L. (1987). *Effective inservice education in Texas public schools.* (ERIC Document Reproduction Service No. ED 290205).

Lieberman, A. (1999). *Teachers—Transforming their world and their work.* New York: Teachers College Press.

Little, J. (1990). Conditions of professional development in secondary schools. In M. McLaughlin, J. Talbert, & N. Bascia (Eds.), *The contexts of teaching in secondary schools: Teachers' realities* (pp. 187–223). New York: Teachers College Press.

McEvoy, B. (1987, February). Everyday acts: How principals influence development of their staff. *Educational Leadership, 44,* 73–77.

Mell, B., & Mell, C. (1990). An experience in Anchorage: Trials, errors, and successes. In B. Joyce (Ed.), *Changing school culture through staff development* (pp. 229–242). Alexandria, VA: Association for Supervision and Curriculum Development.

Mohlman, G., Kierstad, J., & Gundlach, M. (1982, October). A research-based inservice model for secondary teachers. *Educational Leadership, 40,* 16–19.

Mohr, N. (1998, April). Creating effective study groups for principals. *Educational Leadership, 55,* 41–44.

Moore, D., & Hyde, A. (1981). *Making sense of staff development: An analysis of staff development programs and their costs in three urban school districts.* (ERIC Document Reproduction Service No. ED 211629).

Morocco, C., & Solomon, M. (1999). Revitalizing professional development. In M. Solomon (Ed.), *The diagnostic teacher* (pp. 247–267). New York: Teachers College Press.

National Center for Education Statistics. (1993). *America's teachers: Profile of a profession.* Washington, DC: U.S. Department of Education.

North Dakota State Department of Public Instruction. (1986). *Professional development model: A wholistic approach.* Bismarck, ND: Author. (ERIC Document Reproduction Service No. ED 286868).

Olivero, J. (1982, February). Principals and their inservice needs. *Educational Leadership, 39,* 340–344.

Pitner, N. (1987). Principles of quality staff development: Lessons for administrator training. In J. Murphy & P. Hallinger (Eds.), *Approaches to administrative training in education* (pp. 28–44). Albany: State University of New York Press.

Schlechty, P., & Crowell, D. (1983). *Understanding and managing staff development in an urban school system.* Washington, DC: National Institute of Education. (ERIC Document Reproduction Service No. ED 251519).

Shanker, A. (1990). Staff development and the restructured school. In B. Joyce (Ed.), *Changing school culture through staff development* (pp. 91–103). Alexandria, VA: Association for Supervision and Curriculum Development.

Showers, B. (1985, April). Teachers coaching teachers. *Educational Leadership, 42,* 43–48.

Showers, B., Joyce, B., & Bennett, B. (1987, November). Synthesis of research on staff development: A framework for future study and a state-of-the-art analysis. *Educational Leadership, 45,* 77–87.

Smylie, M., & Conyers, J. (1991, Winter). Changing conceptions of teaching influence the future of staff development. *Journal of Staff Development, 12,* 12–16.

Solomon, M., & Morocco, C. (1999). The diagnostic teacher. In M. Solomon (Ed.), *The diagnostic teacher* (pp. 231–246). New York: Teachers College Press.

Sparks, B. (1983, November). Synthesis of research on staff development for effective teaching. *Educational Leadership, 41,* 65–72.

Stallings, J. (1985). *How effective is an analytic approach to staff development on teacher and student behavior?* Nashville: Vanderbilt University, Peabody College. (ERIC Document Reproduction Service No. ED 267019).

Tucker, M., & Codding, J. (1998). *Standards for our schools.* San Francisco: Jossey-Bass.

Wade, R. (1984/1985, December/January). What makes a difference in inservice teacher education? A meta-analysis of research. *Educational Leadership, 42,* 48–54.

9

Evaluating Employee Performance

Evaluation of performance is a fact of life in most work settings, and even though it may be carried out in a routine and perfunctory manner, few individuals approach the experience with indifference. All employees potentially stand to gain or lose from evaluation, but in schools, it is not only teachers and other personnel who have something at stake. Parents and students can also benefit from evaluation, since evaluation procedures properly carried out lead to improved instruction.

In many schools, teacher evaluation has little effect on teacher performance. It is carried out to fulfill the requirements of state statutes, board policy, or union contracts. In such cases, evaluation

> does little for teachers except contribute to their weariness and reinforce their skepticism of bureaucratic routine...[and] does little for administrators except add to their workload. It does not provide a mechanism for a school system to communicate its expectations concerning teaching. (Darling-Hammond, 1986, pp. 531–532)*

Two of the most common problems in teacher evaluation are the relative infrequency of classroom observations and the unrealistically high ratings teachers receive. A majority of teachers report they are observed by an evaluator no more than twice a year, and a substantial number (about one in six) say they have never been observed. Elementary school teachers and younger teachers, including those with less experience, are observed slightly more often than teachers in middle and high schools and those who have been teaching longer (Educational Research Service, 1985).

All employees tend to rate themselves high on performance and are disappointed when they receive lower ratings from superiors than they feel they deserve. On the whole, however, teachers are rated high. One study showed that

---

about 41 percent of teachers surveyed viewed themselves as belonging in the top 10 percent of all performers (a striking finding in itself); however, an even larger proportion (48 percent) reported that their superiors rated them among the top 10 percent. Put another way, the evaluators rate teachers even higher than they rate themselves (Educational Research Service, 1985).

There is nothing inherently wrong with high ratings, and it is human nature to prefer to avoid giving others low ratings. The problem is that personnel who receive higher ratings than they deserve may be lulled into believing that they have no need for further improvement.

Plan of the Chapter

This chapter deals with the following topics: (1) new directions in performance evaluation, (2) purposes of performance evaluation, (3) criteria for evaluating school personnel, (4) models of teacher evaluation, (5) characteristics of successful evaluation programs, (6) state-mandated evaluation systems, (7) legal considerations in personnel evaluation, and (8) evaluation of administrative and support personnel.

New Directions in Performance Evaluation

Teacher evaluation has evolved in new directions in recent years, and one result has been that the line between professional development and evaluation is blurring. The advantages of coupling evaluation with staff development have been obvious, but until now the connection was seldom made. Another change that is underway is the recognition that evaluation of probationary teachers should differ from evaluation of teachers with several years of experience. Beginners now receive more support than they have had in the past, but at the same time the standards they are expected to meet are more demanding, and the evaluation procedures are more intensive. Evaluation of beginning teachers is usually carried out in conjunction with a mentoring program that teams new teachers with veterans who are prepared to help them acquire the skills they need to be successful. More sources of data are used in evaluating teachers, including classroom observations, personal journals, portfolios, and comments of parents and other teachers (Brandt, 1996). In some cases, student evaluations and performance are also taken into account.

A kind of consensus has been reached on what constitutes the basic teaching skills that all teachers should be expected to master, and beginners are expected to have mastered those skills when they start teaching. Interesting new developments are underway with regard to the teachers' and principals' roles in evaluation. Principals are now seen as both evaluators and facilitators, responsible for helping as well as evaluating teachers, particularly those who are new to the profession. At the same time, there is a movement toward placing more responsibility for teachers' professional growth on the teachers themselves.

Team evaluation is gaining adherents. In this plan, a team of teachers prepares a long-range plan, usually covering a period of two to three years, and ending with the development of a product. The product might be a new curriculum, a series of instructional units on related topics, or collections of high-interest artifacts for students. The principal meets with the group periodically to help teachers carry out their plan and monitor its development. Unions have agreed to participate in new evaluation procedures as long as they are not expected to provide data on teacher performance (Brandt, 1996).

While these new developments have been occurring, some other proposals that have received attention in the past appear not to be catching on. Evaluation by peers involves many logistical problems that at the present time seem insurmountable, and self-directed teacher evaluation seems to be fading for lack of interest (Brandt, 1996).

Purposes of Performance Evaluation

The Joint Committee on Standards for Educational Evaluation (1988) has identified the following purposes for evaluation of educational personnel: "Evaluation of educators should promote sound education principles, fulfillment of institutional missions, and effective performance of job responsibilities, so that the educational needs of students, community, and society are met" (p. 21).

This chapter examines two types of evaluation for educational personnel. *Summative evaluation* refers to assessment carried out for accountability purposes. This type of evaluation is usually conducted annually or semiannually, and the results are used to make decisions about individuals, such as whether to grant tenure, to seek termination or transfer, to place an individual on a career ladder, or to make a salary adjustment (Educational Research Service, 1978). *Formative evaluation* serves a developmental function. Its purpose is to help an individual employee improve his or her effectiveness on the job by providing feedback and coaching (Educational Research Service, 1978).

The formative and summative sides of performance evaluation are sometimes in conflict. Formative evaluation relies on the creation and maintenance of a bond of trust between the employee and the evaluator. Summative evaluation, because of the high stakes involved and the emphasis on judging, risks undermining the trust that is essential to helping employees learn new job-related behaviors (Wise, Darling-Hammond, McLaughlin, & Bernstein, 1984). Some authorities believe that formative and summative evaluation cannot be reconciled in the same evaluation system and suggest that the two functions should be separated (Knapp, 1982).

Although formative and summative evaluation are the most common reasons for conducting performance evaluations, other purposes are served as well. Evaluation is sometimes used to validate selection criteria, to provide a basis for career planning, and to select individuals to receive merit pay awards or promotions to positions of greater responsibility (Educational Research Service, 1978).

Selecting Summative Instruments

Care must be exercised in selecting or constructing instruments to be used for summative evaluation. When they are used for decisions about individuals, instruments should have high reliability and criterion or predictive validity. *Criterion validity* refers to the degree of relationship between scores on an instrument and employees' subsequent performance on the job.

Reliability refers to whether different evaluators agree in their ratings of the same teacher and whether an individual evaluator is consistent in his or her ratings. Training of evaluators is necessary in order to ensure reliability. Instruments used for summative purposes should also be tested to ensure that they do not discriminate on the basis of teacher gender or race, or produce different results when applied to teaching situations involving variations in subject matter, class size, or type of student (Smith, Peterson, & Micceri, 1987).

Criteria for Evaluating School Personnel

Workers are evaluated on the basis of possessing certain personal characteristics, demonstrating behaviors associated with successful performance, or producing specified results. The characteristics, behaviors, and results used to judge performance are called *criteria*. To identify criteria for use in evaluating an individual in a position, the job model for that position (see Chapter 3) is a logical place to start. The "Priority Actions" and "Results Sought" sections of the job model are useful sources of criteria for performance evaluation. The "Results Sought" section lists outcomes the employee is expected to achieve, and the performance evaluation should be based on the degree to which the employee has successfully attained those results.

Teachers are asked to perform a number of tasks, but none is more important than instruction. For both formative and summative evaluation, attention to instruction is prominent. Accordingly, the main emphasis in this chapter is on evaluating performance of instructional tasks. The model of student learning depicted in Chapter 1 (Figure 1.1) showed that student learning results from teacher behaviors, which in turn are influenced by teacher knowledge and motivation. If the bottom line is student outcomes, why not measure those results directly rather than relying on indirect indicators of teaching effectiveness?

In some occupations, results are readily available and are easily measured. In sales, for example, the best indicator of employee performance is the number of units sold or the dollar value of sales completed during a given period of time. To the sales manager, a salesperson's personal characteristics are less important than the revenue the employee generates. In manufacturing operations, the quantity of a product produced is a measure of employee performance, and in clerical work the number of letters typed or the number of customer questions answered are measures of employee productivity.

However, the "product" of teaching is the content of children's minds. This output is not tangible, nor is it easily attributed to the efforts of a single teacher, since the learner's responses in a given situation are influenced by all previous experiences. Learning outcomes are not easily measured, and cause-effect relationships between teacher behavior and learning are far from clear. Learning gains achieved by a child during the course of a year result in part from the efforts of the current teacher and in part from the child's previous teachers and from experiences outside of school.

Selecting Criteria

The criteria selected for use in evaluating teachers should be supported by research and experience showing they are related to desirable learning outcomes. The evaluator has the task of determining whether a teacher uses validated teaching behaviors and must also judge whether the behaviors are used in appropriate situations. Teaching behaviors cannot be prescribed as a physician would prescribe a drug for an infection; the teacher must understand when a particular behavior is called for and must be able to call it forth at that moment. This decision must take into consideration the teacher's instructional objectives, the types of students in the class, and the situation in the classroom at a given moment (Knapp, 1982).

The evaluator must consider two questions in assessing teaching performance: Is the teacher able to perform the behavior in question? and Does the teacher use the behavior when it is appropriate to do so and not use it when its use is inappropriate? The first question is a matter of knowledge; the second is a matter of judgment.

Five criteria commonly used to evaluate instruction are knowledge of subject, preparation and planning, implementing and managing instruction, student evaluation, and classroom environment. Exhibit 9.1 provides sample items for each of these criteria that are appropriate for summative evaluation purposes. Some of the items in Exhibit 9.1 are behaviors that teachers are always expected to display. Being fair and impartial in dealings with students, making profitable use of class time, and providing a safe classroom environment are behaviors that are always appropriate. Other items from the instrument represent behaviors that teachers should use most of the time but may elect not to use in certain situations. An evaluator must decide whether the decision to use or not to use one of these behaviors was a sound one.

Effective Teaching Research

Some of the items in Exhibit 9.1 are based on effective teaching research, which identifies teacher behaviors associated with student learning. A summary of that research was presented in Chapter 1. For example, setting instructional goals and communicating them to students, monitoring students' progress, and providing

EXHIBIT 9.1   *Sample Items for Summative Evaluation of Teachers'*
Instructional Effectiveness

Knowledge of Subject
1. Teacher demonstrates understanding of the subject being taught.
2. Teacher helps learners to understand the significance of the topics or activities studied.

Preparation and Planning
1. Teacher prepares instructional plans on both a daily and long-term basis.
2. Teacher makes advance arrangements for materials, equipment, and supplies needed for instruction.
3. Teacher develops teaching procedures to match lesson objectives.
4. Teacher prepares plans for use by substitute teachers in case it is necessary to be absent.
5. Teacher works cooperatively with colleagues in the school and district to develop curriculum and select instructional materials.

Implementing and Managing Instruction
1. Teacher makes the goals of instruction clear to all students.
2. Teacher monitors students' performance and adjusts the pace and difficulty level of instruction as needed.
3. Teacher reviews material previously learned before introducing new concepts.
4. Teacher maintains student interest and attention by using a variety of instructional modes.
5. Teacher frequently checks students' understanding of new material and reteaches when indicated.
6. Teacher makes use of students' ideas to introduce new concepts and reinforce previously learned material.
7. Teacher allocates instructional time to activities that produce the highest rates of student learning.
8. Teacher asks content-related questions that most students are able to answer correctly.
9. Teacher summarizes important points.

Student Evaluation
1. Teacher regularly assigns, collects, and evaluates students' homework.
2. Teacher uses both teacher-made and standardized tests to check student progress.
3. Teacher provides feedback to students.
4. Teacher uses results of student evaluations to modify the pace or scope of instruction.
5. Teacher provides detailed directions for completing assignments and evaluates students' work on the basis of specified criteria.

Classroom Environment
1. Teacher is fair and impartial in dealings with all students, including those of different races and nationalities.
2. Teacher behaves toward all students in a friendly and accepting manner.
3. Teacher displays high expectations for the amount and quality of work to be performed by students and expresses confidence in their ability.
4. Teacher maintains a businesslike learning climate without being humorless or repressive.
5. Teacher informs students about classroom rules and procedures.
6. Teacher provides a safe, orderly, and attractive environment.
7. Teacher uses nonpunitive and preventive techniques for minimizing disruption and maintaining learner involvement.

---

feedback are all derived from this research. Teacher expectations for the amount and quality of work produced by students has also been found to be related to increased learning (Brookover et al., 1982). Obtaining information to rate a teacher on these items usually involves classroom observation. Information on other criteria may be obtained from other sources, including conversations with the teacher and others and student test scores (Ryan & Hickcox, 1980).

Surprisingly, teachers often are not sure what standards are used to assess their performance. Almost one-half of teachers in one study reported they did not know what criteria were used to evaluate them, yet the principals in the schools in which these teachers taught indicated that their teachers knew the criteria (Natriello & Dornbusch, 1980/1981). The authors wrote:

> Informing teachers of the criteria used to evaluate them is of prime importance if procedures for teacher evaluation are to have any impact on modifying and improving teacher performance. If teachers are unaware of the criteria and standards used to judge their performance, they are in no position to direct their energies along lines desired by the school organization. (p. 2)

Site-based management (SBM) introduces a new element into evaluation of teachers. This technique is based on the assumption that greater autonomy for teachers will translate into increased learning for students. However, that will happen only if teachers are willing to use their new freedom to experiment with new ways of doing their jobs and are willing to abandon techniques that do not work and retain those that do. Teachers who prefer to be told what to do and who will not accept responsibility for the success or failure of their efforts do not fare well in SBM schools. In these schools principals must include among the criteria for evaluating teachers the extent to which teachers assume leadership for improving instruction (Prasch, 1990).

Flags and Alerts

One way to make teachers aware of criteria of effective teaching (and also of practices that should be avoided) has been developed by a school district in Colorado (Maglaras & Lynch, 1988). Desirable practices are labeled "green flags," and those that are to be avoided are called "red alerts." Examples of green flags in mathematics classes include heterogeneous grouping, high student interest and teacher enthusiasm, applying mathematics to real-life situations, use of manipulatives, and availability of enrichment activities for all students.

Red alerts are practices that "if seen consistently, call for explanation; they should usually be avoided" (Maglaras & Lynch, 1988, p. 59). Some examples of red alerts from mathematics are giving no homework or excessive amounts of homework, chalkboard work for no purpose, teacher grading papers while students do homework, no diagnostic testing, students not understanding the purpose of homework assignments, and no use of calculators.

Models of Teacher Evaluation

There are several models of teacher evaluation in use in schools. The assumptions about teaching, and about evaluation of teaching in particular, vary from one model to another. Four models that are in widespread use in schools will be examined in this chapter. They are the remediation, goal-setting, portofolio, and assessment models. Exhibit 9.2 presents a brief summary of the major points about each model, including the purpose, objectives, assumptions, and typical methods of operation.

Remediation Model

In districts that use the remediation model, teachers who receive unsatisfactory summative evaluation readings are required to participate in formal remediation sessions to correct identified weaknesses (Pfeifer, 1986). Assistance is provided to the teacher either by the principal or assistant principal or by other teachers or supervisors from the district office. The assistance usually consists of two parts: didactic instruction and classroom practice. The teacher tries new techniques with students while an observer provides performance-related feedback.

Under the remediation model, teachers who fail to meet performance standards may be required to demonstrate improved proficiency in specified areas or face termination. Assistance is provided to help teachers expand their skills, and if no improvement is noted after a reasonable time, action is taken. In some programs a committee of observers, including peers, evaluates the teacher's performance and makes a recommendation for continued employment or termination. In other districts the evaluation process is carried out in the usual way, with the principal observing and rating the teacher's performance and recommending appropriate action.

An assumption upon which the remediation model is based is that individuals can become effective teachers by mastering a limited number of teaching behaviors identified in the research literature as related to student learning. The object of such a program is to bring all teachers to a minimal level of competence using specific instructional criteria such as those shown in Exhibit 9.1.

The remediation model works best with teachers who have correctable problems, who are motivated, and who have the ability to profit from instruction. Classroom management is an example of a problem for which teachers can usually be helped by the remediation approach. The model is most successful when specific corrective techniques can be prescribed and when support is provided to help teachers expand their skills.

The model requires evaluators to spend a good deal of time observing teachers and providing feedback. A few spaced observations over the course of a school year are not sufficient for solving most problems. For severe problems, observations should be scheduled two or more times per week, but for mild deficiencies, biweekly or monthly visit should suffice. Because of these time demands, the remediation model is usually not practical for use with more than a small number of teachers.

EXHIBIT 9.2   *Comparison of Four Evaluation Models*

Remediation Model

Purpose:	Correct identified weaknesses.
Objective:	Bring all teachers to a minimum level of performance.
Assumption:	It is possible to specify effective teaching behaviors and teach them.
Method:	Assess, provide feedback, and reassess.
Works best with:	Teachers with correctable teaching problems.
Evaluator skills:	Ability to provide clear, specific directions.
Possible problems:	Heavy demands on evaluator's time; offers no challenge to more competent teachers; deemphasizes variety in teaching.

Goal-Setting Model

Purpose:	Involve teachers and administrators in choosing individualized evaluation criteria.
Objective:	Increase teacher autonomy and commitment.
Assumption:	Teachers are professionals and able to assess their own developmental needs.
Method:	Teacher prepares annual goals statement; principal reviews, approves, or amends it and evaluates teachers' attainment.
Works best with:	Experienced, motivated teachers.
Evaluator skills:	Ability to help teachers write relevant performance objectives and guide teachers into productive channels; ability to evaluate on individualized criteria.
Possible problems:	Weak or overly ambitious goals; lack of consensus on what constitutes attainment of objective.

Portfolio Model

Purpose:	Base teacher evaluation on documented evidence of effective performance.
Objective:	Encourage teachers to cooperate in formulating high standards of practice.
Assumption:	Teachers will be able to assemble a collection of evidence that will present an accurate picture of teaching skills.
Method:	Teachers maintain a file of handouts, tests, reports, student evaluations, documentation of teaching practices, and other information and submit it to the evaluator.
Works best with:	Experienced teachers in a variety of areas; especially well suited to teachers of art, music, and vocational subjects.
Evaluator skills:	Ability to synthesize a profusion of details into a meaningful assessment of an individual's performance.
Possible problems:	Teachers: Time required to prepare portfolio; temptation to impress with flashy packaging. Administrators: Amount of time required to review portfolios; need to equate evidence from many different sources.

Assessment Model

Purpose:	Base teacher evaluation on amount of student learning.
Objective:	Determine amount of learning attributable to teacher's effort.
Assumption:	Each teacher contributes to students' accumulating knowledge.
Method:	Use pre- and posttests to measure student growth each year.
Works best with:	Teachers of subjects that have well-defined cognitive outcomes.
Evaluator skills:	Able to interpret and understand the limitations of achievement tests; able to take into account uncontrolled factors.
Possible problems:	Inflexible application of procedure results in loss of credibility; method does not identify teacher behaviors that affect learning.

A variation of the remediation model that has received relatively little attention to date is to use professional development to remediate identified deficiencies. This approach helps overcome some of the problems with the model of individual remediation described earlier by reducing somewhat the demands on principals' and supervisors' time (Knapp, 1982).

Goal-Setting Model

Goal-setting models of teacher evaluation involve teachers in selecting the criteria for evaluation. In this approach, each teacher selects developmental goals and identifies strategies for achieving them. These strategies might include observing other teachers, coursework, workshop attendance, or readings (Darling-Hammond, 1986). This approach is used most often for formative evaluation purposes. Goal statements are prepared individually but usually reflect a current schoolwide or systemwide emphasis. A typical goal-setting plan requires a participating teacher to meet with the evaluator near the beginning of the school year to establish the year's goals. The principal may approve the proposed workplan as submitted or amend it by adding additional goals or by revising those submitted by the teacher.

Once a goal statement has been agreed to by both parties, it becomes part of the teacher's personnel file and constitutes a contract between the teacher and the district. In most such plans the principal meets with the teacher once or twice during the year to check on progress. If necessary, the goals may be amended or revised at these meetings.

The goal-setting model presumes that teachers are able to identify their own developmental needs. It is not well suited for teachers who are having difficulty with classroom management or instructional organization, and in some schools that use goal-setting plans, teachers with identified deficiencies do not participate (Tesch, Nyland, & Kernutt, 1987).

The plan is most effective when teachers' efforts are coordinated. When all teachers in a school work together toward improving questioning techniques, for example, the impact on students is far greater than when each teacher works independently of colleagues.

Several problems may be encountered in implementing a goal-setting evaluation plan. One potential problem is disparities in the difficulty of the goals chosen by teachers. Some teachers select goals that require little or no effort, whereas others identify objectives so ambitious that they exceed the time and other resources available to accomplish them. Both cases require the evaluator to exercise critical judgment in reviewing proposed workplans.

A second problem may arise at the end of the year when teachers are evaluated on the attainment of their approved goals. Unless the evaluator and teacher have agreed beforehand what will constitute evidence of achievement of goals, disagreements may occur. Evaluating goal attainment is further complicated by questions of equity when a teacher who has set ambitious goals fails to attain them, while another teacher proposes and easily achieves a modest list of accomplishments. Should the evaluator rate the more ambitious teacher lower for failing to reach all of the proposed goals, or should the difficulty of the outcomes be taken into account in evaluating the teachers?

The major strength of the goal-setting approach is that it gives teachers autonomy in identifying and working toward attainment of professional objectives. Autonomy is a key to building commitment (Hawley, 1982). Goal-setting plans involve considerably more teacher input than the remedial plan (described earlier) and allow for flexibility in the determination of the criteria upon which teachers are evaluated. Their success is dependent on whether teachers approach the program seriously. This approach is most likely to be successful when used with teachers who are experienced and willing to assume responsibility for their professional development.

Portfolio Model

Portfolios are used to document changes in students' academic performance over time, and the idea has been borrowed for use as a device in evaluating teachers. Teachers prepare a portfolio by assembling a variety of information pertaining to their teaching, normally for the purpose of applying for board certification or to renew a professional license. When used for evaluation, the portfolio is presented to the principal, who reviews the information and prepares an evaluation report on the teacher.

Portfolio evaluation appeals to teachers because it gives them more control of the evaluation process, but many teachers find that collecting the information they need to assemble a file is onerous. The process is somewhat less burdensome if specific guidelines are available showing what to include and what to omit. In most portfolio plans, teachers receive a checklist or outline of the materials they are expected to include in the portfolio. Items on the list include the following (Bird, 1990; Wolf, 1996*):

- Resumé
- Educational philosophy and teaching goals
- Professional activities
- Letters of recommendation
- Formal evaluations
- Lesson plans
- Sample tests
- Sample handouts

- Samples of completed student work
- Grade distributions
- Student evaluations
- Parent comments
- Teaching license or certificate
- Professional development activities
- Documentation of teaching practices, including videotapes of class sessions

*"Developing an Effective Teaching Portfolio" by K. Wolf, March 1996, *Educational Leadership, 53,* pp. 34–37. Reprinted with permission of the Association for Supervision and Curriculum Development. Copyright © 1996 by ASCD. All rights reserved.

The resumé contains information about educational background, professional experience, and professional leadership activities. Leadership activities include serving as an officer for a professional association or taking part in regional or statewide service activities such as serving on accreditation teams. District leadership activities that are included on the resumé include chairing committees for staff development or textbook selection. Activities for the school, such as serving as a mentor to another teacher or serving as grade-level chair or department head, are also featured.

Portfolios will be used as one part of the process of assessment leading to national certification of teachers by the National Board for Professional Teaching Standards. The portfolio to be prepared by teachers seeking national certification would document teachers' planning, evaluation, and classroom discussion skills. A written test covering knowledge of the teaching field and a series of assessment exercises would also be required (National Center for Education Statistics, 1993).

Teacher Assessment Model

This approach to evaluating teaching performance establishes a more exacting standard of teaching effectiveness than the three approaches just described by measuring teachers' ability to help students master challenging subject matter. Teacher assessment requires that teachers be able to demonstrate that students have actually gained knowledge from instruction.

Assessment links learning objectives and instruction so that it is possible to determine how much students have learned and whether the observed gains are attributable to an individual teacher's efforts. One other element that is considered in teacher assessment is whether the objectives that students attempt to master are worthwhile (Darling-Hammond, 1998). In practice, that often means confirming that the objectives of instruction are from a set of state-approved standards.

Characteristics of Successful Evaluation Programs

McLaughlin (1990) pointed out that improving evaluation requires increasing the district's capacity by equipping principals and other supervisory staff members with the skills and strategies needed to carry out effective evaluation processes. Few principals are able to maintain evaluation systems that result in improved teaching outcomes without encouragement and backing from district personnel. Human resources managers need to ensure that evaluation processes are integrated in a seamless web with staff development and curriculum development, so that knowledge gained from one process informs the others. District leadership is one of several factors identified as characteristic of successful evaluation programs (Wise et al., 1984).

A second feature of effective evaluation programs is training for evaluators. Training should prepare evaluators to recognize and avoid psychometric errors, such as halo errors, first-impression errors, and leniency errors (Milkovich & Newman, 1996).

Guidelines adopted by the Connecticut State Board of Education to provide guidance for school districts to use in developing teacher evaluation plans contain some elements that are present in any well-designed evaluation plan. The Connecticut guidelines state that general responsibilities and specific tasks of a teacher's position should be available and should serve as a frame of reference for evaluation of the teacher. The guidelines also specify that teachers should be informed about and understand the means by which they will be evaluated and that the evaluation should take into account any factors that affect evaluation results. According to the Connecticut guidelines, evaluation should be more formative than summative and should be implemented in such a way that teachers are encouraged to be creative in their approach to instruction (Iwanicki & Rindone, 1995).

Peer Evaluation

Other attributes of successful teacher evaluation plans are that all participants understand how the system works and are aware of the rationale for the criteria upon which they are evaluated. Understanding and awareness are most easily attained by active teacher participation in the design and implementation of evaluation procedures. Although teachers' unions have traditionally opposed peer evaluation, some have agreed to participate in pilot tests of programs that place teachers in an active role in the evaluation process (Buttram & Wilson, 1987). Most successful evaluation plans distinguish between teachers who have demonstrated competence or mastery and those who are inexperienced or who have identified deficiencies (Conley, 1987).

Cycle of Evaluation

Evaluation of teaching personnel occurs in a regular cycle, although the phases of the cycle vary somewhat from district to district. It is helpful if teachers who are new to the system understand the timing and focus of each of the phases of the cycle and the purpose for each. In most districts, a distinction is made between evaluation that takes place in the first year or two in the classroom and that carried out in subsequent years.

Evaluation for teachers in their first two or three years in the classroom is more intensive and, as a rule, more frequent than for teachers with more experience. Observations made at this stage are usually diagnostic in nature and are intended to provide feedback to help beginning teachers improve their effectiveness. A secondary purpose is to document observations of teachers who may be at risk of being dismissed at the end of the probationary period.

Teachers with three to nine years of service follow a different pattern as compared to teachers near the beginning stages of their careers. Tenured teachers continue to be evaluated on a regular basis, but the process is more relaxed. These teachers may be observed only every other year rather than every year. The purpose of evaluation for these teachers is to ensure that they continue to be effective.

For experienced teachers who have consistently been effective over time, evaluation is aimed at encouraging professional growth and development. The emphasis is on finding opportunities for these teachers to explore new interests, try out new strategies, or take on new leadership responsibilities. The teacher and evaluator usually jointly develop a long-range plan of professional growth activities, which might call for the teacher to work toward an advanced degree or seek national board certification. The plan might include granting leave to allow the teacher to conduct research on a topic related to his or her subject field.

Evaluating Evaluation Systems

The purpose of performance evaluation is to improve a school's ability to accomplish its mission (Stronge & Helm, 1991). If the system in use fails to do that, it should be changed or replaced. When educators consider ways of improving performance evaluation, they often assume that problems with the system can be resolved by developing a better observation instrument or rating form. In fact, what is usually needed is agreement among those who have a stake in performance evaluation regarding its purpose and uses.

Two types of performance evaluation were described earlier in the chapter. Formative evaluation helps to improve an individual's performance on the job, and summative evaluation is used for decision-making purposes. The process of evaluating a performance evaluation system should begin by determining which of the two types is needed. If both are required, then a decision must be made about whether to attempt to combine both into one plan.

If the evaluation plan is intended primarily to assist in making personnel decisions, the evaluation of it should consider how well it performs that function. Are the recommendations clear-cut and free of ambiguity, and do they result in actions that are sound and defensible? If not, the plan may need an overhaul, or those who administer it may need to be better trained in its use.

A good summative evaluation system specifies minimally acceptable performance, and employees are aware that if their performance does not measure up, they may be in jeopardy of a demotion, a cut in pay, or termination. If the reason for an individual's failure to attain a minimally acceptable level of performance is lack of skill, then consideration should be given to providing training and assistance to help correct the deficiency (Guzzo & Gannett, 1988).

If, on the other hand, the evaluation plan was meant to help improve individual performance, an evaluation of the system should consider first whether it is being used for that purpose. Evaluation plans are sometimes subverted for uses other than the intended ones, and it is not uncommon for data from a formative evaluation system to be used for summative purposes. When that happens, employees lose confidence in the evaluation program and either ignore it or resist participating in it.

If it is determined that the information collected from performance evaluations is being used as intended, the next question is whether individuals are able to perform better as a result. If evaluators can point to specific instances of increased individual effectiveness that can be traced directly to evaluation feedback, it is fair to conclude that the evaluation plan is working. But if no specific evidence is available—even though participants may feel positive about the plan—there is a question about its value. In that case, consideration must be given to ways of changing the operation of the evaluation system in order to bring it into line with the stated purpose.

Characterictics of the evaluator and the quality of information provided to teachers influence the extent to which workers benefit from performance evaluation. An evaluator's credibility, relationship to the employee, and ability to model suggestions have all been found to be positively correlated with the appropriate use of evaluation information. Characteristics of the information received by teachers from evaluation sources, including the quality of suggestions and the persuasiveness of the evaluator's rationale for improvement, are also related to the value of the evaluation process for teachers (Duke & Stiggins, 1990).

Both types of evaluation plans are more likely to be successful if they are accepted and supported by those who are evaluated. Teachers look for three features that they regard as indicators that an evaluation plan is likely to be beneficial. First, teachers consider whether it encourages self-improvement. Second, they judge whether evaluators demonstrate, both in their personal attitudes and in the mechanics of evaluating an individual's performance, appreciation for the complexity of teaching. Finally, they consider whether the procedures employed are fair and likely to provide protection of their rights (Darling-Hammond, Wise, & Pease, 1983).

Administrators should not overlook the motivating potential of performance feedback. Knowledge of results is an important motivator, and feedback sets the stage for new learning by pinpointing areas in which improvement is needed. Performance evaluation is one of the few ways by which teachers receive information about the results of their efforts. They gauge their success in the classroom by how their teaching is rated.

The design of evaluation instruments should take their potential motivating effects into account. Teachers pay heed to the criteria on which they are evaluated and adjust their performance accordingly (Hoenack & Monk, 1990).

State-Mandated Evaluation Systems

The law in most states requires regular evaluations of teaching and is explicit in describing the types and frequency of procedures used. Some states provide guidelines for tenured and nontenured teachers or establish performance standards by which teachers are to be judged. In addition, some state statutes specify roles for peer or external evaluators and require training for evaluators (Duke, 1995).

Mandatory state programs for teacher evaluation differ somewhat from state to state, but they tend to have some common features. In Tennessee, evaluation is tied to a statewide career ladder program (Furtwengler, 1985). Teachers who are candidates for advancement to Career Levels II and III are observed and evaluated by three evaluators using a uniform evaluation system developed by the state. For lower-level positions, district administrators and supervisors evaluate teachers in compliance with state guidelines that specify six criteria for judging teaching effectiveness. The criteria are planning, teaching strategies, evaluation, classroom management, professional leadership, and communication.

The Texas Education Agency developed the Texas Teacher Appraisal System to serve several purposes. Data from teacher observations are used for decisions about contract renewal or placement on a career ladder. The information also serves as an indicator of the need for staff development programs related to particular teaching skills (Barnes, 1987).

The instrument developed by the state education agency in Kentucky for use with that state's teacher career ladder is similar to one used in Texas. The Kentucky instrument consists of six functional areas (planning, management of student conduct, instructional organization and lesson development, presentation of subject matter, verbal and nonverbal communication, and evaluation of students). Unlike the Texas instrument, which consists of items describing behaviors associated with greater student learning or higher student satisfaction, the Kentucky instrument contains both positive and negative indicators.

The California Formative Assessment and Support System is a state program that establishes standards for practice in teaching and uses evaluation for the purpose of improving practice. Teachers cooperatively work through a series of activities involving assessment of their teaching. They observe classrooms and conduct research on creating an environment for learning in their classrooms (Olebe, Jackson, & Danielson, 1999).

Because of the states' greater resources, teacher evaluation instruments developed at that level are frequently of higher quality than those that originate at the district level. Evaluation instruments developed in the state of Florida, for example, use research-based items focusing on instructional processes. During the development process, items were tested to establish reliability and job-relatedness and to permit future studies of predictive validity (Florida Coalition for the Development of a Performance Measurement System, 1983).

A study by the Southern Regional Education Board (SREB) (1991) of state-sponsored teacher evaluation systems identified several strengths and weaknesses of these programs. Among the strengths identified by the SREB were the use of research on effective teaching; requiring beginning teachers to demonstrate satisfactory classroom performance prior to initial licensure; introducing a set of common terms and concepts with which to discuss teaching performance; and linking evaluation of teaching with professional development.

The SREB (1991) report also identified some weaknesses of state-sponsored teacher evaluation programs. Among these were the absence of attention to teachers' knowledge of the subject they teach; an overreliance on classroom observation and little use of other means of documenting teaching effectiveness; the failure to assess the relationship between teachers' practices and student outcomes; and the lack of attention to developing ways of identifying the most competent teachers.

Legal Considerations in Personnel Evaluation

Because of tenure, teacher evaluation decisions more often provoke legal challenges than evaluations of other personnel. To protect teachers' rights to procedural fairness, most states impose specific requirements for conducting performance evaluations. Some states require that teachers be notified in advance of the criteria upon which they will be evaluated, and, in case deficiencies are found, that teachers be informed of the nature of the problems. Other requirements establish a minimum number of classroom observations as part of the evaluation process or specify a deadline for completing the process (Webb, 1983). Districts are allowed latitude in establishing performance criteria (McCarthy & Cambron-McCabe, 1987).

Negotiated contracts also contain provisions regulating teacher evaluation. Board negotiators generally prefer to limit such provisions to general descriptions of evaluation procedures and to avoid committing principals to make a specific number of observations, meet specified deadlines for completion of the evaluation process, or notify teachers of performance deficiencies (Deneen, 1980).

However, specifying evaluative criteria either in the contract or in a policy statement has advantages for both the board and for teachers. Publicizing the standards on which teachers will be judged allows teachers to prepare to meet them and allows administrators to assess them. It also avoids reliance on unreliable, invalid, and legally indefensible criteria (Gross, 1988).

Training for evaluators should include information about applicable provisions of state law, state or district policy, and the master contract that affect evaluation. Failure to comply with these requirements can nullify a district's attempt to terminate or place a teacher on probation. Issues related to termination of teachers are examined in more detail in Chapter 15.

Performance Criteria

Legal challenges to evaluation decisions most often take the form of questions about the performance criteria used. Basing unsatisfactory ratings on criteria for which direct links to student learning do not exist are likely to invite legal challenge. Two examples of questionable criteria that are still in use in some districts are appearance or grooming and personal lifestyle. Unless the district is able to show that a teacher's appearance or behavior outside of school has a direct relationship to teaching effectiveness or poses a threat to students, it is unlikely to be successful in a court test (Deneen, 1980).

In reviewing district actions, courts have taken into account, in addition to the factors already enumerated, whether teachers are given an opportunity to correct their weaknesses and whether they are provided with assistance and sufficient time for implementing improvements. Courts may also consider the question of whether the reasons given teachers for unsatisfactory ratings are stated clearly enough to provide direction for correcting deficiencies (Webb, 1983).

The use of student achievement gains to assess teacher performance raises legal questions that are not at issue when other criteria are employed. The use of student test results in teacher evaluation is relatively uncommon, judging by the small number of dismissal cases in which such evidence has been used to document unsatisfactory teacher performance. One authority recommends that student achievement data be used only as supporting evidence for dismissal, not as the sole or primary reason for the action (Groves, 1984, cited in Carter, 1985).

Evaluation of Administrative and Support Personnel

Exhibit 9.3 shows seven criteria that are used to evaluate school administrators. These are generic criteria that can be applied with appropriate adaptations to all administrators, from assistant principal to superintendent. Some of the criteria in the exhibit are taken from the Texas statute that prescribes evaluation of school administrators in that state. For each position to be evaluated, a specific list of duties or results expected would be prepared, and the administrator's performance would belated against that list.

The scope of duties for which administrators are responsible varies. Principals and superintendents are responsible for all areas, but the director of personnel is primarily responsible only for personnel administration.

Administrators are evaluated by their immediate superiors, and the superintendent is evaluated by the board. Principals in small districts are usually evaluated by the superintendent. In larger districts, they may be evaluated by an assistant or associate superintendent.

Some administrator evaluation plans provide for input from subordinates or others who work with the individual. For example, teachers may be asked to evaluate the principal's instructional leadership or community relations skills. In some systems, administrators design their own evaluation form to collect information from subordinates, and they are encouraged to construct items that will be of use to them in planning professional development activities.

There are sound reasons why subordinates' opinions should not be the sole basis for judging administrative performance, but there are equally convincing arguments in support of giving subordinates a voice. Administrators must on occasion make decisions that leave some subordinates unhappy, and they need to be buffered from the resentment that follows such actions. Nevertheless, information from subordinates can provide a perspective on administrative performance that is not available from other sources.

Since most district office personnel provide support services for the schools, it makes sense to ask teachers and principals to evaluate their performance. Teach-

EXHIBIT 9.3 *Performance Criteria for Administrators*

1. *Instructional management:* Improves instruction by (a) monitoring student achievement and attendance and using the data to improve programs, (b) assisting teachers to design effective instructional strategies and select appropriate instructional materials, (c) providing mechanisms for articulation of the curriculum, and (d) supporting programs designed for students with special needs

2. *School/organizational improvement:* Brings about improvement in school programs by (a) collaborating to develop and achieve consensus for an organizational mission statement, (b) organizing to permit and encourage teamwork among staff members pursuing common goals, (c) encouraging an attitude of continuous improvement in curriculum, instruction, and operations on the part of all staff members, (d) arranging for and promoting opportunities for professional development designed to meet identified needs of staff, and (e) providing current information about innovative programs and technologies to staff members

3. *School/organizational climate:* Fosters a positive climate by (a) assessing and planning for improvement of the environment, (b) reinforcing excellence, (c) promoting an atmosphere of caring and respect for others, and (d) encouraging broad participation in decisions about school programs and operations

4. *Personnel management:* Manages personnel effectively by (a) recognizing exemplary performance, (b) encouraging personal and professional growth, (c) administering personnel policies and regulations consistently and fairly and recommending changes when needed, (d) securing necessary personnel resources to meet objectives, and (e) periodically evaluating job performance of assigned personnel

5. *Management of facilities and fiscal operations:* Responsibly manages facilities and fiscal operations by (a) compiling budgets and cost estimates that enable the organization to accomplish its mission, (b) ensuring that facilities are maintained and upgraded as needed, and (c) overseeing school operations, including attendance, accounting, payroll, and transportation

6. *Student management:* Promotes positive student conduct by (a) developing and communicating guidelines for student conduct that help students feel safe and valued, (b) ensuring that rules are enforced consistently and without favor, (c) appropriately disciplining students for misconduct, and (d) effecting collaboration among teachers and parents in managing student conduct

7. *School/community relations:* Ensures community support by (a) clarifying the mission of the school(s) to members of the community, (b) taking an active part in deliberations of school councils and advisory committees, (c) seeking support for school programs from the community, and (d) participating in activities that foster rapport between schools and the community

ers are a valuable source of information about curriculum supervisors and instructional specialists, since they are the recipients of the services provided by those personnel. Principals are also in a position to evaluate at least some aspects of the operations of departments of transportation and maintenance.

Summary

Evaluations of educators should promote sound education principles, fulfillment of institutional missions, and effective performance of job responsibilities, so that the educational needs of students, community, and society are met (Joint Committee on Standards for Educational Evaluation, 1988). Performance evaluation may be either formative or summative in nature. Formative evaluations are intended to help individuals perform more effectively; summative evaluations support decisions on promotion, transfer, and termination.

Four models of teacher evaluation used in schools are the remediation model, goal-setting model, portfolio model, and assessment model. Each serves specific purposes. Successful evaluation programs are characterized by strong district support, including training for teacher evaluators. Legal challenges to evaluation decisions are less likely when teachers are informed about the procedures and the evaluation policy is carefully followed by those responsible for implementing it.

Suggested Activities

1. Three characteristics of evaluation plans that are valued by teachers are (a) protection against arbitrary or biased evaluations, (b) recognition of the complexity of teaching, and (c) provision for professional growth. Describe how you would develop a design for a teacher evaluation plan incorporating these features.

2. Below are goal statements written by four teachers in a school. Imagine that you are the principal of the school and that you use the goal-setting model of evaluation. Prepare a brief response for the author of each goal statement indicating whether the statement is acceptable as written and, if so, how you propose to measure goal attainment. If the statement needs to be amended, suggest how it might be improved.

   Teacher A: "I plan to try to have a perfect attendance record this year."
   Teacher B: "I will contact the parents of all my students during the first grading period to let them know how their child is doing in school and to offer suggestions on how they can help their child to do better work at school."
   Teacher C: "I will attend a professional conference this year (either the teachers' association meeting in April or a conference on teaching talented and gifted students sponsored by the State Department of Education in November)."
   Teacher D: "I will take part in a staff development workshop on teaching thinking skills for science in October. I will try out three of the techniques in my class and will share what I learn with other teachers in my department."

3. One of the problems with portfolio evaluations is deciding how to use the information submitted by a teacher in a portfolio. Select three or four items from the list of items to be included in a teacher evaluation portfolio and be prepared to discuss what you might learn from each piece about a teacher's instructional effectiveness if you were the teacher's evaluator. (*Example:* Suppose a teacher includes examples of classroom tests in a portfolio. What could you learn about his or her teaching from examining these tests?)

4. A frequently heard complaint about summative evaluation plans is that they seldom lead to dismissal of incompetent teachers. Do you agree? If so, explain why you believe it is true. Do you believe the problem is lack of training for those who administer teacher evaluations, opposition from teacher unions contesting the dismissal of members, or courts that are inclined to support teachers' rights over administrators' efforts to improve school performance?

Online Resources

Current practices and new trends in teacher evaluation are examined in the websites listed below.

Teacher Evaluation: New Directions and Practices (www.teacherevaluation.net)
This site includes forms that parents, students, and administrators may use to evaluate teachers. It also offers an extensive bibliography of articles and books about teacher evaluation.

ERIC Digest. (www.ed.gov/databases/ERIC_Digests/ed429052.html)
This digest (New Directions in Teacher Evaluation) discusses using criteria adopted by the National Board of Professional Teaching Standards to select Board Certified teachers as the basis for evaluation of all teachers.

Montgomery County (MD) Public Schools (www.mcps.k12.ind.us/departments/personnel/TE)
This site discusses a new teacher evaluation system adopted by Montgomery County Schools. It includes an evaluation handbook prepared by the county and a discussion of the philosophy and design of the evaluation system.

New York State Education Department (www.emsc.nysed.gov/development)
These standards, introduced in the report *Teaching to Higher Standards: New York's Commitment,* identify the knowledge and skills teachers must have to meet the learning needs of students.

References

Barnes, S. (1987). *The development of the Texas Teacher Appraisal System.* Paper presented at the annual meeting of the American Educational Research Association, Washington, DC. (ERIC Document Reproduction Service No. ED 294323).

Bird, T. (1990). The schoolteacher's portfolio: An essay on possibilities. In J. Millman & L. Darling-Hammond (Eds.), *The new handbook of teacher evaluation* (pp. 241–256). Newbury Park, CA: Sage.

Brandt, R. (1996, March). On a new direction for teacher evaluation: A conversation with Tom McGreal. *Educational Leadership, 53,* 30–33.

Brookover, W., Beamer, L., Efthim, H., Hathaway, D., Lezotte, L., Miller, S., Passalacqua, J., & Tornatzky, L. (1982). *Creating effective schools.* Holmes Beach, FL: Learning Publications.

Buttram, J. L., & Wilson, B. L. (1987, April). Promising trends in teacher evaluation. *Educational Leadership, 44*, 4–6.

Carter, B. (1985). *High expectations: A policy paper on setting standards for student achievement.* Stanford, CA: Stanford University School of Education, Education Policy Institute.

Conley, D. T. (1987, April). Critical attributes of effective evaluation systems. *Educational Leadership, 44*, 60–64.

Darling-Hammond, L. (1986). A proposal for evaluation in the teaching profession. *Elementary School Journal, 86*, 532–551.

Darling-Hammond, L. (1998, February). Standards for assessing teaching effectiveness are key. *Phi Delta Kappan, 79*, 471–472.

Darling-Hammond, L., Wise, A., & Pease, S. (1983). Teacher evaluation in the organization context: A review of the literature. *Review of Educational Research, 53*, 285–328.

Deneen, J. (1980). Legal dimensions of teacher evaluation. In D. Peterson & A. Ward (Eds.), *Due process in teacher evaluation* (pp. 15–43). Washington, DC: University Press.

Duke, D. (1995). Conflict and consensus in the reform of teacher evaluation. In D. Duke (Ed.), *Teacher evaluation policy* (pp. 173–188). Albany: State University of New York Press.

Duke, D., & Stiggins, R. (1990). Beyond minimum competence: Evaluation for professional development. In J. Millman & L. Darling-Hammond (Eds.), *The new handbook of teacher evaluation* (pp. 116–132). Newbury Park, CA: Sage.

Educational Research Service. (1978). *Evaluating teacher performance.* Arlington, VA: Author.

Educational Research Service. (1985, September). *Educator opinion poll.* Arlington, VA: Author.

Florida Coalition for the Development of a Performance Measurement System. (1983). A *study of measurement and training components specified in the Management Training Act.* Tallahassee, FL: Author.

Furtwengler, C. (1985). *Evaluation procedures in the Tennessee Career Ladder Plan.* Paper presented at the annual meeting of the American Educational Research Association, Chicago. (ERIC Document Reproduction Service No. ED 259012).

Gross, J. (1988). *Teachers on trial: Values, standards, and equity in judging conduct and competence.* Ithca, NY: Cornell University, New York State School of Industrial and Labor Relations.

Guzzo, R., & Gannett, B. (1988). The nature of facilitators and inhibitors of effective task performance. In F. Schoorman & B. Schneider (Eds.), *Facilitating work effectiveness* (pp. 21–41). Lexington, MA: Lexington.

Hawley, R. (1982). *Assessing teacher performance.* Amherst, MA: Education Research Associates.

Hoenack, S., & Monk, D. (1990). Economic aspects of teacher evaluation. In J. Millman & L. Darling-Hammond (Eds.), *The new handbook of teacher evaluation* (pp. 390–402). Newbury Park, CA: Sage.

Iwanicki, E., & Rindone, D. (1995). Integrating professional development, teacher evaluation, and student learning: The evolution of teacher evaluation policy in Connecticut. In D. Duke (Ed.), *Teacher evaluation policy* (pp. 65–98). Albany: State University of New York Press.

Joint Committee on Standards for Educational Evaluation. (1988). *The personnel evaluation standards: How to assess systems for evaluating educators.* Newbury Park, CA: Sage.

Knapp, M. (1982, March). *Toward the study of teacher evaluation as an organizational process: A review of current research and practice.* Paper presented at the annual meeting of the American Educational Research Association, New York.

Lawler, E. (1973). *Motivation in work organizations.* Monterey, CA: Brooks/Cole.

Maglaras, T., & Lynch, D. (1988, October). Monitoring the curriculum: From plan to action. *Educational Leadership, 46*, 58–60.

McCarthy, M., & Cambron-McCabe, N. (1987). *Public school law: Teachers' and students' rights.* Boston: Allyn and Bacon.

McLaughlin, M. (1990). Embracing contraries: Implementing and sustaining teacher evaluation. In J. Millman & L. Darling-Hammond (Eds.), *The new handbook of teacher evaluation* (pp. 403–415). Newbury Park, CA: Sage.

Milkovich, G., & Newman, J. (1996). *Compensation* (5th ed.). Chicago: Irwin.

National Center for Education Statistics. (1993). *America's teachers: Profile of a profession.* Washington, DC: U.S. Department of Education.

Natriello, G., & Dornbusch, S. (1980/1981). Pitfalls in the evaluation of teachers by principals. *Administrator's Notebook, 29,* 1–4.

Olebe, M., Jackson, A., & Danielson, C. (1999, May). Investing in beginning teachers—The California model. *Educational Leadership, 56,* 41–44.

Pfeifer, R. (1986). *Integrating teacher evaluation and staff development: An organizational approach.* Stanford, CA: Stanford University, Institute for Research on Educational Finance and Governance. (ERIC Document Reproduction Service No. ED 270506).

Prasch, J. (1990). *How to organize for school-based management.* Alexandria, VA: Association for Supervision and Curriculum Development.

Ryan, D., & Hickcox, E. (1980). *Redefining teacher evaluation.* Toronto: Ontario Institute for Studies in Education.

Smith, B., Peterson, D., & Micceri, T. (1987, April). Evaluation and professional improvement aspects of the Florida performance-measurement system. *Educational Leadership, 44,* 16–19.

Southern Regional Education Board. (1991). *Teacher evaluation programs in SREB states.* Atlanta: Author.

Stronge, J., & Helm, V. (1991). *Evaluating professional support personnel in education.* Newbury Park, CA: Sage.

Tesch, S., Nyland, L., & Kernutt, D. (1987, April). Teacher evaluation—Shared power working. *Educational Leadership, 44,* 26–30.

Webb, L. (1983). Teacher evaluation. In S. Thomas, N. Cambron-McCabe, & M. McCarthy (Eds.), *Educators and the law* (pp. 69–80). Elmont, NY: Institute for School Law and Finance.

Wise, A., Darling-Hammond, L., McLaughlin, M., & Bernstein, H. (1984). *Teacher evaluation: A study of effective practices.* Santa Monica, CA: Rand.

Wolf, K. (1996, March). Developing an effective teaching portfolio. *Educational Leadership, 53,* 34–37.

10

Compensation and Rewards

Education is a labor-intensive enterprise. A larger share of school funds is spent to pay personnel than for any other purpose. Estimates of the proportion of school budgets allocated for personnel costs range from 60 to 90 percent. Personnel funds are expended in accordance with a compensation plan that, if well designed, can help schools achieve their strategic goals.

Compensation plans have three broad objectives—to attract, retain, and motivate qualified and competent employees (Cascio & Awad, 1981). It is desirable that a compensation plan be acceptable to taxpayers, who seek assurance that cost-effective compensation procedures are being followed, and to employees, who are concerned that compensation practices are orderly, fair, and consistent.

Plan of the Chapter

Fair and adequate compensation are important issues in human resources management. Districts that offer competitive salaries and benefits are able to attract and hold well-qualified teachers, and equitable compensation plans help them to maintain employee morale and motivation. This chapter deals with the following topics: (1) sound compensation plans, (2) externally competitive salary plans, (3) adequacy of teacher pay, (4) balance in teachers' salaries, (5) equity and the single salary schedule, (6) forms of incentive pay, (7) keeping costs under control, (8) administrators' salaries, and (9) constructing a salary schedule.

Sound Compensation Plans

Sound compensation plans have six features. They are externally competitive, are internally equitable, are internally balanced, offer incentive, limit cost, and provide adequately for employees' needs (Cascio & Awad, 1981). These six features help achieve three organizational imperatives described by Katz (1973): attracting and

164

retaining members, obtaining commitment, and motivating members to perform role-related behaviors and respond with innovative behavior when appropriate.

Competitiveness improves a district's ability to attract and retain workers; adequacy and balance are important for increasing employee commitment and retention; and equity and incentive help a district to motivate members to perform role-related tasks and to respond with innovative behavior. The sixth factor, cost, impinges on a district's ability to sustain a compensation program.

Externally Competitive Salary Plans

A district's compensation is externally competitive when the district is able to attract a sufficient number of qualified applicants to fill all of its vacancies. Typically, districts in the same regional labor market offer salaries that are reasonably close. One district may offer salaries that are lower than the prevailing level in the region and yet be able to attract the employees it needs if it has offsetting advantages that help compensate for the lower salaries.

Offered salary is probably the single-most important factor that applicants consider in making a decision about a job. There is some evidence that salary plays a more important role in decisions of beginning teachers than it does for experienced teachers (Jacobson, 1989). A possible explanation is that new teachers lack the information to make knowledgeable judgments about such factor as fringe benefits and working conditions.

Single Salary Schedules

It has been estimated that 99 percent of all teachers in the United States teach in districts that use single salary schedules (Murnane & Cohen, 1986). A single salary schedule uses only two factors in determining the salaries of all employees in each job classification: experience and level of education. Historically, the single salary plan is fairly young. The first use of the idea occurred in 1920, when Lincoln (Nebraska), Denver, and Sioux City (Iowa) put single salary schedules into effect. The idea spread rapidly; by 1927, 165 cities had adopted the plan (Morris, 1972).

Teachers' organizations pushed for the adoption of the single salary plan as a way of achieving a more professionalized teaching force. Supporters argued that the plan would encourage professional growth, contribute to a feeling of unity and satisfaction among teachers, equalize pay for men and women, increase tenure, attract better-quality teachers to elementary schools, and encourage teachers to teach at that level rather than aspire to teach in high school.

Critics suggested that the single salary plan was contrary to the law of supply and demand and that it was a "subterfuge" invented by administrators who wished to be freed of the burdensome task of rating teachers on merit. Those who were against the idea argued that elementary teachers did not need extensive educational preparation and that educational attainment in itself was not a criterion of teaching ability. Their bottom-line argument was that the cost of the single salary proposal was excessive (Morris, 1972).

Districts that use the single salary schedule sometimes provide a fixed dollar increment at each step. The increment represents a proportionally larger adjustment for teachers near the bottom of the scale as compared to those near the top. To provide step increments that are proportionally equal, many districts use indexed schedules in which the dollar amounts vary but the rate of increase is fixed.

In most districts with single salary schedules, regular increases are provided for the first 12 or 15 years a teacher is employed, although a recent survey by the American Federation of Teachers (1999) found that the number of steps in salary scales in the 100 largest city school districts in the United States ranged from 8 to 45. After a person reaches the top of the scale, longevity increases are granted about once every five years. Practically speaking, however, teachers in the United States reach the peak of their earning power within 15 years of entering the field. This is in contrast to most other occupations, in which salaries continue to rise throughout most of one's working life.

Since attrition is highest in the first few years after an individual is hired (Mark & Anderson, 1978), it would seem to make sense to provide proportionally larger raises to teachers near the low end of the scale and smaller increases to those at the top in order to hold teachers who might otherwise leave. However, the evidence for the effectiveness of such an approach is not strong. Jacobson (1987) found that in the two regions of New York state that he studied, proportionally larger increases in the middle of the scale were more strongly related to retention of teachers than were adjustments at either top or bottom.

A salary schedule may be made more competitive by increasing salaries across the board or by providing targeted increases. If the district is losing experienced teachers, it may decide to provide targeted increases at the upper end of the salary schedule. On the other hand, if it is having problems attracting beginning teachers, the decision may be made to raise salaries at the bottom end of the schedule.

Another approach is to add more steps to the schedule. Experience increments might be scheduled for 20 rather than 15 years. Experience increments average about 4 percent per year (Bacharach, Lipsky, & Shedd, 1984), so adding 5 additional steps onto a 15-step scale, each providing a 4 percent increase, results in a top-of-the-scale compounded figure that is 21.7 percent higher than the 15-step maximum. However, as long as teachers' salaries lag behind those in other occupations, administrators will be under pressure to maintain or decrease the number of steps in the schedule rather than to increase them.

Critics claim that the single salary schedule lacks motivational power. None of the three motivational theories described in Chapter 6 would predict that the single salary schedule would be an effective motivator. Since the single salary schedule provides equal compensation for teachers with similar levels of experience and education without regard to effort, equity theory would regard it as demotivating for highly productive teachers.

Expectancy theory suggests that incentives must be contingent on performance in order to have a motivating effect on employees, but most single salary plans grant salary increases automatically as employees gain additional experience. Raises are not contingent on performance. Thus, expectancy theory would predict a dampening effect on motivation from a single salary pay plan.

Only goal-setting theory would regard the single salary schedule as neutral in its effect on motivation. In goal-setting theory, compensation is important to motivation only if it serves to make goals clearer. Since there is no strong relationship between performance goals and single salary plans, the theory would predict no motivational effect on employees.

Defenders of the single salary schedule acknowledge that it has weaknesses, but argue that there is no alternative approach that does not have even more problems. Later in this chapter, three proposals for changing the way teachers are compensated will be examined. These alternatives are merit pay, incentive pay, and career ladders.

It is unlikely that the single salary schedule will disappear. Its widespread use and strong appeal to teachers and many administrators militate against its being replaced. However, we can expect to see new models of teacher compensation being adopted by school districts.

The salary increases won by teachers during the 1980s and 1990s moved teaching into a slightly more competitive position with respect to other occupations, but salaries for teachers continued to lag behind those of most fields that require a bachelor's degree. In 1990–91, college graduates with degrees in teaching were paid on average $10,000 less those individuals who majored in computer science and $6,100 less than persons with degrees in mathematics or physical science. However, teachers fared better in comparison with graduates holding degrees in biology, communications, and public affairs. Biology majors averaged annual salaries that were about $1,400 more than teachers, but individuals with degrees in communications or public affairs both earned slightly less, on average, than teachers (National Center for Education Statistics, 1993b).

Reasons for Low Salaries

To what can the disparity between teachers' salaries and the salaries of workers in other occupations with comparable educational requirements be attributed? In part, the decline in teachers' salaries during the 1970s was the market's response to an oversupply of teachers. However, even during periods of short supply, teachers make relatively lower salaries than members of most other comparable occupations.

Teachers, of course, work fewer days per year than full-time employees in most other fields. They are on the job between 182 and 190 days per year (Educational Research Service, 1985), compared to about 225 days per year for most other workers—a difference of about 17 percent. But teachers salaries' appear to be lower than expected, even when this difference is taken into account.

One factor that appears to contribute to low salaries in teaching is the composition of the teaching force. Bird (1985) used Census Bureau data to compare salaries of teachers to those of persons with similar levels of education employed outside of teaching. Mean income from wages for the nonteaching group was 39 percent higher than teachers received. The nonteaching group had somewhat less education (16.3 years compared to 17.7 years) but included more males (60.2 percent versus 20.0 percent) and more whites (88.6 percent versus 79.0 percent).

On an annualized basis, teachers did about as well as a nonteaching group of workers with characteristics similar to those found in teaching, but they did less well than nonteachers with different demographic characteristics. Bird's conclusion was that sex discrimination accounted for the lower salaries in teaching and concluded that "the challenge facing education policymakers today is to seek a new teacher pay comparability strategy to fit a market in which the results of a history of sex discrimination may be disappearing" (Bird, 1985).

Adequacy of Teacher Pay

Adequacy refers to whether employees receive sufficient pay and benefits to permit them to maintain a decent standard of living. Workers whose salaries are too low to permit them to afford a middle-class lifestyle often take second jobs in order to supplement their earnings. This practice, called *moonlighting,* is more common among teachers than members of other occupations. About one-fourth of teachers in public schools earn income from a second, nonteaching job, and one-third earn money from extra-duty assignments for the school system, including coaching athletic teams or sponsoring student clubs. Teachers earned an average of $4,400 from nonteaching jobs and $1,900 from school-related extra-duty assignments in the 1990–91 school year (National Center for Education Statistics, 1993a).

There has been relatively little research on the extent of moonlighting among teachers or of its effects on the individual's attitudes toward the primary job. In one of the few studies of this phenomenon, researchers found that about 13 percent of the 329 Texas teachers they surveyed held second jobs after school or on weekends and holidays. They worked nearly 13 hours a week and earned slightly more than $3,500 a year at the second job. About 31 percent of the respondents also worked during the summer breaks, with average earnings of about $1,900. Teachers who moonlighted year-round thus increased their income by about $5,400 on average (Henderson & Henderson, 1986).

The most common type of outside employment among teachers in the Texas study was sales, reported by 35 percent of respondents. Next in frequency of mention were school-related work (24 percent) and music (15 percent).

Cross-National Comparisons

How do U.S. teachers fare economically in comparison with their counterparts in other parts of the world? One study compared the economic situations of teachers in the United States and Japan (Barro & Lee, 1986). The findings showed that beginning teachers in Japan make 20 to 25 percent less than the average beginning teachers in U.S. schools, but that the lower starting salaries are balanced by long-term gains.

A Japanese teacher with the equivalent of a bachelor's degree who remains in teaching will eventually earn three times the beginning salary, compared to two times or less in most school districts in the United States. The reason for this substantial difference in the long-term rewards of teaching in the two systems has to do with the "topping out" of teachers' salaries. After about 15 years, U.S. teachers no longer qualify for annual increments, but Japanese teachers continue to receive increases each year until retirement.

Balance in Teachers' Salaries

Although salaries are the most visible part of personnel costs and the item that employees most often consider in deciding whether to accept a job offer, they are only part of the total compensation package. Fringe benefits are an important part of the compensation picture. Benefits include immediate and deferred payments employees are entitled to receive by virtue of working in a particular organization. The best known benefits are various kinds of leave, medical and hospital insurance, and retirement contributions.

Three types of benefits are common in school districts:

1. *Collateral benefits:* These are direct and indirect forms of compensation that are received without expenditure of additional effort. Examples are sick leave, medical insurance, and retirement contributions. More than 95 percent of public schools in the United States offered medical insurance to teachers in 1990, retirement benefits were available to teachers in 99 percent of the schools, and dental insurance was offered by 67 percent of the schools (National Center for Education Statistics, 1993a).

2. *Nonsalary payments:* These are supplementary payments made to individuals who perform duties above and beyond their regular assignments. Coaching and sponsoring various activity groups are the most common examples of nonsalary payments. Data from the National Center for Education Statistics (1993a) showed that public school teachers who performed extra-duty assignments earned $1,940, on average, during the 1990–91 school year.

3. *Noneconomic benefits:* This category includes any features of a job that make it more attractive, whether or not the employer thinks of them as benefits. Intrinsic rewards are included here. Examples of noneconomic benefits are small class size, duty-free lunch, a planning period, and motivated students.

The cost of fringe benefits for workers in the private sector has increased dramatically. In 1959, for example, benefit costs for employees averaged less than 25 percent of the total payroll for industrial firms in the United States, but by 1993, that figure had increased to more than 40 percent (Milkovich & Newman, 1996). Educational personnel typically receive fewer fringe benefits than employees in the business world. (Geisert and Lieberman [1994, p. 227], however, claim that fringe benefits received by teachers are 10 to 20 percent higher than for workers in other fields.)

One reason for the increase in the cost of fringe benefits has been the surge in the cost of health care. In Minnesota schools between 1986 and 1991, the cost of medical insurance for professional staff members rose 58 percent, almost four times the rate of increase in salaries in that state over the same period (How Is Minnesota..., 1993).

In certain situations, increasing fringe benefits may be an alternative to raising salaries. For employees who would like to reduce their income tax, an increase in fringe benefits valued at $1,000 may be more attractive than a pay increase of that amount, since taxes on fringe benefits may be deferred or taxed at a lower rate than a salary increase. Fringe benefits are also attractive because they offer services that could not be purchased as cheaply by individuals. Group medical insurance is a good example. Although premiums for group plans are not cheap, they cost considerably less than individuals would pay for comparable coverage. Surprisingly, employees are often poorly informed about the types and value of the fringe benefits they receive, and when they are offered a job, few of them investigate fringe benefits before deciding whether to accept. Exhibit 10.1 lists examples of fringe benefits to which school employees may be entitled. The exhibit classifies benefits into three categories: collateral, noneconomic, and nonsalary payments.

Equity and the Single Salary Schedule

The Equal Pay Act of 1963 requires employers to refrain from discriminating against female employees by paying them less than males are paid for performing the same or similar jobs. Few cases involving teachers have been decided by the courts under the Equal Pay Act, since teachers' salaries are commonly assumed to be gender neutral. However, a study of teachers' salaries found that female teachers in public high schools school earned $1,134 less, on average, than their male counterparts. The discrepancy in salaries of female and male teachers was even greater in private high schools.

The disparity persisted even when differences in educational attainment, experience, and teaching field were taken into account. The researchers concluded that the differences were the result of male teachers receiving more credit for previous teaching experience than females (Bradley, 1989).

In the few cases involving charges of unequal pay for female teachers under the Equal Pay Act, courts have held that schools may not pay female coaches less than male coaches for assignments that involve similar levels of effort. In one case, a plan to provide a salary supplement for male heads of household was struck down (McCarthy, 1983).

EXHIBIT 10.1 *Examples of Employee Benefits Grouped by Type*

Benefit	Beneficiary	Type
Health insurance*	Employee and family	Collateral
Dental insurance*	Employee and family	Collateral
Term life insurance	Designated	Collateral
Sick leave	Employee	Collateral
Retirement contribution*	Employee	Collateral
Tax sheltered annuity*	Employee	Collateral
Leaves of absence		Collateral
Family leave	Employee and family	
Maternity leave	Employee	
Illness	Employee and family	
Military service	Employee	
Sabbatical	Employee	Noneconomic
Tenure	Employee	Noneconomic
Supplemental income Coach, club sponsor, summer school instructor, etc.	Employee	Nonsalary payment
Holidays and vacations	Employee	Collateral
Automatic deduction for professional dues	Employee	Collateral
Travel to professional meetings	Employee	Collateral

*Employee may be required to share cost.

Since the passage of the Equal Pay Act, some progress has been made in closing the gap between men's and women's incomes, but discrepancies remain. Women who work in occupations that are dominated by women, including teaching, nursing, and secretarial work, generally earn less than men. However, a female employee has no redress under the Equal Pay Act unless her employer pays a male more to do a similar job.

Comparable Worth

In an attempt to address discrepancies that are based on occupational groupings, some women have sued, charging discrimination under Title VII of the Civil Rights Act. In one of these cases, nursing supervisors in Denver claimed they were discriminated against because they were grouped for pay purposes with other jobs held predominantly by women rather than being placed in a class of jobs that included more males. The nursing supervisors claimed that they performed work that was equal in importance to that performed by men and should be paid equally.

The concept involved in this case is comparable worth. To date, courts have avoided requiring a comparable worth standard (Landy, 1985).

Aside from adequacy, employees value equity more highly than any other feature of compensation. Opposition of teachers to merit pay is based on a fear of potential inequity. There is no widely accepted objective measure of equity, since people's perceptions vary depending on their definitions of their own and others' contributions and rewards. Moreover, objective judgments of equity are difficult when individuals have access to incomplete information about an organization's compensation policy and practices.

Forms of Incentive Pay

Employers use a variety of compensation plans designed to increase employee motivation and commitment or to strengthen the relationship of pay to performance. Business corporations use compensation to help them achieve certain strategic objectives. Pay-for-performance plans, group and individual incentive plans, profit sharing, and various types of bonuses are widely used by private employers.

The field of education has been more cautious than the private sector about adopting alternative pay arrangements. The forms of alternative compensation used most widely in schools are merit pay, incentive pay, and career ladders. These plans are described in detail here.

Taxpayers are in favor of providing differentiated pay for teachers. In their report entitled *Time for Results*, the National Governors Association recommended developing compensation plans that would recognize differences in function, competence, and performance of teachers (Alexander, 1986). However, taxpayers and politicians often are not aware of the difficulties involved in implementing alternative pay plans.

There is confusion regarding terminology in discussions of alternative pay plans. Terms such as *pay-for-performance, incentive pay, merit pay,* and *career ladder* are used interchangeably and without precision in the media. The terms to be used in this chapter will be defined by reference to features that differentiate them from other types of compensation plans. You should be aware that the descriptions given here are pure types and that in practice a particular plan may incorporate features of two or even three of these types.

Merit Pay

Merit pay is a form of compensation that pays individuals on the basis of their performance on the job. Merit pay awards in education are usually based on performance ratings by principals and may be given either as a one-time bonus or as a salary increase for a specified period of time (American Association of School Administrators, 1983a).

Merit pay was widely adopted in the United States in the 1920s and 1930s but its use faded when districts converted to single salary schedules. A 1978 survey showed that about 4 percent of districts had merit pay plans in effect for teachers and that another 4.7 percent were considering instituting such plans (Thornton, 1986). Jacobson (1996) argued that the reason that merit pay has not been more successful in the United States is because it exacerbates the conflict between closely held values about teaching. He believes that teachers are responsive to monetary incentives such as those offered by merit pay, even though they profess to have chosen teaching out of altruistic motives. Jacobson suggests that the contradiction between teachers' stated values and their behavior creates dissonance that ultimately sabotages merit pay programs.

Proponents believe that merit pay motivates teachers to improve their teaching practices and that, as a result, students benefit. The available research offers little evidence to support that conclusion, but some studies have suggested that merit pay does influence other work-related behaviors, including recruitment, attendance, and retention (Jacobson, 1996).

Objections to merit pay for teachers focus on the subjective nature of teacher evaluation and the divisive nature of the competitive motives merit pay is believed to arouse. Since there are few truly objective measures of effective teaching performance, merit pay plans usually rely on principals' judgments regarding which teachers deserve merit raises. This requires trust on the part of teachers in the principal's ability to fairly and accurately rate their performance. Some teachers lack confidence that principals can be trusted to administer merit pay plans equitably, but most administrators themselves believe they are capable of doing so.

Another objection to merit pay is voiced by those who fear that the competition for salary increases will demoralize employees and destroy cooperation. This threat is felt to be especially great in pay plans with a predetermined limit on the number of workers who qualify (Ballou & Podgursky, 1993).

A number of school districts in the United States have tried merit pay and abandoned it after a short time. One of the few plans to survive more than a few years is located in a St. Louis County (Missouri) school district, where it has been in operation since 1953. An important feature of the plan, and one that probably contributes to its longevity, is the attention given by administrators to teacher evaluation procedures. Principals' evaluation reports are carefully reviewed by district officials, who suggest ways that principals can improve their assessment procedures (Natriello & Cohn, 1983).

Compensation experts point out that the amount and timing of a merit increase have an effect on its motivational value, but little is known about how to structure merit pay plans in order to produce gains in worker output (Milkovich & Milkovich, 1992) or employee acceptance of the philosophy of merit pay. Research is needed to clarify these questions.

Expectancy theory and goal-setting theory (Chapter 6) propose two possible explanations for merit pay's potential effectiveness as a motivator. Goal-setting theory suggests that merit pay and incentive pay plans motivate employees by making goals and expectations clear. Expectancy theory implies that employees are motivated to obtain the incentive (in this case, increased salary).

Incentive Pay

Incentive pay is a salary supplement or bonus paid to teachers who fulfill specified conditions established by the district to help it attain certain goals or solve particular problems (American Association of School Administrators, 1983a). Examples include payments to teachers who are willing to teach in schools with high concentrations of educationally disadvantaged children or who are in fields with teacher scarcity, such as special education, mathematics, and science. Incentive pay is also given by some districts to teachers who attain certain educational or professional growth objectives. The amount of these awards varies. For teaching in a difficult school, a teacher may receive a bonus of $1,500 to $2,000 per year, and for achieving professional growth objectives, the payment is often equivalent to the cost of tuition for a graduate college course.

Houston Independent School District successfully used an incentive plan to recruit teachers with scarce subject specialties. The Houston plan paid salary supplements ranging from $600 to $1,000 per year for teachers of mathematics, science, bilingual classes, and special education.

Career Ladders

The best-known example of a career ladder is that adopted statewide in Tennessee in 1984. That plan provides five levels of teaching competence: Probationary, Apprentice, and Career Levels I, II, and III. Teachers on the top three rungs of the ladder earn from $1,000 to $7,000 per year in salary supplements (Thornton, 1986). Advancement in the Tennessee plan is based on performance and experience. Teachers move from the Probationary to the Apprentice stage in one year and remain at that level for three years. A minimum of five years of experience at Career Levels I and II is required before a teacher can advance to the next higher step. All promotions on the ladder require demonstration of satisfactory performance and a review of performance conducted by assessment teams that consist of teachers, principals, and supervisors (Thornton, 1986).

Most career ladder plans, including the one in Tennessee, assign additional responsibilities to teachers as they advance up the ladder. These duties may include supervising other teachers or planning and leading curriculum or staff development activities.

Advantages and Disadvantages

All compensation plans have both advantages and disadvantages. Single salary schedules have the advantage of being easily administered and acceptable to most teachers. These plans also have one major weakness: They fail to attract and hold enough high-quality teachers.

Merit pay plans have three potential advantages. By rewarding employees who have above-average productivity, they help attract quality employees, provide an incentive for greater effort by current employees, and reduce the level of attrition among more productive employees (Bishop, 1986).

However, any plan that bases compensation on performance evaluation is likely to encounter problems. It is expensive to obtain data on worker productivity, and the information that is obtained is often low in reliability. Even in industry, supervisory ratings are often used to assess productivity, and research shows that those ratings are not very reliable. An added complication of the use of merit pay for teachers is the evidence that teacher performance is not consistent over time. Teachers who achieve above-average learning gains with their students one year may be average or even below average the next.

Aside from the technical difficulties involved in implementing merit pay, there are questions about the soundness of the psychological assumptions on which it is based. Some researchers (Deci, 1972) have found that activities that are intrinsically motivating—that is, those that are performed only for the pleasure of performing them—lose some of their intrinsic motivation if a reward is offered for performing them. Moreover, the research has shown that individuals who are given tangible rewards for engaging in activities that are intrinsically motivating engage in the activities less often after they are rewarded. Some educators interpret these findings to mean that teachers who derive pleasure from teaching may experience less satisfaction from it when merit pay is implemented, and hence may lose interest in teaching well.

One other potential problem with merit pay was cited by Bishop (1986). He noted that monetary rewards and promotions increase an employee's visibility and make the person more attractive to other employers, thus raising the possibility of increased turnover among more productive workers. He proposed using less visible incentives, including praise, desirable job assignments, increased autonomy, participation in selecting coworkers, and opportunities for travel, in place of financial rewards.

Nonsalary rewards may have greater motivational potential for teachers than salary bonuses, according to a study of teachers' preferences of performance rewards (Kasten, 1984). That study involved 26 teachers, 15 of whom reported no interest in merit pay. "Strong interest" in tuition grants was reported by 20 of the teachers, and 21 were strongly interested in the opportunity to have time off to attend conferences. The opportunity to work with student teachers was also of strong interest to 20 of the teachers, and 21 reported a strong interest in receiving money to be spent on classroom enrichment.

One of the problems with merit pay is that many more employees believe they should receive awards than qualify for them. A study of teachers' ratings of themselves and their colleagues (Hoogeveen & Gutkin, 1986) found that teachers rated themselves higher than they rated their peers and that their self-ratings were higher even than the average ratings given all teachers by the principal.

A question investigated by Hoogeveen and Gutkin (1986) had to do with whether teachers agree on the identity of superior performers. In all three of the small elementary schools involved in the study, one teacher was nominated by more than one-half of his or her colleagues as deserving merit pay. This finding suggests that there is a reasonably high degree of consensus in some faculties. Whether similar results would be obtained in larger elementary schools or in high schools, however, is not known.

Career ladders are meant to provide opportunities for teachers to move through a series of positions of expanding responsibility, greater task variety, and increasingly attractive monetary rewards. They are designed for the purpose of attracting and retaining able teachers. However, career ladders, like merit pay, are more expensive to operate than single salary schedules and, if not adequately funded, can result in greater competition and less cooperation among teachers. Moreover, if advancement on a career ladder is based on the results of performance evaluation, teachers are likely to experience the same concerns that they report for merit pay (Timar, 1992).

Incentive pay has the advantage of being effective in attracting better quality applicants for positions that are normally difficult to fill. Incentive pay has no effect on teacher performance, except indirectly, and it is more costly than the single salary schedule (although potentially less expensive than merit pay or career ladders).

Keeping Costs under Control

A critical criterion by which a compensation plan is judged is cost. If the cost is excessive, proposed increases will have little support from either taxpayers or board members. Whether the cost of a proposed pay plan is reasonable or excessive depends on one's point of view. What is reasonable to the members of a union may be considered excessive by the board. The objective must be to maximize the five criteria described earlier in this chapter while at the same time maintaining acceptable cost limits.

The American Association of School Administrators (1983b) reported that beginning salaries for teachers would have to be increased an average of 35 percent in order to attain the goal of making teachers' salaries competitive with those paid in other professions with similar educational requirements. The increases required to reach such a goal would have ranged from a low of 14.2 percent to a high of 58.5 percent in the 28 districts surveyed.

The cost of merit pay and other similar programs depends on the size of the awards and the number of teachers who qualify for them. The problem is illustrated by the experience of Fairfax County (Virginia) school officials. During a one-year pilot test of a proposed merit pay program, school officials discovered that the number of teachers who qualified for a 10 percent salary increase on the basis of performance evaluations exceeded the predicted number by 3.4 percent. The additional cost to the district, had the plan been in effect, would have exceeded one-half million dollars ("Fairfax Officials," 1987).

The Educational Research Service (1983) reported that districts with operational merit pay plans gave awards to teachers ranging from $28 to $6,000. The average of the lowest amount received by a teacher in the surveyed districts was $804, and the average of the highest amounts was $1,738. An average of 26 percent of teachers received awards. The definition of merit pay used in that survey differs from the one presented in this chapter, and the costs would have varied somewhat if the definition used here had been applied.

A rough estimate of the cost of merit pay can be obtained by multiplying the anticipated average award by the number of teachers expected to qualify. Using the midpoint of the high-low award range reported by Educational Research Service as the average award size and 26 percent as the number of recipients, a district could anticipate investing about $24,300 per year for each 100 teachers employed ($934 × .26 × 100). Giving larger awards or giving awards to more teachers would increase the cost, and smaller or fewer awards would lower it.

Administrators' Salaries

Salaries for administrators represent about 8.5 percent of the average district budget, according to one study (Chambers, 1978). Table 10.1 shows the minimum (starting) salaries for nine administrative positions in 1993–94 for districts with the largest (25.000+) and smallest (300–2,499) enrollments.

The data in Table 10.1 show that for five of the six district office positions in the table, administrators in large districts earned higher salaries than those who worked in the smallest districts. However, principals and subject-matter supervisors in small school districts had higher starting salaries than their counterparts in

TABLE 10.1   *1993–94 Minimum Salaries of Selected Administrators in Large and Small School Districts and Ratios*

	Large Districts	*Small Districts*	*Ratio*
Superintendent	$107,954	$73,738	1.46
Asst. Superintendent	62,051	53,282	1.16
Director of Instruction	53,716	44,779	1.20
Director of Finance	53,877	36,412	1.48
Director of Personnel	52,509	41,799	1.26
Instructional Supervisor	40,539	44,003	.92
Elementary Principal	45,691	47,737	.96
Middle School Principal	40,580	44,336	.92
High School Principal	42,421	47,161	.90

Note: Large districts are those with enrollments of 25,000 or more students; small districts enroll between 300 and 2,499 students.

Source: Salaries Paid Professional Personnel in Public Schools, 1993–94. Arlington, VA: Educational Research Service, 1994. Reprinted by permission.

the large districts. Superintendents and directors of finance in large districts earned almost 1.5 times the salaries of their counterparts in small districts, whereas principals in large districts earned 4 to 10 percent less than principals in small districts.

Merit pay for administrators is more common than for teachers. A 1978 study found that 15.3 percent of school districts offered merit pay for administrators, compared to only 4 percent with merit pay plans for teachers (Kienapfel, 1984). At least one state has adopted a statewide career ladder plan for administrators and supervisors (North Carolina Department of Public Instruction, 1984). The North Carolina plan consists of four steps, beginning with Provisional status and advancing through Career Statuses I, II, and III.

An individual must spend a minimum of two years at each step before being eligible to advance to the next higher level. Advancement is based on satisfactory performance and demonstrated professional growth, including completion of continuing education credits appropriate for the position and related to the needs of the individual (Kienapfel, 1984). Advancement from one career status level to the next results in a salary increase of 10 percent in addition to the normal 5 percent step increment.

Some districts have abolished salary schedules for principals and offer only minimum and maximum salaries. Salaries are determined individually, based on several factors such as the size of the school served and the quality of the individual's performance.

Constructing a Salary Schedule

Salary schedules are usually developed by firms that specialize in employee compensation. The task is one that requires a considerable amount of expertise and a great deal of data. The first decision to be made in developing a salary schedule is the number of grades or levels to be included. Henderson (1985) defined *pay grades* as convenient groupings of a wide variety of jobs that are similar in difficulty and level of responsibility but with little else in common. The number of grades to be incorporated into a schedule varies depending on the number of employee specialties and the extent to which the district administration wishes to be able to make small distinctions in compensation.

Each grade is subdivided into 10 to 15 steps to provide for differences in experience and level of educational attainment. The difference between the lowest step in adjacent grades in school district salary schedules typically ranges from 2.5 to 4 percent, and there is obviously considerable overlap across grades.

The procedure used to establish salaries for dissimilar jobs is *job evaluation* (Landy, 1985). A job evaluation involves these steps:

1. Select the jobs to be evaluated and choose the evaluation factors. The factors should be skills or abilities that are required to varying degrees in all of the positions and for which salary differences can be justified. An example of a factor that is frequently used is education; people who hold jobs requiring

higher levels of education receive higher salaries than those whose jobs require less education, other things being equal.

2. Collect information about the positions from a variety of sources, including interviews, job descriptions, and observations.
3. Using information collected in step 2, rate the jobs being evaluated by assigning points for each criterion. Sum the points to obtain a total for each position. This activity is normally carried out independently by members of a committee who compare their ratings after they are completed and discuss differences until a consensus is reached.
4. Rank the positions by point totals agreed upon in step 3. Select a few key positions and assign salaries to those by investigating salaries for similar positions in nearby districts.
5. Assign salaries to the remainder of the positions by comparing the point totals for those positions to the point totals for the key positions.

Job evaluation should result in a salary schedule that is internally consistent and externally competitive. It is necessary to repeat the procedure about every 10 years because jobs change over time and their relative importance to the district shifts. As duties evolve and new specialties emerge, some positions must be moved up or down on the scale to preserve internal competitiveness.

Summary

A well-designed compensation plan should help a district to accomplish the objectives of attracting and holding employees and helping employees engage in reliable task-related behavior and, when appropriate, to be spontaneous and innovative in carrying out a job. Six features of a sound compensation plan are competitiveness, adequacy, balance, equity, incentive, and reasonable cost. A competitive salary structure enables an organization to attract employees; adequacy and balance help to hold them; and equity and incentive assist in motivating employees to higher productivity. Reasonable cost permits the organization to continue to offer an attractive compensation package to its employees.

Most school districts in the United States use single salary schedules, in which teachers are paid on the basis of education and experience. Three other approaches to teacher compensation are being tested in some districts. Merit pay rewards teachers who are judged above average in effectiveness; career ladders establish steps in which teachers may advance in both income and prestige; and incentive pay involves salary supplements for teachers who possess scarce skills or fulfill specific contractual requirements such as accepting a difficult teaching assignment. All of these plans have advantages and disadvantages that should be considered before a decision is made to implement one or more of them.

Job evaluation is a procedure by which a school district equates jobs with different content for purposes of compensation. It is used to eliminate inequities in salaries and to ensure that all salaries are commensurate with level of responsibility.

Suggested Activities

1. In trying construct a salary schedule that is externally competitive, a school district must sometimes sacrifice internal equity. Discuss the relative importance of these two features. Under what conditions is it advisable to increase external competitiveness at the cost of internal equity? What problems may arise as a result?

2. The argument is sometimes made that dollars spent increasing beginning salaries have a bigger payoff for a school district than those spent on raises for experienced teachers. Discuss the merits of that argument and cite reasons why you believe it is or is not true. How do you explain research showing that increases in the middle of the salary schedule have more impact on retention than those at the lower or upper ends?

3. Adding additional steps to existing salary schedules has been proposed as a way to make teaching more competitive with other occupations. However, that idea has little support among teachers. Why do you think teachers do not favor adding steps?

4. A study cited in this chapter showed that some school personnel hold two jobs during the academic year. What are the factors that contribute to teachers and other employees working at two jobs? What is the likely effect of a second job on teachers' effectiveness? What policy should districts adopt with regard to second jobs?

5. One way by which classroom teachers can increase their income is to obtain an advanced degree. However, the salary increase teachers receive from holding a master's degree is relatively small. Estimate the cost to a teacher of obtaining a master's degree and, using the present salary schedule in your district, determine how long it would take a teacher to make back that cost. Is the decision to obtain an advanced degree a rational decision from an economic point of view? What noneconomic factors influence teachers to decide to pursue an advanced degree?

Online Resources

Websites maintained by public schools systems, teacher unions, and research organizations offer a bountiful source of information about teachers' salaries. They make it possible to compare salaries across districts and to review features of alternative forms of teacher compensation.

Salary Expert (www.salaryexpert.com)
> This site lists average salaries of teachers (kindergarten, primary, and secondary) and teacher aides for cities in the United States. It also shows average national salary and fringe benefits. This is a useful source of information for comparing salaries of competing districts.

Teacher Union Reform Network (www. kiva.net/~pdkintl/kappan/kurb0001.htm)
> The Network, composed of local units of the American Federation of Teachers and the National Education Association, takes the position that efforts to improve schools must be supported by changes in teacher compensation plans. The site describes several alternative plans for compensating teachers.

Cincinnati Public Schools (http://98.203/127.5/general/compen.html)
> The Cincinnati Teacher Evaluation and Compensation system provides teachers with opportunities for incentive pay based on acquisition of specialized training, advance degrees, certification in additional content areas, or taking on leadership roles.

Consortium for Policy Research in Education (www.wcer.wisc.edu/cpre/teachercomp/
tchrcompmodel 1a.HTM)
This site has examples of four models of alternative salary schedules for teachers. In one
model, teachers can gain salary increments by obtaining a master's degree, passing a content test, gaining licensure in a second teaching field or in an area of teacher shortage, or
obtaining certification from the National Board of Professional Teaching Standards. Increments may also be given to teachers who increase their computer skills or learn about Reading Recovery or cooperative learning.

References

Alexander, L. (1986). Time for results: An overview. *Phi Delta Kappan, 68,* 202–204.

American Association of School Administrators. (1983a). *Some points to consider when you discuss
merit pay.* Arlington, VA: Author.

American Association of School Administrators. (1983b). *The cost of reform: Fiscal implications of "A
nation at risk."* Arlington, VA: Author.

American Federation of Teachers, Department of Research. (1999*). Survey and analysis of teacher
salary trends 1999.* Available online: www.aft.org/research/survey99/tables.

Bacharach, S., Lipsky, D., & Shedd, J. (1984). *Paying for better teaching: Merit pay and its alternatives.*
Ithaca, NY: Organizational Analysis and Practice.

Ballou, D., & Podgursky, M. (1993, October). Teachers' attitudes toward merit pay: Examining
conventional wisdom. *Industrial and Labor Relations Review, 47,* 50–61.

Barro, S., & Lee, J. W. (1986). *A comparison of teachers' salaries in Japan and the U.S.* (ERIC Document
Reproduction Service No. ED 273630).

Bird, R. E. (1985). *An analysis of the comparability of public school teacher salaries to earning opportunities
in other occupations.* Research Triangle Park, NC: Southeastern Regional Council for Educational Improvement. (ERIC Document Reproduction Service No. ED 256070).

Bishop, J. (1986). *The recognition and reward of employee performance.* Paper presented at a conference
on the New Economics of Personnel, Tempe, AZ. (ERIC Document Reproduction Service
No. ED 268376).

Bradley, A. (1989, December 13). New study finds a gender gap in teachers' salaries. *Education
Week,* pp. 1, 12.

Cascio, W., & Awad, E. (1981). *Human resources management: An information systems approach.*
Reston, VA: Reston Publishing.

Chambers, J. (1978). *An analysis of educational costs across local school districts in the State of Missouri,
1975–76.* Denver: Education Commission of the States.

Deci, E. (1972). The effects of contingent and noncontingent rewards on intrinsic motivation. *Organizational Behavior and Human Performance, 8,* 217–220.

Educational Research Service. (1983). *Merit pay plans for teachers: Status and descriptions.* Arlington,
VA: Author.

Educational Research Service. (1985). *Scheduled salaries for professional personnel in public schools,
1984–85.* Arlington, VA: Author.

Fairfax officials still unsure of the cost of teacher merit pay. (1987, May 13). *The Washington Post,*
p. Bl, B9.

Geisert, G., & Lieberman, M. (1994). *Teacher union bargaining: Practice and policy.* Chicago: Precept.

Henderson, R. (1985). *Compensation management* (4th ed.). Reston, VA: Reston Publishing.

Henderson, D., & Henderson, K. (1986). *Moonlighting, salary, and morale: The Texas teachers' story.*
(ERIC Document Reproduction Service No. ED 269374).

Hoogeveen, K., & Gutkin, T. (1986). Collegial ratings among school personnel: An empirical
examination of the merit pay concept. *American Educational Research Journal, 23,* 375–381.

How is Minnesota spending its tax dollars? (1993). St. Paul, MN: Office of the State Auditor.

Jacobson, S. (1987). *The distribution of salary increments and its effect on teacher retention.* Paper presented at the annual meeting of the American Educational Research Association, Washington, DC.

Jacobson, S. (1989). Change in entry-level salaries and its effect on teacher recruitment. *Journal of Education Finance, 14,* 449–465.

Jacobson, S. (1996). Monetary incentives and the reform of teacher compensation: A persistent organizational dilemma. In S. Jacobson, E. Hickcox, & R. E. Stevenson (Eds.), *School administration: Persistent dilemmas in preparation and practice* (pp. 89–100). Westport, CT: Praeger.

Kasten, K. (1984, Summer). The efficacy of institutionally dispensed rewards in elementary school teaching. *Journal of Research and Development in Education, 17,* 1–13.

Katz, D. (1973). The motivational basis of organizational behavior. In M. Milstein & J. Belasco (Eds.), *Educational administration and the behavioral sciences: A systems perspective* (pp. 319–346). Boston: Allyn and Bacon.

Kienapfel, B. (1984). *Merit pay for school administrators: A procedural guide.* Arlington, VA: Educational Research Service.

Landy, F. (1985). *Psychology of work behavior.* Homewood, IL: Dorsey

Mark, J., & Anderson, B. (1978). Teacher survival rates: A current look. *American Educational Research Journal, 15,* 379–383.

McCarthy, M. (1983). Discrimination in employment. In J. Beckham & P Zirkel (Eds.), *Legal issues in public school employment* (pp. 22–54). Bloomington, IN: Phil Delta Kappa.

Milkovich, G., & Milkovich, C. (1992, November/December). Strengthening the pay-performance relationship: The research. *Compensation and Benefits Review, 24,* 53–62.

Milkovich, G., & Newman, J. (1996). *Compensation.* Chicago: Irwin.

Morris, L. (1972). *The single salary schedule: An analysis and evaluation.* New York: AMS Press. (Original work published 1930).

Murnane, R., & Cohen, D. (1986). Merit pay and the evaluation problem: Why most merit pay plans fail and a few survive. *Harvard Educational Review, 56,* 1–17.

National Center for Education Statistics. (1993a). *Schools and staffing in the United States: A statistical profile, 1990–91.* Washington, DC: U.S. Department of Education.

National Center for Education Statistics. (1993b, March). Teacher salaries–Are they competitive? *Issue Brief,* pp. 1–2.

Natriello, G., & Cohn, M. (1983). *Beyond sanctions: The evolution of a merit pay system.* Paper presented at the annual meeting of the American Educational Research Association, Montreal.

North Carolina Department of Public Instruction. (1984). *North Carolina career development plan for administrators, supervisors and other certified personnel.* Raleigh: Author.

Thornton, R. (1986). Teacher merit pay: An analysis of the issues. In R. Thornton & J. Aronson (Eds.), *Forging new relationships among business, labor and government* (pp. 179–199). Greenwich, CT: JAI Press.

Timar, T. (1992). Incentive pay for teachers and school reform. In L. Frase (Ed.), *Teacher compensation and motivation* (pp. 27–60). Lancaster, PA: Technomic.

11

Creating Productive Work Environments

"In fundamental ways, the U.S. educational system is structured to guarantee the failure of teachers" (McLaughlin, Pfeifer, Swanson-Owens, & Yee, 1986). That indictment was not written by a disgruntled teacher. It was authored by four educational researchers in one of the nation's leading universities, who reached that conclusion after interviewing 85 teachers about the conditions of their work. Despite evidence that the charge is not true in many schools, it is difficult to deny that in too many cases it accurately describes reality.

Why do many people find psychological success in their work so elusive? To what extent are structural conditions in schools responsible for the sense of frustration and defeat that teachers and members of support staffs experience? What can administrators do to make schools more conducive to success? These are questions that are addressed in this chapter.

Plan of the Chapter

Chapter 6 described three theories of employee motivation and their effect on human performance. However, working conditions in many schools are such that even motivated employees are unable to achieve maximum productivity. This chapter examines how environments in schools inhibit employee productivity and it suggests ways of creating more productive work environments. The chapter considers four topics: (1) psychological success and work environments, (2) qualities of productive work environments, (3) teacher stress and burnout, and (4) employee assistance programs in schools.

Psychological Success and Work Environments

All human beings strive to experience psychological success. One way by which they are able to do that is by performing competently in some personally valued task (Hall & Schneider, 1973). Teachers as well as students gain self-esteem when they believe they are performing capably a task that they value, and they experience satisfaction from the feeling that they are using their abilities appropriately and effectively (McLaughlin et al., 1986).

The environments in which people work may either increase or decrease the likelihood that they will experience psychological success. When conditions in the work environment prevent them from meeting their expectations, disappointment and frustration follow. Self-esteem suffers and the individual withdraws emotionally and perhaps physically by leaving the organization (Hall & Schneider, 1973). If the employee is not able to change jobs, continued frustration produces stress that may eventually lead to job burnout.

Unfortunately, the work environment in some schools does little to help employees experience psychological success. Surveys have shown that teachers believe that working conditions in schools limit their effectiveness and contribute to feelings of frustration (Corcoran, 1990).

Among the conditions about which teachers have expressed most concern in these surveys are low salaries and limited opportunities for advancement; heavy workloads; limited contacts with colleagues; shortages of materials and supplies for teaching; limited input into school decisions; lack of support from administrators; unfair or unhelpful evaluation practices; unavailability of stimulating professional development opportunities; run-down or outdated facilities; and lack of respect from administrators, students, and parents (Corcoran, 1990). Similar concerns are expressed by other school employees, including counselors, aides, nurses, and secretaries. Many of the conditions that limit employee productivity in schools are so common that they are taken for granted as characteristic of these occupations.

Some conditions found in schools prevent employees from doing their best work, whereas others simply make it more difficult to do a good job. Many teachers manage to be effective in spite of large classes by taking work home on evenings and weekends, and they overcome the lack of materials and supplies by buying them from their own funds. Other employees cannot solve their problems as easily, however. A counselor who is assigned to an office in which his or her conversations with students can be overheard by others is unable to conduct confidential counseling sessions with students, and a teacher who cannot be confident of receiving support from the principal must avoid teaching topics that offend sensitive parents.

Fortunately, the prospects for creating and sustaining productive work environments in schools have improved as our knowledge of the factors that contribute to employees' feelings of psychological success have increased. Based on recent research, we can identify elements of the work setting that employees rank as most important, and it should come as no surprise that some of these are factors about which teachers expressed concern. The elements identified by employees as most important were having a good relationship with one's supervisor; being treated as an important person; receiving adequate and fair compensation; working in a safe, healthy, and stress-free environment; having a job that is socially relevant; and having opportunities for growth and development (Bruce & Blackburn, 1992). Other job factors to which employees attach importance are good relationships with co-workers, having a job with variety, being involved and informed, and being able to maintain a balance between work and family responsibilities (Bruce & Blackburn, 1992).

School administrators, in general, and personnel administrators, in particular, need to find ways to create more productive working environments in schools. Although it may be true that administrators have little or no control over some conditions that cause psychological stress for employees, they are able to influence others.

Qualities of Productive Work Environments

Productive work environments are those that enable employees to perform their jobs effectively and to experience psychological success while doing it. These environments generally have six characteristics:

1. Continuous learning culture
2. Supportive administrative leadership
3. Opportunity to work collaboratively with others
4. Respect for people as individuals
5. Opportunity to use one's knowledge and skill and to receive feedback on one's performance
6. Necessary resources to do the job

When one of these conditions is missing, teachers are less likely to be able to carry out their work successfully and hence are not as likely to experience psychological success.

Continuous Learning Culture

In organizations that value learning, employees share ideas about new techniques and procedures that may help to increase productivity. The culture of these organizations encourages employees to listen to one another's ideas and to try out those that sound promising. Learning organizations provide extensive learning opportunities for employees, either through internal training and professional development programs or by supporting employee access to external opportunities (London, 1998).

Employees who take advantage of the learning opportunities provided by the organization are recognized by supervisors, and those who use the knowledge gained from those experiences to develop new approaches to their work or perfect existing ways of performing their jobs are rewarded. The organization's evaluation system is tied to employees' efforts to increase their knowledge and skill and to apply what they learn on the job (London, 1998).

Supportive Leadership

Leaders achieve results by influencing members of the group to work toward attaining group goals. Four types of leadership behavior may be involved (House, 1971):

1. *Directive leadership:* The leader spells out expectations to subordinates.
2. *Supportive leadership:* The leader treats subordinates as equals and shows concern for their well-being.
3. *Participative leadership:* The leader involves subordinates in advising about or actually making decisions concerning their work.
4. *Achievement-oriented leadership:* The leader identifies challenging work-related goals and communicates to subordinates confidence in their ability to achieve them.

Supportive, participative, and achievement-oriented leadership are the critical elements of a productive work environment. Directive leadership is also necessary on occasion. Leaders must be able to determine which type of leadership is needed in a given situation and to exhibit the behaviors associated with that type. They may differ in the types of leadership they prefer. Some principals rely primarily on participative leadership to achieve results, by delegating instructional duties to department heads and teachers. Others identify a small group of innovative teachers and use achievement-oriented leadership to encourage them to try new ideas and share with other teachers those that work (Little & Bird, 1987).

A large body of research suggests that when workers are given the opportunity to make decisions about how to organize and carry out their work, their satisfaction and commitment increase. In most cases, their performance also improves, but occasionally changes are limited to reductions in sick days, turnover, and other indirect indicators of performance (Louis & Smith, 1990).

Participative leadership is particularly important in schools, but the evidence indicates that few teachers believe they have much influence over decisions about their work. Data collected nationally in 1990–91 showed that fewer than 40 percent of teachers in public schools reported they had a great deal of influence over decisions about discipline policy, in-service training, ability grouping, and curriculum development. However, the level of self-reported influence varied somewhat across district types (National Center for Education Statistics, 1993b).

The number of teachers who reported having a lot of influence changed slightly between 1987 and 1990, increasing by a small amount in two areas, decreasing slightly in another, and remaining unchanged in the fourth (National Center for Education Statistics, 1993a). This finding was surprising, since during this time school-based management was widely adopted in U.S. schools (Caweiti, 1994).

Although a participative style of leadership has several important benefits, there are limitations to be considered. Participative decisions take more time than directive decisions, and if employees are called on to make decisions for which they lack the necessary interest, knowledge, or experience, the quality of their decisions is likely to be poor (Landy, 1985).

Increasing Trust. Supportive leadership helps build trust between administrators and employees. Leaders gain employees' trust by exhibiting consistent and predictable behavior and by demonstrating a commitment to helping individuals do a better job. Trust is important; without it, administrators' efforts to influence employees' behavior are likely to fail. Workers who trust their boss are more willing to accept his or her influence since they believe the supervisor will not suggest a course of action that will harm them.

Principals use a variety of strategies to demonstrate support for teachers, including involving them in important decisions; doing things with them; being positive, cheerful, and encouraging; being available and accessible; and being honest, direct, and sincere. They also exercise supportive leadership by collecting and disseminating information to staff members, assisting teachers with their tasks, facilitating communication within the school and between the school and community, and establishing procedures to handle routine matters (Leithwood & Montgomery, 1986).

Principals who wish to become more effective in supportive leadership should make a point of talking with teachers often about their personal and instructional interests and concerns. Teachers would like opportunities to discuss a variety of issues, including their own career plans and training needs, their concept of education, and the content of their courses. However, most teachers have relatively few chances to talk with administrators even about issues of immediate concern, including adjustments in work assignments, their own performance, their need for materials and supplies, instructional problems, and teacher/parent relationships. On only two topics do teachers report having fairly frequent conversations with principals. Those are student achievement and behavior (Bacharach, Bauer, & Shedd, 1986).

Administrators exhibit achievement-oriented leadership by alerting employees to new practices and encouraging them to experiment. They help obtain the resources employees need in order to try out new ideas, and they provide advice on implementation of innovative practices. Principals who make opportunities for teachers and other professional employees to attend conferences are also exhibiting achievement-oriented leadership.

Some principals hesitate to initiate discussions about teaching for fear of being perceived as intruding (Corbett, 1982). They consider teachers to be autonomous professionals who know their work and need no direction from an administrative superior. However, most teachers do not share that view of their role. They think of principals as colleagues with expertise in dealing with a variety of teaching problems, and welcome the chance to talk with them.

Teachers' morale is higher in schools in which principals provide support by offering constructive suggestions, displaying interest in improving the quality of the educational program, encouraging superior performance standards in the classroom, maintaining egalitarian relationships, offering social and managerial support, and standing behind teachers in conflicts with students and parents (Gross & Herriott, 1965).

Even though the press of managerial duties limits the time available for principals to perform as instructional leaders (Deal, 1987) and even though involving teachers in a participative style of leadership makes sense, the principal must retain the title of leader both symbolically and in fact. No other individual carries the authority to speak for the school as a whole in resolving differences of opinion regarding allocation of resources and in making decisions regarding goals. The role of instructional leader is one that the principal can and should carry. A participative mode of decision making, when appropriate, enhances the principal's instructional leadership rather than detracts from it.

Collaborative Work Arrangements

In schools with site-based management (SBM), the responsibility for student success moves from the central office to the schools. One of the first jobs that must be undertaken by SBM schools is team building. This involves helping employees to envision new roles that permit and encourage collaboration between and among staff members, students, parents, and the community (Payzant, 1992). Even noncertified staff, such as custodians and food service workers, assume new roles in SBM schools and assume more responsibility for accomplishing the school's mission (Prasch, 1990). Site-based management does not guarantee that communication will be better or that teachers, counselors, and other employees will cooperate more closely, but it does provide an opportunity to create conditions under which these things are possible.

Under school-based management, decisions about curriculum that were formerly made at the district level are made by the faculty and staff of the school. Each school must decide how to allocate the resources it receives. Schools have the freedom to hire more aides and fewer teachers if they choose to do so, or they may divert some of the money from teachers' salaries into technology.

Teachers often describe the schools in which they work in terms of how close teachers are to one another and how willing they are to work together. Working together encompasses many activities—discussing, planning, designing, analyzing, evaluating, and experimenting (Little, 1981).

Most teachers look for opportunities to share with colleagues what they are doing in their classrooms, but many prefer to speak with those whom they know well and for whom they feel an affinity. Few are willing to speak out in faculty meetings unless group norms supporting such sharing exist. However, the Internet opens an avenue for teachers to share with others in an atmosphere that greatly reduces feelings of vulnerability. These *learning communities,* as they are called (Lieberman, 1996), give teachers an opportunity to interact on the Internet with colleagues in other states and even other nations to manage their own learning by selecting topics for discussion, asking questions, and sharing discoveries. Networks nurture a culture that encourages inquiry and values sharing.

Scholars have begun to recognize the importance of teacher communities for the development of true professionalism. The term *community* refers to a group of people who have something in common that becomes the basis for their association with one another. In the case of a professional community, the something that ties people together is their common interest in their work. Although we tend to think of communities as consisting of people who have physical contact with one another, using the Internet makes it possible to create virtual communities.

The importance of teacher communities was described by Talbert and McLaughlin (1996) in this passage:

> We expect that strong teacher communities foster a shared knowledge base or technical culture, shared commitment to meeting the needs of all students, and durable professional identities and commitments. Conversely, without opportunities to acquire new knowledge, to reflect on practice, and to share successes and failures with colleagues, teachers are not likely to develop a sense of professional control and responsibility. (p. 133)

Accepting a collaborative mode of operation in schools requires first adopting an attitude that improvement is necessary and desirable. If teachers have not fully accepted that value, the principal should make its adoption the first priority. After that, administrators can suggest activities that will permit teachers to work collaboratively for more effective instruction. Some examples of ways teachers collaborate appear in Exhibit 11.1.

Respect for Individuals

Teachers and other school employees desire respect from others, including their colleagues on the job, administrators, parents, students, and the community at

---

EXHIBIT 11.1   *Examples of Collegial Cooperation in Teaching*

Design and prepare instructional material
Design curriculum units
Research material and ideas for curriculum
Write curriculum
Prepare lesson plans
Review and discuss existing lesson plans
Persuade others to try a new idea or approach
Make collective agreements to test an idea
Invite other teachers to observe one's classes
Observe other teachers
Analyze practices and effects
Teach others in formal inservice
Teach others informally
Talk publicly about what one is learning or wants to learn
Design inservice sessions
Evaluate the performance of the principal

Source: The Power of Organizational Setting: School Norms and Staff Development by J. W. Little, April 1981. Paper presented at the annual meeting of the American Educational Research Association, Los Angeles. ERIC Document Reproduction Service No. ED 221918.

large. Lack of respect has led many teachers to believe that their work is unimportant and unappreciated (Louis & Smith, 1990).

Lack of respect for others is demonstrated in a number of ways, both obvious and subtle. Behavior that indirectly shows disrespect erodes an individual's self-confidence and sense of efficacy, whereas more overt manifestations can lead to an individual's experiencing a threat to his or her psychological security. The potential power of lack of respect on individuals is evident in the results of a recent survey of employees' work-related fears.

Employees who experienced fear related to their work reported that their concerns had created negative feelings about the organization or about themselves or had a negative impact on the quality or quantity of their work. Some reported that, as a result of the fear, they were taking more care to avoid actions that might expose them to repercussions or were engaging more often in politically oriented behavior by cultivating "connections" with powerful individuals in the organization. Others reported that they were contemplating a transfer to a job outside the organization or had engaged in petty revenge or sabotage (Ryan & Oestreich, 1991). The researchers also found that employees who reported being fearful less often put forth extra effort to complete a task, more often attempted to hide mistakes, and less often engaged in creative thinking or risk-taking behavior on the job (Ryan & Oestreich, 1991).

Supervisory behaviors are a source of anxiety for many employees. Behaviors that are especially likely to arouse fear, whether the supervisor intends it or not, are silence, glaring, abruptness, insults and put-downs, blaming, yelling and shouting, and an aggressive, controlling manner.

Suggestions for administrators that will help lessen the level of fear in an organization include recognizing its presence and harmful effects and avoiding behaviors that are known to increase it. Administrators who wish to lower the level of anxiety are also advised to reduce ambiguous behavior, to talk about sensitive issues that are likely to arouse fear and that employees may be embarrassed to bring up on their own, and to welcome criticism (Ryan & Oestreich, 1991).

Using Knowledge and Skill

Few experiences are more important for employees' feelings of well-being than holding a job that allows them fully to use their knowledge and skill. Most young workers are less satisfied in their jobs than more experienced individuals, and the reason is that entry-level jobs tend to be less demanding and offer fewer opportunities for these workers to use the knowledge and skill they have acquired from their training.

Employees who are required to stretch in order to meet challenging aspects of their jobs are generally happier in their work and more productive than those for whom the job is a familiar routine. Of course, mastery is partly a function of one's experience, and the longer an individual is in a job, the less likely it is that he or she continues to be challenged by it. For that reason, the opportunity to move into new positions or take on demanding new duties that force the employee to acquire new skills and knowledge are important for maintaining employee interest and involvement.

For many school employees, school-based management provides such challenges. Teachers, counselors, and other employees who are unaccustomed to participating in decisions outside of their own immediate area of responsibility must learn new skills in order to participate fully in the operation of the school once SBM is introduced. Among these skills are developing and implementing a school improvement plan; learning to work effectively as a member of a team; and gathering, analyzing, and reporting data. Training in these skills can produce benefits in the form of a more efficient and effective transition to SBM (Holcomb, 1993).

Facilities and Resources

In many schools, the building itself is a hindrance to effective teaching (Olson, 1988). Buildings that are not kept clean or in which maintenance work is neglected, either because of lack of funds or employee indifference, are less pleasant places to work than those in which facilities are clean and well maintained.

Although amount of space is a more common problem, the quality of space is also a concern of teachers (Bacharach et al., 1986). *Quality* refers to availability of electrical outlets, running water, telephone, adequate lighting, and privacy. It also encompasses furnishings, including desks, and electronic equipment such as computers.

Good teaching is hindered by the shortage of textbooks, equipment, and supplies. It is not uncommon for teachers to have too few microscopes, maps, and computers for their classes, and in some schools even textbooks must be shared. Adequate facilities and resources do not by themselves guarantee teacher satisfaction or effectiveness, but they help (McLaughlin & Yee, 1988).

Teacher Stress and Burnout

Teachers have historically been attracted to the profession because of their desire to work with children, and that factor is still an important motivation for teachers. In the last 30 years, however, a number of changes in families and society have made it more difficult for teachers to reach students as effectively as they could in the past, with the result that some teachers feel their work is less rewarding. Today's teachers have less freedom to decide what to teach and how to teach it, and they feel more pressure from administrators and parents. Much of what they teach is prescribed, and teachers are held accountable for preparing students to pass standardized tests on the prescribed content. Teachers feel less like professionals who exercise their judgment and more like clerks who carry out directives from superiors (Provenzo & McCloskey, 1996).

Some teachers are better prepared, both by temperament and training, to deal with stress, but excessive and prolonged stress saps any teacher's energy and sharply reduces productivity. Administrators should be especially sensitive to work conditions that contribute to teacher stress. Among these conditions are heavy workloads, interpersonal problems with colleagues, scarcity of resources, lack of decision latitude, and physical factors such as noise and crowding (Guglielmi & Tatrow, 1998).

The stress experienced by teachers varies depending on the type of teaching position a person holds and the extent to which the individual is able to shrug off job-related stressors. Teachers with large classes and many disruptive students are likely to experience more stress than those with smaller classes and more well-behaved students. Yet, even in comparable teaching situations, two individuals may experience different levels of stress because of variations in the tolerance for stress. Thus, no action is likely to reduce stress for all teachers, although some actions have more promise for relieving stress than others.

Types of Stress

There are at least four sources of stress in schools (Albrecht, 1979). *Time stress* occurs when the time allotted for completing a task is insufficient or when inflexible dead-lines are established for completion of work assignments.

Situational stress arises when the situation in which a person is placed creates a psychological threat that exceeds the individual's ability to cope (Albrecht, 1979). Special education teachers are especially susceptible to situational stress because much of their work is bound by imposed restrictions. In one recent study, two-thirds or more of special education teachers reported spending between 10 and 30 percent of their time on required paperwork or individual education plan (IEP) team meetings and less than one hour per week working one-on-one with students. One teacher wrote: "I am supposed to keep perfect paperwork, collaborate with regular education teachers, train and grade peer tutors, keep in constant touch with parents, and still find time to teach my students!" (Sack, 2000).

Encounter stress is experienced when a person is forced to deal with other individuals whose behavior is unpleasant or unpredictable (Albrecht, 1979). An example of encounter stress is a teacher who is confronted by a student who is angry about a grade received on a test or a parent who is hostile and abusive.

Anticipatory stress occurs when an individual experiences anxiety about an upcoming event (Albrecht, 1979). Teachers may experience anticipatory stress prior to issuing report cards or before a classroom observation visit by the principal.

Symptoms of Stress

The experience of stress is manifested in feelings of fear, anxiety, depression, and anger. The individual subjected to prolonged stress experiences fatigue, reluctance to go to work, withdrawal, hypersensitivity to criticism, and hostility and aggression toward others (Cedoline, 1982).

Stress also produces physiological effects, such as changes in skin conductance, heart rate, and blood pressure. Individuals are unlikely to be aware of physiological changes except when the level of stress experienced is quite high.

However, the physiological manifestations of stress exact a cumulative toll on mental and physical health.

Stress can also affect cognitive functioning. Some stress is desirable for optimal performance, but exposure to unrelenting stress results in a marked decrease in performance (Lazarus, 1968).

Over time, the frustration, anger, disappointment, and guilt that teachers experience have a cumulative effect on their feelings about themselves and about their work that results in a condition known as *burnout*. Burnout has been defined as a form of alienation characterized by the feeling that one's work is meaningless and that one is powerless to bring about change that would make the work more meaningful. The experience of meaninglessness and powerlessness is intensified by the feeling that one is alone and isolated (Dworkin, 1987). Teachers who are experiencing job burnout often exhibit cynicism and negativism. They are likely to be inflexible and rigid and to demonstrate reduced concern for students and fellow workers.

Factors in Burnout

Factors that contribute to teacher burnout are role ambiguity (having a job in which duties are not clearly spelled out); responsibility/authority imbalance (having insufficient authority to carry out the responsibilities one has been assigned); a workload that is either too heavy or too light; inability to obtain information needed to carry out one's responsibilities; and job insecurity (Milstein, Golaszewski, & Duquette, 1984). Interactions with superiors can also lead to stress for some teachers. Teachers who receive no performance feedback from principals and who feel that they are unable to influence the administrators' decisions about their work are more likely to experience stress (Litt & Turk, 1985).

Administrators can help reduce the stress teachers experience by following some commonsense precautions:

1. Reduce time pressures by alerting teachers early to upcoming deadlines and by providing directions and assistance to help teachers complete paperwork requirements.
2. Assist teachers in obtaining help for students with emotional and psychological problems; if district resources are not available, appeal to community service agencies and service clubs for help.
3. Provide training to help teachers deal with disruptive students and, when necessary, provide support for teachers who are experiencing problems with student behavior.
4. Remove the dread of performance evaluation by pointing out that everyone can improve in some area; give teachers the opportunity to evaluate the school administration.
5. Provide feedback to teachers on their classroom performance, including specific suggestions that will help them be more effective teachers.
6. Offer to participate in parent conferences when teachers request it; provide training in planning and carrying out parent conferences.

7. Make time for informal conversations with teachers and give them a chance to talk about whatever they wish to talk about, bearing in mind that the most conscientious teachers are most subject to burnout.
8. Plan faculty outings that provide a break from the routine and allow teachers to have a good time with colleagues.
9. Help discouraged teachers maintain perspective by reminding them of past successes. Invite former students who have done well back to the school to talk about their successes and how their teachers helped them succeed.

Teacher Absenteeism

One of the symptoms of excessive stress on the job is absenteeism. Although not all absences can be attributed to on-the-job stress, when chronic absenteeism is encountered, administrators should consider the possibility that teachers are under excessive stress. A number of factors are involved in absenteeism, including individual characteristics, characteristics of the job, motivation to attend, and ability to attend (Steers & Rhodes, 1978).

Individual factors that may contribute to absence from work include gender, age, marital status, and size of family. An employee may be unable to attend work because of illness, transportation problems, or family responsibilities. Job characteristics that have an impact on employee absences are work-group size, peer relations, and the scope of work. Individuals who work with a small group of people are likely to feel a greater sense of responsibility to the group and thus miss work less often. Peer relations have a similar effect; employees who like and get along with fellow workers will tend to have more regular attendance than employees who do not feel as close to other workers.

Motivation to attend is related to sick-leave policy (whether one receives wages for days missed because of illness), work-group norms, an individual's personal work ethic, and his or her commitment to the organization.

Job satisfaction does not appear to be closely tied to employee attendance. Individuals who are members of cohesive groups with high satisfaction have low absenteeism, but when a group of cohesive workers express dissatisfaction with the job, absenteeism is usually higher (Steers & Rhodes, 1978).

Does teacher absenteeism translate into loss of student learning? The research on this question shows mixed results. Some studies show that students of teachers who miss school frequently have lower achievement test scores than those whose teachers were regular in attendance, whereas other studies found no relationship between the variables. However, there are at least two good reasons why excessive teacher absences should be discouraged and efforts made to reduce them. First, absenteeism costs the district money. A district with 500 teachers and a 4 percent absenteeism rate that pays substitutes $90 a day incurs additional costs of $324,000 a year for substitutes. Second, teacher absenteeism is related to student absences. Students of teachers who miss school frequently tend to have poor attendance records, too, and since school funds are usually distributed on the basis of attendance, schools with poor attendance receive less money from the state (Steers & Rhodes, 1978).

Of course, some absenteeism is legitimate and necessary. No employee should be encouraged to go to work when he or she is ill. To do so puts other workers at risk and increases the chances that the employee's condition will worsen. There are also times when a "mental health" day is in order. Taking a day off to rest can help a teacher feel relaxed and improve his or her ability to concentrate.

Principals of schools in which teachers are absent frequently can work to change the culture that permits or encourages absenteeism. During World War II, workers were reminded that missing work hindered the American war effort. This appeal to patriotism reduced the amount of time lost to absences and improved the output of both military and civilian goods. In the same way, if teachers understand that their contributions to student learning are important, most will respond to appeals to maintain continuity of instruction by reducing unnecessary absences.

Employee Assistance Programs in Schools

Employees' productivity may be affected by problems that originate on the job or elsewhere. In the past, supervisors could suggest that an employee with problems seek help, but if the worker chose not to do so, there was little the supervisor could do about it. Individuals with medical problems were usually willing to seek help because in most cases the employer provided insurance to cover the cost of medical care. But when the problem was not a medical one, many employees did not know where to go to find help, or if they did, they avoided going. Many of these cases involved individuals with problems of alcohol abuse, for which treatment was expensive and not readily available.

A number of companies instituted counseling programs to assist individuals whose work was affected by alcohol or drug abuse and other mental health or personal problems. Gradually, these programs came to be known as *employee assistance programs.* They are now widespread in industry and are becoming more commonplace in school districts.

An employee assistance program consists of policies and procedures for identifying and assisting employees whose personal or emotional problems hinder their job performance. Counselors in an employee assistance program also provide a valuable service by advising principals and other administrators about how to work more effectively with employees who have various kinds of mental health or personal problems (Hacker, 1986). Most administrators are not trained to work with problem employees, and they can perform their jobs more effectively if they have access to professional advice on dealing with such workers.

Wellness Programs

Because of escalating costs of all types of health care, many industrial concerns and some schools districts are now offering wellness programs, which emphasize good health practices for all employees. The idea of a wellness program is to help employees prevent illness by using sound judgment in decisions on nutrition, weight control, exercise, and use of drugs, tobacco, and alcohol.

Summary

All human beings want to experience psychological success. One of the most common ways by which they seek to do that is by performing competently in some personally valued task. Schools are structured in such a way that teachers frequently experience failure in their efforts to help children grow and develop.

Productive working environments are characterized by a continuing learning culture; supportive administrative leadership; opportunities to work collaboratively with others and receive respect from others, including administrators, colleagues, and parents; opportunities to use one's knowledge and skill and to receive feedback on one's performance; and the resources one needs to do the job.

Four types of leadership used by administrators to achieve desired results are directive, supportive, participative, and achievement-oriented leadership. All four types are appropriate in particular situations. Directive and achievement-oriented leadership behaviors provide clear guidelines for teachers to follow and make goals more salient. Supportive leadership increases trust between teachers and administrators and helps to foster norms of collegiality, which in turn facilitate the introduction of participative leadership. Participative leadership increases commitment to group decisions.

Teachers often experience stress because of the conditions under which they work. Conditions that are particularly conducive to stress are pressure to produce learning gains and disruptive and disrespectful students. Prolonged stress leads to physical and emotional symptoms characterized by a loss of interest in work and in the welfare of others. Administrators should be sensitive to the need to provide supportive leadership to alleviate teacher stress.

Employee assistance programs help individuals whose job performance is affected by personal or mental health problems. Wellness programs are designed to help all employees avoid illness by observing sound health practices.

Suggested Activities

1. An item that almost always shows up on lists of desirable characteristics of work environments in schools is *supportive administrative leadership.* Explain what is meant by that phrase and give one or two specific examples of it from your own experience. Tell what you think are the necessary ingredients of supportive leadership and why school employees attach so much importance to it. Are school personnel different from people in other occupations in this respect?

2. Suppose you are preparing for an interview for the position of assistant principal in a school. Write a list of questions you might ask the principal or other personnel in the school that would yield useful information about the environment of the school. Explain what you would expect to learn from the questions you wrote.

3. A number of people have observed that some stress is desirable and that the total absence of stress makes life boring. Nevertheless, individuals vary in their tolerance for stress. Is some stress acceptable to you? Think of one or two situations in which

you have experienced "pleasant" stress and an equal number in which you have experienced "unpleasant" stress. What is the difference between the two? Do you deal with "pleasant" stress differently from the way you handle "unpleasant" stress? If so, why? Do you agree that teaching is a "stressful" occupation? Why or why not?

4. Individuals value opportunities to work collaboratively with one another, but in schools such opportunities are few in number. Tell what action you might take as a school administrator to create an environment in a school that would increase the number of opportunities for personnel to work together.

Online Resources

Many educators are motivated less by salary and benefits than by the desire to perform a useful public service and work with children. Aside from that difference, however, teachers and workers in other occupations have very similar responses to conditions in the workplace. These sites are a source of useful information on factors that have a salutary effect on employee morale.

U.S. Bureau of Labor Statistics (stats.bls.gov/opbhome.htm)
> The BLS website contains extensive information about compensation, retirement planning, health and safety, and regional and national data on the employment outlook in a variety of occupations.

Roper Center for Public Opinion Research (www.ropercenter.uconn.edu/pubper/pdf/pp115c.pdf)
> This site reports the results of national surveys of workers' attitudes toward their jobs, their work, and their employers. Respondents to the surveys were from all kinds of occupations, and their responses suggest actions that deserve consideration in schools. Factors identified in the surveys that affect workers' satisfaction on the job include receiving recognition for accomplishments, availability of medical leave benefits, opportunity for promotion, salary level, and minimal levels of job-related stress.

Business.com (www.business.com/directory/human_resources/index.asp)
> This site is a rich source of full-text articles on many issues related to human resources management. Examples of topics covered are compensation and benefits, hiring and retention, labor law, and health and safety.

University of Oregon (eric.uoregon.edu/publications/digests/digest120.html)
> ERIC Digest 120 discusses factors that affect teacher job satisfaction and proposes steps to raise the morale of school employees.

References

Albrecht, K. (1979). *Stress and the manager.* Englewood Cliffs, NJ: Prentice Hall.

Bacharach, S. B., Bauer, S. C., & Shedd, J. B. (1986). The work environment and school reform. *Teachers College Record, 88,* 241–256.

Bruce, W., & Blackburn, J. (1992). *Balancing job satisfaction and performance: A guide for human resource professionals.* Westport, CT: Quorum.

Cawelti, G. (1994). *High school restructuring: A national study.* Arlington, VA: Educational. Research Service.

Cedoline, A. J. (1982). *Job burnout in public education.* New York: Teachers College Press.

Corbett, H. D. (1982). Principals' contributions to maintaining change. *Phi Delta Kappan, 64,* 190–192.

Corcoran, T. (1990). Schoolwork: Perspectives on workplace reform in public schools. In M. McLaughlin, J. Talbert, & N. Bascia (Eds.), *The contexts of teaching in secondary schools: Teachers' realities* (pp. 142–166). New York: Teachers College Press.

Deal, T. E. (1987). Effective school principals: Counselors, engineers, pawnbrokers, poets . . . or instructional leaders? In W. Greenfield (Ed.), *Instructional leadership: Concepts, issues, and controversies* (pp. 230– 245). Boston: Allyn and Bacon.

Dworkin, A. G. (1987). *Teacher burnout in the public schools: Structural causes and consequences for children.* Albany: State University of New York Press.

Freudenberger, H. (1977). Burn out: Occupational hazard of the child care worker. *Child Care Quarterly, 6,* 90–99.

Gross, N., & Herriott, R. (1965). *Staff leadership in public schools: A sociological inquiry.* New York: Wiley.

Guglielmi, R. S., & Tatrow, K. (1998, Spring). Occupational stress, burnout, and health in teachers: A methodological and theoretical analysis. *Review of Educational Research, 68,* 61–99.

Hacker, C. (1986). *EAP: Employee assistance programs in the public schools.* Washington, DC: National Education Association. (ERIC Document Reproduction Service No. ED 281267).

Hall, D. T., & Schneider, B. (1973). *Organizational climates and careers: The work lives of priests.* New York: Seminar Press.

Holcomb, E. (1993). *School-based instructional leadership: A staff development program for school effectiveness and improvement.* Madison, WI: National Center for Effective Schools.

House, R. L. (1971). A path-goal theory of leader-effectiveness. *Administrative Science Quarterly, 16,* 321–338.

Landy, F. J. (1985). *Psychology of work behavior.* Homewood, IL: Dorsey.

Lazarus, R. S. (1968). Stress. In D. L. Sills (Ed.), *International encyclopedia of the social sciences* (Vol. 15, pp. 337–348). New York: Macmillan.

Leithwood, K. A., & Montgomery, D. J. (1986). *Improving principal effectiveness: The principal profile.* Toronto: Ontario Institute for Studies in Education.

Lieberman, A. (1996, November). Creating intentional learning communities. *Educational Leadership, 54,* 51–55.

Litt, M. D., & Turk, D. C. (1985). Sources of stress and dissatisfaction in experienced high school teachers. *Journal of Educational Research, 78,* 178–185.

Little, J. W. (1981, April). *The power of organizational setting: School norms and staff development.* Paper presented at the annual meeting of the American Educational Research Association, Los Angeles. (ERIC Document Reproduction Service No. ED 221918).

Little, J. W., & Bird, T. (1987). Instructional leadership "close to the classroom" in secondary schools. In W. Greenfield (Ed.), *Instructional leadership: Concepts, issues, and controversies* (pp. 118–138). Boston: Allyn and Bacon.

London, M. (1998). *Career barriers: How people experience, overcome, and avoid failure.* Mahwah, NJ: Erlbaum.

Louis, K., & Smith, B. (1990). Teacher working conditions. In P. Reyes (Ed.), *Teachers and their workplace: Commitment, performance, and productivity* (pp. 23–47). Newbury Park, CA: Sage.

Maslach, C., & Pines, A. (1977). The burn-out syndrome in the day care setting. *Child Care Quarterly, 6,* 100–113.

McLaughlin, M. W., Pfeifer, R. S., Swanson-Owens, D., & Yee, S. (1986). Why teachers won't teach. *Phi Delta Kappan, 67,* 420–426.

McLaughlin, M. W., & Yee, S. M. (1988). School as a place to have a career. In A. Lieberman (Ed.), *Building a professional culture in schools* (pp. 23–44). New York: Teachers College Press.

Milstein, M. M., Golaszewski, T.J., & Duquette, R. D. (1984). Organizationally based stress: What bothers teachers. *Journal of Educational Research, 77,* 293–297.

National Center for Education Statistics. (1993a). *America's teachers: Profile of a profession.* Washington, DC: U.S. Department of Education.

National Center for Education Statistics. (1993b). *Schools and staffing in the United States: A statistical profile.* Washington, DC: U.S. Department of Education.

Olson, L. (1988, September 28). Work conditions in some schools said "intolerable." *Education Week,* pp. 1, 21.

Payzant, T. (1992). Empowering teachers and enhancing student achievement through school restructuring. In L. Frase (Ed.), *Teacher compensation and motivation* (pp. 454–481). Lancaster, PA: Technomic.

Prasch, J. (1990). *How to organize for school-based management.* Alexandria, VA: Association for Supervision and Curriculum Development.

Provenzo, E., & McCloskey, G. (1996). *Schoolteachers and schooling: Ethoses in conflict.* Norwood, NJ: Ablex.

Ryan, K., & Oestreich, D. (1991). *Driving fear out of the workplace.* San Francisco: Jossey-Bass.

Sack, J. (2000, October 25). CEC report tracks "crisis" conditions in special education. *Education Week,* 15.

Steers, R., & Rhodes, S. (1978). Major influences on employee attendance: A process model. *Journal of Applied Psychology, 63* (4), 391–407.

Talbert, J., & McLaughlin, M. (1996). Teacher professionalism in local school contexts. In I. Goodson & A. Hargreaves (Eds.), *Teachers' professional lives* (pp. 127–153). London: Falmer.

12

Legal Issues in Human Resources Management

The legal authority to employ, assign, transfer, suspend, and terminate teachers is assigned by the states to local school boards, and the boards are given wide latitude in the exercise of that power (Hudgins & Vacca, 1995). The large majority of personnel decisions are made by school boards on the recommendation of an administrator. For that reason, principals and district administrators who are involved in human resources management activities should be aware of legal ramifications of personnel decisions.

Although they delegate considerable power over personnel matters to school boards, the states set professional preparation requirements for teachers, counselors, and administrative personnel. The states also prescribe other qualifications for those positions, including age, moral character, and citizenship (*Education Law*, 1989).

Most of the actions taken during the process of recruitment, selection, and placement of employees—including advertising, preparation of application forms, and conducting interviews—are potential areas of legal vulnerability. Also included under the aegis of the law are decisions to transfer, promote, discipline, or dismiss employees. The best protection against violating these laws is to be well informed about statute and case law relating to the various facets of human resources management, which is the subject of this chapter.

Plan of the Chapter

This chapter covers the following topics: (1) state legislation and school boards, (2) antidiscrimination legislation, (3) types of discrimination, (4) defending personnel practices, and (5) affirmative action and reverse discrimination.

State Legislation and School Boards

The states delegate to school boards the authority to hire and assign or reassign and terminate employees. The states also establish rules governing the preparation and certification of professional personnel, including teachers, counselors, school social workers, school psychologists, and administrators. State laws and regulations specify the course of study that the various personnel must complete and stipulate licensing procedures, including tests of general or professional knowledge. School boards may establish higher standards than those specified by the state, but they may not lower the standards.

Most states require school personnel to be free of communicable diseases, and school boards sometimes establish other policies dealing with employee health. Some states prohibit school boards from establishing a residency requirement, but where it is permitted, courts have usually upheld residency rules as long as the boards were able to establish a rational basis for the policy (*Wardwell* v. *Board of Education of the City School District of Cincinnati,* 1976).

School boards have authority to assign teachers to a school, grade level, or subject, and may transfer teachers at will, as long as the individual is qualified to hold the position to which he or she is assigned. In some states the law places limitations on the board's freedom to transfer a teacher from a higher-paying to a lower-paying job or from a position of more to a position of less responsibility. In Colorado, for example, state law allows transfers of teachers upon the recommendation of the chief administrative officer of the district, provided the teacher's pay is not reduced from its current level for the remainder of that school year. Arizona, like many other states, permits governing boards to reduce salaries or eliminate positions in order to save money, but a board may not lower the salary of a certified teacher who has been employed by the district for three years, unless all salaries are reduced by a commensurate amount.

State laws also provide a number of safeguards and incentives for teachers, including the protection against a reduction in salary. Michigan law invalidates any contract or agreement between a teacher and a board under which the teacher would agree to waive any rights or privileges granted by state law. It also forbids school districts from assigning a teacher to more than one probationary period, thus denying districts the option of extending the probationary period for a teacher whose performance is not satisfactory. It is common for states to require that probationary teachers be notified by a certain date if their contracts will not be renewed for the following school year. If a district fails to notify a teacher that he or she will not be renewed, the contract is automatically extended for one year.

Alaska is one of the more generous states in providing incentives and protections for teachers. The law of that state requires school boards to provide information on the availability and cost of housing in rural areas and to assist teachers in finding a place to live; school districts are even empowered to lease housing in order to rent living space to teachers. Alaska law also guarantees a 30-minute duty-free lunch period for teachers in schools with four or more teachers and requires districts to pay moving expenses for teachers who are involuntarily transferred to a school that is more than a 20-minute drive from their current location. In Arizona, a teacher who returns to teaching in public schools after a stint in charter schools is protected against loss of certification, retirement, salary status, or any other benefit provided under the law or school board policy.

Some state legislation also provides incentives for substitute teachers. In Michigan, a substitute who teaches for 60 days in one assignment is granted the same privileges as full-time teachers, including leave time and a salary equal to or higher than the minimum salary on the district salary scale.

Antidiscrimination Legislation

Antidiscrimination legislation is intended to protect identified groups from bias in selection, salary, and promotion decisions. The federal government, most states, and many localities have laws that prohibit discrimination on the basis of race, color, religion, sex, disability, or national origin. Discrimination based on age, marital status, and sexual preference is also prohibited under some state laws (Hauck, 1998).

These laws make it illegal to recruit employees in such a way that protected groups are discouraged or prevented from applying. Employers may decide to recruit new workers by asking current employees to tell friends and relatives about a vacancy, but they may not legally limit recruiting to that method, since workers seldom recommend people of a different race. The employer is expected to advertise the vacancy widely so that all qualified prospects have a chance to learn about it (Sovereign, 1999). Discrimination occurs when decisions about selection, placement, promotion, compensation, discipline, or dismissal of individuals are made on the basis of characteristics other than qualifications, ability, and performance (McCarthy, 1983). A number of state and federal statutes, regulations, and executive orders forbid discrimination in recruiting, selecting, placing, promoting, and dismissing employees. In this section, some of the more important federal statutes relating to discrimination will be reviewed.

Civil Rights Act of 1964 and Pregnancy Discrimination Act of 1978

The most significant piece of legislation dealing with discrimination in employer/employee relations is the Civil Rights Act of 1964, as amended. Title VII of that act covers all employers with 15 or more employees, including state and local governments as well as schools and colleges. Religious institutions are exempt with respect to employment of persons of a specific religion.

The law prohibits discrimination with respect to compensation and terms, conditions, or privileges of employment on the basis of race, color, national origin, sex, or religion. The legislation also prohibits limiting, segregating, or classifying employees or applicants for employment in any way that deprives an individual of employment opportunities or otherwise adversely affects his or her status as an employee.

Title VII is administered by the Equal Employment Opportunity Commission (EEOC), which administers most federal legislation dealing with employment rights. Title VII requires that a charge of discrimination be investigated by a state or local agency if the employer is covered by a state or local fair employment practice law. Most states have such laws, which prohibit discrimination by employers on the basis of color, religion, sex, or national origin. Some also ban discrimination related to age, disability, marital status, physical appearance, sexual preference, and political affiliation (Hauck, 1998). The EEOC has no adjudicatory authority, but most claims of discrimination under Title VII must be reviewed by the EEOC before legal action is taken against an employer. If, following an investigation, the Commission concludes that the law has been violated, it attempts to persuade the employer to eliminate the illegal practice. If this approach does not work, the Commission will issue a finding confirming that a basis for legal action exists (van Geel, 1987).

The Pregnancy Discrimination Act of 1978 extended the protections of Title VII of the Civil Rights Act to pregnant employees. This law requires employers to treat pregnancy the same as other temporary medical condition. Except where state law establishes conditions that make separate policies necessary, school divisions are advised to establish a single policy on medical leave, including maternity leave (Hubbartt, 1993).

Title VII of the Civil Rights Act was amended by the Civil Rights Act of 1991. One of the amendments made it unlawful for an employer to adjust scores on employment tests or to set different cut-off scores for the purpose of benefiting applicants of a particular race, color, religion, sex, or national origin. Some affirmative action plans had adopted these practices for the purpose of giving minorities a slight advantage in selection, but Congress has outlawed that practice.

Age Discrimination in Employment Act of 1967

The Age Discrimination in Employment Act (ADEA) of 1967, as amended in 1986, enjoins discrimination against individuals above the age of 40 in hiring, assignment, training, promotion, and the terms and conditions of employment (McCarthy & Cambron-McCabe, 1992). Under the ADEA, employers may offer incentives to induce employees to retire early as long as such plans are not used to circumvent the intent of the legislation.

The legislation makes it unlawful to give preference to a younger person over an older one if the older person is within the protected range. For example, a district that promotes a 45-year-old employee rather than a 60-year-old because of the latter's age when the two are equally qualified would be guilty of age discrimination, just as it would be for promoting a 25-year-old employee over an equally qualified

40-year-old. The act offers no protection against discrimination based on age for individuals who are outside the protected range. Thus, refusing to hire a 21-year-old applicant on the basis of age is not unlawful.

An employer charged with violating the Age Discrimination in Employment Act may disprove the charge by showing bona fide occupational qualification (BFOQ). For example, a director hiring an actor to play the part of a 25-year-old man in a play could lawfully select a younger person over an applicant within the protected age range solely on the basis of age. An employer who uses age as a qualification for employment must be able to show a reasonable relationship between the requirement and job performance. This is usually done by citing a connection between employee age and safe performance (van Geel, 1987).

In the Civil Rights Act of 1991, Congress expressed a preference for submitting claims under ADEA to arbitration rather than litigating those charges in the courts. Employers have followed that advice as a way of reducing litigation costs (Thorne, 1996).

Equal Pay Act of 1963

The equal Pay Act of 1963 forbids an employer from paying higher wages to employees of one sex than it pays to those of the opposite sex for jobs that require equal skill, effort, and responsibility and that are performed under similar working conditions. Employers may not attempt to comply by reducing the wages of any employee. Exceptions are allowed for wages that are based on a seniority system or a merit pay plan. The Equal Pay Act applies to federal, state, and local governments as well as to private commercial and industrial firms. Enforcement of the act became the responsibility of the Equal Employment Opportunity Commission in 1979, but the statute is less frequently used than Title VII since a violation of one is also a violation of the other and most attorneys prefer to bring suit under Title VII (McCulloch, 1981).

A question that frequently arises in litigation having to do with equal pay is how similar duties must be in order for two jobs to be considered as meriting equal pay. Courts have not always been consistent in defining the degree of required difference (Schlei & Grossman, 1976). It is common for female custodians to be assigned tasks that are less physically demanding than those assigned to males. For example, male custodians may be responsible for removing snow from school sidewalks and driveways, whereas female employees escape that duty. Males may be required to climb a ladder to change lightbulbs, install wiring, repair air conditioning equipment, and perform other tasks that female employees are not asked to perform.

Given these differences in assigned duties, is it justifiable to pay higher wages to the male employees? In the cases that have been tried under the Equal Pay Act, the answer to that question given by the courts has most often been *no*. The courts have held that the differences in the duties required of male and female custodians were not great enough to justify wage differences favoring males.

As a general rule, wage differences in favor of one sex are more likely to be sustained by the courts if the additional duties of the higher paid sex require a significant percentage of the employees' time or if they can be shown to require significant extra effort (Schlei & Grossman, 1976). For example, a school board could justify paying a male soccer boys' coach more than it pays a female girls' soccer coach if it could show that the boys' team played more games and spent more time practicing than the girls' team.

Rehabilitation Act of 1973 and Americans with Disabilities Act of 1990

The Vocational Rehabilitation Act (VRA) of 1973 and the Americans with Disabilities Act (ADA) of 1990 prohibit discrimination in employment decisions against qualified individuals with disabilities. The VRA applies to federal contractors and agencies that receive financial assistance from the federal government, whereas the ADA applies to most employers with 15 or more employees.

Both acts provide that an individual with a disability who is able to perform the "essential functions" of a position, with or without reasonable accommodation, is qualified for consideration for a position and may not be refused employment solely on the basis of the disability. *Essential functions* are defined as primary duties that are intrinsic to a specific job, not including those of a peripheral nature (Jacobs, 1993).

Three questions that are used to help identify essential functions of a job are (Fersh & Thomas, 1993):

1. Does the position exist to perform the function?
2. Are there only a limited number of employees available to perform the function?
3. Is the function so highly specialized that the person holding the position is hired for his or her ability to perform that particular function?

To help answer those questions, consider information obtained from written job descriptions, estimates of time devoted to various functions, suggested consequences of not performing a particular function, and the terms and conditions of collective bargaining agreements (Fersh & Thomas, 1993).

Some jobs have a limited number of essential functions. For a school nurse, essential functions include the ability to apply first aid and make decisions regarding follow-up actions when a child is ill or injured—for example, whether to contact parents to take the child home or call emergency services. Other jobs have multiple essential functions. School counselors discuss problems of personal adjustment with students and work with them to find solutions. But counselors also help students locate information about prospective careers, calm anxious or upset parents, prepare and mail transcripts, and administer and interpret standardized tests. All of these functions are essential, but the position of counselor does not exist solely to perform one of these functions to the exclusion of the others.

The EEOC defines *reasonable accommodation* as a modification or adjustment in the way a job is ordinarily performed that enables a qualified individual with a disability to perform the job without imposing an undue hardship on the employer (Schneid, 1992). Examples of accommodations are providing entrance ramps to allow access to persons in wheelchairs, granting time off for medical treatments or physical therapy, and purchasing special equipment or adapting existing equipment to enable people with disabilities to perform a job.

Other forms of accommodation include hiring an assistant to perform the tasks that the employee with disabilities is unable to perform and restructuring work assignments to limit those employees' responsibilities to tasks that are within their capabilities. An employer is not required to make accommodations that are unduly costly or disruptive to the operation of the business or agency (Schneid, 1992).

A person is considered to be disabled if he or she has a physical or mental impairment that substantially limits one or more major life activities or is regarded as having such an impairment. Individuals who have undergone drug rehabilitation are considered to be disabled, but those who are currently using drugs are not. Homosexuality is not considered a disabling condition, but AIDS is (Schneid, 1992).

The law does not require an employer to hire a person with disabilities who is less qualified than a person with no disabilities, but it forbids employers from refusing to employ individuals solely on the basis of their possessing a disability. Employers may legally refuse to hire an applicant with disabilities whose employment in a particular position would result in creation of a safety hazard for the employee or others when it is not possible through reasonable accommodation to eliminate the danger (Gordon, 1992). However, the employer should be prepared to produce evidence that the claimed hazard is real and not simply a pretext.

Deciding whether to employ individuals with disabilities as teachers requires administrators to consider the safety and well-being of students as well as the rights of the disabled. Districts that are able to show that they have carefully weighed a disabled applicant's qualifications to perform the job with reasonable accommodation against the potential risk to students created by hiring the person stand a good chance of prevailing in court.

On the other hand, districts that refuse to consider a disabled applicant's qualifications are almost certain to lose a legal challenge. A district that declined to allow a blind applicant to take a qualifying examination for a teaching position on grounds that her blindness made her incompetent to teach sighted students lost its suit and was required by the court to hire the teacher and provide back pay and retroactive seniority (*Gurmankin v. Costanzo*, 1997).

Interviewers should ask applicants with disabilities to indicate how they will perform essential functions of the position for which they are applying and what accommodations they will need in order to carry out their duties. Requests for accommodation should be treated on an individual basis and decisions should take in account both the expected cost and the potential for creating hardships for other employees (Sovereign, 1999).

One question that is still largely unanswered is to what extent the law protects employees who contract contagious diseases. The Eleventh Circuit Court held that the legislation did not exclude persons with such conditions as long as their presence did not pose a risk to other people. The case involved a teacher who had been dismissed from her job because she had tuberculosis (*Arline* v. *School Board of Nassau County*, 1985).

Family and Medical Leave Act of 1993

The Family and Medical Leave Act (FMLA) was enacted to allow families to balance the demands of their jobs with the needs of their families. The act grants eligible employees up to 12 weeks of unpaid leave during a 12-month period to care for a newborn child, adopted child, or foster child; for personal illness; or to care for a parent, spouse, or child with a serious health problem. The legislation covers private employers with 50 or more employees and state and local government employers without regard to the number of people they employ. A *serious health condition* is defined by FMLA as a condition that requires in-patient care or continuing treatment by a health care professional. An individual may have a serious health condition under FMLA without qualifying for coverage under the Americans with Disabilities Act of 1990.

School Safety

In recent years, violent attacks against teachers and students by other students and, in a few cases, by intruders in schools, have raised public awareness of the importance of implementing measures to make schools safer. In 1994, Congress passed the Improving America's Schools Act, which included Title VII, known as the Safe and Drug Free Schools and Communities Act. The purpose of this legislation was to prevent violence in and around schools and to strengthen programs designed to prevent illegal use of alcohol, tobacco, and drugs. The legislation provides funds for programs designed to achieve those goals.

Several states have also enacted legislation intended to reduce the threat of violence in schools. Kentucky established a Center for Safe Schools, which collects data on school violence, conducts research, and disseminates information about successful school safety programs. The center also provides technical assistance to local schools in the state and administers grants to school districts. The center maintains an extensive clearinghouse on issues and best practices in school safety. The Internet address for the clearinghouse appears in the Online Resources section of this chapter.

Colorado law requires school boards to adopt and implement a safe school plan and mandates that principals report annually in writing about the learning environment of their schools, including attendance figures; dropout rate; disciplinary violations; possession of dangerous weapons, alcohol, drugs, or tobacco; and destruction or defacement of school property. The Colorado law also directs boards of education to adopt procedures to be followed in case a teacher is assaulted, harassed, or falsely accused of child abuse. The law requires that all new school employees be screened for previous criminal activity. The legislation is contained in Section 22-32-109.1 of Colorado Revised Statutes and can be accessed online.

Constitutional Protections

All U.S. citizens have certain protections under the Constitution. Freedom of speech, association, and religion are guaranteed by the First Amendment, and the rights of due process and equal protection are secured by the Fifth and Fourteenth Amendments, respectively. Privacy rights also derive from the Constitution (Sorenson, 1987).

The Supreme Court has held that the free speech right of school employees must be balanced by consideration for the efficient operation of schools. In reviewing a case in which a teacher was dismissed for making public statements critical of the school board and the administration (*Connick* v. *Myers*, 1983), the Supreme Court held that discussion of issues related to public concerns was protected under the First Amendment but that comments about issues of a personal nature were not so protected. Unfortunately, the distinction is clearer in theory than in practice.

Criticism by teachers of student grouping practices and of the quality of the educational programs have been held to be matters of public concern and thus entitled to protection (*Cox* v. *Dardanelle Public School District*, 1986; *Jett* v. *Dallas Independent School District*, 1986). However, statements that were critical of school officials for changing registration procedures and for delays in purchasing teaching materials were judged to be matters of personal concern and thus not protected (*Ferrara* v. *Mills*, 1986; *Daniels* v. *Quinn*, 1986).

The Seventh Circuit Court held that a district action prohibiting teachers from holding prayer meetings at school before the school day started did not infringe on the teachers' right of free speech (*May* v. *Evansville-Yanderburgh School Corporation*, 1986). The right to privacy has been cited as protecting women who choose to bear a child out of wedlock from adverse employment decisions (*Eisenstadt* v. *Baird*, 1972). Policies that require pregnant teachers to begin mandatory maternity leave at a specific point in the pregnancy have been held to deny teachers' rights to equal protection under the Fourteenth Amendment (Director, 1973).

Types of Discrimination

Title VII of the Civil Rights Act of 1964 prohibits overt discrimination, also known as *disparate treatment*. This is the most flagrant and, fortunately, also the least common form of discrimination. It occurs when an individual who is a member of a protected group and who qualifies for or holds a job is discriminated against for legally indefensible reasons.

A more common form of discrimination is *adverse impact,* which occurs when employment practices that are neutral in intent have a discriminatory effect on a protected group. This is the most common form of discrimination (Miner & Miner, 1978). Among actions that can lead to charges of adverse impact are using screening tests on which members of one group score lower than other groups and establishing educational or experience requirements that adversely affect members of a protected group.

Once an adverse impact claim is established, the district must show that the practice is valid for the purpose intended. This is a "business necessity" defense. The Supreme Court accepted such a defense in allowing the use of the National Teachers Examination (NTE) for teacher certification and to determine employee salaries (*United States* v. *State of South Carolina,* 1978). However, in *Griggs* v. *Duke Power Company* (1971), the Supreme Court held that the use of a test of general intelligence for selection purposes was discriminatory because the test had an adverse impact on minority applicants and had not been validated for use in employee selection. The use of an arbitrary cutoff score as part of a selection process without prior investigation of the potentially harmful effects of such a decision is likely to be successfully challenged (Beckham, 1985).

Perpetuation of past discrimination refers to the lingering effects of discriminatory practices after the practices themselves have ended. Under segregation in the South, for example, African American staff members were assigned to schools that enrolled only African American students. These were often schools with outdated facilities and limited budgets. After integration took place, the effects of previous personnel assignment practices lingered until districts took action to reassign personnel in order to achieve balance in the racial distribution of staff members.

The fourth type of discrimination is *failure to make accommodation.* Section 504 of the Rehabilitation Act of 1973 and the Americans with Disabilities Act of 1990 require employers to make reasonable accommodations in order to enable employees who have disabilities to perform a job. Reasonable accommodations include improving accessibility, restructuring jobs, modifying work schedules, designing flexible leave policies, adjusting or modifying examinations and training materials, and providing qualified aides or assistants (Fersh & Thomas, 1993).

Sexual Harassment

When it occurs on the job, sexual harassment is considered discrimination and is prohibited under Title VII of the Civil Rights Act. Charges of job-related sexual harassment may be analyzed under either the disparate treatment or adverse impact theories, depending on the situation (Lindemann & Kadue, 1992).

Sexual harassment claims are usually one of three types: unwelcome sexual advances, gender-based animosity, or a sexually charged workplace. *Quid pro quo* discrimination occurs when an employee is the object of sexual advances that involve explicit or implicit promises of employment benefits in return for sexual favors. Hostile environment discrimination results from other employees or supervisors engaging in conduct that is offensive to an employee because of his or her gender, even if the conduct is not sexual in nature. For example, a woman who joins a previously all-male work group may be subjected to hostile comments and treatment by the male members of the group because of her gender (Lindemann & Kadue, 1992). Even if the actions of employees are not sexually suggestive, they constitute sexual harassment if the intent is to embarrass or humiliate another employee or to prevent that individual from doing his or her best work.

The Supreme Court, in *Meritor Savings Bank* v. *Vinson* (1986), held that sexual harassment violates Title VII's prohibition against sex discrimination even if the loss incurred by the offended employee is psychological and not financial. *Meritor* involved a sexual harassment claim against a supervisor by a female employee. The woman admitted that she had voluntarily had sexual relations with her boss on numerous occasions. The bank argued that the voluntary nature of the liaison freed the bank from liability, but the Supreme Court held that the test for sexual harassment was whether the woman had indicated that the sexual advances were unwelcome (Lindemann & Kadue, 1992). In *Harris* v. *Forklift Systems, Inc.* (1993), the Court clarified somewhat the conditions under which sexual harassment creates a hostile or sexually charged working environment. In the Court's words:

> Whether an environment is "hostile" or "abusive" can be determined only by looking at all the circumstances, which may include the frequency of the discriminatory conduct, its severity, whether it is physically threatening or humiliating..., and whether it unreasonably interferes with an employee's work performance. The effect on the employee's psychological well-being is relevant in determining whether the plaintiff actually found the environment abusive. But while psychological harm, like any other relevant factor, may be taken into account, no single factor is required.

In a more recent case, the Court found an employer to be liable for the actions of its employees. In *Faragher* v. *Boca Raton* (1998), the Court reversed an Eleventh Circuit decision after a female lifeguard quit her job, charging that two male supervisors, by unwelcome touching and suggestive remarks, had created a sexually hostile workplace. The question was whether the employer (the city of Boca Raton, Florida) was liable for the actions of the supervisors. The lower court held that the city was not liable, but the Supreme Court reversed the appellate court, ruling that, since the employer had failed to exercise "reasonable care" to prevent and promptly correct any sexually harassing behavior, it was liable for the supervisors' actions. Increased litigation involving charges of sexual harassment has led to greater awareness of this problem but has also created confusion about what types of behavior are appropriate in the workplace.

If one is not already in effect, a policy should be developed by school districts designating an individual who is responsible for investigating charges of sexual harassment. The individual assigned to investigate should be someone who will treat the charges in a serious and professional manner, and the procedures followed should be thorough, prompt, and impartial.

The policy should also describe alternative procedures for investigating and acting on charges made by an employee against his or her immediate supervisor that do not require the employee to confront the supervisor. Care should be taken to avoid retaliating against employees who file charges of sexual harassment (Hubbartt, 1993).

Administrators must also be prepared to investigate charges of sexual harassment made by students against teachers, counselors, or other school personnel and, if a school employee is found guilty of harassment, to take prompt disciplinary action. Charges by students against school personnel are difficult to judge because of the strong emotions such charges arouse and because of the difficulty of proving or disproving them. Sexual attention from a teacher is often flattering to a young person, but it also produces feelings of confusion and guilt. Students occasionally lodge false charges of sexual advances against teachers in retaliation for something the teacher has done.

When the person charging sexual harassment is a student, the investigator must first establish that the student understands sexual harassment and is not simply misinterpreting harmless behavior. Most children today have a pretty clear idea about the types of behavior that are acceptable and unacceptable, but occasionally a child will misinterpret an innocent gesture by an adult. As a result, many teachers, counselors, and other personnel avoid touching students out of fear that they may be falsely charged with sexual harassment.

If the initial investigation establishes that the child understands sexual harassment and is not simply seeking revenge, the investigator's first concern must be to protect the child and any other children who might be at risk. If there is reason to believe that the child's charges have a basis in fact, police should be contacted. School personnel have a responsibility to protect children in their care from exploitation. No other responsibility is more important.

Defending Personnel Practices

If a district is charged with discrimination in hiring practices, it may be able successfully to defend its actions by showing that the relevant characteristics of the applicant pool are comparable to the characteristics of the employees hired. Thus, for example, if 15 percent of applicants are members of a protected group and the district can show that an equal or greater percentage of persons hired were members of that group, that constitutes *prima facie* evidence of the absence of disparate treatment.

A more stringent test involves a comparison of the characteristics of those hired with the characteristics of members of the labor pool. This was the test used by the courts in the *Hazelwood* case. Hazelwood School District was charged by the Justice Department with violating Title VII of the Civil Rights Act by failing to recruit and employ African American teachers. The district's attorneys argued that, since the percentage of African American teachers employed by the district equaled or exceeded the percentage of African American students, the district was in compliance. The Supreme Court ultimately ruled that the relevant comparison was not the ratio of teachers to students but rather the ratio of minority teachers employed by the district to the number of qualified minority persons in the labor pool in the St. Louis metropolitan area. Hazelwood lost the suit and was required to hire and give back pay to minority applicants who had previously been rejected (*Hazelwood School District* v. *United States*, 1977).

Preventing discrimination before it happens is preferable to correcting it after it has occurred. School districts can help prevent discrimination by adopting an equal employment opportunity policy and publicizing it in advertisements and employee handbooks and by ensuring that personnel practices conform to the policy. Adopting practices that advance the goal of equal opportunity ensures that the policy will have its intended effect.

Human relations personnel should be reminded periodically that all records—including personnel files, correspondence, and computer files—are subject to subpoena when a suit is filed against the district. Even email messages can be obtained by attorneys in the search for evidence that the district has performed actions that are illegal. A standard rule for human relations personnel should be: Never place anything in an employee's personnel file unless the individual has seen the document and signed a statement indicating that he or she is aware that it will be part of the personnel file. It is also recommended that employees have access to their personnel files periodically (Thome, 1996).

Establishing a Defense

Personnel practices that have disparate impact may nevertheless be allowed by the courts, provided that the district is able to show a bona fide occupational qualification (BFOQ) or business necessity. One school district was upheld by the courts after hiring a male applicant without a master's degree over a female with the degree by arguing the male could be hired at a lower salary and could also perform coaching duties. To successfully use business necessity as a defense, an employer must be able to show that the practice is necessary for the efficient operation of the district and that no acceptable alternatives with lesser adverse impact are available (Valente, 1980).

Exclusion refers to the degree of pervasiveness of a particular practice. If personnel practices occasionally result in adverse impact to members of protected groups, there is a lower level of legal vulnerability than if the practices consistently result in adverse impact upon those groups. Employers are most likely to win a legal challenge when a practice involves a low degree of exclusion and a high degree of business necessity. Employers are most vulnerable when exclusion is high and business necessity is low (Schlei & Grossman, 1976).

Other factors that are sometimes considered in discrimination cases are the degree of potential risk to human health and safety or the potential for economic loss resulting from employee performance. An airline company may be able to justify exclusionary selection practices in hiring pilots by showing that the practices are necessary to reduce the chance of injury or death to passengers resulting from performance of inadequately trained employees. A hospital might support exclusionary hiring practices by showing that they are necessary to protect the health of patients. Exclusionary practices may also be defended by showing that they reduce the amount of potential economic loss to the employer resulting from employees who lack essential skills. Employers whose work involves lower levels of risk would be held to a correspondingly lower level of exclusionary practice in hiring.

Accurate and detailed records are a necessity to a successful defense if a district is charged with discrimination in employment practices. It is recommended that the district human resources office maintain charts showing the age, race, color, sex, and national origin of all applicants and similar information about those hired. Since collecting such information on the application form itself may itself constitute *prima facie* evidence of discriminatory intent, it is advisable to use a pre-employment inquiry form to collect that data. This is a form that all applicants are asked to complete and return separately from the application form itself. The applicant has the option of filling out the preemployment inquiry anonymously in order to avoid the possibility of being identified.

The *Uniform Guidelines on Employee Selection Procedures* were developed jointly by the Equal Employment Opportunity Commission, the Departments of Justice and Labor, and the Civil Service Commission to meet the need for consistency in personnel selection. The guidelines apply to both private and public employers who are covered by federal equal opportunity legislation (*Uniform Guidelines*, 1978).

Affirmative Action and Reverse Discrimination

The intent of affirmative action is to open job opportunities that have traditionally been closed to minorities and women. The purpose is not, as some have assumed, to achieve "proportional representation through preferential hiring" (Fullinwider, 1980, p. 159). There is little disagreement on the need for and importance of providing educational and employment opportunities to members of groups that have been subject to discrimination. However, preferential hiring, which is one element of affirmative action, arouses strong feelings from both proponents and opponents (Fullinwider, 1980).

Amendments to Title VII of the Civil Rights enacted by Congress in 1991 made it unlawful for an employer to adjust scores on employment tests or set different cut-off scores for the purpose of benefiting applicants of one race, color, religion, sex, or national origin. Such actions are known as *reverse discrimination,* and the Supreme Court has placed limitations on programs with such provisions unless they serve a "compelling governmental interest" and are "narrowly tailored" to correct specific instances of past discrimination. Thus, any program that gives preference in hiring to minorities on the basis of generalized past discrimination is likely to be viewed by the Court as violating the constitutional guarantee of equal protection.

The Supreme Court upheld California's ban on affirmative action in programs of that state by refusing to review a decision of the appellate court, which had ruled that giving an advantage to members of one group in employment would penalize other groups. The appellate court held that Proposition 209 was constitutional, and the Supreme Court affirmed the decision. The California law adopted after the passage of Proposition 209 states that "the state shall not discriminate against, or grant preferential treatment to, any individual or group on the basis of race, sex, color, ethnicity or national origin in the operation of public employment, public education or public contracting."

Reverse discrimination occurs when members of a protected group such as African Americans or females are given preference in employment decisions in order to correct the effects of previous discrimination. These actions have been approved by the courts when they have been designed specifically to correct past discrimination and do no unnecessary harm to the rights of other employees.

Actions by school districts to protect the jobs of minorities when layoffs occur were the subject of Supreme Court review in *Wygant* v. *Jackson Board of Education* (1986). In that case, the Board of Education of Jackson (Michigan) and the Jackson Education Association had agreed that the district would maintain a constant proportion of minority workers, which meant that white employees with more seniority were laid off while less senior minority employees kept their jobs. The district argued that this remedy was necessary because of the severity and duration of societal discrimination. The Court ruled that racial classifications must be justified by a compelling state purpose and that societal discrimination alone is not a sufficient justification.

Summary

Local school boards have the authority to employ, assign, transfer, suspend, and terminate teachers, and they are given wide latitude by the courts in the exercise of that power. States require teachers to have a valid teaching certificate. Boards may assign teachers to schools as long as there is no violation of the bargaining agreement or the teachers' contract. Reassignments are subject to legal challenge if they involve a demotion, but most courts have upheld the board in these cases.

Title VII of the Civil Rights Act affords protection against discriminatory employment decisions based on race, color, sex, religion, and national origin for all employees. The Pregnancy Discrimination Act extended the same protections to pregnant employees. The Age Discrimination in Employment Act protects employees above the age of 40 from age discrimination in personnel decisions, and the Equal Pay Act requires employers to pay women the same as men who perform similar jobs. The Rehabilitation Act and Americans with Disabilities Act make it illegal for employers to refuse to hire persons with disabilities because of their disabilities and require employers to make reasonable accommodations for such employees. The Family and Medical Leave Act of 1993 allows employees to take time off from work when they have illness in the family or a newborn or adopted child.

Restrictions on affirmative action have been put in place by Congress and the Supreme Court. It is now illegal to adjust test scores for the purpose of giving an advantage to minorities or other groups, and state laws limiting affirmative action have been upheld by the Supreme Court.

Suggested Activities

1. Examine the State Code of your state and identify the qualifications for teachers, counselors, and administrators. What qualifications are listed besides educational ones?

2. All states require teachers and other professional personnel to be licensed. They also provide for revocation of the license. What are the conditions in your state for which a professional license may be revoked? Does the State Code spell out due process rights of employees whose licenses are revoked? If so, what are they?

3. Obtain a copy of a sexual harassment policy for a school district and answer these questions:
   a. What actions does the policy require a supervisor to take when he or she first learns about a charge of sexual harassment by a person whom he or she supervises?
   b. What procedures are recommended to ascertain the facts about a harassment charge?
   c. What corrective actions are suggested or required when a charge of sexual harassment is confirmed?

4. Suppose that you are the principal of a middle school. One of your teachers belongs to a religious group that requires its members to observe six holy days each year. Members are required to be absent from their work on those days. The bargaining agreement provides for three religious holidays and three days for conducting "necessary personal business." Personal business days are granted only if the employee can demonstrate need. The teacher in your school asks that he be allowed to use the personal business days for religious observance. This has not been done previously in the district. What will you tell the teacher? (The Supreme Court decided a similar case in *Ansonia Board of Education* v. *Philbrook*, 1986).

5. Read Case Study II (at the end of the book) and answer the questions following the case.

Online Resources

These sites provide information on legal issues in human resources management.

Centers for Disease Control (www.cdc.gov/ncipc/dvp/yvpt/partner.htm)
   This resource provides links to organizations and agencies that supply information on and assistance in preventing and coping with youth violence.

Equal Employment Opportunity Commission (www.eeoc.gov/index.html)
   This site contains information on federal laws prohibiting job discrimination enforced by EEOC. News of recent EEOC decisions and information on technical assistance and training are also given.

Findlaw (www.findlaw.com)
> Searchable databases of state statutes and court decisions as well as federal laws and court rulings are provided. Advice on various aspects of human resources management is given at (http://smallbiz.biz.findlaw.com).

Kentucky Center for Safe Schools (http://kysafeschools.org/clear/index.html)
> The Clearinghouse locates and evaluates information on school safety practices and disseminates the information through the Internet and by CDs, print, and email newsletters.

Library of Congress (lcweb.loc.gov/global/state/stategov.html)
> The Library of Congress website contains full texts of state statutes as well as legislative updates.

References

Ansonia Board of Education v. *Philbrook,* 478 U.S. 1034, 1047 (1986).

Arline v. *School Board of Nassau County,* 772 F.2d 759 (1985).

Beckham, J. (1985). *Legal aspects of employee assessment and selection in public schools.* Topeka, KS: National Organization on Legal Problems of Education.

Connick v. *Myers,* 461 U.S. 138 (1983).

Cox v. *Dardanelle Public School District,* 790 F.2d 668 (1986).

Daniels v. *Quinn,* 801 F.2d 687 (1986).

Director, J. (1973). Mandatory maternity leave, rules or policies for public school teachers as constituting violation of equal protection clause of Fourteenth amendment to Federal Constitution. *American Law Reports federal cases and annotations* (17 ALR 768). Rochester, NY: Lawyers Co-operative Publishing.

Education law (Vol. 2). (1989). New York: Matthew Bender.

Eisenstadt v. *Baird,* 405 U.S. 438 (1972).

Faragher v. *Boca Raton,* 111 F.3d 1530 (1998).

Ferrara v. *Mills,* 781 F.2d 1508 (1986).

Fersh, D., & Thomas, P. (1993). *Complying with the Americans with Disabilities Act: A guidebook for management and people with disabilities.* Westport, CT: Quorum.

Fullinwider, R. (1980). *The reverse discrimination controversy: A moral and legal analysis.* Totowa, NJ: Rowman & Littlefield.

Gordon, P. (1992). The job application process after the Americans with Disabilities Act. *Employee Relations Law Journal, 18,* 185–213.

Griggs v. *Duke Power Company,* 401 U S 424 (1971).

Gurmankin v. *Costanzo,* 556 F.2d 184 (1977).

Harris v. *Forklift Systems, Inc.* 510 U.S. 17 (1993).

Hauck, V. (1998). *Arbitrating sex discrimination grievances.* Westport, CT: Quorum.

Hazelwood School District v. *United States,* 433 U.S. 299 (1977).

Hubbartt, W. (1993). *Personnel policy handbook.* New York: McGraw Hill.

Hudgins, H., Jr., & Vacca, R. (1995). *Law and education: Contemporary issues and court decisions* (4th ed.). Charlottesville, VA: Michie.

Jacobs, R. (1993). *Legal compliance guide to personnel management.* Englewood Cliffs, NJ: Prentice Hall.

Jett v. *Dallas Independent School District,* 798 F.2d 748 (1986).

Lindemann, B., & Kadue, D. (1992). *Primer on sexual harassment.* Washington, DC: Bureau of National Affairs.

May v. *Evansville-Vanderburgh School Corporation,* 787 F.2d 1105 (1986).

McCarthy, M. (1983). Discrimination in employment. In J. Beckham & P. Zirkel (Eds.), *Legal issues in public school employment* (pp. 22–54). Bloomington, IN: Phi Delta Kappa.

McCarthy, M., & Cambron-McCabe, N. (1992). *Public school law: Teachers' and students' rights* (3rd ed.). Boston: Allyn and Bacon.

McCulloch, K. (1981). *Selecting employees safely under the law.* Englewood Cliffs, NJ: Prentice Hall.

Meritor Savings Bank v. *Vinson,* 106 S.Ct. 2399 (1986).

Miner, M., & Miner, J. (1978). *Employee selection within the law.* Washington, DC: Bureau of National Affairs.

Schlei, B., & Grossman, P. (1976). *Employment discrimination law.* Washington, DC: Bureau of National Affairs.

Schneid, T. (1992). *The Americans with Disabilities Act: A practical guide for managers.* New York: Van Nostrand Reinhold.

Sorenson, G. (1987). Employees. In S. Thomas (Ed.), *The yearbook of school law* (pp. 1–44). Topeka, KS: National Organization on Legal Problems of Education.

Sovereign, K. (1999). *Personnel law.* Upper Saddle River, NJ: Prentice Hall.

Thome, J. (1996). *A concise guide to successful employment practices* (2nd ed.). Chicago: CCH Inc.

Uniform Guidelines on Employee Selection Procedures. (1978). Available online: www. uniformguidelines.com/uniformguidelines.html.

United States v. *State of South Carolina,* 434 U.S. 1026 (1978).

Valente, W. (1980). *Law in the schools.* Columbus, OH: Merrill.

van Geel, T. (1987). *The courts and American education law.* Buffalo, NY: Prometheus.

Wardwell v. *Board of Education of the City School District of Cincinnati,* 529 F.2d 625 (1976).

Wygant v. *Jackson Board of Education,* 476 U.S. 267 (1986).

13

Collective Bargaining in Schools

The work of most teachers in schools in the United States is governed by negotiated contracts between teachers' organizations and boards of education. The process by which the parties reach agreement on a contract is known as *collective bargaining*. Collective bargaining originated early in the twentieth century as industrial unions fought successfully for better working conditions and the right to participate in decisions about their work.

The National Education Association (NEA), the larger of two national organizations that represent teachers, is not affiliated with the labor movement, preferring the designation "professional organization." However, in its actions, NEA resembles industrial unions; its tactics and objectives are quite similar to those of the American Federation of Teachers (AFT), which is the other, smaller organization for teachers. The AFT is affiliated with the national labor movement.

Board negotiators are sensitive to the dollar costs of union proposals but pay less attention to their potential impact on instructional quality. The unions seek provisions to protect job security, establish satisfactory conditions of work, and guarantee generous salaries and benefits. These and other similar provisions may create barriers to improved instruction by limiting the district's power to dismiss or transfer employees, change job descriptions, or alter staffing patterns. Once incorporated into the contract, they are difficult to change, and improving instruction becomes dependent on the willingness of the union to accept modifications in the contract.

Plan of the Chapter

This book advocates an approach to collective bargaining that encourages negotiators to consider the potential effects on instruction of contract proposals, in addition to the usual attention given to issues of cost and security. The following topics

218

are covered in this chapter: (1) background on collective bargaining in schools, (2) scope of bargaining, (3) new forms of collective bargaining, (4) negotiating processes, and (5) impact of collective bargaining on schools.

Background on Collective Bargaining in Schools

Collective bargaining has been called one of the three most significant developments in public education in the past half century (Mitchell, Kerchner, Erck, & Pryor, 1981).* (The other two are desegregation and the introduction of categorical aid programs by the federal government.)

In 1959, Wisconsin became the first state to pass legislation governing collective bargaining between teacher unions and school boards (Cresswell & Murphy, 1980). Since that time, about 80 percent of the states have enacted enabling legislation. These laws vary in the degree of regulatory specificity and in the types of rights accorded unions. Some statutes provide an opportunity for teachers' unions to "meet and confer" with school boards, whereas others contain detailed and specific lists of what may and may not be negotiated.

The right to "meet and confer" gives employees' organizations an opportunity to meet with the board to argue for improvements in worker security, conditions of work, and benefits. The board is obligated to hear the teachers' presentation but is free to ignore their suggestions. "Meet and confer" is based on an assumption of commonality of interests of teachers and board members and it is the first stage in the evolution of a stable relationship between unions and boards.

The first stage breaks down when teachers realize that their goals are in conflict with those of the board, and teachers turn to militant tactics to win concessions, leading to acrimonious exchanges and occasional strikes (Jessup, 1981). Out of the conflict and strife emerges a second stage in the relationship, characterized by more equitable distribution of power (Mitchell et al., 1981).

This "second generation" of labor relations is characterized by acceptance by boards of teachers' right to bargain and by reduced conflict between the parties, leading to a period of relative stability (Mitchell et al., 1981). Teachers' organizations frequently wield considerable power during this stage.

A more mature "third generation" of labor relations begins when parents begin to demand action to improve instruction and removal of incompetent teachers, or when the board decides on its own to initiate such actions. At this stage, boards are generally more sensitive to teachers' rights to due process and are aware of past neglect of those rights. When boards with a strong commitment to quality education demonstrate a willingness to involve teachers in decisions on curriculum and instruction, significant progress can result (Mitchell et al., 1981).

*Material from D. Mitchell, C. Kerchner, W. Erck, and G. Pryor reprinted from "The Impact of Collective Bargaining on School Management and Policy," *American Journal of Education, 89,* 147–188. © 1981 University of Chicago Press. Used by permission.

Private Sector Bargaining

Collective bargaining in the private sector is regulated by the National Labor Relations Act, but there is no comparable federal statute governing bargaining involving public employees. Collective bargaining for public employees is governed by state statutes, case law, and administrative regulations (Cresswell & Murphy, 1980). Some state statutes are comprehensive, applying to all public employees, but others apply only to teachers.

There is general agreement on several points, however:

1. Strikes of public employees are unlawful or, if permitted, are closely regulated. Nevertheless, strikes among teachers are fairly common.
2. Bargaining units may not represent members of more than one employee group (Cresswell & Murphy, 1980). Both teachers and administrators may negotiate with the board, but they may not be represented by the same organization.
3. Parties are allowed to negotiate a procedure for resolving impasses and disagreements regarding interpretation of the contract. In some cases, the state requires binding arbitration if the parties are not able to arrive at a contract (Cresswell & Murphy, 1980).
4. When one organization represents all workers, it is called an *exclusive representative;* if each organization represents only its own members, it is called a *proportional representative.*

Scope of Bargaining

Topics of discussion between teacher organizations and boards of education are determined by the legal framework governing bargaining, the history of the relationship between the parties, and their willingness to negotiate an issue (Cresswell & Murphy, 1980). Legislation may specify mandatory topics (those about which the parties must negotiate) and exclude others from the bargaining table. Any topic that is not specifically mandated or forbidden is subject to negotiation if the parties agree. A list of items that are often included in teacher contracts appears in Exhibit 13.1.

Unions like to widen the scope of the negotiations to cover as many aspects of the work situation as possible. However, management generally prefers to limit the scope of the talks in the belief that anything not covered in the contract remains a prerogative of management (Mitchell et al., 1981). In addition to negotiating salaries and conditions of work, teacher unions favor including in the contract policies relating to the curriculum, student placement, and teacher selection and assignment. Almost half (46 percent) of agreements in effect during the 1981–82 school year contained provisions on curriculum. About 64 percent had policies on student placement, and 96 percent provided for policies relating to teacher selection and assignment (Goldschmidt, Bowers, Riley, & Stuart, 1984).

EXHIBIT 13.1   *Typical Provisions of Negotiated Agreements between Teachers and Boards of Education*

Recognition
School calendar
Improvement of instructional programs
Parent/teacher conferences
Personnel evaluation
Salary and benefits
Students
   Discipline
   Report cards
Substitute teachers
Teachers' professional rights
   Leave policy
   Professional development
   Privacy rights
   Personal safety and security
Teacher transfer and promotion
Teachers' workload
   Class size limitations
   Extracurricular duties
   Number of preparations
Teaching conditions
   Hours of work
Union rights and activities

Some contract provisions have more impact on instruction than others. Examples of proposals that could have an effect on instruction are shown in Figure 13.1. The figure shows the positions taken by the union and the board of education on each issue. In the middle, a marker indicates the position that would be most likely to promote instructional quality. The nearer the mark appears to the position taken by one of the parties, the greater the likelihood that that party's position is instructionally responsible. The issues are discussed in the paragraphs that follow.

Teacher Evaluation

Through collective bargaining, teachers' unions push to include in the contract restrictions on evaluation practices that they believe are unfair or that might be used by administrators to punish teachers. The restrictions include limiting when and where teacher observations can be held and what data may be included in written evaluations. Unions also seek to write into the contract prohibitions against evaluating teachers on the use of one approved model of instruction, arguing that teachers may achieve equally good results using a variety of approaches (Black, 1993).

FIGURE 13.1   *Location of Most Instructionally Effective Position between Opposing Demands of Teacher Union and Board on Selected Issues*

Issue	Teacher Position
Teacher evaluation	Limited number of classroom observations with advance notice
Transfer and reassignment	More senior teachers have choice of teaching assignments; no involuntary transfers
Selection	Teacher committee decides which applicants are hired
Class size	Specified upper limit; class divided or aide provided if limit exceeded
Preparations	Limit on number; additional planning time provided if exceeded
Extra duty	Duties required only if stated in agreement; pay for all extra duty
Planning time	Minimum number of minutes per week; no exceptions
Curriculum and textbook committees	Teachers volunteer and are paid extra
Reduction in force	Enrollment loss and program change only basis for reduction
	Reductions absorbed by attrition whenever possible; otherwise seniority governs
Working conditions	Require daily preparation period for elementary and secondary teachers; limit classroom interruptions; provide teaching supplies and individual desk, filing cabinet, and storage space for all teachers
Safety and security	District will reimburse all teachers for medical expenses and loss or destruction of property from a physical attack occurring on or near school property; district will take action leading to arrest and conviction of individuals involved in physical attack on a teacher

The negotiated agreement between Seattle Public Schools and the Seattle Education Association contains examples of provisions dealing with teacher evaluation that are commonly found in such contracts as well as one provision that is not often found in these agreements. Article XI of the Seattle agreement states that "a meaningful and effective evaluation process is based on the principles of mutual respect, shared accountability, and continuous improvement." It further states that supervisors "shall conduct an initial meeting" with employees by November 1 for the purpose of discussing the evaluation process and the evaluation criteria and to communicate performance goals and expectations. By the end of May, the evaluator must complete an evaluation form and provide a copy to

FIGURE 13.1   *Continued*

Instructionally Effective Position						Board Position
—	—	—	—	X	—	No limit, no advance notice
—	—	—	—	X		Administrators decide, considering teachers' expressed preferences
—	—	X	—	—	—	Principal decides which applicants are hired
—	—	—	X	—	—	Principal decides optimum number based on teacher skills, budget, and student needs
—	—	X	—	—	—	Principal considers number of preparations but no absolute limit on number
—	—	—	X	—	—	Duties performed as needed upon assignment by principal; pay only if contract requires
—	X	—	—	—	—	Provided within limits of available resources
—	X	—	—	—	—	Teachers volunteer or are appointed; no extra pay
—	—	—	—	X	—	Enrollment loss, program change, budget cutbacks, and other factors allowed
—	—	—	—	X	—	Reductions absorbed by attrition if possible; otherwise seniority and other factors govern
X	—	—	—	—	—	Provide preparation period for secondary teachers when practicable; provide teaching supplies, furniture, and equipment appropriate for the type of instruction
—	—	—	—	X	—	District will provide free insurance to cover medical expenses and loss or destruction of personal property resulting from a physical attack on school property; district will provide assistance of the association attorney in pursuing legal action against an attacker

each employee with the understanding that the employee may add his or her comments to the form.

A less common provision in the Seattle contract states that a joint bargaining committee "will seek to develop a system to be used district wide for measuring the growth in student achievement on a classroom-by-classroom basis and using such measurements in teacher evaluation. The focus in measuring student achievement shall be on the progress students have made over the course of the academic year." The agreement also states that no teacher may be evaluated as unsatisfactory in the first two years the contract is in force on the basis of student achievement alone (Washington Education Association, 2001).

Transfer and Reassignment/Selection

Teacher transfer and reassignment policies have long been an area of contention between boards and unions (McDonnell & Pascal, 1979). Teacher unions prefer limiting involuntary transfers to situations involving declining enrollment or changes in programs and favor making seniority the sole criterion for deciding who is transferred (Cresswell & Murphy, 1980). Board negotiators favor allowing administrators to make these decisions under more general guidelines.

The importance for teacher morale of contractual safeguards against arbitrary decisions on transfer and reassignment should not be underestimated, but neither should the potential negative consequences for the quality of instruction be overlooked. A principal who is prevented from selecting the most qualified teacher is hampered in trying to improve the quality of learning in the school.

As school restructuring efforts proceed, organized teachers in some areas are pressing for authority to play a more active role in personnel decisions, arguing that this empowers teachers. They advocate a more direct voice for teachers in teacher selection and favor assigning teachers responsibility for assisting colleagues who are performing unsatisfactorily and for providing training for mentor teachers in induction programs. Boards generally agree to teacher participation in these matters but view teacher control as intrusion and resist it.

Some negotiated contracts contain clauses prohibiting discrimination against employees by either the union or the board. When discrimination is suspected, the employee has a choice of filing a grievance, which may ultimately be decided by arbitration, or bringing suit under a state or federal statute such as Title VII. The U.S. Supreme Court has on at least one occasion voiced concern about handling discrimination claims through arbitration. Since the procedures used in arbitration are somewhat less formal than those followed in court proceedings, the justices questioned whether arbitration would result in a thorough and fair outcome. As a general rule, transcripts of arbitration proceedings are less complete, and procedures that are routinely followed in a courtroom—such as discovery, cross-examination, and testimony under oath—are often ignored in arbitration hearings. The Supreme Court was concerned that the more lax rules and procedures common to arbitration proceedings might result in questionable decisions (Hauck, 1998).

Class Size/Preparations

Class size is another contentious issue between boards and teacher associations. The union argues that limiting class size facilitates teachers' work, and boards answer that reducing class size by even a small amount is expensive and produces no verifiable increase in student learning. Boards are especially opposed to provisions that require dividing a class or providing an aide if enrollment exceeds a stated limit by only one or two students.

Limits on the number of different preparations a teacher may be assigned make sense from the point of view of instructional effectiveness. Again, however, such a policy is difficult to administer if expressed in absolute terms with no room allowed for administrative judgment.

Extra Duty

Unions prefer that the contract specify the extra duties teachers are required to perform and include rules to ensure fairness in the assignment of those duties. They also favor provisions for additional pay for noninstructional tasks.

Duties that have traditionally been a part of teachers' responsibilities, such as sponsoring clubs and meeting with parents, have become optional under most negotiated agreements. In districts that do not pay extra for them, these jobs are often not done. Even teachers who are willing to donate their time are discouraged from doing so by union officers anxious to preserve the principle of extra pay for extra work (Mitchell et al., 1981).

Some extra duties are necessary for the efficient operation of the school, but an excessive number can interfere with good instruction. It is not always possible to anticipate what duties may be necessary, so some flexibility is needed. Everything considered, the best solution seems to be to include in the contract a statement acknowledging the administration's responsibility for fair and judicious use of extra duty and providing extra pay for the more time-consuming tasks. The statement should also acknowledge teachers' responsibility to perform the duties.

Planning Time

Teachers seek to include in the contract a statement that guarantees a minimum number of minutes of planning time each week. From an instructional point of view, these regulations are desirable, but overly prescriptive rules should be avoided.

Curriculum and Textbook Committees

The majority of contracts contain no provision dealing with curriculum revision and textbook selection committees (Cresswell & Murphy, 1980). These committees perform important functions, and teachers who serve on them should receive payment for their time.

Reduction in Force

Both sides have an interest in limiting the impact of reduction in force on employee morale. Usually both teacher and board negotiators are willing to discuss the order of release, but they sometimes disagree on the criteria to be used. Unions prefer that seniority be the only factor considered, whereas management argues for allowing considerations of performance and program needs in making reduction-in-force decisions (Cresswell & Murphy, 1980).

Reduction in force can impact instruction by depleting the faculty of a school of persons qualified to teacher certain subjects and by triggering bumping, which may lead to less qualified teachers taking over for those who are more qualified. Chapter 15 discusses this topic in more detail.

Working Conditions

Teachers favor required planning periods and ample supplies and materials. These are not unreasonable expectations and are necessary for good instruction. Boards are usually supportive of these requests.

Safety and Security

Teachers are justifiably concerned about their safety and that of the students with whom they work. Although the number of violent attacks in schools is small, the possibility of one is always present, and teachers are reasonable in asking boards to take action to reduce the risk. However, legal action against those who perpetrate attacks is the province of civil authorities and not the school board.

New Forms of Collective Bargaining

In recent years, a search has been undertaken to find new approaches to collective bargaining that will permit the parties to reach agreements more quickly and encourage boards and unions to cooperate in the interest of improving education. Several new models have been tried, with varying degrees of success. Among the new approaches are expedited bargaining, progressive bargaining, the win/win approach, principled negotiations, and strategic bargaining.

In *expedited bargaining,* the parties agree to limit the amount of time available to reach an agreement and the number of issues that will be discussed. The time limit is usually two to three weeks and the number of items to be discussed is usually no more than 10. Expedited bargaining avoids the protracted discussions that have in the past held up school operations and planning while negotiations were underway (National Education Association, 1991).

Progressive bargaining is the opposite of expedited bargaining. Progressive bargaining is intended to permit full discussion of any issue that either party wishes to raise. Because of the number of issues examined and the amount of time spent on each one, progressive bargaining sometimes continues for months. Issues are referred to subcommittees for study, and if a stalemate is reached, fact finding and mediation are used to resolve the impasse (National Education Association, 1991).

Win/win bargaining was developed by a sociology professor, Irving Goldaber, who specialized in conflict resolution and hostage intervention. This form of bargaining is highly structured, and includes detailed rules that govern negotiating sessions. At the outset, participants must agree that the needs of the institution take precedence over individual goals (Booth, 1993). Some authorities describe win/win bargaining as an "attempt to bring civility to teacher bargaining" but criticize it because unions attempt to use the process to increase teacher power at the expense of the board's prerogatives. According to these critics, a school board that accepts limitations on its authority in order to maintain a collaborative relationship with the teachers' union is likely to find itself hamstrung in trying to improve educational quality or introduce efficiency measures (Geisert & Lieberman, 1994).

Principled negotiations was developed by the Harvard University Negotiation Project and is intended for use in any setting, including negotiations between employers and employees. The objective of this approach is to allow both parties to benefit without compromising their interests (Fisher & Ury, 1981, 1988). The principled negotiations approach provides a set of guidelines for negotiators that help remove the most common stumbling blocks to agreement. Among these guidelines are the following (National Education Association, 1991):

1. *Separate the people from the problem.* Negotiators are encouraged to accept emotions expressed by the other side and to allow people to let off steam without reacting angrily. Negotiators are urged to listen actively and speak clearly.
2. *Focus on interests, not positions.* An individual's or group's position on an issue is a way of advancing an underlying interest. By trying to identify the interest, bargaining partners can identify other, more acceptable, positions that may be equally effective at advancing their interests.
3. *Invent options for mutual gain.* The idea here is to create new choices that satisfy both shared and separate interests. This guideline helps avoid situations in which both parties lock in to positions early and refuse to yield. It also helps the parties refrain from the assumption that a win for one side necessarily signifies a loss for the other.
4. *Evaluate options, not power.* The parties to the negotiations should establish a set of criteria by which proposals will be judged. The criteria might include fairness, cost, and practicality. In the absence of criteria, the final outcome is often determined by which party is more unyielding in its positions.

Strategic bargaining is the negotiating counterpart to strategic planning. In this approach, the parties are urged to develop a vision of the future for their organization and to identify potential hurdles that might be encountered in trying to actualize that vision. The power of strategic bargaining is its focus on the future and the underlying assumption that labor and management must contribute to building the future, that neither can do it alone (National Education Association, 1991).

Negotiating Processes

Both sides in collective bargaining know that they have the power to inflict damage on the other. The board can withhold the concessions teachers seek, and teachers can strike. (Even in localities in which strikes are unlawful, unions are sometimes willing to risk them in order to extract concessions.) Most of the time, collective bargaining works because the two sides develop a level of trust that allows them to work cooperatively to reach a mutually acceptable agreement. This trust does not emerge immediately, however. As with most human exchanges, development of trust between negotiators takes time.

Successful negotiations occur in three stages, as depicted in Figure 13.2. In the first stage, demands are heard and the parties agree on the issues to be negotiated and the order in which items are to be taken up (Lipsky & Conley, 1986). Board representatives sometimes try to postpone negotiating economic issues in hopes that the union will make concessions on other items in order to proceed more quickly to wages and benefits (Geisert & Lieberman, 1994). During the second stage, parties come to acknowledge one another's legitimacy and begin developing trust. In the third stage, serious bargaining takes place, with both parties making concessions on less vital issues in order to prevail on more important questions (Lipsky & Conley, 1986).

Both sides learn what the other side hopes to gain from the negotiations early in the process, but it takes longer for them to begin to get a picture of what the other is willing to accept. Bargaining proceeds through a series of give-and-take exchanges with each party yielding on some demands in return for concessions from the other side (Mitchell et al., 1981). Teacher negotiators, for example, may demand a 10 percent salary increase, expecting to settle for 7 or 8 percent and prepared to strike if the board does not come through with at least 6.5 percent. The board, on the other hand, may approach the table prepared to offer 6 percent but preferring to settle for 5.5. Obviously one side must yield if a settlement is to be reached. However, neither side wants to make a concession too early in the process for fear of appearing weak.

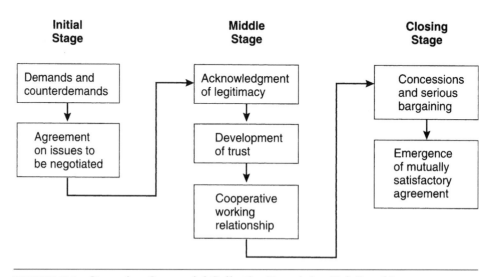

FIGURE 13.2   Stages in a Successful Collective Bargaining Relationship

As the distance between the parties narrows, bargaining becomes more difficult because the negotiators are nearing their final positions. Impasses are not uncommon at this point and are more likely to occur when one or both sides is poorly informed about the other's true position.

When the board signals that it is making its final salary offer, for example, union negotiators must decide whether the board is bluffing or will, under pressure, agree to a higher amount. Teachers' representatives may propose a figure they believe is slightly above the board's predetermined limit in hopes that board negotiators will yield in order to reach a settlement, but this strategy has some risks. If the teachers miscalculate, they may provoke a strike that neither side wants (Mitchell et al., 1981).

If the differences are resolved and an impasse avoided, an agreement is finally reached. The work is now finished unless the teachers or board members reject the settlement. If negotiators have stayed in close touch with their constituencies throughout the process, however, that should not happen.

Processes for New Forms of Bargaining

Negotiating models vary in the degree of importance attached to each of the stages in Figure 13.2. Several of the newer models of collective bargaining attempt to reduce the total amount of time devoted to bargaining. In win/win bargaining, identification of issues takes place prior to the initiation of bargaining. In the process of deciding which issues to negotiate, the bargaining teams begin to develop a cooperative working relationship, so that when negotiations start, the participants are ready to move immediately to the closing stage.

In progressive bargaining, the initial stage is prolonged as members of both teams discuss a variety of issues. These preliminary discussions allow the parties to become acquainted and to develop trust, so that by the time bargaining gets underway, an agreement can be reached quickly.

Expedited bargaining attempts to speed up negotiations by limiting the number of issues discussed and setting deadlines for reaching agreement. However, since this model does not provide for preliminary discussions, the parties are not always able to reach a satisfactory consensus on the issues they wish to resolve.

In its emphasis on principles and deemphasis on power, the principled negotiations model expands the middle stage of negotiations and devotes less time to the initial and closing stages. This approach is particularly effective at building trust and encouraging the emergence of cooperative working relationships.

Strategic bargaining shifts the focus of attention away from current issues toward consideration of the organization's future. It places considerably more emphasis than other models on the middle stage of bargaining. In arriving at an agreement about the future, the parties often are able to develop a trusting, cooperative relationship that permits them to move to the final stage of negotiations with confidence that they will be successful.

Resolving Impasses

The climate of negotiations is affected by several factors, including the personalities of the participants, the pressure each side feels from its constituencies, and the nature of the situation (Cresswell & Murphy, 1980). When trust breaks down and union and management representatives find themselves at an impasse, outside intervention may be needed. Mediation, fact finding, and arbitration are used to resolve differences in such a situation. Compulsory or binding arbitration involves a presentation by each side of its position on the issues they have been unable to resolve. After hearing both arguments, the arbitrator makes a decision that is binding on both sides. An alternative approach is *final offer arbitration*, which involves both sides making final offers to the arbitrator on the issues in conflict. The arbitrator then chooses one of the offers (O'Reilly, 1978).

In preparing for final offer arbitration, each side must consider how the other side is likely to respond. Teacher representatives making a final offer on salaries are aware that if they are unreasonably demanding the arbitrator will be likely to adopt the board's position. Similarly, board representatives must try to anticipate the position the teachers are likely to take in order to present an offer that has a reasonable chance of being accepted. Thus both parties are prevented by self-interest from making offers that are unreasonable or nonresponsive.

Impact of Collective Bargaining on Schools

There is agreement that collective bargaining has had a major impact on the operation of schools in the United States, but there is less consensus on whether schools and teachers are better off or worse off as a result of collective bargaining. Four questions that are frequently asked about collective bargaining are: (1) What effect does collective bargaining have on teachers' salaries? (2) In what ways does it affect the quality of instruction and how much students learn? (3) How does bargaining impact on principals' power? and (4) Is site-based management compatible with collective bargaining? This section will examine answers to these questions.

Teachers' Salaries

Collective bargaining in the private sector results in sizable gains in salary for workers who are represented by negotiators. Seven studies conducted during the 1970s found that the average increase in salaries of workers whose unions bargained collectively with employers ranged from 21 to 32 percent more than the gains received by workers in the same industry who did not bargain (Freeman & Medoff, 1984). Of course, employees of these firms might have received higher salaries anyway, even if they had not had collective bargaining, since other factors, including employee skill and aggressiveness and employer generosity, may have contributed to the outcome. But, even allowing for these factors, collective bargaining appears to lead to salary advantages for private sector employees.

However, findings from research on the effects of collective bargaining on teachers' wages are not so favorable. In one study it was found that the average difference in salaries of teachers in districts that bargain as compared to those without bargaining ranged from 0 to 12 percent (Johnson, 1988). The author of that study concluded:

> Negotiation has increased teachers' salaries modestly, if at all. It seems unlikely that the precise effect will eventually be determined, because further research on this question is increasingly complicated by the expansion of bargaining and the virtual impossibility of identifying comparable bargaining and nonbargaining districts and controlling for spillover effects. (p. 616)

Student Learning

Studies on the impact of collective bargaining on student learning suggest that bargaining is related to increased learning for average students but decreased learning for above and below average youngsters. One of the common concerns about unions is that they hold down productivity, but the reality seems to be somewhat more complicated. One study showed that unionized districts had higher student achievement gains than nonunion districts for average students. The difference in achievement test gains was about 7 percent, favoring unionized districts. However, for students who were above or below average in ability, nonunionized districts did a better job, by about the same margin (Eberts & Stone, 1987).

The authors of that study noted that the latter result was consistent with the view that unions tend to standardize work procedures. They also reported that instructional leadership by principals in union districts seemed to have had a positive effect on learning, but that a negative relationship was found between leadership and learning in nonunion schools. They attributed these results to the unions' role in keeping administrators informed about teachers' needs and concerns.

Potentially, the most damaging result of collective bargaining from the point of view of student learning occurs when negotiators reach an impasse and a work stoppage results. Strikes are traumatic events for school personnel. Everyone loses, and it may take years to repair the damage. Student learning is affected both by the length of a strike and by whether or not striking teachers are replaced by substitutes.

There has been relatively little research on the subject, but the available studies show, as one would expect, that shorter strikes are less harmful than longer ones. Mathematics achievement seems to be more sensitive to loss of instruction than reading. Mathematics is negatively affected both by the length of strike and by the presence of substitute teachers, whereas reading achievement appears to be affected more by the length of a strike than by the presence of substitute teachers (Crisci & Lulow, 1985). That may be because substitute teachers are less likely to be proficient in teaching mathematics.

For principals and human resources managers, the obvious lessons from this research are, first, to take actions that will prevent or limit the length of teacher strikes and, second, if strikes occur to seek to maintain normal instructional routines to the extent possible.

Work of Principals

Negotiated agreements limit the power of principals to make decisions related to administration and organization of the school by forcing the administrators to become interpreters of the contract (Ubben & Fulmer, 1985). District administrators pressure principals to adhere closely to the contract because of fear that leniency by one principal will lead to demands from teachers in other schools for similar treatment (Mitchell et al., 1981).

Principals sometimes express concern about the difficulty of dismissing incompetent teachers, whom they feel are protected by the unions. The teachers' organizations deny the charge and insist that they will support dismissal of teachers whose incompetence is adequately documented.

The truth is probably somewhere between these positions. Most administrators know of cases in which ineffective teachers have managed to keep their jobs with union support. However, it is also true that administrators have occasionally been careless in documenting poor performance or have simply lacked the courage to take action against an incompetent employee out of fear of the union's reaction.

Principals who are accustomed to a free-wheeling style of management may have difficulty adjusting to life under a negotiated agreement. Being successful in such a situation requires an individual with considerable flexibility—one who is careful to abide by the provisions of the master contract, yet able to inspire teachers to give more than the minimum effort in order to increase learning.

Most administrators will admit that collective bargaining has some positive features. Among these are the increased security that teachers feel and the increased clarity of teachers' work responsibilities. Principals who work in districts with contracts that detail duties teachers are expected to perform report that they have no problems in getting those duties carried out (Jessup, 1981).

All in all, administering a school that operates under a negotiated agreement probably require skills that are no different from those required in schools in which there is no agreement in effect. In both cases, the administrator must attend to details and provide leadership to move the faculty toward a goal of improved instruction.

Bargaining and Site-Based Management

Some authorities claim that collective bargaining is incompatible with site-based management (SBM) of schools or that, at the very least, there are likely to be problems encountered in the effort to implement SBM in districts with negotiated contracts. For example, these authorities express concern that teacher members of a school council might refuse to approve layoffs of fellow teachers even when such an action was needed. Some people believe that SBM is a tactic employed by teacher unions to seize control of schools (Walker & Roder, 1993).

However, there is not much evidence that teacher unions are promoting SBM, and some union officials have expressed strong concerns about it. One of the more optimistic union officials concluded that SBM will work if management agrees to share or relinquish some of its power and if the details of the plan have been fully discussed during negotiations (Poltrock & Goss, 1993).

In some districts with SBM, unions have agreed to a provision in the master contract to allow waiving parts of the contract that are in conflict with decisions of school councils. However, before embracing waiver provisions, unions usually insist that principals accept co-equal status with teachers in specified areas of decision making (Poltrock & Goss, 1993). Some union officials are adamant in their opposition to these concessions and warn that accepting waivers will lead to gradual erosion of employee rights (Clark, 1993).

Some school districts have implemented SBM successfully without prior bargaining about operational details. This appears to work in situations in which teachers and administrators are able to develop an informal approach that avoids confrontation over divisive issues. In another tactic that appears to have promise, unions have agreed to permit deviations from the master contract if the principal and a majority of teachers in a school agree on the need for the waiver (Clark, 1993).

Summary

Collective bargaining has been called one of the most significant developments in education in the past half century. The content of negotiated contracts is regulated by state statutes but generally covers compensation and working conditions. Some agreements may impinge on the quality of instruction in schools, and board negotiators should take those effects into account, along with attention to cost and administrative prerogatives, in reaching a settlement.

Negotiations proceed through three stages: (1) an initial stage in which the sides state their positions and agree on the issues to be negotiated, (2) a middle stage in which trust emerges and a cooperative working relationship is established, and (3) a closing stage in which both parties begin to bargain seriously, granting the concessions that are needed to reach a mutually acceptable agreement.

New approaches to collective bargaining are being tried in a number of school districts. Among these approaches are expedited bargaining, progressive bargaining, the win/win approach, principled negotiations, and strategic bargaining. Several new forms of bargaining are designed to speed the negotiation process by setting deadlines for reaching an agreement and limiting the number of issues to be discussed.

When the two sides are not able to reach agreement, outside assistance may be required. Mediation, fact finding, and arbitration are all used to help resolve impasses.

Suggested Activities

1. Following is a statement on class size proposed by the teachers' union. Take and defend a position for or against the proposal as written. (You are not allowed to rewrite it.)

   "We believe instruction is most effective when class sizes are kept small enough to permit teachers to diagnose students' needs and plan instruction to meet them. To permit the level of teacher attention needed for learning to occur, we ask the board to agree to place a limit of 20 students in classes in reading and English in grades 1–12 and to limit all other classes in grades 1–12 (except special education) to no more than 24 students. Each special education student assigned to a regular class will count as two students for purposes of calculating size limits."

2. Principals are sometimes excluded from joining the board's negotiating team because board members believe they might be inclined to side with teachers. Principals argue that they could help the board's representatives understand how proposed contract provisions might affect instruction, and thus avoid language likely to harm learning. Take and defend a position on this proposition:

   "Principals should be represented on the board's negotiating team."

3. Consider the statement on teacher evaluation that follows. If you were a member of the union bargaining team, what changes would you propose in the statement? If you were a member of the board team, what changes would you want made?

   "The union and the board recognize the importance of teacher evaluation for sound instruction. Teachers will be evaluated in the following way: The principal will observe each teacher at least twice during the school year, will evaluate the teacher after each observation, and will inform the teacher of the results. No later than April 15, the principal will prepare a written narrative describing the teacher's strengths and weaknesses and include the statement in the teacher's personnel file. If the teacher is completing the probationary period, the principal shall recommend that the teacher be tenured or terminated."

4. In schools with site-based management, school councils sometimes request waivers of certain provisions in the master contract. Should waivers be allowed? If so, what type mechanism should be used to review and approve such requests? Are there certain parts of the contract that should be sacrosanct—that is, no waivers allowed under any circumstances? If so, which ones?

5. Locate contract provisions from two master contracts relating to one of the topics listed below. Read the provisions from each contract and compare and contrast them. Tell which provision is more favorable to teachers and which is more favorable to the board. (You may wish to use one of the online master contracts listed under Online Resources.)
   a. Evaluation of teachers
   b. Teacher safety and security
   c. Teacher transfer and promotion
   d. Extracurricular duties of teachers

6. Locate additional information about one of the new forms of collective bargaining described in the chapter (expedited, progressive, win/win, and principled). Report

what you find out. Tell how that type of bargaining differs from traditional collective bargaining and take a position on whether implementing that form would be an improvement over current practice.

Online Resources

Master Contracts

These sites contain the complete text of collective bargaining agreements between the teachers' association and the board of education:

Detroit (Michigan) (www.dft231.com/2000_contract.htm)

Fairbanks (Alaska) North Star Borough (www.alaska.net/~fea/agreement.html)

Los Alamos (New Mexico) (http://laps.losalamos.k12.nm.us/person/Certified/pdf)

Metro Nashville-Davidson County (Tennessee) (www.nashville.k12.tn.us/general_info _folder/TeacherAgreement.htm)

Ojai (California) (www.oft.org/oftsite/mc)

Osceola County (Florida) (www.osceola.k12.fl.us/depts/personnel/contracts/index. htm)

References

Black, S. (1993, October). How teachers are reshaping evaluation procedures. *Educational Leadership, 51*, 38–42.

Booth, R. (1993). *Collective bargaining and the school board member.* Springfield, IL: Illinois Association of School Boards.

Clark, R. T. (1993, Spring). School-based management—Problems and prospects. *Journal of Law and Education, 22*, 183–186.

Cresswell, A., & Murphy, M. (1980). *Teachers, unions, and collective bargaining in public education.* Berkeley, CA: McCutchan.

Crisci, P. E., & Lulow, R. J. (1985). The effect of school employee strikes on student achievement in nine Ohio school districts. *Journal of Collective Negotiations, 14*, 197–212.

Eberts, R. W., & Stone, J. A. (1987). Teacher unions and the productivity of public schools. *Industrial and Labor Relations Review, 40*, 354–363.

Fisher, R., & Ury, W. (1981). *Getting to yes: Negotiating agreement without giving in.* New York: Penguin.

Fisher, R., & Ury, W. (1988). *Getting together: Building relationships as we negotiate.* New York: Penguin.

Freeman, R. B., & Medoff, J. L. (1984). *What do unions do?* New York: Basic Books.

Geisert, G., & Lieberman, M. (1994). *Teacher union bargaining: Practice and policy.* Chicago: Precept Press.

Goldschmidt, S., Bowers, B., Riley, M., & Stuart, L. (1984). *The extent and nature of educational policy bargaining.* Eugene, OR: University of Oregon, Center for Educational Policy and Management.

Hauck, V. (1998). *Arbitratrating sex discrimination grievances.* Westport, CT: Quorum.

Jessup, D. (1981). *Teacher unionism and its impact: A study of change over time.* Washington, DC: National Institute of Education.

Johnson, S. M. (1988). Unionism and collective bargaining in the public schools. In N. J. Boyan (Ed.), *Handbook of research on educational administration* (pp. 603–622). New York: Longman.

Lipsky, D. V., & Conley, S. C. (1986, April). *Incentive pay and collective bargaining in public education.* Paper presented at the annual meeting of the American Educational Research Association, San Francisco. (ERIC Document Reproduction Service No. ED277111).

McDonnell, L., & Pascal, A. (1979). *Organized teachers in American schools.* Santa Monica, CA: Rand.

Mitchell, D., Kerchner, C., Erck, W., & Pryor, G. (1981). The impact of collective bargaining on school management and policy. *American Journal of Education, 89,* 147–188.

National Education Association. (1991). *Collaborative bargaining: A critical appraisal.* Washington, DC: Author.

O'Reilly, R. C. (1978). *Understanding collective bargaining in education.* Metuchen, NJ: Scarecrow Press.

Poltrock, L., & Goss, S. (1993, Spring). A union lawyer's view of restructuring and reform. *Journal of Law and Education, 22,* 177–182.

Ubben, G. C., & Fulmer, B. (1985). The relationship of collective bargaining to the decision-making power of the public school principal. *Journal of Collective Negotiations, 14,* 141–150.

Walker, P., & Roder, L. (1993, Spring). Reflections on the practical and legal implications of school-based management and teacher empowerment. *Journal of Law and Education, 22,* 159–175.

Washington Education Association. (2001). *Article XI: Evaluation* (4). Available online: www.wa.nea.org/info/orgnztn/seahomepage/contract/articl03.htm.

14

Managing Conflict in Schools

Conflict occurs in all organizations, and although managers work to resolve or eliminate it, it is important to recognize that some conflict is inevitable and may even have beneficial effects (Pneuman & Bruehl, 1982). Conflict occurs when people disagree regarding values, information, and goals, or when individuals compete for scarce resources (Rahim, 1986). Organizational managers usually become involved when conflict occurs among members of the organization, and managers themselves are sometimes parties to conflict.

Conflict may occur between individuals, within or between groups, or between an individual and a group. The focus of this chapter is with conflict involving school personnel and, in particular, that which involves two teachers or groups of teachers or a teacher and an administrator such as a principal. Conflict involving parties outside of the school is beyond the scope of this book. For example, issues of conflict between teachers and parents will not be addressed, even though many of the principles for handling various types of conflict are identical.

Plan of the Chapter

This chapter deals with the following topics: (1) nature of conflict in organizations, (2) alternative methods of resolving conflict, (3) managing conflict through the grievance process, (4) grievance arbitration in schools, (5) arbitration involving work rules, (6) other issues in arbitration, and (8) effects of arbitration on the district.

Nature of Conflict in Organizations

In any human activity, disagreements and conflict are inevitable. In the workplace, much conflict centers on one of four issues: disagreements about the application of rules and policies, disputes regarding the allocation of resources and privileges,

confusion about duties and responsibilities of employees, and hostility over perceived unfairness in performance evaluation.

Exhibit 14.1 shows examples of these four types of on-the-job conflicts. Example 5 of Exhibit 14.1 deals with the interpretation and application of board policy.
In Examples 1 and 3, the issue is the allocation of resources and privileges. Conflict
about job duties and responsibilities is evident in Examples 2 and 6, and Examples
4 and 7 illustrate conflict related to assessment of individual performance.

The principal or human resources administrator must act as conflict manager
when disputes arise. There are certain actions the administrator may take that are
more likely than others to lead to resolution of the conflict. If the dispute centers on
something the administrator did, then he or she must be prepared to defend that
action by citing the policy or rationale for it. If the decision was made in haste and
not well thought out, it may be necessary for the administrator to change it. After
hearing all sides, however, if the administrator continues to feel that the decision

---

EXHIBIT 14.1   *Examples of Conflict Situations in Schools*

Example 1: A teacher in the mathematics department requests permission to attend a
regional conference sponsored by the state mathematics teachers' association. The
department head has also asked to attend, but there is not enough money in the budget to
pay expenses for two teachers. The principal gives the department head approval to
attend the meeting and denies the teacher's request. The teacher protests this action and
accuses the principal of favoritism.

Example 2: An English teacher protests to the principal that he is being treated unfairly
because he teaches 135 students each day, whereas an English teacher across the hall has
only 119.

Example 3: The business education department requests money to buy two additional
computers to replace two that are worn out. The request is denied, but the industrial arts
department receives money to buy a new jigsaw for the woodworking shop. The business
teacher complains that "the business department never gets any support from the
principal."

Example 4: The principal of an elementary school admonishes a third-grade teacher for
failing to notify the parents of a child whose grades have dropped so that they could
intervene before report cards went home.

Example 5: A special education teacher requests personal leave in order to appear in court
for the final hearing for the adoption of her son. The agreement states that personal leave
may be used "only for unforeseen emergencies." The hearing is not an unforeseen
emergency since the teacher has known about it for two months.

Example 6: The chairperson of the social studies department at a middle school tells the
principal that other teachers in the department are complaining because one of the
teachers in the department fails to show up for department meetings and has not
participated in department committee assignments.

Example 7: A teacher complains that evaluation ratings given by the principal do not fairly
represent the quality of her work.

---

was correct, it should be left intact. Most employees will accept adverse decisions without bitterness if they have received a respectful hearing from a decision maker who has no "hidden agenda" (Yates, 1985).

The role of the principal or human resources administrator in attempting to resolve conflict depends on the nature of the strife. Some conflict involves disagreements about events, as when two witnesses give different accounts of an altercation between two students. Other disagreements are technical in nature, involving arguments over the best way to perform an action. For example, a teacher and supervisor may disagree over the preferred method of teaching reading. Interpersonal conflict occurs when a disagreement between two individuals erupts into threats and recriminations. Disputes about work rules or the correct interpretation of a collective bargaining agreement fall under the rubric of legal conflict (Stitt, 1998).

When disputes center on group competition for resources, there is a temptation for conflict managers to attempt to resolve them by using the strategy of "something for everyone." However, in most school districts at the present time, resources are too scarce to be distributed "casually and generously" (Yates, 1985, p. 164) without regard to the implications for achieving the goals of the district. To preserve the manager's ability to use organizational resources to achieve identified goals, managers must be prepared to cite long- and short-term goals identified earlier through a strategic planning process (see Chapter 2).

Alternative Methods of Resolving Conflict

The most common method of resolving conflict in the workplace is by the use of a grievance procedure. However, several other methods for handling disputes have emerged in recent years and are being used in place of or in addition to grievance procedures. These methods involve cooperative approaches to settling conflicts, which seek to help employees resolve their disagreements and improve their performance on the job. Cooperative conflict theory encourages employees to hear and consider each other's ideas and work to mold them into a mutually acceptable outcome (Tjosvold, 1993).

Four alternative methods for settling disputes are peer review, an ombudsman, mediation, and fact finding. *Peer review* refers employee complaints to a panel consisting of employees and supervisors. An employee with a grievance who is not satisfied after discussing the issue with a supervisor may seek a peer review to conduct an objective examination of the grievance and reach a binding decision. The panel has the authority to correct unfair treatment or the inconsistent application of work rules and policies (McDermott, 1996).

Ombudsmen first appeared in Sweden; corporations, government agencies, and universities in the United States have since adopted the idea. The practice is relatively new in school districts. The ombudsman is an employee of the company or district who is independent and has the authority to investigate complaints that are brought to his or her attention. Ombudsmen receive and handle complaints from customers but also may attempt to settle disputes among employees or between management and labor (McDermott, 1996).

In *mediation,* a neutral third party serves as an impartial channel of communication between the disputants in an effort to achieve a voluntary settlement of the dispute. The mediator acts as a sounding board and confers with both parties in an effort to develop a compromise acceptable to both sides. The parties present the facts of the case as they see them, and the mediator then provides his or her opinion and attempts to persuade the disputants to modify their positions (Stitt, 1998).

Fact finding brings in a neutral third party to hear both parties' positions, study the dispute, and resolve incompatible versions of fact. The fact finder investigates, reviews documents, and interviews witnesses to determine the facts of the situation. He or she then presents a written report to the disputants or to an authority, such as a judge (Stitt, 1998).

Fact finding and mediation are referred to as *interest-based processes* for resolving disputes. Such processes focus on the parties' interests rather than on their rights or power. Since interest-based processes are consensual, conflict can be resolved only if the parties accept the proposed solution. If one of these approaches does not lead to a settlement, then one or both of the parties may resort to the use of power or assertion of their rights to reach a resolution. However, a feminist perspective on conflict suggests that power is most productive when it is used not to coerce others but as an opportunity for parties to a dispute to creatively confront their disagreements in a way that empowers both (Papa & Canary, 1995).

Managing Conflict through the Grievance Process

According to research, conditions in schools are conducive to the production of grievances. Schools have workers with generally homogeneous backgrounds who have similar working conditions and who have common free time during the workday. These conditions contribute to a relative increase in the number of grievances in an organization as compared to other organizations (Lutz & Caldwell, 1979). For this reason, principals must be alert to conditions that lower teacher morale or raise their feelings of frustration. When grievances increase in number, principals may be blamed for the increase even though they had nothing to do with creating conditions that led to it.

Much conflict that occurs in the workplace involves disagreements between employees and supervisors over disciplinary actions and conditions of work. Teachers and school principals agree about most aspects of school operations but disagree about a few. They generally agree that teachers should have a good deal of autonomy in deciding what to teach, in choosing instructional activities and materials, and in the relative emphasis given to instructional topics. They also agree that principals have the responsibility to supervise and evaluate teachers' work.

Disagreements between teachers and administrators most often occur when the administration proposes to change teaching assignments or responsibilities, to prescribe certain instructional procedures, or to require teachers to perform nonteaching duties.

Negotiated contracts normally include a grievance procedure, which is an orderly process for resolving disputes over interpretation and administration of the contract (*Contract Administration,* 1983). Grievance procedures have a long history in industry. The first record of their use dates back to the early years of the twentieth century, but they did not come into widespread use in this country until World War II. A recommendation of the President's Labor-Management Conference that all labor contracts include a procedure for settlement of grievances gave impetus to their adoption. The U.S. Supreme Court gave additional support to their use when it held in a series of decisions that courts should not rule on the merits of disputes between labor and management but should limit themselves to enforcing arbitration awards and reviewing questions of arbitrability (Lovell, 1985)

At the present time, grievance procedures are pervasive in industries with negotiated labor agreements, and they are increasingly used to resolve employee/employer disputes in schools. In districts without negotiated agreements, written grievance policies govern the resolution of disputes. The grievance process is favored by most employers and many unions because it is a quicker and less costly way of settling disputes than strikes and lengthy litigation (Lovell, 1985).

Arbitration has a number of advantages over litigation. Arbitration is faster than pursuing a resolution through the courts and is usually less complicated. The disputants are not required to hire attorneys, and because of the flexibility of the proceedings, facts are obtained more quickly and easily. Decisions arrived at by arbitration are announced soon after the hearing, whereas a court decision may be delayed for several months. Moreover, arbitration decisions are seldom appealed, since courts are inclined to uphold arbitrators' decisions (McDermott, 1996).

One of the most important advantages of grievance arbitration from an employer's point of view is its potential for avoiding strikes. When employees can seek redress from unfair actions of management, they are less likely to walk off the job. If a strike does occur, an employer who has agreed to settle disputes through binding arbitration is usually able to obtain injunctive relief through the courts (*Boys Markets Inc.* v. *Retail Clerks,* 1970).

The grievance procedure is intended to prevent work stoppages by providing a means for employees to have their complaints heard. Grievance procedures usually work well in resolving disputes about work rules, leave time, and job duties, but they are less effective for resolving the types of conflict that are encountered in schools with site-based management.

The operational assumptions of SBM are different from the assumptions used in grievance processes. In schools with SBM, disputes are resolved through informal discussion, cooperation, and compromise. The search for solutions usually takes into account the interests of teachers, students, and parents. Grievance procedures, on the other hand, use an adversarial approach and ultimately rely on an objective outside party to hear the evidence and decide the issue. The procedures focus on faithfully interpreting an agreement rather than seeking the best solution to a problem. Resolving conflict in a school with SBM involves evaluation of options, with attention given to the school's mission and the well-being of the parties involved. Finding a solution often requires compromise.

Some districts with SBM plans have developed, in collaboration with employee unions, a variation on existing grievance procedures that is intended to settle disputes on site rather than appeal them to arbitration. In Dade County (Florida) Schools, a grievance committee composed of administrators and union representatives hears grievances appealed from schools with SBM plans. If a dispute is not resolved by the grievance committee, it is appealed to a two-person panel composed of the district superintendent and a union vice president. Only if the panel fails to resolve the issue does it go to binding arbitration (Fossey, 1992).

Administering Grievance Procedures

A grievance clause in a master contract usually consists of a definition of *grievance*, tells who may initiate a grievance, and establishes deadlines for filing and processing employee complaints. The clause also details the procedural steps that are followed in processing the grievance, including the final step, which in many districts is binding arbitration.

Unions favor grievance plans that include binding arbitration as the final step because they feel that it guarantees employees a fair hearing for their complaints. However, most school boards prefer advisory arbitration, which leaves the final decision on a dispute in the hands of the board (Lovell, 1985). The grievance clause also specifies which parties may file grievances. In some districts, teacher associations and unions are allowed to file, whereas in others only individuals are permitted to grieve the employer's actions.

Steps in Resolving Grievances.   Most grievance policies provide three or four steps through which a grievant may appeal a complaint. Step 1 commonly includes both an informal and a formal stage. The employee initiates action informally by bringing to the attention of the supervisor the decision or situation that originally aroused the employee's concern. If not satisfied with the response received, the employee may then proceed to Stage 2 of Step 1 by formally filing a written grievance with the same supervisor. In the case of teachers, Step 1 involves the principal of the school in which the grievant works.

In most districts, a form is provided on which the employee is asked to (1) describe the incident, decision, or practice that gave rise to the complaint; (2) cite the contract or policy provision that has been violated; and (3) explain what corrective action is being requested. Since there is usually a time limit for filing a grievance, the grievant must specify the date of occurrence of the precipitating event or the date on which the employee first learned about it.

Appeals Procedures.   If the employee is unhappy with the decision at the first step, he or she proceeds to Step 2 by appealing to the next higher level, usually either the director of human resources or an assistant superintendent. Finally, Step 3 involves a hearing before the superintendent if the grievant has not received satisfaction. Step 4 in the grievance procedure is a hearing before the board of education or an arbitrator or arbitration panel. In districts with binding arbitration, the decision of the arbitrator is final, but in districts that use advisory arbitration, the recommendation of the arbitrator is reviewed by the school board, which has the final word about the employee's complaint.

Grievance hearings become more formal as the complaint advances from one administrative level to the next. The only written documentation required at the first step is the supervisor's written decision, but at the final step, a transcript of the hearing is prepared (Salmon, 1983). The transcript, along with the superintendent's written decision on the employee's complaint, is reviewed by the arbitrator or arbitration panel if the grievance is appealed to arbitration.

Grievance Arbitration in Schools

When an employee fails to achieve a satisfactory solution to a grievance after following all of the steps provided in the policy, the final step is arbitration. The rules on arbitration vary, depending on the state in which the individual works and on the provisions of the bargaining agreement. Some states require boards to include binding arbitration in contracts with employees, whereas others leave the decision to the negotiators. A few prohibit binding arbitration.

Certain powers of school boards are nondelegable and are considered nonarbitrable unless state law specifically permits review. Among these are the power to hire, promote, and discharge employees; establish the curriculum; and set standards of service (Lovell, 1985).

Courts generally prefer to allow arbitration procedures to operate without interference, but if nondelegable powers of school boards have clearly been abridged in the process of arbitration, courts are likely to intervene. In some states, the courts are less ready to grant arbitration the acceptance in the public sector that it has traditionally been accorded in the private sector (Lovell, 1985).

Selection of Arbitrators

A grievance may be heard by a single arbitrator or by a panel consisting of several arbitrators. The procedures followed in selection of arbitrators are those established by state legislation or by a professional organization such as the American Arbitration Association or an agency such as the Federal Mediation and Conciliation Service. The usual practice is for the designated organization or agency to submit a list of five to seven names of qualified arbitrators, from which representatives of the grievant and the board alternately delete names until only the required number remains (Ostrander, 1987).

The arbitrators' function is to determine whether the administrative decision or practice to which the employee objects is a violation of the bargaining agreement. Most disputes involve rights that union members claim to have received at the bargaining table and that management denies were granted. The arbitrator thus has the task of determining which interpretation is the one intended by the parties at the time the contract was signed (Ostrander, 1987).

Guidelines for Interpreting the Contract

In arriving at an interpretation of the contract, arbitrators are guided by several rules of contract interpretation. Among them are the following (Elkouri & Elkouri, 1973):

1. If the intent of the parties is clear, it should govern.
2. Words are given their ordinary and accepted meaning unless other meanings are specifically indicated.
3. The meaning given to a passage in the contract should be consistent insofar as possible with the intentions expressed in other parts of the contract.
4. When the agreement specifically includes something, it is assumed that which is left unstated is excluded.
5. When there is a conflict between specific and general language, specific language should govern.
6. When there is no evidence to the contrary and the meaning of a term is unclear, the intentions of the parties should be viewed to be the same as those held during the negotiations that led to the agreement.
7. No consideration should be given to compromise offers or to concessions offered by one party and rejected by the other during the process that led to arbitration.

Exhibit 14.2 contains a summary description of a teacher's grievance. The arbitrator relied on several rules of contract interpretation in arriving at a decision. The arbitrator's decision and the reasoning that led to it are described below, but before you read abut them you may want to test your skill as an arbitrator by reviewing the case and making a decision on your own.

Arbitrator's Reasoning and Decision

In Exhibit 14.2, the arbitrator noted that Subsection A.1 of Article 20 used the term *applicants* without further specifying the meaning of the term and that the statement indicating that when two applicants are equally qualified, the most senior would be appointed suggested that the term was meant to refer only to employees. Since Subsection A.2 referred only to "outside applicants," the arbitrator reasoned that that Subsection A.1 was referring only to employees. He further noted that if outside applicants were meant to be included in Subsection A.1, there would have

EXHIBIT 14.2   *Lexington Local Board of Education and Lexington Support Association*

Background

In February 1998, Lexington Board of Education posted a vacancy for the position of educational aide at Eastern Elementary School. The job involved monitoring the playground, indoor recess, and the cafeteria. Five people applied for the position, three of whom were employees of the school district, including a woman who drove a school bus for the district. After interviewing the five applicants, the principal of the school recommended Kim Olivieri, who was not an employee of the district, for the position.

An applicant who was a district employee filed a grievance claiming that the Board had "violated, misinterpreted, or misapplied" the agreement between the association and the board. The pertinent sections of the agreement were Articles 20 and 21 (summarized below).

The grievant was the senior of the three district employees who applied for the position of aide at Eastern Elementary. According to the principal of the school, who interviewed all of the applicants, the three Board employees were all qualified for the position. The association argued that, since the grievant was the most senior of the three, she should have been appointed.

As the association interpreted the contract, if a member of the bargaining unit qualifies for a position, the position must go to that person. If more than one member is qualified, the position goes to the most senior. The Board disagreed, arguing that the agreement did not grant any particular preference to employees unless two or more applicants were equally qualified, in which case the position was to go to the more senior person.

The Board also argued that the grievant did not have a good attendance record in her position as bus driver, whereas Ms. Olivieri's record showed no problem with attendance. On that basis, the Board argued, Ms. Olivieri was more qualified than the other applicants.

The question presented to the arbitrator was whether the Board had violated Article 20 when it awarded the position at Eastern Elementary School to Kirn Olivieri and, if so, what the remedy should be. The arbitrator stated that the case presented three sub-issues:

1. What is the correct interpretation of Articles A.1 and A.2?
2. What is the proper application of the articles?
3. What should be the remedy if a violation is found?

In answering these questions, the arbitrator noted that if the language of the contract is clear and unambiguous, the arbitrator has no choice but to apply the terms as written. If the terms are not clear, then the arbitrator must rely on other means to discern the meaning of the language. Specifically, he or she refers to past practice and bargaining history for assistance in interpreting the language of the contract.

Relevant Contract Provisions

Article 20

A.1. In determining which applicant will be awarded a vacant position, training, experience, work record, aptitude and ability to work well with other employees with whom the applicant will have contact will be considered. If in the opinion of the Superintendent two or more applicants are equally qualified, then the most senior will be appointed.

A.2. No outside applicant will be hired to fill a vacancy unless the criteria in A.1 of Article 20 has been followed.

been no need for Subsection A.2. He concluded that Subsection A.1 dealt only with applicants from within the bargaining unit and that Subsection A.2 authorized the employers to go to outside applicants only if no unit member qualified for the position.

The arbitrator decided that Subsection 20 A.1 mandated the appointment of the grievant to the vacancy and ruled out the appointment of an outside applicant such as Ms. Olivieri. The arbitrator ordered the Board to award the vacant position to the grievant and to grant her back pay.

Arbitration Involving Work Rules

Many grievances have to do with application of work rules. It has been noted that principals are expected to discuss disagreements concerning work rules with the involved parties and that doing so increases the chances that the principal will be successful in mediating future disputes (Lutz & Caldwell, 1979). Disagreements over work rules usually involve these three questions (Turner & Weed, 1983):

1. What action or activity is covered by the rule?
2. Under what conditions is the activity appropriate?
3. To whom does the rule apply?

Consider a policy that states, "Teachers will confer with parents upon request and at a mutually convenient time regarding students' academic performance." What actions are covered by the rule? If a teacher discusses a child's work with a parent by telephone, does that constitute conferring? What about an exchange of notes? If the request for a conference originates with the principal rather than a parent, does that constitute a "request" within the meaning of the policy?

Under what conditions is the activity appropriate? Suppose a teacher tells an inquiring parent that there is no need for a conference since the child in question is doing well. Has the teacher violated the rule? Suppose the teacher has a second job and cannot arrange a mutually satisfactory time for a conference. Is she exempt from the rule?

To whom does the rule apply? Are both part-time and full-time teachers obligated by the rule? Is a teacher who has a child for one period a day under a mainstreaming arrangement equally as bound by the rule as the child's base teacher? Is an itinerant teacher who spends only three or four hours per week in a school required to meet with parents who request it?

Deciding Which Rule Applies

In some disputes, a question arises regarding which of two or more rules governs. In one such case, the contract between teachers and the board of the Anoka-Hennepin District in Minnesota contained a provision stating that "teachers shall not be disciplined, reduced in rank or compensation without just cause." Teachers who missed school because of snow requested they be granted personal leave for the half-day they missed. The request was denied and the teachers lost one-half day's pay. They filed a grievance that ultimately went to arbitration. The teachers cited the "just cause" clause, but the district argued that its action was justified by a clause governing emergency leave. That provision held that absence from school because of the effects of weather on transportation would not be approved for emergency leave purposes. The arbitrator supported the district in this case (Coulson, 1986).

Interpreting Just Cause

Arbitrators are frequently confronted with the necessity of interpreting "just cause" clauses, such as the one in the Anoka-Hennepin contract. The intent in using this phrase is to allow administrative discretion while protecting employee rights granted by the contract. Several criteria are used by arbitrators to determine whether administrative action meets the "just cause" standard. Among the questions an arbitrator is likely to ask are the following:

1. Was the employee informed of management's rules and expectations?
2. Were management's rules and expectations reasonable?
3. Was adverse action necessary to maintain orderly, efficient procedures in the organization?
4. Was the employee given a chance to improve his or her conduct?
5. Was the imposed penalty reasonable? (Ostrander, 1981, p. 41)

Teachers' Use of Force

Teachers are expected to take action to prevent students from fighting or to stop fights when they occur, yet the rules about the use of force in such situations are often unclear. In a junior high school in Michigan, a teacher who encountered two students fighting sent another child to the principal's office for help. The principal came and stopped the fight, but on the following day the principal placed a letter of reprimand in the teacher's file because he felt she should have been more aggressive and stopped the fight herself (Coulson, 1986).

A teacher in a school in Iowa got into trouble with the school principal for the opposite reason: He was too aggressive in separating two youngsters who were fighting. The teacher grabbed one of the students by the shoulder and pulled him away from the other boy, causing the student to fall and strike his head. He wrapped his arm around the other boy and pulled him into the office. The teacher was reprimanded for excessive use of force (Coulson, 1986).

Both teachers filed grievances seeking to have the reprimands removed from their personnel files. How would you rule if you were the arbitrator? It might help you to know that the first teacher had taught for a total of 30 years, 13 in the same system, and had never been previously reprimanded. The teacher in the Iowa school, however, had been warned by the principal about excessive use of force and had previously received a reprimand for the same offense.

The arbitrator in the first case decided, as you probably did, that the teacher should not have been reprimanded, but in the second case the arbitrator held that the reprimand was justified. In both cases, teachers were operating on the basis of expectations that were not very clear or explicit, but the second teacher, because of the principal's previous warning, was especially vulnerable to disciplinary action. Some use of force in these situations may be required, but a fine line exists between suitable or appropriate force and excessive force. In this case, the teacher crossed that line.

Grievances on Evaluation

A good many grievances filed by teachers concern evaluation procedures. In handling these disputes, administrators must be guided by the language of the contract. When contract language is specific with regard to evaluation procedures, any departure from the provisions will probably be rejected in arbitration. If the language is permissive, then an administrative decision is more likely to be upheld.

Some contracts specify who is responsible for making classroom observations but do not forbid others from observing in classes. It is common for contracts to state that the principal is responsible for making classroom observations as part of the evaluation process. In one case, a principal called in a central office supervisor to make an additional observation of a teacher, and the teacher filed a grievance, claiming that the use of the supervisor for a classroom observation violated the contract. The administration was upheld in that case on grounds that the contract did not specifically forbid the use of observers other than the principal (Ostrander, 1981).

Another complaint that teachers sometimes make is that principals use information for evaluation purposes that was not obtained by means of classroom observations. Arbitrators have held that such use of information from other sources is justified unless specifically prohibited by the contract.

Guidelines for Action

Being aware of the factors that arbitrators consider in deciding disputes over work rules can help administrators make better decisions and avoid some of the emotional cost of confrontations with employees. In disputes that involve employee absence or tardiness, arbitrators look for a pattern of employee behavior and are not inclined to support the board when an employee's infraction is limited to a single incident. Advance notification is also considered. A teacher who fails to notify the principal when she is absent from school is less likely to win an appeal of a reprimand than a teacher who has been more conscientious about notification (Ostrander, 1981).

Negative Norm Setters

Arbitrators also consider an individual employee's behavior in light of the behavior of other employees. A reprimand of a teacher who has accumulated "excessive" absences is unlikely to be sustained if other teachers in the district with equal or greater numbers of absences were not reprimanded. Employees whose behavior is poorest set the standard by which all employees are judged, so administrators must first take corrective action against these negative norm setters.

Noncompliance with work directives is a charge that most often arises in connection with noninstructional duties. Teachers are expected to monitor hallways, cafeterias, and restrooms in most schools. In some schools they also supervise the playground and bus-loading ramps. If the contract defines particular duties as voluntary, teachers may refuse to perform them without being subject to penalty. A question arises, however, when a teacher has agreed to perform a duty and later discontinues the activity before the task is complete. Consider a teacher who agrees to serve as sponsor of a cheerleading squad and resigns at midyear because of an increased workload related to a part-time job just taken on. Would a reprimand issued to a teacher in such a situation be sustained?

There is no way to predict what an arbitrator will decide in a given case, but if the contract is silent on the issue in question, then the arbitrator will use other information, including past practice, in making a decision. In this case, several factors must weigh on the decision. The arbitrator might consider whether the teacher understood that the assignment was for the full year, whether the teacher received supplemental pay for sponsoring the cheerleaders, and whether the teacher gave advance notice of her impending resignation and offered to help train a successor.

Other Issues in Arbitration

Arbitrability

One of the issues that frequently confronts arbitrators is the question of arbitrability. *Arbitrability* refers to whether a grievance is subject to arbitration. Grievances that deal with powers granted to the board by statute are not arbitrable, and those that are not timely are also likely to be judged nonarbitrable. Most grievance policies limit the number of days that may elapse after occurrence of an event before a grievance is filed. If the allowable number of days for filing a grievance is exceeded, it may be declared nonarbitrable unless the teacher failed to learn of the precipitating event until after it occurred.

Arbitrabilty also hinges on definitions of what is or is not arbitrable as stated in the negotiated contract or contained in state statutes. Certain disputes may be grievable but not arbitrable (*Contract Administration,* 1983). In those situations, teachers have no appeal beyond the steps provided in the grievance procedure within the district.

Timeliness

Just as teachers must file a grievance within a specified number of days after the occurrence of the event they are grieving, administrators are required to respond to formal grievances within a few days of receiving them. Even though a grievance may arrive at a time when a principal is overwhelmed with other responsibilities, an answer must be given within the required time or the administration faces the possibility of losing in arbitration because of delay.

Questions of Law

Grievances frequently involve claims that state laws have been violated, but there is no unanimity of opinion regarding whether arbitrators should attempt to interpret the law in settling such disputes. Some people believe that arbitrators should not consider issues of law but should rather confine themselves to interpreting the collective bargaining agreement. Others argue that arbitrators are uniquely qualified to interpret the law as it applies to the parties to a collective bargaining agreement.

Past Practice

Past practice is frequently used by arbitrators as a guide in resolving disputes. If a particular practice has been consistently followed and there is nothing in the contract to indicate that the negotiators intended to change it, then any deviation from the practice by the administration is likely to be rejected. On the other hand, if the bargaining agreement specifies a procedure that is a clear departure from past practice, and the evidence suggests that both parties agreed to the change, then grievances appealing to past practices are unlikely to be upheld.

Problems most often arise when contract language appears to sanction a departure from previous practice but it is not clear that the negotiators meant to initiate the change. In one district, the contract specified that the "principal shall meet with the teacher following each classroom observation to discuss the results." When a new contract was negotiated, the language was changed slightly. In the new version, the provision read: "The principal shall meet with the teacher to discuss the results of classroom observations."

A teacher complained that the principal had not held a postobservation conference with her following a visit to the classroom and had informed her that a conference following every observation was no longer required. When the question reached arbitration, the arbitrator had to decide whether the negotiators had intended to drop the requirement. The board representative argued that such a change was intended, but the teacher representative denied it. In the absence of agreement that a change in practice was intended, the arbitrator held that principals should continue meeting with teachers after every observation.

In some cases, arbitrators have upheld departure from past practice when conditions warranted unusual actions. In one case, teachers participating in a mass "sick-out" to protest an action of the board were required by the administration to produce a physician's statement or have their pay docked for the time they were not at school. The penalized teachers grieved the decision, claiming that it violated past practice. The arbitrator upheld the administration on grounds that the teachers' actions justified the board's response (Ostrander, 1981).

Teacher Allegiance

Some issues are more important to teachers than others, and they will demonstrate flexibility on certain provisions of the contract while holding firm on others. Teachers are most likely to grieve what they believe to be violations of contract provisions affecting job security, transfers, class size, and assignment to noncontractual duties (Johnson, 1984).

However, most teachers feel allegiance to their school and to the principal and will try to work out disagreements before resorting to filing grievances. On occasion, teachers have even overridden the objections of union officials and performed duties that were not required by the contract in order to help facilitate a school's program (Johnson, 1984).

Effects of Arbitration on the District

Arbitrators' decisions can have considerable impact on district personnel policies. For that reason, most district administrators attempt to include in the contract language that narrowly defines which disputes may be taken to arbitration. Some administrators make it a practice never to go to arbitration unless they are certain of winning (Salmon, 1983). There is some wisdom in that position. Although the contract language may appear to be straightforward and clear to district administrators, there is no guarantee that the arbitrator will agree with their interpretation, and once an arbitrator's decision has been announced, it establishes a precedent that may be difficult to change (*Contract Administration*, 1983).

Summary

Conflict in work settings usually involves one of four issues: interpretation and application of work rules, allocation of resources, duties and responsibilities, and assessment of performance. The effort to solve work-related conflict requires clarification and discussion of underlying issues, a search for shared values, exploration of possible solutions, and selection of one solution.

Increasingly, schools are relying on grievance procedures developed through the process of collective bargaining to resolve disputes. Arbitration is a component of the grievance procedure in many districts with bargaining agreements. A grievance process permits employees to have their complaints heard by managers or administrators in the organization and, ultimately in most cases, by an impartial arbitrator. Grievance procedures reduce the cost of settling disputes for both employees and employers by taking issues out of the courts and reducing the time required for resolution.

Arbitrators who review disputes between management and labor must decide whose interpretation of the contract is correct. Guidelines that are used by arbitrators to help them arrive at an accurate interpretation of contract language include the rule of consistency and the rule of intent. Arbitrators must frequently deal with complaints that involve interpretation and application of rules. Questions they must answer include to whom rules apply and what actions are either required or forbidden by a rule. "Just cause" complaints refer to contract clauses in which the administration is prohibited from withholding an employee benefit without good reason. These grievances are usually decided on the basis of reasonableness in behavior.

One of the principles used by arbitrators in resolving grievances is past practice. Unless it is clear that the board and the teachers' union intended to institute a new practice, the arbitrator usually holds that previous practice will remain in effect.

Suggested Activities

1. Read Exhibit 14.3 and prepare to present either the grievant's or the board's case before an arbitration panel. Stage a simulated hearing before three classmates representing the panel. After both sides have presented arguments, the panel will make its decision. You may want to locate the case in *Labor Arbitration Reports* to find how it turned out.

2. The principal of an elementary school informs teachers that he is concerned about student behavior in the cafeteria and proposes that they sit with their students while they eat rather than sitting together at one end of the room. There are strong objections from some teachers. There is no policy or contractual agreement that prevents the principal from directing teachers to sit with their students, but he prefers to avoid conflict if possible. How would you advise the principal to resolve this conflict?

3. Interview a principal or director of human resources to learn more about the types of conflict situations that arise with regard to interpretation and application of work rules and how they are usually resolved.

4. Read the following rule and answer the three questions on page 246 regarding work rules.

   Teachers who plan field trips must secure administrative and parental approval in advance and must take necessary precautions to ensure the children's safety while away from school. No trip will be approved that does not have a logical tie-in with the curriculum. Teachers are responsible for making up any missed class time.

EXHIBIT 14.3   *Chicago Board of Education and Chicago Teachers Union Local 1, AFT*

The grievant, R, was employed by Chicago Public Schools as a substitute teacher in 1987 and four years later was appointed to a full-time position at Gary Elementary School. A new principal (L) was assigned to the school in 1993, and R soon began having problems with the new administrator. L assigned written work for teachers that they had not previously been expected to do, and R was unable to keep up. He asked to take student records home so he could complete his work there, but the principal denied his request.

Although he often worked late at school, R continued to fall further behind. Frustrated by the work and his inability to keep up, R on several occasions became angry or irritated with other teachers. In March 1994, the principal, L, initiated a request for R to undergo a physical examination and psychiatric evaluation, citing Board Rule 4-44. The Board's psychiatrist. Dr. G., found that R's mental and physical conditions were within normal limits. R returned to work, but his behavior did not change, and several staff members complained to the principal, several of them indicating that they were afraid that R might harm them physically. In November 1994, the principal again invoked Rule 4-44 and asked R to undergo a second examination. L could have taken disciplinary action against R, in which case R would have had due process rights, but he explained that he chose not to do so because he felt R needed medical help. A different psychiatrist (Dr. W) examined R on this occasion and reported that R appeared "unstable" and "on the verge of a nervous breakdown" due to stress. She recommended that the teacher seek treatment for anxiety and stress before returning to the classroom.

In December 1994, R was directed by the Board to apply for a medical leave of absence or face possible dismissal. R refused to apply for leave and sought to obtain a hearing before the Board. In the meantime, R had begun meeting with a counselor, B, and reported to L that these sessions were helping him. The union attorney wrote to the district superintendent and later to the principal, stating that R had obtained a "clean bill of health" from his personal physician and asking the superintendent to approve an independent examination of the teacher. Neither administrator responded to the attorney's request.

R worked until the start of the winter holiday in December and at that time was placed on medical leave. In early January, he saw Dr. M, who after an examination of R stated that there was no psychiatric reason he should not be allowed to continue to teach. Dr. M admitted that R had difficulty relating to some of his colleagues and also stated that R had a chronic "adjustment disorder" with underlying obsessional and schizoid features. However, he insisted that these problems would not prevent R from functioning normally as a teacher. Dr. M also criticized Dr. W, whose earlier examination of R he described as "slapdash."

In February 1995, the counselor, B, wrote that R showed "no signs of any psychiatric impairment that would interfere with continuing his duties" as a teacher. This statement was contained in a memorandum that B gave to R to use in the attempt to gain reinstatement. In March 1995, the union attorney again wrote the Board with a request for an independent examination of R and threatening court action if the request was denied. The same request was contained in a letter mailed in June to the Director of Employee Health Services. The attorney received no response from either party. In May 1995, the Board acted to require R to file for medical leave of absence or face dismissal. The Board notified R of this decision but took no further action on it.

R filed a grievance in November 1995, which was denied. In February 1996, a conference was held, and a new examination of R was conducted by Dr. W under the supervision of the Director of Employee Health. Later in the month, R was notified that he had successfully passed the examination and was reinstated in his former position. Immediately the principal, L, prepared an application requesting a medical leave of absence and asked R to sign it. R refused. On July 1, L was replaced as principal of Gary School by the assistant principal, D, who was R's former union representative.

EXHIBIT 14.3 *Continued*

Positions of the Parties

The union contended that the Board was required by state law to initiate a remediation process to correct R's behaviors that were a cause of concern. The union also argued that the board had denied R a due process hearing to challenge the demand that he take medical leave, even though Illinois law stated that R had a property interest which could not be taken without due process. It also pointed out that the Director of Employee Health Services had admitted that in previous cases employees who had requested a second medical opinion were granted it. Finally, the union stated that the Board had denied R the opportunity to participate in the district's employee assistance program which covered stress and emotional problems.

The Board argued that it had a right to order a complete physical examination of the teacher and that, based on the results of that examination, there was a reasonable basis to conclude that R was unfit for duty. The Board also stated that employees did not have the right to request a second examination and that an involuntary medical leave of absence was not the same as termination and therefore did not require a due process hearing.

Relevant Contract Provisions

Board Rule Sec. 4-33

The superintendent shall have authority, subject to approval of the Board, to grant a leave of absence to an employee who shall file a written request and present proof establishing personal illness.

Any employee who is granted an extension of leave shall be required to pass a health examination by a medical examiner selected by the superintendent before return to duty. If the employee does not pass such examination and makes written request to the superintendent for additional medical opinion, the superintendent shall select another medical examiner acceptable to both the employee's personal physician and the superintendent. If the medical opinions are in disagreement, a third medical examiner shall be selected.

Board Rule Sec. 4-44

The superintendent shall have authority to require a health examination by a medical examiner selected by the superintendent of any employee whenever, in the judgment of the superintendent, there seems to exist any disability which might impair the efficiency of such employee.

Issues

1. Whether the Board deviated from policy or violated the collective agreement when it placed R on involuntary leave of absence.
2. Whether the Board deviated from policy or violated the collective agreement when it failed until February 1996 to respond to demands for R's reinstatement.
3. If the board deviated from policy or violated the collective agreement in either respect, what is the appropriate remedy?

Source: Reprinted with permission from *Labor Relations Reporter-Labor Arbitration Reports.* 108 LA 1193. Copyright 1997 by the Bureau of National Affairs, Inc. (800-372-1033).

Online Resources

A number of sites with information on dispute resolution are listed below.

Department of Education (www.ed.gov/database/ericdigest/ed339791.html)
This site provides information on educational resources and guidelines on dealing with conflict resolution within educational institutions.

Equal Employment Opportunity Commission (http://www.eeoc.gov)
Information about the use of alternate dispute resolution in the EEO complaint/appeal process is given on this website.

Office of Personnel Management (http://www.opm.gov/er)
Information is presented about the Office of Personnel Management. The site contains a resource guide for alternate dispute resolution.

American Arbitration Association (http://www.adr.org/publications.html)
This site shares a list of AAA periodicals that address the latest developments in alternate dispute resolution.

CPR-Institute for Dispute Resolution (http://www.cpradr.ord/welcome.htm)
This site provides information about a nonprofit alliance of corporations and firms using alternate dispute resolution.

Mediation Information and Resource Center (http://www.mediate.com)
Information about mediation and a list of mediator resources are given.

Federal Mediation and Conciliation Service (FMCS) (www.fmcs.gov/about fmcs.htm)
FMCS is a federal agency that provides mediators free of charge to parties at impasse in contract negotiations. It also provides parties with lists of grievance arbitrators.

Society of Professionals in Dispute Resolution (SPIDR). (http://www.spidr.org/pubs.htm)
Publications of the Society are listed.

References

Boys Markets Inc. v. *Retail Clerks, Local 770*, 398 U.S. 235 (1970).

Chicago Board of Education and Chicago Teacher Union Local 1, AFT, 108 LA1193 (1997).

Contract administration: Understanding limitations on management rights. (1983). Eugene, OR: University of Oregon, Center for Educational Policy and Management. (ERIC Document Reproduction Service No. ED 271842).

Coulson, R. (1986). *Arbitration in the schools: An analysis of fifty-nine grievance arbitration cases.* New York: American Arbitration Association.

Elkouri, F., & Elkouri, E. (1973). *How arbitration works.* Washington, DC: Bureau of National Affairs.

Fossey, R. (1992). *Site-based management in a collective bargaining environment: Can we mix oil and water?* (ERIC Document Reproduction Service No. ED 355644).

Johnson, S. (1984). *Teacher unions in schools.* Philadelphia: Temple University Press.

Lexington Local Board of Education and Lexington Support Association, 111 LA 411 (1998).

Lovell, N. (1985). *Grievance arbitration in education.* Bloomington, IN: Phi Delta Kappa.

Lutz, F., & Caldwell, W. (1979). Collective bargaining and the principal. In D. Erickson & T. Reller (Eds.), *The principal in metropolitan schools* (pp. 256–271). Berkeley, CA: McCutchan.

McDermott, E. P. (1996). *Alternative dispute resolution in the workplace.* Westport, CT: Quorum.

Ostrander, K. (1981). *A grievance arbitration guide for educators.* Boston: Allyn and Bacon.

Ostrander, K. (1987). *The legal structure of collective bargaining in education.* New York: Greenwood Press.

Papa, M., & Canary, D. (1995). Conflict in organizations: A competence-based approach. In A. Nicotera (Ed.), *Conflict and organizations* (pp. 153–179). Albany: State University of New York Press.

Pneuman, R. W., & Bruehl, M. E. (1982). *Managing conflict.* Englewood Cliffs, NJ: Prentice Hall.

Rahim, M. (1986). *Managing conflict in organizations.* New York: Praeger.

Salmon, H. (1983, April). *A superintendent's perspective of the grievance process.* Paper presented at the annual meeting of the National School Boards Association, San Francisco. (ERIC Document Reproduction Service No. ED 251927).

Stitt, A. (1998). *Alternative dispute resolution for organizations.* Toronto: John Wiley.

Tjosvold, D. (1993). *Learning to manage conflict.* New York: Lexington.

Turner, S., & Weed, F. (1983). *Conflict in organizations.* Englewood Cliffs, NJ: Prentice Hall.

Yates, D., Jr. (1985). *The politics of management.* San Francisco: Jossey-Bass.

15

Termination and Reduction in Force

The emphasis in this book has been to improve on how teacher quality and performance through the application of sound principles of human resources management. This positive approach, when carried out consistently over time, will produce significant gains in the quality of instruction in schools.

However, there are times when less pleasant actions must be taken. When enrollments decline or funds are lost, reductions in force may be necessary, and when a teacher who appeared promising proves to be unable to manage a classroom successfully, termination must be considered. These actions are the subject of this chapter.

Plan of the Chapter

This chapter deals with the following topics: (1) carrying out a reduction in force, (2) reduction in force and employees' rights, (3) discipline of school personnel, (4) incompetence in the classroom, (5) dismissal and nonrenewal, (6) documenting unsatisfactory performance, and (7) rights of dismissed teachers.

Carrying Out a Reduction in Force

The purpose of a reduction-in-force (RIF) policy is to permit the district to achieve necessary cutbacks in the number of employees on the payroll without disrupting services. That outcome is most likely to be achieved if a policy providing fair, efficient, and consistent procedures for carrying out cutbacks has been developed in advance of the need (DeKalb County School System, 1979).

The need for reductions in the number of employees can arise in several ways. Developments that most often result in layoffs are declining enrollments, funding shortfalls, discontinuation of programs, and reorganization or consolidation of school districts. About four-fifths of the states have legislation that legitimizes reductions in force for one or more of those reasons (Zirkel & Bargerstock, 1981).

If a state statute does not expressly identify a particular factor as a legitimate basis for laying off an employee, then the school district may be on shaky ground if it implements reductions for that reason. A Pennsylvania court reinstated a teacher who had been laid off by a district that had experienced a budget shortfall because financial exigency was not identified in the state statute as an acceptable reason for laying off employees (Zirkel & Bargerstock, 1981). However, some state courts have held that declining enrollments in one program may justify staff reductions, even though total enrollments are not declining (Caplan, 1984). The seven steps involved in carrying out a reduction in force and the individual or department responsible for each are shown in Exhibit 15.1 and discussed in the sections that follow.

Determining That a Surplus Exists

The first step in carrying out a reduction in force is determining that layoffs are needed. If enrollment drops or funding is cut, the district may need fewer employees. When the number of excess personnel is small, normal attrition may achieve the needed reductions, but if it doesn't, other possibilities, including reduction in force, must be considered. The decision to lay off personnel is made by the district superintendent after consultations with other administrators. Among the factors to

EXHIBIT 15.1   *Steps Involved in Implementing Reduction in Force*

Step	*Responsible Individual or Department*
1. Determination that surplus exists	Superintendent (in consultation with principals and other administrators)
2. Identification of position classifications and certification fields affected	Human resources department (or official designated by superintendent)
3. Review of alternative actions	Superintendent, human resources department, finance department, and principals
4. Identification of a potential reduction-in-force pool	Human resources department, director of instruction, and union officials
5. Rank individuals in the pool using criteria established by law and policy	Human resources department with assistance from principals and others
6. Review of ranked list to remove protected individuals and groups	Human resources with assistance from superintendent, principals, and other administrators
7. Implementation of reduction in force	Superintendent, human resources department, and principals

be considered before a final decision is made are enrollments, state statutes, accreditation standards, financial condition, court rulings, and program priorities (DeKalb County School System, 1979).

Identifying Classifications Affected

Once the superintendent has declared a personnel surplus, the human resources department is faced with the task of determining surplus personnel by position classification and certification field. If enrollments have dropped in business education courses, for example, the human resources department may declare a surplus of business education teachers. The number of surplus teachers will depend on the size of the enrollment decline, the number of teachers with business education certification employed by the district, and the number of teachers required to maintain the program.

Reviewing Alternatives

Layoffs are a traumatic experience for individuals involved. When layoffs occur, even employees who are not directly affected may experience feelings of depression and anxiety out of empathy for colleagues who are being laid off and feelings of concern for their own future security. It is sometimes possible to avoid the stress of layoffs by taking action to postpone or avoid the need to carry out a reduction in force. Among the actions to be considered are early retirement, unpaid leaves of absence, half-time employment, assistance in finding alternative employment, and retraining.

Early Retirement.   Early retirement is one of the most widely used methods for avoiding reductions in force because it solves the problem of surplus personnel without the trauma of layoffs. On the other hand, early retirement is expensive and is not always a satisfactory solution. It works best when enrollments are declining at an equal rate in all grade levels and programs and when the district has a relatively large number of employees nearing retirement age. If personnel surpluses are concentrated in a few programs or grade levels or if few individuals are close to retiring, early retirement is less likely to be a viable solution.

Leaves of Absence.   Unpaid leaves of absence have the advantage of allowing employees to continue in-force insurance policies that are provided by the district. An employee is thus able to secure health insurance for self and family at rates below those that are available to individuals. Normally, the individual must pay the premium for the policy, but in some instances that cost is borne by the district. Employees on unpaid leave will be reinstated if a position is available at the expiration of the leave. Unpaid leaves offer psychological support at a crucial time by letting employees know that the district still values their contributions and wishes to continue the employer/employee relationship.

Part-Time Employment. Half-time or substitute positions are sometimes offered to employees who otherwise would be laid off, in the belief that most people would rather work part time than not work at all. If one position is assigned to two half-time employees, both have some income, whereas an employee who is laid off receives no income. As a temporary measure to give employees time to find alternative employment, half-time work helps.

Job-Hunting Assistance. Providing assistance to help individuals who are laid off to find new jobs is a psychologically sound strategy, since it motivates these employees to take action and move forward. Employees who receive layoff notices are sometimes immobilized by the hope that they will quickly be recalled. Rather than try to find another job, they sometimes waste months waiting for a recall notice. Beginning a systematic and wide-ranging job search can help them cope more realistically with their situation by assessing their strengths and examining their options.

Retraining Teachers. Retraining teachers who are about to be laid off is a viable strategy if enrollments in the subjects in which they are retrained are expected to remain stable. Teachers who are near to being certified in critical subjects are sometimes allowed to begin teaching classes in those subjects on temporary teaching certificates while they continue to take courses to qualify for full certification. However, teachers who lack the necessary subject matter competence should not be permitted to teach until they acquire it.

Identifying the Potential Pool

If alternative actions are not feasible, or if after such actions are taken an oversupply of teachers remains, the district then begins the crucial step of preparing a list of employees who are subject to being laid off. The list is prepared by reviewing personnel files of all individuals in the affected positions, using criteria established by the reduction-in-force policy. In the example used earlier, the pool might include all business education teachers or, in a large district, business education teachers with fewer than a specified number of years seniority.

It is wise to involve the director of instruction early in the process. Some programs require teachers who are certified in certain subspecialties in order to operate effectively, and the director of instruction can provide that information. A good example is a music program that involves offerings in chorus, band, and orchestra. A school with several tenured band teachers and no tenured chorus or orchestra teachers may end up with an oversupply of band teachers if seniority is the sole criterion for making reduction-in-force decisions. The director of instruction can identify needed adjustments in the pool in order to maintain a well-balanced instructional program.

Rank Ordering the Pool

Personnel files of employees who are included in the pool are reviewed and any who are considered essential for the continued operation of school programs are protected by being moved out of the pool. A teacher who is endorsed in a subject in which shortages exist or one whose teaching duties cannot be assumed by others in the department may be removed from the pool. This is a good time to review the bargaining agreement and state statutes to ensure that those documents are not violated in the process of carrying out the reduction in force. If there is a question about the interpretation of contract or statutory provisions, union officials and the board attorney should be consulted.

Factors that may be taken into account in determining which employees are assigned to the pool, in addition to seniority and tenure status, are performance ratings, extra-duty assignments, and additional certification areas. Teachers who perform extra duties, such as department head or cheerleader sponsor, may be protected from layoff over teachers with more seniority who do not perform extra duties.

Reviewing of Ranked List

At this point, a final review of the ranked list is carried out, with involvement of principals and various district staff members. The purpose of the review is to make deletions and additions that may be needed in order to avoid violating provisions of state law, negotiated agreements, and district policy, and to provide safeguards against disruptions of programs and unnecessary harm to program quality. When the review is complete and the superintendent has signed off, the list goes to the human resources department, which initiates the process of notifying affected employees.

Implementing Reduction in Force

The final step in the process is to notify the individual employees who are to be laid off from their jobs. This is usually done by letter from the superintendent or the director of human resources. The letter identifies the date that the reduction in force becomes effective and outlines the employee's rights under the law and the bargaining agreement.

Reduction in Force and Employees' Rights

Collective bargaining agreements and state statutes grant certain rights to employees who are subject to being laid off. These rights include privileges earned through seniority, the opportunity to continue health insurance in effect at the employee's expense, and future reinstatement when funding permits.

In general, more senior workers are protected against layoffs when other employees with less seniority hold the same job. However, administrators sometimes decide to lay off a teacher with more seniority while retaining one with less seniority. When that happens, the district may expect to face a court challenge.

An example involved a Pennsylvania school district. The superintendent retained a teacher with less seniority as coordinator of a program for gifted students and laid off teachers who had more seniority. The administrator's rationale was that the teacher who was retained was more qualified for the position because she had been involved with the program since its inception, had more experience with arts and humanities, and was better at interacting with students and members of the community. Those arguments might have prevailed in some states, but the Pennsylvania Supreme Court held that the law of that state required the district to lay off employees with the least seniority (*Dallap* v. *Sharon City School District*, 1990).

Under collective bargaining agreements in force in many school districts, employees who are threatened with layoffs may replace or "bump" an employee with less seniority. However, this right has limitations. The bumping teacher must possess a valid certificate to teach the subject taught by the teacher being bumped and must have more seniority than the bumped teacher. It is common to require teachers who bump other teachers to have had recent and successful experience teaching the subject to which they are requesting to transfer. In some districts, the bargaining agreement gives the principal of the school receiving a replacement teacher the prerogative of reviewing the transferring teacher's credentials to determine whether that individual's qualifications are sufficient to maintain program quality (Johnson, 1982). In districts with such a policy, a teacher who received certification to teach a subject many years earlier but has never taught in that field and has taken no recent coursework would not be permitted to replace a teacher with more up-to-date credentials and experience.

Protection for Minorities

Minority employees who have been hired under affirmative action programs often have the least seniority in their districts and therefore are most vulnerable to reductions in force. Bargaining agreements sometimes provide protection from layoffs for these individuals. In one case involving such a policy, the Supreme Court held that the board failed to show a "compelling purpose" in arguing that past societal discrimination justified the plan and so rejected it. The Court stated:

> Societal discrimination alone is [not] sufficient to justify a racial classification. Rather, the Court has insisted upon some showing of prior discrimination by the governmental unit involved before allowing limited use of racial classifications in order to remedy such discrimination. (*Wygant* v. *Jackson (MI) Board of Education*, 1986)

However, in a case tried under Title VII of the Civil Rights Act, the Supreme Court upheld a plan that benefitted individuals who had not been identified as actual victims of discrimination (*Geier* v. *Alexander*, 1986).

Layoffs in Site-Based Schools

Most reduction-in-force policies were developed for districts in which uniform personnel allocation formulas are in effect in all schools, but under site-based management, staffing patterns may vary from school to school. Schools are allowed to decide whether to use established staffing ratios to decide how many teachers and other staff members to hire or to adopt alternative formulas and, for example, hire fewer teachers and more technicians and aides (Odden & Picus, 1992).

Alternative staffing practices raise complex questions when a layoff is necessary. Suppose a school has given up one teaching position in exchange for three instructional aides. If the school is scheduled to lose a teaching position in a reduction in force, should it have the option of releasing either one teacher or the three aides?

A similar question might arise in a school that uses computer-based instruction and hires a computer technician in place of a teacher to assist in producing instructional materials. Suppose that a RIF takes place and the faculty decide that they cannot operate the program without the technician's assistance. Should the technician be retained and a teacher laid off? When a reduction in force occurs, the district specifies the departments and subjects that will lose staff. Since the technician assists teachers in all subject areas but is not assigned to any one department, is he or she immune from being laid off?

In some localities, school councils are given the option of transferring funds across budget categories and may reallocate money from one account to another (Clune & White, 1988). Suppose that teachers in a school agree to teach larger classes and apply the salary savings to the purchase of books and materials. Since the school has in effect already reduced its staff size, should it be immune from further personnel cuts during a reduction in force?

In all of these situations, the answer to the question depends on board policy, past practice, and the collective bargaining agreement. When districts adopt school-based management, employee unions are often asked to agree to permit waivers of certain provisions of the master contract (Poltrock & Goss, 1993). Some have agreed to do that, but other unions have refused to permit any deviation from contract language related to reduction in force (Clark, 1993). Districts need to develop clear and specific guidelines governing layoffs, so that when questions such as these arise they can be answered.

Staffing Adjustments Required

When a reduction in force takes place, principals are required to make adjustments in staffing by redistributing instructional and noninstructional assignments among the remaining staff members. In the case of elementary schools, this may involve nothing more than reducing the number of classes in the affected grade levels and reassigning students, but it often involves much more. In middle and high schools, principals are faced with making adjustments in the master schedule to reflect shifting enrollment patterns brought about by the elimination of some course offerings.

For example, if fewer classes are offered in the business education department because of staff reductions, existing classes in that department as well as in other departments may increase in size, as a result of the reduced number of elective options available to students.

These changes in enrollment patterns also have implications for the purchase of equipment, materials, and supplies. If available business education classes increase in size, it may be necessary to purchase additional computers to accommodate the increased enrollment.

If teachers who were laid off were sponsors of student clubs or activities, it will be necessary for the principal to arrange to recruit other teachers to take over those duties rather than let the programs languish. If the layoffs involved nonteaching personnel, such as guidance counselors, the principal must see to it that the workload is redistributed equitably among remaining staff members.

The decision to carry out a reduction in force is not an easy one, but it is simple compared to the difficulty and distress that faces an administrator who attempts to terminate a teacher. The next section addresses the topic of teacher discipline and termination.

Discipline of School Personnel

On occasion, disciplinary action must be taken against a school employee who has been guilty of breaking the law or violating board policy. In a progressive disciplinary system, the action taken depends on the seriousness of the incident and whether it is a first-time offense. For a minor offense, the usual disciplinary action is an oral reprimand. For example, an oral reprimand would be an appropriate response for a teacher who oversleeps and arrives late for school but fails to call ahead to notify the office.

A more serious disciplinary response is a written reprimand, which is issued after an employee has broken a rule several times, or, in the case of a more serious infraction, after the first offense. A written reprimand would be appropriate when a school bus is involved in a minor traffic accident as a result of carelessness on the part of the driver of the bus. The next disciplinary steps, in order of progressive severity, are suspension with or without pay and nonrenewal or termination. In addition to these actions, in some states salary adjustment is used for disciplinary purposes.

The contents of an oral or written reprimand are similar. In both cases, the administrator issuing the reprimand identifies the action that is the basis for the reprimand and cites the policy that has been violated. The employee is reminded to refrain from the action in the future and warned of the consequences of failing to do so.

Exhibit 15.2 shows an example of a written reprimand issued by a principal to a tenured teacher who engaged in an altercation with a student. The administrator describes the actions for which the reprimand is issued, cites the policy that was violated, and admonishes the teacher to refrain from future violations. One copy of

EXHIBIT 15.2   *Letter of Reprimand to a Teacher*

Ms. Wanda Olson
Price Elementary School
Clearfield, OH 43236

Dear Ms. Olson:

On Thursday, October 11, you engaged in an argument with a student, Mary Anne Carter, during which you admit calling her a "lame brain" and making derogatory remarks about her appearance. When Mary Anne's mother called you to complain, you admit that you refused to discuss the incident with her and suggested that she call me.

Let me remind you that board policy states that teachers in Clearfield Schools will avoid harsh, abusive, and profane language in front of students. The policy also states that teachers will, when asked, arrange to meet with parents to discuss questions and concerns. In the incident described above, you were in violation of this policy.

I realize that the student's behavior was provocative, and I have taken appropriate disciplinary measures with the student. However, the child's behavior, while not acceptable, does not excuse your actions. Therefore, I am issuing this reprimand and directing you to avoid further violations of this policy. If you ignore this directive, more serious measures will be taken. I hope and trust that you will exhibit professional behavior in all future dealings with students and parents. A copy of this letter will be placed in your personnel file, but if you finish the school year without further violations of board policies, the letter will be removed.

Sincerely,

Mark W. Williams
Principal

---

the written reprimand goes to the employee, and a second copy is placed in his or her personnel file. The file copy may be removed after a time if the employee has no further infractions.

When a teacher or other school employee is involved in a serious infraction of a rule or law, the disciplinary action is proportionately more severe. As a general rule, an employee who is arrested and charged with possessing or selling drugs will be suspended without pay pending a court decision. If the individual is found guilty, he or she can expect to be terminated.

When an employee is disciplined for breaking a law or school board policy, the action is often challenged by the individual, who charges either that the severity of the punishment is disproportionate to the seriousness of the crime or that the employer obtained the information illegally. A number of state and federal statutes limit employers' access to and use of private information about employees. It is important to be aware of this legislation in considering disciplinary actions against employees.

Among federal safeguards against unauthorized release of private information about employees is the Electronic Communications Privacy Act of 1986, which protects electronic communication, such as email, from unauthorized disclosure. However, the law does allow employers to disclose information transmitted by electronic means if the government requests the information. Thus, the Federal Bureau of Investigation is able to access personal email records of an employee it suspects of breaking the law or having information about a violation. The Drug-Free Workplace Act, passed by Congress in 1988, provides that employers who receive federal grants or contracts are required to notify the government if an employee is convicted of a drug violation that occurs in the workplace. The employer must also take corrective action to prevent a recurrence. The Health Insurance Portability and Accountability Act of 1996 provides for a fine of up to $250,000 and/or imprisonment for an employer who discloses information about the health of an employee without authorization (Hubbartt, 1998).

State laws must also be considered before decisions are made about discipline of employees. Right-to-privacy laws in some states place limits on the collection or use of nonjob-related information about employees, and legal protections exist in a number of states to safeguard employees from false charges of drug use resulting from unreliable tests. State laws also place limits on employers' use of arrest records in making employment decisions where the arrested individual was never convicted of a crime (Hubbartt, 1998).

Most states have laws governing the collection and management of information about employees. Commonly, these laws specify the types of information that employers may and may not collect and grant to employees the right to access their personnel files and request copies of records on evaluation, compensation, and discipline (Hubbartt, 1998).

Incompetence in the Classroom

Some observers believe that the greatest impediment to the improvement of instruction in schools is the quality of teachers. It has been argued that teacher competence is the most severe problem facing the schools and that school administrators have been lax in failing to take firm and prompt action to dismiss teachers who are not performing satisfactorily (Johnson, 1984). Bridges (1985) has argued the point forcefully:

> Most teachers in our nation's schools are competent, conscientious, hard-working individuals. All too often their efforts are overshadowed by the poor performance of a relatively small number of incompetent classroom teachers. These incompetents must be identified and assisted, and if they fail to improve, they must be dismissed. (p. 19)

Scriven (1980) took an even more critical position:

The current state of teacher personnel policies is that they are reasonably fair to teachers—a great improvement over the pre-union situation—and extremely unfair to students, parents and taxpayers. They protect all, but they *excessively* protect the congenital incompetent, the once-but-no-longer competent and the competent non-performer....We have teacher policies that ruthlessly sacrifice productivity for equity. Productivity without equity is morally intolerable; equity without productivity is socially irresponsible. (p. 2)

How accurate are these charges? Is quality of teachers a critical problem in the schools? Are administrators remiss in failing to act to remove incompetent performers? Are we overly concerned with protecting the rights of poorly performing teachers at the expense of students? These are important questions that will be examined in this section.

Views of Teacher Quality Problem

The public has a more sanguine view of the quality of public school teachers today as compared to a decade ago. The 2000 Gallup Poll of the public's attitudes toward the public schools reported than only 4 percent of respondents cited difficulty in hiring "good" teachers as one of the biggest problems facing public schools. Concerns cited by a larger percentage of respondents were lack of financial support for schools; poor discipline; overcrowding; fighting, violence, and gangs; use of drugs; crime and vandalism; and concern about standards and the quality of student learning. Items that were tied with teacher quality in frequency of mention were parents' lack of interest and support for schools, low teacher pay, and too few teachers (Rose & Gallup, 2000). Previous surveys had found that teacher quality was cited as a problem by 7 percent of respondents in the 1993 Gallup Poll and by 11 percent in 1988 (Elam, Rose, & Gallup, 1993; Gallup & Elam, 1988).

Not surprisingly, teachers are less likely than parents and administrators to agree that teacher quality is a major concern. However, even teachers agree that a problem exists, and those who teach with incompetent teachers often report that they feel demoralized. Some are discouraged because they feel they try hard to do a good job while some of their colleagues do nothing more than the minimum (Johnson, 1984).

Administrative Responsibility

Few teachers are willing to take a personal position on incompetence in the profession or to pressure union officers to do so. However, many of them believe that administrators should set high standards for teacher performance and take action against teachers who do not meet those standards (Johnson, 1984).

Many administrators and some teachers believe that unions protect both incompetent teachers and those who have lost interest in teaching but remain in the classroom. However, others, including many administrators, believe that poor teachers can be removed from classrooms if the procedures that are available are put into use by principals (Johnson, 1984).

One of the concerns expressed by administrators and union leaders alike is that in the current concern for school productivity, teachers' rights are likely to be overlooked. Gross (1988) pointed out the danger and suggested a possible solution:

> Requiring fact rather than assumption as a basis for disciplinary action may appear on the surface to make it more difficult to dismiss immoral or incompetent teachers. On the contrary, identifying and eliminating unfairness in the current disciplinary system for tenured teachers will require school districts to develop hiring, evaluation, promotion, and disciplinary policies and practices that can be validated with competent evidence. (p. 2)*

If selection and evaluation procedures are in place and working well, there should rarely be a need to dismiss teachers. Yet, even when care and thought are exercised in selecting and placing teachers, and when opportunities for professional growth are provided, there will still be a few who do not perform the job satisfactorily or who lapse into substandard performance after a time. Districts should monitor the performance of all teachers and be prepared to take action against those few who fail to meet their standards of performance.

School boards review recommendations for dismissal of school employees and decide whether the action is warranted. Traditionally, boards have also heard appeals of a decision to dismiss an employee. Teachers believe that school boards have a conflict of interest that lessens the chance that a person who is terminated will receive a fair hearing. As a result of these concerns, legislatures in more than half of the states have in recent years enacted laws to change the procedures by which termination decisions are made and appeals heard (Lopez & Sperry, 1994).

A variety of alternative practices for ensuring due process to teachers who have been terminated have emerged to replace the practice of lodging all authority with school boards. In most of the states that have revised their procedures, hearing officers or panels, usually individuals with legal training who are not employees of the board, serve as objective fact finders, and school boards determine whether the facts justify dismissal of an employee. In a small number of states, school boards have been removed from the process of teacher termination altogether (Lopez & Sperry, 1994).

Administrators sometimes argue that the protections enacted to safeguard teachers' academic freedom make it difficult or impossible to dismiss incompetent teachers. They claim that the elaborate and time-consuming procedures required to document poor performance and the cost of hiring attorneys to handle court actions arising from termination decisions discourage them from trying to remove poor teachers from classrooms. To achieve balance, legislatures in several states have adopted laws eliminating or restricting tenure for public school teachers. In some cases, teachers receive a renewable one- or two-year contract and may be terminated with or without cause upon expiration of the contract (Hirsch, 1998).

Dismissal and Nonrenewal

Many employers operate under an employment-at-will doctrine that allows the employer to terminate an employee at any time for any cause or no cause. The employer who is protected by the doctrine incurs no legal liability for terminating an employee. The exception to employment-at-will occurs when an employee is under contract or is protected by statute (Sovereign, 1999). Nontenured teachers are usually employed under contract, and if a district determines that the teacher's performance is not satisfactory and acts to terminate his or her employment before the contract expires, the district generally must be prepared to defend its action. The exception occurs if a teacher is hired without a written or implied contract.

Nonrenewal occurs when a nontenured teacher's contract expires and the district chooses not to renew it. No reason need be given, and the teacher generally has no recourse. Administrators should exercise care not to imply to an employee that his or her contract will be renewed. Suggesting that a contract will be renewed is referred to as an *implied contract* and may require that the district furnish reasons for its decision not to renew the individual's contract (Sovereign, 1999).

State statutes and board policies identify the basis on which tenured teachers may be dismissed from their jobs and prescribe the procedures to be followed in carrying out a decision to terminate. An administrator who recommends termination of a tenured employee should be careful to adhere to every requirement of the law and policy or have sound reasons for any failure to do so. Since most termination decisions end up in court, the district must be prepared to defend its actions by showing that the decision to dismiss was neither arbitrary nor capricious. If the district fails that test, there is a good chance that the court will direct the district to reinstate the teacher with back pay.

The first step for an administrator contemplating dismissing a teacher is to become thoroughly familiar with the applicable policy and/or statute and to carefully follow the procedures outlined therein. In general, policies and statutes deal with the kinds of behavior that are regarded as justifiable grounds for dismissal, time lines, the type of notification to be given to the teacher, hearing procedures, and due process protections. If the teacher is tenured, the due process guarantees are more elaborate than for a teacher who is still on probation.

Arizona law states that a teacher who is charged with unprofessional conduct, conduct in violation of laws or rules, or inadequate classroom performance must be given specific examples of the actions or omissions that led to the charge and a list of the rules or laws that the teacher is alleged to have violated. The purpose of this provision is to allow the teacher to prepare a defense. Arizona also grants any teacher receiving such a notice the right to a hearing (Dismissal of Certificated Teacher, 2000).

A district should not allow any information to be included in any employee's personnel record unless the individual has seen it. If a document is to be included in an employee's personnel file, it is advisable to ask the employee to sign a statement verifying that he or she has seen the document and is aware that it will become part of the personnel file. One of the first things defense attorneys ask for when they initiate legal action against an employer is the employee's personnel record. If they find information in the record that the employee has never seen, they can use that discovery to persuade the court that the employee's superiors were biased (Sovereign, 1999).

An employee who is dismissed may go to court and charge wrongful discharge, defamation, or discrimination. To avoid these possibilities, care should be taken to fully explore the basis for any such possible claims. If an employee is covered by a negotiated agreement between management and labor, human resources personnel should ensure that no provision in the agreement is violated by the dismissal. Similarly, if a written or oral contract exists with the dismissed employee, the action to dismiss should be designed not to violate terms of the contract. An employee may have grounds for a charge of defamation of character if attorneys can produce a statement by the employer that disparages the employee's appearance, work, attitudes, or behavior. Charges of discrimination are likely to be upheld in court if it can be shown that an individual member of a protected class was passed over for promotion or given smaller-than-average salary increases because of his or her gender, religion, racial or ethnic background, or physical disability status (Sovereign, 1999).

The district's chances of prevailing in litigation by a discharged employee are enhanced if the district has adopted reasonable rules and regulations and these have been communicated to all employees and enforced consistently and fairly. It is also helpful if any employee who has been charged or disciplined for any reason is given adequate opportunity to present his or her side and, if necessary, given time and assistance to improve his or her job performance (Sovereign, 1999).

State statutes identify specific causes for which teachers may be dismissed. The most common grounds for dismissal are incompetence or neglect of duty, immorality or unprofessional conduct, and insubordination. Some states allow dismissal for "good or just cause" and "inefficiency" (Neill & Custis, 1978).

Dismissed teachers have been charged, among other things, with failing to maintain classroom control, abuse of students, excessive tardiness, failure to maintain self-control, and refusing to accept supervision. Dismissals have also been based on failure to use up-to-date teaching methods, failure to use tact in dealing with students and co-workers, and low student achievement. In most cases of incompetence, teachers fall short of an acceptable standard of performance in several areas.

Incompetence or Neglect of Duty

Incompetence covers a broad range of conditions and behaviors. Physical or mental incapacity and lack of knowledge of subject are examples of behaviors that have been successfully cited as evidence of incompetent teaching. Other examples include failure to maintain appropriate discipline, mistreatment of students, failure to adopt new teaching methods, lack of cooperation, and personal misconduct in or out of school (Valente, 1980).

Courts generally interpret statutes on teacher dismissal to favor teachers, which places on the district the burden of assembling substantial documentation to show that the teacher was guilty of persistent dereliction of duty or lack of cooperation. Testimony of department heads, supervisors, other teachers, parents, and even students may be introduced to establish incompetence and to show a connection between the teacher's conduct and his or her performance as a teacher. If the board is not successful in convincing the court of the teacher's incompetence, it may be ordered to reinstate the teacher and pay lost wages and damages *(Education Law,* 1989).

Physical disability may not be used as the basis for dismissal of an employee except when the individual has a contagious disease or is so severely impaired that even with reasonable accommodation he or she is unable to perform effectively in a job. *Reasonable accommodation* is defined by the Equal Employment Opportunity Commission (EEOC) as modifications to the manner in which a job is customarily performed that enable a qualified individual with a disability to perform the essential functions of that position (Schneid, 1992).

When a district contemplates terminating a tenured teacher for incompetence, it must explain to the teacher in what areas his or her performance is deficient. Time must then be given to the teacher to correct his or her problems. As a rule, a single incident of poor judgment or incompetent behavior is not sufficient to justify termination of a tenured teacher. Courts look for patterns of behavior, and if none is found, they are likely to support reinstatement.

An example of one such case involved a teacher from Maine who worked outside of school as a gunsmith. The teacher inadvertently brought a revolver and some ammunition to school in a jacket pocket. The jacket, with the weapon inside, was stolen and the teacher was later dismissed by the school committee, which argued that bringing the revolver and ammunition to school were evidence of grave lack of judgment that justified dismissal. The court reversed the committee's action, noting that dismissal was not justified when the individual's ability to teach effectively was not in question *(Wright* v. *Superintending School Committee,* 1976).

Immoral or Unprofessional Behavior

Dismissing a teacher on grounds of immoral or unprofessional conduct places on the board the burden of showing that the teacher's behavior had an adverse impact on students or other teachers. There is no absolute standard against which such behavior is judged. Rather, the courts take into account such factors as age and maturity of the students, degree of adverse impact, motive for the behavior, and the likelihood that it will be repeated (Alexander & Alexander, 1985).

Teachers have been discharged on grounds of immoral behavior for engaging in sexual misconduct with students. Some courts have held that when sexual involvement occurs between teacher and student, a presumption of adverse impact is justified without additional proof (McCarthy & Cambron-McCabe, 1987). Other examples of immoral behavior for which teachers have been discharged are physical abuse of students, use of profanity, misconduct involving drugs or alcohol, and misappropriation of funds.

Homosexual behavior has been allowed as grounds for dismissal in some courts, but not in others (Landauer, Spangler, & Van Horn, 1983). As a general rule, private sexual behavior, whether homosexual or heterosexual, is regarded by the courts as grounds for dismissal only to the extent that it affects the individual's effectiveness as a teacher. But it should also be noted that teachers are regarded as exemplars and that their actions "are subject to much greater scrutiny than that given to the activities of the average person" (*Chicago Board of Education* v. *Payne*, 1982).

A teacher who is convicted of a crime of moral turpitude may be dismissed. However, an arrest alone is not usually sufficient grounds for dismissal, although it may be justifiable grounds for suspension. Sexual crimes are considered irremediable and are sufficient to justify dismissal. Use of drugs can justify immediate suspension pending dismissal (*Education Law*, 1989).

Insubordination

Insubordination is a lawful cause for dismissal of teachers in many states. Actions that may be construed as insubordinate include failing to follow rules and regulations pertaining to use of corporal punishment, absenteeism, tardiness, and failing to complete required reports.

Insubordination also includes a teacher's refusal to perform properly assigned duties. Administrators may assign duties that are not specified in a bargaining agreement as long as they are reasonably related to the instructional program and are not unduly time consuming or burdensome. However, a teacher may not lawfully be dismissed for refusing to perform duties for which he or she lacks competence or that are unrelated to the school program (*Education Law*, 1989).

Some courts have held that a single incident of insubordination is sufficient to justify dismissal. A teacher in Kansas was dismissed after he had his wife call the school to report that he was ill while he was actually in Texas interviewing for another job. The teacher had earlier requested and been denied leave. The principal of the school at which the teacher taught learned of the deception when the principal of the Texas school in which he interviewed called for a recommendation. The Kansas Court of Appeals upheld the decision to terminate the teacher's contract, noting that a single incident of insubordination could be sufficient to justify termination (*Gaylord* v. *Board of Education*, 1990). A similar conclusion was reached by the Colorado Supreme Court, which held that a district was justified in dismissing a teacher who had used profanity in front of several students after having been ordered by the superintendent to refrain from doing so (*Ware* v. *Morgan County School District*, 1988).

A board is most likely to win a legal test of a decision to dismiss a teacher for insubordination if it can show that the teacher knew about but repeatedly violated a rule, regulation, or directive, thereby causing harm to the school. The board's case will be further buttressed if the teacher's behavior is considered irremediable (Landauer et al., 1983).

Documenting Unsatisfactory Performance

Most teachers occasionally violate school rules and policies, but most of those violations are minor and many of them are ignored by principals. When serious or repeated violations occur, the principal is obligated to take action. This involves preparing written documentation of the teacher's actions and the actions taken by the principal or others to remediate the problem, sending a copy to the teacher, and placing a copy of it in the individual's personnel file. Performance evaluation reports and descriptions of classroom observations are also included in the personnel file.

Five types of records prepared by principals are involved in documenting unsatisfactory performance: specific incident memoranda, private notes, descriptions of classroom observations, evaluation reports, and summary memoranda. If a teacher takes an action (or fails to take action) that constitutes violation of policy, the principal should immediately hold a conference with the teacher to discuss the infraction and to remind the teacher of the policy that has been violated. If the teacher's behavior is serious enough, this conference may be followed by a specific incident memorandum in which the principal summarizes the actions taken by the teacher that violated policy and describes any corrective action the principal has taken, including issuance of a reprimand (Frels & Cooper, 1982).

Specific Incident Memoranda

The specific incident memorandum should contain an objective description of the teacher's act or failure to act, a comment on the detrimental effect of the action on students, a description of suggestions or directives given the teacher by the principal or supervisor, and a statement indicating whether the teacher complied with the directives or followed through on suggestions (Neill & Custis, 1978).

It is advisable to ask the teacher to acknowledge receiving the memorandum by signing a copy to be placed in the individual's personnel file. The teacher should also be given the opportunity to prepare a written response explaining circumstances surrounding the incident and presenting the teacher's version of the facts. This response is also placed in the personnel file (Frels & Cooper, 1982).

Private Notes

Brief private notes about teachers may be kept by a principal as reminders for follow-up action but should be destroyed as soon as possible. For example, a principal may make a note to remind a teacher that students must be given at least one day's notice before being assigned to after-school detention in order to allow them to arrange transportation home. If the teacher continues to violate the rule after meeting with the principal, the administrator may reprimand the teacher or may place a note in a private file that serves as a reminder to comment on the teacher's actions in the performance evaluation report (Frels & Cooper, 1982).

Observation Reports

In most school districts, principals are required to observe teachers' classroom performance and to note the results of these observations in a memorandum or on a form provided by the district. These records are retained in teachers' personnel records and, if a teacher is dismissed, are used as part of the documentation. Notes prepared by the principal should be as detailed as possible, since relying on memory to recall events from an observation that occurred several months or years earlier is extremely risky.

Evaluation Reports

Evaluations of teachers' performance become part of a permanent documentary record. Evaluations are usually based on classroom performance but may include ratings on other aspects of a teacher's work. Some teachers may perform satisfactorily in the core tasks of teaching, such as planning and presenting instruction, but have problems working with administrators, teachers, and parents. These problems should be noted in the evaluation summary since they may be central to a subsequent action to dismiss.

Most teachers receive satisfactory performance ratings, even though their performance does not always justify them. It is extremely difficult to convince a court that a teacher's performance falls below the minimally acceptable standard when over a period of years the teacher has consistently received satisfactory performance ratings from principals. This problem is not exclusive to schools; it happens in most organizations (Bridges, 1984). However, organizations that do not grant tenure to their employees have more discretion in discharging unsatisfactory performers. When the decision is made to terminate a tenured teacher, the district should be able to produce evidence over a period of at least three years showing a pattern of unsatisfactory performance. Moreover, the board should be prepared to show a connection between identified deficiencies and loss of learning (Barton, 1984).

Summary Memoranda

A summary memorandum outlines the results of several incidents or classroom observations. It is used when the principal wishes to call to the teacher's attention several related instances of rule or policy violations or to summarize several classroom observations. The summary memorandum is used when the individual actions are not serious enough to warrant writing a specific incident memorandum but which, taken together, constitute a pattern of behavior that requires attention.

The documentary record should be a complete, accurate, and specific compilation of facts about an individual's performance. Complete and accurate records benefit both the district and the individual, since courts will uphold a termination action when documentation exists to show that a teacher's performance fails to meet the standards required by the district. Courts will dismiss the action when documentation is not available to substantiate the charge.

Principals who are documenting unsatisfactory performance by a teacher should be prepared to write objective, factual descriptions about what is observed in classrooms or in other areas of the school. Global descriptions are likely to be challenged in court and should be avoided. In their place, principals should use specific descriptions of classroom events or teacher actions. Sample descriptions of both types are provided in Exhibit 15.3.

Rights of Dismissed Teachers

A district may refuse to renew the contract of a nontenured teacher without stating reasons for the decision, except in states with statutes that require notification. Tenured teachers, however, are entitled to certain protections prior to dismissal. Successful dismissal of a tenured teacher requires that the district strictly observe these procedural requirements.

EXHIBIT 15.3   *Global versus Specific Documentation*

Global	*Specific*
Had poor classroom management procedures	Three students were out of their seats and four others were talking, ignoring the teacher.
Violated the school policy on collection of payment and fees	Failed to issue receipts to three students who paid $5 locker fee.
Inadequately prepared for teaching	Had not prepared a lesson plan for the class; used part of class time to show a movie that was only tangentially related to the topic being studied.
Classroom appearance poor	Bulletin board displays unchanged for six months; books and papers piled atop bookcases and teacher's desk.

The following list enumerates the due process protections that are provided tenured teachers by various state statutes (Cambron-McCabe, 1983):

1. A statement of charges
2. Access to evidence and names of witnesses
3. A choice of an open or closed hearing
4. Opportunity to be represented by counsel
5. Opportunity to introduce evidence, call, and cross-examine witnesses
6. A transcript of the hearing upon request
7. A written decision
8. Right of appeal

A teacher may be suspended without a hearing if his or her presence in the school represents a potential threat to students or other persons, or if the individual is charged with a crime involving moral turpitude.

Constitutional Protections

The Constitution grants certain rights to all American citizens, and employees are protected from employers' actions that infringe on those rights. The Fourteenth Amendment provides that government shall not "deprive any person of life, liberty, or property without due process of law." Tenured teachers and nontenured teachers under contract have potential property and liberty interests that are jeopardized by termination, and thus they are entitled to procedural due process before being terminated. Due process involves, at a minimum, notice of charges and an opportunity for a pretermination hearing at which evidence must be presented to show that the charges are true and support the proposed action (Hill & Wright, 1993).

The First Amendment guarantees freedom of speech, but the Supreme Court has held that right must be balanced with employers' interest in maintaining an efficient operation. In *Pickering* v. *Board of Education* (1968), the Court held that speech that interfered with employee performance, created disharmony, or undercut supervisory authority was not extended the same protections as other forms of expression.

In *Connick* v. *Myers* (1983), the Court held that to be protected, an employee's statement must deal with public—and not merely private—concerns. Determining which issues are private or public involves considering whether the expression advances a purely personal or community interest and whether or not there is general public interest in the issue (Frels & Schneider-Vogel, 1986).

A legal challenge under the First Amendment is likely to occur when an employee is terminated after openly criticizing district policy. The district may argue that the decision to dismiss was based on performance deficiencies and not on the employee's statements, but if the two events are proximate in time, questions are certain to be raised about the district's true motives (Frels & Schneider-Vogel, 1986).

In 1990, 40 states required prospective teachers to pass a test in order to be certified (National Center for Education Statistics, 1993), and a few states have enacted legislation that requires testing of practicing teachers. Both types of laws have been challenged in court.

In Texas, state law requires public school teachers and administrators to pass the Texas Examination for Current Administrators and Teachers (TECAT), which tests basic reading and writing skills. An organization representing teachers and administrators challenged the law, claiming that it was an unconstitutional impairment of teachers' and administrators' contracts. The Texas Supreme Court rejected the claim and upheld the test (*State* v. *Project Principle*, 1987).

In Alabama, the required test was the National Teachers' Examination (NTE). The Supreme Court of that state held that the board had properly refused to renew contracts of 106 teachers who had failed to attain the required score on the examination (*York* v. *Board of School Commissioners*, 1984).

Teachers who are threatened with dismissal are often given the option of resigning in order to avoid embarrassing and damaging publicity. Administrators should use care in attempting to persuade a teacher to resign, because courts may view the resignation as coerced and order the teacher reinstated. Courts have held that when an employer makes working conditions so unpleasant that an employee resigns rather than continue to work under such adverse conditions, the employer's action is unfair. Employers can avoid such an outcome by counseling and, if necessary, disciplining employees for cause rather than trying to force them to resign. If an employee can demonstrate that an employer's actions were taken for the purpose of forcing the employee to resign and conditions were so bad that the employee had no choice, then the employer may be held liable (Thorne, 1996).

Remediation

A question that is often raised in dismissal cases is remediability. If the behavior for which a tenured teacher is dismissed is considered remediable, then the board has an obligation to permit the teacher the opportunity to correct the behavior before it takes action to dismiss. The board's decision on the question of remediability is subject to judicial review. If there is a question about remediability, administrators are wise to assume that the behavior in question is remediable and to permit the teacher the opportunity to correct it. There is no absolute standard for judging how much time should be allowed for remediation. Although five weeks was found to be insufficient in one case, eight weeks was considered adequate by another court (Landauer et al., 1983).

Eight types of remediation are provided for teachers whose performance is judged to be unsatisfactory. They are listed in Exhibit 15.4 along with examples of actions appropriate for each. The first six remediation actions in Exhibit 15.4 should be carried out together. Although districts sometimes take one of these actions alone (for example, goal setting or instructional input), the chances of success are much greater if all six are used.

EXHIBIT 15.4   *Actions and Examples for Teacher Remediation*

Goal setting:	Help the teacher establish instructional and behavioral goals for students.
Instructional input:	Arrange for the teacher to take a class or attend a workshop to learn new skills.
Modeling:	Provide released time for the teacher to observe a colleague who has the skills the teacher is learning.
Practice:	Arrange time for the teacher to practice new skills in a nonthreatening environment.
Feedback:	Provide feedback to the teacher who is attempting to master new skills.
Reinforcement:	Provide rewards, including praise, for correct use of newly learned skills.
Therapy or counseling:	Arrange for intensive emotional support for the teacher who has severe emotional problems.
Environmental change:	Arrange for the teacher to transfer to a different assignment.

Source: Managing the Incompetent Teacher by E. M. Bridges, 1984, Eugene: University of Oregon ERIC Clearinghouse on Educational Management.

Goal setting was discussed in Chapter 6 as a motivational technique. In working with a teacher who has significant deficiencies in instructional performance, it is advisable to help the individual establish learning and behavior goals to achieve better classroom control and increased student achievement.

Instructional input equips the teacher with the knowledge and skill needed to achieve the goals. Modeling, practice, feedback, and reinforcement help the teacher to refine the skills and acquire facility and confidence in their use. Teachers who are having difficulty implementing instruction effectively may need to be reminded about the conditions under which learning occurs. Teachers help students to learn by establishing clear learning objectives, choosing appropriate learning tasks, expressing confidence in students' ability, providing rewards to practice new skills, and creating conditions under which transfer of learning can occur (Tyler, 1985).

Therapy/counseling and environmental change are less often used. They may be applied together, in conjunction with other techniques, or alone, depending on the nature of the teacher's problem. Teachers whose problems are related to their life situation may profit from therapy or counseling, and those whose difficulties emanate from their work assignment often perform better in a different setting. Sometimes it is necessary to provide psychological support along with environmental change.

Summary

Reductions in force and termination of employees are occasionally necessary personnel actions. Policies governing both contingencies should spell out the actions to be taken and define the rights of employees involved. The purpose of a reduction-in-force policy is to permit the district to achieve necessary cutbacks in the number of employees on the payroll without disrupting services. Reduction-in-force policies should describe a procedure for declaring that a surplus of employees exists and for identifying the employee classifications and positions affected. It should also specify alternatives that may be taken to avoid layoffs. Preparation of a layoff pool should be done in consultation with the director of instruction in order to avoid harm to instructional programs.

Teachers may be dismissed for reasons related to incompetence, immoral or unprofessional behavior, and insubordination. Tenured teachers who are dismissed must be accorded due process rights, and all teachers are protected against loss of constitutional rights.

Principals anticipating the need to dismiss a teacher should prepare a detailed documentary record of the individual's performance deficiencies. Specific incident memoranda, private notes, observation and evaluation reports, and summary memoranda are all used to establish a record of evidence. An effort must be made to provide remedial assistance to tenured teachers if the deficiency is considered remediable.

Suggested Activities

1. What action would you, the principal, take in the following situations? Give reasons for your decision.
   a. A teacher tells you that she observed a male eighth-grade teacher from your school attending a movie with one of his female students the previous evening.
   b. At a basketball game, you observe the coach walking unsteadily as enters the gym with his players. As you approach him, you can smell alcohol on his breath.
   c. A teacher from your school gives a speech to a local environmental organization criticizing the superintendent and school board for deciding not to introduce an environmental education program into the curriculum.

2. Research a state statute that provides for appointment of a hearing officer to hear the appeals of teacher termination decisions and answer the following questions. (*Note:* Refer to Lopez & Sperry [1994] for a list of relevant state statutes.)
   a. Does the legislation identify qualifications for hearing officers? If so, what are they?
   b. What duties does the hearing officer (or panel) have under the law?
   c. What are the school board's duties?

3. Review the actions used for teacher remediation (Exhibit 15.4). Explain under what circumstances goal setting would be the best approach for helping a marginal

teacher improve his or her performance. When would instructional input and environmental change be most appropriate?

4. Read Case Study III (at the end of the book) and answer the questions that follow the case study.

Online Resources _____

Information on disciplinary actions and employee termination is readily available online, although much of what one finds is aimed at the business world. Since many employment laws and regulations apply to both public and private enterprises, these websites can be a useful source of information.

WetFeet (www.wetfeet.com?employer/articles/article/asp?aid=389)
> This site features an article entitled "Best Practices for Employee Termination" that is recommended reading for administrators who face having to terminate an employee.

eCompanyNow (www.ecompany.com/eCompany/0,1632,,00.html)
> This searchable site is designed for human resources managers in the business world, but some of the material is applicable to schools as well. The site features 281 articles on employee termination. In searching for information, bear in mind differences in terminology between *education* and *business*. A search for "reduction in force" produced documents about the effects of interest rate reductions by the Federal Reserve Bank on the stock market.

Employment Law Channel (www.uslaw.com/channel.tcl?channel_id=41)
> This site provides information on age discrimination, employee termination, sexual harassment, and wrongful discharge. The U.S. Law Library has information for both employers and employees on rights of employees with disabilities.

U.S. National Institutes of Health (wwwl.od.nih.gov/ohm)
> This site is maintained by the Office of Human Resource Management of the National Institutes of Health. It contains a searchable database with information of interest to human resources managers in many settings. A search using the descriptor "employee discipline" produced nine sites. The topics included an overview of employee discipline, conducting administrative inquiries, and types of offenses. It also offered an adverse action worksheet and explained what to include in a disciplinary case file. Although the policies apply only to NIH, some can easily be adapted for schools.

Shasta (California) Office of Education (www.shastalink.k12.ca.us/csca/Contracts/Article16.html)
> Article 16 is the policy on employee discipline of the Shasta Schools. Other policy statements can also be accessed from this site.

References _____

Alexander, K., & Alexander, M. (1985). *American public school law* (2nd ed.). St. Paul, MN: West.

Barton, M. (1984, April). *What you ought to know about termination and due process.* Paper presented at the annual meeting of the National School Boards Association, Houston. (ERIC Document Reproduction Service No. ED 247641).

Bridges, E. (1984). *Managing the incompetent teacher.* Eugene: University of Oregon, ERIC Clearinghouse on Educational Management.

Bridges, E. (1985, January). It's time to get tough with the turkeys. *Principal, 64,* 19–21.

Cambron-McCabe, N. (1983). Procedural due process. In J. Beckham & P. Zirkel (Eds.), *Legal issues in public school employment* (pp. 78–97). Bloomington, IN: Phi Delta Kappa.

Caplan, G. (1984). Current issues in reduction-in-force. In T. Jones & D. Semler (Eds.), *School law update . . . preventive school law* (pp. 15–22). Topeka, KS: National Organization on Legal Problems of Education. (ERIC Document Reproduction Service No. ED 244321).

Chicago Board of Education v. *Payne*, 430 N.E.2d 310, 315 (111. App. 1982).

Clark, R. T. (1993, Spring). School-based management—Problems and prospects. *Journal of Law and Education, 22,* 183–186.

Clune, W., & White, P. (1988). *School-based management.* New Brunswick, NJ: Rutgers University, Center for Policy Research in Education.

Connick v. *Myers,* 461 U.S. 138 (1983).

Dismissal of Certificated Teacher, Ariz. Rev. Stat. ss 5-15-539-E (2000). Available online: www.azleg.state.az.us.

Dallap v. *Sharon City School District,* 571 A.2d 368 (Pa. 1990).

DeKalb County School System. (1979). *A policy and administrative procedure for reduction in force.* Decatur, GA: Author. (ERIC Document Reproduction Service No. ED 228690).

Education law (Vol. 2). (1989). New York: Matthew Bender.

Elam, S., Rose, L., & Gallup, A. (1993, October).The 25th annual Phi Delta Kappa/Gallup Poll of the public's attitudes toward the public schools. *Phi Delta Kappan, 75,* 137–152.

Frels, K., & Cooper, T. (1982). *A documentation system for teacher improvement or termination.* Topeka, KS: National Organization on Legal Problems of Education.

Frels, K., & Schneider-Vogel, M. (1986). *The First Amendment and school employees: A practical management guide.* Topeka, KS: National Organization on Legal Problems of Education.

Gallup, A., & Elam, S. (1988). The 20th annual Gallup Poll on the public's attitudes toward the public schools. *Phi Delta Kappan, 70,* 33–46.

Gaylord v. *Board of Education, School District 218,* 794 P.2d 307 (Kan. App. 1990).

Geier v. *Alexander,* 801 F.2d 799 (1986).

Gross, J. (1988). *Teachers on trial: Values, standards, and equity in judging conduct and competence.* Ithaca, NY: ILR Press.

Hill, M., & Wright, J. (1993). *Employee lifestyle and off-duty conduct regulation.* Washington, DC: Bureau of National Affairs.

Hirsch, E. (1998, February). Teacher policy: A summary of current trends. *State Legislative Report, 23* (5), 1–10.

Hubbartt, W. (1998). *The new battle over workplace privacy.* New York: AMACOM.

Johnson, S. (1982, March). *Seniority and schools.* Paper presented at the annual meeting of the American Educational Research Association, New York. (ERIC Document Reproduction Service No. ED 221931).

Johnson, S. (1984). *Teacher unions in schools.* Philadelphia: Temple University Press.

Landauer, W., Spangler, J., & Van Horn, B., Jr. (1983). Good cause basis for dismissal of education employees. In J. Beckham & P. Zirkel (Eds.), *Legal issues in public school employment* (pp. 154–170). Bloomington, IN: Phi Delta Kappa.

Lopez, C., & Sperry, D. (1994). *The use of hearing officers in public educator termination actions.* Salt Lake City: University of Utah, Utah Education Policy Center.

McCarthy, M., & Cambron-McCabe, N. (1987). *Public school law: Teachers' and students' rights* (2nd ed.). Boston: Allyn and Bacon.

National Center for Education Statistics. (1993). *Digest of education statistics.* Washington, DC: U.S. Department of Education.

Neill, S., & Custis, J. (1978). *Staff dismissal: Problems and solutions.* Arlington, VA: American Association of School Administrators.

Odden, A., & Picus, L. (1992). *School finance: A policy perspective.* New York: McGraw-Hill.

Pickering v. *Board of Education,* 391 U.S. 563 (1968).

Poltrock, L., & Goss, S. (1993). A union lawyer's view of restructuring and reform. *Journal of Law and Education, 22,* 177–182.

Rose, L., & Gallup, A. (2000, September). The 32nd annual Phi Delta Kappa/Gallup Poll of the public's attitudes toward the public schools. *Phi Delta Kappan, 82,* 41–58.

Schneid, T. (1992). *The Americans with Disabilities Act: A practical guide for managers.* New York: Van Nostrand Reinhold.

Scriven, M. (1980, October). *Teacher personnel policies: Equity, validity, and productivity.* Paper presented at the Midwest Policy Seminar, St. Louis. (ERIC Document Reproduction Service No. ED 206741).

Sovereign, K. (1999). *Personnel law.* Upper Saddle River, NJ: Prentice Hall.

State v. *Project Principle,* 724 S.W.2d 387 (Tex. 1987).

Thorne, J. (1996). *A concise guide to successful employment practices* (2nd ed.). Chicago: CCH, Inc.

Tyler, R. (1985). Conditions for effective learning. In M. Fantini & R. Sinclair (Eds.), *Education in school and nonschool settings* (pp. 203–229). Chicago: University of Chicago Press.

Valente, W. (1980). *Law in the schools.* Columbus, OH: Merrill.

Ware v. *Morgan County School District,* 748 P.2d 1295 (Colo. 1988).

Wright v. *Superintending School Committee,* 331 A.2d 640 (Me. 1976).

Wygant v. *Jackson Board of Education,* 476 U.S. 267 (1986).

York v. *Board of School Commissioners of Mobile County,* 460 So.2d 857 (Ala. 1984).

Zirkel, P., & Bargerstock, C. (1981, January). Reduction-in-force. *A Legal Memorandum,* pp. 1–8.

Case Studies

Case I

Allison Hamrick looked over the application form filled out by Judy Worth, who was applying for a third-grade vacancy. Hamrick, principal of Aspen Grove Elementary School, needed a third-grade teacher to replace Lucy Howe, a beloved teacher who had taught at the school for almost forty years and had retired the previous year. Parents and students alike were sad to see Ms. Howe leave, and they voiced the hope that her replacement would be equally as good. At first, Hamrick thought she might have found the replacement she wanted when she first reviewed Worth's application. Now she wasn't so sure.

Worth had taught fifth grade for five years at an elementary school in the small community of Barclay, 200 miles to the south. Her educational background was solid, with a bachelor's and a master's degree from the state university and additional hours of credit from summer coursework. She appeared to have a wide range of interests, including geography, science, and the environment. Hamrick had been reminded often enough by Clarence Davis, the assistant superintendent for instruction, that she needed to work to upgrade the quality of instruction in science and math at Aspen Grove School. Most of the teachers at the school had begun teaching at a time when less emphasis was placed on math and science, and they concentrated on reading, spelling, and language arts. They did a good job in those subjects, but these days that wasn't enough.

Hamrick again picked up Worth's application form. In responding to the question, "What are your main reasons for wanting to teach in Converse County?" Worth has written, "My parents are in poor health, and I would like to be closer to them. I grew up in Converse County and have always have had a desire to return there. Even though I've been away more than 20 years, it still feels like home." Worth's application was accompanied by two letters of reference, one from Worth's principal and the other from a fellow teacher. Both were positive regarding Worth's teaching. The principal described Worth as "a creative and competent teacher who seeks out opportunities to expand her knowledge and skill." The teacher had written, "It's been a pleasure to teach with Judy, and I hate to see her have to leave."

Hamrick laid the reference form aside and reached for an unsigned letter she had received just two days before. The letter bore no signature and appeared to have been written hurriedly in a difficult-to-read scrawl. It was postmarked Barclay, the town where Worth taught. It said, "You ought to know that Judy Worth changed the answers on her students' answer sheets on state tests. She was caught and agreed to resign so they wouldn't fire her. A friend."

Hamrick was puzzled. She wondered if the unsigned letter could be true, and if it was, why the principal of Worth's school wouldn't have said something about it when he wrote the reference. She wondered if it might be a dirty trick thought up by another teacher who disliked Worth for some reason. She pondered what she ought to do. She could call Clarence Davis and ask for his advice, or she could contact someone in the Human Resources Department to see what advice they would give. She might even call Judy Worth and ask her about the information contained in the letter.

Questions for Case I

1. What advice would you give Allison Hamrick? Why do you suggest that?
2. In general, what policy would you take with regard to unsolicited (and anonymous) information about applicants for a teaching vacancy? Should such information be ignored or investigated? Suppose you investigate such a report and are not able either to confirm or disprove it. How would that affect your decision about hiring a person such as Judy Worth?
3. If it is confirmed that Ms. Worth did indeed change students' answers to test questions, should that disqualify her from further consideration for a position at Aspen Grove? Why or why not?
4. If a teacher admits changing test scores, should he or she be allowed to resign rather than face the possibility of being dismissed? What ethical obligations does a personnel administrator have in such a case?

Case II

Jerry Marks and Linda Cross, members of the human resources staff, had been asked by Dr. Martin Overstreet, assistant superintendent, to prepare a draft policy on drug and alcohol use by employees to be presented to the board at its next meeting. The two are meeting to discuss the contents of the policy.

The need for such a policy became clear earlier in the year when two employees who were suspected of drinking on the job were treated differently. In one case, the employee—a school custodian—was placed on suspension for five days and a letter of reprimand was placed in his file. He was warned that more severe disciplinary action would be taken if the behavior was repeated. In the second case, a cafeteria worker was sent home for the remainder of the day with a verbal warning, but no further action was taken.

"Drinking on the job wasn't a persistent problem for either of these people, as far as I know," Linda said. "A five-day suspension for a first-time offense seems kind of severe."

"I don't think so at all," Jerry replied. "It's important to send a message to people."

"What about drug use?" Linda asked. "Suppose someone comes to work after using marijuana or meth? Shouldn't the penalty for that be more severe than for alcohol use?"

"It's no different," Jerry said. "If you can't do your job, you should be disciplined."

"Drugs are illegal; alcohol is not," Linda noted.

"Well, I think we refer anyone who is suspected of using drugs to the county attorney for prosecution," Jerry said. "The county doesn't prosecute people for using alcohol unless they commit a crime."

"How do you know someone has used marijuana?" Linda asked. "Don't you have to do a blood test? And can we authorize medical tests in the policy?"

"I'm sure we can," Jerry said. He went on: "Here's a statement from a drug and alcohol policy from a school district in Kansas. See what you think." He began to read: "'The unlawful possession, use, or distribution of alcohol and controlled substances on school property is prohibited. Employees whose work is affected by the use of drugs, alcohol, or other substances or who possess or distribute them on school property will be subject to disciplinary action, including reprimand, suspension, and termination of employment.'"

"No distinction made between drug use and alcohol use, or between using and selling?" Linda asked.

"I think you can make a distinction," Jerry said, "but it's a matter of judgment—determining how serious the offense is and then taking appropriate action."

Linda frowned. "I think the policy ought to be more specific, maybe listing possible disciplinary actions for each offense," she said.

"It actually makes it harder to apply the policy if you try to make it too specific," Jerry replied. "There has to be room for judgment."

"But that's what happened with the two employees earlier in the year," Linda said. "One principal thought a suspension was in order, and the other just sent the employee home for the day. Too much room for judgment and you get uneven results."

"What about different groups of employees?" Jerry asked.

Linda frowned. "I'm not sure what you mean."

"Isn't it more serious for a teacher to use alcohol or drugs than, say, a custodian. Or what about a bus driver?"

Linda thought a moment. "I think bus drivers ought to be tested periodically whether they are suspected of drug use or not," she said. "But I wouldn't penalize teachers more than a custodian."

Jerry looked at his watch. "We need to talk about some other issues," he said. "We can come back to these questions another time."

"Sounds good," Linda said. "What other issues do you have in mind?"

"I think the policy should say that employees are required to report previous drug or alcohol offenses," Jay observed.

"The application form has a space to list felony convictions," Linda said. "Isn't that enough?"

Jerry responded: "Maybe not. They may have misused alcohol or drugs without being convicted of a felony."

"But I don't think it's legal to ask if they have been arrested unless they were convicted," Linda said.

"You may be right about that," Jerry said. "I'm not sure."

"I think it would be a good idea to check the law, especially the Drug Free Workplace Act and the Drug Free Schools and Communities Act, and see what they say," Linda added.

"You're right," Jerry said. "Good idea. If you will check one, I'll take the other. When can we meet again?"

Questions for Case II

1. Take and defend a position on this question: Should a policy on drug and alcohol use by school employees include specific sanctions for each offense?
2. Do you agree with Linda that all school bus drivers should be tested regularly for drug and alcohol use and that other employees should not be tested unless there is reason to believe they may be using illegal drugs? How do you justify your position?
3. If you were writing a policy on employee use of drugs and alcohol, what provision would you make for medical tests for employees suspected of using illegal drugs or alcohol?
4. What sources would you consult in drafting a policy on drug and alcohol use besides policies adopted by other school districts? Explain why you believe those sources would be useful.

Case III

Donald Becker, principal of Lawson High School, wrote a sentence on the sheet of paper in front of him and reread it silently. He thought about the words briefly and then scratched them out. After a moment, he discarded the paper and pulled a fresh sheet from his drawer.

"Dear Ms. Diamond," he wrote. He paused, reflecting on the events of the previous two days.

In his mind he went back to the telephone call he had received the previous Sunday from Pat Simmons, orchestra teacher at the school. Ms. Simmons had told him that Abby Diamond had called her Friday night and asked her to take her place at the regional band competition on Saturday. Ms. Simmons said that she had reluctantly agreed to do so because students would have been terribly disappointed if the trip had been cancelled.

Abby Diamond was the band teacher at Lawson High. It was her first year at the school. She had transferred to Lawson from a middle school in the district where she had taught for three years, and she had caused problems for Mr. Becker almost from the day she arrived.

On Monday, Mr. Becker had stopped Ms. Diamond in the hall before classes to ask her why she had not made the trip with the band. She had told him that she was ill and hadn't felt like accompanying the band to the competition. "You had a responsibility to call and let me know if you weren't going," he had said. "In the future, let me know if you are unable to meet your responsibilities."

"Pat Simmons agreed to go in my place," Ms. Diamond had replied. "I knew she would do a good job with the band."

"The band isn't Pat's responsibility," Mr. Becker told her. "You are the band teacher. What would have happened if Pat couldn't have gone?" Ms. Diamond had shrugged and walked away.

The trip was the latest in a series of actions by Ms. Diamond that Mr. Becker felt showed indifference toward her responsibilities. He had decided to write a letter for her personnel file to impress on the teacher the importance of being more conscientious about her work and to warn her to avoid a repetition of Saturday's incident.

He felt that it was important to reiterate to Ms. Diamond that, as band teacher, she was expected to accompany the band on all trips and that if she was unable to go, she was to notify him. He sat for a minute deep in thought, recalling months of frustrating experiences with Ms. Diamond.

Earlier in the year, Mr. Becker had learned from several students that Ms. Diamond had on several occasions placed a student in charge of the class and left the room. They had told him that the first time or two it happened she had returned near the end of the period but that on one occasion she didn't return to the class at all. One parent had even called him to complain about Ms. Diamond leaving the band class unsupervised.

Mr. Becker had explained to Ms. Diamond that board policy required teachers to remain in the classroom at all times when students were present or to arrange for a teacher or aide to supervise the class if they had to leave. She had assured him that she would observe the policy in the future. But a week later, when he had gone into the teachers' lounge in the middle of a period, she had been sitting there with a soft drink in her hand, leafing through a magazine. "Who's taking care of your class?" he had asked.

"I left Yolanda in charge for just a minute," Ms. Diamond had replied. "I have a migraine headache, and I needed to get away for a few minutes. I'm going right back."

Mr. Becker warned Ms. Diamond that she was not to leave her classroom unattended and that if she did so again she would be reprimanded. Ms. Diamond had assured him that it would not happen again.

Unsupervised classes and missed trips weren't the only problems Mr. Becker had had with the teacher. One parent had complained that she was treated rudely when she called to ask Ms. Diamond to help her daughter locate some sheet music that the girl said she had returned to the teacher. Ms. Diamond insisted that the music had not been returned and told her that she would have to pay for it. When the parent asked her to see if she could locate the sheet music, the teacher had replied, "That's not my responsibility. These kids have to learn to take better care of their things."

Other parents had complained about Ms. Diamond's choosing the same small group of students to perform for school programs and PTA meetings. Mr. Becker assured the parents she was choosing the better musicians for special events, but some of the parents disputed that. "She only selects her favorites," one parent charged. "There are some excellent musicians in the band who are never picked to perform on programs."

Mr. Becker was puzzled. Ms. Diamond was a likable person, but he had never known a teacher who took responsibilities so lightly or who could find so many ways to evade her obligations. He wondered if she had behaved that way when she was teaching at the middle school before coming to Lawson and, if so, how she could have received tenure. Ms. Diamond had arrived at Lawson High with a favorable recommendation from the principal of the middle school, and Mr. Becker wondered if the principal had simply given a good reference in order to get rid of a problem teacher.

With a sigh, he picked up his pen and prepared to finish the letter.

Questions for Case III

1. Is a letter of reprimand an appropriate response for Abby Diamond's failure to make the trip to the regional band competition? What other disciplinary options might Donald Becker have considered? What action would you recommend? Should the principal have taken disciplinary action sooner? Explain.
2. What should Mr. Becker say in the letter of reprimand? Besides the band trip, should he also mention parents' complaints about the teacher? Why or why not?
3. Draft a letter of reprimand to Abby Diamond for Donald Becker's signature.
4. Consider the ethical and legal issues involved when a principal is asked to make a recommendation for a teacher seeking a transfer to another school. If the teacher's performance is marginal, is the principal ethically obligated to report that fact to the principal of the receiving school? What are the legal implications of reporting such information?

Index

D0537181

EGYPT
UNCOVERED

EGYPT
UNCOVERED

VIVIAN DAVIES AND RENÉE FRIEDMAN

STEWART, TABORI & CHANG
NEW YORK

CONTEN

First published in 1998 by British Museum Press a division of The British Museum Company Ltd 46 Bloomsbury Street, London WC1B 3QQ

Published and distributed in the U.S. in 1998 by Stewart, Tabori & Chang a division of U.S. Media Holdings, Inc, 115 West 18th Street, New York, NY 10011

Distributed in Canada by General Publishing Company Ltd. 30 Lesmill Road, Don Mills, Ontario, Canada M3B 2T6

Egypt Uncovered is an international television coproduction by S4C (Wales). Produced by John Gwyn Productions for S4C in association with Discovery Channel (USA) and La Cinquième (France).

Designed by Harry Green

ISBN: 1-55670-818-1 Library of Congress Catalog Card Number: 97–62390

Printed in Great Britain by Butler & Tanner Ltd, Frome and London Color separations by Radstock Reprographics

10 9 8 7 6 5 4 3 2 1

TITLE PAGE: Scene showing King Seti I (*c.*1294–1279 BC). Temple of Seti I, Abydos.

OPPOSITE ABOVE: Statue of Thutmose III (1479–1425 BC).

OPPOSITE BELOW: Vignette from 'The Book of the Dead', belonging to a man called Ani. Nineteenth Dynasty.

PREFACE

There is a huge popular fascination with the ancient Egyptians and their great civilization, but also a common misconception that there is little left to be discovered about them. Nothing could be further from the truth. The Nile Valley and its adjacent deserts continue to be enormously productive archaeologically. Important new discoveries, enhancing our knowledge and transforming our views, are being made on a regular basis, both in the field and in the laboratory; indeed with such frequency that even Egyptologists now struggle to keep pace and popular syntheses often lag far behind.

Focusing on some (by no means all) of the key archaeological sites in Egypt and the Sudan and on a number of representative scientific projects, this book reviews major aspects of ancient Egypt and Nubia in the light of the latest advances in knowledge and with the full collaboration of the experts concerned. It has been written to accompany a five-part television series – a co-production between S4C (Wales), Discovery Channel (USA) and La Cinquième (France) – which covers the same topics, in a refreshingly responsible but still accessible and entertaining way. Of late, ancient Egypt has been very ill-served in the media, with an alarming number of television programmes purveying bizzare and misleading nonsense, some of it masquerading as serious Egyptology. The public deserves better. The reality is so much more interesting, rewarding and exciting than the fantasy. Egypt's story is a celebration of human ingenuity and skills, of resilience and adaptability, and of truly gigantic achievements; the story of a people, with recognisable concerns and worries, seeking to understand and control their world and doing so, in their uniquely distinctive way, for over three thousand years. It is a tale with a surprising twist, as the remains of these very people are now making a contribution to the modern world in a capacity that goes well beyond their Egyptological relevance.

The book could not have been produced without the co-operation of a large number of institutions and individuals (see Acknowledgements). Special thanks are due to the officials of the Supreme Council for Antiquities of Egypt and the National Corporation of Antiquities and Museums of the Sudan respectively, who gave us every assistance in visiting sites and in taking photographs; to colleagues in the field and in various museums and other institutions, who allowed us generous access to their material; and to the staff of the Department of Egyptian Antiquities, British Museum, who have been enormously supportive. A good proportion of the photographs was taken by Peter Hayman and Jim Rossiter of the British Museum Photographic Service. The line illustrations were drawn or adapted by Claire Thorne of the Department of Egyptian Antiquities. The computer graphics are the work of 4:2:2 Videographics of Bristol. The book has been designed, with customary skill and flare, by Harry Green. The final editing and processing, done with commendable calm and efficiency, under unusually hectic conditions, have been the responsibility of Coralie Hepburn and Julie Young of British Museum Press.

VIVIAN DAVIES AND RENÉE FRIEDMAN

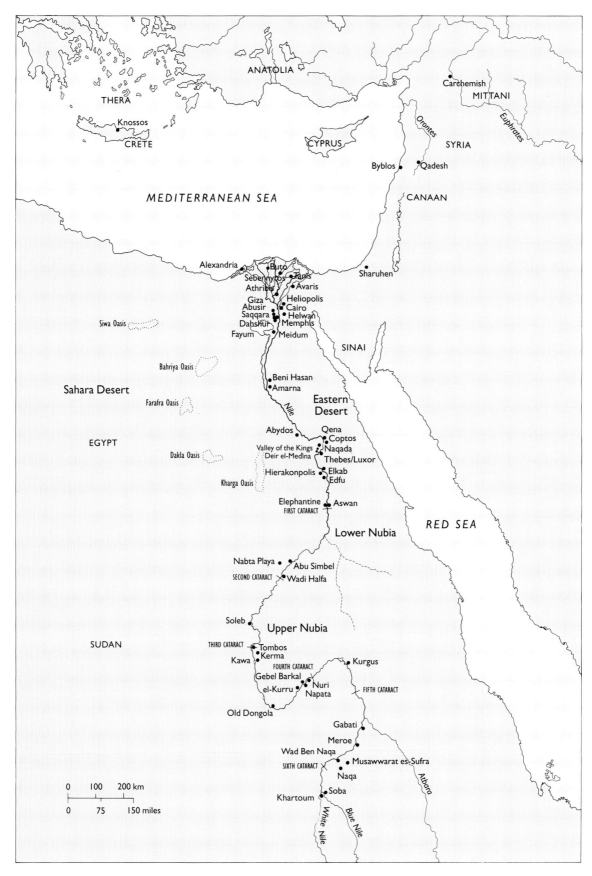

THERA

Knossos
CRETE

ANATOLIA

Carchemish
MITTANI

CYPRUS

SYRIA

Orontes

Euphrates

MEDITERRANEAN SEA

Byblos ● Qadesh

CANAAN

Alexandria
Buto
Sebennytos Tanis
Athribis ● Avaris
Heliopolis
Giza Cairo
Abusir ● Helwan
Saqqara ● Memphis
Dahshur
Fayum Meidum

Sharuhen

SINAI

Siwa Oasis

Bahriya Oasis

Beni Hasan
Amarna

Eastern
Desert

Sahara Desert

Farafra Oasis

Nile

EGYPT

Dakla Oasis

Abydos
Qena
Coptos
Naqada
Valley of the Kings
Deir el-Medina Thebes/Luxor
Hierakonpolis Elkab
Edfu

Kharga Oasis

Elephantine Aswan
FIRST CATARACT

RED SEA

Lower Nubia

Nabta Playa ● Abu Simbel
SECOND CATARACT Wadi Halfa

Soleb
Upper Nubia

SUDAN

THIRD CATARACT Tombos
Kerma
Kawa
FOURTH CATARACT Kurgus
Gebel Barkal
el-Kurru Nuri
Napata FIFTH CATARACT

Old Dongola

Gabati
Meroe
Wad Ben Naqa
SIXTH CATARACT Musawwarat es-Sufra
Naqa
Khartoum Soba

Atbara

0   100   200 km

0   75   150 miles

White Nile

Blue Nile

ACKNOWLEDGEMENTS

The authors are indebted to the many colleagues who have helped in various ways during the preparation of this book.

For sharing the fruits of their research and providing advice, access and information: Salah Mohammed Ahmed, Gus Alusi, Carol Andrews, Dorothea Arnold, Morris Bierbrier, Manfred Bietak, Charles Bonnet, Betsy Bryan, Joao Campos, Alfredo Castiglione, Angelo Castiglione, David Counsell, Deborah Darnell, John Darnell, Rosalie David, Anna-Maria Donadoni, Peter Dorman, Josef Dorner, Günter Dreyer, Arne Eggebrecht, Mohammed El-Saghir, Siddig Mohammed Gasm Elseed, Dina Faltings, Adel Farid, Richard Fazzini, Joyce Filer, Hans-W. Fischer-Elfert, Lesley Fitton, Joann Fletcher, Fawzy Gaballah, Ulrich Hartung, Ali Hassan, Fekri Hassan, Zahi Hawass, Fritz Hinkel, Hassan Hussein Idriss, Nasri Iskander, Peter Jánosi, David Jeffreys, Ray Johnson, Michael Jones, Tim Kendall, Mark Lehner, Jaromir Malek, Ian Mathieson, Theya Molleson, Mary Anne Murray, Paul Nicholson, Frank Norick, David O'Connor, Svante Pääbo, Richard Parkinson, Gillian Pyke, Stephen Quirke, John Ray, Mohammed Saleh, Romuald Schild, Louise Schofield, Sylvia Schoske, Abdeen Siam, Isabella Welsby Sjöstrom, Jeffrey Spencer, Rainer Stadelmann, Eddie Tapp, John Taylor, Jonathan Tubb, Patricia Usick, Miroslav Verner, Christopher Walker, Roxie Walker, Derek Welsby, Fred Wendorf, Helen Whitehouse, Dietrich Wildung, Jean Yoyotte, Christiane Ziegbo.

For invaluable logistical support and practical assistance: Jerry Baker, Caroline Biggar, Tony Brandon, Herma Chang, Reg Davis, Darrel Day, Bob Dominey, El-Tahir Adam El-Nur, Tony Fellowes, Sue Giles, Alan Goulty, Ben Green, John Hayman, Tim Healing, Mary Helmy, Romany Helmy, Ed Johnson, Jane Johnson, Howard M. Jones, Yarko Kobylecky, Judy McKeehan, Margaret Massey, Claire Messenger, Jim Putnam, David Rawson, Don Sloan, Christopher Sykes, Yolanda Sykes, Rowen Unsworth, Tania Watkins, Ken Wildsmith.

For making the project possible in the first place and for ensuring its successful conclusion: Huw Jones, Cenwyn Edwards and Ian Jones of Sianel Pedwar Cymru (S4C), Mike Quattrone, Steve Burns, Tomi Landis and Georgann Kane of Discovery Channel, and John Gwyn and his production team. On behalf of all the archaeological and scientific projects mentioned in this book, we thank the various funding and sponsoring agencies without whose support such work could never take place.

CHAOS AND

KINGS

When the Greek historian Herodotus visited Egypt four and a half centuries before the birth of Christ, he was awestruck. 'The wonders were greater than those of any other land', he observed. There were pyramids taller than any man-made structure on earth, avenues of sphinxes, half-man, half-beast, colossal statues of long-dead pharaohs and all around the enigmatic symbols of Egypt's sacred writing. But two things intrigued him more than any other: Egypt's great antiquity and its most remarkable of rivers, the Nile.

Here along the banks of the Nile was a civilization that had flourished since time immemorial. To the ancients, Egypt was already ancient. Even the Egyptians, with the oldest recorded history in the world, had merged their beginnings with myth. It was a culture so old that its origins remained shrouded in mystery.

Herodotus said that Egypt was a land given to the Egyptians by the Nile. Its power to be 'contrary in nature' to all other rivers, by flooding its banks in summer, was a great puzzle to him and others after him. So it was to remain until Victorian explorers discovered its sources in two parts of East Africa. From Lake Victoria in present-day Uganda, the White Nile flows northward and is joined in the Sudan by the Blue Nile and Atbara River, both rising in the highlands of Ethiopia. After a journey of almost 3400 miles (5470 km), the river reaches the Egyptian Nile Valley to create an oasis 650 miles (1050 km) long through a pitiless desert. For its last 100 miles (160 km) it fans out into a broad delta plain before spilling into the Mediterranean Sea. Once a year, swollen by the summer monsoon rains in Ethiopia, the river flooded its banks, depositing nutrient-rich soil which the Egyptians called 'The Black Land'. Without it Egypt would be barren. With it, it was one of the most fertile regions on earth.

Left Colossal statues of Ramesses II (1279–1213 BC). Temple of Abu Simbel.

It is no surprise that the Nile had a profound effect on all aspects of the Egyptians' lives. Their calendar of twelve months, each of thirty days, the model for the one we use today, was based on it. They divided the year into three seasons: the time of the summer flood was called 'Inundation', 'Emergence' was when the water receded and crops could be planted, and the 'Dry Time' in the spring was the time of harvest. The division of the seasons meant the division of labour: the flooding of the land released a huge workforce that, while waiting for the waters to recede, could be employed on the major public building projects for which Egypt is so famous.

Opposite The Nile, the world's longest river and Egypt's lifeblood.

It seemed to Herodotus that there were no people in the whole world who gained from the soil with so little labour: 'the river rises of itself, waters the fields, and then sinks back again; thereupon each man sows his field and waits for the harvest.' But the Egyptians knew this was not always the case. Life on the Nile could be precarious, the climate could change dramatically and the river was unpredictable. Too high a flood and villages could be destroyed, too low a flood meant famine as the land turned to dust. Despite

Right Reaping grain. From the tomb of Mereruka, Saqqara. Sixth Dynasty, c.2330 BC.

Left A stela marking the level of the Nile in year twenty-three of the king of Upper and Lower Egypt, Amenemhet III of the Middle Kingdom (1831 BC). The line through the oval at the bottom indicates the 'mouth' or height of the annual Nile flood waters. Taxes were levied according to the height of the inundation and the amount of land that would be watered and fertilized by it.

13

Above The conflict between Seth, the god of chaos and confusion, here depicted as a mythical creature with a pointed snout, and Horus, the falcon god of the sky, is reconciled in the person of the pharaoh, on whom they confer their blessings. From the temple of Ramesses II, Abu Simbel.

Opposite The delicate balance of the universe rested in the hands of the pharaoh in the form of his sister, the goddess *Ma'at*, seen here seated and wearing her characteristic feather headdress. From the temple of Ramesses II, Abu Simbel.

the fact that the Nile was more constant than any other of the world's great rivers, it is estimated that one Nile flood in five was either too low or too high.

The Egyptians called such events 'chaos' – the release of powerful forces which could disrupt their ordered world. To protect themselves from chaos, the Egyptians envisioned a ruler or pharaoh who was a living god, the earthly manifestation of Horus, the falcon ruler of the skies. Pitted against him was the unruly god of the desert, Seth, the harbinger of chaos, a force that needed to be controlled but could never be defeated. The reconciliation of the conflicting powers of order and chaos was the king's chief role. This delicate balance was so important to the Egyptians that they deified the concept as *Ma'at*, a goddess with the feather of truth on her head. *Ma'at* was the favourite daughter of the creator god and the wife of the god of wisdom. Since creation she had lived among humans on earth entrusted to the care of her brother, the pharaoh. It was his responsibility to look after her and to maintain her with justice, piety and, if need be, by force. Those who took good care of their sister were rewarded, but those who did not risked the vengeance of the gods.

This eternal conflict between order and chaos was a central concern of Egyptian civilization. The battle to harness the powers of nature, both cosmic and human, lies at the heart of Egypt's unique development. But the

true story of how it all came about had vanished in antiquity and is only now reappearing with the help of the archaeologist's trowel.

In the twilight of Egypt's greatness around 300 BC, an Egyptian priest named Manetho began to compile a history of Egypt for his new monarch, Ptolemy, a Macedonian Greek successor to Alexander the Great. It was to be a complete history beginning with creation, and in it Manetho organized the pharaohs into thirty dynasties or royal families down to his own time. His history, however, has been preserved only in the works of later authors, who for the most part wished only to refute his claim of Egypt's vast heritage. Unfortunately these copies are often contradictory and rife with errors. Only tattered fragments remain of the detailed records Manetho must have examined, and we can only imagine the wealth of information they once contained. Yet a faint hint can still be gleaned from the walls of some of Egypt's most sacred places.

Above King-list from the temple of Ramesses II at Abydos, a similar version to that of his father, Seti I. Such lists, though selective in content, have been invaluable for building up an internal chronology for Egyptian history.

Chronology

Manetho organized his history of Egypt prior to the beginning of Greek administration into thirty dynasties of kings. Today the dynasties are grouped into broader kingdoms or periods of strong or weak government and cultural cohesion. Some dynasties overlap.

Predynastic and Dynasty 0	c. 4500–3100 BC	
Dynasties 1–2	c. 3100–2686 BC	Early Dynastic
Dynasties 3–8	c. 2686–2125 BC	Old Kingdom
Dynasties 9–10	c. 2160–2025 BC	First Intermediate Period
Dynasties 11–13	c. 2125–1650 BC	Middle Kingdom
Dynasties 14–17	c. 1750–1550 BC	Second Intermediate Period
Dynasties 18–20	c. 1550–1069 BC	New Kingdom
Dynasties 21–24	c. 1069–715 BC	Third Intermediate Period
Dynasties 25–30	c. 747–332 BC	Late Period
Macedonians/Ptolemies	332–30 BC	Greek administration
Roman emperors	30–642 AD	Roman/Byzantine administration

One thousand years before Manetho was born, King Seti I (1274–1279 BC) built a temple at Abydos dedicated to Osiris, the god of the dead. In a special 'Hall of the Ancestors' Seti is carved in exquisite low relief in the act of making offerings, while his young son, the future King Ramesses II, reads from a papyrus roll. The content of this document is carved on the wall before them – seventy-five of their revered royal ancestors listed in chronological order. The name of each king is encircled by a stylized coil of rope, a symbol signifying eternal protection that is called by Egyptologists a cartouche. It was the exclusive preserve of royalty: only the names of kings and queens were placed in a cartouche (the realization of this fact was critical for the decipherment of hieroglyphics in modern times). At the very end, Seti proudly adds his name to this continuous tradition of kingship spanning over 2000 years of Egyptian history. But where did it begin?

The earliest name in the list is King Menes, who, according to Manetho, founded Egypt's first dynasty, reigned sixty years, advanced his army beyond the frontiers of his realm and won great renown before being carried off by a hippopotamus. Yet Manetho, as Seti before him, knew that the beginning of Egyptian history was not the work of just one man. Before Menes, Manetho

Above Among the Spirits of the Dead who reigned before Menes were the falcon-headed Souls of Buto and the jackal-headed Souls of Hierakonpolis. Their presence was required to legitimize all royal functions throughout Egyptian history. Bronze. Late Period, after 600 BC.

relates, Egypt was ruled by the demigods also called the Spirits of the Dead, their names long forgotten. Among them were the falcon-headed Souls of Buto and the jackal-headed Souls of Hierakonpolis, the spirits of the deified dead kings of two towns in two very different parts of Egypt.

The Nile flows from south to north, and the narrow river valley in the southern portion of the country is thus called Upper Egypt. This is where Hierakonpolis is located. The flat alluvial plain of the Delta in the north was called Lower Egypt; here was Buto. The landscape of these two regions was strikingly different to the Egyptians, so much so that they considered their country as the 'Two Lands', each with its own heraldic flower, protective goddess, distinctive crown, royal title, capital and demigods, all brought together and unified through the power of the king.

Egyptologists have long pondered whether these dualistic divisions are merely manifestations of the Egyptians' love of symmetry, as seen in their art and architecture and ever apparent in the natural landscape. Or could there be encapsulated within them, fragments of half-forgotten fact about Egypt's beginnings? Archaeologists are now finding out. Remarkably, however, the story doesn't start along the banks of the Nile, but in the wilderness of the Sahara desert

Above Egypt was composed of the 'Two Lands', each with its own symbolic imagery. The Nile Valley of Upper Egypt was the land of the lotus, the kingdom of the White Crown, protected by the vulture goddess Nekhbet. The papyrus plant, the Red Crown and the snake goddess Wadjet symbolized the Delta in Lower Egypt. Coffin of Nesmut, c.950–900 BC.

Nabta Playa

The southwest corner of Egypt is the most arid place on earth. In this part of the Sahara desert less than one millimetre of rain falls each year, but it evaporates before ever hitting the ground. Yet here, for more than twenty years, an international team led by Professor Fred Wendorf of Southern Methodist University, Dallas, and Dr Romuald Schild of the Polish Academy of Sciences has been investigating the scattered remains of people who just may be the distant ancestors of the pharaohs. For the Sahara desert was not always so inhospitable. Some 10,000 years ago, Africa's summer rain belt shifted northward, increasing the amount of rain and allowing seasonal lakes or 'playas' to form in low-lying areas.

One such former lake is called Nabta Playa. Once the largest basin in the southeastern region of the Sahara, it lies about 60 miles (100 km) west of Ramesses II's famous temple at Abu Simbel. The water it collected from the summer rains provided the moisture for a grass-covered savannah-like plain shaded by drought-resistant trees such as acacias. On and off, for over 4000 years, it was the home for a nomadic people who learned to cope with this harsh and unpredictable environment. Now it is a remarkable laboratory for investigating how environmental stress contributed to social and cultural innovation.

Almost from the beginning the early inhabitants of Nabta had learned to herd cattle, perhaps the first to do so in all of Africa. They used them as renewable resources, living on their milk and blood rather than their meat. This made life in the desert possible. By 8000 years ago, a tightly organized way of life had developed which allowed them to remain in the desert all year long. Excavations in one lakeside village in 1974–7 by Wendorf and his team have revealed at least fifteen large oval houses originally made of sticks and reeds arranged in three parallel rows. Around the hearths and in nearby

Right Ten thousand years ago the Sahara desert was a grassy plain with numerous seasonal lakes or playas filled by summer rains. One of the largest lakes in the southeastern region was Nabta Playa.

Below Excavation along the former edge of the lake at Nabta Playa revealed the remains of oval houses with hearths, storage pits and walk-in wells.

storage pits, some forty-four different varieties of grains, fruits and roots were recovered, as well as some of the oldest pottery in Africa. Three deep walk-in wells attest to a certain amount of community spirit in both their construction and use. Yet the key to the inhabitants' survival was the ability to predict when and if the rains would come, for after the last well ran dry, two days at most separated life from death.

In 1992 the team discovered the ingenious way in which the ancient Nabtans solved this problem. A circle of small upright stone slabs, only 4 m (13 ft) in diameter, looks like a miniature version of Stonehenge and was used perhaps in a similar way, but over 2000 years earlier. Co-director Romuald Schild explains how this, the oldest calendar ever found, worked:

Above Stonehenge in miniature. Co-director of the excavation Romuald Schild examines the world's earliest calendar.

'Four pairs of slabs in the circle are longer and set closer together than the others. These are called gates. Two pairs on opposite sides of the circle are aligned exactly north–south, while the other two are aligned at 70 degrees east of north. This direction points to the position of the sun on 21 June. That is the beginning of summer and was the beginning of the rainy season in this belt of Africa.'

Waiting for the summer solstice and counting the days until it rained must have been a serious business. But when the rains finally came, it was a time of celebration. Not far from the calendar circle, atop a high dune, is the place where the entire population must have gathered for the annual festivities. Over the years they left behind over 2 m (6.5 ft) of refuse and more cattle bones than anywhere else in the Sahara. It was a time for cattle slaughter, a rare and probably religiously charged event, both for consumption and also sacrificial burial, perhaps as offerings to the gods who brought the rain.

More intriguing still, the festival grounds also included a complex alignment of ten large standing stones and a series of thirty mounds crowned with huge stones, perhaps to mark the graves of important people. Remarkably, these stones, some weighing over one and a half tonnes, had been dragged into position from a quarry more than a mile away. Yet beneath one of these mounds was buried not a fallen ruler, but what appears to be an early sculpture. It is still possible to see how the sandstone was shaped: by making grooves and then using a wedge, the workmen were able to strike off the flakes at the exact points they wished. With its sharp edges and smooth faces, this sculpture is an impressive piece of stoneworking and according to Wendorf, 'may well mark the beginning of Egyptian fascination with working large stones'.

These monuments are the first evidence of the emergence of leaders who could command the building of large-scale public architecture. Their construction required a degree of skill, organization and commitment previously unknown at such an early date. It would seem that the stresses of survival in an unpredictable desert led to this unprecedented degree of social organization. For to survive in the difficult environment in which they lived, the people needed rulers who could make the life-or-death decisions on which their existence depended.

These remarkable early advances in technology and society seem, ironically, to correspond to the beginning of the end for these desert dwellers. Slowly the rains diminished and became more intermittent. Finally, around 6000 years ago, they ceased entirely and the Sahara desert became the barren waste it is today. What happened next is still unclear, but it is possible that when the last ruler made the decision to abandon the desert and led his organized band eastward to the life-giving waters of the Nile, they brought with them to Egypt many of those features that would soon distinguish this region from anywhere else on earth.

Above The sculpted stone found buried in a large pit beneath one of the mounds.

The Move to the Nile

The Nile waters that nourish and the silts that fertilize also bury and wash away. Whatever evidence there is for the interaction of the desert folks and the indigenous hunters and fishermen who lived along the Nile at that period is now deeply buried. We may never know exactly what happened, but within a short time, amazing things began to occur. Soon the first glimmerings of Egyptian civilization appear within the graves of the prehistoric, or Predynastic, inhabitants of the Nile Valley. In them are found some of the finest and most elegant pottery vessels ever produced in Egypt. Later came

Above Around 4000 BC some of the finest and most elegant pottery ever produced in Egypt began to appear in Upper Egyptian graves.

animal-shaped palettes for grinding cosmetics, carved out of stone from distant quarries. In the most wealthy and élite tombs were flint knives so expertly ground and flaked that they have never been equalled. They could only have been made by dedicated master craftsmen.

First discovered in 1895, these Predynastic graves reveal the long history of the ancient Egyptian belief in an afterlife into which the dead could take with them both their wealth and their status. The conspicuous consumption evident in the rich graves of a minority shows that already by 4000 BC there

Right Animal-shaped palettes of slate for grinding cosmetics, c.3300 BC.

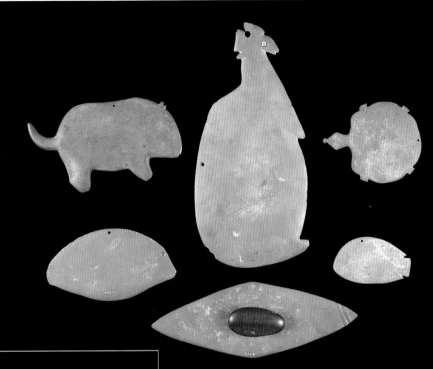

Below Finely crafted flint knives, c.3600–3200 BC.

were the rulers and the ruled. No longer was the Nile Valley a land of hunters and gatherers. It could well be that the lessons learned earlier in the desert gave the Upper Egyptians the competitive edge against their neighbours and set them on the path that would ultimately lead to the birth of the Egyptian nation. But how they adapted these lessons and developed them into a distinctive civilization cannot be discerned in the graves alone. For the full picture, one has to investigate their settlements.

Hierakonpolis

The ancient site of Hierakonpolis, a Greek name meaning 'city of the falcon', was long venerated by the ancient Egyptians as the early capital of the Kingdom of Upper Egypt and the home of the falcon Horus, the patron god of kingship. The discovery a hundred years ago of rich caches of discarded temple furnishings on a low mound within the modern village seemed to confirm the ancient traditions about the site. But it was not until the American Expedition, formerly led by Dr Michael Allen Hoffman, took to the field

in 1978 that the true foundation of its importance started to emerge. A century ago, archaeologists thought that all that the desert surrounding the site contained was a plundered cemetery not worth exploring. Little did they know that hidden beneath its crater-pocked surface was a wealth of new information on one of the most significant chapters in Egyptian history.

Recent explorations have shown that by 3500 BC Hierakonpolis was the most important settlement along the Nile – a vibrant, bustling city already equipped with many features that would later come to typify Egyptian culture and form the basis of its economy. Stretching for over 2 miles (3 km) along the edge of the floodplain, it was a city of many neighbourhoods, filled with farmers, potters, craftsmen and officials.

In 1978 the Hierakonpolis Expedition uncovered the house and workshop of one particular potter who produced cooking pots for his neighbourhood clientele. He signed his pots by impressing a crescent-shaped thumbprint into the wet clay just below the rim. Five thousand years later, fragments of these pots – some 300,000 of them – still covered the ground where the potter worked. Dwellings from the Predynastic era rarely survive, but this small, semi-subterranean rectangular house, measuring only 4.0 × 3.5 m (13.1 × 11.4 ft), once composed of posts and mud-coated reeds, can be

Opposite The house of the potter. The charred remnants of the posts that held up the roof still lie just as they fell when burned over 5500 years ago.

Below The appearance of the potter's house can be reconstructed with accuracy from the charred remains.

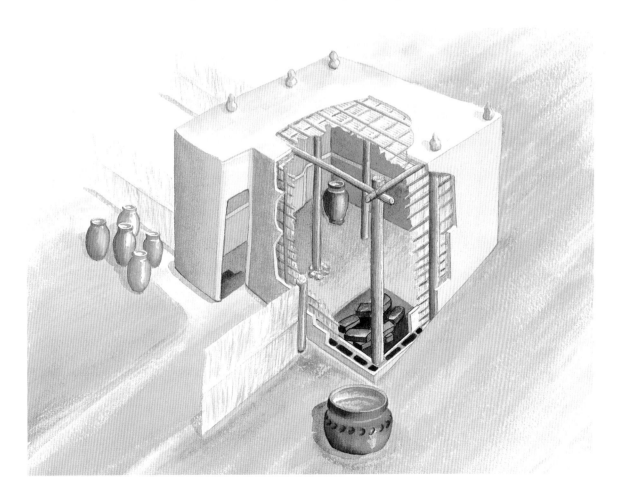

reconstructed due to a fortunate (for us) industrial accident. It would seem that the potter worked a little too close to where he lived, and one day a shift in the wind caused the fire from his pottery kiln, located just over 5 m (16 ft) away, to travel the short distance to the house, setting it alight. The fire reddened and hardened the soil and mud bricks that formed the lower portion of the house and reduced the posts and mats of its walls to charcoal and ash, found by the archaeologists just as they had fallen. Evidence does suggest that the potter wisely rebuilt his house in stone.

On the north side of the town stretched a large industrial zone. Excavations here in 1989 revealed an installation of huge pottery vats for brewing wheat-based beer. This thick and nutritious, only mildly alcoholic, brew was bottled in a range of standardized beer jars, manufactured near by. It is estimated that this brewery, Egypt's earliest, could produce about 1365 litres (300 gallons) of beer a day. At that rate, the brewery could supply a daily ration for over 200 people, and so far only a small fraction of this quarter has been investigated. The centralized collection and redistribution of such resources were ways of saving up against famine and vagaries of the Nile, guarding against chaos, but in good years they could make a king very rich.

Opposite Time has reduced the Predynastic temple at Hierakonpolis to a paved area, large post-holes and trenches, but by carefully recording these remains it is possible to reconstruct its original appearance.

Above Reconstruction of the Predynastic temple at Hierakonpolis. Huge timber pillars formed the façade of the temple's central shrine, which was made up of colourful woven mats on a timber frame.

Nowhere is the power of the early king more evident than in the centre of this vast town, where in 1985 Egypt's earliest temple began to emerge from beneath the sand. Although post-holes and trenches are all that remain, careful excavation and analysis of the finds leave little doubt about the nature of the complex. In a large oval courtyard stood a solitary pole displaying the image of the god, while at its base, on makeshift platforms, the early kings of

Above Exotic stones were gathered from the far reaches of the desert and transformed into luxury items such as these in the workshops surrounding the temple.

Upper Egypt viewed their bounty and the slaughter made for the falcon god: new-born goats, cattle, crocodiles and even fish, some up to 2 m (6 ft) in length and weighing over 175 kg (386 lb). Around the courtyard, in little workshops, trained craftsmen transformed raw materials gathered from the far reaches of the realm into luxury goods for their princely patrons and their gods; ivory boxes, polished stone jars, jewellery and ceremonial weapons.

The temple's centrepiece was a three-room shrine, its façade made up of four huge timber pillars. From the depth and size of the holes that anchored these pillars we can estimate that they would have been at least 12 m (20 ft) high. To build such a structure, conifers from the forests of Lebanon may have been imported and floated down the Nile. Lavishly appointed with coloured mats for walls, the shrine must have dominated the temple complex and the town of Hierakonpolis as a whole. Destined to become the prototype for later Egyptian temple architecture, it was a potent symbol of the power of the king and Horus, patron god of Egyptian kingship for the next 3000 years.

Above Until recently the only visible remains at Buto dated to the New Kingdom and later, suggesting to some that the kingdom of Lower Egypt was a myth. Buried below metres of debris, excavations are now finding the remnants of an early culture very different from Upper Egypt.

Buto

The Lower Egyptian counterpart of Hierakonpolis was the city of Buto, and here archaeologists are finding an early community of a very different character. The fact that they are finding anything at all from this period is itself noteworthy.

Today the remains of ancient Buto cover over half a square mile (1 sq. km), but none of the visible ruins, in some places up to 24 m (80 ft) tall, dates to the early periods. As a result, some scholars considered the legend of the 'Souls of Buto' and the existence of a Predynastic kingdom in Lower Egypt to be a myth, and the Delta at that time to have been an uninhabitable swamp. But in 1983 a team from the German Archaeological Institute determined to test this assumption. The main problem was that if early sites existed, they must be buried below several metres of silt brought by the annual Nile flood and the debris of millennia of later occupation.

Geological drill-cores allowed archaeologists to examine the lowest layers below the mound of Buto. Not only did they find the earliest settlement, some 3 m (10 ft) below sea level, but they also discovered that the Delta was not always the well-watered place it is today. In fact, in prehistoric times, parts of the Delta were practically desert. Although various branches of the Nile cut through the Delta plain, it was only in the fifth millennium BC, shortly before the first inhabitants came to Buto, that a rise in the level of the Mediterranean Sea backed up the Nile, causing it to flood its banks. When this occurred, the high tops of sand dunes made a perfect place to escape the inundation, and it is upon a long-buried dune, some 7 m (23.5 ft) below the surface, that the first settlement at Buto was discovered. Well below the water-table, excavation of the early levels could only be done with the help of diesel water pumps. This was difficult and dangerous work: the pumps had to run continuously day and night, since one break in the vacuum suction would allow the water to rush back in minutes.

It is now clear that Buto was the site of continuous Predynastic occupation for over 500 years. The stratified accumulation of debris, mostly hundreds of thousands of pottery sherds, has allowed the expedition director, Dina Faltings, to study the nature of this culture over time. By 'reading' the pottery she can tell that, in striking contrast to the Saharan influences that affected their Upper Egyptian contemporaries, the early Butites looked to the east. Distinctive pots, expertly made on a turning device and decorated with bands of white paint, point to a connection with early cultures in the Negev desert. This interaction was, however, short-lived and the Butites returned to making pottery by their traditional, rather unsophisticated, hand-made methods. They mixed Nile clay with straw or strands of flax, fashioned a lump of clay for the bottom, added some upright slabs and then squeezed it all together to make a pot. After a vessel dried, its surface was rubbed with a pebble, making it more watertight and attractive. But as soon as pottery from Upper Egypt began to appear, its elegance and superior quality were obvious. A makeshift pottery kiln found at Buto in 1995 shows that the Lower Egyptians tried to imitate the Upper Egyptian forms in their own local materials and with their own techniques, but without the specialized knowledge of the Upper Egyptian craftsmen – it wasn't a very successful undertaking.

Less than a hundred years later, these differences had ceased to matter. The indigenous pottery of the Delta had all but vanished and had been replaced with vessels made in Upper Egyptian shapes and in the Upper Egyptian way. The Delta houses were no longer made of bundled papyrus and mats but with mud bricks, as in the south. Moreover, although no cemeteries have yet been located at Buto, the evidence from other Delta sites indicates that even the most traditional of religious beliefs had changed to mirror the Upper Egyptian practice of including valuable grave-goods. This may represent one of the rare cases of archaeological evidence for a political event. It would certainly appear that the 'Two Lands' were not a myth: the Delta and the Valley were originally different lands with different cultures, but by the beginning

Opposite By 'reading' the pottery, Buto expedition director Dina Faltings can trace the development of Predynastic culture in the Delta over time.

of Egyptian history, at about 3100 BC, they had become one. How did this occur? Did Upper Egyptian culture take over the Delta via peaceful commercial contacts, or was it imposed with the help of lethal weapons?

Narmer's Palette

Since its discovery a century ago, the Palette of Narmer has influenced the way we view the unification of Upper and Lower Egypt and the birth of the world's first nation state. Found in a cache of temple offerings at Hierakonpolis in 1898, it was dedicated by King Narmer, possibly the same figure as the legendary King Menes, Egypt's first pharaoh. On one side it depicts Narmer wearing the bulbous 'White Crown' of Upper Egypt about to strike down a prone prisoner in the presence

Above The exquisite slate Palette of King Narmer. On one side Narmer, wearing the White Crown of Upper Egypt, stands with upraised mace about to smite the enemy chief whose name, written in hieroglyphs beside his head, is 'Wash'. The outcome is elucidated by the falcon grasping a symbol of the land and people of the papyrus plant. The meaning is clear: Horus, the patron god of kingship, now controls the Delta. Yet the presence of the foot-washer and sandal-bearer behind the king has suggested to some scholars that the action depicted here is ritual rather than historic.

On the other side Narmer, now wearing the Red Crown of Lower Egypt, marches in procession in the company of high officials to inspect two rows of decapidated foe at a place called the 'door of Horus'. The king's name, written as a catfish (*nar*) and a chisel (*mer*), appears before his face and again in the top

registers within a panel that represents the gate of the royal palace, or 'great house'. Below, the serpentine necks of the two captive lions frame the dish in which cosmetics were ground, perhaps to dress the divine image of the god. They portray the control and balance of powerful opposing forces vested in the person of the king. Below, as a raging bull, the king tramples town walls and gores its inhabitants to maintain this balance.

Right The 'White Crown' and the 'Red Crown' worn together form the 'Double Crown', the symbol of the king's dominion over the 'Two Lands' of Egypt.

of the falcon god Horus. On the other side, Narmer, wearing the distinctive 'Red Crown' of Lower Egypt, moves in a procession towards two rows of decapitated prisoners. Below, the lions with their serpentine necks intertwined symbolize the unification.

The key element for understanding the palette has always been the crowns. For the first time, one king is shown wearing both the Red and the White Crown. The message seems unambiguous: in about 3100 BC King Narmer of Upper Egypt smites his enemies with the help of his patron god, defeats the Lower Egyptian kingdom and assumes its crown and control – the decisive act of one man.

For the next 3000 years, the same images would reappear. In due course the two crowns would become entwined to form the 'Double Crown', signifying that the pharaoh was the lord of the 'Two Lands', and it would grace the head of every king until the end of Egyptian civilization. The image of the smiting king was inscribed on temple façades throughout Egypt to reinforce his conquest of enemies, both real and metaphoric. However, the

continuous ritual significance of these images has caused some scholars to question the historic interpretation of the Narmer Palette. Could just one object be trusted to tell us so much? New discoveries at Abydos in Upper Egypt are now clarifying this issue.

Abydos

At the mouth of the dramatic canyon at Abydos, which the Egyptians believed to be the entrance to the underworld, lay the tombs of the kings of the first two dynasties. Over 1000 years later, one of these tombs was to be mistaken for that of Osiris, the god of the dead, and for another 1000 years pilgrims would leave millions of little offering vessels in his honour. For this reason, the area is now called in Arabic the 'Omm el Gaab', 'Mother of Pots'.

In 1977 Dr Günter Dreyer of the German Archaeological Institute began reinvestigating the cemeteries at Abydos to fill in blanks left by inadequate and hasty nineteenth-century excavations. Using the exacting standards of modern archaeology, Dreyer has revealed remarkable new finds that are forcing us to re-evaluate the site of Abydos and the early history of Egypt as a whole.

Since the royal tombs were repeatedly pillaged in antiquity and excavated twice in modern times, one wouldn't expect there to be much left to find. Yet new clearance around the tomb of Narmer revealed a tiny ivory label of great importance. On it the name of the king comes alive. As the '*nar*' or catfish (the first element of his name), Narmer smites an enemy out of whose head sprout the papyrus reeds of the Delta marshes. As Dreyer explains:

> 'Such labels served to indicate the date of oil shipments. At that time, dates were indicated by the names of years and these names were chosen after the most important events of that year. In this case, it's a victory of King Narmer over the Delta people and obviously it is the same event as depicted on the Narmer Palette. From this we may conclude that the Narmer Palette indeed refers to an historical event which took place in a certain year.'

Confirmation that Narmer's victory was an actual event rather than a ritual one is welcome new information. However, further discoveries at Abydos show that this event was only one, but perhaps the last, step in a process of unification that had begun at least five generations before Narmer was born.

Excavating in 1988 in an area that had been long neglected to the east of the royal cemetery, Dreyer and his team happened upon a surprisingly

Left Recent excavations have revealed that even earlier kings were buried at Abydos; kings of a previously unknown dynasty, Dynasty 0.

Writing

One of the world's most beautiful scripts, the Egyptian hieroglyphic writing system consists of hundreds of different signs – pictures of natural and man-made things. However, the script is not a primitive 'picture writing' but a sophisticated system capable of communicating complex information. The Egyptians had different types of signs: some stand for complete words, usually the object they represent (word signs); but most signify sounds or combinations of

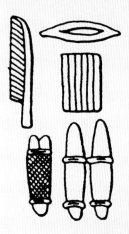

Left Group of five hieroglyphs, including different types of sign. The top three are 'sound signs', writing the word 'irp' meaning 'wine'. Below them are two 'determinatives' representing wine jars, which make the meaning of the word clear.

Above right Clay tablet with early Mesopotamian writing, c.3000 BC.

sounds (sound signs), like our alphabetic characters. For example, the reed leaf stands for the sound 'i', the mouth for the sound 'r', the mat for 'p'. Together these signs phonetically spell 'irp' the word for wine. In addition, a picture of wine jars with no phonetic value could be appended to help determine the sense of the word and prevent any ambiguity. Signs used in this way are called 'determinatives'.

Until recently it was thought that the earliest writing system was invented by the Sumerians in Mesopotamia towards the end of the fourth millennium BC and that the idea was borrowed by the Egyptians at the beginning of the First Dynasty (c.3100 BC). However, recent discoveries at Abydos have shown that the Egyptians had an advanced

system of writing even earlier than the Mesopotamians, some 150 years before Narmer. Remarkably, there is no evidence that this writing developed from a more primitive pictographic stage. Already, at

the very beginning, it incorporated signs for sounds.

Unlike Mesopotamian writing, which can be shown to have gradually evolved through a number of stages, beginning as an accounting system, Egyptian writing appears to have been deliberately invented in a more-or-less finished form, its underlying principles fully in place right from the outset. A parallel for such a process is known from more recent times: in AD 1444 the Korean script (still widely regarded as one of the world's most efficient) was invented by order of the king, who assembled a group of scholars for the purpose.

In Egypt this invention corresponds with the birth of the Egyptian state, and its growing administrative and bureaucratic needs. Some of the earliest uses of this writing system were to record the receipt of tax, and denote the origin of commodities and their production date. It was not until much later that surviving works of literature and historical records were composed, but the capacity to create such texts was already in place at this early time.

A cursive form of the hieroglyphic script, called hieratic, was soon developed for day-to-day use, when it was normally written in ink on papyrus.

elaborate brick-lined tomb with twelve rooms fitted out as a house for eternity, complete with doors and windows. But this tomb, which they called U-j, was not just a house but a palace. An ivory sceptre, of the kind that formed part of the standard royal regalia of later times, indicates that its owner was clearly the ruler of a previously unknown dynasty, a Dynasty 0, who reigned in about 3250 BC. More importantly, in one of the rooms were 150 small labels

Right Tomb U-j at Abydos was not just a house for eternity but a palace, complete with doors, windows, storerooms and bedchambers, for one of the kings of Dynasty 0, c.3250 BC.

Below Labels from Tomb U-j testify to the existence of a developed writing system over 150 years earlier than previously attested. The label in the lower left-hand corner may spell out the name of the Delta town Bubastis, suggesting that taxes were already being collected from the 'Two Lands' in Dynasty 0.

Below From its inception, the hieroglyphic system used signs for sounds. On the two labels on the left, the tall 'lightning bolt' spells out the word for '*grh*' or 'darkness'; the snake is the letter '*dj*' which together with the mountain sign below writes '*djw*', the word for 'mountain'. On the other three labels, the word for mountain appears again, but this time with a crested ibis, which spells '*akh*', meaning 'lightness'. Together these inscriptions can be read as the 'mountains of darkness' and the 'mountains of light', or the western and eastern mountains.

of ivory or bone, many of which appear to have been attached to bolts of linen. Carved on some of them are numbers indicating amounts or size, but on others are recognizable and readable hieroglyphic signs which spell out phonetically the names of places from which these goods originated. Small and laconic as they are, these labels testify to the existence of a developed writing system over a hundred years earlier than we ever expected.

What is equally surprising about the labels from this tomb is that some of the named places are in the Delta, suggesting that taxes and tribute were already being collected from Lower Egypt. In addition, hundreds of wine jars imported from Canaan, stacked three deep in one of the tomb's stone rooms, indicate that a well-established trade, passing through Lower Egyptian territory, was now firmly in the hands of this Upper Egyptian king. But who was this ruler, perhaps one of the earliest to rule the two lands of Egypt? Dreyer suggests that his name be read as Scorpion, as many pottery vessels had this name written in ink on them. But there were other names as well, simple names written with an animal sign: sea-shell, dog, lion and elephant – perhaps the members of a royal dynasty that even the Egyptians were later to forget or only vaguely remember as demigods. Further research may yet make them mortals.

Memphis

To crown the achievement of a unified nation, the early kings moved their capital to a suitable place from which to administer the Two Lands. They chose a spot at the southern apex of the Delta so strategic that it remained the administrative centre of the country until Roman times. Located a little to the south and across the river from modern Cairo, the Greeks called it Memphis. To the Egyptians it was appropriately 'The Balance of the Two Lands'. It was also called 'The White Walls', probably in reference to the gleaming walls surrounding its most important landmark, the king's palace. It is possible that the founding of this magnificent city marked the beginning of recorded factual history about Egypt's early kings, but the proof of this depends on finding the actual remains of the first city at Memphis. These, however, have remained elusive until recently.

Spreading around the modern village of Mit Rahina, the visible mounds and later ruins of Memphis have always been thought to cover the spot of its first foundation. When an expedition of the Egypt Exploration Society, now headed by David Jeffreys, began to survey the massive ruin fields in 1982, the results were surprising. They found that, unlike sites such as Buto, for example, Memphis was not a giant layer cake with superimposed levels of continuous occupation stretching back in time. Instead, the city appeared to be constantly, if sometimes only gradually, shifting. The reason for this was the Nile. In ancient times, the course of the river was not set, and after a high flood the Nile could retreat to a different channel. Over time it moved

further and further to the east, and with it moved the city. When the expedition located the New Kingdom city in one place and the town of the Middle Kingdom further to the west, it became clear that the evidence for the first 1000 years of the city's life had to lie even closer to the desert's edge, but where?

Considering the northern location of the numerous First Dynasty cemeteries in the Memphite region, David Jeffreys realized that the first city had to be somewhere close by. As the first to use the Saqqara plateau, site of the ancient necropolis for Memphis, the early officials had an unlimited choice of places to build their impressive tombs, and Jeffreys assumed they would have chosen locations close to home. Geological corings are beginning to verify this assumption. Remnants of the early town have been found some 2 miles (3 km) northwest of the Memphis ruin fields and close to the western escarpment. Unfortunately they are buried several metres down and well below the water-table, so it may be many years before excavations can expose the marvels of the first national capital. Yet dozens of laboriously hand-turned corings do provide a picture of the deposits buried beneath the modern topsoil and have revealed another surprising twist to the story of early Memphis.

Alternating bands of silt and sand in the cores testify to a series of climatic changes when the Nile floods were alternately low or high. Too high and the town was flooded, houses of unfired mud brick collapsed and cattle drowned; too low and the sands from the west blew in and carpeted the valley floor with a taste of the desert. These were the forces of chaos at work, and it was the king's job to control them by providing the appropriate disaster relief, either by feeding the famine-stricken or marshalling the manpower

Below Over time – from its first foundation to modern times – the city of Memphis shifted its position as the river altered its course.

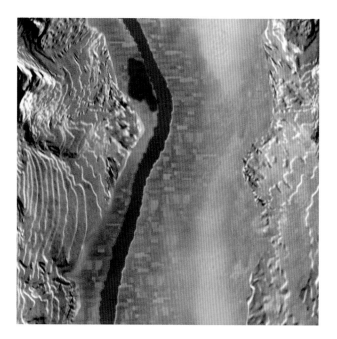
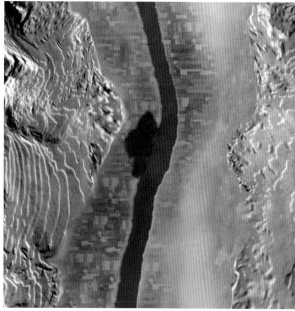

for rebuilding. But above all, it was his responsibility to propitiate the gods who caused such chaos and to redress the all-important cosmic balance.

The Famine Stela inscribed on Sehel Island at the First Cataract of the Nile describes such an event. In it, King Djoser, a Third Dynasty king who is famous as the builder of the Step Pyramid, gives his thanks in the form of rich gifts to the gods of the cataract region for ending the distress caused by seven years of low Nile floods. Although carved over 2000 years after Djoser's reign to bolster the claim of the priesthood to certain revenues, in light of the new evidence from Memphis, it may actually be based on historic fact.

Above The Famine Stela at Sehel Island near the First Cataract of the Nile describes a seven-year famine during the time of King Djoser. Ptolemaic Period.

In this case and others, the king was apparently able to handle the crisis. Yet the geological cores reveal that at the end of the Old Kingdom, approximately 1000 years after its founding, early Memphis was engulfed by a huge sand-dune, evidence of a sustained period of low Nile floods and searing heat. This was just one of the many disasters that befell all of Egypt at this

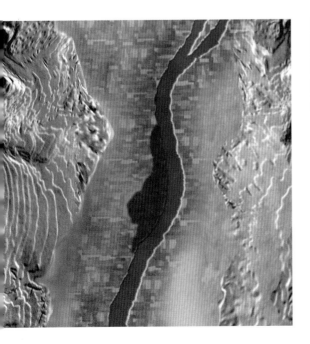

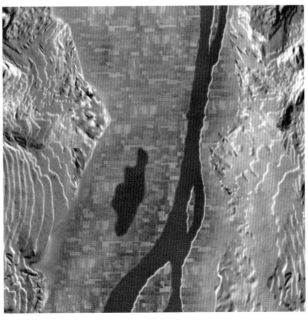

Above The 'Dam of the Pagans' at Helwan was the first great attempt at flood control in history, but unfortunately it was destroyed by water before it was completed. Fourth Dynasty, c.2600 BC.

time, disrupting the unity of the land and bringing the country to its knees. Sometimes, despite the efforts of the kings, chaos won.

The Helwan Dam

Pharaohs were expected not simply to react to the powers of chaos when disaster struck, but to be proactive as well. To protect Memphis from the Nile, Herodotus relates that its founder, the legendary King Menes, built dikes and dams. The truth of this remains to be ascertained, but near Helwan, about 20 miles (32 km) south of Cairo, the ruins of the world's oldest dam testify to the civil engineering abilities of the pharaohs at the very dawn of the Pyramid Age.

Seth, the chief god of chaos and confusion, was appropriately also the god

of the desert and the thunderstorm, for within hours the occasional thunderstorm in the desert can produce a flash-flood of terrifying and destructive intensity. It was to control such flash-floods that the dam was constructed. Called 'Sadd el-Kafara', or 'Dam of the Pagans', it was discovered in 1885 about 7.5 miles (12 km) into the desert. Yet it had to wait almost a hundred years before engineers and archaeologists uncovered its full story.

A remarkable engineering feat, the dam consists of three parts: a loose filling of rubble, encased between two roughly built walls, which were each faced with dressed blocks of stone. Over 98 m (321 ft) wide at the bottom and 56 m (184 ft) across at the top, the dam was designed to be 14 m (46 ft) high and 110 m (361 ft) long. Günter Dreyer of the German Archaeological Institute, working with hydraulic engineers from the Technical University of Braunschweig, estimates that it took about 500 workmen to build it. These men were housed in barracks, which Dreyer helped to uncover on the northern side of the dam in 1982. A good 75 per cent of the workforce must have been engaged in hauling the rubble and stone – some 80,000 cubic metres (104,640 cubic yards) of it – probably on a seasonal basis during the three months of the Nile flood. The remainder – supervisors, stone cutters and food providers – may have worked on a year-round basis for up to ten or twelve years.

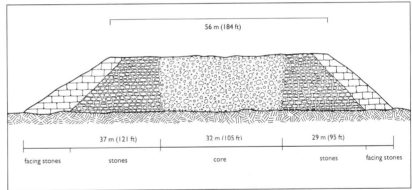

Above right The dam consisted of three parts: a filling of rubble in the centre, held in place by rough masonry walls, which were then covered with dressed stone blocks, still visible today.
(After Gaarbrecht and Bertram)

By modern calculations, the dam was over-designed, but nevertheless based on sound hydrological knowledge. It would have served its purpose had it been completed. Unfortunately, with 70 per cent of the construction complete, the first great dam in history was destroyed by the chaos it was built to control, when a massive flash-flood swept the unfinished central section away. The intensity of this flood must have had catastrophic consequences downstream in the quarrying and loading docks which the dam was meant to protect. Perhaps with these installations now in ruins, there was little point in continuing the construction of the dam and all work was abandoned. Tragically, it was just a matter of three years on either side. Had it rained three years earlier, before the construction had reached the *wadi* (dry valley) bed, little of the work would have been washed away. Had it rained three years later, the flood would certainly have been contained by the completed edifice. In the end, ten years' labour was for nought, and it would be many more years before the Egyptians tried something like this again.

Weni

The ability of the pharaoh to command a large workforce to fight chaos was not limited to the occasionally unsuccessful battles to control the forces of nature. Chaos in a human form also threatened the delicate balance that it was the pharaoh's role to maintain. Although there are numerous visual tributes to the victories won by the kings of the early dynasties over a human foe, it is not until later that texts are preserved which give a more detailed picture of the king's power.

In about 2280 BC a senior court official named Weni recorded the notable events of his life on a monolithic slab of limestone set into his tomb at Abydos. Weni relates how his pharaoh, King Pepi I of the Sixth Dynasty, dealt with the marauding powers of chaos.

'When his majesty took action against the Sand Dwellers of the east, his majesty made an army of many tens of thousands from all over Upper Egypt...There were counts, seal-bearers, chieftains and mayors, chief priests and desert scouts...I was the one who commanded them all...This army returned in safety. It had ravaged the Sand Dwellers' land, it had sacked its strongholds, it had thrown fire into all of its mansions...His majesty sent me to lead this army five times, to attack the land of the Sand Dwellers as often as they rebelled... His majesty praised me for it more than anything.'

While the protection of his citizenry and his borders were of foremost concern to the pharaoh, it would appear that the chief benefits of these bellicose campaigns related to the king's economic interests. The Egyptians professed a horror for the chaos of the desert, the land of Seth, and a strong distaste for those lands and peoples beyond the borders of their own well-ordered world. Yet that never stopped them from going to these places, for they had many things to offer. The desert to the east of the Nile Valley, in particular, had great mineral wealth: not only gold and copper, but also fine stones and semi-precious gems with which to feed the Egyptians' ever-growing appetite for beautiful things. Exploited already in Predynastic times, a new discovery in the Eastern Desert shows that, by the beginning of the First Dynasty, the desert's bounty may well have been under the king's control.

Wadi Abu Had

Below At Wadi Abu Had, in the wilderness of the Eastern Desert, excavations show that rock crystal, amethyst and malachite were collected, processed and prepared for shipment to the Nile Valley.

About 30 miles (50 km) west of the Red Sea coast is the Wadi Abu Had. It is a wide valley bisected by white limestone ridges and occasional green groves of acacia trees, bounded by majestic red granite peaks which contrast with the black basalt hills. Overwhelmed by this colour combination of spectacular beauty, the casual traveller in this wilderness wouldn't cast a glance at the low ridge near the *wadi* centre. Here it was, however, that during an intensive survey in 1993, Ann Bomann of the American School of Oriental Research

spotted a series of interlocking semicircular rough-stone walls in a depression cut out of the soft limestone. Two seasons of excavation showed that inside these walls and beneath their once tent-like roofs, desert resources were collected and processed. Cobbles of basalt were heated and crushed to give up their veins of malachite, a green powder of copper, used as eye make-up. Rock crystal was gathered and flaked. Rough amethysts, mined in nearby granite cliffs, were collected, and the precious purple crystals were refined. While a small band of workmen here prepared their harvest for shipment to the Nile Valley, the marks on the pottery vessels found within the complex indicate that supplies from centralized government storehouses kept them alive.

This collection station was ideally situated at the confluence of three passes through the desert within easy access of transport caravans bringing back any of a number of other treasures. It was one in a network of trading depots, and possibly even colonial administrative centres, which stretched across northern Sinai and half way up the Levantine coast. But by the end of the First Dynasty, all were abandoned for reasons unknown. It would be another millennium before the Egyptians could sustain such a broad imperial vision. In the meantime, it would seem that it was more efficient to send out expeditions, sometimes on a large scale, to get what they wanted by whatever means necessary.

Harkhuf

To lead an expedition beyond the boundaries of the ordered world required bravery and skill. Such men were highly regarded and well compensated. Among the most famous of them was a man named Harkhuf. He was based at Elephantine, at the First Cataract of the Nile – the perfect place from which to launch, at his majesty's bidding, expeditions to the south to bring back for him the exotic treasures of Africa. In his tomb in the cliffs at Qubbet el-Hawa overlooking his town, Harkhuf relates the notable events of his four expeditions into Nubia, 'to bring the produce of all foreign lands to his lord', by casting the 'dread of Horus into the foreign lands'. He boasts of the donkey-loads of incense, ebony, oils, panther skins, elephant tusks and throwsticks he procured in the south lands, but he is most proud of a far more exotic acquisition: a dancing pygmy.

When apprised of the news, King Pepi II himself (c.2278–2184 BC), the last king of the Sixth Dynasty, who was a boy of no more than nine years of age at the time, was compelled to write to Harkhuf in his own hand. A royal

Left The brave men who led expeditions into Africa to bring back its treasures for their king were buried in cliffs overlooking the First Cataract of the Nile.

letter was an honour so rarely bestowed that Harkhuf placed a verbatim copy of its text, grammatical mistakes and all, on the façade of his tomb. In it the boy king's anticipation is palpable:

> 'Come north to the palace at once! Hurry and bring with you this pygmy whom you brought from the land of the horizon dwellers who does the dances of the gods. When he goes with you into the ship, place worthy men around him on deck, lest he fall into the water! When he sleeps, surround him with worthy men in his tent. Inspect him ten times a night. My majesty wishes to see this pygmy more than the gifts of the mine-lands. Orders have been given to the town mayors and overseers of priests that supplies are to be furnished for you from every storage depot and every temple.'

In theory, if not in reality, the king owned everything and it was his to command at his will. In return he maintained the balance of the universe with justice and piety, and did battle with the undefeatable powers of chaos, be they natural phenomena, social upheaval or supernatural forces. With the skills perhaps forged by distant ancestors facing a hostile environment in the desert and honed over the centuries along the banks of an ever-changing Nile, the pharaohs had learned how to raise an army, organize a workforce or prepare a trading expedition. They knew how to gather taxes in times of plenty and distribute supplies in times of need. The longevity of Egyptian civilization is testimony to their abilities.

But each king met one final challenge, one final battle with chaos – the battle for eternal life. For although the king was a god, he was also a man, and he was going to die. The afterlife waited, but it was in no way guaranteed, and the way there was fraught with danger. The chaotic elements from which recreation could be forged had to be confronted, negotiated and controlled for the king's resurrection to be complete.

By 2700 BC the stage was set for the maximum test of all the king's skills for this ultimate challenge. Men began hauling huge stone blocks to the desert's edge. A new type of monument arose to keep chaos at bay. The age of the pyramids had begun.

Below Detail of Harkhuf's copy of the royal letter, carved on the façade of his tomb. The hieroglyphs that spell out the word for 'pygmy' occur twice in this section.

ION MACHINE

I t was the hope of every Egyptian to be reborn after death, to attain an afterlife with the sun-god Ra and be resurrected with each sunrise, and to join with Osiris in the cyclical regeneration of nature and plant life with the receding of the annual Nile flood. These are not opposing beliefs, but a complementary interweaving of the varying cycles of creation with which the Egyptians linked their own eternal rebirth. However, neither the annual rise of the life-giving waters of the Nile nor the re-emergence of the sun each morning was guaranteed. Eternal night and the cessation of plant life were constant threats which had to be averted so that creation could begin again. In the same way, formidable obstacles had to be overcome for resurrection to be achieved.

The journey to the next world was perilous: demons waited to sidetrack the unprepared, judgements were made. Most people had to depend on their family to provide the proper equipment and chant the appropriate spells to help them attain the afterlife. But the king could call upon the resources of the entire country in his bid for immortality. The greatest manifestation of this is seen in the pyramids of the Giza Plateau.

The three pyramids at Giza are the most visited attraction in Egypt, if not the world. The Great Pyramid of the Fourth Dynasty king Khufu, the ultimate 'resurrection machine', is the largest

Left The pyramids at Giza. The middle pyramid built by Khafra is actually half a metre (2 ft) smaller than its neighbour (to the right), the Great Pyramid of Khufu, but built on higher ground it appears to dominate the plateau.

Above left An enormous support system was needed to create and maintain the pyramids, including ancillary staff to produce food, pottery and building supplies. Servant statues from Giza. Old Kingdom, c.2500 BC.

pyramid ever built. It stands with its neighbours, the pyramids of Khafra and Menkaura, as the last remaining of the Seven Wonders of the Ancient World. The immense size of these pyramids invites comparison with the most ambitious human projects of any age, and they have never ceased to fire people's imagination. The first surviving description of them is by the fifth-century BC Greek traveller Herodotus, who also began the tradition of fantastic stories which surround them still today. Herodotus is called the father of history, but the emphasis was on the story – after all he had an audience to entertain, both as readers and on the lecture circuit.

In one tale of whimsy, Herodotus relates that King Cheops, the Greek name for Khufu, was so evil a man that for lack of money to build his massive pyramid he confined his own daughter to a chamber, where she had to receive clients and exact payment for her services. She, in addition, demanded that each man give her one stone so that she could build her own pyramid, this being identified as one of the three queen's pyramids in front of the Great Pyramid today. Herodotus also reports that his guides said that both Cheops and Chephren (Khafra) shut the temples to divert payment to their tombs, placing the land in such great misery that in his day their memory was hated. Be that as it may, power has never before or since been so massively concentrated or so physically expressed as in the pyramids of these Fourth Dynasty kings.

Both Herodotus and Egyptian texts explicitly state that pyramids served as tombs, and the archaeological evidence confirms this beyond doubt. Nevertheless, from the nineteenth century onwards, bizarre theories about their function have proliferated, insisting that the Great Pyramid in particular served a hidden, more exalted purpose. Interpreted variously as an astronomical observatory, sundial, the embodiment of secret knowledge about the past and the future, the Great Pyramid has been held to be the perfect structure and the product of divine inspiration. Such 'pyramidiocy' has sometimes been promoted for political reasons. For example, calculations (not necessarily accurate) revealed that the basic unit of measure used in the construction of the Great Pyramid was remarkably similar to the English inch. As the perfect unit in a divine creation, to abandon the inch for the metric system, as Parliament was considering in 1874, would be a blasphemous and pagan act; and indeed, partly for this reason among others, the move was rejected.

In more recent times, pyramidiocy has resurfaced in various updated forms. As our horizons have broadened, it is not just secret biblical knowledge that has been discerned encrypted in the form and dimensions of the Great Pyramid, but extra-terrestrial intelligence as well. Yet even the most bizarre theories concerning master races and alien origins for these supreme Egyptian creations in their way pay tribute to the Fourth Dynasty rulers, simply by expressing incredulity that they could organize and complete so colossal a task.

The Pyramid Builders of the Old Kingdom

Third Dynasty	
Djoser	c. 2686–2667 BC
Sekhemkhet	2648–2640
Khaba	2640–2637
Huni	2637–2613

Fourth Dynasty	
Snefru	c. 2613–2589 BC
Khufu	2589–2566
Djedfra	2566–2558
Khafra	2558–2532
Menkaura	2532–2503

Fifth Dynasty	
Userkaf	c.2494–2487 BC
Sahura	2487–2475
Neferirkara	2475–2455
Shepseskara	2455–2448
Raneferef	2448–2445
Niuserra	2445–2421
Menkauhor	2421–2414
Djedkara-Isesi	2414–2375
Unas	2375–2345

Sixth Dynasty	
Teti	c.2345–2323 BC
Pepi I	2321–2287
Merenra	2287–2278
Pepi II	2278–2184

Right A total of ninety-seven pyramids of the kings and queens of Egypt dot the landscape from the Delta to the First Cataract, but even more pyramids are to be found in the Sudan.

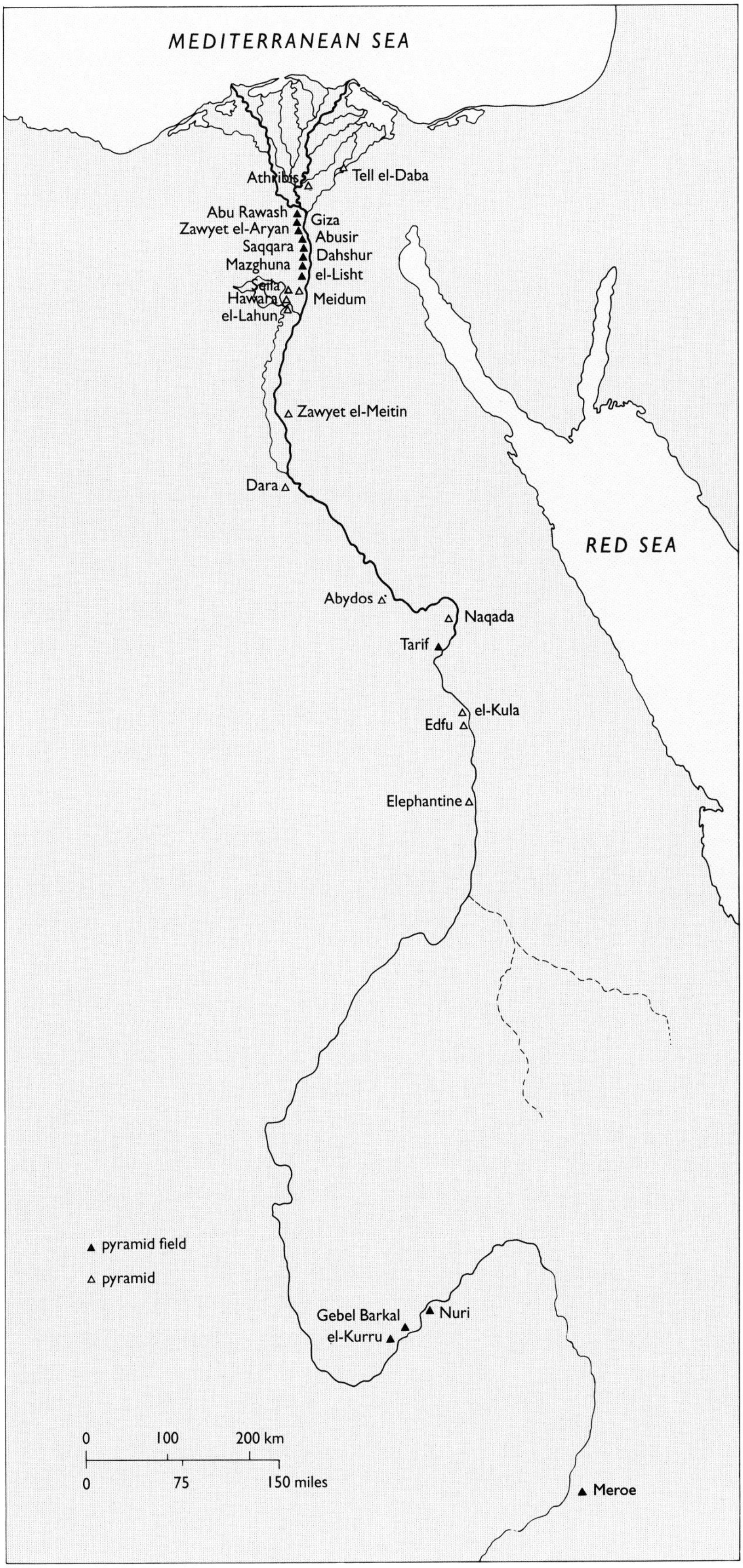

MEDITERRANEAN SEA

Athribis

Tell el-Daba

Abu Rawash

Giza

Zawyet el-Aryan

Abusir

Saqqara

Dahshur

Mazghuna

el-Lisht

Seila

Hawara

Meidum

el-Lahun

Zawyet el-Meitin

Dara

RED SEA

Abydos

Naqada

Tarif

el-Kula

Edfu

Elephantine

▲ pyramid field

△ pyramid

Gebel Barkal

Nuri

el-Kurru

0   100   200 km

0   75   150 miles

Meroe

Pyramids, however, are not restricted to Giza, nor are they phenomena only of the Fourth Dynasty. The origins of the pyramid begin well before the 'Pyramid Age' of the Old Kingdom and end long after. For over one thousand years Egyptian kings built tombs for themselves and their queens in the form of pyramids. There are in fact over ninety 'royal' pyramids in Egypt, dotting the landscape from the apex of the Delta to the First Cataract of the Nile. Remarkably, at least twice as many again are to be found further south, in modern day Sudan, the ancient land of Kush. Some 2000 years after the first pyramid was constructed, the native Sudanese kings of Kush returned to the pyramid form for their tombs, ushering in yet another millennium of pyramid building. Revived and reinterpreted in a style strictly their own, the Kushite kings kept the pyramid alive long after the culture which invented it was moribund. In fact, it was not until the introduction of Christianity and a distinctly different view of how the afterlife might be attained that the venerable art of pyramid building on the African continent finally came to an end.

▨ The Resurrection Machine

To understand the origins of the pyramids one must go back to the very beginning, the beginning of the world as the Egyptians saw it. For at this time there was only a watery void called Nun, which contained the essence of all creation. Out of this chaotic yet creative soup arose a mound, just as the mounds of fertile silt teeming with life emerged as the waters of the annual Nile flood receded. On that mound of creation appeared the sun god Ra–Atum, embodiment of life and goodness, the source of energy, light and warmth. From him the rest of creation issued forth as he rose in the sky, only to plunge back into the chaotic void with every sunset to be re-created again. For the Egyptians, creation unfolded not once, but continuously. By linking up with this cosmic cycle, they too could emerge reborn.

The pyramid was essentially this mound of creation, a cocoon in which the king underwent the transformation or recreation into an eternal transfigured spirit called an *akh*. Journeying to the sky, he was united with the gods and resurrected each morning.

But the pyramid itself was only one part of the resurrection machine. Like all gods, the king was in permanent need of the sustenance and offerings which were provided to him on earth. Thus the pyramid alone was not enough to ensure a good afterlife. In time elaborate complexes developed which incorporated the pyramid and offering places, ranging from small chapels to a vast series of interconnected temples and estates, to service the needs of the deceased pharaoh on earth. No pyramid or pyramid complex is exactly like another. Their continuous development can be understood not only in terms of technological innovation and evolving religious beliefs, but also of the desire to ensure the absolute and eternal power of the resurrection machine to do its job.

The Prehistory of Pyramids

By the beginning of the First Dynasty, if not earlier, the mound of sand and rubble heaped on top of a grave, perhaps initially as a marker, had become associated with the primordial mound of creation.

Out in the desert at Abydos, the first kings of Egypt were buried in deep brick-lined tombs topped with square or rectangular mounds of sand which Egyptologists call 'mastabas', due to their resemblance to the benches that once stood in front of modern Egyptian village homes. So important was the mound over these royal tombs, that by the middle of the First Dynasty, the

Above In the First Dynasty tomb of King Den (c.2950 BC) the remnants of the retaining walls that once held the mounds are still visible.

Right The early kings constructed two mounds over their deep, brick-lined tombs: one directly above the tomb itself, but still below ground; and one above ground to cover and protect the one below.

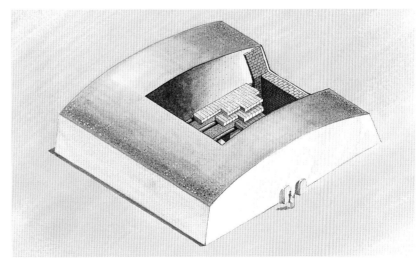

57

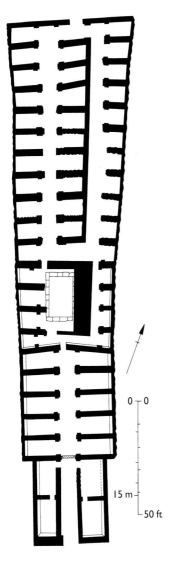

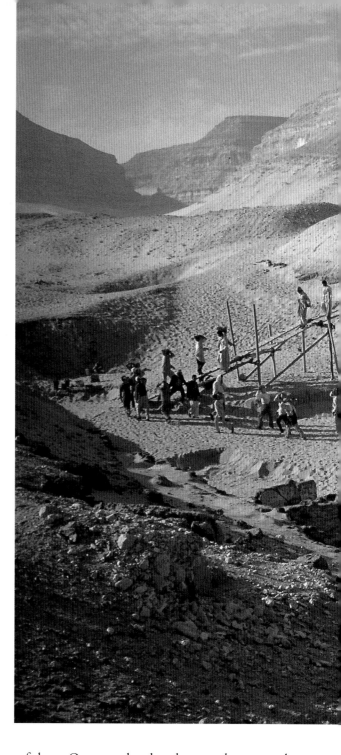

Left A plan of Khasekhemwy's tomb made after its first excavation almost a hundred years ago.

builders constructed two of them. One was placed underground, supported by a retaining wall, directly over the stout roofing beams that covered the increasingly elaborate tombs. The second mastaba, encased in a mud-brick wall, was placed above ground, directly over the first. Clearly the early kings had come to see that various chaotic forces, such as rain or flash-floods and wind storms, could destroy the burial mound and interrupt resurrection much in the same way they feared chaos could interfere with the actual cycle of cosmic creation. The upper mastaba was designed to protect the lower mastaba and doubled the chances of survival in this world and the next. This

Above Uncovering the tomb of King Khasekhemwy at Abydos.

reinforcement and multiplication of the mound later played a part in the genesis of the pyramid.

With each generation the royal tombs became more elaborate, containing a huge number of sumptuous offerings and surrounded by the graves of wives, household retainers, servants and even pets. The largest and the last royal tomb to be built at Abydos is that of King Khasekhemwy, the last king of the Second Dynasty who ruled Egypt to about 2686 BC. Since 1995 Dr Günter Dreyer of the German Archaeological Institute has been re-investigating his tomb, clearing away the sand that has covered it since its initial

Above Khasekhemwy's funerary enclosure is today called 'Shunet es-Zebib', the 'Storehouse of the Flies', a name derived from the local legend that it was one of the granaries that Joseph used for storing the harvest against the seven lean years, as related in the Bible. The decoration of recesses or niches on the exterior walls of Khasekhemwy's palace of eternity imitates the appearance of the palace he used in life.

excavation a century ago. Completely unlike the tombs of his predecessors, Khasekhemwy's tomb is trapezoidal in shape and impressively large. In a trench dug deep in the sand, it was constructed of mud brick and measures almost 69 m (230 ft) in length, varying in width between 17.6 m (56 ft) and 10.4 m (33 ft).

After two seasons, Dreyer has succeeded in clearing again the first part of the tomb, which was made up of thirty-three storage rooms for offerings and funerary equipment laid out in three rows. His careful study of the architectural remains has revealed a fascinating story of structural collapse which protected valuable burial equipment from the robbers who burrowed through the walls to get at it; further large-scale pillaging was followed by pious restoration in the Middle Kingdom, many centuries after the tomb was built. However, Dreyer has yet to reach the really interesting part of the tomb, the burial chamber – a room built entirely of dressed stone blocks. At the time of

its initial discovery, this chamber was the earliest stone construction then known, and, although earlier examples of stone masonry have since been found, Khasekhemwy's remains the finest of its age. New research suggests it is but a mere hint of what he was capable.

While such tombs were the private chambers of the king for eternity, at the edge of the desert about half a mile (1 km) away each king built for himself an eternal palace of state; a place where the official and ritual business of a king could be undertaken for eternity, and where eternal tribute and nourishment would be supplied.

No doubt based on the actual palace that the king used during his lifetime, many of these massive mud-brick enclosures were decorated on their outer surface with a series of niches or recesses to create a panelled effect. Professor David O'Connor of the Institute of Fine Arts, New York, has been studying these enclosures for many years. Although most have been reduced to a scant few courses of brickwork, traces of a whitewash coating are still preserved. The result must have been dazzling, as an intricate pattern of light and shadow was reflected across these brilliant white-panelled walls over the course of the day. It is not surprising therefore, that this architectural style was to have a lasting influence in Egypt. Before the invention of the cartouche to enclose a king's name (see page 16), the image of the niched façade of the royal palace was used. The king's name was inscribed as if on the lintel over an elaborately panelled gateway in a device called a *serekh*. Subsequently, the whole design of panels, recesses and doors became the fixed scheme for the carved stone sarcophagi of royalty and the élite alike throughout the Old Kingdom and later. In effect, the sarcophagus became each person's individual palace of eternity.

Khasekhemwy's is the only one of these palaces of eternity at Abydos still clearly visible. In fact, it is hard to miss. Still standing in places to its full original height of 11 m (36 ft), with walls 5.5 m (18 ft) thick, it is one of the oldest standing mud-brick structures in the world. It measures 122 m (400 ft) in length and 65 m (213 ft) wide and is surrounded by a low curtain wall. Unfortunately, little remains within the structure to help determine how it might have functioned, since buildings of temporary and perishable materials have vanished. However, clearance of a portion of the vast enclosed space in 1988 by O'Connor and his team uncovered a large mound of sand and gravel covered with a brick skin near the centre of the structure. Its

Right King Khasekhemwy wears the White Crown of Upper Egypt on one of the most ancient datable statues in the world and possibly the earliest representation in the round of a known historical personage. One of a pair of statues from Hierakonpolis. Limestone, *c.*2690 BC.

Above On the funerary stela of the First Dynasty king Wadje, the niched façade of his palace is reproduced as the device called a *serekh* to hold his name, *c.*2980 BC.

significance is not entirely clear. Perhaps it formed another 'mound of creation', signifying the presence of the king's resurrected spirit; and as such it is another step toward the birth of the pyramid.

This king's ability to marshal a workforce to construct such a massive tomb and vast mortuary palace is as impressive as the structures themselves. Millions of mud bricks were involved, some of which had to be hauled over a mile into the desert to be put in place. But Khasekhemwy didn't just build one of these palatial enclosures, he built another at Hierakonpolis. Only one-third the size of the enclosure at Abydos, it was nevertheless no mean feat, and it too still stands to its original height, a testament to its builders' construction skills. The real story of the pyramids begins here, in terms of the organizational aspect alone.

Khasekhemwy, although little known, was the first major builder among the pharaohs, but he didn't stop with the building of tombs. The accomplished relief carving on the hard stone architectural features that embellished both his enclosure and the temple of Horus at Hierakonpolis, as well as the two stone statues of himself that he dedicated there, anticipates the formal style and poses of Egyptian art which were to follow. Khasekhemwy had taken Egypt to the cusp of the Old Kingdom, the first great flowering of Egyptian civilization. Massive constructions of mud brick and refined carving of hard stone were well within his control. But it seems that Khasekhemwy may have had even greater aspirations, further north, at Saqqara.

The Step Pyramid

Saqqara was the site of the necropolis of ancient Memphis. It is dominated by the Step Pyramid of King Djoser, the first of Egypt's pyramids and one of the most remarkable architectural achievements of the ancient Egyptians. Constructed entirely of stone, the pyramid is surrounded by a complex in which the originally wooden and mud-brick structures of the palace were faithfully rendered in stone. This was truly a palace of eternity, built for the first time in the world entirely of imperishable stone. The careful restoration of the complex over the past fifty years by the French architect Jean-Phillipe Lauer allows one to experience some of the awe felt by ancient Egyptian tourists who visited the site over one thousand years after it was built. Ancient graffiti record their impressions and admiration:

> 'The Scribe Ahmose came to see the Temple of Djoser. He found it
> as though heaven were inside it, Ra rising within, heaven raining
> myrrh and incense dripping upon it.'

It is, in fact, from these graffiti that the owner of the pyramid, a mysterious King Netjerikhet, could be equated with King Djoser, known from the historical king-lists.

Captured in the permanence of stone was a moment in time for the king's eternal use. Not just any moment, but the festival of rejuvenation the king would have celebrated in his lifetime in his thirtieth year on the throne. Assembled are the shrines of the gods from all over the country to welcome

Above Khasekhemwy's enclosure at Hierakonpolis, the oldest standing brick building in Egypt.

Right A graffito left by an ancient Egyptian tourist who visited the Step Pyramid one thousand years after it was built.

Above Imhotep, King Djoser's architect, was later deified as a god of architecture and medicine. Bronze statuette. Late Period, after 600 BC.

Opposite The Step Pyramid and its associated structures form the first monumental funerary complex built entirely of stone.

him and acclaim him after completing a ritual test of his virility. Offices of state and an extensive temple fill the north end of the complex, and all are surrounded by a niched stone wall.

The magnificence of this complex earned Djoser immortality, but greater fame went to its architect, a man of learning named Imhotep, who was credited with the invention of working in hewn stone, major works of medicine and literature, and although a common man was later deified as a saint.

The Step Pyramid complex represents a dramatic increase in technical progress and artistic accomplishment – advances made in a remarkably short period of time. Even today, this quantum leap from the use of stone for details such as the stone-lined chamber in the tomb of Khasekhemwy to the raising of huge monuments built exclusively of this material has been attributed to Imhotep's vision and aptitude. However, new work suggests that the way, in fact, had already been paved.

Gisr el Mudir

To the west of the Step Pyramid, the desert looks barren, but emerging from the drift sand here and there are the stone masonry walls of rectangular enclosures. The largest of these mysterious monuments is called the Gisr el Mudir, or 'enclosure of the boss'. First noted in the nineteenth century, the full extent of this enclosure was not appreciated until aerial photographs in the 1920s revealed it to be enormous, and it has intrigued Egyptologists ever since. Measuring about 350 × 650 m (1150 × 2130 ft), it is almost twice the size of the Step Pyramid enclosure. However, the excavation of such an immense complex, its walls stretching to the horizon, is a task only slightly less daunting than building it in the first place, and as a result, its age, purpose and accurate dimensions long remained a subject of speculation. Only recently have cost-efficient means for answering these questions been developed.

Ian Mathieson of the National Museums of Scotland is using some of this new technology. With an electric resistivity meter, which measures the resistance of buried features to an electrical current passed through the ground, he is mapping the subsurface topography of the Gisr el Mudir without ever shifting a shovel of sand. In this way, excavations can be directed to specific parts of this vast area which show special promise for answering the many outstanding questions. After particularly high readings, selected areas along the face of the walls were chosen for further investigation. Here Mathieson uncovered fifteen courses of limestone masonry, a stone wall still about 4.5 m (15 ft) high. The intended height must have been much greater, as the walls are an astounding 15 m (49 ft) thick, composed of rubble fill with a masonry skin for the majority of their length, but solidly built of roughly dressed stone at the corners. According to Mathieson, the enclosure must have been the largest stone construction that anyone could have built at that time in history. It is especially impressive, as pottery recovered from these excavations

Above An electric resistivity meter is used by Ian Mathieson and his team to detect features buried beneath the vast area of the Gisr el Mudir.

indicates that the enclosure's construction predates King Djoser by some years. It, not the Step Pyramid complex, may in fact be the oldest building in stone, although it was apparently never completed. Exactly who was responsible for it still remains unknown, but it is hard to imagine anyone other than the great builder King Khasekhemwy who, at the end of his reign, may have made an even bigger and better bid for immortality, this time in stone.

Right Excavations along the west and north walls of the Gisr el Mudir revealed the incredible size of its stone walls.

Opposite The enormous rectangle to the west of the Step Pyramid has puzzled Egyptologists ever since it size was made clear from aerial photographs. It is called the Gisr el Mudir, 'the enclosure of the boss'.

The probability that Khasekhemwy was responsible for the Gisr el Mudir is strengthened by a recent discovery from his tomb at Abydos. Although Khasekhemwy is known to have been the last king of the Second Dynasty, the identity of his successor long remained unclear. Working at the north entrance to the tomb, however, Günter Dreyer came upon an area that had never been cleared before. Here, around the door, he found several seal impressions of King Djoser. Clearly, Djoser must have buried Khasekhemwy, closing his tomb and placing upon it his royal seal. Burying one's predecessor was the duty of every king, and for the first time we now know that King Djoser must have been the immediate successor to Khasekhemwy and may even have been his step-son. What this new discovery shows is that, probably not for the first time and certainly not for the last, a ruler has been given credit for advances made by his predecessor.

The Step Pyramid and its Descendants

According to Dreyer, this succession is important for understanding the development of the Step Pyramid. With the ability to quarry, transport and lay large quantities of stone already developed, Imhotep's true innovation appears to have been combining the two elements of the tomb and the funerary palace in a new way. As Dreyer explains:

> 'When Djoser built his tomb he decided to bring the two
> elements, tomb and large enclosure, together but what happened?
> He built his tomb shaft, the chamber and the mound above, the
> initial mastaba over that and then the enclosure wall was built
> around it. But now the important mound, the mastaba, was no
> longer visible. I think to solve this problem they built several
> smaller mastabas on top of the first one.'

This solution to the problem was not, however, achieved all at once. In fact, it took six changes of plan before the Step Pyramid reached its final form. Because at almost every one of these stages, the builders added the finishing touch of facing the local masonry with gleaming white limestone before deciding to build again, it is possible to distinguish the various alterations in places where the pyramid has since subsided. Beginning as a mastaba measuring about 63 m (207 ft) on each side, it soon became a larger and larger mastaba, and only later a monument rising in four levels. The engineering of these levels was perhaps Imhotep's true innovation, and the ultimate result was Egypt's first pyramid; a pyramid comprised of six steps reaching a height of 63.7 m (209 ft), quite visible above the enclosure wall, and a towering symbol of King Djoser's eternal life and power.

Left Dreyer suggests that it was the desire that the king's tomb be visible above the enclosure wall which led to the development of the world's first pyramid.

In these changes are manifest not only the

pharaoh's power, but also his will to create continuously for as long as this life permitted. This is an urge he seems to have inherited from his predecessor. For Khasekhemwy, this desire led to ever bigger and better structures in three different locations. Djoser, on the other hand, concentrated his creative powers in one place with remarkable results.

Not surprisingly, this new type of monument made a strong impression on the Egyptians. Soon the pyramid became not only a resurrection machine for the pharaoh, but also a striking symbol of royal power in this life and the next. Although none of Djoser's successors in the Third Dynasty were able to complete their pyramid tombs, the last king of the dynasty, a ruler named Huni, was successful in erecting some if not all of the eight smaller step pyramids which curiously dot the landscape from Athribis in the Delta to Elephantine at Egypt's southern border. All are essentially similar in size, most being approximately 18 m (60 ft) square at the base, and there is no evidence that any of them served as tombs. Instead they appear to be emblems of royal presence throughout the land. Much like the mound or 'protopyramid' within the funerary enclosure of Khasekhemwy at Abydos, the little step pyramids may have been focal points for posthumous veneration and offerings for the king. However, the distribution of these little pyramids at or near provincial administrative centres suggests that they also had significance during the king's life. It is possible that each of these places once contained a provincial palace for the king's use during his tour of the country for the purposes of tax collection and census counts. This tour took place every other year and in the early Old Kingdom the years of a king's reign were recorded according to the number of times this census and collection took place. How often the king himself actually took part in this process is unknown, but with the enduring symbol of his authority ever-present, his physical attendance may not have been required. The function of these intriguing pyramids is, however, still a matter of speculation. While some have been known for a while, others, like the one at Athribis, have only recently been discovered. Still others that may lie concealed under the sand could prove capable of shedding further light on their true purpose and meaning.

Snefru

The greatest builder of the Pyramid Age was King Snefru, the first king of the Fourth Dynasty, during whose reign the biennial tax levy may have become a more frequent event. As a result, it is difficult to assess the true intensity of Snefru's creative power. He is accorded a reign of twenty-four or twenty-nine years in the ancient king-lists, yet the recent discovery of an inscription mentioning the twenty-fourth occasion of the census suggests he may have reigned as long as forty-eight years, if the taxes were still collected every other year. But regardless of his total years, his reign is distinguished by the number and sheer magnitude of the works he carried out. The owner of

Left The Bent Pyramid at Dahshur would have surpassed the height of the Great Pyramid had it been completed as designed, but the foundations could not support the weight and the plans had to be changed.

Far Left Snefru's first pyramid at Meidum was originally constructed as a step pyramid. The king later transformed it into a true geometric pyramid.

three full-sized pyramids and probably two smaller ones, he shifted one-third more stone – some 3,600,000 cubic metres (4,708,800 cubic yards) of it – than his son and successor Khufu, the builder of the Great Pyramid.

Snefru's reign represents an important period in Egyptian history, a period of transition in art and architecture. It was a time when developments in the rendering of the human form and major advances in the working of stone were crystallized and perfected. To him belongs the credit for the first geometrically true pyramids ever attempted in Egypt, as well as major and long-lasting changes in how the resurrection machine functioned. It was his experiments with its conception and form that set the stage for the remarkable achievements at Giza.

Previously believed to belong to Huni, simply because no one could conceive of one king building so much, the pyramid at Meidum is now recognized as the first of Snefru's projects. Its bizarre shape, the result of later stone-robbing, has earned it the Arabic name 'Haram el Kaddab' or 'The False Pyramid'. It was, however, built – again after several changes of plan – as a step pyramid, the only full-sized one after Djoser's to have been completed. Snefru then decided to try his hand at something completely different.

For his second great project, Snefru chose the previously unused plateau at Dahshur further to the north. He selected the site for his pyramid, now known as the 'Bent Pyramid', for obvious reasons. Here was a large flat area with good-quality stone near by and a gorge that could serve as a natural transport ramp from the Nile. It appeared to be very suitable place to build a new eternal abode of a great ruler. This turned out, however, to be a crucial mistake.

The underlying sands and shales eventually proved unable to support the weight of the pyramid, the first to be designed as a true geometric pyramid and one that would have surpassed the height of the Great Pyramid had it been completed as planned. Although various theories have been proposed to explain the curious change in angle which gives the Bent Pyramid its name, the most convincing reason for its shape was the necessity to remedy the cracks and fissures caused by subsidence which began to appear even while this pyramid was being built.

Dr Rainer Stadelmann, Director of the German Archaeological Institute, has been studying the pyramid for many years to determine exactly what went wrong. As the Bent Pyramid retains more of its original smoothed outer casing blocks than any other pyramid, it is not easy to discern the ancient problems and the methods used to solve them. The best evidence is actually found on the inside of the pyramid within its internal passages and chambers. By studying the cracks and repairs in these areas, Stadelmann has been able to recreate the unfortunate chain of events.

The original plan was to build a true pyramid with a rather steep slope of about 60 degrees, but about half-way through construction the outer casing began to crack. To prevent further subsidence, additional masonry was added to all four sides, reducing the angle of inclination to 54 degrees. Yet it was too late. Fissures in the blocks of the completed internal chambers appeared. They tried everything: plaster patches, a new lining of masonry, and even imported cedar logs to shore up the walls.

It was clear that drastic measures were necessary to save the pyramid, the largest monumental building attempted since the beginning of the Egyptian state, but what more could they do? Ultimately, the architects decided that a radical reduction of the angle and a change in the method of laying the masonry were required. The upper half of the pyramid was completed at an angle of 43 degrees to a height of 105 m (344 ft) with smaller stones laid in horizontal rather than inwardly sloping courses to diminish the weight of the mass. Then Snefru started again.

Two and a half miles (4 km) to the north lies Snefru's third pyramid. Called the 'Red Pyramid' after the rusty tinge of the local limestone of its core, it would become Snefru's final resting place. Quick to learn from their mistakes, this time the king's architects laid a foundation platform of several courses of fine white limestone to prevent the problem of subsidence from recurring. The lesson of the Bent Pyramid also encouraged them to construct the pyramid with stones laid in level, rather than inclined, courses at the similarly modest angle of 43 degrees to a not insubstantial height of 104 m (341 ft), making it the fourth highest pyramid ever built. With its construction, pyramids left the arena of experimentation and finally achieved the distinctive and proper geometric form they would retain until their building ceased.

The perfection achieved on the exterior of the Red Pyramid is matched by the elegance of its internal chambers. A long descending corridor entered from the north side of the pyramid led to three rooms, over 12 m (40 ft) high and built of enormous limestone blocks. Two connecting chambers were at ground level within the base of the pyramid, but the third was shaped within the masonry of the pyramid itself. It could only be entered via a carefully concealed passage in the wall of the second chamber, some 7.6 m (25 ft) above its floor. According to Rainer Stadelmann, 'With this marvellous sequence of large and high rooms, King Snefru finally had achieved a burial place he could be happy and content with. It was his eternal residence, built with absolute perfection.' The most stunning aspect of these rooms is the corbelled ceilings, the blocks of which were placed in eleven to fourteen layers, each one protruding out over the room about 15 cm (6 in) on all four sides until a pyramid-shaped roof was obtained. In this ingenious way, the weight of the pyramid could be supported. More than two million tonnes of stone rested on these ceilings, yet there are no cracks, no subsidence. Not only had the architects tackled the vexing problems of construction, but by creating a pyramid within a pyramid, they reinforced the king's chances of resurrection.

For over twenty years Rainer Stadelmann has been excavating around the

Below This isometric drawing of the Red Pyramid shows the internal system of three chambers entered by a sloping corridor from the north side.
The temple complex on the east of his pyramids was another of Snefru's innovations.
(After Rainer Stadelmann)

Red Pyramid. His discoveries have added considerably to our understanding of Snefru's reign and vision. But one discovery in particular has helped to answer the age-old question of how long it took to build a pyramid. Stadelmann explains:

> 'When we started excavating here we found part of the outer casing still preserved, but a lot of blocks had fallen or were displaced. On the reverse of these loose stones we found inscriptions in red paint naming the working gangs who constructed the pyramid, for examples, the "Green gang" or the "Western Gang". We also found the name of Snefru in a cartouche. I would say about every twentieth stone was inscribed, but the most exciting thing was that dates were also written on the backs of these blocks.'

From these dates, Stadelmann has been able to determine the sequence of work. An inscription on one of the foundation blocks dates the beginning of construction to the fifteenth census count undertaken during Snefru's reign,

perhaps equivalent to his twenty-second or twenty-ninth year on the throne. Two years later, six layers of stone had been laid. Within four years 15 m (49 ft), or about 30 per cent, of the pyramid were already completed. When studied together, the inscriptions show that it took about seventeen years to construct the entire pyramid.

To celebrate its completion, the proud builders added a solid limestone pyramid-shaped capstone, called today a 'pyramidion'. To the Egyptians, it was the *benbenet*, the very tip of that mound of creation where the creator god stood when he created the world. Placed on top of these soaring mounds of masonry, it joined the earth with the sky. Few pyramidions from the Pyramid Age survive, possibly because many were gilded with precious metals. The earliest one now known was discovered in fragments around the base of the Red Pyramid. After painstaking restoration, Stadelmann found that each side had a slightly different angle; even with all of their experience in construction, the Egyptians had trouble reaching the top without some readjustments. Such mistakes remind us of the human elements in these austere piles; nevertheless, the error is extraordinarily small – only 2 degrees over 102 m (335 ft), almost 160 courses of stone! Such a minimal readjustment is, in fact, a true testimony to the abilities of Snefru's architects.

To complete such a pyramid in seventeen years is an even more impressive feat when one considers that at the same time Snefru was hedging his bets by filling in the steps of the pyramid at Meidum, transforming it too into a geometric pyramid, a shape for which he and his architects deserve full credit. But with this change in shape also came a transformation of the concept of the afterlife and a modification of the complex necessary to ensure it.

The shape and orientation of the pyramid complexes of Snefru's ancestors suggest they looked to the stars, linking their journey to the afterlife with the never-setting circumpolar stars, 'the imperishable ones', as they called them. But while they ascended their staircase to the stellar sphere, Snefru trod a ramp of gleaming white limestone like the sun's rays to heaven. To reinforce this connection Snefru laid out his temples along a new east–west alignment in accordance with the course of the sun. This new emphasis on the sun led to the adoption of an entirely new name, a new manifestation, of the king on his ascension to the throne as the 'Son of Ra', the son of the sun god, a father he would join in the afterlife. Snefru pioneered his new axial design for his resurrection machine at all three of his pyramids, but his son and successors at Giza perfected it.

Giza

Equipped with the accumulated experience of his father Snefru, Khufu concentrated his creative energies at the northern edge of the Giza plateau. His Great Pyramid is remarkable not only for its sheer size, rising some 146 m (479 ft), but also for the extreme accuracy of its orientation and the precision

Opposite Rainer Stadelmann with the reconstructed pyramidion of the Red Pyramid.

Above The valley temple of Khafra. In the view below, ramps lead from the harbour into the valley temple enclosure. Beside it, the Sphinx and Sphinx temple are unique to Khafra.

of its construction. Despite its undeniable majesty, time has been kinder to its neighbour, the pyramid of Khafra, a structure only 0.6 m (2 ft) smaller. The network of buildings at its base represents the best preserved of all the Old Kingdom pyramid complexes. It is here that the component parts which make up this new type of solar resurrection machine can best be understood, a type which would become the standard.

Above Reconstruction of Khafra's pyramid complex. The pyramid and mortuary temple were linked to the valley temple by a long causeway.

Numerous architectural features define a pyramid complex, but the most prominent are the valley temple, causeway, mortuary temple and of course, the pyramid itself. At the edge of the cultivated plain, probably fronted by a canal or harbour stood the monumental entrance to the complex, which Egyptologists call the valley temple. Khafra's was built of local limestone but encased in colossal granite blocks. Two doors gave access to this portal within

Avove The Sphinx presides over the Giza necropolis as the colossal guardian of the horizon, the living image of Khafra reborn as the sun god.

Opposite The false door allowed the spirit of the deceased, whether king or commoner, to come out and partake of the daily offerings placed before it. Royal false doors were made of red granite. Those of non-royal people were usually made of limestone, often, as here, painted red in imitation of granite. From the tomb of Mehu, Saqqara. Sixth Dynasty, c.2300 BC.

which were twenty-three life-sized statues of the king. Connecting the valley temple and the mortuary temple, linking the life-giving waters and the desert plateau, was a covered causeway or entrance corridor almost 495 m (1624 ft) long. The mortuary temple, which abutted the east side of the pyramid, was an elaborate complex of rooms and courtyards which mirrored the king's palace. The principal part was a large open courtyard surrounded by a pillared cloister and shrines in which the king's sacred image was housed. Here the rituals and prayers for the king were performed and the sustenance and offerings due to him were laid out on an altar in the open courtyard lined with brilliant alabaster. From the private chambers deep within the pyramid, where his mummified body lay encased in its granite sarcophagus, the spirit of the king would emerge to partake of these daily offerings via a niched panel called a 'false door'. Often carved out of hard red granite, it copied the panelled door-jamb, lintel, rounded wood support and double-leaved door of domestic architecture. As the sun rose each morning, its rays illuminated the polished white limestone of the pyramid's eastern face, filling the open court of the temple with light, so that the king's spirit was reborn afresh. Sacred boats symbolically docked outside the mortuary temple and alongside

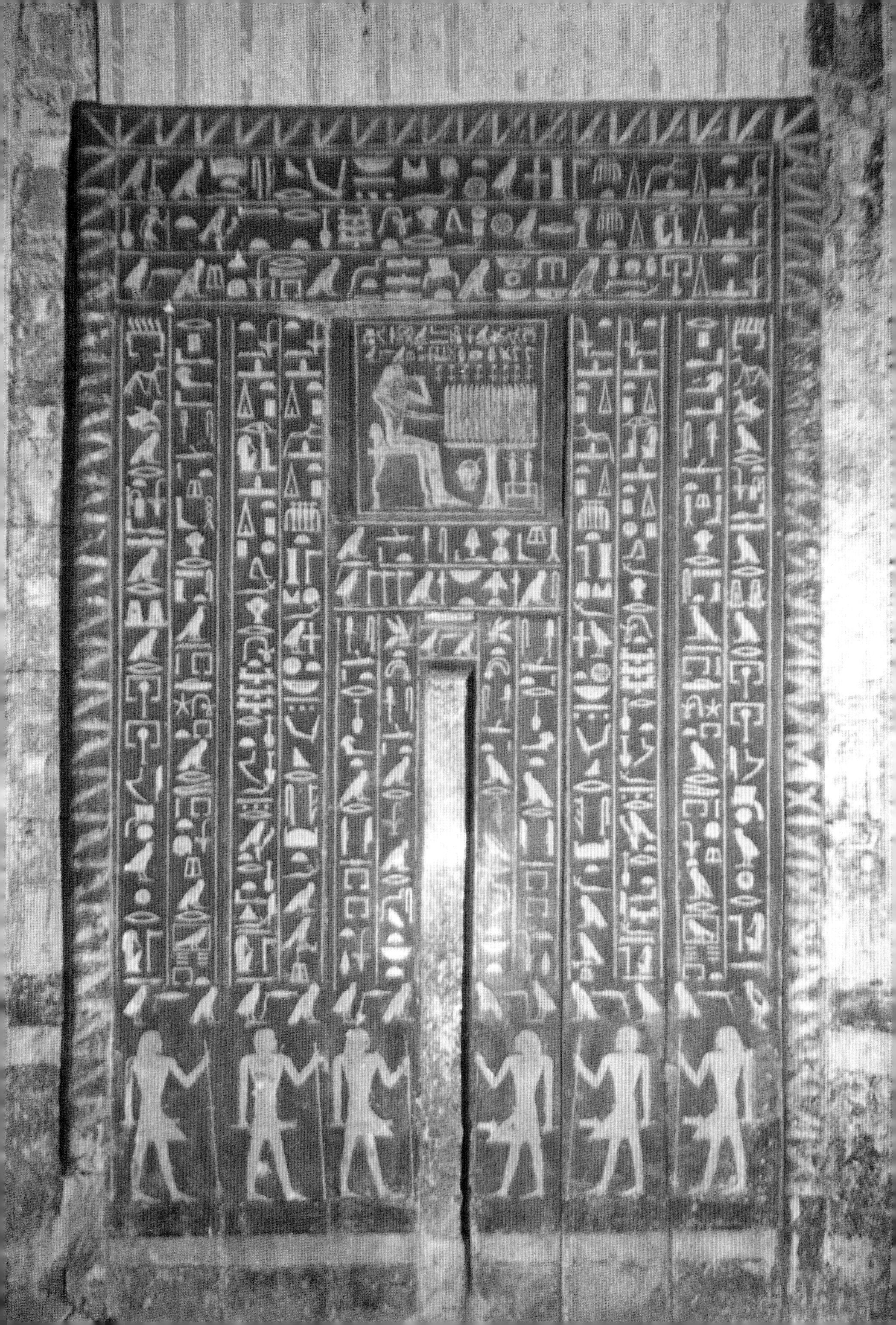

the pyramid were ready to carry him on his journey through the sky. From the reign of Snefru onward, all kings desired to build such a complex. But Khafra added something unique.

This was the Sphinx, which presides over Giza (and art history) as the first colossal royal statue in Egypt. A composite of a lion's body with the king's head, it is a manifestation of Khafra reborn as the sun god, a powerful creature who guards the necropolis as he guards the horizons. Although it seems that the sphinx (or to the Egyptians *shesep ankh* meaning 'living image') and the temple at its base were never entirely completed, this does not mean that they were an afterthought. Both are intimately connected with Khafra's causeway and valley temple, and had been designed together with them. It was not by chance that the knoll of living rock from which the Sphinx was carved was left in place after the stones for the valley temple were quarried. Although the Sphinx's temple may never actually have functioned, it was designed to serve the sun god. Like a giant sun clock with pillars representing the twelve hours of the day and night, it was oriented so that on the spring and autumn equinox, the rays of the rising sun would illuminate its inner sanctum.

What role the architectural features of the pyramid complex played in the actual funeral of the king remains unresolved. Their major purpose for eternity was two-fold: to serve as a palace for a resurrected king, and as a temple to an immortal god. Unlike the buildings surrounding the earlier Step Pyramid, these complexes were not frozen in time, but dynamic and active institutions. But in order to function, they needed both provisions and personnel.

Pyramid Power

To build and maintain the pyramids, an enormous support system must have existed. Production facilities for food, pottery, building materials and supplies, storage depots, and housing for the workmen and those responsible for servicing the pyramid temples were necessary. This is perhaps where we see the true power of the pyramid: as the centre of a vast engine of production and a key element of the redistributive economy that bound people to the king and kept Egyptian civilization alive for a very long time.

Since the reign of Snefru, an entire town was associated with each pyramid, full of people employed to maintain the king's afterlife. New villages and agricultural estates were founded in the hinterlands specifically for supplying the pyramid cult and those who worked for it. This flow of resources from the peripheries to the pyramid, and thus to the very centre of the state, was in large part responsible for making Egypt into the most powerful centralized nation of its time. The organizational skills each pyramid represents are phenomenal. While skilled craftsmen and management staff worked year round, farmers would come from the provinces during the inundation

The Workmen's Bread

Modern techniques are now making it possible to discover how the bread baked in the pyramid workers' village would have tasted. The taste would have depended on the grain used to make it, and this was the job of archaeobotanists such as Mary Anne Murray to find out. Seeds and other botanical material are separated from the dirt, using a flotation tank, a vat full of flowing water. As its name suggests, this is designed to allow the lighter organic material to float to the top as the dirt and stones sink to the bottom. In this way the frag-

ments of barley and emmer wheat ground to make the bread were recovered. Such grain contains little of the gluten that makes modern bread light and crispy. The loaves were baked over an open fire in large bell-shaped pots. Attempts at reproducing the recipe and the seemingly strange baking technique resulted, not surprisingly, in massive cake-like loaves, high in calories and starch, which could have fed several people at one meal. Far more economical than producing any kind of flat bread, by baking this type of bread in pots the Egyptians had developed a way to feed several hundred or even several thousand people quickly and efficiently.

Mary Anne Murray separates the precious botanic material from the dirt using a flotation tank.

Above The low benches and troughs plastered with fine white clay turned out to be part of a fish-processing plant.

period to do the heavy work. It is estimated that in all, some 200,000 people took part in the construction of a pyramid. But until recently it seemed as if all evidence of their existence had inexplicably vanished. In fact, it was simply a matter of looking in the right place.

To the south of the Giza pyramids lies a featureless tract about 15.8 hectares (39 acres) in extent, as yet unengulfed by the sprawling suburbs of Cairo. Here in 1988 Dr Mark Lehner of Harvard University began to uncover unprecedented glimpses at what it really took to build the pyramids. When Lehner first excavated a rectangular building with a series of curious

pedestals along each wall, he thought he had found a simple granary. But when mud sealings, originally from doors, bags and jars, turned up mentioning the *wabet* or embalming place of Menkaura, the builder of the third pyramid at Giza, he knew he had found something more. Yet before he could investigate further, the modern world intruded.

In 1991 a mechanical digging machine gouged out a huge trench to the east of this building. Out of that trench came thousands of pot-sherds dating from the time of the pyramids. When Lehner and his team examined the trench, they found two intact bakeries; the large bell-shaped pots in which the bread was baked still littering the floor. Ancient tomb scenes show offering bearers carrying large conical loaves of exactly the same shape as these pots would have produced.

The bakery was attached to a larger building, the focus of investigation since 1995. Within it, Lehner explains,

> 'we found these very curious low benches and troughs paved very carefully with clean desert clay. We had no idea what they were for until we started paying very close attention to the last few millimetres of the deposit over the floor. Scraping that back, sometimes with Swiss army knives, we found very fragile fibrous deposits that turned out to be the gills, fins, cranial parts and vertebrae of fish. So we believe we are in a fish processing centre. Somehow these benches and troughs were serving to process and dry fish on a very large scale. So, at the base of the pyramids, we have loaves and fishes.'

During further examination, the bones were identified as the remains of catfish, a fish particularly abundant in the waters of the inundation, but one not especially prized for its taste. Exquisite scenes of drag-nets teeming with a wide variety of fish being hauled ashore grace the tombs of the nobles of the Pyramid Age, yet the evidence suggests that fish of any type were not considered appropriate offerings for the deceased, perhaps because of their often unattractive odour. However, payment of labourers with fish is well attested. The conclusion seems inescapable: here is the long-sought facility for feeding the army of workmen who built or maintained the Giza pyramids.

Once the construction of the pyramid was completed, the area then became a cemetery for those who stayed on to support the pyramid cult, and further insights into the once unknown lives of these workmen come from this cemetery. A tourist riding a horse around the pyramids literally stumbled across it, her horse's hoof puncturing what turned out to be the intact vaulted roof of a tomb. Crude hieroglyphs scrawled on the false door identified the tomb-owners as Ptah-shepsesu and his wife. Built of mud brick and scraps of stone left over from the pyramid construction, the tomb is not grand when compared to the mastabas of the nobles laid out near their sovereign at the base of the Great Pyramid. Yet it is a mirror of that arrangement, as

Right Built of left-over stone from the pyramid construction, little mounds of creation cover the graves of some of the workmen.

the tombs of those who worked under Ptah-shepsesu are arranged all around his tomb beneath miniature mastabas of their own. Even in death, status no matter how modest was respected. Since 1990, excavations under the supervision of Dr Zahi Hawass, Director of the Giza Plateau, have revealed over 600 smaller graves grouped around the thirty larger tombs of their masters.

These tiny tombs come in a variety of forms: square, stepped, vaulted and domed to evoke a pyramid-like shape. Made of mud, rubble and construction debris, most are less than a few feet square. Some are fitted out with miniature false doors, and in a few, even of the smallest, statues were found, but most are unfortunately anonymous and without grave goods. Buried without the benefit of mummification, which at this period was still a prerogative of the élite, the bones contained in these tombs tell their story of a life which, though generally healthy, was full of toil. Arthritis and degenerative joint disease, particularly in the back, indicate heavy and sustained labour. These people were not slaves, but their ration of bread and fish was probably well earned.

In the slope immediately above, tombs built of dressed stone belong to a wealthier class; their owners bear titles such as Director of the Draughtsmen,

Below Zahi Hawass examines one of the workmen's tombs. It was outfitted with miniature false doors and a tiny courtyard.

Inspector of the Craftsmen, and Overseer of the Masonry. One of the more interesting tombs is that of a man named Nefer-thieth. One wall in his chapel is beautifully carved with scenes of the tomb-owner and his extensive family, and from it we can reconstruct a little bit more of the lives of these intriguing people. Nefer-thieth had two wives, with whom he had eighteen offspring. Although the specific post he held is never clearly stated, his chief wife, Nefer-hetepes, was a weaver, and indeed, a little extra income may have been useful with all those children, eleven of whom were hers. Because of the number of scenes depicting the making of bread and beer, Zahi Hawass

Above The 'Wall of the Crow' separated the sacred precinct of the Giza pyramids from the town of the living that supported them.

believes Nefer-thieth may well have been the supervisor of a bakery. It is perhaps in this capacity that he could have arranged for the fourteen different types of bread and cakes listed on this wife's funerary offering menu to be delivered on special holidays and for eternity.

In its heyday this area south of Giza must have been a hive of activity, although perhaps not all activities were appropriate in the precinct of the god-kings. To separate the sacred from the profane, a huge stone wall was constructed, now called the 'Wall of the Crow'. According to Lehner, 'anywhere else in the world it would be a national treasure. Actually it has been somewhat ignored at Giza because it is dwarfed by the Pyramids and the Sphinx. But it is much bigger than you think.' Clearance of the drift sand against its southern face revealed it to be 10 m (33 ft) high and more than 12 m (39 ft) thick at its base. The gateway alone is 7 m (23 ft) high and capped with three enormous limestone lintels. It may actually be one of the largest surviving gates in the ancient world.

Left The so-called 'Unfinished Pyramid', the first step of a pyramid built of small blocks and covered with gravel. It was originally considered to have been abandoned and never used.

Below Papyrus documents found in the pyramid temple of Raneferef detail the practical workings of the 'resurrection machine'. This document records daily deliveries of produce for the temple and its priests.

Below Painted limestone statue of King Raneferef (*c*.2448–2445 BC) discovered in the pyramid mortuary temple.

It will take many more seasons of digging to unlock all the secrets in this unexpected place, but already it offers an exceptional window into the perhaps unremarkable lives of the ordinary people who made and maintained some of the world's most extraordinary monuments. It is not, however, the only source of information available to us on this subject.

Abusir

At Abusir, not far to the south of Giza, the tombs of kings of Egypt's Fifth Dynasty (*c*.2494–2345 BC) are the 'Forgotten Pyramids'. Robbed of their fine limestone casing in the Roman Period, they cannot compete with their

colossal neighbours, yet it is here that unique documentary evidence for how the pyramids functioned was found.

In 1893 local farmers digging in the ruins stumbled across over 300 fragments of papyrus from the pyramid complex of King Neferirkara (*c.*2475–2455 BC), which were then sold and distributed around the world. This unique archive contained the duty rosters of the pyramid temple personnel, inventories of the pyramid's equipment, accounts of its income and even reports on inspections of its physical condition over the years. Yet this extraordinary collection, written in ink in hieratic (a cursive form of the hieroglyphic script), remained unpublished for seventy-five years.

As a result, the first archaeologists to excavate at Abusir did not have the benefit of these documents to guide them. However, the Czech mission which has been exploring the site since 1976 has made full use of them. One scrap in particular caught the attention of Professor Miroslav Verner, director of the Czech Mission. It mentioned the mortuary temple of a little-known king, Raneferef (c.2448–2445 BC), whose tomb had never been found. Verner immediately realized it meant that this king's tomb and temple must be somewhere at Abusir, but where? The logical place to begin was at the so-called 'Unfinished Pyramid', the lowest step of a pyramid core which was believed to have been abandoned unoccupied. Using sub-surface sensing techniques, the Czech archaeologists were amazed to discover that a complete and once active mortuary temple had been built in front of this unfinished pyramid.

More surprising still was what they discovered when they began excavating this temple. Amongst the tumbled walls was the largest cache of Fifth Dynasty royal sculpture in existence, including a fine painted limestone statue of King Raneferef, his head shielded by his protector, the falcon god Horus. But this was not all: gratifyingly, another collection of rare papyrus documents detailing the working of this king's temple cult were uncovered.

It seems that King Raneferef died prematurely, when the underground chambers of the pyramid were complete but only the lowest step of the superstructure constructed. What happened next provides a revealing insight into how the Egyptians viewed the workings of a resurrection machine. After his death, his successor Niuserra (c.2445–2421 BC) quickly turned the unfinished pyramid into a makeshift mastaba, encasing it in fine limestone and topping it with gravel – it is little wonder that it is called 'the mound' in the contemporary papyri. To it he attached a mortuary temple for Raneferef's

Right The priests' duties were to assist in the daily rituals and to help transport, maintain, guard and inventory the provisions and possessions of the pyramid complex. Relief from the tomb of Ankhmahor, Saqqara, showing offerings being brought for the consumption of the deceased. Sixth Dynasty, c.2300 BC.

Above Miroslav Verner directs the clearance of the burial shaft. He hopes that some remnant of Raneferef's funeral equipment may still be found.

eternal nourishment. Originally of mud brick and fitted-out with the bare necessities of a red granite false door and an altar, the mortuary temple was later enlarged into a sprawling complex of halls, courts, storerooms and even a slaughterhouse called the 'Sanctuary of the Knife'. Although burial beneath a pyramid was every king's ideal, each king clearly had to build his own. For those unlucky enough to die before completing theirs, a lesser mound of creation would suffice, but for the practical business of resurrection a working mortuary temple was indispensable.

The Abusir documents give us a detailed picture of how these mortuary temples worked. We now know that, in addition to a permanent staff of priests, purifiers and scribes, each mortuary temple was manned by a team selected from a cross-section of the inhabitants of the associated pyramid town. The higher-status members were called 'servants of the god', while the others were simply referred to as 'those before the irrigation basin', or towns-folk. This non-permanent priesthood was divided into five groups called by Egyptologists *phyles* or tribes. There were perhaps forty priests per phyle and they were subdivided into two groups of twenty. Each sub-group served in the temple one month in ten. This system allowed a large number of people to be involved in and benefit from the service of their departed sovereign.

The duty of these priests was to assist in the daily rituals for the king and to help transport, maintain, guard and inventory the possessions and provisions of the pyramid complex. Some were so punctilious at their job they recorded even the fact that a ball of incense was not in its proper place in a box. Each morning and every evening the sacred rites took place. Before the royal statues, the ceremony of re-animation called 'the opening of the mouth' was performed (see page 209). The townsfolk would unveil, bathe and dress the statues, while the servants of the god chanted the sacred formulae and fumigated with incense. Now the king's spirit was ready for the ritual meal. The documents reveal that the king enjoyed an extensive menu, and so did the priests. For once the king's spirit had partaken of the essence of the offerings, the priests partook of their physical presence. There seems to have been plenty to go around: according to one papyrus from the archive of Raneferef, 130 bulls were slaughtered in the course of just one ten-day festival – all this to honour a relatively short-lived king.

In effect, the pyramid complexes functioned as part of a massive redistribution scheme and one that was highly successful. As at the pyramids of other more important kings, Raneferef's cult was maintained until the end of the Old Kingdom and was then revived briefly in the Middle Kingdom 400 years later. Far from sapping the resources of Egypt, the pyramids nourished the nation as well as the king's spirit.

As long as the mortuary temple was up and running, the king's resurrection and successful afterlife were assured. But the last king of the Fifth Dynasty took out an additional insurance policy.

Pyramid Texts

Lavish and colourful reliefs embellished the walls of the pyramid temples and the causeway, but within the pyramid itself the burial chamber of every king, with the exception of Djoser, had remained unadorned. King Unas, the last king of the Fifth Dynasty, changed all that. Erecting his pyramid at Saqqara, directly adjacent to the Step Pyramid complex of Djoser, he followed his neighbour by decorating his internal chambers, but in an entirely new way.

Around his black basalt sarcophagus, evocative of the fertile earth, he placed white alabaster slabs incised and painted to resemble the matting of a divine purification tent, open to a sky in the form of a gabled ceiling decorated with golden stars against a field of deep blue. Intricately carved all around this were the words of the oldest religious literature in the world. Called the Pyramid Texts, they are spells and ritual utterances drawn from a body of sacred knowledge, some immeasurably old and others newly invented. Some are spells to keep away danger, to protect the king from noxious snakes and insects; others are tabulations of the food, drink and clothing required for eternity. Some are hymns to the gods and litanies of their sacred names. But others, complete with instructions for words to be spoken or ritual actions to be performed, must have been incantations recited at the king's funeral and during the daily ritual in the pyramid temple. Together

Opposite The burial chamber of King Unas (c.2375–2345 BC), the walls inscribed with the first ever 'Pyramid Texts', the oldest religious literature in the world.

Left The tomb of Thutmose I (c.1504– 1492 BC) was carved deep into the rock in a hidden place in the Valley of the Kings.

they chart the journey of Unas into the afterlife, free from misdeed, able to fly past all obstacles to the sky, where his homecoming is celebrated by the gods among whom he thrives for all eternity.

The arrangement of the spells within the pyramid chambers has long been a puzzle. Some scholars think it might reflect the order of the funeral ritual performed over the body of Unas, but a new interpretation suggests that Unas arranged his spells for him to read himself. As added insurance in case the ritual cycle in the pyramid temples should break down, Unas, rising from his sarcophagus, and moving with the spells out to the east toward the sunrise, could transform himself into an effective and immortal spirit.

The kings who followed also made use of this body of texts, sometimes choosing different spells and creating new ones. In all, over 700 different spells are known and no two pyramids contain the same selection. Over the centuries these spells were adapted to changing conceptions and modified to serve the needs of a wider audience. Eventually, inscribed on a papyrus roll and called 'The Spells for Going Forth by Day' or today the Book of the Dead (see page 179), they would become a potent guide for negotiating the afterlife and attaining resurrection for anyone who could afford a copy.

End of the Pyramid Age

The Old Kingdom was the great age of pyramid building in Egypt. Pyramids would continue to be built for another 500 years, but priorities were changing. At the beginning of the New Kingdom, the pyramid form was turned over to the officials of the realm to build over their rock-cut tombs. The king had different plans.

In about 1500 BC King Thutmose I instructed his architect, Ineni, to build him a different kind of tomb. On the west bank of the Nile opposite Thebes, Egypt's most important religious centre in the New Kingdom, he found the perfect spot: a deep canyon dominated by a more enduring monument, a huge pyramid-shaped mountain, today called el-Qurn. Even more compelling, this peak and the massif of which it was a part, when viewed from the city of the living, resembled the hieroglyphic sign for the horizon, specifically the western horizon and the entrance to the underworld. Behind it was the perfect place to build a city of the dead. Here Ineni burrowed deep into the rock; long stepped corridors spiralled down to a burial chamber, a winding way symbolic of the landscape of the underworld. Certain that the body of his pharaoh would be secure, he left a touching inscription on the walls of his own tomb at Thebes. It reads, 'I supervised the excavation of the tomb of His Majesty alone, no one seeing, no one hearing.'

Nearly thirty pharaohs would eventually be buried in what is now known as the Valley of the Kings. At the edge of the cultivated fields each king built his palace of eternity, or Mansion of Millions of Years as it was called, reviving a tradition dating back to Egypt's first kings.

Above Royal pyramids ceased to be built in the New Kingdom. Instead the pyramid-shaped mountain called el-Qurn towers over the royal burial ground of the New Kingdom in the Valley of the Kings at Thebes.

Immortality was now reinforced by the stunning array of texts and pictures which decorated their distant tombs and was assured in the increasingly elaborate mortuary temples and temples of state, where the king was portrayed both with and as the god Amun–Ra, the chief god of Thebes. These new mounds of creation, embellished with the tribute from a far-flung empire, would become the focus of the king's creative urge, and would now speak of his power and the glory. And like the pyramids, they continue to stun and amaze.

But this is far from being the end of the story. Centuries later the royal pyramid would make a dramatic reappearance, this time not in Egypt but much further south in Nubia (in present-day Sudan), in a kingdom known to the Egyptians as Kush – until recently one of history's best-kept secrets.

Below View of Gebel Barkal from the south with its distinctive pinnacle at one end. It was called 'the pure mountain' by the Egyptians, who believed it to be the home of a southern, ram-headed manifestation of Amun–Ra, their pre-eminent god and the source of all kingship.

The Pyramids of Kush

The story of the pyramids of Kush goes back to the New Kingdom, to when Egypt had a great empire abroad. For centuries Egypt had coveted the wealth of Nubia, the homeland of the Kingdom of Kush; it had vast resources of gold and other minerals, and dominated the principal trade routes into the heart of Africa. In the Eighteenth Dynasty the Egyptians invaded Nubia, and after a protracted struggle conquered the first Kingdom of Kush (see Chapter

3, Age of Gold). Under King Thutmose I (1504–1492 BC) the Egyptians sacked and burned the Kushite capital, then located at Kerma near the Third Cataract, and under Thutmose III (1479–1425 BC) extended their control southwards to the Fourth Cataract. Here, on the site of an old Kushite settlement, they founded a new city called Napata, which marked the southernmost point of their occupation of Nubia. Napata was strategically located at a point on the Nile where several important desert roads converged. Of even greater significance was the presence near the site of a sacred mountain, one of the Nile Valley's most spectacular landmarks. Known today as Gebel Barkal, the Egyptians called it 'the pure mountain'.

Standing in the desert about a mile from the north bank of the Nile, Gebel Barkal is a flat-topped sandstone outcrop, over 91.4 m (300 ft) high,

Below Tim Kendall in the rock-cut temple built by King Taharqo directly beneath the pinnacle of Gebel Barkal. The scene on the wall shows the ram-headed Amun–Ra seated within 'the pure mountain'. Kendall points at the uraeus represented as rearing from the mountain's front.

its most distinctive feature a soaring free-standing pinnacle on its west corner, itself 82 m (270 ft) high. Beneath the sheer southern face of the mountain are the remains of a large number of temples built and rebuilt, over a period of over 1500 years, by Egyptian and later Kushite kings. Gebel Barkal was clearly a very sacred place, but why? Recent work on the site and its temples by Dr Tim Kendall of the Museum of Fine Arts, Boston, has gone a long way to addressing the question. Kendall believes the answer lies in the

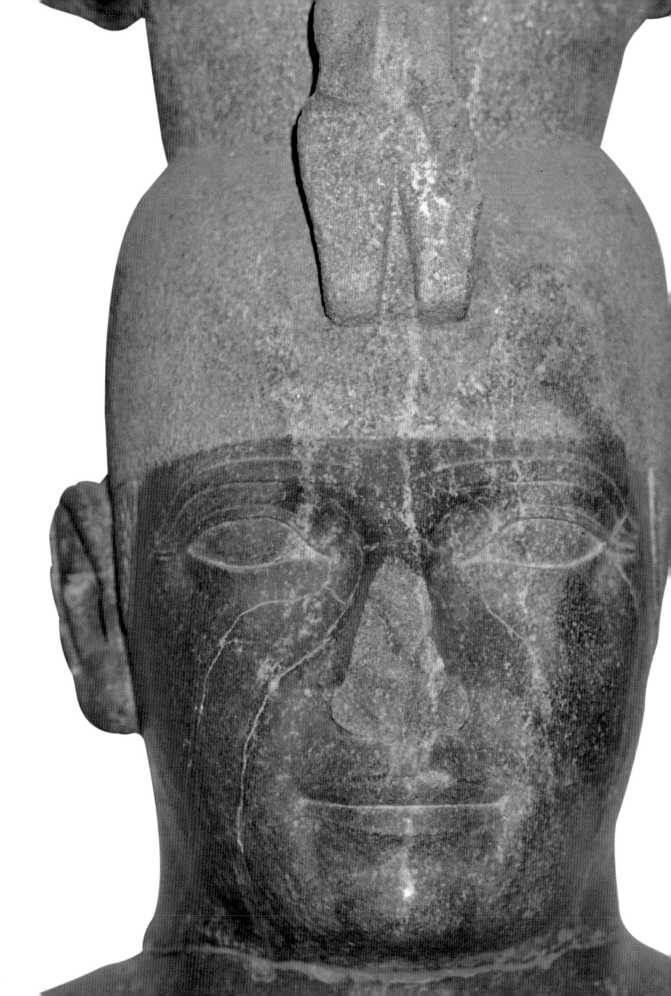

shape of the mountain, in particular in the form of the pinnacle. He points out that inscriptions of Thutmose III from the site indicate that the Egyptians saw Gebel Barkal as a symbol of the primeval mound of creation and the dwelling-place of a southern version – ram-headed – of their state god, Amun–Ra of Thebes. He believes they were first led to this idea by the peculiar shape of the pinnacle:

> 'When the Egyptians came here, they saw in this strange rock formation the image of a very familiar symbol, a rearing cobra or uraeus, the symbol of kingship which the kings wore on their crown. The cobra seems to be wearing the White Crown of the south, symbolizing kingship over the south. So they believed the great god, Amun–Ra of Karnak, the source of all kingship, lived here inside the rock in an alternate form, conferring kingship over the south and the authority to rule over Nubia.'

Opposite Head from a colossal standing statue of King Taharqo, the greatest of the Kushite kings. Made of grano-diorite. From Gebel Barkal.

Thus, conveniently for the Egyptians, they had divine sanction for the conquest and occupation of Nubia. The latter had always really been part of Upper Egypt. The Egyptian king, traditionally 'the lord of the Two Lands', was now legitimately the lord of Egypt and Nubia. Ironically, this formulation was later to rebound on the Egyptians, when the reverse situation occurred – the authority of Amun–Ra of Gebel Barkal being invoked to legitimize Kushite rule over Egypt.

After a hiatus of several hundred years, during which the Egyptians abandoned Nubia, a new independent kingdom of Kush arose during the eighth century BC, its capital at Napata, its cult-centre at Gebel Barkal devoted still to the worship of Amun–Ra. The native kings, proclaiming themselves the true heirs of Thutmose III and other great pharaonic ancestors, laid claim to the throne of Egypt, which they conquered under King Piye (c.747–716 BC) and ruled for over fifty years as Egypt's Twenty-fifth Dynasty.

The most famous and powerful of Piye's successors was King Taharqo (690–664 BC), whose reign marks the high-point of Kushite empire and achievement. Taharqo was a great builder, erecting temples, shrines and statues throughout the Nile Valley, and turning Gebel Barkal into an architectural showpiece, its central temple a southern version of Karnak in Thebes, though on a smaller scale. High up on the great pinnacle he had an inscription recording his dominance carved in hieroglyphs and sheathed in gold – to be visible far and wide, no doubt a spectacular sight as it glistened in the sun. Directly beneath the pinnacle he had another, smaller temple hollowed out of the rock, which contains scenes of the king offering to the gods, one of which confirms Kendall's view of the religious meaning of the mountain and the pinnacle. The scene shows the king standing before a representation of Gebel Barkal. It is painted reddish brown, like sandstone, and has a flat top with a sloping front, attached to which is a large rearing uraeus. Within

Overleaf The remains of the main temple dedicated to Amun–Ra, seen from the top of Gebel Barkal. First constructed by the Egyptians in the Eighteenth Dynasty, it was rebuilt and extended by the Kushite kings to be their 'southern Karnak'.

Opposite The pyramids of Nuri, King Taharqo's prominent among them.

it sits the ram-headed Amun–Ra. The accompanying inscription, in Kendall's words,

> 'actually tells us that he's in the mountain, that he's Amun–Ra, lord of the thrones of the Two Lands, who is in the pure mountain, which is what they called Gebel Barkal, and you see how they represented the pinnacle as a giant rearing cobra with a sun-disc on its head…the way they imagined it from the west side of the mountain.'

Below Pyramid-fields at Meroe. In the foreground lies the southern cemetery; in the distance, the northern. There is also a western cemetery. Together they contain the remains of over a hundred pyramids.

Seeing themselves as the restorers of order after a period of chaos, the Kushites, while enthusiastically embracing pharaonic iconography, sought models – for their art, architecture and rituals – in the hallowed past, at the same time imparting to them a distinctive style of their own. The most prominent of their revivals was the pyramid – a tomb form long abandoned in Egypt. Beginning with King Piye, a new period of pyramid building was inaugurated, which, astonishingly, was to last for over a thousand years, sur-

viving not only the expulsion of the Kushites from Egypt in about 662 BC but also the move of their royal cemetery from Napata to Meroe in the south just after 300 BC. During this period an extraordinary number of pyramids was erected, both around Napata, at the cemeteries of El Kurru, Nuri and Gebel Barkal, and in Meroe, which contains the largest single concentration of pyramids in the Nile Valley. The total number of Kushite pyramids known to date is 223, far exceeding the number attested from Egypt, though they are, of course, in general much smaller and not all are royal, since the privilege of owning a pyramid-tomb was extended in due course to members of the private élite.

The largest of the Kushite pyramids, by some distance, is Taharqo's at Nuri, which in its final, enhanced form stood to a height of over 49 m (160 ft) and is thought to have been inspired by the pyramids of the Old Kingdom near Memphis. More typically, Kushite pyramids are relatively slender with steep sides, sometimes with moulded edges. Unlike their Egyptian counterparts, they do not end in a pyramidion but have truncated tops surmounted by an angular capstone. In their finished form, they were covered in white plaster, sometimes painted red and white, with a band of stars around the base and with circular plaques made of blue faience inserted in their surface. The earlier pyramids are built throughout of stone, while the later examples, like those at Meroe, consist of a core of debris enclosed by a stone casing; some of the very latest are made of red brick or just rubble.

The most important pyramids in Meroe are those of the so-called northern cemetery, which was reserved for the exclusive use of the royal

Right The northern cemetery at Meroe, a royal burial ground which includes the pyramids of thirty kings and eight ruling queens.

Above Workmen of the Sudanese Antiquities Service in the process of reconstructing one of the pyramids in the northern cemetery, using a lifting-device called a *shaduf*.

family. Thirty kings, eight ruling queens (called *kandake* – the origin of the modern name Candace), and three princes or co-regents were buried there. The exact methods of building these pyramids have recently been investigated by the German architect Friedrich Hinkel, who worked with the Sudanese Antiquities Service to stabilize and reconstruct a number of them. Quite unexpectedly, in four of them he discovered the remains of a vertical post, made of cedar-wood, which he believes functioned as the shaft of a giant *shaduf*, a traditional lifting device commonly employed in the Nile Valley for raising water for irrigation, here adapted for lifting stone blocks for the casing of the pyramid. To prove the point Hinkel reconstructed one of the pyramids using just such a *shaduf*. It worked perfectly. Based on his experiment, Hinkel has been able to determine that the steep incline of the sides follows necessarily from the use of the *shaduf*, and that to erect one of the larger pyramids, standing to a height of about 30.5 m (100 ft), would have taken about a year.

Unlike many of their Egyptian predecessors, these pyramids were never intended to house a burial within their structure. They marked the presence of a tomb, rather than being the tombs themselves. The burial chambers, accessed directly from above or from the east by means of a descending staircase, are always subterranean. These different elements were not built concurrently but represent quite separate phases in the construction process. In some cases, the owner of the pyramid built only the underground chamber, in which he or she was buried; the construction of the pyramid itself was begun only after the funeral and was the responsibility of the successor, who was also duty bound to complete the remainder of the mortuary complex. The most important element here was the cult chapel on the east side, decorated internally, in egyptianizing mode, with scenes of the deceased in the company of various funerary gods, giving and receiving offerings. From the outside, the chapels, fronted by pylons (towers flanking a temple gateway), look like miniature temples. They too, like the pyramids, were plastered and painted.

The occupants of the tombs were buried with the traditional rich trappings of royalty, though only fragments and scraps of their original contents have survived, almost all the burial chambers having been thoroughly plundered in antiquity. Externally the pyramids remained in very good condition until the nineteenth century, when they were subjected to the

Right and opposite Jewellery, in the form of an armlet and a shield-ring, from the treasure of Queen Amanishakheto (late first century BC), found in her tomb in the northern cemetery at Meroe. Made of gold with glass inlay, the decorative technique and style, combining Egyptian and Kushite motifs and insignia, are typically Meroitic. The central motif on the shield-ring is the head of the Kushite lion god, Apedemek. On the armlet is the Egyptian funerary goddess Isis.

most appalling damage. In 1834 an Italian adventurer, Guiseppe Ferlini, began to dismantle some of them, searching for hidden treasure. He struck lucky, finding a collection of stunning gold jewellery in the pyramid or tomb of Queen Amanishakheto, who ruled in the late first century BC. It is the largest and most important cache of Meroitic jewellery ever discovered, containing many rare items and types otherwise known only from representations. All are wonderful examples of the goldsmith's art, their complex iconography, combining Meroitic, Egyptian and Hellenistic motifs, bearing eloquent testimony to the cosmopolitan world that the Kushites inhabited. Tragically, the discovery sparked a great wave of treasure hunting. The pyramids were systematically vandalized and some almost totally destroyed.

Today, the ruined pyramids of Meroe form one of the most evocative and poignant landscapes to have survived from antiquity. Including in their midst the last pyramid ever built on the African continent – erected in AD 370 and now reduced to a humble heap of rubble – they mark the end of an awesome tradition, one which survived for over 3000 years and has given the world its most enduring symbol of the ancient past.

Right Head of a figure of Amun–Ra, the king of the gods, made of solid gold, the 'flesh of the gods'. Probably a cult statue from a temple shrine. From Thebes. New Kingdom–Third Intermediate Period, c.1400–850 BC.

Far right Scene showing Nubians – chiefs, princes and a princess – doing obeisance and bringing gold to to the Egyptian court. From the tomb of Huy, Viceroy of Kush under King Tutankhamun, Thebes, 1336–1327 BC.

AGE OF GOLD

Left Gold bracelets inlaid with carnelian, turquoise and blue frit, inscribed with the name of King Thutmose III. Part of the jewellery buried with three of his queens. From Thebes. Eighteenth Dynasty, c.1450 BC.

During the New Kingdom (1550–1069 BC), and especially the Eighteenth Dynasty (1550–1295 BC), the Egyptians ruled a great empire, stretching northwards into the Near East as far as the Euphrates and southwards deep into present-day Sudan, to the Fourth Cataract of the Nile and beyond. It was an empire forged initially by military might but sustained in the end by diplomacy and the gift of gold. The most beautiful and precious

of all materials, gold was universally sought-after, and Egypt was its main source. Egypt had access to seemingly inexhaustible supplies, from the deserts east of the Nile Valley and from Nubia. In Egypt gold was reputed to be as 'common as dust'.

But gold was not simply a precious commodity. It was valued by the Egyptians for reasons beyond its intrinsic worth. The colour of the sun, untarnishable, unaffected by time, gold was a symbol of eternity. Transformed by ritual, gold became the flesh of Ra and the other immortal gods. To be bedecked with gold was to partake of its divine qualities, and to be buried with gold – ideally wearing a gold mask, encased in gold coffins, like Tutankhamun

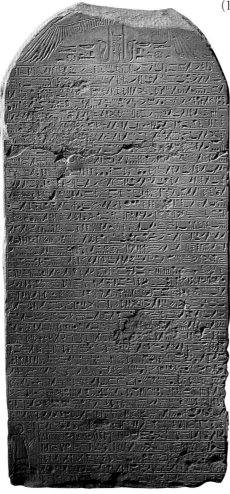

(1336–1327 BC) – was to be ensured eternal life. In royal tombs, the burial chamber was known as the 'house of gold'.

In the New Kingdom, the Egyptians acquired, buried and disbursed gold in unprecedented quantities and enjoyed unparalleled wealth, power and prestige. The age of empire was a golden age in every sense. Yet it had sprung from very inauspicious circumstances, during a period when Egypt, for the first time in its long history, was ruled by foreigners.

■ The Hyksos and the Theban Revolt

Following the collapse of Egypt's Middle Kingdom, the country had fallen under the domination of the so-called Hyksos, 'foreign rulers', who held sway for over a hundred years during the Second Intermediate Period (c.1650–1550 BC). Originally immigrants into Egypt from Canaan, the Hyksos had forged a strong power-base in the northeast Delta, an area of great strategic importance, where they established their capital, Avaris (called *Hwt-waret* in Egyptian texts). From this stronghold they were well-placed to control the lucrative trade routes, by land and by sea, with the Near East and the Mediterranean world. To secure their southern border and trade with Africa, they formed an alliance with the powerful kings of Kush, who from their capital at Kerma near the Third Cataract ruled the gold-rich land of Nubia.

Above Stela of King Kamose, which commemorates a successful Theban campaign against the Hyksos king Ipepi. From the Temple of Karnak, Thebes. Seventeenth Dynasty, c.1555 BC.

Right Base of a scarab, decorated with a scene of King Thutmose I standing in a horse-drawn chariot and slaying a foreign enemy with an arrow shot from his great bow. The horse, chariot and composite bow were originally foreign imports into Egypt, but during the New Kingdom they became standard elements in the iconography of the Egyptian king as all-conquering hero.

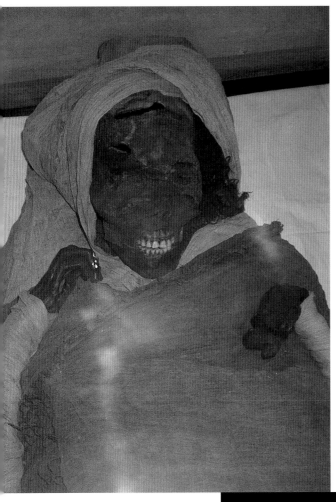

The whole of Egypt paid obeisance to the Hyksos overlords but with increasing reluctance and disaffection, especially in Thebes in Upper Egypt. Here a family of local rulers eventually rebelled, styling themselves as the true kings of Egypt – known to us as the Seventeenth Dynasty (*c*.1650–1550 BC) – and began a war of independence.

Initially the Hyksos had a substantial advantage in the form of better weaponry and superior military technology. They had the horse and chariot, giving them greater mobility, and a new type of bow, the 'composite' bow, of laminated construction and of great tensile strength, which could shoot arrows over a much longer distance than an ordinary wooden bow. Nevertheless, learning and adapting, the Thebans turned the tables on their erstwhile masters, with such success, in fact, that the horse-drawn chariot and the composite bow, both of foreign origin, soon become icons of Egyptian military dominance, of the pharaoh as the all-conquering hero. But the road to liberation was far from smooth, and at least one Theban king appears to have paid with his life. A mummy excavated at

Above Mummy of King Seqenenre Tao. The wounds in his skull, made by Hyksos weaponry, are plainly visible.

Right Hyksos battle-axe, with cast socket and narrow chisel-shaped blade: a formidable piercing weapon. Second Intermediate Period, c.1650–1550 BC.

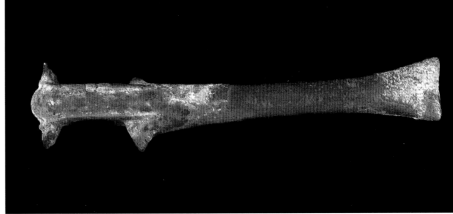

Thebes, now in the Cairo Museum, belongs to King Seqenenre Tao (*c*.1560 BC), one of the first Theban rulers actively to oppose the Hyksos. The king bears wounds in his skull, which to judge from their shape, were made by weapons peculiar to the Hyksos, one of them a distinctive chisel-shaped battle-axe. It is very probable he was slain in battle.

Greater success was enjoyed by Seqenenre's successor, King Kamose

Above Excavations in progress at Tell el-Daba/Avaris, here uncovering a palatial complex of the early Eighteenth Dynasty, previously hidden underneath the cultivation.

(*c.*1555–1550 BC). A famous commemorative inscription, the Kamose Stela, gives an account of a Theban campaign led by Kamose against the Hyksos king Ipepi, from which was brought back much valuable plunder, including chariotry and battle axes. Kamose boasts of taunting Ipepi before the walls of Avaris:

> 'Behold, I have come, I am successful…As the mighty Amun endures, I will not leave you alone, I will not let you tread the fields without being upon you. O wicked of heart, vile Asiatic, I shall drink the wine of your vineyard…I lay waste your dwelling place, I cut down your trees.'

But where exactly were the walls of Avaris? And how great a stronghold really was it? For a long time it was impossible to answer these questions. Avaris was a lost city, its precise location unknown, its remains hidden beneath deposits of Nile silt and modern cultivation. The only evidence for its existence was its mention in Egyptian texts – that is until recently, when an Austrian expedition, led by Professor Manfred Bietak of the University of Vienna, in one of the most important archaeological discoveries of modern times, finally located the site of Avaris, in the eastern Nile Delta near a modern village called Tell el-Daba.

Though the city is much ruined, systematic excavation over a period now of more than twenty years has slowly but gradually revealed its infrastructure – its houses, palaces, tombs and temples – and shown how it changed and developed through time. Beginning as a small Egyptian settlement in the Middle Kingdom, Avaris was gradually occupied by an increasingly large and thriving Canaanite community, eventually emerging as a great cosmopolitan city, the capital of the Hyksos, in the Second Intermediate Period. The work has shown that at its zenith Avaris was even more formidable than we might have imagined. Extending over an area of 0.96 square miles (2.5 sq. km), it was one of the largest cities in the eastern Mediterranean world, an international centre of commerce and trade. Bietak estimates that scattered over the

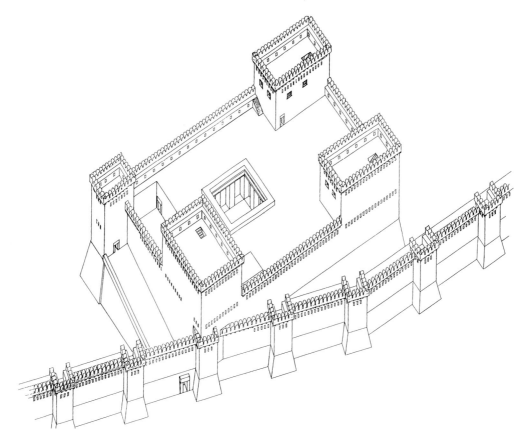

Above Reconstruction of the palatial fortress of the early Eighteenth Dynasty, built on the site of the earlier Hyksos citadel. *(After Manfred Bietak)*

site are the remains of over two million pottery containers for imported wine, oil and other commodities.

We now know that Avaris was defended by an impressive buttressed wall, made of mud brick, over 8 m (26 ft) thick, and a huge fortified citadel, which had been strategically located at a bend in one of the ancient Nile channels, now disappeared. Associated with the citadel was a garden for growing vines, the very vineyard, Bietak believes, threatened with appropriation by Kamose. Confirming the testimony of the Egyptian texts, the archaeology shows that the citadel was abandoned at the end of the Hyksos period and was subsequently modified by the Egyptians in the early Eighteenth Dynasty. That the culture of the inhabitants was indeed Canaanite or western Asiatic is clearly indicated by the style of architecture of the temples and palaces, by the nature of the burial customs, and by the types of artefact found in the graves. Many of these graves belonged to warriors, who were buried with a set of weapons, distinctive among them the form of battle-axe from which Seqenenre Tao received his fatal wounds.

▨ The Desert Routes

A major goal for the Thebans would have been to prevent a military alliance between the Hyksos to their north and the kingdom of Kush to the south. They appear to have thwarted this threat by carrying out a pre-emptive strike against the Kushites and by disrupting communications between the two allies. The Kamose Stela recounts that the Hyksos king, Ipepi, had sent a letter to the king of Kush, reminding him of their mutual interests and urging him to launch an attack from the rear while Kamose was occupied in the Delta:

> 'He [Kamose] chose the two lands to persecute them, my land and yours, and he has ravaged them. Come, navigate downstream, do not be afraid. Behold he is here with me. There is no one who will be waiting for you in this Egypt, for I will not let him go until you have arrived. Then we shall divide the towns of this Egypt, and the land of Khent-hen-nefer [Nubia] will be in joy.'

Right Map showing desert routes and location of major caravan stops in the Qena Bend. *(After John and Deborah Darnell)*

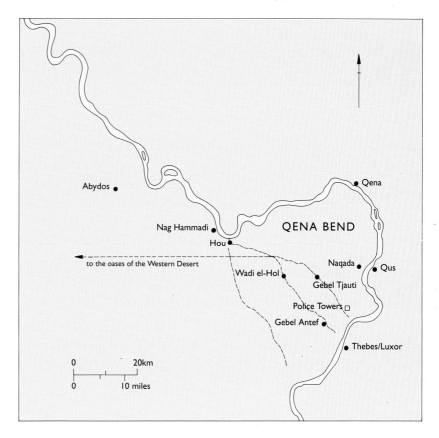

Above John and Deborah Darnell examining petroglyphs (rock inscriptions and pictures) at Gebel Tjauti, assisted by a workman who holds a mirror to reflect sunlight onto a shaded area. This part of the cliff, with its overhang offering welcome shade, appears to have functioned as a regular rest-stop for desert travellers.

Perhaps crucially for the outcome of the war, the letter never arrived, for the messenger carrying it was intercepted on his desert route by one of Kamose's patrols. His capture is unlikely to have been simply a piece of good fortune; more likely it was the result of a deliberate policy by the Thebans of monitoring and policing desert routes.

It is becoming increasingly clear that the Egyptians' use of the desert – for travel, trade and general communication – was much greater than has previously been thought, and that control of the desert routes would have been especially vital during periods of conflict. Important new light on the subject has been shed by two American archaeologists, Dr John and Deborah

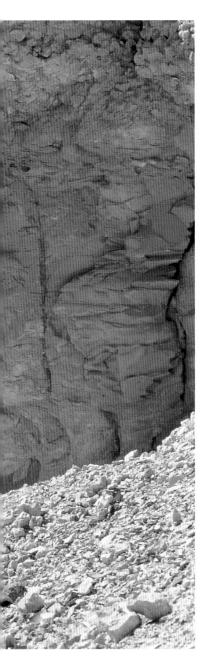

Darnell of the University of Chicago, who over the last six years or so have been carrying out a systematic survey of the desert west of Thebes. Their findings have been extraordinary, revealing a hitherto unmapped system of ancient roads, short-cutting the Qena Bend of the Nile and linking with other routes to the great oases in the west and to Nubia in the south. The routes are littered with pot-sherds, of many different periods, showing that they were in heavy use over several millennia. At points along the routes, the Darnells have discovered the sites of major caravan stops, marked by hundreds of rock inscriptions and drawings, left by the travellers.

The inscriptions are written in a variety of scripts, mostly hieroglyphic and hieratic, but also demotic, Coptic, Greek and even Proto-Sinaitic. Typically of such inscriptions, they are not always easy to read and interpret, as they tend to be rather crudely incised and are often superimposed on each other in a confusing manner. To produce an accurate record of the material has taken the Darnells many seasons of painstaking documenting and copying. Concentrated at two sites in particular, in the Wadi el-Hol on the road between Thebes and Hou and at the so-called Gebel Tjauti on the Alamat

Above right Hieroglyphic inscription of the 'police official Aam's son, the overseer of metal workers, Renseneb', incised underneath the rock-hang at Gebel Tjauti, *c.* 1700 BC. It is superimposed on a picture dating from probably nearly 1300 years earlier, while below it are two graffiti in the Coptic script, dating from over 2000 years later.

Tal road, these petroglyphs are far from being simply the ancient equivalents of 'Kilroy was here'; they bear eloquent witness to the many and varied activities in which the travellers were involved and show how busy and important such desert routes were. Many of the petroglyphs are religious in nature, taking the form of prayers to the gods, in particular to the goddess Hathor, who had special significance in the context of the desert. Some commemorate special journeys or events: a royal visit to Thebes or an astronomical observation. Most consist simply of a name and title; among these, policemen, whose task it was to patrol the desert, figure prominently. One of the drawings may well depict a policeman in the process of apprehending a

Above Remains of a watch tower which guarded the Theban end of one the major desert routes and was probably also used as a base for the desert police force.

miscreant. Most important historically, a number of texts testify to military activity and to the strategic importance of those routes. One such text, dating significantly from the Hyksos Period, appears to eulogize a Theban ruler for slaying foreigners in the desert and for striving selflessly to train the desert guards.

This preoccupation with security in the desert is further confirmed by one of the Darnells' most remarkable archaeological discoveries – the remains of two substantial watch towers, 12.2 m (40 ft) in diameter, of rubble and mud brick with drystone ramps along the sides, which guarded the Theban end of the Alamat Tal route and would probably also have served as a base for the roving desert patrols in the region. They were built during the late Second Intermediate Period, the time when the war between the Hyksos and the Thebans was beginning to escalate at the hands of Kamose.

The Beginnings of Empire

Despite his triumphs, Kamose died before he could attain his ultimate goal. The final defeat of the Hyksos and their expulsion from Egypt were to be the achievements of his younger brother, who succeeded him on the throne, Ahmose (1550–1525 BC), the first king of the Eighteenth Dynasty and founder of the New Kingdom. We know this to be the case as the achievement is recorded in a biographical inscription relating to a man who had been a contemporary witness to the events as a serving soldier in King Ahmose's army. The man's name was also Ahmose, son of Ibana, and his biography, one of the longest and most important historical inscriptions to have survived from ancient Egypt, is inscribed on the walls of his tomb at the site of Elkab, his home town in Upper Egypt, south of Thebes. He had a long and distinguished military career, serving under three successive kings, Ahmose, Amenhotep I and Thutmose I, spanning a period of fifty years or so, during which he rose from the junior ranks to be Admiral of the Fleet.

He gives an account of several campaigns, with particular reference to his own acts of bravery – the slaying of enemies and the taking of prisoners – and to the recognition and rewards he received, in the form of gold, slaves and land. The highest accolade that could be bestowed upon a soldier in ancient Egypt was the award of the so-called 'gold of bravery' by the king. Ahmose, son of Ibana, was given this award no fewer than seven times. He must have been one of the great military heroes of his age as well as a very wealthy man at the end of his career. A representation of him in the tomb shows him proudly wearing some of his gold.

Right Biographical inscription of a soldier named Ahmose, son of Ibana, in his tomb at Elkab in Upper Egypt. It gives an account of his military career, spanning the reigns of three successive kings, during the early Eighteenth Dynasty. Starting out as an ordinary soldier, like his father before him, Ahmose was much decorated and ended up as an admiral of the king's fleet. Early in his career he fought under King Ahmose against the Hyksos. The man himself is depicted to the left of the inscription; the smaller figure is that of his grandson, Paheri, who was responsible for the tomb's decoration.

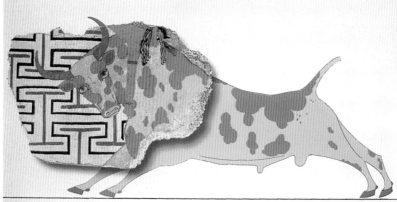

Above Minoan fresco-fragment showing part of a bull-leaping scene with a maze pattern in the background. Such a scene is otherwise known only from the royal palace of Knossos in Crete. Its presence in an Egyptian royal palace suggests a strong link between the Egyptian and Minoan royal courts. From Avaris/Tel el-Daba.

We are told that four of these acts of bravery for which he was specially rewarded took place in the war against the Hyksos under King Ahmose, the first three in battles around Avaris, which was eventually captured and sacked, and the fourth during the subsequent successful siege of the town of Sharuhen, a Hyksos stronghold in Canaan, a campaign which laid the foundations for the Egyptian empire in western Asia.

Following the defeat of the Hyksos, Egypt was now unified under a strong native king for the first time in over a hundred years. But clearly there was no room for complacency. It has been suggested that King Ahmose feared that the Hyksos and their allies might eventually counter-attack and as a result

Right Manfred Bietak examining a fragment from a bull-leaping scene.

forged an alliance with another great Mediterranean power. The evidence for such a development comes from an astonishing discovery made by the Austrian expedition at the site of the citadel of Avaris – the remains of wall-paintings of superb artistic quality and breathtaking beauty, but completely un-Egyptian in style, content and technique. On close examination, they were recognized as fragments, many thousands in number, of Minoan frescoes, the first ever to be discovered on Egyptian soil. Manfred Bietak believes they once decorated the walls of a new royal citadel, which King Ahmose built on the site of the old Hyksos fortress (see page 114).

The scenes strongly recall the famous frescoes painted on the walls of houses on the island of Thera and in the royal palace at Knossos, the Minoan capital, on Crete – human figures involved in various ritual and sporting activities, including acrobats and bull-leapers, landscapes with plants and animals, including antelope, leopards and lions in flying gallop, and decorative motifs such as rosette-friezes and maze-patterns.

The most important tableau, of which several fragments survive, showed a wonderful scene of bull-leaping. This sport had great ritual significance for the Minoans, expressing, it has been suggested, man's dominance over the power of animals. It is a subject otherwise represented only in the palace at Knossos and appears to have strong royal connotations. The presence of these prestigious Minoan paintings on the walls of an Egyptian palace presupposes a close relationship between the two royal courts, and Manfred Bietak believes that the two powers may well have forged an alliance, cemented perhaps by an inter-dynastic marriage. As the foremost sea-power of its time, Minoan Crete would have provided Egypt with protection against invasion from the sea; in exchange the Minoans would have received gold, African exotica and other luxury commodities, to which Egypt, a growing land-empire, had increasingly ready access.

The Kingdom of Kush

During the Eighteenth Dynasty, gold become a major tool for promoting Egyptian interests and securing important allies. Egypt had some gold mines of its own in its eastern desert, but by far the greatest number and the most productive lay to the south of Egypt, in the eastern deserts of Nubia and along the Nile Valley in the area of the Third Cataract in present-day Sudan. For the new imperial Egypt the possession of those mines became an absolute priority.

With the northern border secured, King Ahmose directed his army southward towards Nubia, most of which was still under the control of the Hyksos' old ally, the ruler of Kush. The roots of the Kushite capital, Kerma, go back to remote antiquity; there is evidence for a settlement in the area as far back as the fourth millennium BC. Subsequently, three major historical phases may be distinguished, each marked by distinctive developments in

Above Reconstruction of the fortified inner city of Kerma, showing clearly the enormous central temple, the *deffufa*, and the conical royal residence of the Middle Kerma Period.

funerary customs and material culture. These phases are known as Ancient Kerma (*c*.2500–2050 BC), Middle Kerma (*c*.2050–1750 BC), and Classic Kerma (*c*.1750–1500 BC). Throughout these periods, Kush was often in conflict with Egypt, resisting the latter's attempts at territorial expansion. Kush proved to be a formidable opponent, its warriors enjoying a legendary reputation for their skills with the bow and arrow. The civilization reached its zenith during the Classic Kerma period, significantly when Egypt was under the rule of the Hyksos.

Though generally portrayed in Egyptian texts as barbaric and of little substance, in reality Kushite culture was highly developed, with a strong and stable economic base and complex political and religious institutions. True appreciation of its nature and achievements has been made possible by the recent excavations of a Swiss team led by Professor Charles Bonnet of the University of Geneva, which has been investigating Kerma, building on the work of a previous American expedition. They have shown that Kerma was no simple settlement, nor, as was once thought, an Egyptian frontier outpost, but a substantial city, the earliest and largest in Africa outside Egypt, which covered at its height a total area of about 26.3 hectares (65 acres).

Right Charles Bonnet examining the beautifully worked marble altar of the *deffufa*.

Below The *deffufa* at Kerma, as it is today, from the west, looking at its main entrance, beyond which a staircase ascends to an altar-chamber, and then to the roof, where open-air rituals were conducted. The temple is made of solid mud brick, its pylons to the right rising to above 20 m (65 ft).

Above View from the roof of the *deffufa* looking south-west. In the foreground are the remains of a large circular hut-like building, believed to have been the royal residence or audience hall during the Middle Kerma Period, c.2050-1750 BC.

Architecturally, it must have been very striking, as impressive in its own way as the contemporary city of Avaris in the north. Its core was surrounded by a massive wall of mud brick, over 9 m (30 ft) high, which had projecting rectangular towers, four fortified gates, and a deep dry ditch in front. This wall enclosed and protected the palace of the king, the houses of the nobility, gardens, and a large religious complex. The centre was occupied by a huge white temple called nowadays the *deffufa* (a traditional Nubian term for any large building made of mud brick), which occupied over 325 sq. m (3500 sq. ft) and whose pylons reached to over 20 m (65 ft) in height – a substantial building even by Egyptian standards. Around it was a secondary religious complex, isolated from the rest of the city by a 5 m (16 ft) high wall, consisting of a number of small chapels, quarters for priests, storerooms and bronze workshops. The great temple, shorn of its white plaster and ravaged by time, is still today a dominating presence, three and a half thousand years after the Egyptians sought the city's destruction.

Above Examples of African products prized by the Egyptians: seen here are logs of ebony, exotic animals and animal skins, a large ivory tusk and ostrich eggs. Thebes, tomb of Rekhmire. Eighteenth Dynasty, reign of Tuthmose III (c.1479–1425 BC).

Above Charles Bonnet and Salah Mohamed Ahmed, Director of Excavations of the National Corporation of Antiquities and Museums of the Sudan, in the dighouse at Kerma, examining a fine ceramic bowl, recently excavated.

At first glance, the *deffufa* resembles an Egyptian temple, but is actually very un-Egyptian in concept and structure. It is a solid mud-brick construction with a single monumental gateway to the side. This entrance gives access to a stairway leading up to a small chamber, which is occupied by a great circular altar of white marble, on which sheep and goats were sacrificed. From the altar chamber, a further staircase, to the left, leads up to the roof, where it is thought that open-air rituals, probably connected with the worship of the sun god, took place. Today, the roof offers a wonderful vantage point from which to view the remains of the city below, the plan and internal organization of which Bonnet has been able to work out in some detail.

One striking vestige, the outline of which can be clearly discerned a little to the southwest, is that of a large round hut, once fitted with a conical roof, whose walls, made of mud brick with wooden supports, stood to a height of at least 9 m (30 ft). A quintessential piece of African architecture, of a scale and type unparalleled elsewhere in the ancient Nile Valley, its size and location suggested to Bonnet that it was the residence or audience hall of the king during the Middle Kerma period. During the succeeding period, a new, larger palace, more elongated and roughly rectangular in plan, was built further to the west and centred on an axis directly aligned with the entrance to the *deffufa*. It was a complex structure, which included a long entrance corridor at the side, storage areas for foodstuffs and other commodities, and an archive room, in which Bonnet discovered the remains of thousands of small mud blanks for making seals, for the marking of goods or sealing of messages, a clear indication that business of some considerable scale was transacted at the site. At the centre of the palace was an imposing audience hall, where the king, seated on a throne placed on a raised platform, received delegations. Its roof was supported by several large columns, estimated to have been about 7.6 m (25 ft) high. This was the palace of the last kings of Kerma. The remains of its walls bear the evidence of burning, and Bonnet believes it was finally destroyed by fire, together with much of the rest of the city, by the invading Egyptian forces led by King Thutmose I (see page 129).

During its heyday, the kingdom of Kerma or Kush controlled not only the gold mines but also major trade routes, both north–south and east–west, with the rest of Africa, from which such highly prized commodities as ivory, ebony, incense, animal-skins and slaves were obtained. It had a sophisticated society, served by highly skilled specialized craftsmen producing a wide range of goods from a variety of different materials. Its most distinctive product was an exquisite pottery, coloured black and red and eggshell thin, among the finest ceramic produced in the ancient world. The kingdom's prosperity

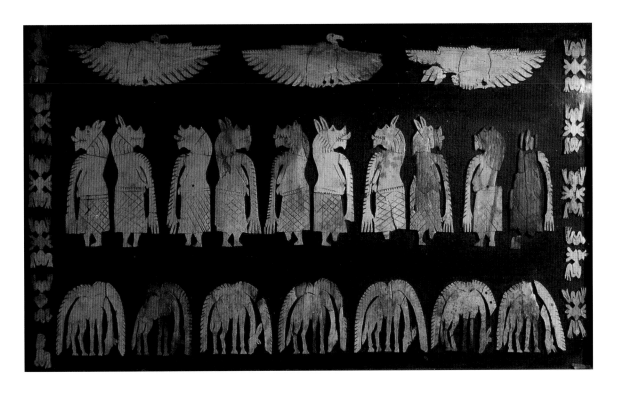

Above Ivory furniture inlays in the forms of animals and birds. From the royal tombs at Kerma. Classic Kerma Period, c.1750-1500 BC. Excavated by an expedition from the Museum of Fine Arts, Boston and Harvard University (1913–1916).

is clear from the wealth of material found in the city's cemetery, which contains over 30,000 burials. During the Classic Kerma period, the kings were buried in huge tumulus tombs over 80 m (262 ft) in diameter, filled with huge quantities of luxury and prestige goods – pottery, jewellery, weaponry, inlaid furniture – mostly of local manufacture but with some Egyptian imports, such as stone sculptures and vessels. Buried with the kings were hundreds of sacrificed animals and human attendants – priests and concubines – to serve them in the afterlife, clear if gruesome testimony to their great status and power. Erected near to the tombs were massive mud-brick chapels (one of them is known as the eastern *deffufa*), where their funerary cults were carried out, the internal chambers finely decorated with faience tiles and painted scenes. The kingdom of Kush was no cultural backwater.

One of the great puzzles surrounding Kush has been the question of how its population and livestock were sustained. To feed the capital city and the population of the kingdom would have required a substantial agricultural base. Yet, most of Kerma's hinterland consists of desert – to all appearances a barren waste punctuated by occasional clumps of trees. Thanks to a recent discovery by a team of archaeologists led by Dr Derek Welsby of the British Museum, however, we now know that this is an entirely misleading picture.

Welsby has been carrying out a detailed survey of the desert region in the Dongola Reach to the south of Kerma for the Sudan Archaeological Research Society. In an area covering about 700 square miles (1813 sq. km), which was previously an archaeological blank, his team has located over 400 ancient sites, settlements and cemeteries, most of them dating from the Kerma Period. When these were plotted on a map, it became clear that many of them fell into a linear distribution, along the banks of what were evidently two old branches of the Nile, still plainly visible in places, where their banks

Below Derek Welsby (on the left) and one of his team, Simon Mortimer, investigate the remains of a stone and timber building, once probably fitted with a raised wooden floor, designed, Welsby believes, for the storage of grain which was destined for the capital city at Kerma. There are many such buildings, dating from the Classic Kerma Period, in this once well-watered area of the Dongola Reach.

are marked by lines of vegetation. Confirming Welsby's results, the northern continuation of these channels has been independently traced by Jacques Reinold of the Sudan Antiquities Service's French Archaeological Unit. Quite remarkably then, what is now desert was once a fertile tract of land, watered by two additional Nile channels. Eminently suitable for the growing of crops and the pasturing of animals, the region supported large numbers of thriving agricultural communities. Significantly, many of the settlements contain the remains of stone and timber buildings, with what may have been raised wooden floors, probably for the storage of grain and other produce. Such buildings are not found in Kerma itself. Welsby believes they may well have formed part of a network of collection points, from which the capital would have been supplied.

But this prosperity did not last, as nature appears to have turned against the kingdom of Kush. The archaeological evidence at present suggests that the two Nile channels began to dry up towards the end of the Classic Kerma period, a change in conditions which would have had serious consequences for the food supply and the viability of the population in the region. If this is the case, it could not have happened at a worse time. Egypt, the colossus to the north, was resurgent, fresh from conquests in Canaan and bent again on southward expansion.

Conquest and the Gold-fields

Beginning with a campaign under King Ahmose, the Egyptian army took Lower Nubia with little resistance. But, despite their internal problems, the Kushites, from their base at Kerma in Upper Nubia, provided stubborn opposition, and it took many campaigns by a succession of Egyptian rulers before they were finally subdued. The decisive blow was struck by Thutmose I (1504–1492 BC), one of Egypt's great imperial kings. Early in his reign, he penetrated to beyond the Third Cataract, the first Egyptian king ever to do so, and inflicted a crushing defeat on a Kushite army. A long inscription, carved on a huge rock at Tombos just north of Kerma, commemorates the victory: 'he has overthrown the chief of the Nubians; none of them has survived. The Nubian archers are fallen in slaughter, are spread over the plains, their entrails fill their valleys, their blood pours down like rain.' It is probable that the sacking and burning of Kerma, witnessed in the charring of its walls, soon followed.

According to his inscription at Elkab, Ahmose, son of Ibana, actually served in the campaign. He speaks proudly of his own feats of bravery in traversing the rapids of the Cataract, as a result of which he was promoted to troop commander. He tells us that Thutmose I himself slew the enemy chief with the first arrow shot from his great bow (see page 110) and that the king sailed back triumphantly to Egypt with the corpse of his enemy hung upside down from the prow of his boat, the arrow still stuck in his chest!

Having broken the power of Kush, Thutmose I and his successors, especially Thutmose III (1479–1425 BC) and Amenhotep III (1390–1352 BC), firmly established and extended Egyptian control over the Nubian goldfields. The most productive mines were located deep in the Eastern Desert of Sudan, over 150 miles (241 km) from the Nile, in dried-up river valleys or *wadis*, especially the Wadi Allaqi and the Wadi Gabgaba and their tributaries, between the Nile and the Red Sea. Over a hundred mines and goldworking sites are known from these *wadi*-systems. They are currently being explored by an Italian expedition led by Alfredo and Angelo Castiglione. In order to withstand the harsh conditions of the desert, where the days are burning hot and the nights can be freezing cold, this expedition travels in specially designed and equipped vehicles.

Gold occurs in alluvial deposits and in veins in quartz rock. The Castigliones have found plentiful evidence of surface and underground mining for the quartz. They have also found hieroglyphic inscriptions left by ancient Egyptian officials along the routes and at the locations of mines. The

Right The location of gold mines in the Eastern Desert and along the Nile. *(After Vercoutter)*

Overleaf A section of the Wadi Allaqi in the Eastern Desert of Sudan, a region of hugely productive gold mines; in the middle foreground can be seen the remains of buildings belonging to the Graeco-Roman mining town of Berenice Panchrysos.

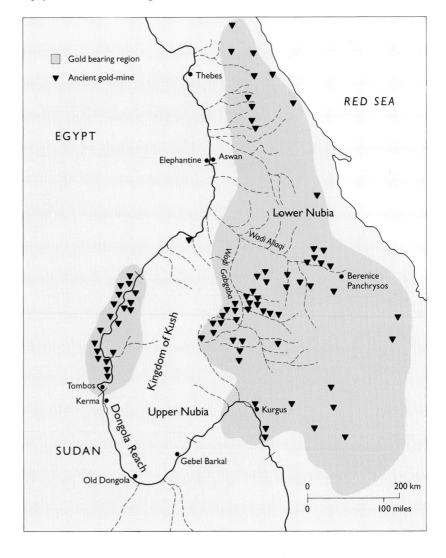

Right Detail of the biographical inscription of Ahmose, son of Ibana, from a passage describing how the chief of the Nubians was slain by the first arrow shot from Thutmose I's bow and how his body was then taken back to Egypt, hung upside down from the prow of the king's boat. One of the hieroglyphs here depicts the chief upside down, the king's arrow still stuck in his chest.

Above This large sloping rock, located near the village of Tombos at the Third Cataract, bears on its upper face a long victory inscription of King Thutmose I, commemorating his defeat of a Kushite army. On the rear is a smaller, later stela of the Viceroy of Kush, Merymose (see page 136).

Above Gold jewellery, in the form of rosettes, scarabs, flies and arms: part of a robber's loot, dating mainly from the second century BC. From the Wadi Terfowi, a branch of the Wadi Gabgaba.

exploitation of the mines was ruthless and sustained. It is thought that the actual mining was carried out mostly by slaves, prisoners of war and convicts, condemned to hard labour, which many would never survive. Water was in extremely short supply, and we know from Egyptian texts that expeditions might lose substantial parts of their workforce from thirst alone, if they failed to locate or dig wells. The extraction of the quartz must have been back-breaking. Chunks of it had first to be detached and then transported to the surface. Here it was crushed and ground to a fine powder, which was washed with water on a sloping surface to separate the gold. The remains of the implements used by the workers – pestles and mortars and grindstones – are still scattered around in the vicinity of the mines.

The Castigliones have been able to show that the exploitation of these gold-fields continued over centuries. Among their most remarkable discoveries, they have located the site of a long-lost town, Berenice Panchrysos, mentioned by classical writers as a goldworking centre. It is a substantial settlement, one and a quarter miles long (2 km), consisting of two strongholds, administrative offices and houses. The population is estimated to have been at least 10,000. Berenice Panchrysos was the headquarters of the gold industry in this region in the Graeco-Roman and medieval periods. Its

Below Statue of Thutmose III (1479–1425 BC), the grandson of Thutmose I, who extended Egyptian control deep into Upper Nubia. Inscriptions from his reign in the Temple of Karnak at Thebes record the receipt of enormous quantities of gold from Nubia.

existence and its size provide clear testimony of the long productivity of the mines of the Nubian desert.

In the vicinity of the mining sites, the Castigliones have found graves of different dates, some evidently belonging to the native Bedouin who traversed the region and also benefited from its mineral wealth. Hidden in one disturbed grave was a bag containing a tomb-robber's loot – exquisite gold jewellery, including gold scarabs and gold flies, remarkably similar in form to Egyptian jewellery.

Colonial Rule

Enormous quantities of gold poured into the treasuries of the pharaohs from the mines of Nubia. Inscriptions from the time of Thutmose III, the grandson of Thutmose I, record that during three years of his reign an aggregate of 9277 *deben* of gold was received from these sources. A *deben* was a basic unit of weight, equivalent to 91 g (3.2 oz). The total gold recorded is therefore equivalent to 1830 lb (794 kg) weight, worth many millions of dollars at today's prices. These same texts also record the receipt of huge quantities of other much-coveted commodities, such as ivory, ebony, cattle and slaves. Little wonder that the Egyptians were not content merely to conquer Nubia but sought to make it a permanent part of Egypt itself.

As later empires were to do with their subject peoples, the Egyptians cleverly adopted a policy of assimilation and indoctrination. The sons of Nubian chiefs were taken to Egypt to be educated at the Egyptian court and be imbued with Egyptian culture. They learnt the Egyptian language, wore Egyptian clothes, and even took on Egyptian names. Thoroughly 'Egyptianized', they returned to their native land to serve as part of the governing élite in the Egyptian administration.

At the head of the colonial government was a powerful official designated as the Viceroy of Kush, an Egyptian drawn from the pharaoh's inner circle and directly answerable to

Right Weighing gold: the gold, in
the form of rings, is placed in one
side of the balance; on the other
side are metal weights, cast in the
form of different animals, which
represent units of the *deben*.
From the tomb of Rekhmire, the
vizier of Thutmose III, Thebes.

Opposite Head of the inner
sarcophagus of Merymose, made
of grano-diorite. From Thebes.

Below Stela of the viceroy
Merymose, shown adoring two
cartouches containing the names
of his master, Amenhotep III, which
surmount the bound figures of
two Nubian captives – a clear
symbol of dominance. The stela is
carved on the back of a huge rock
at Tombos (see page 131).

him. As 'director of the gold lands of Amun', another of his titles, the viceroy
was charged above all with securing a regular supply of that most valued commodity. One of the most famous and successful of these viceroys was Merymose, who served under King Amenhotep III. Merymose's name appears
everywhere, most notably in a stela carved on the back of the huge rock at
Tombos which bears on the front the great victory inscription of Thutmose I.
Here he is pictured with his arms raised in adoration before the names of his
master, Amenhotep III. The stela functions as a symbol of the pharaoh's domination and as a tribute to his great ancestor, who had first conquered the
region over a century before. Merymose served Amenhotep III as Viceroy of
Kush for thirty years. He was ultimately rewarded for his services with a tomb
at Thebes, which included, quite exceptionally for a non-
royal person, three magnificent hard-stone sarcophagi,
beautifully carved with religious scenes and inscriptions.

The long reign of Amenhotep III (1390–1352 BC) was
the acme of the imperial age, a period of unparalleled
peace and prosperity, which saw great artistic achievements
and religious developments. The king initiated a vast
building programme, which transformed the architectural
landscape of the Nile Valley. He made major additions to
the great Temple of Amun–Ra at Karnak, built the magnificent new temple of Luxor, and erected hundreds of
statues of the gods and of himself, some of them on a
gigantic scale, such as the so-called Colossi of Memnon,
which stood in front of his mortuary temple at Thebes.
Calling himself 'Egypt's Dazzling Sun', Amenhotep III
even aspired to be identified with the sun-god Ra himself,
as his embodiment on earth.

Abroad, the pharaoh's prestige had never been higher. Egypt's wealth was the envy of the ancient world. As we know from the famous cache of diplomatic correspondence called the 'Amarna Letters', rulers great and small wrote to the Egyptian king, pleading for gold, of which Egypt had so much:

> 'Great King, King of Egypt, my brother...
> Gold in your country is like dust; one simply
> picks it up. Why are you so sparing of it? I
> am building a new palace. Send me as much
> gold as is required for its adornment.'
>
> *(Letter from the King of Assyria to Amenhotep III)*

> 'May my brother send me in very great quantities unworked gold...and much more gold
> than he sent to my father. In my brother's
> country gold is as plentiful as dust...
> Whatever my brother requires for his house,
> let him write and take it.'
>
> *(Letter from the King of Mittani to Amenhotep III)*

Above Clay tablet inscribed in cuneiform with a letter from Tushratta, King of Mittani, to Amenhotep III, one of a series detailing negotiations for a marriage between Tushratta's daughter, Tadukhipa, and the Egyptian king. As a bride-price, Tushratta asks for 'gold in very great quantity', adding that 'gold is like dust in the land of my brother'. From Amarna.

In return for gold, the Egyptians were able to acquire prestige commodities, which they coveted but lacked, prominent among them lapis lazuli and conifer wood such as cedar. To judge from the correspondence, foreign princesses were the top of Amenhotep III's list, to swell his harem and strengthen alliances through inter-family marriage.

Houses for Eternity

The élite who served the king well – administrators, priests, soldiers, scribes – shared in the state's wealth and luxury. They were able to commission fine statues of themselves and magnificent tombs. The creation of a tomb, a 'house for eternity', suitably decorated and reflecting their elevated status in life, was every Egyptian's highest aspiration.

The greatest concentration of private tombs belonging to Egypt's imperial age is found carved into the limestone hills overlooking the west bank of the Nile at Thebes. One of these tombs – a particularly interesting one – has recently been the subject of detailed study by Professor Betsy Bryan, Egyptologist and art-historian, of Johns Hopkins University, Baltimore. The tomb belonged to a man called Su-em-niwet, who occupied a high office, that of 'royal butler', under King Amenhotep II (1427–1400 BC). It is one of a

Above Betsy Bryan carefully recording on transparent plastic a painted scene showing the tomb-owner, Su-em-niwet.

group of élite tombs belonging to high-ranking officials of the period which are so positioned in the necropolis as to overlook their king's funerary temple below. It was the custom to decorate the superstructure or chapels of private tombs with coloured scenes, some illustrating the owner engaged in daily-life activities, others showing episodes from his funeral. If the rock in which the tomb was cut was sound enough, the decoration would be carved in relief and then painted; if not, as in the case of Su-em-niwet's tomb, the scenes would be executed in paint on a base of white plaster. Su-em-niwet must have died before his tomb was quite finished, as the painted scenes were abandoned in varying stages of completion. Undesirable as this would have been for an ancient Egyptian, it is what makes the tomb so interesting to modern art historians, as it provides a wonderful opportunity to study painting techniques and methodology, the details of which are largely concealed in a piece of finished decoration.

By close study of the walls, Professor Bryan has been able to determine that a large team of artists, of varying levels of competence, were employed in painting the chapel's three chambers, their work marked by characteristic features of style and technique. She has found that some artists or groups of artists specialized in certain types of composition, some even in certain types of colour. The unfinished state of the paintings has been particularly revealing as to how pigments were mixed to extend the colour range and how compositions were built up, and certain desirable hues achieved, by the careful application of layers of different-coloured paint, placed one upon the other.

The work of one artist, regarded as a true master by Betsy Bryan, stands out from the rest. Interestingly, his work occurs only in the chapel's front chamber – the best-lit in the tomb – and is confined to scenes of a prestigious or unusual nature, for example representations of statues of the king and queen. It is of superb artistic quality, all the more admirable as it was done freehand. In composing a scene, Egyptian artists usually employed a conventional background grid to help them proportion and space the main elements in a scene, but the Su-em-niwet master required no such aid. Using a tiny, slender brush, he drew by eye alone, with enormously practised ease and to wonderful effect, producing perfectly proportioned figures, which he then coloured with great skill and subtlety.

On the other side of the scale is the artistry displayed in the tomb's innermost chamber, the area where the owner's funeral was depicted. Here, in the darkest part of the tomb, the work was assigned to some of the least competent artists, including perhaps apprentices and the more elderly workmen now past their best. One of them worked solely in yellow paint and in a very slapdash fashion: he had no facility to paint consistently to an outline and often obscured or spoiled an otherwise nicely finished detail by covering it with yellow paint. Another kind of error is observable in a depiction of funeral attendants. Closely grouped together, the figures are given different-coloured skins, alternating light and dark red – a commonplace device in Egyptian art for distinguishing between individuals in such contexts. In one area, confusion or lack of attention on the part of the artists has led to two adjacent figures being painted incorrectly, each being shown with a light upper half and dark bottom half.

The growing private affluence of Egypt's imperial age and the increasing demand for finely decorated tombs would have placed a high premium on the services of a master artist. Among other things, Professor Bryan's work has raised questions as to how such artists were recruited for private work. There is no doubt that the very best craftsmen would have been employed in the royal service, primarily in the tombs in the Valley of the Kings. It is possible that some of them might on occasion have been allowed to undertake other commissions for favoured courtiers, or simply did so in their own spare time.

Almost all the kings of the New Kingdom, covering a period of over 400 years, were buried in the Valley of the Kings, from Thutmose I in the early Eighteenth Dynasty down to Ramesses X in the late Twentieth Dynasty. Tutankhamun was buried in a small makeshift tomb, never intended for a king, but otherwise the royal tombs, as befitting the status of their occupants

Opposite Unfinished decoration showing registers of offerings, including military equipment and royal statuettes. The work of a master artist, the scene was drafted free-hand, without the aid of a grid. Tomb of Su-em-niwet; front room, north wall.

and their function as symbolic representations of the great and mysterious underworld, are substantial structures, many times larger and more complex than the contemporary private tombs. Some of them are real giants, the most finished and the finest being the tomb of Seti I (1294–1279 BC), second king of the Nineteenth Dynasty, which is about 100 m (330 ft) long, the walls and ceilings of its many passages, chambers and side-rooms decorated throughout to a uniform standard of excellence. The workmen who built these tombs were not recruited *ad hoc* but were part of a permanent work-force, a select band of craftsmen, specially attached to the royal tombs – a system which had been in operation for 200 years by the time of Seti I. These craftsmen were the élite of their kind – everyone a master – and were treated as such. They lived with their families apart from the rest of the population in a walled village, of about seventy houses, some distance from the Valley at

Below Figure of the goddess Hathor, where a 'specialist' in yellow paint has carelessly painted over the finished detail of her eye. Tomb of Su-em-niwet; corridor, south wall.

Above Ceiling of the burial chamber of King Seti I, magnificently decorated in black and yellow paint, showing the twelve hours of the night and the heavenly constellations represented in various human and animal forms. Valley of the Kings, c.1280 BC.

Overleaf View, from the south, of the village of Deir el-Medina, which housed the community of artists who worked in the royal tombs in the Valley of the Kings. New Kingdom, c.1504–1099 BC.

a place called today Deir el-Medina. The ancient Egyptians called the village 'the Place of Truth' and the workmen 'servants in the Place of Truth'.

Fortunately for us, they were an unusually literate community and left behind copious records of their activities, especially from the periods of the Nineteenth and Twentieth Dynasties, written in hieratic sometimes on papyrus but more usually on bits of broken pottery or limestone called *ostraca*. We know from these that the workmen of a tomb were divided into two gangs, a right and a left, who probably worked the two sides of a tomb simultaneously, each in the charge of a foreman. There was also a 'scribe of the tomb', who kept a daily record of progress and a register of attendance. The normal number of workmen was about sixty, though this could vary as appropriate. They consisted of stonemasons, carpenters, sculptors, draughtsmen and painters. Posts in the workforce were generally hereditary, passing down from father to eldest son, sometimes over several generations. They worked an eight-hour day with a break in the middle and had a day off every ten days, though they were also entitled to special holidays on the occasions of festivals to the gods. The intitial hollowing out

Above Scene showing King Ramesses II in his chariot at the Battle of Qadesh, truimphantly leading his forces and slaying the Hittites. From the temple of Abu Simbel, c.1270 BC.

of a tomb appears never to have taken more than two years or so. Its decoration, on the other hand – the composition of the scenes, the relief sculpting, the painting – would have taken a great deal longer, which is why most of the tombs were unfinished at the king's death. Seti I's tomb is one of the few exceptions.

Money as we know it did not exist in ancient Egypt. The workmen's pay consisted of rations of grain, supplemented by supplies of fish, vegetables, wood for fuel, pottery and occasional treats of meat, wine and beer. Any surplus could be exchanged for other products, using a system of relative values

expressed in *deben*. There are many records of such transactions, involving payment for household and funerary furniture, livestock and luxury commodities, showing that this was an affluent community, something that is also evident from the size and quality of some of their own tombs.

Decline and Collapse

Two hundred years after Egypt's first imperial conquests, the records of Deir el-Medina and the splendour of tombs such as that of Seti I present a picture of continuing domestic prosperity. Abroad, however, dark clouds had long been gathering on Egypt's imperial horizons. Another great military power, the Hittite empire, based in Anatolia (now Turkey), had arisen in the north and now threatened Egypt's domination. The conflict came to a head during the reign of Seti I's son, Ramesses II (1279–1213 BC), when a great battle took place in 1274 BC between the two powers near a town called Qadesh in Syria.

Though widely celebrated on Egyptian temple walls as a great victory for Ramesses, the outcome was at best a draw. Ultimately Ramesses was obliged to relinquish a great deal of the northern territories and to sign a peace treaty with the Hittite king. The Egyptian empire in the Near East had been delivered a blow from which it was never fully to recover. The story thereafter is one of gradual decline, punctuated by periods of brief resurgence, with Ramesses' successors fighting a series of rearguard actions against a variety of hostile forces coming from different directions. Within a century or so of his death the empire had completely gone.

During the same period, significantly, the supply of Nubian gold appears to have diminished. The routes to the desert mines were more difficult to traverse, owing probably to the increased aridity already evidenced in the drying up of the Nile channels in the Dongola Reach (see pages 128–9). Records appear to indicate that under the last great pharaoh of the New Kingdom, Ramesses III (1184–1153 BC), second king of the Twentieth Dynasty, only a few *deben* of gold were dedicated annually to the temple of Karnak, a paltry amount when compared to the vast sums donated by his predecessors at the height of the empire.

From the same king's reign we have further evidence of economic decline. An official document records that payment to the Deir el-Medina workmen was delayed for a period of six months resulting in them marching in protest, demonstrating and withdrawing their labour on the king's tomb – the first recorded strike in history. The same document states that a number of workmen were charged with attempting to enter illegally a number of royal tombs with a view to plundering them. They were caught before any harm was done, but others were later to succeed, as is clearly shown by the transcript of a court case during the reign of Ramesses IX (1126–1108 BC) recording the testimony of a stonemason, Amenpnufer, who was charged with tomb-robbery and confessed after having been 'beaten with sticks' and having his 'feet and hands twisted':

> 'We went to rob the tombs in accordance with our regular habit, and we found the pyramid tomb of King Sekhemreshedtawy, Son of Ra, Sobekemsaf, this being not at all like the pyramids and tombs of the nobles which we habitually went to rob. We took our metal tools and forced a way into the pyramid of this king through its innermost part. We found its underground chambers, and we took lighted candles in our hands and went down. Then we broke through the rubble...and found this god lying at the back of his burial-place. And we found the burial-place of Queen Nubkhaas, his queen, situated beside him...We opened their sarcophagi and their coffins...and found the noble mummy of this king...We collected the gold we found on the noble mummy of this god together with that on his amulets and jewels...We collected all that we found upon her likewise and set fire to their coffins...Thus I, together with the other thieves who are with me, have continued down to this day in the practice of robbing the tombs of the nobles and people of the land who rest in the west of Thebes. And a large number of people of the land rob them as well, and are as good as partners of ours.'

Amenpnufer and his gang were found guilty and would have suffered, in penalty, the cruellest of deaths, impaling on a stake. But despite the severe penalties, sporadic tomb-robbery continued, encouraged by administrative corruption and laxity, as the Twentieth Dynasty drew to a close in the midst of economic and political turmoil. Central authority collapsed and the country split into two, into a northern and southern kingdom, each under its own ruler. The southern kingdom fell under the effective control of the High Priest of Amun–Ra in the temple of Karnak, who had become an enormously powerful figure, more powerful than the king himself. The last king of the Dynasty, Ramesses XI (1099–1069 BC), had begun a tomb in the Valley of the Kings but, fearing for its ultimate safety, had left it unfinished and moved elsewhere in the country. After 400 years of continuous occupation, the community of workmen abandoned Deir el-Medina, never to return. No royal tomb would ever again be built in the Valley of the Kings.

Crisis followed crisis, as the Viceroy of Kush, a man called Panehsy, rebelled successfully against the authority of the southern kingdom. Nubia became independent again and the gold mines were lost. Egypt's Age of Gold had truly come to an end.

These events sealed the fate of the royal tombs. Full of gold bullion and other precious commodities, they offered an irresistible temptation, and not just to tomb-robbers. The Egyptologist Dr Nicholas Reeves has recently suggested that the greatest threat came from the State itself. While campaigning against Panehsy in Nubia, the High Priest and General Piankh wrote a letter to a senior official in Thebes ordering him to 'uncover a tomb amongst the tombs of the ancestors and preserve its seal until I return'. The implications seem clear: in these times of need, it had become official practice to enter sealed tombs and recycle their contents for the State's purposes, in the case of Piankh probably to fund the war against Panehsy.

With the security and integrity of the necropolis so compromised, the policy was adopted of removing the royal mummies from their original tombs, rewrapping them where necessary, and reinterring them in new locations. Eventually two secret caches were created, in reused tombs, one inside and one outside the Valley. Here the mummies were reburied without any of their original burial equipment or precious accoutrements. The threat posed by tomb robbers was no doubt one reason for this policy of collective reinterment. But Reeves believes that in these straitened economic times the

Right Letter in the hieratic script on papyrus to the High Priest and General Piankh from necropolis officials, confirming that they have carried out his instructions to 'uncover a tomb amongst the tombs of the ancestors and preserve its seal until I return' – an indication, scholars now believe, that it had become official policy to enter the royal tombs in the Valley of the Kings and strip them of their valuables for the use of the State. From Thebes, Twentieth Dynasty, c.1071 BC.

situation suited the authorities very well, providing a convenient pretext for entering the tombs, removing the owners and systematically appropriating whatever gold and other treasure lay within. Only Tutankhamun escaped – the location of his tiny tomb no doubt long forgotten – to give us a tantalizing glimpse of what vast riches the tombs in the Valley of the Kings must once have contained.

Whatever the motives, it is a policy for which we today should be enormously grateful. The secret caches remained hidden and undisturbed for

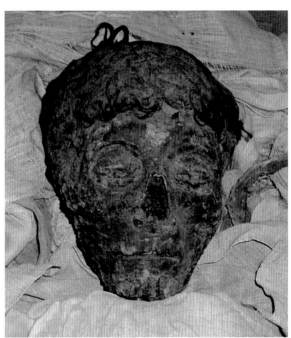

Left The burial chamber, the 'house of gold', of King Tutankhamun, with its stone sarcophagus and the king's outer coffin, made of gilded wood, which contains the royal mummy. Tutankhamun was originally buried wearing a gold mask within a nest of three coffins, the innermost one made of solid gold. The mask and the other two coffins are now in the Cairo Museum. Thebes, Valley of the Kings, Eighteenth Dynasty, c.1327 BC.

Above Head of the mummy of King Ahmose (c.1525 BC). From Thebes.

nearly three millennia until their discovery in the last decades of the nineteenth century. When examined, they were found to contain some seventy bodies in total, including the mummies of most of the pharaohs of the New Kingdom, over twenty in number, many still in very good condition. As a result, we can gaze at the actual faces of some of the greatest names of the Age of Gold: of Ahmose and Thutmose I, who helped to create it, of Seti I and Ramesses II, who fought to maintain it, and of Ramesses III and his successors, under whom it fell into final decline.

DEITIES AND DEMONS

The images on the tomb walls of the ancient Egyptians portray an idyllic existence along the banks of the Nile, but in truth it was also a life full of uncertainty. To understand and manage their world, the Egyptians populated it with an ever-growing array of divine beings – deities and demons who exercised influence on every aspect of life in this world and the next, and who had to be appeased, controlled and sometimes threatened.

Hathor, the great cow deity and mother of pharaoh, was the goddess of fertility and love; but when angered she could also destroy humanity. Sekhmet, the lioness, symbolized the nurturing warmth of the sun, but she also evoked its scorching heat and deadly pestilence. Selket, the scorpion, could give or take breath away; her sting gave her the power to grant life or death. Khnum, a ram-headed god, brought forth the life-giving waters of the Nile flood, yet he could also hold it back.

The appearance of the gods stemmed from the observation of nature. Certain creatures were perceived to embody special qualities – strength in the lion, virility in the ram, speed and sight in the falcon. The dualistic qualities of the gods derived from the experience of life: the universe had its good side and its bad and it had to be constantly kept in balance. To maintain this delicate equilibrium, which the Egyptians called *ma'at*, they needed to ensure the benevolence of the gods who made up their universe – gods born at the beginning of time and created with creation.

Below The scorpion goddess Selket, a guardian of the living and the dead. Bronze. Late Period, after 600 BC.

Right Sekhmet, the lady of life, was a lioness personifying the warmth of the sun, but she could also scorch and burn. Grano-diorite. Reign of Amenhotep III (c.1390-1352 BC).

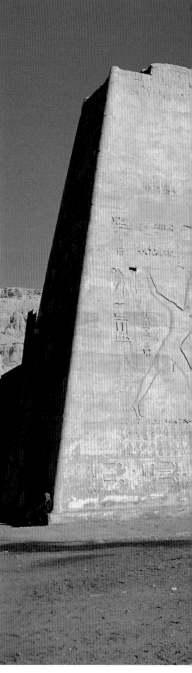

Above The great snake of the underworld, Apep, symbolized the primeval forces of chaos. Described as over 16 m (52 ft) long, his front part made of flint, he tried to capsize, ground and swallow the sun boat as it passed through the night. Tomb of Seti I (c.1294–1279 BC), Valley of the Kings.

Above Apep was so dangerous that even his name had to be magically killed. Here a knife severs the neck of the hieroglyphic determinative of his name. Tomb of Seti I, Valley of the Kings.

To the Egyptians, creation was not a single, isolated event but an ongoing cycle of renewal to be repeated daily with the rising of the sun, as the sun god emerged anew from the mound of creation victorious over the demons of the netherworld who sought to destroy him each night. Chief among these demons and agents of chaos was the giant snake Apep, who tried to hinder the progress of the sun boat with the coils of his writhing body. Every god played a part in warding off Apep's attacks throughout the night and ensuring creation each morning. Only by constant and correct obser-

Above The massive ceremonial gateways, called pylons, at the front of each temple, represented the moutains of the horizon. Mortuary Temple of Ramesses III (c.1184–1153 BC) at Medinet Habu.

vance of their cults could the creative cycle be guaranteed and the forces of chaos kept at bay.

The cult of the gods took place in temples that were carefully designed to mirror the cosmos at that first perfect moment of creation, and the rituals that took place within them were a metaphor of the process of creation itself. At the height of Egypt's greatness in the New Kingdom (1550–1069 BC), temples were built to embody creation on a grand scale. At the front of each temple stood a soaring monumental gateway, called a pylon. Aligned so that

the sun rose or set between its twin towers, it represented the horizon. On each tower scenes of pharaoh overwhelming his enemies served as powerful sentinels, conferring protection against the imperfection and threats of the exterior world. Each morning just before dawn, priests, ritually purified, shaven of all hair and clad only in the purest linen, entered through this gate into the festival courtyard, open to the sky, decorated with the kings' exploits undertaken on the god's behalf. From here, as the floor level rose and the ceilings became lower, the priests travelled from the outermost edges of the ordered world to the inner core of creation – the mound.

One ramp led up to a semi-lit hall filled with columns shaped like the papyrus and lotus plants which grew in the primeval marsh surrounding the

rising mound. Then another took them into the inner sanctum and the pitch blackness of the holy of holies, the pinnacle of creation. Here in his shrine the deity rested in his cult statue in the pure silence and darkness of pre-existence. Breaking the seal on the door to this sanctuary, the priests entered the holy place chanting prayers and burning incense. As the sun rose the god was roused and the cosmos was reborn.

On the temple walls, every need of the god was shown attended to by the king. It was the king who bathed, adorned, and anointed the statue of the god. It was the king, too, who laid out sumptuous feasts for the god's nourishment. In reality a cadre of priests enacted the rituals in the name of their master, declaring to the god, 'It is the king who sends me'. This was not a matter of self-aggrandizement on the part of the king, but a necessary part of the mainte-nance of the Egyptian world. The king was the representative of mankind. Offering the fruits of the earth to the god enabled the god to reciprocate by offering important things back to the king, such as years of eternity upon the throne, stability in government, strength and success. In this fashion the offer-ings would reconfirm the creation of the world as the Egyptians knew it.

Unlike a modern house of worship, Egyptian temples functioned more like machines engineered to keep the cycle of the universe in motion. This was a technical operation that required a qualified staff and specialized knowledge, thereby excluding the majority of the population, in order to ensure that the crucial task of survival was never impaired. The fact that the people couldn't go in, however, did not mean that the god couldn't come out.

Oracles

The Egyptians put their faith in what at first glance appears to be a baffling number of divine beings. Although not all had temples, there were gods of the physical world, including the earth and sky; gods who embodied abstract ele-ments such as wisdom and love; and gods of specific locations. Throughout history every town and village in Egypt had a local deity. If the town produced a line of pharaohs, the prominence of that local god rose. And so it was in Thebes: beginning with the New Kingdom around 1550 BC, the local god Amun united with the sun god Ra to reign as the king of the gods, just as the princes of Thebes now reigned as kings of Egypt. The cult statue of Amun–Ra resided in the main temple of the state, the magnificent temple at Karnak, the largest temple ever built. Yet, like everyone, he enjoyed getting out now and again to visit the other temples and shrines that filled ancient Thebes.

Left The king, as representative of all mankind, is shown tending to every need of the god, here Ra–Harakhty, to ensure the smooth running of the universe. Temple of Ramesses II (1279–1213 BC), Abu Simbel.

Overleaf The temple of Karnak at Thebes, mansion of the state god Amun–Ra. In the foreground is the sacred lake in which the priests purified themselves.

Above Amun–Ra came out on festival days in his travelling boat, carried on the shoulders of priests. Too sacred and powerful an image to be viewed directly, his statue is hidden by a curtain. From Karnak, the Red Chapel of Hatshepsut (*c.*1479–1457 BC).

For the majority of the population the most direct encounter with this great god of state occurred when his cult statue came out of its sanctuary on the occasion of major festivals. The most important of these was the 'beautiful feast of Opet', when the statues of Amun, his wife Mut and their son Khonsu were escorted in a great and joyous procession down an avenue of sphinxes, 2 miles (3.2 km) long, to the temple of Luxor to relive their honeymoon.

It was an event eagerly anticipated. A riot of activity erupted when they appeared at the door of the temple in their ceremonial travelling barques hoisted on to the shoulders of priests. Soldiers and citizens chanted hymns of praise, others kneeled in adoration and kissed the ground. Musicians,

Nubian dancers and acrobats performed for the gods, priests clapped their hands and women shook rattles. Along the route specially built chapels filled with offerings provided rest stops for the god and the priests, while vendors lined the way supplying food to the masses.

Such occasions also provided the opportunity to ask the god for his judgement, for an oracle. As the procession drew near, a petitioner would dash in front of the barque and beg a consultation. If the god agreed, the procession halted to hear a yes or no question posed to the god: 'Will an unpopular foreman be removed from the job? Will a loved one return from a journey safely? Should I buy this cow? Are these things true?' A step forward meant yes, a step back no.

If the reply was unsatisfactory, it was possible to consult another oracle or even ask the same god again on another occasion. A papyrus in the British Museum records the remarkable case of Petjau-em-di-amun who was picked out by the oracle as a thief responsible for stealing five tunics. Denying the allegation, he took his own case to another oracle which confirmed the verdict. After appealing unsuccessfully two more times, he finally, after a certain amount of physical inducement, confessed his guilt. Following an additional one hundred lashes of the cane, he also promised not to retract his confession. Interestingly, it still remains unclear whether the garments were ever recovered.

The use of oracles was not confined to the ordinary populace. They were also consulted by kings, when divine approval or ratification was required for some extraordinary decision, course of action or series of events. Nothing could have been more extraordinary, in terms of the Egyptians' view of the correct order of things, than the ascension to the throne of Queen Hatshepsut following the death of her husband, Thutmose II, in 1479 BC. Since the legitimate successor, Thutmose III (his son by another queen), was too young to rule in practice, it was arranged that his step-mother Hatshepsut should act as regent during the boy king's minority. Within two years, however, she had assumed the throne herself and been crowned as king, a position she occupied for twenty years. During this period, Thutmose III was officially co-ruler but was very much the subordinate partner. Whether this course of events arose out of personal ambition, as has traditionally been thought, or (more likely) was dictated, at least initially, by some political necessity, is uncertain. But one thing is clear: a female on the throne of Egypt ran contrary to *ma'at*. Horus, the king, had always to be a man.

Sanction for such a drastic departure could only come from Amun–Ra, the king of the gods, and it was here that the device of the divine oracle was invoked. In an inscription carved on her famous 'Red Chapel' at Karnak, the official line was promoted that, during a festival procession in the temple of Luxor, Amun–Ra had prophesied Hatshepsut's ascent to the throne through 'a very great oracle…proclaiming for me the kingship of the Two Lands, Upper and Lower Egypt'. A series of scenes in the same chapel actually depicts Amun–Ra crowning her as king – an iconographic programme designed to confirm her legitimacy. After an initial period when she had been represented as a woman, she is now consistently shown dressed as a king with the body of a man (though interestingly the texts accompanying the scenes persist in some-

Above As the oracle ordained, Hatshepsut, depicted with the body of a man, is crowned king by Amun–Ra, with the goddess Hathor in attendance. The Red Chapel, Karnak.

times referring to her as a female). The special sanction was not, however, to last much beyond her reign. The strength of centuries of convention was too great, and the Hatshepsut episode was so fundamentally at variance with *ma'at* that its record could not be allowed to survive. In due course, her image and cartouches as king were systematically erased or removed from view.

It is unlikely that common folks could approach Amun–Ra during such an important time as the Opet Festival. There were numerous lesser shrines

Right The queen who would be king: statue of Hatshepsut, shown in her more feminine guise from early in her reign, yet still in the full regalia of kingship. From Thebes, Deir el-Bahri.

whose deities could be consulted. Nevertheless, new evidence indicates that the great gods of Thebes came out more often than previously thought. In fact, it now emerges that Amun–Ra left his house every ten days; his destination was a little temple across the river, whose small size belies its importance.

Medinet Habu

In the northeast corner of the huge enclosure surrounding the mortuary temple of Ramesses III, called today Medinet Habu, stands a small temple which was already old when Ramesses was born. Long after his sprawling temple had fallen into disuse, this temple continued to attract the attention of kings who restored it and added to it for over 1500 years. Since 1994 a

Above Peter Dorman records the reliefs in the sanctuary of the 'genuine mound of the west', the home of the primeval gods of creation. Hatshepsut Temple at Medinet Habu.

team of Egyptologists from the University of Chicago's Oriental Institute has been restoring and recording its fine inscriptions and reliefs, and working to unlock the secret of its holiness and its history.

Probably a sacred site since the Middle Kingdom, its earliest surviving structure, the sanctuary, was built by Queen Hatshepsut. As Director Dr Peter Dorman explains:

> 'Like all monuments built by Hatshepsut, the temple exhibits extensive recarving, renovation and repainting. Hatshepsut suffered a posthumous historic revision at the hands of her stepson

Thutmose III, and her names throughout were altered. In other places her figure was entirely effaced and replaced by a fully laden table of offerings. However, through the layers of later paint and plaster, traces of her original figure may be seen to varying degrees, often accompanied by devotional inscriptions.'

The significance of the temple can be determined from several inscriptions. To the Thebans, it marked the spot where the original mound of creation came into being. Proclaimed 'the genuine mound of the west' and called 'the mound of the fathers and mothers', it was the home of the eight primeval gods who, according to one myth, existed before creation and came together to form the creation mound. Called the Ogdoad or 'Group of Eight', they were four pairs of male and female deities representing the primordial elements, one of whom was Amun, the god of hidden power.

But why here? The edge of the desert seems an odd location for a mound

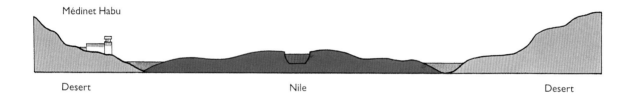

Médinet Habu

Desert   Nile   Desert

Above Cross-section of the Nile Valley at Thebes. Because the flood plain is higher than the low desert which surrounds it, before the Nile overflowed its banks the rise in the water-table was evident in the desert margins. *(After Marc Gabolde)*

Right The side entrance to the genuine mound of the west Hatshepsut Temple at Medinet Habu.

Above The well-preserved remains of some of the houses in the famous village of the royal tomb-builders at Deir el-Medina.

arising out of the water, but new research on the geomorphology of the Nile Valley makes it in fact the natural place. With each inundation the Nile deposited a layer of silt on its banks, and over the millennia this silt has built up to make the flood-plain higher than the low desert which surrounds it. Long before the Nile would have actually flooded its banks each year, a rise in ground water would be noticed in the low desert, particularly where the high plateau of the desert was close by. The water and marsh plants which surrounded the temple before the flood, and probably for a while thereafter, gave it its visible and long-lasting sanctity.

Amun–Ra came to this spot to commune with his brethren every ten days, or once a week according to the Egyptian calendar. This must have provided

ample opportunities for oracles from even this great god. But for day-to-day life, the gods and their power could be found closer to home.

Deir el-Medina

Deir el-Medina, as it is now called, was the home of the craftsmen who built the kings' tombs in the Valley of the Kings (see pages 142–7). Hidden away in the desert on the west bank of Thebes, both to protect the craftsmen's intimate knowledge of the royal tombs and to provide easy access to work, the dry environment has preserved it well.

Today, the outlines of seventy houses can still be counted, arranged to either side of a central path. Housing was provided by the state and was fairly standard in plan, although over the years individual touches were added. Despite certain variations in size and the number of rooms according to the status of the occupant, the typical house consisted of an antechamber or front room and a living-room characterized by a brick couch. Off that were two smaller rooms, possibly a bedroom and a kitchen. Conditions must have been cramped, but with food, water and even laundresses provided by the state, the lives of these skilled and literate craftsmen were probably not uncomfortable. Just beyond the town walls to the west, the craftsmen turned their skills to the construction and decoration of their own tombs, dug into the rock and topped with little pyramid-shaped chapels. When royal tomb-building ceased at the end of the Twentieth Dynasty the workers and their families stayed on, but marauding nomads soon forced them to abandon their village rapidly, never to return, leaving behind personal possessions, and most importantly, written documents. Uniquely preserved, Deir el-Medina, more than any other place in Egypt, has provided a glimpse into the everyday lives of the ancient Egyptians – lives which were touched by deities and demons from the cradle to the grave and beyond.

Birth

The greatest threat to life came at birth. The day of birth was a day of joy, but like the creation of the world itself, it too was fraught with peril. It was a dangerous interface of life and death, when demons conspired to cause harm and deities had to use all their protective powers to prevent it. As was the case until quite recently, the mortality rate at birth for both mother and child was high; a special cemetery at Deir el-Medina for infants and young children contained over a hundred graves.

To prevent the demons who were massing from overrunning the house, on the day of delivery the mother-to-be retired to a special place. Here mother and child would remain in seclusion for about two weeks after the birth, during which time attendants looked after them, adorning the mother, purifying her, making her ready to rejoin the community as a vibrant and healthy new mother. In the more spacious surroundings of rural farmsteads or the

villas of city officials, birth took place in an airy tent-like pavilion hung with vines and festive bowers erected in the garden, but in the crowded village of Deir el-Medina, an enclosed platform in the front room of the house may have served this purpose.

Found in almost half of all the houses at Deir el-Medina, this structure is called a 'birth-box'. It was a rectangular construction of mud brick, partially or fully enclosed, except for an opening on its long side, which was approached by set of steps and was originally plastered and painted with the bizarre images of two powerful deities, the god Bes and the goddess Tawaret.

Bes was a bandy-legged dwarf with the mane and tail of a lion, his tongue protruding over sharp teeth in a gesture meant to intimidate enemies. Bes is actually a convenient name for nearly a dozen different gods, all represented in almost identical ways. He could be Aha, the fighter, or Hayet or Tetetenu, all of whom safeguarded women in labour and young children. His images on headrests, beds, furniture legs and mirrors served to keep demons away throughout the house, and as an amulet worn around the neck his frightening likeness provided constant protection.

Above An *ostracon* shows a healthy new mother with her hair specially dressed, clad in jewels and special sandals, enjoying the festivities as she rejoins the community after her period of seclusion. From Deir el-Medina. New Kingdom, *c.*1300–1100 BC.

Right An enclosed raised platform in the front room of a house at Deir el-Medina may have served as a 'birth box'.

Opposite above Tawaret was a powerful protectress of women in childbirth. From Deir el-Medina. Nineteenth Dynasty.

Opposite below Squatting on bricks in the 'birth box', a woman gives birth with the support of Hathor, the cow-headed goddess of love and fertility. Relief from the Temple of Hathor at Dendara, now in Cairo Museum. Graeco–Roman Period.

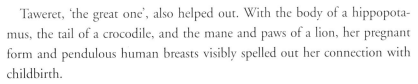

Taweret, 'the great one', also helped out. With the body of a hippopotamus, the tail of a crocodile, and the mane and paws of a lion, her pregnant form and pendulous human breasts visibly spelled out her connection with childbirth.

As the birth drew near, the labouring woman kneeled or squatted on special 'birth bricks' attended by midwives representing the goddess Isis, the epitome of the good mother, and her sister Nephthys. The goddess Hathor, the great cow goddess of love, fertility and birth, was also invited to attend – not surprisingly, she was one of the most important deities in ancient Egypt. From her great udder she nourished the kings of Egypt, and amulets from her sanctuary could prevent prolonged labour. Meanwhile, practitioners of the sacred arts, equipped with magical spells, amulets and medical prescriptions, were called in to perform special incantations and dances, invoking the gods to ensure a safe and speedy delivery.

A short distance from Deir el-Medina, but separated from it by 500 years, was a tomb apparently belonging to one of these practitioners in the late Middle Kingdom. The tomb shaft, found below a much later storeroom of the Ramesseum, the mortuary temple of

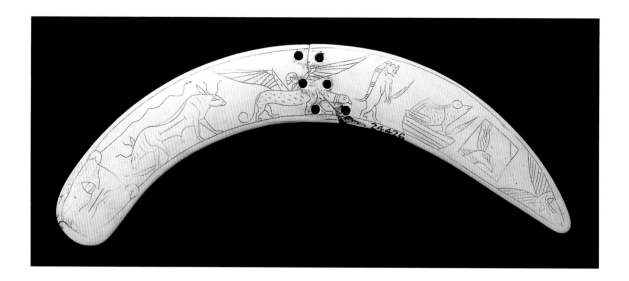

Top Magical knife for protecting mother and child. Hippopotamus ivory, c.1800 BC.

Above A pair of ivory clappers for frightening away demons. From Lahun in the Fayum, c.1900–1750 BC.

Right By donning this (much used) painted-canvas mask, an attendant channelled the power of Beset during the delivery rites for mother and child. From Lahun in the Fayum, c.1900–1750 BC.

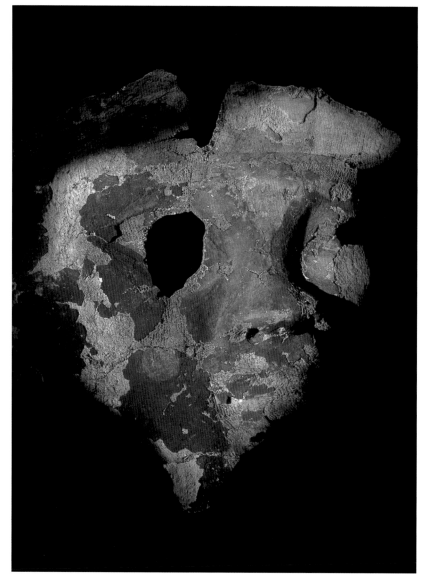

Ramesses II, led to a much disturbed burial chamber, but within it was a wooden box containing his remarkable kit.

The box contained twenty-three fragmentary papyrus rolls, a bundle of reed pens, and a unique collection of amulets, figurines and implements that were used to protect mother and child. There were ivory clappers in the shape of hands to frighten away evil spirits, female figurines to ensure the mother's safety and continued fertility, and a set of four magical wands or apotropaic (i.e. evil-averting) knives, made from hippopotamus tusk. These were used to draw a circle of protection around the mother-to-be and later, the sleeping child. Too powerful to be placed in the grave intact, they were broken in antiquity, but show evidence of extensive use. Inscribed on such wands are figures representing a mixture of malevolent and protective elements. To be effective, the child was identified with the young sun god Ra, who battles the forces of chaos. As Ra emerges victorious over his enemies to achieve his own birth each morning, so too, through the use of such a wand, would the child. At one tip is a canine head, a sign denoting the ancient Egyptian word for 'power'. The severed head of a donkey represents chaos defeated with the help of the gods: the frog goddess Heket, another goddess of childbirth; Tawaret, who wields her knife; and other composite deities.

Among the most extraordinary objects found in this kit were a wooden statuette of Beset, the female counterpart of Bes, holding a bronze snake staff in each hand just as she is often depicted on the knives, and an actual snake staff of bronze originally discovered entangled in a mass of hair to strengthen its personal effect. Although not found among the equipment in this box, in another contemporary but less extensive kit unearthed in the Fayum, a life-size and much-used mask transformed a priestess or attendant into a conduit for the divine and protective strength of Beset, just like the statuette, to empower the spells written on the papyrus rolls.

There was a spell 'to release a child from the belly of its mother', 'to make protection for a child on the day of its birth', tests to determine whether the baby would live or die, and other incantations to restore health to the mother herself.

Left This rare statuette of Beset acted as a conduit for her protective power. From Thebes, magician's kit, c.1850–1750 BC.

But the Ramesseum practitioner dealt not just with birth. Other papyri in his box contained spells and prescriptions for treating muscular pain and diseases of the eye, as well as texts for funerary rituals and hymns in praise of the king. A 'knower of things', as the Egyptians called him, he was no itinerant magician. The decoration on the lid of his box identifies him as a *hery seshta*, 'one who is over the secrets', a title of a specific priestly rank within the state temples. And the magic that he used to assist in childbirth was no different from the magic that made the gods awake in their temples. Magic, or *heka*, was what made creation possible and carried none of the unsavoury connota-

Below The embodiments of perception, Sia, and magic, Heka, accompany the god Ra and help pilot his boat through the dangerous landscape of the underworld. Tomb of Seti I, Valley of the Kings.

tions it has acquired in modern times. Magic was what kept the universe going. Personified as a god, in the company of Sia (wisdom or perception) and Hu (divine pronouncement), Heka helped pilot the boat of the sun god Ra through the treacherous terrain of the underworld to achieve rebirth each morning.

Magic and Myth

Egyptian magic worked in a very specific way. First the problem had to be perceived and then the power or *heka* of the gods invoked. The Egyptians

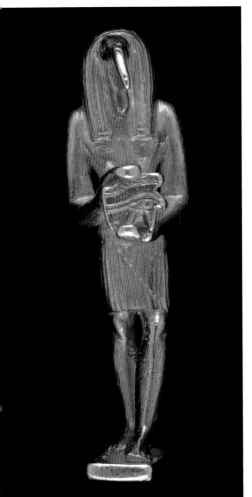

maintained a belief that the perils of this life could be overcome through indentifying with the gods who overcame their own hardships. By far the most popular for assuaging personal afflictions were Osiris, Isis and Horus. The epic saga of their ordeals would form the basis of many Egyptian beliefs and practices.

When Ra wearied of ruling the earth, he retired to heaven, leaving his successors to reign in their turn. When Osiris attained kingship of the earth with his sister and wife Isis at his side, a golden age ensued, but it was not destined to last long. His brother Seth, jealous of his popularity, savagely murdered him, introducing death to the world. Isis revived him long enough to conceive a son, but despite her great powers, Osiris became the god of the dead.

Now alone in the world, Isis went into hiding in the marshes of the Delta, where she bore and raised her son, Horus, to avenge the murder of his father and reclaim his rightful throne. The marshes were full of the emissaries of Seth – venomous snakes and scorpions, and deadly disease – but Isis, a dedicated mother, used all of her power to protect Horus by learning their names. To know something's name was to understand its essence, and thus to have control over it. Isis's exemplary care for her child, combined with her magical skills, made her the ideal deity to be invoked for cures and protection.

Episodes in the intricate myth of Isis and Horus became the active force behind many spells and amulets. Small stone stelae which became popular around 700 BC show Horus as a child standing on crocodiles and holding snakes, scorpions and other dangerous animals in each hand as their master, now made immune from their poison by the power of Isis. These were powerful amulets and the Egyptians believed that water poured on them was endowed with healing powers over bites and stings for those who drank it.

One of the most popular and distinctive Egyptian amulets was the Wedjat or eye of Horus. The universal symbol of healing and wholeness, it represents the eye that Horus lost during the battle with Seth to avenge his father's murder. Luckily, the ibis-headed god of

Left Using his great wisdom, the ibis-headed god Thoth was able to restore the eye that Horus lost while avenging his father's death. Called a Wedjat, the eye became a universal symbol of health and wholeness as well as piety and self-sacrifice. Gold amuletic figurine, c.1000 BC.

Above left The hardships Isis endured to raise her son Horus made her the ideal mother whose immense curative powers were frequently invoked. Edfu Temple. Graeco-Roman Period.

175

wisdom, Thoth, was able to retrieve the eye, and as the moon waxed he slowly put it back together and restored it to health. In the same way, the Egyptians believed that injuries incurred without blame could be cured with the wisdom and the power of the divine.

Based on years of observation and experience, the Egyptians had also developed a body of medical knowledge, which they did not distinguish clearly from magic. Medical care followed the same three basic steps that made magic effective: observation of the patient's condition; diagnosis of the problem; and active treatment which could take the form of a prescription of herbs, a medical procedure or an incantation or spell.

When illness struck, the Egyptians called in a priest or physician, often one and the same, who consulted medical papyri, his reference manuals for treatment. One literate inhabitant of Deir el-Medina named Kenherk-hopeshef, however, had his own set of texts in his exceptionally extensive library and preferred to take care of himself. One of his self-treatments survives. Troubled by a particularly nasty headache, he wrote the following spell on a piece of papyrus to expel the demon responsible for it:

'Turn back Sahekek, demon which came forth from heaven and earth, whose eyes are in his head and whose tongue is in his buttocks. He feeds on excrement…he lives on dung…I know the name of your mother, I know the name of your father. I am the two hands of the headrest. Stay away from me.'

Complete with the instructions that the word be recited four times over arrows made of flax stems, the wear patterns on the papyrus suggest that it was then folded up and placed as a pillow on his headrest, which also survives.

Below The demon Sahekek is depicted as a nude child in the pose of someone with a very bad headache. He was said to originate from the far ends of Nubia. Ostracon, New Kingdom, thirteenth century BC.
(After Gardiner and Černy)

Right Headrest of the scribe Kenherkhopshef, decorated with figures of various protective deities, among them the god Bes, who warded off evil demons from the headrest's owner as he slept. Limestone. Nineteenth Dynasty, thirteenth century BC.

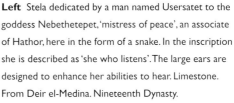

Left Stela dedicated by a man named Usersatet to the goddess Nebethetepet, 'mistress of peace', an associate of Hathor, here in the form of a snake. In the inscription she is described as 'she who listens'. The large ears are designed to enhance her abilities to hear. Limestone. From Deir el-Medina. Nineteenth Dynasty.

Below Shrine, probably for holding a stela or ancestor-bust, in the main room of a house at Deir el-Medina.

Above Stela, probably from a household shrine, showing the 'Servant in the Place of Truth Pen-men-nefer' offering to the god Ptah, a patron of craftsmen. Painted limestone. From Deir el-Medina. Nineteenth Dynasty.

The cause of an illness or adversity was not always clear. Perhaps the gods had been offended, or demons let loose. To keep the balance in their life, like the balance of the universe, the craftsmen at Deir el-Medina worshipped the gods. Around the exterior of the village were small chapels to gods and goddesses, places for group ritual observances with the workmen themselves serving as priests. But in the main living room of each house there was also a shrine, with a stela either set into the wall or placed on a pedestal, to the gods of their choice. Especially favoured, for obvious reasons, were Ptah, the patron god of craftsmen; Thoth, the god of writing; and the deified king Amenhotep I and his wife, founders of the village. The gods could be vengeful but forgiving. One stela reads, 'I am a man who swore falsely by Ptah and he made me go blind…He caused me to be like a dog in the streets, I being a man who had sinned against his Lord. Righteous was Ptah toward me, when he taught me a lesson. Be merciful to me, look on me in mercy!'

They also worshipped a goddess of more local significance. Poisonous snakes were common in their desert home, and one way to protect themselves from this danger was to venerate snake-deities. One of them, Meretseger, 'She who loves Silence', was to become a popular patron of the village, for in the Egyptians' dualistic view of the world, that which worked against you could also be cajoled to work on your behalf. Snakes made of clay placed at the doors of the house were also popular means for providing protection from deadly snakes as well as frightening nightmares.

This is an idea which has a long history; even the humble tombs of the people who built the pyramids at Giza invoked the destructive powers of dangerous creatures to protect them from intruders. On a false door recently discovered in this cemetery, its owner threatens: 'If anyone will disturb my tomb he will be eaten by a crocodile, a hippopotamus and a lion.' His wife threatens the same but adds snakes and scorpions to the list.

Ancestors

The dead could also be powerful allies. Because the afterlife was the realm of both deities and demons, the villagers at Deir el-Medina set up household shrines in their living-rooms where offerings were made to the busts and stelae portraying their ancestors. Now equipped with divine powers themselves, the dead had direct access to the gods and could intervene on behalf of their respectful family.

To communicate with them the Egyptians wrote 'letters to the dead' on papyrus and on the interior of bowls once heaped with offerings. These messages covered everything from legal problems to domestic strife and even chatty greetings. Couched in the form of a reciprocal agreement, one son implored his deceased father to exert some influence on the outcome of a court case, supply him with a healthy new son, and punish some maidservants, possibly also deceased, who were currently annoying his wife. And while he was at it, another healthy child for his sister would also be welcome.

But not all ancestors were willing to intercede. Those who may have been slighted in death, or bore a grudge in life, could come back to haunt the family. In 1200 BC a man stalked by misfortune thought it might be the doing of his dead wife. To reproach her he wrote a letter reminding her that he'd been a caring husband, and it really wasn't his fault that he was away on business when she died. Whether she was guilty or not remains unknown. Identifying malevolent spirits and pernicious demons by name was a tricky business at best, but on the final journey into the afterlife, there was no room for error.

Below So-called 'ancestor-bust', the focus of a domestic cult at Deir el-Medina. The bust represented a recently deceased family member, who had attained a blessed state in the afterlife and was therefore well placed to act as a mediator between the family and the gods. Painted limestone. Nineteenth Dynasty.

The Dead

Above Painted scene in the burial chamber of the 'Servant in the Place of Truth, Pashedu' at Deir el-Medina. The large seated figure is the god of the dead Osiris, his green skin symbolic of new growth and rebirth. The tomb-owner is shown behind him, as a small figure kneeling in adoration. Nineteenth Dynasty.

Overleaf The deceased and his wife pause before the gates of the underworld, which are guarded by an array of demons. Passage is possible only through knowledge and recitation of their secret names: 'I know you, I know your name….' Book of the Dead of Ani. Nineteenth Dynasty.

To become as one with Osiris, the god of the dead, and travel in the solar boat with Ra, entailed a dangerous journey. There were obstacles and traps to be negotiated, monsters and demons to be avoided or confronted. Doom and eternal damnation awaited the ignorant or unwary. For these reasons, the Egyptians developed a compilation of spells called the 'Spells for Going Forth by Day', now known as the 'Book of the Dead'.

A virtual guidebook to the afterlife, it was written on papyrus or linen and placed with the body to help the deceased recognize the inhabitants and landscape of the underworld so as to be able to pass through it unharmed. It was potent magic. Success was guaranteed: 'Whoever knows these texts is one who on the day of resurrection in the other world arises and enters in.'

The Book of the Dead contained spells for fetching a ferry-boat in the sky; for passing by the dangerous coils of Apep; for being transformed into any shape one might wish to take; and for guiding one through the proper responses in the hall of judgement.

But in order to attain bliss in the Egyptian version of heaven, the 'Field of

Left Head of a demon-figure, in the form of a hippopotamus with teeth bared, one of the inhabitants of the underworld and here an embodiment of disorder and danger. Wood coated with black resin. Probably from Thebes, Valley of the Kings, New Kingdom, c.1479–1108 BC.

Reeds', one had first to get past the demons who guarded its many gates. Each gate was a danger, a challenge, an obstacle, guarded by demons who would devour the souls of those destined for damnation. The key to disarming them was again to know their secret names: there was 'the barker', 'the raging one with hippopotamus face', 'he who devours filth from his hind parts', 'the unapproachable', 'the bloodsucker' and 'he whose eyes spew fire'. The deceased would approach each one and proclaim, 'I know you and I know your name.'

Dreams

The deceased were not the only visitors to the realm of the dead. At night sleepers could, through their dreams, enter the world beyond and commune with the gods. A dream was believed to be a revelation of truth, an omen of good or bad, though its meaning was not always clear. To help, people

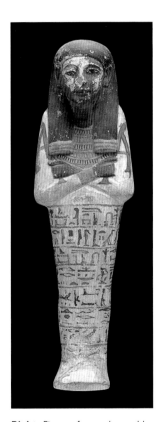

Below Shabti-figure of the scribe Kenherkhopshef, one of the great 'personalities' of the community of royal workmen. From his tomb, as yet unidentified, at Deir el-Medina. Thirteenth century BC.

Right Figure of an underworld demon, facing frontwards, pulling at his beard, his legs curiously in profile. The unconventional pose and action evoke his chaotic nature. Wood coated with resin. From Thebes, Valley of the Kings. Twentieth Dynasty, c.1108 BC.

Above Section of the 'Book of Dreams', a unique composition, once part of the library of Kenherkhopshef. It contains a list of dreams, each one identified as 'good' or 'bad', with an explanation of their true meaning. Written in the hieratic script on papyrus. From Deir el-Medina. Nineteenth Dynasty, thirteenth century BC.

known to be gifted at interpreting dreams could be consulted, whether priests attached to temples or a local 'wise person' who had built up a reputation in the field. The scribe Kenherkhopshef of Deir el-Medina owned his own 'Book of Dreams', the only work of its kind to have survived to modern times, though one imagines there must have been others like it. It is a handy compendium listing many different types of dream, in each case with an explanation of how it was to be interpreted, though it must be said that some are rather vague and hedging, very much like modern horoscopes:

> 'If a man sees himself in a dream dead –
>   Good. It means a long life.'
> 'If a man sees himself in a dream, his bed catching fire –
>   Bad. It means driving away his wife.'
> 'If a man sees himself in a dream drinking warm beer –
>   Bad. It means suffering.'
> 'If a man sees himself in a dream looking out of a window –
>   Good. It means the gods hear his cries.'
> 'If a man sees himself falling off a wall –
>   Good. It means the issuing of a favourable edict.'
> 'If a man sees himself looking after monkeys –
>   Bad. It means change awaits.'

Kenherkhopshef himself was one of the great characters of Deir el-Medina, much mentioned in the records and not always to his credit. An assertive and self-confident man, he held the influential position of scribe of the workforce for over forty years during the Nineteenth Dynasty. Respected by his seniors, he was very unpopular with his subordinates for being autocratic, showing little appreciation of their work, and for abusing his position of power. Often absent from work, he was in the habit of removing men from their official duties in the royal tomb to carry out his own private commissions. He was twice indicted for bribery, though he got off on both occasions.

Though clearly a rogue, Kenherkhopshef appears nevertheless to have been an erudite man, and documents of his suggest that he had an interest in literature and history. We have no idea when or how he acquired the dream-book but it would have been an enormously valuable possession – to be used, no doubt, by himself and his family but also perhaps more widely. Given the importance attached to dreams and to their correct interpretation, possession of the compendium would surely have provided a commercial opportunity which someone of Kenherkhopshef's character would not have been slow to seize. On application, and for suitable recompense, he might well have been willing to make its contents available to the community at large.

When already well into his fifties, Kenherkhopshef married a girl, Naunakhte, over forty years his junior (she may have been as young as twelve at the time). The marriage was childless, and after his death most of his property, including the dream-book, passed to his wife. In due course, the book became the property of one of her sons by a second marriage, now a prized family heirloom, to which he proudly added his name.

Above John Ray at work transcribing a group of *ostraca* bearing texts in the demotic script, similar to those in the archive of Hor.

In the following centuries, dreams, as communicative and revelatory experiences, came to play an increasingly prominent role, at all levels of society, in the practice of people's religion and in the ordering of their lives. By the Ptolemaic period (305–30 BC), when Egypt was under Greek rule, dreams and their interpretation had become a lucrative industry, and dreaming a professional calling. People regularly paid specialists to interpret their dreams or even to dream for them.

One of the most successful of these dreamers was a priest called Hor, who worked at the great cemetery of sacred animals at Saqqara, near the ancient city of Memphis, during the reign of King Ptolemy VI (180–145 BC). We know a great deal about Hor, as he left behind an archive of documents, a collection of about sixty-five texts written in ink on *ostraca* (pot-sherds) in Egyptian demotic, the script (a cursive form of hieroglyphs) developed for

Above View of the inside of one of the ibis galleries at Saqqara. Dr Nick Fieller, an archaeological statistician, examines one of the pottery jars containing an ibis mummy.

day-to-day use during the later periods of Egyptian history. Originally stored in a small chapel attached to the burial catacombs of the sacred ibis, the archive was discovered by an expedition of the Egypt Exploration Society in the 1960s and early 1970s. It has since formed a major focus of study for John Ray of the University of Cambridge, one of the world's leading authorities on demotic texts. Ray's work has shown that the documents record various events in Hor's career over a period of about twenty years up to 147 BC.

Hor began his career in the service of the goddess Isis in his home town near Sebennytos in the Delta. We learn from one of the texts that his life changed dramatically one night, in October 166 BC, when he had two dreams. One of them was humorous, the other more serious. In the first he dreams that he's walking up the great avenue between the temples where he works. It is night and he's surrounded by tombs. In the middle of the avenue

he is confronted by a ghost, who throws him into a panic by asking, 'Have you brought the food for 60,000 ibises?' In the other dream, he is working in a labour-gang, unpleasant work for a man of his standing. The foreman of the gang comes up to him and pays money for him to be released. Hor goes back to his home town, but the people of the labour-gang chase after him. They catch up with him and won't let him go. Suddenly the foreman appears and says, 'I am not a foreman, I am a god. Do not worship anybody except me.' And Hor replies, 'I will never do that again.' The god in question was Thoth. These dreams marked a turning-point in Hor's life. As a result of them, he moved from the Delta to Saqqara to serve the cult of the ibis god, Thoth, in the sacred animal necropolis.

Hor would have found no difficulty in making the move, as he was already a celebrated sage. Two years previously he had made a telling intervention at a time of national crisis. In 168 BC Egypt had been invaded by the Seleucid king of Syria, Antiochos Epiphanes. At the moment of maximum danger, Hor, who was attached at the time to the Egyptian army, had an important dream. Hor was granted an audience with Ptolemy himself, and assured him that all would be well, as indeed it turned out to be. His reputation was made.

The Sacred Animal Necropolis

The sacred animal necropolis at Saqqara is a huge burial complex, in the form of a series of underground galleries, containing vast quantities of mummified animals – baboons, cats, cows, dogs, hawks and ibises, each animal identified with a certain god, who was the subject of a cult. During the late first millennium BC, it was a great place of pilgrimage, with temples and shrines to which people came from far afield to make offerings and to commune with the gods, principally by paying for an animal or bird of their choice to be mummified and deposited, often enclosed in a pot, in one of the galleries. For a price, Hor was available for consultation by such pilgrims. Seeking divine guidance on matters of personal concern, perhaps a medical problem or a course of future action, they would pay Hor to have the god Thoth appear in one of his dreams and impart advice to them, a practice known as incubation. Hor would request the god to appear by reciting a special 'dream-invocation'. The god was not always prompt. Sometimes Hor had to wait several days.

John Ray regards such practices as serving an important social need, akin in some ways to modern-day therapy. The sacred animal cults belonged to the world of 'the ordinary guy', for whom the great temples remained inaccessible: 'Here you had something much more human, much more personal. Here you had gods who were interested in the little man, who could actually help him to sort out his problems.'

The priests, however, did not always do right by their customers. In addition to the accounts of his dreams, Hor's archive also contains records of an administrative nature, which shed fascinating and sometimes unfavourable light on the management and day-to-day practice of the animal cults. One particularly interesting document records an investigation into a corruption scandal, which centred on financial irregularities and the swindling of pilgrims, the latter process apparently involving the depositing of empty jars

Above The central shrine in the temple complex of the sacred animal necropolis at Saqqara, where Hor worked as a priest and dreamer. Along the cliff-face on either side are the entrances to a number of subterranean galleries where the sacred animals were buried in their millions.

rather than ones filled with bird mummies, for which the pilgrims had paid. A commission of inspectors was formed, and eventually six men, 'servants of the ibis' and 'servants of the hawk', were arraigned and imprisoned. As a result, the commission ordered a complete review of the arrangements for the burial of the sacred birds.

That such skulduggery was taking place has been borne out by modern examination of the bird mummies, recently carried out by Dr Paul Nicholson of the University of Cardiff, who has been investigating anew the galleries and their contents for the Egypt Exploration Society. Among other things, he has been carefully tracing the processes involved in the nurturing and preparation of the birds before their final deposition. It is known that the ibises were bred on a nearby lake, and examination of their remains has shown that in life they were well fed and looked after. When required by a pilgrim, they were killed (probably by breaking of their necks) and cursorily mummified, sometimes being desiccated and dipped into bitumen, before being wrapped in linen bandages and then placed in a pottery container, closed with a saucer-shaped lid. They were finally taken to the galleries, where they were stacked in various side chambers. This was not done on a one-by-one basis. One of Hor's documents indicates that a mass burial was performed once a year, when with appropriate ceremony the galleries would be specially opened for the occasion and then resealed. The ibis cult must have been one of the most popular. It is estimated that the galleries once held over four million ibises.

Nicholson and his team have found that, in general, the ibis mummies do indeed contain ibises. The same does not, however, hold true for the hawk mummies. A good proportion of these turn out to be 'pseudo-hawk mummies', shaped on the outside to look like hawks, but inside containing neither a hawk nor any kind of whole bird. He describes these pseudo-mummies as being varied in content:

> 'Some include parts of birds of prey, the bulk being made up of packing, sticks, or other bones; others contain large rodents, such as the Egyptian giant musk shrew. Ibis bones were sometimes used to supplement or substitute for the birds of prey, and in one instance ibis mandibles were used longitudinally to make a kind of frame around which linen was wrapped to form the mummy shape.'

Above left Paul Nicholson examining the mummy of an ibis. Preparation of the bird for burial involved dipping the body into some black resinous matter before wrapping it in linen. It was then placed in a pottery jar for final deposition in the galleries.

Left Bird mummy, skilfully wrapped and shaped to look like a hawk. Some specimens, when unwrapped, have turned out to be 'pseudo-mummies', containing little or no hawk remains. Late Period, after 600 BC.

Nicholson believes the explanation for this rampant cheating in the case of the hawk mummies lies in the fact that, unlike ibises, birds of prey are very difficult to breed in captivity and would, therefore, have needed to be trapped for use in the cults. The inevitably limited supply of such birds meant that a single specimen might be shared out among several mummies, while sometimes a mummy had to be completely faked.

One animal cult at Saqqara stands out from the rest in terms of both its importance and its meaning. This was the cult of the dead Apis bull, the origins of which probably go back to the earliest dynasties. Regarded while alive as a manifestation of Ptah, the creator god of Memphis, there was only one Apis at any one time, selected on the basis of colouring and certain other markings. The bull had to be black with, among other features, a white diamond-shaped mark on its forehead. He lived in pampered luxury in a special stall in the precincts of the great temple of Ptah in Memphis, served by a special cadre of priests, solicitous to his every need. He was the source of oracles and prophecies, certain aspects of his behaviour being regarded as significant for these purposes, and, like the king, he had a special window, from which he made public appearances.

The death of the Apis was an occasion for great national mourning, the corpse being afforded many of the rituals appropriate to the passing of the king. It was fully embalmed and purified in a special complex, some of whose structures have been identified close to the temple of Ptah. Among the most prominent features are a number of beautiful stone beds decorated with leonine heads and legs and with spouts and containers at one end for the discharge and containment respectively of liquid. These are often thought to have been the actual platforms on which the bulls were eviscerated and embalmed, but recently Michael Jones, an archaeologist working for the American Research Center in Egypt, has come to a different conclusion. He believes that, because the platforms are made of alabaster (calcite), a stone associated in the Egyptian mind with cleanliness and purity, the actual 'dirty work' of mummification must have been carried out elsewhere. For him, these magnificent beds would have been used only for the ritual purification of the mummies:

'the priests would have brought the completed mummy on a wooden carrying frame, placed it on top of the bed and poured libations of water over it…The water would have flowed out through the spout at the end and collected in the basin, whose enormous size gives some idea of the quantity of liquid needed for the purification process. The water could not be allowed to run anywhere. Having flowed over the body of the god, it was powerfully charged.'

Below Bronze figure of an Apis bull, with the characteristic mark on its forehead. Late Period, after 600 BC.

Above Stone platform used for the purification of the Apis-bull mummies. The vessel to hold the discharged liquid is still in place. Memphis. Late Period, after 600 BC.

Duly embalmed, the bull's body was transported along the processional way which linked Memphis and Saqqara for burial in a large stone sarcophagus, set in a vast underground catacomb specially reserved for the Apis bulls and known as the Serapeum. Just like humans, they were buried with various accoutrements, among them little *shabti*-figures, some with bull's heads to serve them in the afterlife. In death the Apis was identified with the god of the dead Osiris, to become the unity known as Osorapis.

The growth of the sacred animal cults represents an extraordinary religious development, the causes of which have been much debated. John Ray and others believe that, since it gained strength during a period of increasing political decline, towards the end of pharaonic history, and reached its zenith during a period of foreign occupation, the development may perhaps be best explained as the response of a native culture – dominated by foreigners and threatened with loss of identity – seeking to emphasize what was fundamentally and peculiarly its own. The Egyptians might have lost their independence and their position in the world, but they still had their own culture, their own special demons and deities. This made them different. This made them Egyptian.

The Nobility and Gentry, Visiters and Inhabitants of BATH and its Vicinity, are respectfully informed, that

TWO EGYPTIAN
MUMMIES,
A MALE AND FEMALE,

In the highest State of Preservation, *with various other Relics,*

BROUGHT TO THIS COUNTRY BY

Mr. BELZONI,

The celebrated Traveller, are now open for Exhibition at

10, New Bond-Street.

The MUMMIES are of the first Class: the Inspection of them it is presumed must be highly satisfactory to every Person, as exhibiting two distinct Specimens; the Bandages of the Male having been entirely removed from the Body, which is perfect, while the mode of applying them is beautifully illustrated in the Envelope of the Female.

The CASES are covered with Hieroglyphics, enriched with Ornaments most elaborately executed; the Interiors containing the Histories of the Lives of their very ancient Occupiers, in Egyptian Characters, as fresh as when inscribed by the Hand of the Artist, after a Lapse of probably

THREE THOUSAND YEARS.

" Perchance that very Hand, now pinioned flat,
" Has hob-a-nob'd with Pharaoh glass to glass,
" Or dropp'd a halfpenny in Homer's hat,
" Or doff'd its own to let Queen Dido pass,
" Or held, by Solomon's own invitation,
" A torch at the great Temple's dedication."

AMONG THE OTHER RELICS WILL BE FOUND

A MUMMY OF THE IBIS,
THE SACRED BIRD OF EGYPT;

An Urn with Intestines from Elei; an Inscription on the far-famed Paper of Egypt (the Papyrus); a massive Fragment of Granite with Hieroglyphics from Memphis; a variety of Idols in Stone, Clay, and Wood, from the Tombs of the Kings in the Valley of Beban-el-Malook, and the Ruins at Carnac; Urns, Vessels of Libation, Bronzes, Coins, &c. &c.

N.B. A few EGYPTIAN and other ANTIQUITIES for SALE.

Admittance, One Shilling each.

☞ PURCHASERS WILL BE ALWAYS RE-ADMISSIBLE.

A DESCRIPTIVE ACCOUNT of this COLLECTION will be published in a few Days.

WOOD and CO. Printers of the Bath and Cheltenham Gazette, UNION-STREET, BATH.

1842

othing about the ancient Egyptians has captured the modern imagination more than their preserved remains: mummies. There is something indescribably fascinating about peering into the face of a person who departed this earth several thousand years ago, and few things make the ancient Egyptians come more to life than their corporeal remains in death. This is not only because of the pathos their remnants may evoke, but because modern scientific examination of them is providing exciting new insights into the conditions under which they lived.

Mummification evolved from the concept of preserving the body as a receptacle for the vital life force which survived death. To the ancient Egyptians, the preservation of the body by desiccating with salts, anointing with resins and wrapping in bandages was an important factor in attaining and maintaining an afterlife. To modern-day Egyptologists and scientists, it is a godsend of preserved material.

Although we are all familiar with mummies, they have been an underestimated and ill-used resource. From medieval times well into the nineteenth century untold numbers of mummies were ground up for medicine. Their tissues, blackened by embalming oils, were believed to have the same medicinal powers as *mumia*, or bitumen, better known as asphalt, which was then found only in limited quantities in the Near East. The word 'mummy' comes from this use of the ancient bodies, but it now describes the body itself that has been either naturally or artificially preserved.

In the early nineteenth century, inspired by the discoveries that accompanied Napoleon's Nile campaign of 1798–1801, Egyptomania – the passion for anything Egyptian – swept Europe, and mummies became big business in a different way. To stock museums and the 'curiosity cabinets' of the well-to-do, a lucrative trade in Egyptian artefacts, including mummies, arose. The unwrapping of a mummy acquired on a young gentleman's tour of Egypt was an excuse for a fashionable soirée. Public exhibitions of mummies became popular sensations, and with the growth of tourism to Egypt, the desert hills were scoured for mummies to sell as *antikas*. There were plenty to find. The Italian adventurer Giovanni Belzoni, who made his fortune in the antiquities trade excavating monuments and tombs, recounts his exploration in the Theban hills: 'Every step I took I crushed a mummy in some place or another. Thus I proceeded from one cave to another, all full of mummies piled in various ways, some standing, some lying and some on their heads.'

Such discoveries led to a glut of mummies, and soon a more practical use

Above Following the opening up of Egypt after the Napoleanic expedition (1798–1801), mummies were exported in great numbers as 'curiosities'. Only later was their scientific significance appreciated. (*After Augustus Granville*)

was found for them. When faced with a severe shortage of rags for paper-making due to the American Civil War, an enterprising paper manufacturer in Maine named Isaac Augustus Stanwood had the idea of importing mummies from Egypt for their linen wrappings. Arriving by the boatload, the mummies were unwrapped and their bandages reduced to pulp in vats. The resins and oils used in the embalming process had stained the cloth, resulting in a heavy brown paper which proved to be especially suitable for meat wrapping. Stanwood was able to buy and ship tonnes of mummies for three cents a pound – less than half the price of buying rags at home. Reportedly covered in almost 30 lb of linen each, an entire mummy cost about a dollar. Stanwood would have continued this lucrative arrangement, had not a local outbreak of cholera, which included among its victims employees of Stanwood's paper-mill, brought it to a halt. Although the mummies were blamed for the epidemic, the tradition of brown paper in meat markets can still be found today.

But perhaps the most ignominious use of Egypt's legacy was as firewood. Mark Twain, in his humorous travel tale *The Innocents Abroad*, recounts seeing a railway engineer who, while stoking the furnace of a steam train with the shrivelled remains of the ancient Egyptians, exclaimed, 'Damn these plebeians, they don't burn worth a cent! Pass out a king!'

After surviving thousands of years, just how many mummies were lost during this episode is impossible to determine. Luckily, by the early nineteenth century the scientific potential of mummies had begun to be realized. In 1825 the young British physician Augustus Granville performed a scientific autopsy on the mummy of a woman named Irtyersenu, and published the results. He was able to determine that the woman had died in her fifties, had borne children, had a disease of the scalp and an ovarian cyst, but due to his careful storage of her remnants we now know that she probably died of pneumonia. It soon became clear how much could be learned from mummies.

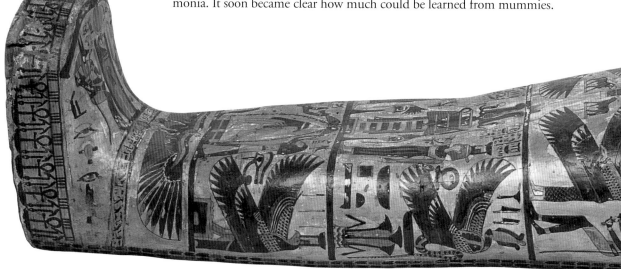

Radiography

The invention of radiography (X-rays) in the 1890s marked an important new stage in the investigation of mummies. Unwrapping a mummy, even in a laboratory for the best scientific reasons, is an act of destruction. Henceforth, mummies could be examined non-invasively and their integrity preserved. However, while the potential of the technique was quickly realized, its application to mummies remained sporadic until the 1960s, since when its use has become standard. Mummies in museum collections are still unwrapped, but generally these days only in appropriate cases, for example when the condition of a mummy is known to be deteriorating.

Radiography allows an enormous amount of useful information to be gathered non-destructively. It reveals whether there is actually a body inside the wrappings, its sex, whether it suffered from injuries or certain diseases, and the likely age at death. It can also tell us a great deal about the techniques of mummification, but it has always had one major limitation. In a conventional X-ray plate, all of the internal features are superimposed, sometimes making their interpretation very difficult. Fortunately, in recent years a new enhanced form of radiography, making use of advanced computer technology, has been developed, which has no such limitation. This is the technique of computerized axial tomography, in short 'CAT-scanning' or 'CT-scanning'.

The value of CT-scanning in the examination of Egyptian mummies has been demonstrated by a number of collaborative projects carried out between the British Museum and various medical research departments in London hospitals. One of these projects involved the mummy of a 'chantress of Amun' who lived during the Twenty-second Dynasty (about 900 BC) named Tjentmutengebtiu. The mummy was examined in 1991–2 at St Thomas's Hospital, using a programme developed by Dr Stephen Hughes, Senior Medical Physicist. The Museum was represented by Dr John Taylor.

Below The intricately decorated case enveloping the mummy of Tjentmutengebtiu is made of cartonnage, a delicate material consisting of linen or papyrus stiffened with plaster. Direct examination of the mummy would entail destruction of the case. Twenty-second Dynasty, c. 900 BC.

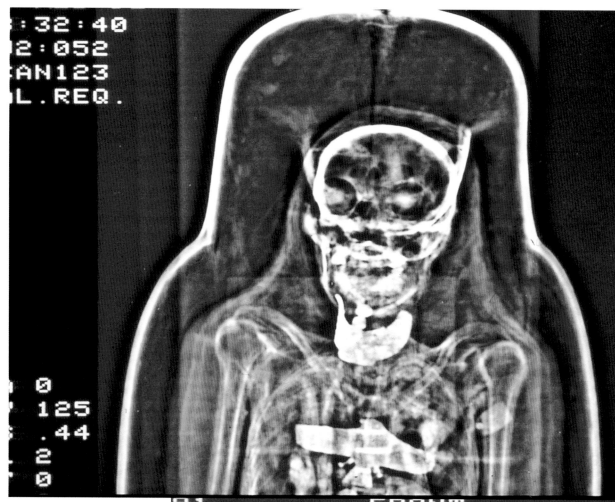

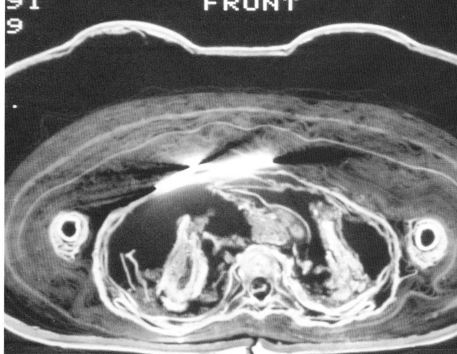

Above Scientists have been able to look through the mummy case of Tjentmutengebtiu and examine her body with the use of sensitive CT-scans. In addition to her bones and wrappings, the scans reveal her false eyes, an ornament around her neck and a large falcon amulet on her chest.

Right A CT-scan section through her chest shows the heart inside the body cavity and, to either side, the wrapped bundles of the individually mummified internal organs, which were returned to the body. The metal falcon amulet resting on her chest appears as a patch of intense white.

A CT-procedure involves the radiographic scanning of the body, from top to bottom, in a series of lateral slices or cross-sections. The data from the scan is stored in a digital format for use in a computer to create a three-dimensional image of any part of the body which can be viewed clearly in isolation and rotated on screen to be seen from any angle. Because the scanner's beams are highly sensitive to the differing densities of structures and objects within the body, bone, soft tissue such as skin or internal organs, embalming substances and other funerary objects such as amulets or papyrus, even wax figurines, can be easily distinguished. As so strikingly shown in the case of Tjentmutengebtiu, the computer can be used to reconstruct on screen a three-dimensional image of the lady's head, showing the linen packing in her cranium and the amount of soft tissue still preserved.

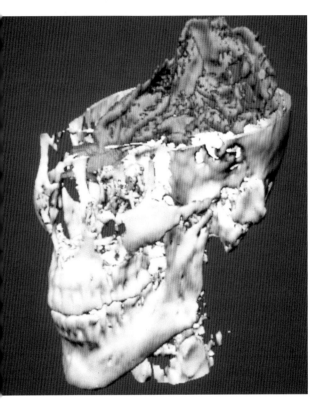

Above The data from the CT-scans can be used to generate a three-dimensional model of any part of the body. Here a cut-away view of Tjentmutengebtiu's skull reveals the linen packing (coloured purple) inserted into her cranium after the removal of the brain.

From conventional X-rays, previously taken, it was estimated that she died sometime between the ages of twenty-five and forty. The highly detailed data recovered from the CT-scan on the state of her teeth and the mineral density of her bones now allows a more precise determination of her age at death at between nineteen and twenty-three years, although the cause of death is still unknown.

Another project, organized by Joyce Filer, a physical anthropologist from the British Museum, has been devoted to the examination of mummies from Egypt's Roman period, dating a thousand years later than Tjentmutengebtiu. Mummies of this period are sometimes fitted with wooden panels decorated with painted portraits of their owners instead of the traditional Egyptian mask. The portraits pose an intriguing question: do they reflect the actual age and appearance of the deceased at or near the time of death, or were they painted at some time prior to that event? The use of CT-scanning has helped to answer this query.

A case in point is one of the most famous of these portrait mummies, that of a man called Artemidorus, dating from about AD 100–120. His portrait represents him in his early twenties, but was this his actual age at death? A recent CT-scan, carried out by a team from the Royal National Throat, Nose and Ear Hospital led by Dr Gus Alusi, indicates that it probably was. Particularly diagnostic for his age is the state of his dental development, especially the wisdom teeth which had not yet erupted. His skeleton, which was not quite fully grown, also indicates that he was a young man at the time of his death.

After having determined that the youthful appearance of the portrait corresponded with the age of its owner, another member of the team, Joao

Right One of the finest examples of its kind, the mummy case of Artemidorus incorporates a portrait of its owner painted in a Roman style, while the gilded decoration over the body reflects the traditional Egyptian hope of resurrection with the god Osiris. From Hawara. Roman Period, AD 100–120.

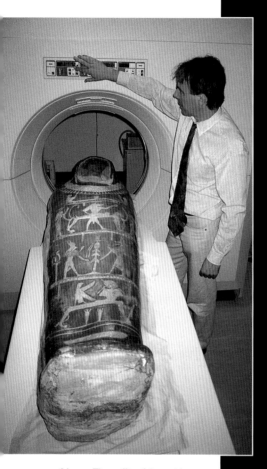

Above The coffin of Artemidorus enters the CT-scanner under the supervision of David Rawson of the Royal National Throat, Nose and Ear Hospital, London.

Opposite High-resolution radiographic images showing the mummy of Artemidorus within his coffin. The skeleton is complete, with much soft tissue surviving. The internal organs and the brain have been removed.

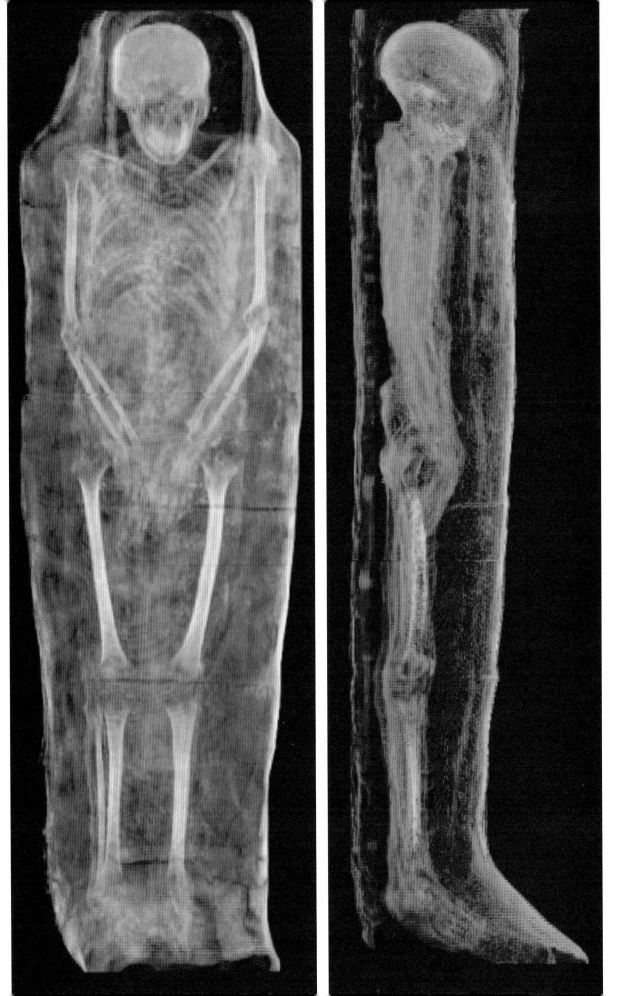

Campos, used the CT-data to see if the handsome likeness mirrored the living reality. To the computer-generated model of Artemidorus' skull, he has added a layer of flesh, using measurements developed in forensic science to help identify anonymous crime victims, appropriately varying in thickness according to the bone structure of the head. After that process is completed,

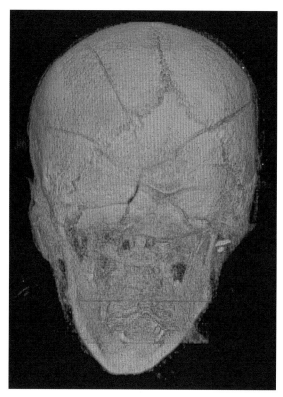

Above Computer reconstruction of the back of Artemidorus' skull, clearly revealing the radiating fractures – the result of a blow by a 'blunt instrument.'

as Campos explains: 'what we do is map the portrait that we've got from the case of the mummy on to the reconstructed face, so we have the real texture of the eyes, eyebrows, lips and skin, and the result is a very realistic view of the face in three dimensions.' The result came as somewhat of a surprise. The true Artemidorus apparently had rather chunky, prominent features, and his striking portrait, although clearly of the same face, was a rather idealized view.

The CT-scan of Artemidorus has revealed another especially intriguing aspect of this young man's life. There is substantial damage to the back of his skull, fractures which Alusi and Filer believe could only have been caused by a 'big blow on the head by a large, heavy object...the proverbial blunt instrument'. Since there are no signs of healing, these injuries, if inflicted on him while still alive, 'must have happened close to the time of death, and may even have been the cause of death'. Further, the number of loose vertebrae and dislocated ribs suggest that the body was already in a state of decomposition when he was mummified. Was Artemidorus the victim of foul play, his body found only sometime later, or simply subjected to rough and careless handling at the embalmer's workshop? Analysis of the scans has not yet been completed, and the final answer to this ancient mystery will have to await the full publication of the project.

It is clear that these new scanning methods can be used to peer through the wrapping of mummies to reveal a wide variety of things, among them details of the craft of the embalmer. The scans have shown us how they did their job, and sometimes how they did not.

Mummification

The process of mummification was held sacrosanct, so the details of exactly how it was done were never publicly recorded by the Egyptians. The earliest written account is by the Greek traveller Herodotus, who visited Egypt in about 450 BC. Over the centuries the techniques of mummification changed considerably, and Herodotus' account can only be used to reflect the customs of his time. According to him, the most expensive method, which involved several stages over a seventy-day period, was well beyond the reach of the ordinary citizen. Later, in the Roman period in which Artemidorus lived, the oils, resins and spices for embalming alone cost 65 drachmas, the equivalent of the average wage for two months' work. The cost of the labour is unknown.

Above At the embalmer's workshop the liver, lungs, stomach and intestines were removed and mummified separately. They were then placed in special containers called canopic jars which were protected by four gods, the Sons of Horus. Even when it became customary to return the organs to the body, canopic jars were still considered necessary equipment, and solid or dummy jars like these wooden ones were made. c.1000 BC.

At an embalmer's workshop, the body would be laid out. First the brain would be removed through the nostrils with an iron hook and discarded as unimportant. The CT-scan of Artemidorus shows this clearly: to penetrate to the brain, the ethmoid bone, which separates the roof of the nose from the cranial cavity, was broken through, and pieces of this bone and part of the brain can still be seen within the skull. But modern science has shown that this was not the only way: the brain could also be extracted through a hole made at the base of the skull, or even via the eye sockets.

Next, an incision in the abdomen, usually on the left side, was made to remove the internal organs. Here timing was critical. Because of their high water content, internal organs are the first parts of the body to decompose. Modern scans have shown that the skill of the embalmer varied from case to case, but the evisceration of the body was rarely perfect or complete, and organs were frequently left behind. Nevertheless, special care was generally taken to retrieve the liver, lungs, stomach and intestines. These organs were mummified separately by dehydrating them with a naturally occurring salt called natron, a mixture of sodium carbonate and sodium bicarbonate (baking powder). Placed in containers called canopic jars or, as in the case of Tjentmutengebtiu, returned to the body as wrapped parcels, these organs were reunited with the body by magic.

The body was then covered from head to toe with natron, to remove the moisture from the tissue and so prevent decay. The mummy of Artemidorus

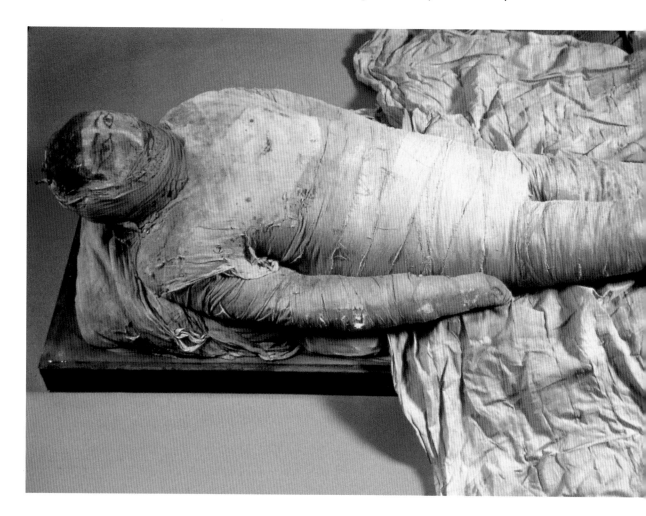

Above One of the oldest preserved mummies, dating from the end of the Fifth Dynasty (*c.*2400 BC). Huge quantities of linen were used to wrap each individual limb separately. The face is covered with a mask painted directly onto the bandages.

is a fine example of the effectiveness of this treatment, as the scans reveal the preserved state of his ears, nose and probably his tongue. So sensitive are these scans that even the crystals of natron still adhering to his skin can be discerned.

After about forty days the natron was removed and the body washed, and in some cases padded out with linen or sawdust to improve its appearance. Rubbed with oils and coated with resins, it was now ready to be wrapped in linen, sometimes in several hundred metres' worth. One mummy of the early Middle Kingdom, about 2000 BC, had over half a mile (0.75 km) of linen wrappings. The intricate bandaging of the body and the placement of a multitude of amulets within the wrappings could be a time-consuming activity, for aside from lack of vigilance, there is no other explanation for the large

Below right A heavy stone scarab was placed on the chest to prevent the heart from incriminating its owner in the underworld's Hall of Judgement. New Kingdom, c.1180 BC (?).

Overleaf In the final judgement, the heart of the deceased was weighed against truth, depicted as a goddess with a feather on her head, while the seated judges look on. Anubis adjusts the scales, while Thoth, the god of wisdom, records the verdict. Ammut, 'the devourer', stands ready to gobble up the hearts of those who do not pass the test. Vignette from the papyrus of Anhai, Twentieth Dynasty, c.1180 BC.

number of insect eggs and small rodents often found beneath the wrappings. Indeed, an elaborate shroud could hide a multitude of sins. For example, while the head of Tjentmutengebtiu had been packed with linen and her body adorned with amulets, for Artemidorus only a small piece of cloth pushed up his nostrils seems to have sufficed to give the appearance that full padding had taken place. This is not the first time modern techniques have revealed a bit of skulduggery on the part of the embalmers.

Artemidorus' mummy contained no amulets of the kind commonly found in earlier Egyptian mummies. It was evidently felt that the funerary scenes depicted on his mummy case sufficed to ensure the afterlife that mummification helped to attain. The fashion in mummy cases and coffins varied widely over time; in Artemidorus' day, while portrait panels were a popular innovation, many still preferred the more traditional funerary mask – one that was gilded if possible, for gold, the flesh of the gods, signified that the deceased

had made it to the afterlife and had become one with the gods. However, attainment of the afterlife was not quite that easy.

The heart, deliberately left in place within the body, was believed to be the source of human personality and the centre of emotions. It was also the key player in the hall of judgement, the last hurdle before entering eternal paradise. Placed on a pan and weighed against the feather of truth, the heart's balance was checked while the deceased proclaimed his or her innocence of forty-two heinous crimes, such as murder, theft or blasphemy. One failure to keep in balance with truth and the heart was eaten by the 'devourer'. Dying this second death was what the Egyptians feared most, and to make sure that it didn't happen, special scarabs made of hard and heavy stone were placed over the heart in the wrappings. Inscribed on the back was a spell, 'Oh, my

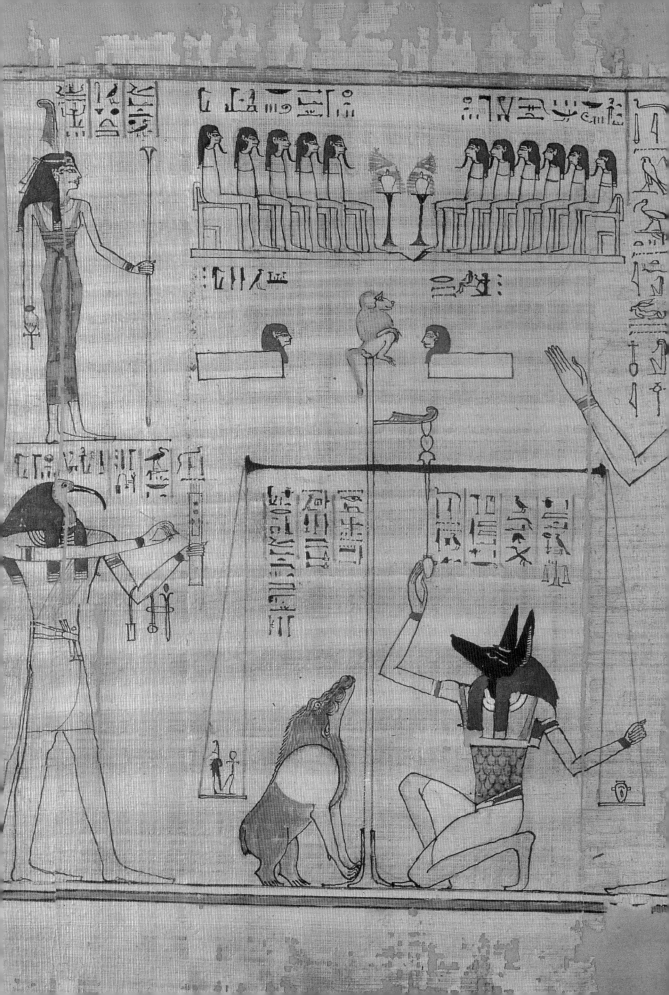

heart which I had from my mother. Do not stand up as a witness against me in the judgement hall…do not tell them what I've really done.'

The most expensive form of mummification, when properly carried out, was undoubtedly very effective. The lifelike remains of the mummified kings of the New Kingdom stand as silent witness to this. They are so well preserved that the sores, possibly of smallpox, are still visible on the face of Ramesses V, the white roots at the base of Ramesses II's dyed red hair can still be seen, and the family resemblance to his father Seti is still quite noticeable.

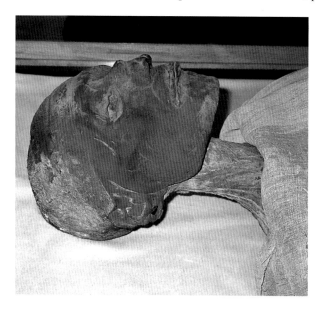

Above The bodies of the kings were treated with the best embalming techniques of their time. The skin of the mummy of Ramesses V is so well preserved that sores, possibly from smallpox, are still visible on his face. Twentieth Dynasty, c.1143 BC.

Opposite Beneath the reed mat, the intact body of a young man was found with linen bandages wrapped around his head and hands. This new discovery at Hierakonpolis suggests that the first step towards mummification had already been taken place in Predynastic times, c.3500 BC.

Origins of Mummification

For the Egyptians, the preservation of the body was essential for the spirit, the *ka*, to find sustenance in the afterlife. Without a body, the spirit would go hungry. It has commonly been thought that this concept was a by-product of the burial customs of the Predynastic Period (*c.*4000 BC), when the dead were placed in shallow graves in the hot, dry sand of the desert, which preserved their bodies naturally. When the graves were disturbed by animals or looters, revealing the nearly lifelike appearance of their ancestors, the Egyptians came to believe that the preservation of the body was important. But as the graves became deeper and more elaborate, partly in an attempt to protect the body from disturbance, the contact with the desiccating heat of the desert was lost and decomposition set in. Thus the practice of mummification was considered to derive from trying to do artificially what hot dry sand did naturally, and by the middle of the First Dynasty (*c.*2950 BC), the date of the earliest preserved artificial mummy, this took the form of wrapping the body in bandages. However, new discoveries at Hierakonpolis in Upper Egypt are revising this view.

In 1997 a team of archaeologists and physical anthropologists under the direction of Dr Renée Friedman of the University of California, Berkeley, began excavating a previously unexplored cemetery at the site of Hierakonpolis. There, about 1 m (3 ft) beneath the desert surface, they found dozens of well-preserved graves of its Predynastic inhabitants, buried in a crouched position and wrapped in matting. Miraculously, these graves had escaped the widespread plundering of the nineteenth century, when cemeteries were pillaged for saleable artefacts and trinkets. This does not mean they had never been disturbed, and it soon became clear that plundering had taken place not long after burial, in the Predynastic Period. The robbers knew exactly who was buried where and what it was they wanted – something evidently located

at the neck. As a result, throughout the cemetery, there had been disturbance to the area of the head, while the remainder of the body was untouched. In some cases, the robbers tunnelled down with such accuracy that only a small slit in the matting at the neck is evidence of their work.

The activities of the grave robbers would certainly have been obvious to the family of the deceased, who would have tried to take preventive measures. What one of these measures may have been became evident with the discovery of two different graves. One was an intact burial of an adult male, aged twenty to thirty-five, who was found still covered in matting and surrounded by seven pots filled with food offerings. As the upper mat was pealed away, the man, who had died at about 3500 BC, emerged. Surprisingly, his head had been wrapped in narrow strips of linen, as were his hands and arms. A similar practice was observed in a heavily plundered burial of a woman, whose long hair was extremely well preserved beneath the linen

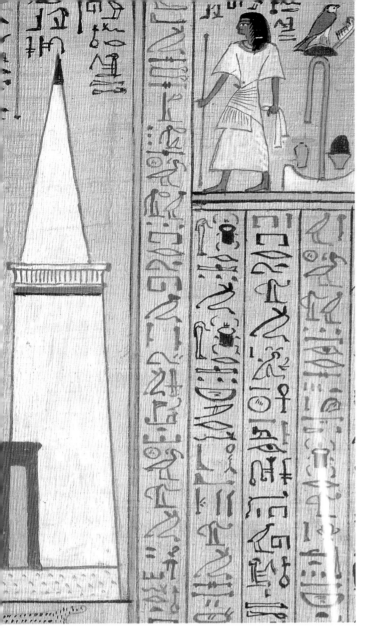

Above In the New Kingdom the ceremony to re-animate the mummy, called 'the opening of the mouth' was performed in front of the tomb. While a priest clad in a leopard skin offered incense, several different implements were held to the orifices of the head to restore the senses. Vignette from the papyrus of Hunefer. Nineteenth Dynasty, c. 1250 BC.

bandages. In her case, the upper body had been padded with cloth bundles over 10 cm (4 in) thick, perhaps to attain a more life-like appearance. In addition to this padding and wrapping of the body, the surprising discovery of what may be resin on the skin and linen in these and other burials found in this cemetery suggests that, already in Predynastic times, methods of artificial mummification were being tried out, some five hundred years earlier than previously thought. Significantly, the focus of the protective wrapping was the head, essential for identification of the corpse by the spirit, and the hands, the means by which the spirit was fed. This new discovery of Egypt's first mummies suggests that the importance placed upon preserving the body was a concept as old as Egyptian culture itself.

Life and Afterlife

Prior to the funeral, during the period of embalming, the body was considered an empty shell. To re-animate the corpse and restore its senses, a ritual ceremony called 'the opening of the mouth' was performed. During the ceremony, a priest would touch all the orifices of the head with a set of ritual implements. Because these utensils resemble tools used in carpentry, it is thought that the ceremony was originally employed only on statues to animate them with the royal or divine spirit. Already during the first dynasties, however, corpses were revivified in this way. Once restored to his or her senses, the deceased could partake of offerings which were physically present or, from the Old Kingdom onward, magically provided by the myriad of workers depicted on the tomb walls. These tomb paintings depict the deceased as eternally youthful, beautiful and well nourished. The servants, however, were not always so lucky; they could be shown more realistically, suffering from the diseases, deformities and life of toil which their corporeal remains confirm.

The condition of people's bodies can tell us not only how they died but how they lived and to what social class they belonged. Roxie Walker of the Bioanthropology Foundation has for many years been engaged in a study of human remains from excavations in Egypt, part of the research collections of The Faculty of Medicine of the University of Cairo. Among them, two bodies, both female but one belonging to a commoner the other to a queen, form an interesting contrast. Roxie Walker has established that both had died young – one was about twenty, the other eighteen – but had lived very different lives. The anonymous commoner, dating from about 1450 BC, had been involved in manual labour from an early age:

'Her thoracic vertebrae show early arthritic changes due probably to carrying heavy weights. Her arms are robust and show evidence of muscle development indicating that she lifted and carried things. There is substantial wear to the teeth, caused by the standard poor person's diet consisting of coarse bread, onions, vegetables and very little meat.'

The other body is that of a lady named Ashait, one of the queens of Mentuhotep II (2055–2004 BC), the king who founded the Middle Kingdom. It bears no indications of stressful physical activity:

'Her thoracic vertebrae are unmarked by any sign of strain, of effort or of hard work. Her teeth show no wear. There is no evidence for muscular development on her arms, which are long and slender. Her well-preserved hand is gracile and elegant, her nails beautifully manicured and stained red with henna.'

Ashait was a refined lady, who had lived a privileged and pampered life, albeit a short one. Even had we not known her name and circumstances, this much could have been deduced from examination of her body alone.

Above Roxie Walker examines the skull of an anonymous commoner in the museum in the Faculty of Medicine of Cairo University. Social class can often be determined from the study of human remains.

Right The beautiful manicured and henna-dyed nails on the delicate hand of Queen Ashait indicate that she led a life of leisure; c.2020 BC.

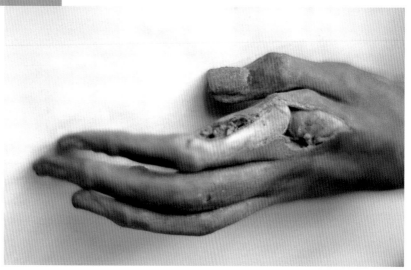

The same collection contains some of the finest examples of human hair to have survived from antiquity. Hair, potentially a rich source of information on a wide range of cutural and medical issues, is a relatively neglected subject, now receiving productive attention from Dr Joann Fletcher of the University of Manchester. By examining hair samples microscopically, for example, she has shown that head lice were common among the ancient Egyptians. Though lice are certainly a health hazard, as they can carry certain diseases and cause skin infections, contrary to popular belief they are not the result of poor hygiene: 'They thrive in clean short hair, where they have easy access to the host's blood supply, feeding several times a day…and the louse is no respecter of class, being quite at home in the hair of pharaohs and farm-

ers alike.' The frequency of lice in fact suggests that the Egyptians washed their hair routinely. To prevent an infestation some relied on regular combing and the use of oils; others shaved their scalps and wore wigs, which also protected their heads from the sun. Ultimately, the way you dressed your hair in public and the kind of wig you wore were significant social markers. The more important you were, the more elaborate the style.

Dr Fletcher's research is shedding especially interesting new light on the question of the colour of hair. She has determined that,

'the wide range of shades portrayed in Egyptian art does, to a large extent, reflect the diverse range found in reality. The most common hair colour, then as now, was a very dark brown, almost black colour, although natural auburn and even (rather surprisingly) blonde hair are also to be found.'

As today, it was commonplace to disguise grey hair with a dye, normally a form of henna. Greying locks could also be hidden with extensions of human hair braided carefully into the owners natural hair. It was a vanity which was not only indulged in life but also extended to the afterlife: hair could be elaborately styled after death, as one would want to look one's best for the most important of all journeys.

Above Hair is a rich source of information about the ancient Egyptians. Detailed examination by Joann Fletcher of the hair of Hat-nufer, who died about 1450 BC, has shown that the braided plaits are actually extentions that had been woven into the natural greying locks of the elderly lady after her death. These were then fashioned into an elaborate bouffant style such as that worn by the goddess Hathor.

Disease

Bones, hair and teeth contain important evidence of lifestyle and of the many afflictions that affected the ancient Egyptians, but many ailments leave no mark on the bone. For determining a wider range of health patterns in ancient Egypt, as well as the ancient Mediterranean world, the tissues preserved in mummies are a unique resource.

Dr Rosalie David, Keeper of Egyptology at the Manchester Museum, has

been at the forefront of mummy research for many years. Over her career she has investigated a number of the health problems the Egyptians faced, and she is currently interested in tracing the pattern of one disease called schistosomiasis (bilharzia) over a 5000 year period from ancient to modern times. Schistosomiasis is a debilitating and ultimately fatal condition caused by a parasitic worm present in the sluggish waters of irrigation canals. The worm enters the human body by penetrating the skin and grows to maturity in the liver; it then moves to the bladder and intestines to breed, laying thousands of spiky eggs which trigger painful inflammation in its human host. The disease is endemic today in Egypt, and it was probably prevalent in ancient times, but because accurate diagnosis has been dependent on finding the actual remains of the parasite in the liver or intestines (organs often removed in the mummification process), the extent of the disease in ancient times has been difficult to ascertain. However, a new laboratory test recently developed for rapid diagnosis of living patients may be equally useful in diagnosing sufferers long dead. Called the ELISA test, it detects the antigen released by the body into the bloodstream specifically to fight off the schistosomiasis worm.

As a first step toward determining the incidence of this disease in antiquity, Dr David must validate this new test on ancient mummified remains. To do this she has chosen 'Manchester Mummy 1766', the body of an anonymous young woman who died in the first or second century AD. Her gilded mask, covering her head and chest, is adorned with modelled snake-bracelets, rings and necklaces inlaid with glass imitations of semi-precious stones. Although she appears to be a lady from a well-to-do family, unlikely to suffer from such a disease, an X-ray examination of her mummy in 1972 revealed evidence of calcification of the bladder, one of the common results of virulent schistosomiasis infection.

On 2 November 1997 Mummy 1766 was wheeled into the Neuro-radiology Department of the Manchester Royal Infirmary for her first test. Here, doctors inserted through an existing hole in the mummy a narrow tube fitted with a miniature camera called an endoscope to guide them in the recovery of tissue samples from deep inside the body. According to Rosalie David, 'the use of the endoscope was a breakthrough, which the Manchester team pioneered back in the mid-eighties, because with it we are virtually non-destructive in our examination of the mummies.' Directed by multi-sectional X-ray images, the endoscope was able to penetrate deeper into the body than ever before and retrieve several uncontaminated samples not only for use in the study of schistosomiasis but also for further research on, among other topics, pain relief.

Dr David Counsell, Consultant Anaesthetist at Victoria Hospital in Blackpool, has had a lifelong interest in ancient Egypt. Combining his passion with his training, he is now investigating the use of pain-relieving drugs in ancient Egypt. He hopes that the samples from Manchester Mummy 1766

Opposite The gilded mask of 'Manchester Mummy 1766' indicates that this young woman was from a wealthy family. X-rays suggest that she suffered from a painful parasitic infection, but only a test on tissue sample will confirm this. Roman Period, first–second century AD.

Overleaf Endoscopic examination of Mummy 1766 by the Manchester team, from left to right, Drs David Counsell, Rosalie David, Eddie Tapp and Ken Wildsmith. The results are visualized on the screen on the left. Before and during the procedure, a series of rotating radiographic images which helped to locate the internal organs accurately were taken by the Manchester Royal Infirmary's state-of-the-art multi-sectional X-ray machine, on the right.

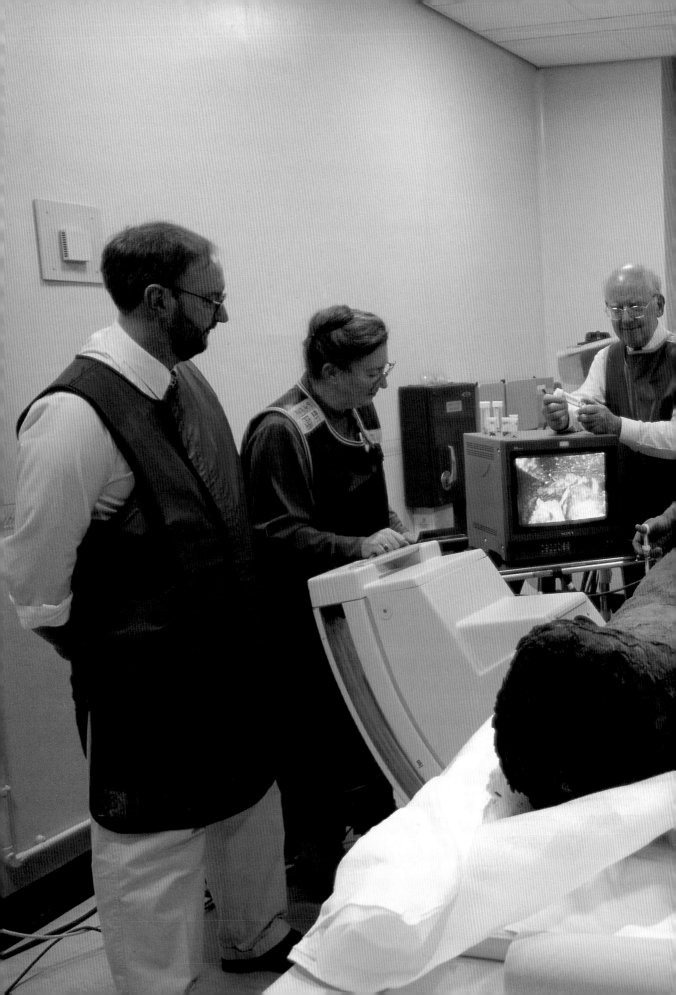

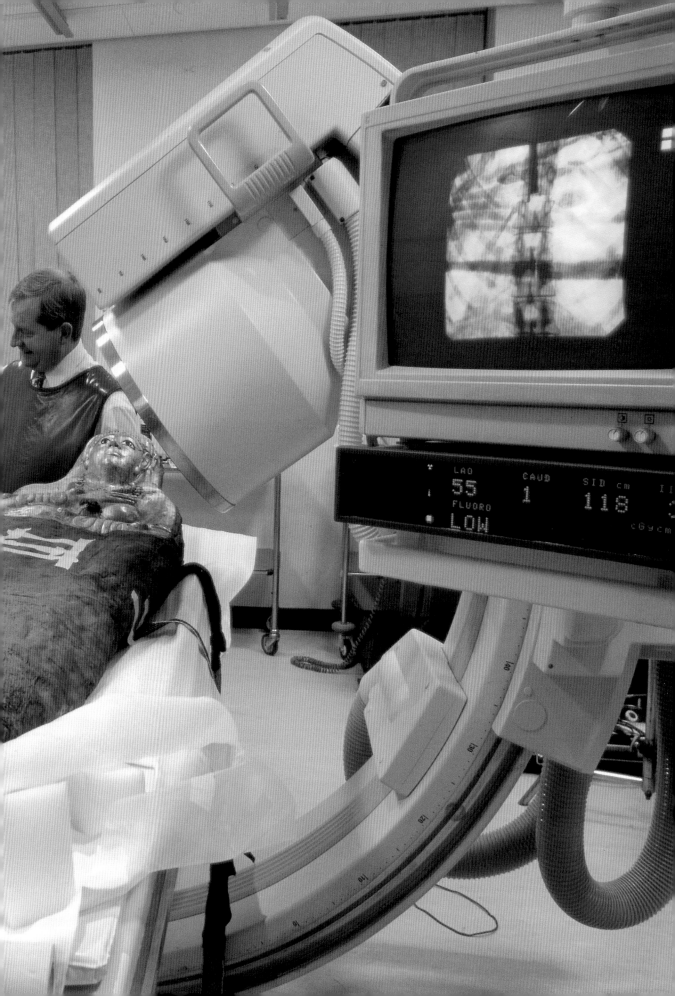

Right The poppy from which the drug opium is derived is not native to Egypt. It is thought, however, that the ancient Egyptians may have imported it from Cyprus, where the flower grows wild, in small juglets that seem to imitate in their form the poppy's seed capsule (right). To date, these jars are the only evidence to suggest the Egyptians used this drug, but new analytic methods may produce scientific proof.

in particular will shed some light on this topic, because the condition of the bladder indicates that the lady must have suffered greatly. As Dr Counsell explains:

> 'We know a lot about the traditions of medicine in ancient Egypt, and we also know that the ancient Egyptians were likely to have known about some of the powerful plant-based drugs the we still use in modern medicine today. We'd be particularly interested in drugs such as morphine and codeine, which are both powerful pain-killers and both derive from the opium poppy. It is quite clear that drugs such as opium were in widespread use at around the time of Christ. There is written evidence describing opium, the harvesting of opium, its use as a pain-killer and indeed its side-effects. But what we don't know is how or if it was used before that time.'

At the Medimass Laboratory in Manchester, a laboratory which specializes in forensic and chemical identification, a minute sample from Mummy 1766 will be analysed using gas chromatography and mass spectroscopy to find out. If any narcotics are present, they will be detected by their mass and weight. These very accurate techniques can also determine if the drugs were actually taken in life and metabolized, or whether they are contaminants or by-products of the mummification process. According to Dr Counsell,

> 'These techniques have been applied in a wide range of archaeological circumstances over the past few years, but I think we've only just scraped the surface of the possibilities that are available…From my own point of view, the important aspect of this work is to push back the boundaries of history.'

But it is not just to satisfy our fascination with the ancient Egyptians that this scientific work is done. Techniques honed in the analysis of Egyptian mummies are now being used to perfect the scanning and evaluation of living patients, saving money and saving lives.

Contribution to Modern Medicine

While new scientific techniques are producing fresh insights, otherwise largely unattainable, into how the ancient Egyptians lived and died, there has also been a reciprocal benefit to modern medicine. Mummies are proving to be valuable 'guinea-pigs' in the refining of techniques before they are used on live human beings.

The CT-scanning of Artemidorus, which yielded so much useful Egyptological information, was part of such a process. Many of the surgical operations carried out at the Royal National Throat, Nose and Ear Hospital, London are targeted on the base of the skull in an area containing major arteries and nerves. Dr Gus Alusi and his colleagues have been investigating ways of eliminating the risk of damaging these delicate structures during surgery and of safely reducing the time required to perform operations in this complex area of the body. Artemidorus has been enormously helpful to the team in achieving the desired end:

> 'One of the more difficult aspects of the research has been actually getting preliminary data of a high enough resolution that we could use for more accurate visualization. The Egyptian mummy, encased and wrapped in bandages, challenged us and provided us with problems that we had to solve in order to be able to see certain parts of the anatomy more accurately…The kind of data required to determine how best to produce optimal quality images could not have been obtained from scans on living patients as it would have meant a very large and potentially lethal dose of radiation.'

The Chantress of Amun, Tjentmutengebtiu, has made an equally significant contribution to modern health, in her case by helping the scientists at St Thomas's Hospital, London to generate an improved and safe method of monitoring difficult pregnancies. After the experience gained in 1992 from calibrating the scanner to electronically unwrap the mummy and examine her internal organs, it occured to Dr Stephen Hughes, 'that the same computer technique, adapted for ultra-sound, could be used to scan babies in the womb, measure their limbs and monitor the growth of their organs'. One of the first young mothers to benefit from this new procedure was Mrs Yolanda Sykes, who had suffered difficulties during a previous pregnancy. But in 1994 she gave trouble-free birth to a healthy boy, Christopher, and expressed her gratitude publicly: 'Knowing problems would be picked up by the scan

Above Mrs Yolanda Sykes and her son
Christopher visiting the mummy of
Tjentmutengebtiu in the British Museum:
'I never thought I'd have cause to be
grateful to someone who had been dead
for 3000 years.'

was great…I never thought I'd have cause to be grateful to someone who had been dead for 3000 years. But we've all got good reason to be thankful to Christopher's other mummy.' Many a mother and child have since had occasion to be thankful to this new technique. Fascinatingly, the Egyptians' quest for rebirth in the next world has helped make possible safe birth in this one.

But the contribution of mummies to modern medicine promises to go well beyond simply playing the role of the guinea-pig. In 1985 the Swedish scientist Dr Svante Pääbo successfully cloned DNA extracted from the tissue of an Egyptian mummy and thereby helped to initiate the brand-new field of 'molecular archaeology'. Ancient Egypt, with its huge quantities of well-preserved human and animal remains spanning several millennia, offers an unparalleled wealth of raw material for palaeobiological studies and has been at the forefront of such research. The unique 'genetic fingerprint' encoded in an individual's DNA offers the prospect of establishing the existence of relationships between one person and another, between one family and another, and between entire populations – information of fundamental historical and demographic importance which cannot be certainly retrieved from any other source. In the field of medicine, molecular archaeology offers the possibility of identifying the ancestors of certain diseases, through the DNA of the relevant pathogen, and of tracing their evolution through time, a process which, experts believe, could assist in the development of antidotes. Hepatitis B and malaria are among several major diseases which have been targeted for such study. To date, ancient DNA research has been beset by methodological difficulties and there is no question that extravagant claims have been made on the basis of flawed or contaminated samples. But as these difficulties are resolved and techniques of retrieval and analysis are improved, more sure progress, and some important breakthroughs, can be expected.

One very popular image of the Egyptian mummy is that of the vengeful monster of the horror movie. In reality, however, mummies are no joke, nor is any curse attached to them. Properly approached and treated, they are eloquent witnesses to the past and rich repositories of scientific information, of potential benefit to the whole of mankind.

FURTHER READING

Adams, B. and Cialowicz, K., *Protodynastic Egypt*, Princes Risborough 1997

Andrews, Carol, *Egyptian Mummies*, London 1984

Andrews, Carol, *Amulets of Ancient Egypt*, London 1994

Andrews, Carol, *Ancient Egyptian Jewellery*, London 1996

Andrews, Carol (ed.), *The Ancient Egyptian Book of the Dead* (trans. by Raymond O. Faulkner), London 1989

Arnold, D., *Building in Egypt: Pharaonic Stone Masonry*, New York 1991

Baines, J. and Malek, J., *Atlas of Ancient Egypt*, Oxford 1980

Bierbrier, M., *The Tomb-Builders of the Pharaohs*, Cairo 1989

Bietak, Manfred, *Avaris: Capital of the Hyksos. Recent Excavations*, London 1996

Bowman, Alan K., *Egypt after the Pharaohs*, London 1996

Capel, Anne K. and Markoe, Glenn E. (eds), *Mistress of the House, Mistress of Heaven: Women in Ancient Egypt*, New York 1996

David, R. and Tapp, E. (eds), *Evidence Embalmed: Modern Medicine and the Mummies of Ancient Egypt*, Manchester 1984

David, R., and Tapp, E. (eds), *The Mummy's Tale: The Scientific and Medical Investigation of Natsef-Amun, Priest in the Temple at Karnak*. London 1992

Davies, W.V., *Egyptian Hieroglyphs*, London 1987

Donadoni, S. (ed.), *The Egyptians*, Chicago 1997

Filer, Joyce M., *Disease*, London 1995

Forman, Werner and Quirke, Stephen, *Hieroglyphs and the Afterlife in Ancient Egypt*, London 1996

Germer, R., *Mummies. Life after Death in Ancient Egypt*, Munich/New York 1997.

Hart, G., *Egyptian Myths*, London 1990

Hawass, Z., *Silent Images. Women of Pharaonic Egypt*, Cairo 1995

Hoffman, M.A., *Egypt Before the Pharaohs: The Prehistoric Foundations of Egyptian Civilization*, revised and updated, University of Texas 1991

Hornung, E., *Idea into Image: Essays on Ancient Egyptian Thought*, New York 1992

James, T.G.H., *Egyptian Painting*, London 1985

James, T.G.H. and Davies, W.V., *Egyptian Sculpture*, London 1983

Kemp, B.J., *Ancient Egypt: Anatomy of a Civilization*, London 1989

Kendall, Timothy, *Kerma and the Kingdom of Kush 2500–1500 B.C.: The Archaeological Discovery of an Ancient Nubian Empire*, National Museum of African Art, Washington 1997

Kitchen, K.A., *Pharaoh Triumphant: The Life and Times of Ramesses II, King of Egypt*, Warminster 1982

Lehner, M., *The Complete Pyramids,* London 1997

Lesko, L.H. (ed.), *Pharaoh's Workers: The Villagers of Deir El Medina*, Cornell University Press 1994

Malek, J., *In the Shadow of the Pyramids: Egypt during the Old Kingdom*, London 1986

Manley, B., *The Penguin Historical Atlas of Ancient Egypt*, Harmondsworth 1996

Moran, W.L., *The Amarna Letters*, Baltimore 1992

Nunn, John F., *Ancient Egyptian Medicine*, London 1996

O'Connor, D., *Ancient Nubia: Egypt's Rival in Africa*, Philadelphia 1993

Parkinson, R.B., *The Tale of Sinuhe and other Ancient Egyptian Poems 1940–1640 BC*, Oxford 1997

Parkinson, Richard, *Voices from Ancient Egypt: An Anthology of Middle Kingdom Writings*, London 1991

Parkinson, Richard and Quirke, Stephen, *Papyrus*, London 1995

Pinch, Geraldine, *Magic in Ancient Egypt*, London 1994

Quirke, Stephen, *Who Were the Pharaohs? A history of their names with a list of cartouches*, London 1990

Quirke, Stephen, *Ancient Egytian Religion*, London 1992

Quirke, Stephen and Spencer, Jeffrey (eds), *The British Museum Book of Ancient Egypt*, London 1992

Reeves, N., *The Complete Tutankhamun: The King, The Tomb, The Royal Treasure*, London 1990

Reeves, N. and Wilkinson, R., *The Complete Valley of the Kings: Tombs and Treasures of Egypt's Greatest Pharaohs*, London 1996

Robins, Gay, *Women in Ancient Egypt*, London 1993

Robins, Gay, *The Art of Ancient Egypt*, London 1997

Shaw, Ian and Nicholson, Paul, *British Museum Dictionary of Ancient Egypt*, London 1995

Spencer, A.J., *Early Egypt: The Rise of Civilisation in the Nile Valley*, London 1993

Spencer, Jeffrey (ed.), *Aspects of Early Egypt*, London 1996

Stead, Miriam, *Egyptian Life*, London 1986

Taylor, John H., *Unwrapping a Mummy*, London 1995

Taylor, John, *Egypt and Nubia*, London 1991

Verner, M., *Forgotten Pharaohs, Lost Pyramids: Abusir*, Prague 1994

Walker, C.B.F., *Cuneiform*, London 1987

Walker, Susan and Bierbrier, Morris (eds), *Ancient Faces: Mummy Portraits from Roman Egypt*, London 1997

Welsby, Derek A., *The Kingdom of Kush: The Napatan and Meroitic Empires*, London 1996

Wente, E., *Letters from Ancient Egypt*, Atlanta 1990

Wildung, D. (ed.), *Sudan: Ancient Kingdoms of the Nile*, Paris/New York 1997

Williams, Jonathan (ed.), *Money: A History*, London 1997

A number of periodicals provide up-to-date reports on current archaeological fieldwork and research projects. Especially recommended are *Egyptian Archaeology. The Bulletin of the Egypt Exploration Society* (London), *KMT. A Modern Journal of Ancient Egypt* (Sebastopol), and *Sudan and Nubia. The Bulletin of the Sudan Archaeological Research Society* (London). For membership/subscription details, contact respectively The Egypt Exploration Society, 3 Doughty Mews, London WC1N 2PG, UK; KMT Communications, 18 Lucero Road, Santa Fe, NM 87505–8845, USA; and The Sudan Archaeological Research Society, c/o Department of Egyptian Antiquities, British Museum, London WC1B 3DG, UK

INDEX

Numbers in *italics* refer to
illustration captions

Abusir, 88–92
Abydos, 16, 35–8, *35,* 46, 57–61, 69, 70
afterlife, belief in, 22, 50, 53, 179, 193,
 203, 206, 211
Aha, 170
Ahmed, Salah Mohamed, *126*
Ahmose, King, 119, *119,* 120, 122, 129,
 151, *151*
Ahmose, son of Ibana, 119–20, *120,* 129,
 131
akh, 56
Alamat Tal road, 117, 119
Alexander the Great, 16
Alusi, Dr Gus, 197, 200, 217
Amanishakheto, Queen, 107, *107*
Amarna Letters, 138, *138*
Amenhotep I, King, 119, 177
Amenhotep II, King, 138
Amenhotep III, King, 130, 136, *136,* 138,
 138
Amenpnufer, 147–8
amethysts, *47,* 49
Ammut, *203*
amulets, *175,* 175–6, *196,* 202, 203
Amun, 99, 159, 162, 164, 166, 167, 168–9
 see also Amun–Ra
Amun–Ra, 96, *96, 97,* 99, *99,* 102, *108,*
 159, *159, 162,* 163, 164
 see also Amun; Ra
Anatolia, 147
ancestors, *177,* 178, *178*
Ani, *179*
animal necropolis, Saqqara, 185,187–91
Anubis, *203*
Antiochus Epiphanes, King of Syria, 187
Apep, 154, *154,* 179
Apis bulls, *190,* 190–1, *191*
art, 62, 73, 139–40
Artemidorus, mummy of, 197–200, *198,*
 200, 201, 202, 203, 217
artists, 139–40
Ashait, 210, *210*
Asia, western, 120
Assyria, King of, 138
Atbara River, 11
Athribis, 70
Avaris, 110, 112, *112,* 113–5, *114,* 120,
 120, 122

bakeries, *83,* 85
basalt, 49
battle-axe, chisel-shaped, 111, *111,* 115
Bedouin, 135
beer, 27
Belzoni, Giovanni, *192,* 193
Bent Pyramid, *70,* 73, 73–4
Berenice Panchrysos, *130,* 134–5
Bes, 170, 173, 176
Beset, *172,* 173, *173*
Bietak, Professor Manfred, 113, 114, *121,*
 122
bird mummies, *186,* 188–90, *189*

birth, 169–73, *170, 172, 173*
'birth box', 170, *170*
'birth bricks', *170,* 171
Blue Nile River, 11
Bomann, Ann, 47
Bonnet, Professor Charles, 123, *124,* 126,
 126, 127
'Book of the Dead', 95, 179, *179*
'Book of Dreams', 184, *184,* 185
bow, composite, *110,* 111
brain, extraction of, 201
bread, 83, 85
brewery, 27
British Museum, 128, 163, 195, 197
Bryan, Professor Betsy, 138, 139, *139,* 140
bull-leaping scene, *120, 121,* 122
burial
 animal, 187–91
 human *see* graves; pyramids; tombs
Buto, 17, 29–32, *29*

Cairo Museum, 111, *170*
calendar
 based on Nile, 13
 Nabta Playa, 20, *20*
Campos, Joao, 200
Canaan/Canaanites, 32, 110, 114, 120, 129
canopic jars, *201,* 202
cartouche, 16, 61, *136*
Castiglione, Alfredo and Angelo, 130, 134,
 135
cattle, 18, 20
causeway, 79, *79,* 80
cemeteries *see* graves; pyramids; tombs
chaos, 14, *14,* 42–3, 44, 46, *46,* 50, 58
chapels, 106, 128, 139, 140
chariot, horse-drawn, *110,* 111, *146*
Cheops, King *see* Khufu (Cheops), King
Chephren, King *see* Khafra (Chephren),
 King
Classic Kerma Period, *127, 128*
cobra/uraeus, 99, 102
Colossi of Memnon, 136
copper, *47,* 49
Counsell, Dr David, 213, *213,* 216
craftsmen, tomb, *80,* 142–7, 169, 177
 see also Deir el-Medina
creation
 ideas about, 56, 154
 mound of, 56, 57, 96, 99, 154, 157, 167
 and temples, 155, 157, 159, 167
Crete, *120,* 122
crowns, *18,* 32–3, *33, 61,* 99
cuneiform, *138*
CT-scanning, 195–200, *196, 197, 198,* 217
Czech Mission, 90

Dahshur, 73
'Dam of the Pagans' (Helwan Dam), 44–6,
 44, 45
Darnell, Dr John and Deborah, *116,*
 116–7, 118
David, Dr Rosalie, 211, 213
dead, the, 178, 179–83 *see also* graves;
 pyramids; tombs

Den, King, *57*
deffufa, 123, 124, 125–6
Deir el-Bahri, *165*
Deir el-Medina, 143, *143,* 147, 148, *168,*
 169, 170, *170,* 171, 176, 177, *177,* 178,
 178, 184, *184*
deities *see* religious beliefs; names of deities
Delta, 11, 17, 29, 30, 32, 35, 38, 70, 110,
 113, 175, 186, 187
demons, 154, 169, *176, 179, 182,* 183, *183*
demotic script, 185–6
desert, 46, 47, 49 *see also* desert routes;
 Eastern desert; Negev desert; Sahara
 desert
desert routes, *115, 116,* 115–19, *118, 119*
determinatives, 36, *154*
disease, *206,* 211–17, *213*
Djedfra, King, 54
Djedkara-Isesi, King, 54
Djoser, King, 43, 54, 63, 64, 67, 69, 70,
 73, 92
DNA, 219
Dongola Reach, *128,* 128–9, 147
Dorman, Dr Peter, 166, *166*
Double Crown, 33, *33*
dream-invocation, 187
dreams, 183–7, *184*
Dreyer, Dr Günter, 35, 38, 45, 59, 60, 69
drugs, 216
dynasties
 grouped into kingdoms/periods, 16
 Dynasty 0, *35,* 36, *37*
 Dynasty 1, 36, 42, 47, 49, 57, 206
 Dynasty 2, 59, 69
 Dynasty 3, 43, 54, 70
 Dynasty 4, *44,* 53, 54, 54, 56, 70
 Dynasty 5, 54, 88, 90, 92
 Dynasty 6, *13,* 46, 49, *50,* 54, *80, 90*
 Dynasty 13, *176*
 Dynasty 17, *110,* 111
 Dynasty 18, 96, *99, 108, 112, 114,* 109,
 114, 119, 122, *126,* 140
 Dynasty 19, 142, 143, *170, 176, 177,*
 178, 179, 184, 185
 Dynasty 20, 140, 143, 147, 148, *149,*
 169, *183*
 Dynasty 22, 195, *195*
 Dynasty 25, 99

Early Dynastic Period, 16
Eastern Desert, 47, 130, *130*
Egypt Exploration Society, 38, 186, 188
Eighteenth Dynasty, 96, 109, *112,* 114,
 114, 119, 122, *126,* 140
electric resistivity meter, 64, *67*
Elephantine, 49, 70
ELISA test, 213
Elkab, 119, 129
El Kurru, 103
el-Qurn, 95, *95*
embalming process, *201,* 201–2, *206*
endoscope, 213, *213*
Ethiopia, 11
Euphrates, 109
expeditions, 49

221

ILLUSTRATION ACKNOWLEDGEMENTS

Ägyptisches Museum und Papyrussamlung, Berlin: 107.

Ashmolean Museum, Oxford: 46, 61.

Manfred Bietak: 120 (below).

Bristol Museum and Art Gallery: 192.

British Museum, London, courtesy of the Trustees of the British Museum:
Contents page (below), 16, 17, 18, 22, 23 (above & below), 28, 32
(casts of original in Cairo Museum), 36 (right), 64, 109 (copy), 110 (below),
111 (below), 119, 137, 138, 149, 152, 153, 170 (above), 172 (above), 175
(below), 176, 180–81, 182, 183 (left and right), 184, 189 (below), 190, 193,
194–5, 198 (right), 201, 203, 204–5, 208–9.

Alfredo and Angelo Castiglione: 132–3, 134.

John and Deborah Darnell: 117, 118 (above and below).

Vivian Davies: 20, 29, 31, 34, 39, 52, 59, 72, 73, 76, 80, 81, 83, 84, 86
(below), 87, 94 (above & below), 96, 100–101, 102, 103, 105, 111
(above; Cairo Museum), 121, 125, 131 (left and right), 134, 136 (below),
151 (Cairo Museum), 168, 185, 188, 189 (above), 191, 198 (right), 206
(Cairo Museum), 218.

Egypt Exploration Society: 186.

Joann Fletcher: 210 (below).

Werner Forman Archive, London: 93, 172 (below right), 173.

Renée Friedman: 12, 13 (above & below; Hearst Museum), 40–41, 43
(above), 47, 48, 53 (Hearst Museum), 57, 60, 62 (above), 62 (below; Louvre,
Paris), 63, 65, 68, 71 (Cairo Museum), 86 (above), 90, 112–13, 144–5, 157,
171 (below; Cairo Museum), 172 (below left; Manchester Museum), 175
(above), 177 (right), 212 (Manchester Museum), 216 (Manchester Museum).

German Archaeological Institute, Cairo: 37 (above, centre & below),

Peter Hayman: title page, contents page (above), 10, 14, 15, 44, 50, 51, 91,
97, 98, 110 (above; Luxor Museum), 116, 124 (above and below), 126
(above and below), 127 (Khartoum Museum), 128, 135 (Luxor Museum),
136 (above), 139, 143, 146, 150, 154 (above and below), 155, 156, 158,
160–61, 162, 164, 166, 167 (below), 170 (below), 174, 179, 210 (above),
211.

Hierakonpolis Expedition Archive: 24, 26, 207.

Friedrich Hinkel: 104.

Yarko Kobylecky: 120 (above).

The Manchester Museum, The University of Manchester: 214–15.

Ian Mathieson: 66, 67 (above & below),

The Metropolitan Museum of Art, New York: 108 (above; Purchase,
Edward S. Harkness Gift, 1926 [26.7.1412]), 108 (below; Fletcher Fund,
1926 [26.8.125, 127]), 165 (Rogers Fund and Contribution from
Edward S. Harkness, 1929 [29.3.2]).

Museo Egizio, Turin: 171 (above), 177 (above left and below left), 178, 202.

Royal National Throat, Nose and Ear Hospital, London: 199, 200.

S4C (graphics by 4:2:2 Videographics, Bristol): 19 (above), 27, 33, 42, 43
(below), 78–9, 123.

St Thomas's Hospital, London: 196–7.

Staatliche Sammlung Ägyptischer Kunst, Munich: 106.

Miroslav Verner: 88 (above, centre & below), 89.

Fred Wendorf: 19 (below), 21.